D1238261

# THE STRUGGLE FOR
# THE HOLY LAND

# The Struggle for the Holy Land

## Arabs, Jews, and the Emergence of Israel

William Hare

**MADISON BOOKS**

*Published by Madison Books*
*4720 Boston Way*
*Lanham, Maryland 20706*

*3 Henrietta Street*
*London WC2E 8LU, England*

*Distributed by National Book Network*

*⊖™ The paper used in this publication meets the minimum requirements of*
*American National Standard for Information Sciences—Permanence of*
*Paper for Printed Library Materials, ANSI Z39.48–1964.*
*Manufactured in the United States of America.*

*Library of Congress Cataloging-in-Publication Data*

*The struggle for the Holy Land : Arabs, Jews, and the emergence of*
*Israel / William Hare*
*p. cm.*
*Includes bibliographical references and index.*
*1. Jewish–Arab relations. 2. Israel–Arab conflicts. 3. Israel—*
*History. 4. Zionism—History. 5. Palestinian Arabs—Politics and*
*government. I. Title.*
*DS119.7.H358 1995 956.94—dc20 95-3019 CIP*

*ISBN 1–56833–040–5 (cloth : alk. paper)*

# Contents

# Introduction

Of all the challenges confronting humanity at this crucial moment of world history, standing in the forefront is the seemingly insoluble challenge of the Middle East, an area whose volatility and geopolitical complexities have overwhelmed some of the brightest minds.

Biblical scholars are familiar with the dire prophecy in Revelation calling for the final battle on earth to take place in the Middle East, bearing the reference of Armageddon. The conflagration described in Revelation has been considered to resemble nuclear war as described with increasing vividness by scientists in recent years. The questions therefore arise as to what bearing this prophecy might hold for humanity and if there is a way to prevent such a mammoth conflagration.

In order to provide any kind of meaningful examination of the Middle East in its numerous ramifications and widespread volatility, it is imperative to do more than study the region along with the divergent beliefs of the people inhabiting it. It is necessary to analyze the Middle East from its very roots, extending as far back as tribal days, observing customs and beliefs of the peoples as they evolved. These developing psychological roots must then be carried forward all the way to the present, so as to provide a clearer picture of the region by examining the beliefs of its residents, which extend from the traditional to the contemporary, and by comparing and contrasting how their patterns of thought and behavior have been nurtured.

Another important factor to be considered in a definitive Middle East analysis is the influence of other countries in the region. The roles of such nations as Great Britain, the United States, and Russia have left an indelible mark on the Middle East and have helped to shape the forces of change through the years.

When embarking on any study of the Middle East, one must also remember that religious and sociological concepts, along with the shaping of historical forces, result from the thinking of individuals. Too often, unfortunately, historians analyze the subject by looking at the fascinating yet perplexing forest that lies beyond them without making a solid effort to describe and evaluate the various components of the numerous trees in their midst.

The critical element in any historical evaluation lies in the care with which the components of the trees are studied. Metaphorically, the trees represent individuals. It was individuals who held sway over masses of people through their ideas. Such ideas most certainly did not develop in vacuums. They sprang from environmental roots and processes of conditioning, which inevitably govern the developmental makeup of all individuals. These myriad nuances of thought, these varying life experiences, govern what individuals believe as well as the course of action they take in every aspect of their life.

To arrive at understanding, it is imperative, particularly in the case of a complex regional entity such as the Middle East with its numerous patterns of belief, that one study with great care the individuals who helped to shape the destiny of the region. To achieve peace in the region, one must come to grips with what people believe and with the ideals and concepts they hold near and dear to them. We must push beyond the concepts themselves and seek both to understand the individuals who propounded the concepts and to learn how and why they came to believe what they did.

Such a task is far from easy, but yet it must begin, for unless human beings with dedication and purpose explore the issues concerning peaceful stability in the Middle East, we will be left with the painful alternative of ignorance and the hostilities that ultimately spring from it. In a nuclear world that possibility is earth-shattering in its dimensions.

# 1

# The Unfinished Sentence

He was a quiet man, disdainful of public recognition and its inevitable disruptions to tranquility. The power of this man's trailblazing intellect coupled with his unswerving civility toward humans of every creed and national origin rendered him a giant revered by people all over the world for his ability to perceive the larger picture while lesser individuals became enmeshed in a mire of minutiae.

On April 18, 1955, the entire civilized world fell into mourning over that rarest of losses, that of a universal man of conscience capable of grasping the total picture of civilization with microscopic clarity. To achieve that unique world vision requires the combination of retaining the human touch while developing acute analytical skills and at the same time advancing beyond the stage of normal human capabilities through acquiring the powers of a mystic. By applying human characteristics while at the same time transcending beyond them into a mystical world, such a rare individual has one foot on the planet and the other in the cosmos. Achieving a harmonious blend of not one but two rarely cognizable worlds is the kind of grand feat scarcely ever achieved by one individual. Quite naturally, this type of person, combining enough of the practical to ascertain humanity with sufficient components of the mystic to rise above it in the pursuit of something lying beyond, possesses the potential to uplift humans beyond the ranks of mere mortals by tapping into an infinite conscience.

Albert Einstein was such a man, and his passing on April 18, 1955, produced the same kind of international shock waves that had rever-

1

berated seven years earlier with the passing of another universal giant, Mohandas Gandhi. After Gandhi's death at the hands of an assassin on January 30, 1948, Einstein issued a statement for a memorial service to be held in Washington, D.C., for the man who, more than any other individual, was credited with energizing the movement toward independence in his native India, which reached fruition in 1947. Einstein's statement contained the following: "It was his [Gandhi's] unshakable belief that the use of force is an evil in itself, to be shunned by those who strive for absolute justice. . . . The veneration in which Gandhi has been held throughout the world rests on the recognition, for the most part unconscious, that in our age of moral decay he was the only statesman who represented that higher conception of human relations in the political sphere to which we must aspire with all our powers. We must learn the difficult lesson that the future of mankind will only be tolerable when our course, in world affairs as in all other matters, is based upon justice and law rather than the threat of naked power, as has been true so far."[1]

Einstein believed that Gandhi held "the most enlightened views of all the political men of our time"[2] and profoundly felt that the concept of revolution without violence, which he utilized to attain independence in India, needed to be practiced on a large scale to achieve the objective of bringing peace to the world on a supranational scale. Never one to dodge a confrontation in which basic individual liberties were at stake, Einstein incorporated Gandhi's concepts into another arena, that of congressional investigations into the beliefs of suspected political nonconformists at the height of the Cold War hysteria of the early and mid-fifties.

In response to a letter from a Brooklyn teacher who was a target of congressional inquiry, Einstein quickly replied, stating his view unequivocally and in the process granting permission to publicize his position if the inquiry target deemed it appropriate. Einstein's response was published in the *New York Times* on June 12, 1953. The strategy recommended by Einstein was that of following Gandhi's concept of noncooperation rather than resorting to the response of many inquiry targets by which they refuse to answer questions on the basis of the constitutional protection of a witness against self-incrimination as delineated in the Fifth Amendment.

The gist of Einstein's position was his belief that "it is shameful for a blameless citizen to submit to such an inquisition and that this kind of inquisition violates the spirit of the Constitution."[3] His position as a civil libertarian therefore deemed it preferable to endure a jail term for contempt of Congress rather than avail oneself of the protective safeguards of the Fifth Amendment, thereby avoiding prosecution.

Like Gandhi, Einstein was also a self-described and committed pacifist but emphasized that he was a convinced rather than an absolute pacifist. Einstein felt compelled to make the distinction relative to his pacifism as a result of divergent patterns of conduct in the First World War as opposed to the Second World War. Like his long-standing friend and also acknowledged pacifist, philosopher, and mathematician Bertrand Russell, after refusing to condone or participate in any way in World War One, which ultimately led to his departure from his native Germany, Einstein drew the line on pacifism with the rise of Hitler and his aggressive posture, which brought on World War Two.

He carefully explained that whereas he remained a convinced pacifist, there were circumstances in which he deemed the use of force justifiable. The principal basis for such action was resisting an enemy bent on destroying him and his people. In all other instances he regarded the use of force as a means of settling conflicts among nations to be impermissible. Rather than regarding his pacifism as springing from a thoroughly reasoned analytical process, Einstein defined it as an instinctive feeling, an outgrowth of his abhorrence at the thought of taking another human life.

There was one other basic similarity between Einstein and the man he considered to be the premier political thinker of his time, Mohandas Gandhi: a burning aspiration to achieve freedom and tranquility for his people. Gandhi was the great architect of freedom for his native India following many years of British colonial rule. For Einstein the burning dream during most of his adulthood, that of seeing his own Jewish people achieve homeland status, became a reality with the creation of the nation of Israel in 1948, the same year that the man whose wisdom he so dearly revered, Gandhi, was assassinated by a religious fanatic while en route to a prayer session.

Just as the movement spearheaded by Gandhi had been long and arduous, entailing great human sacrifice amid much bloodshed, the achievement of independence by the Jewish people occurred after much struggle and bloodshed, with many lives perishing in the process.

By 1919, the year that the Zionist movement vigorously sought to enlist the support of Einstein, he had become the most famous scientist in the world. The man who had burst into international fame at the tender age of twenty-six in 1905 upon publication of his essay regarding the theory of relativity, written while he was a clerk in a Zurich, Switzerland, patent office, was a visible world presence despite his frequently expressed desire for solitude and public obscurity. In that he was Jewish it was understandable that the Zionist movement, seeking to effectively employ any asset at its disposal, would labor assiduously to bring the world-renowned scientist under its organizational umbrella.

Rather than eagerly accept entrance into the ranks of the Zionists, however, Einstein entertained misgivings. The basis of his cautious reluctance was one he shared with a number of other Jews. Reaction to the expressed Zionist goal of achieving homeland status for the Jewish people resulted in a dichotomy, one that pitted Jews of varying opinion one against the other. It is common in times of diligent effort that a tide of turmoil often results in an excess of zeal, which precipitates confusion. Even a cursory study of the history of any nation will bring numerous examples to the fore. The result of such overzealous effort, in which many seek to proselytize the ranks of the uncommitted to achieve a common goal, frequently consists of polar opposite viewpoints. Instead of clarifying the group's basic posture, misunderstandings arise, and widespread debate is provoked both within and outside of the ranks.

In the case of Zionists, an oversimplification process was occurring in which two equally dedicated schools of thought tugged mightily at each end of the ideological spectrum while thoughtful observers such as Albert Einstein watched from the sidelines.

One viewpoint stoutly denied that the Jews represented a nation at all. This group was adamantly and vocally opposed by a contrasting entity, which held that the Jews were a nation and nothing else, but a nation that had been deprived of its national territory.

In 1911, Einstein declared his belief that Zionism was more of a dream than a tangible reality. He was also intellectually uncomfortable with any movement that embraced nationalism. This feeling was strengthened during the World War One period, when Einstein along with equally courageous colleagues opposed Germany's participation in the conflict at a time when he was a professor at the University of Berlin. At a point wherein world opinion was reacting angrily against Germany for violating the neutrality of Belgium, some of Germany's leading intellectuals published a public declaration supporting their nation's conduct in what was called a "Manifesto to the Civilized World."[4] The manifesto denied that Germany had engaged in wanton aggression in violating Belgium's neutrality, asserting that the course had been taken in Germany's self-protection in the anticipating the war plans of the Allied powers and that to have refused to take action would have been suicidal. It further declared that Germany was defending the white race from the likes of "Russian hordes . . . allied with Mongols and Negroes." The manifesto closed on a note of shrill-pitched nationalism with the assertion that Germany was doing no more than fighting to preserve its national culture, the treasured legacy of Goethe, Beethoven, and Kant, and that its stalwart protector, standing arm in arm with the people, was the German military.

A sensitive pacifist such as Einstein would find numerous reasons for apprehensive concern over such a pronouncement, buttressed because it bore the signatures of ninety-three of the nation's leading intellectuals from virtually every artistic and professional walk of life. Included in their ranks were Ernst Hackel, the famous evolutionist; Wilhelm Röntgen, the discoverer of X rays; Paul Ehrlich, the great biochemist; Engelbert Humperdinck, the composer of *Hansel and Gretel*; and Max Reinhardt, the pioneer of the modern theater. The prominence of the names supporting such a militant national pronouncement was cause enough for concern, but what troubled Einstein and others like him beyond that fact was the realization that the manifesto's viewpoint was shared by the nation's populace at large.

Despite the strong popularity of the positions advanced by Germany's cultural elite in the manifesto, a challenge was promptly undertaken. Within days of the manifesto's publication, a noted German pacifist, Georg Friedrich Nicolai, circulated his response among faculty members at the University of Berlin, where he held a chair in physiology. The work was entitled a "Manifesto to Europeans"[5] and its author understandably encountered great difficulty in his enlistment of sponsorship, because he was bucking a strong tide of German nationalism. Only three cosigners could be found. One of them was Einstein, in what emerged as the first political document to bear his signature.

The "Manifesto to Europeans" took the position that vigorous military action unleashed throughout Europe was not promotive of culture and indeed threatened the growth of culture as a result of the barbarous impact of war. It called for all countries to exert a cohesive effort to achieve a peace treaty that would prevent further wars from erupting, then concluded by calling for the creation of a League of Europeans to promote the cause of peace.

The "Manifesto to Europeans" could be classified as vintage Einstein in its formulations and objectives when measured with Einstein's writing and statements throughout his life. Up to the time of his death, the undiluted message revealed by Einstein was that of man's posture in the world community, the shrinking globe as evinced by the advent of advanced technology, the potentially destructive nature of much of that technology, and the vital need to achieve a foothold for the preservation of peace through international law. As he moved closer to his death in 1955, Einstein's focus became more centralized on one basic objective—the creation of an international body designed to preserve peaceful order in a troubled world community. In order to achieve such an objective, Einstein would ruefully lament, it would be necessary for individuals to sacrifice a measure of national sovereignty to secure a desired international result. His pessimism, as displayed in letter after letter to fellow peace activists, resulted from what he perceived as great reluctance on the part of citizens of individual nations to grasp the total picture. Just as Einstein realized during the turbulent period surrounding World War One from his vantage point in a militantly nationalistic Germany that Europe was becoming a shrinking continent and that war could be circumvented by the concerted action of a League of Europeans, by the mid-fifties he looked at an entire globe that had been reduced in size by the wave of advancing technology. His response to the ugly specter of nuclear war was accordingly the same as his response to Europe's travails in World War One, only on a broadened scale. Concerted action was more necessary than ever through what he viewed as the only feasible vehicle, a vitally functioning world body in which nations would willingly accede to a diminution of sovereignty in pursuit of a broader purpose, that of international order.

So on the one side Albert Einstein remained that rarity of human beings, an international citizen with a world view who always looked beyond chauvinistic considerations. On the other he was also a Jew, a heritage he regarded with pride.

Two factors caused Einstein to become more amenable to the Zionist viewpoint, generating a departure from his 1911 posture that Zionism embodied a dream rather than a tangible practical objective. In 1917, the Balfour Declaration was issued, being a statement by the British foreign minister that His Majesty's Government looked with favor upon the creation of a Jewish homeland in Palestine and would use its best efforts to bring about such an objective. The second factor was more personal for Einstein, a visceral concern for his fellow Jews in the wake of firsthand observation. When he moved from Switzerland to Berlin, he observed anti-Semitism at work, about which he stated that young Jews were being prevented from moving up the ladder of society. Until that time, Einstein had maintained there was "nothing that called forth any Jewish sentiments in me."[6]

The responsibility of recruiting Einstein to Zionism fell to Kurt Blumenfeld, who met with him in 1919. According to Blumenfeld, despite Einstein's scientific eminence, at the time that he was initially recruited to the Zionist cause, major worldwide response to his persona and ideals had not yet commenced on any notable scale. When Zionism was emphasized as a national movement, Einstein responded by stating it was not necessarily a good idea to remove Jews from their spiritual calling. He wondered aloud whether, as a result of a religious tradition that had evolved outside Palestine, Jews had become too estranged from the country and country life. He pointed out to Blumenfeld that an innate spirituality could have been the likely catalyst that had resulted in so many scientific accomplishments by Jews. He therefore could not help but be troubled by Zionism's emphasis on nation building by taking Jews from other regions, including Europe, out of their natural habitat and making farmers and laborers out of them.

A few days later, when Einstein met again with Blumenfeld, he told him that Hermann Struck, the etcher, had tried to interest him in the Bible and the Jewish religion but that he had declined to pursue such an interest, explaining that he did not know about his religious feelings, that he had always felt comfortable in knowing what he must do, and that he was in no further need of inner fortification.

Shortly thereafter, Einstein's thoughts took a promising turn in Blumenfeld's favor. Blumenfeld quoted Einstein as saying:

"I am against nationalism but in favor of Zionism. The reason has become clear to me today. When a man has both arms and he is always saying I have a right arm, then he is a chauvinist. However, when the right arm is missing, then he must do something to make up for the missing limb. Therefore I am, as a human being, an opponent of nationalism. But as a Jew I am from today a supporter of the Jewish Zionist efforts."[7]

The logical apparatus of Einstein's powerful intellect continued turning the question of Zionism over in his mind. While he continued adhering to the concept of Zionism as a necessary practical reality, he parted company with those who sought to incorporate it into a grand national scheme at the expense of eliminating traditional roots.

On the question of whether or not there was an entity that one could classify as a Jewish faith, Einstein responded:

"If I catch sight of an expression like 'German citizens of Jewish faith' I cannot help smiling a little sadly. What is there to be found in this pretty label? What is Jewish faith? Does there exist a kind of unbelief by virtue of which one ceases being a Jew? There is not. But it suggests that the right people believe two things, i.e., (1) I don't wish to have anything to do with my poor (East European) Jewish brethren, and (2) I do not want to be taken for a child of my own people, but only as a member of a Jewish community."[8] Einstein went on to add that he was neither a German citizen nor a member of what could be termed a Jewish faith but that he was a Jew and happy to belong to the Jewish people, even though he did not consider them to be in any way God's elect.

To Einstein's way of thinking, a German Jew who works for the Jewish people and for the Jewish home in Palestine is as much of a German as a Jew who becomes baptized and changes his name ceases to be a Jew. He stated the crux of his belief as follows: "He who remains true to his origin, race and tradition will also remain loyal to the state of which he is a subject. He who is faithless to the one will also be faithless to the other."[9]

Although many looked upon the Zionist goal as embodying a Jewish political state, Einstein saw the fruition of the Zionist goal in cultural means. As late as 1938, he wrote that the value of the Zionist undertaking stemmed from the cultural impact of an "educating and unifying effect on the Jews of different countries. I am not for the striving for a Jewish state, mainly because I am against the secularization (or becoming worldly) of Jewry."[10]

While many Zionists were calling for mass emigration to the promised land, Einstein favored a cautious approach, recognizing the stark reality of Arab opposition. Despite his misgivings and qualifications, however, Einstein's support of Zionism increased in the period immediately following World War One. He recoiled at the humiliations being accorded to Jews from the east at the hands of Berliners. The recently successful upheaval in Russia and the acquisition of power on the part of the Bolsheviks through revolution prompted displays of anti-Semitism on the part of many of the German populace in that the Russian Revolution was perceived as having a Jewish influence.

Under the prodding of German Zionist Kurt Blumenfeld, Einstein agreed to go to America in 1921 with Chaim Weizmann, the most visible figure in the world Zionist movement, for purposes of raising funds for a projected American Hebrew University. Through the efforts of Weizmann and Einstein, among others, the goal became reality, and the institution still functions under the name of Brandeis University.

Men of vision such as Einstein see problems well in advance of even the most generally well-informed members of the populace. From the very outset, while committing himself to the Zionist cause, he was able to observe potential danger signals from an important quarter. At a time when General Edmund Allenby's victories in the Middle East were establishing British hegemony in the area as Turkish troops were driven into retreat, the principal focus on the part of Zionists was concentrated on developing a favorable influence on the British. The most significant movement in that direction was the Balfour Declaration of 1917. Einstein complained that too much emphasis was being placed on dealing with the British and not enough on dealing with the Arabs. At a time when Jews were smarting over confrontations with Arabs in Palestine, Einstein preached reconciliation, concluding that unless the Jews were capable of achieving peace with Arab forces in the area, the British could be expected to drop their support of their cause.

In a letter of November 25, 1929, to Chaim Weizmann, Einstein sounded a prophetic note: "Should we be able to find a way to honest cooperation and honest pacts with the Arabs, then we have learned absolutely nothing during our 2,000 years of suffering, and deserve all that will come to us."[11]

This farsighted man of vision recognized the importance of bipartisan cooperation between Jews and Arabs in the region. He knew that unless a way could be found to bring about a proper measure of conciliation, then strife would have to inevitably result because each side felt a strong natural bond with the land it occupied. Therefore without a proper measure of understanding, strife would be the inevitable result, as has been exemplified graphically in the more than six decades that have elapsed since Einstein's letter was written.

Many Zionists disagreed with Einstein's position, feeling that Arab provocations had generated appropriate responses on their part. Einstein, in the manner of the pacifist, was willing to overlook provocations of the moment as he looked at what he deemed to be the total picture. Violence would beget violence, and the longer and more intense such conflict became, the harder it would be for the divergent forces to lay down their arms and achieve a peaceful solution in the interests of both.

At the advent of the 1930s, however, whatever differences Einstein had with certain people in the Zionist movement receded as he saw a sharp rise of anti-Semitism occurring in Europe. Concurrent with that rise was the appearance of ominous war clouds, which would ultimately plunge the world into armed conflict.

For Einstein it was a time to make a statement and identify with his group, so on the evening of January 29, 1930, he appeared at a Berlin synagogue and played his violin in a white skullcap to raise contributions for a Jewish community welfare center.

As the perilous thirties unfolded, the sensitive pacifist and quiet, unassuming man of science had every right to feel as if the whole world was closing in on him. As the conflict in the European theater grew grimmer and the onrushing march of Hitler's forces became deafening, Einstein, like so many German intellectuals both Jewish and Gentile, saw the ugly, approaching specter and left the country.

When Einstein arrived in America, he fell into an acutely sensitive category as the best-known scientist in the world in a period in which technological advancements would push humanity to new heights of punishing devastation in pursuit of military victories.

Here was a man who had opposed World War One and had spent much of his time during that conflict crisscrossing Europe and participating in the vast, pacifist intellectual underground, taking pride in the numerous messages he had succeeded in smuggling into prisons where so many outspoken opponents of the war had been incarcerated.

Here was a renowned pacifist who said he had come by his own feelings not by intellectual analysis but by instinct. He simply could not bear to think of killing a human being.

Now he saw an increasingly troubled world. As the crushing surge of Hitler and his allies continued, the agonizing question surfaced in Einstein's mind as to whether pacifism was the answer. What if the Third Reich were to swallow up mankind itself? What if, after the smoke of battle cleared, amid the destructive rubble of war, humanity found itself stripped of hope and meaning and forced to endure whatever grand scheme Hitler and his henchmen concocted, with total discipline enforced by gun or bayonet?

On the other side of the coin, there was the manifest reality that with technological advancements having reached the point they then occupied, a war would render more cumulative destructiveness than had all previous conflicts combined.

By the summer of 1939, after Einstein had spent better than five years in the United States and was firmly established at Princeton University, his main concern was in his own research and his attempt to develop a unified field theory. His mind had shifted away from contemporary physics problems, but it was Leo Szilard, a noted Hungarian émigré who had previously taught at the University of Berlin and had known Einstein in Europe, who brought him into immediate touch with the present.[12]

Working with Enrico Fermi at Columbia University, where Szilard enjoyed guest status in performing laboratory experiments in physics, Szilard established that in the course of releasing vast amounts of energy through nuclear fission, extra neutrons were emitted that might be capable of producing a chain reaction. When this discovery was linked to the possibility that uranium could be used as an explosive to liberate a million times as much energy as any known explosive, the stark potential would then exist to construct a superinstrument of warfare, an atomic bomb.

Amid such apprehensive speculation there existed highly disturbing information on the world scene. Germany had seized control of Czechoslovakia in the spring of 1939, and it refused to sell to other countries of the world any of the uranium it garnered from that source. They also existed the very real possibility that Germany would seek to tap the vast potentials of the world's richest uranium source, the fertile Union Minière mining deposits of Belgium.

Szilard's words doubtlessly reverberated like a stinging slap. If Germany seized control of the world's uraniumn deposits and simultaneously achieved a successful scientific result by developing an atomic bomb, the entire world would be at its mercy. The grand design of Hitler would then have a strong likelihood of achievement. Einstein also realized the awesome potential of science in his native land of Germany, and no doubt this record of impressive achievement made the sense of urgency even more paramount.

After much discussion over the wisest course of action to pursue, it was ultimately decided that two letters would be written—one to the Belgian government warning of the dangerous consequences of Germany's acquiring significant amounts of uranium, and one to President Franklin D. Roosevelt delineating the nature of the threat to the United States as well as the rest of mankind should a German scientific achievement of such magnitude be realized.

On the question of providing the means of getting the president's ear on such a vital matter, a New York friend of Szilard's, Dr. Gustav Stolper, an economist who was a German refugee and a former member of the Reichstag, recommended that they consult Alexander Sachs, a prominent economist and a close confidant of Roosevelt's.

On the subject of submitting a letter to the Belgian government,

Szilard sent out a proposed draft to Einstein, but there the process apparently ended. It is to be assumed that Szilard and Einstein decided instead to concentrate their focus on making contact with President Roosevelt.

With respect to Alexander Sachs, he agreed to deliver a letter into the president's hands once he had been provided with it. The process was completed after Szilard winnowed down a rough draft from Einstein. After receiving Einstein's signature, it was then delivered to Sachs.

The letter, bearing the date of August 2, was not actually delivered to Roosevelt until October 11. During the nervous interval between its receipt by Sachs and its delivery to the president, Szilard mournfully informed Einstein that it was possible that Sachs was not their man and that he might be useless to them. Sachs later explained the delay as resulting from his fear that, should he press Roosevelt at a time when he was preoccupied with the outbreak of the war and the neutrality laws, the letter would be passed down to a subordinate. Instead, Sachs felt that it was worth the risk to wait until he had time to make the proper personal contact with Roosevelt.

In his meeting with President Roosevelt, Sachs not only read the Einstein communication but also read one of his own stressing the need for funds to finance a much-needed project.

"Alex, what you are after is to see that the Nazis don't blow us up,"[13] was Roosevelt's response.

By evening of that say day, a committee had been instituted headed by Dr. Lyman J. Briggs, director of the U.S. Bureau of Standards, for the purpose of investigating the potentialities of nuclear fission.

When efforts failed to transpire at the brisk pace that Einstein, Szilard, and Sachs had envisioned, it was decided that fresh impetus was needed. A letter was sent off under Einstein's signature to Sachs, with the purpose of having him then transmit it to Roosevelt. The urgency of the matter was stressed by Einstein's reference to the research efforts in the uranium field by chemists at the Kaiser Wilhelm Institute of the Institute of Chemistry in Germany.

With Sachs generating additional pressures that were sparked by the second Einstein letter, the Briggs committee was placed under the control of the National Defense Research Committee, which Roosevelt created, and a special committee of the National Academy of Sciences set up to inform the government of any developments in nuclear fission that might affect defense. This effort in turn led to the creation of the

Manhattan Project and the development of the atomic bombs, which were used on Japan.

It was the fear that the Germans would first acquire an atomic bomb that catalyzed Einstein into action, and yet, in retrospect, the confirmed pacifist had misgivings toward the end of his life.

"I made one great mistake in my life—when I signed the letter to President Roosevelt recommending that atom bombs be made," he told Nobel Prize–winning biochemist Linus Pauling, "but there was some justification—the danger that the Germans would make them."[14]

So World War Two was fought, the Atomic Age was born, and Einstein was left to feel the cutting edge that a supersensitive man like himself would encounter in responding to the destruction of war. One notable point of sorrow was the grave tragedy encountered by his fellow Jews in the Holocaust, as the unceasing boot of the Third Reich sought to exterminate the Jewish population of Europe.

The man who had supported the Zionist cause since 1919 saw the dream of a Jewish state become a reality with the creation of Israel in 1948. Though he was coaxed by friends to emigrate there, particularly when his disenchantments with the spread of the Cold War and the ugly specter of McCarthyism and its threat to individual liberties reached a peak, he deferred, deciding to remain in Princeton, New Jersey, to pursue his scientific studies.

When Chaim Weizmann, Einstein's old colleague in the Zionist movement and Israel's first president, died in 1952, the offer was made to Einstein by Abba Eban, Israeli U.S. ambassador, to accept the position. It was explained to Einstein that the position of president was largely a ceremonial office in Israel and that every effort would be extended to provide him with facilities of the highest order to carry out his important scientific research.

Einstein declined the position, explaining that as a scientist he had spent his entire life dealing with objective matters and therefore lacked the aptitude and experience to deal with people and to exercise functions, and he cited his advancing age as well.

"I am the more distressed over the circumstances [of declining the position] because my relationship to the Jewish people has become my strongest human bond," Einstein noted, "ever since I became fully aware of our precarious situation among the nations of the world."[15]

While Einstein continued registering support for Israel, he remained mindful of the deeply rooted antagonisms between Arabs and Israelis, fully recognizing the inherent dangers not only for the Middle East but the entire world. In a letter to Zvi Lurie, a prominent member of the

Jewish Agency in Israel, he stated, "The most important aspect of our [Israeli] policy must be our ever-present, manifest desire to institute complete equality for the Arab citizens living in our midst, and to appreciate the inherent difficulties of their present situation . . ."[16]

The critical nature of Middle East politics in 1955 had made such a profound impact on peace lover Einstein's mind that, when he was asked by the Israeli consul in New York to make a statement on the occasion of the forthcoming anniversary of Israel's independence, he agreed, but with one proviso. He was asked to write about the cultural and scientific accomplishments of Israel, with particular emphasis on the peaceful uses of atomic energy. Einstein suggested that, in view of Israeli-Arab difficulties, a statement focusing on that overriding issue would be far timelier than to write about scientific achievements and would exert a greater impact on public opinion.

Ambassador Eban and Consul Reuven Dafni visited Einstein at Princeton to confer with him about his statement, which was to be delivered over an Israeli television and radio network. When he felt that further consultation was needed, consul Dafni revisited him two days later.

The notes Einstein made on that occasion are not available, and two hours after the meeting he was fatally stricken.

During the last four days of Einstein's life, he ordered to his bedside the notes he had compiled concerning his statement to the people of Israel, hoping that he might finish a responsibility he deemed to be of great importance.

At his death shortly after midnight on April 18, 1955, he left just one page of notes he had made prior to his final meeting with Consul Dafni.

He wrote about the conflict between Israel and Egypt, stating that while some might consider it to be an insignificant problem, such was far from the case. "In matters concerning truth and justice there can be no distinction between big problems and small,"[17] he explained.

After then discussing the problems existing between the communist and noncommunist world, he devoted what proved to be the final survivable paragraph of his life to the question of conflict, a problem that had concerned him with unceasing devotion throughout his life, and particularly with the advent of atomic power.

He stated the following:

In essence, the conflict that exists today is no more than an old-style struggle for power, once again presented to mankind in semireligious trappings. The difference is that, this time, the development of atomic power has imbued the struggle with a ghostly character; for both parties know and admit that, should the quarrel deteriorate into actual war, mankind is doomed. Despite this knowledge, statesmen in responsible positions on both sides continue to employ the well-known technique of seeking to intimidate and demoralize the opponent by marshaling superior military strength. They do so even though such a policy entails the risk of war and doom. Not one statesman in a position of responsibility has dared to pursue the only course that holds out any promise of peace, the course of supranational security, since for a statesman to follow such a course would be tantamount to political suicide. Political passions, once they have been fanned into flame, exact their victims . . ."[18]

The combination of a commanding intellect and acute sensitivity enabled Einstein to see the world stripped bare to its roots, like a tree shorn of its leaves in autumn. He saw his concept of relativity utilized and expanded until man developed the capability of destroying the planet, which he mourned greatly. As a Jew, Einstein identified closely with the plight of his people, particularly during the dark days of World War Two, when some six million of them along with an equivalent number of non-Jews lost their lives in Nazi death camps. And then, once a Jewish nation had become a realized entity with the creation of Israel, a conflict immediately developed pitting the Israelis against Arab forces.

Einstein realized only too clearly that the world had become a tinderbox, a dry forest in which, by striking an ill-timed match, everything would go up in smoke. He had lived through two destructive world conflicts, had seen Arabs and Isralis thrown immediately into battle after the creation of the nation of Israel, and wished with every ounce of his being for a world devoid of strife.

He recognized the potential for world conflict in the Middle East, given its strategic geopolitical location and the deeply rooted antagonisms of the various contesting groups.

So it was only natural that at the time of his death, this perceptive man of the world would be working on a message to the Israeli people emphasizing the danger of war and stressing the imperative of developing means of consultation and conciliation in place of the time-tested and flaw-ridden concept of confrontation.

The unfinished sentence of the statement Einstein was diligently working on at the time of his death carries a resounding ironic note. It embodies the unresolved nature of world conflict and the crying urgency of bringing diplomacy to bear in the world's tinderbox of the Middle East.

# 2

# The Roots of Zionism

"What has gotten into him?" was the concerned question that reverberated throughout the Jewish community in Vienna.

Whenever an individual engages in an act that is seemingly out of character with past activities, tongues are certain to wag, and concern will be raised.

At any rate, Theodor Herzl's conduct was being questioned in mid-February of 1896, and many a Jewish friend and colleague wondered whether he had taken leave of his senses.

The subject of worried concern on the part of the Jewish community in Vienna was a pamphlet being displayed in the windows of the stores of Breitenstein, Viennese booksellers. The pamphlet was entitled *Der Judenstaat* and would be published in English under the title of *The Jewish State: An Attempt at a Modern Solution of the Jewish Question.*[1]

The basis for concern was not that such a pamphlet had been written. There were polemicists in Vienna as well as other cities of Eastern Europe, and had one of them written *Der Judenstaat,* it is doubtful that shock waves would have either resulted or most certainly if they had, been of the same degree of magnitude.

What caused shock waves to reverberate throughout the Jewish community of Vienna was not the nature of the work, but the identity of the author.

Theodor Herzl was an example of someone who had been fully assimilated into the fabric of Viennese culture. Therefore, the question

17

immediately arose as to why he would rock the boat by writing the kind of pamphlet that he had. Another question was also being asked, one that made those who knew him wonder even more strongly if Herzl had not taken leave of his senses. Not only in their eyes was there no reason for a successfully assimilated product of Viennese culture such as Theodor Herzl to run the risk of incurring displeasure by publishing such a controversial work, but what puzzled them even more, particularly those who knew Herzl well, was why he had chosen to make a sudden quantum leap into the realm of politics, a world that had theretofore been professionally alien to him.

Herzl, who was born in Budapest in 1860 and moved in his youth with his family to Vienna, had experienced a culturally assimilated background in Vienna. His father was in the clothing business and had provided young Herzl with not only a comfortable living standard but a good education as well, which culminated in a law degree with a specialty in Roman law and acceptance into the Viennese bar.

He practiced law for a short time but ultimately opted for a career in the field that had always been his first love, that of writing. Even during the years when he was studying law, Herzl had found the time to write plays and essays. Now he turned his efforts into the literary and journalistic domains with great vigor.

In the realm of playwriting, he achieved only a modicum of success, a reality that would frustrate him throughout his life, in that it was his unyielding belief that his preponderant gifts were literary and that it was the public's as well as his own misfortune that they had not been sufficiently appreciated. In the journalistic sphere, however, he achieved appreciable recognition, carving out a niche by free-lancing for a leading Berlin newspaper and later by contributing articles to Viennese journals.

In October 1891, a pivotal event in Herzl's short but highly eventful life occurred. He was appointed Paris correspondent for *Neue Freie Presse*. To a true cosmopolitan such as the Vienna-bred Herzl, such an assignment filled him with a flourish of creative zest. Here was a chic and elegant city at a moment of cultural zenith being made available to an enterprising young journalist to whom the arts and the overall question of culture assumed the highest importance.

Given the aforementioned, it is understandable that Herzl's sudden launch into the field of political pamphleteering produced shock waves among those who knew him. Although most of Herzl's friends during his early and formative years were Jewish and he was known to have resigned from Albia, the student fraternity to which he belonged in college, because it was about to embrace anti-Semitism, there was nothing in his subsequent background to provide even a hint of the spark that needed to surface within Herzl to motivate him to write *Der Judenstaat*. Hence, the recurring question "What got into Herzl?" which reverberated throughout Viennese Jewish society was logical and deserved a similarly reasoned response.

The catalytic springboard that prompted Herzl to take a long and scrutinizing look into his Jewish heritage and from which the correlative question "Where do the Jews go from here?" arose resulted from an event that occurred in Paris while he was there and that preoccupied the hearts and souls of seekers of justice throughout the world.

The trial of Alfred Dreyfus, a captain in the French Army who was accused of treason, attracted worldwide attention. Dreyfus, of Jewish descent, was convicted in a trial that had demonstrated blatant disregard for justice, substituting for it a glutting dose of prejudice.

Herzl watched the trial in horror, unable to believe what he was seeing, and the resulting outbursts of anti-Semitism that he witnessed in Paris as an immediate outgowth of the trial sickened his sensibilities even more.

The jolting shock, the painful blow to Herzl's sensibilities, stemmed from his belief that he had been working in the city that represented the very pinnacle of European sophistication and tolerance. It was one thing for Jews to experience difficulties in places such as Berlin, Germany, his own Vienna, and throughout Russia, with periodic keen outbursts of anti-Semitism to send his people scurrying underground in a state of uncertainty. These incidents were tragic, but they were at least expected. On the other hand, however, to see these very same destructive forces take root and flourish in presumably liberal, supposedly culturally advanced Paris made one thing painfully clear to the journalist: Jews were not safe from anti-Semitic outbursts, in Paris or anywhere else.

The Dreyfus trial brought home with ringing impact on Herzl the stark reality that, although the Jews might have been liberated from a ghetto existence in Paris, they remained a separate and frequently ostracized group. He learned that there was indeed a discernible correlation between the physical ghetto, the shackles of which had been removed, and a more deeply rooted, less tangible but clearly real psychic ghetto.

After Herzl had spent some time grappling with the realities of the Dreyfus case and the painful surge of anti-Semitism that followed it, one all-embracing idea began to take shape in his mind. The only way for Jews to become truly free, the only means of throwing off the shackles of both the physical and the psychical ghettos, lay in eliminating world Jewry. The only way to achieve that objective stemmed from establishing fresh roots in a new environment by locating Zion somewhere where the old Jewish heritage that had been lying dormant through ghettoization and periodic attempts at assimilation, none of which ever seemed to bear ultimate fruit, could flourish.

Writing with a sense of moral outrage and embracing an impassioned idealism as he polemically lobbied for a cause near and dear to him, Theodor Herzl believed that his message was an original one. Despite his apparent absence of historical research prior to his undertaking, had he been thinking in a universal sociological context, Herzl would have realized that the passionate Zionist strains released within him, catalyzed by the Dreyfus case and its aftermath through the writing of *Der Judenstaat*, had already been experienced by others extending far back in time. The reason was simple. Given a recurring set of experiences in numerous social settings, coupled with a common heritage along with concurrent acceptance of and studies in Judaism, it was virtually inevitable that others would fathom beliefs identical to those Herzl forcefully articulated in *Der Judenstaat*.

For at least twenty-one centuries, Jews have been living in Europe, and for a period nearly that long, organized Jewish congregations were to be found there. The Zionist concept of returning to the Palestinian homeland, which was activated in political terms by Theodor Herzl at the close of the nineteenth century, was a response to the Diaspora, or dispersion, of Jews away from their native homeland to other nations, notably ones in Europe.

Scholars have pinpointed the beginnings of the vast initial Diaspora as stemming from the destruction of the second Temple by Titus in 70 C.E. The Jews initially fled to Egypt and all the other countries in the Middle East, then across North Africa to Spain. Even though they settled in nations such as Ethiopia, India, and China as well, the main body of the migrating waves of Jews located predominantly in Eastern Europe, with a lesser number settling in Central Europe. And though a small remnant remained in Palestine, Europe became the new center of Jewish population and culture. It remained so until the time of the Holocaust of World War Two.

Certain scholars believe that the Jewish dispersion was a natural phenomenon and reject the Diaspora theory as myth, contending that the majority of Jews voluntarily left Palestine before the destruction of the Temple to live as Roman citizens in the Roman cities. Some sources maintain that one out of ten Roman citizens was Jewish.

All the same, whether one chooses to believe the Diaspora account or not, the ultimate result of the massive Jewish migration set into motion elements of frustration and alienation, in which the settlers incurred the dual sufferings of physical and psychical ghettoization.

An example of the stern reality encountered by Jews in Europe was provided by the late-nineteenth-century writings of Sholom Aleichem. His story "The Town of the Little People" was about the Jewish people of the Russian town of Kasrilevka and the great pride they took in their cemetery. Not only did the cemetery contain the remains of Jews embracing all walks of life from the town, but the dominant theme of Aleichem's story was that the cemetery became the town's social vortex, the people's springboard to pride and identity within Kasrilevka. Why would a cemetery be placed on such a plateau? Because it was seen as the piece of land of which the Jews were indisputably in charge. Since the grass and the trees and the air unquestionably belonged to them, they consequently felt a measure of freedom there that was not present anywhere else.[2]

Had such a story been written by an anti-Semite who was eager to level literary barbs at Jews, then one could pinpoint the author's motivation as thoroughly negative and could either dispute the conclusions or at least consider the distinct possibility of exaggeration. Rather than being anti-Semitic or unsympathetic to the Jewish cause, however, the author, Sholem Aleichem, was known as the "Jewish Mark Twain," noted, as was Twain, for combining trenchant humor along with social perception. Aleichem was a superb humorist with a deeply abiding reverence for his fellow Jews.

Rather than writing about the hapless and luckless encounters of his fellow Jews, Aleichem was doing no more and no less than any perceptive writer whose works are destined to endure, such as his have. He was recording what was transpiring around him, with pen and paper serving as a microscopic camera's eye.

One recurring hero of Aleichem's is the luckless schlemiel, a Yiddish word describing an unlucky bungler or chump. The literary critic Ruth Wisse, in discussing the presence and the impact of the schlemiel in Jewish literary works by Aleichem as well as others, pictures the schlemiel as a "challenge to the accepted notion of heroism."[3] In that it was within the nature of the schlemiel to question the feasibility of traditional heroism and subdue any desires within that direction, Wisse detected in this quality a unique kind of strength.

Ruth Wisse's theory of the schlemiel as a "challenge to the accepted notion of heroism" sounds much like that recent vogue of cinema activity devoted to the phenomenon of the antihero. The cinematic concept of the antihero as depicted on the screen most notably by Paul Newman and Steve McQueen revolves around somebody standing outside the traditional mainstream of life. In this respect, the antihero has something in common with the schlemiel of Aleichem and other Jewish literature.

The main disparity between the antihero so ably presented on the screen by Paul Newman, Steve McQueen, and others and the schlemiel of Jewish literature is evidenced by the manner in which each responds to the outsider status into which the character has been placed.

In the case of the cinematic antihero, one finds a life immersed in struggle. The outsider, despite recognizing the impossibility of the situation, vows nonetheless to buck the odds and battle tenaciously. The result is that the antihero is ultimately overcome by the impossible odds and loses, but not before waging a furious struggle.

The response of the schlemiel to being relegated to the role of the outsider was markedly different. In place of launching a struggle against the numerically overwhelming forces of society, the schlemiel instead accepts the role of lucklessness, even injecting humor into the plight.

A particularly interesting dichotomy manifested on numerous occasions by Jews in Europe was to portray the image of the luckless schlemiel in society and then, in the privacy of one's living quarters or in the confines of ghetto society when dealing strictly with Jews, of embracing traditional teaching concepts of Judaism. The result was the creation of the quasi-schizophrenic existence of the luckless, plodding schlemiel on the one hand and the alert and proud manifester of a long cultural tradition, of which Jews remained proud, on the other. The developing pattern of Jews who perform the role of the schlemiel for outward consumption while pridefully extolling a cultural tradition in their own domain came about over a lengthy period of time. Like any cultural development's impact on people, so much was dependent on conditioning and on the manner of treatment directed toward Jews as minority members of the cities and nations in which they resided.

At the beginning of the nineteenth century, there were approximately two and a half million Jews in the world. Of this number, roughly 90 percent lived in Europe.

Despite the fact that some prominent Jewish banking families prospered enormously in early nineteenth-century Europe, the most notable example being the Rothschilds, significant changes did not occur within the ranks of German Jews until the great influx of young Jews into professional ranks.

As Jews began to ease up the ladder and move from small towns into the mainstream of city life to prosper and become intrinsic parts of the cultural fabric in Germany, a nation containing a large Jewish population, some virtually inevitable sociological reactions began to occur. In order to prosper in predominantly Christian Germany, a nation with a long and proud cultural tradition of its own, it was necessary for Jews to willingly accept at least some form of cultural assimilation. As this occurred, certain old bonds with the Jewish tradition of their forefathers weakened.

The process of dilution of old ties was understandable in view of several circumstances. The first factor was that of pressure being directed from without. If non-Jews were to allow Jews to be absorbed into the social and economic mainstream of German society, then, according to their viewpoint, it was not asking too much to expect Jews in return to consider themselves to be Germans first and to de-emphasize, if not renounce altogether, their ties with their ancient cultural past. A second element militating toward dilution or rejection of old Jewish ties stemmed from the fact that the greater the period of time that passed and the longer that Jews remained a part of German culture, the more distant their old ties became. As families from generation to generation fought for economic and social recognition, the more intense the focus inevitably became to be absorbed into the predominantly Christian society and away from their traditional roots, which correspondingly atrophied. A third reason was that Judaism as a religion had little if any attraction for Western-educated people in general, a phenomenon that had a cultural impact on the mind of particularly successful Jews who had worked their way into the mainstream of German society. The last movement that had seized the attention of the Jewish world to any discernible extent was the messianism of Shabtai Zvi and his pupils, which had long before faded from the scene.

Another historical event that produced a major impact on Jews both in Germany and throughout Europe was the Enlightenment, which changed the face of Europe intellectually and culturally with its flowering of philosophy, literature, and the arts. The more solidly that the impact of the Enlightenment was felt throughout Europe, the greater the pressure that was brought to bear on Jews to part company with their traditional religious and cultural roots in the interest of assimilation.

On the surface, the idea of the Enlightenment's working as a negative factor against the Jews might seem puzzling. After all, the most highly visible of the Enlightenment thinkers was Voltaire, whose acerbic wit was frequently directed at traditional Christian thought, the prevalent religious concept of European society. Even if Judaism were to catch flak as a result of the Enlightenment's propensity toward the secular, it would have seemed to make logical sense that Jews, with considerably lesser visibility than their Christian counterparts, would escape close scrutiny through a heavier emphasis being placed in another direction. In addition, because much of the reaction to Enlightenment thought involved concentrating less on the religious and more on the secular, it might have been expected that Jews would be under attack to a lesser rather than a greater extent.

In the resulting intellectual brushfire started by Voltaire and others, Christianity did receive wounds, particularly in its more traditional forms, but on careful scrutiny it is readily comprehensible to see why Jews suffered even more.

In Germany, what with the careful scrutiny being placed on previously accepted modes of Christian thought and in the onrushing tide toward secularism, there was more emphasis on the great secular thinkers and artists who excelled in Germany and had filled the German people with sturdy nationalistic pride. There were towering philosophers such as Kant and Hegel. There was the great playwright, statesman, and thinker Goethe, along with the awesome presence of that brooding composer of towering genius, the indomitable Beethoven.

The presence of these greats interwoven into the fabric of German culture gave its largely Christian population a philosophical underpinning in response to the great upheaval created by Enlightenment thought.

On the other hand, what did the Jews have to offer on their own behalf? The ancient rabbinical tradition, extending back to a distant region from a distant period in time and devoid of cultural chauvinism and immediacy, left Jews an all too frequently vulnerable target for derision.

It must be remembered as well that, whereas Voltaire and others had an impact on the thinking of Christians, particularly those given to intellectual secularization, it was therefore understandable that certain

Jews, particularly among the more successful and assimilated, would also react when their Jewish religious roots were concerned.

Goethe stated that Jews could not be given a part in a civilization whose very origins they negated, and the philosopher Fichte propounded an even stronger viewpoint, declaring his opposition to making Jews full-fledged citizens on the rationale that they constituted a state within a state and were permeated with a burning hatred of all other people. He concluded by asserting that he would instead rather have sent them back to Palestine or cut off their heads overnight and replaced them with non-Jewish heads.

During the early part of the nineteenth century, all the great hostesses of Berlin became Christians. Even the daughter of Moses Mendelssohn, the famous German Hebrew theologian, became a Christian.

Perhaps the most interesting account of a religious transformation during the Enlightenment period is represented by the Levi family of Germany.

Herschel Levi's father, along with his grandfather, had been rabbis in the Rhineland. Their entire lives had been spent within the sheltered walls of the Jewish community as they sought to fortify themselves against the often hostile attitudes of the Christian community.

The intellectual upheaval of the Enlightenment precipitated stirrings within Levi, however, and after reading Voltaire along with certain of his German disciples, he became committed to the secular modes of thought embodied in the Enlightenment period. Eventually he cut himself off from his traditional Jewish roots, even from his own family. He changed his surname, developed a new retinue of friends and associates, and achieved a modest level of success in his law practice until he was confronted by a dilemma outside his realm of control.

With the passage of the anti-Jewish laws in Germany, Herschel Levi saw his livelihood spontaneously cut adrift.

By then Levi had abandoned his ties with Judaism, embraced mildly deist theological views, and no doubt was able to make an easy and relatively smooth transition as he embraced the somewhat enlightened Lutheranism of his Prussian neighbors.

Herschel Levi officially embraced Lutheranism in 1817, just one year before his wife gave birth to a son. Relations between father and son were, from all accounts, uniformly intimate despite the markedly dissimilar makeups of the two individuals. The father was decidedly tranquil. Though well educated, he had never had a strong liking for social causes. His ideal eminence of state was Frederick the Great, an enlightened prince who shared the same revulsion for ideologues as

Napoleon Bonaparte. The son was mercurial in temperament and possessed an intellect rooted in intense curiosity.

The mild-mannered father changed his name to Heinrich Marx, and his son, with his insatiable intellectual curiosity and mercurial temperament, went on to become the best-known political revolutionary in the world today.

An analysis of the numerous writings on Karl Marx reveals a sharply antagonistic view of religion in general and of Judaism in particular. It is eminently plausible that the process his father underwent to achieve equality in a society in which Jews were legally and socially inferiors left a permanent bitter taste in his mouth.

The bitterness that the conversion process of his father generated within Karl Marx was by no means an isolated case. Throughout Europe, Jews, as a means of achieving legal and social equality, reacted by renouncing the beliefs handed down to them. Even in instances in which great success resulted, there remained an inextinguishable psychological burden that was never totally surmounted.

In England, Benjamin Disraeli converted from Judaism to Episcopalianism. In spite of his celebrated success in which he vaulted from a prominently read novelist to the position of prime minister of Great Britain, he remained sensitively aware of his peculiar status throughout his life, along with the fact that he remained a target to be used by his enemies as a result of the decision he had made.

Disraeli, despite his conversion, periodically revealed visions of the grandeur of the Jews' leading them toward a great future while believing that Jews should be given full civic rights on the basis that they represented a superior race.

Another Jew by birth, the famous socialist thinker Ferdinand Lassalle, expressed a vituperative viewpoint, referring to the Jews as "the degenerate descendants of a great tradition who had acquired the mentality of slaves during centuries of servitude." He expressed with pungent hostility his hatred of the people from whom he descended, stating to them, "Cowardly people, you don't deserve a better lot; you were born to be servants."

At the very time when Karl Marx was seeking through his writings to awaken the workers of the world by encouraging them to launch a communistic revolution to overthrow their masters, Lassalle was leading his own socialist movement. Marx, the revolutionary, was disposed to loathe socialist thinkers like Lassalle, who favored a more gradualist approach. It was therefore far from unusual that he would sharply attack Lassalle in an exchange of letters with his cohort and financial benefactor Friedrich Engels. What makes the attack psychologically revealing is that Marx, the descendant of Jewish rabbis, saw fit to attack Lassalle in vehement personal terms on the basis of his Jewish roots. Marx lacerated Lassalle to Engels as a "Jewish Nigger" and attributed flaws to the socialist thinker that included lack of tact, vanity, and impatience, along with other "typically Jewish" traits of character.

The conscientious reader is compelled to stand back in a state of numbed bewilderment about the circuitous routes taken by Jews suffering identity crises in the ideologically tortuous setting of nineteenth-century Germany in particular and other parts of Europe in general.

Here was Karl Marx, descended from rabbis, denouncing Lassalle as a "Jewish Nigger" while this same Lassalle had referred to Jewish descendants bearing the same roots as his own as "cowardly people," terminology so disparaging that it could have come from Joseph Goebbels's Third Reich propaganda machine.

The Jewish question disturbed Marx to the point where he felt compelled to write about it, no doubt hoping that in the process the long shadow he continued to acutely feel would recede into the past.

In 1844, Marx wrote an essay in the form of a rebuttal to a series of articles by Bruno Bauer on the subject of the Jewish question. Bauer's position held that the Jews lagged one stage behind Christianity in historical progression. His conclusion was that Jews needed to be baptized as a prerequisite to receiving full civil emancipation. Marx disputed Bauer's conclusion, asserting that Jews were no longer a racial or a religious entity. Remaining consistent with his view regarding exploitation of the masses through the capitalist system, Marx thereby concluded that Jews were solely an economic entity, that they had been forced into usury and other forms of negative behavior as a result of the treatment they had received within the system, and that accordingly they would be emancipated in the same manner as non-Jewish Europeans by throwing off the yoke of economic exploitation and oppression. Marx ridiculed the idea of Jews' achieving emancipation through baptism. He saw such a practice as embodying futility, an instance of trading one set of chains for another. To provide Jews with political liberties would also, in Marx's view, consist of nothing more than perpetuating the self-delusion of liberal reformers that society could be significantly improved through means less comprehensive than his own revolutionary prescription.

The dominant philosophical thinker during the period of Marx's formative years and thereafter within Germany was G. W. F. Hegel, who wrote, "Judaism was the world of the wretched, of misfortune and ugliness, a world lacking inner unity and harmony."

Marx utilized Hegel's philosophy of history to a point, then discarded his basic conclusions for a substituted series of concepts of his own. Hegel's posture was that of a historical idealist: once civilizations pass through a given series of dialectical transformations, the ultimate result is a positive absolute. Marx concluded that if Hegel's dialectical theory could be "turned on its head" and given the kind of materialistic ideological spin that his own formula would provide, then one would have a sound and workable historical framework. Through the dialectical materialism concept inherent in Marxism, the forces of history would proceed through a series of conflicts, moving from a system such as mercantilism toward capitalism, with the ultimate result being a people's revolution and the dictatorship of the proletariat through communism. The ultimate achievement of communism represented Marx's version of the Hegelian absolute.

The influence of Marx caused a variety of reaction among both Jews and non-Jews in the sensitive intellectual environment of nineteenth-century Germany and throughout the rest of Europe as well. Despite Marx's stern disavowal of any link to his Jewish roots, many in the non-Jewish world continued to see him as a Jew and criticized his thinking as exhibiting a Talmudic craftiness, which anti-Semites abhorred. Some adherents of both Jewish and non-Jewish backgrounds pointed with satisfaction to Marx as a descendant of the Jewish prophets and focused on the messianic element in Marxism. Understandably, detractors made the same arguments, but giving them a negative rather than positive interpretation.

The case of Karl Marx and the various reactions to him both positive and negative, along with Marx's own stinging disavowal of his own Jewish heritage, contributed to the pattern of confusion and uncertainty within the Jewish community in Germany. So did the confusion from other quarters involving numerous messages of disavowal by promiment individuals with Jewish roots, sometimes including vicious attacks on Judaism.

It was just such an environment, producing numerous conflicting messages on the part of Jews along with many instances of anti-Semitism generated within the majority Christian community, that caused the schlemiel character of Sholom Aleichem to wander in a state of social instability.

Given the variety of problems encountered by Jews in the Germany of the nineteenth century, it would seem inevitable that someone or some force would rise to the surface eventually to diligently labor on behalf of Jews, as was finally exemplified in the launching of the Zionist movement.

As we move further along in the nineteenth century and switch the scene of focus from Germany to Russia, the manifestation of Zionism becomes perhaps even more readily comprehensible.

Prior to 1881, there had been skirmishes in Jewish communities in Russia, most notably in Odessa in 1859 and 1871, but little significance had been attached to such clashes and they were essentially looked upon as similar in nature to others that had occurred periodically.

Beginning with the year 1881, however, pogroms became an almost permanent feature of Russian society. The sweeping transformation that caused Russia to change from a nation in which a liberal policy toward Jews prevailed to one with aggressive hostility revolved around a change of leadership. Czar Alexander I had pursued a relatively liberal policy under which Jews could enter public schools and were able to buy land and settle on it. Alexander II had abolished serfdom, and, although restrictive laws against Jews were not abolished, a spirit of tolerance pervaded the Russian landscape and Jews were hopeful that eventually full civil rights would be conferred upon them.

That hopeful optimism held by Jews that the future offered potential for improvement in their lives was quickly dashed when Alexander II was murdered. He was succeeded by Alexander III, at which point the situation turned dramatically against the Jews. In accordance with the "provisional laws" of May 1882, tens of thousands of Jews were expelled from the villages in which they had settled and also from cities outside the areas of settlement.

The pogroms that took place from April through June of 1881 following the murder of Alexander II were more vicious in nature than those that had previously been experienced. The word "pogrom" is derived from the Russian verb *pogromit,* meaning to destroy, and the forces of destruction ran amok mainly in southern Russia, in cities such as Elizavetgrad, Kiev, and Odessa, where Jews had enjoyed a greater measure of prosperity compared to Poland and White Russia. The pogroms continued in 1883 and 1884, extending into other cities as well. Jews were killed by fanatical mobs and much of their property was destroyed. Although the attacks ceased in 1884, a fresh wave surfaced two decades later, the onslaught reaching its climax in October 1905, when 810 Jews were killed in a period of twelve days in riots all over western and southern Russia.

When one analyzes the ideological uncertainty that prevailed among

Jews in Germany during the nineteenth century along with the brutality to which they were subjected in Russia in that same period, one would anticipate some form of ideological reaction within the Jewish communities of Europe. The fruition of this ideological upheaval did not occur until Theodor Herzl launched the Zionist movement, but there were two other spirited architects who had laid earlier groundwork.

Moses Hess, born in Bonn, Germany, and raised in Cologne, was a publicist by trade whose intellectual predilections led him into the sociopolitical realm. He spent a great deal of time in intellectually fertile Paris, developing a deeply rooted belief in socialism and a fervent belief that justice could be achieved on a comprehensive scale only by supplanting the institution of private property with a system in which all property reverts into public hands.

Hess's strong socialist convictions prompted him to make the acquaintance of Karl Marx in Germany, and his meeting with Marx filled him with awestruck devotion.

"He [Marx] is the greatest, perhaps the one genuine philosopher now alive, and will soon . . . draw the eyes of all Germany. . . . He combines the deepest philosophical seriousness with the most biting wit. Imagine Rousseau, Voltaire, Holbach, Lessing, Heine, and Hegel fused into one person—I say fused, not thrown together in a heap—and you have Dr. Marx."

Hess, whose own brand of socialism was a curious fusion of ardent traditional Judaism with idealist humanitarianism and Hegelian ideas, preached the primacy of economic over political factors. The concept of private property was the root of all economic evil, and the masses could never be truly emancipated until not only all private property was abolished, but also national property. Hess advocated removing national frontiers in the midst of forging a new international society structured on a rational, collectivist economic basis.

Though his belief in the abolition of private property and the creation of a collectivist society would be acceptable to Marx, there were other aspects of Hess's concepts that ran counter to Marx's stated principles. Hess was one of the utopian socialists whose beliefs were formed in Paris, a group that Marx caustically assaulted in his *Communist Manifesto* as ". . . steeped in the dew of sickly sentiment, a Philistine, foul and enervating literature."

Whereas Hess was primarily a romanticist, a believer in the goodness of humanity and in the ability of humankind to surmount its obstacles in achieving a utopian society, the coldly rational pessimist Marx saw humankind as an institution that needed to be liberated from itself. Whereas Hess took on the image of the idealistic messianic reformer, Marx was the coldly calculating social scientist who believed that sentimentality was a dangerous weakness to be avoided and sharply ridiculed.

Despite his lack of respect for Hess's beliefs, Marx nonetheless decided that his best interests could be served by utilizing to his own advantage Hess's passionate zeal for the socialist cause. It was Hess, laboring on Marx's behalf, who succeeded in motivating a group of liberal industrialists in the Rhineland to finance the publication of a radical journal containing articles on political and economic subjects that criticized the policies of the Berlin government. Published in Cologne, *Reinische Zeitung* embraced a policy supportive of the rising bourgeois class.

Moses Hess, in his role of fervent missionary, made one young convert to his cause who would eventually occupy a ranking of the first order in world revolutionary politics. It was none other than Friedrich Engels who fell under Moses Hess's influence before meeting Marx, the man whose cause he would champion both financially and polemically in the pursuit of communist revolution.

After laboring assiduously in thc socialist vineyards seeking to promote change, Hess abruptly retired from politics to devote himself to the study of natural sciences.

Ten years after his retirement from politics, in 1862 at the age of fifty, Hess unleashed a bombshell in intellectual circles by publishing a book that was to have been entitled *The Revival of Israel* but became known under the less symbolic *Rome and Jerusalem, the Last Nationality Question.*

Hess, who, unlike Marx, had been born into a family in which the Jewish tradition remained alive, began his work with an apologetic confession that he had been estranged from his people for twenty years but was eager to return. He then launched into his central treatise, the idea of a dramatic return to the Holy Land by the Jewish people to launch a new state in Palestine, which would function as a socialist entity.

In this work, Hess embraced a pessimistic view of anti-Semitism at a time when almost all of his contemporaries on the left were convinced that it was a dying institution of the old order. Hess went on to assert that the racial antagonism of the Germans toward the Jews was a deep, instinctive force that overwhelmed rational argument. In view of such profound prejudices, Hess accordingly believed that reform and assimilation designed to obliterate any outward Jewishness would not produce the desired result.

"We shall remain strangers among the nations," Hess asserted.

On the subject of the acutely sensitive racial issue, Hess believed that Germans were deeply prejudiced without even being aware of it.

As to the major difficulty confronting Jews, Hess defined it as homelessness, the remedy for which was a land of their own, specifically a return to their Palestine origins.

"Without soil a man sinks to the status of a parasite, feeding on others," Hess asserted.

Hess criticized the reformers who sought to make Judaism more broadly acceptable by seeking to merge certain of its concepts with Christianity and the kind of rationalist thought that had gained great credence during the Enlightenment period. He denounced those teachers who sought to educate intolerant Christians about Judaism, insisting that a successful synthesis in Jewish teaching could result only from being situated in a nation of their own, which they controlled politically.

Despite his boundless enthusiasm for the creation of a Jewish state, Hess adopted the conviction of a seasoned realist in conceding that most Jews, particularly those who had achieved a measure of success in their respective nations, would not desire to pick up and leave in the interest of pursuing an idealistic adventure in a distant land. He did believe, however, that many Eastern European Jews would accept the opportunity to emigrate to Palestine if given the chance.

It was Hess's ultimate conviction that such a state was needed for two reasons: to serve as a spiritual center and to serve as a base for political action.

*Rome and Jerusalem* was criticized for stylistic defects, along with oversimplification in both the political and religious spheres, but yet it remains a model of prescient insight into both the field of anti-Semitism and the quest for Zion. Like so many authors who are ahead of their time, Hess did not always receive the most positive audience attention. Indeed, sometimes he received no attention at all, as evidenced by the fact that only some 160 copies were said to have been bought by one year's time after the book's publication, after which the publisher suggested that Hess buy back the remaining copies at a reduced price. On the other hand, sales figures alone would not be a fair index of the impact of Hess's ideas on the intellectual community, where fresh ideas are swapped and microscopically examined with simultaneous spontaneity.

Hess's *Rome and Jerusalem* marked the high watermark of his involvement in Zionist activity because after 1862 he again devoted the thrust of his attention to the socialist movement. In Paris, he became a leader in Lassalle's new party and a member of the First International, eventually dying a forgotten man in 1875.

The circuitious ideological link consisting of Hess, Marx, and Lassalle provides illustrative insight into the exensive and convoluted vortex of thought in Jewish Eastern European intellectual circles in the nineteenth century, in which every strain of thought seemed to be tugging simultaneously, often in disparate directions.

Here was Hess, an adherent of Hegel, who embraced utopian socialism with idealistic underpinnings, ultimately sowing some of the initial polemical seeds of Zionism as he argued persuasively for the creation of a Jewish nation in Palestine after self-admittedly short-shrifting his own Judaic roots for a large part of his life.

Here was Marx, the descendant of rabbis, who strove mightly to eliminate every vestige of Jewishness in his makeup, going so far as to refer to Lassalle, who, like Marx, was trying to renounce his Jewish background, as "Jewish Nigger."

Here was Lassalle, denounced along with Hess by Marx for falling into what the father of communism deemed an odious school of thought that avoided the practical and sought to merge utopian socialist concepts of France with German tradition, in turn heaving an insulting diatribe at Jews by referring to them as "cowardly people" who deserved perpetual servant status.

Perhaps this type of chaotic admixture of ideas was the inevitable result of a besieged people's reactions to a freqently discomforting minority status within Eastern European nations. Some sought to assimilate to the point of thoroughly denouncing their Jewish origins. Others sought to remain true to their traditions, often at the expense of great ridicule and monetary loss. And there were those who staked out an intermediate position, adhering to certain Jewish concepts while seeking to modify them to comfortably embrace certain Christian and other nationalistic beliefs but running the risk of being denounced by Jews and Christians at the same time.

Just as Theodor Herzl, the father of political Zionism, had been spurred into action as a response to the injustice of the Dreyfus trial and its aftermath in Paris, events in the devastating pogrom phase in Russia in 1881 brought to the fore a leading early advocate of a Jewish state.

Like Herzl, Leo Pinsker's background was that of a successful assimilationist. Just as Herzl and his family occupied a comfortable station in Viennese society, the same would also have to be said for Pinsker, but with even greater emphasis.

A physician with a distinguished background, Pinsker was the son of a renowned Jewish scholar. A graduate of Moscow University, he established his reputation in intellectual circles by assuming a position of advocacy of cultural assimilation. Like most of the leading Jewish intellectuals in the Europe of that period, Pinsker had believed both that the route toward success for Jews resided in understanding and that the ugly specter of anti-Semitism should be approached through education, which would then quash prejudices rooted in ignorance and lack of comprehension.

Pinsker would adhere to this posture until the vicious attacks on Jews in 1881, at which point he announced that he was parting company with his former assimilationist allies. He had begun entertaining misgivings about the value of assimilationism during the riots in his hometown of Odessa in 1871. Now, ten years later, he began to seek answers outside the ambit of the assimilationist circle to which he had belonged in Odessa.

The result of Pinsker's thoughtful reflection was a book, *Autoemanzipation*; his radical departure from the comforting position of assimilation, in which the community's intellectuals would assure their Jewish cohorts that anti-Semitism could be stamped out through a solid education program, which in turn would eradicate the foundation of ignorance from whence it had sprung, was what made his effort noteworthy.

Pinsker was sixty years old when *Autoemanzipation* was published, and it is doubtful that anyone other than a person of broad social and intellectual experience could have contributed the type of work he set forth.

He sought to dash the optimism of the liberals and socialists concerning the eventual uprooting of anti-Semitism by declaring that it existed as an inevitable consequence of the unique position that Jews held in European society.

Stripped to its internal roots, anti-Semitism was the result of what Pinsker saw as an immutable sociological law. Yes, Jews had failed to achieve equal rank in Europe despite the fact that many had been willing to renounce their heritage and backgrounds. According to Pinsker, no nation has a predilection for foreigners. The reason why Jews experienced greater difficulty than did members of other groups was that they had no country of their own. Whereas members of other groups could move into a nation in the form of a guest from elsewhere, Jews, having no nation, were in the position of being beggars rather than guests.

As a result of such permanent outsider status, which Pinsker maintained was the fate of Jews, not even legislative emancipation could remedy this immutable fact. The yoke could not be removed so long as Jews were seen as wandering nomads, vagrants unable to provide a satisfactory account of where they had come from and where they would go.

Pinsker's analysis of anti-Semitism resulted in the following dour definition of the Jew:

"For the living, the Jew is a dead man; for the natives an alien and a vagrant; for the property holders a beggar; for the poor an exploiter and a millionaire; for patriots a man without a country; for all classes, a hated rival."[4]

Once Pinsker had finished laying out his gloomy perspective of where the Jew stood in society, he set out to provide a course of action to remedy the existing situation.

For Jews, looked upon in Pinsker's view as vagrants and perennial outsiders, what was needed was self-respect. In that the Jew suffered alien status as a result of not having a national identity, the logical conclusion for Pinsker was that the Jew should achieve that sort of identity that was so painfully and glaringly absent.

The subject of emigration was briefly considered but rejected on the basis that the type of widespread departure desirable to achieve Jews' ends would be denied them. No other country was likely to open its gates to widespread emigration from Russia, which Pinsker deemed necessary in order for the Jews to be able to shed their parasite image.

Pinsker's next conclusion would put him in the same context with Hess before him and Herzl afterward. What Jews needed was an opportunity to secure land in order to launch a nation of their own. He recommended that a national congress be convened for the purpose of purchasing land for that reason.

At the time he published his pamphlet, he was a territorialist rather than a Zionist. He warned Jews that their goal should not be "restoring ancient Judea" but establishing a territory of their own. He mentioned North America and Asiatic Turkey as possibilities.[5]

It was not until Pinsker's last years that he embraced the Zionist concept of establishing a Jewish nation in the Holy Land as a leading member of the Lovers of Zion the forerunners of Political Zionism.

Despite the earlier writings of Hess and Pinsker, the person designated as the father of Zionism was Theodor Herzl. The title was invested in him because, whereas Hess and Pinsker toiled mightily in the theoretical vineyards, it was Herzl who made the quantum leap from the realm of theory into that of practical politics.

Herzl reacted in the manner of a man hit with a bolt of lightning in 1896, when, in reaction to his great frustration over the tragic Dreyfus affair, he turned his life completely around, moving in a fresh direction with a messianic fervor that dazzled all who knew him.

Up until the time of the publication of *Der Judenstaat*, Herzl's career objective appeared to be that of establishing himself as a cultured man of the arts through his plays and essays. By being selected as Paris representative for a leading Viennese journal, his career realization had seemingly moved closer. His main concern was to see that his plays along with the novels he also periodically wrote received the kind of serious attention he felt they deserved. It was Herzl's lifelong belief that his greatest talents resided in the creative arts, and to the end of his days he would insist that these abilities exceeded his organizational skills as the world's leading spokeman for Zionism.

Perhaps the definitive point of irony among those who knew Herzl was that he made his mark by moving a cause that had been immersed in the theoretical world, that of Zionism, into that of the practical. The reason was his propensity for radical solutions that fell into a strongly romantic vein. Perhaps because of his strong creative urges, and compounded by his frustration over not being accorded what he felt was his rightful position in letters, Herzl's instincts appeared grounded in the grandiose to the frequent exclusion of the pragmatic. An interesting case in point was his belief in 1893, just three years before the publication of *Der Judenstaat*, that what was needed for Jews was a widespread baptism of their children. He recommended that they submerge themselves in the people and wished to appeal to the pope. In exchange for the pope's assistance in helping to squelch anti-Semitism, Herzl would in turn lead a movement among the Jews for voluntary conversion to Christianity. This effort would culminate in a solemn procession to St. Stephen's Cathedral in Vienna. The procession would be led by the adult leaders of the Jewish community, who would then remain outside the church while the others would embrace Christianity.

*Der Judenstaat* offered a polemical mix, which embodied some of the old grandiose Herzl concepts along with a pragmatic framework that manifested his new facet as an organizer. Herzl the grand idealist surfaced in his declaration of a utopian state. In that he did not feel that nations were then ready for democracy, his preference was for a democratic monarchy or an aristocratic republic in which no member of the state would be discriminated against. Though opposing the creation of a theocracy, priests would receive the highest honors but would not be permitted to interfere with administration of the state. Herzl's appreciation for ceremony was exemplified by his mention of the attire of priests in the new state. They would be clad in impressive robes, and cavalry members would be bedecked in yellow trousers and white tunics, with officers wearing silver breastplates. The emergent practical side of Herzl was revealed through a detailed blueprint of the future Jewish state he hoped to lead into existence. *Der Judenstaat* contained chapters entitled "Workers' Dwellings," "Purchase of Land" and "Unskilled Laborers" in which were detailed the means of effectuating the reality of a Jewish state along with the functions of the citizens who would populate it.[6]

According to Herzl's blueprint, two agencies would initiate the embryonic structuring of the new nations. The "Society of Jews" would provide a scientific plan and political guidance, and the "Jewish Company" would assist emigrants while organizing trade and commerce.

On the question of where the new state would be situated, Herzl's pamphlet was as notable for what it did not say as for what was specifically revealed. The book contains not one reference to Arabs at all, and certainly not so much as a hint that Palestine was occupied by them.

This absence of specific analysis of the then geopolitical realities in Palestine has prompted many sage observers to focus on the point that Herzl, in his blueprint for the creation of a Jewish state, felt that the goal could be realized through settling in any one of a number of areas.

In the Zionist Congress of 1931, the man who was destined to become Israel's first president and who is generally regarded to be the world's leader of practical Zionism following Herzl's death, made an interesting observation relative to Herzl's posture on where the Jewish state should be situated.

"In all of Herzl's declarations," Chaim Weizmann said, "the idea of the Jewish state appears only in his book, *Der Judenstaat*. When he wrote this book, Herzl was far from certain that Palestine was the land where his plan would probably be realized."[7]

In Weizmann's mind, Herzl regarded the Palestine plan as something academic, and there was no certainty that his vision of a Jewish state applied specifically to Palestine.

"The whole style of his book makes it probable that while writing it [*Der Judenstaat*] he was thinking about another land [Argentina]," Weizmann further revealed, "and that he added the passage about Palestine later on, just to make his Zionist friends feel good."

Politics is defined as the art of the practical, and Herzl's fence-straddling approach on the issue of where the Jewish state would be located has the distinctive ring of a leader seeking to achieve a consensus without alienating potential followers. Herzl sought to inculcate as broad an audience as possible with the concept of launching an exodus to another land as a means of establishing an independent entity for Jews. By achieving this newly acquired independence, European Jews could surmount the ponderous difficulties of anti-Semitism and assimilation. By not breaking down any of the existing questions pertaining to settlement in Palestine, Herzl could then hold out his options regarding where the new state he was advocating could be situated. On the other hand, recognizing the strong urges on the part of many prospective followers for that nation to be located in Palestine due to deeply seated religious convictions, Herzl saw to it that their desire was expressed by mentioning Palestine within the context of being the focus of the new state.

The renowned Jewish philosopher and theologian Martin Buber saw in Theodor Herzl a countenance that was lit with the glance of the Messiah. Herzl's demeanor was indeed imposing. With his long black beard and intense, dark-eyed look of stern, imposing intelligence, he looked like a no-nonsense rabbi intent upon converting all who fell within range of his voice.

However, despite the urgency of his message and the fact that he was stating principles with which Jews could be expected to feel at least some level of identification, the response within the Jewish community to *Der Judenstaat* was far from uniformly positive. Many Jews regarded the pamphlet as a revival of medieval messianism.

One of Herzl's sternest critics was none other than the chief rabbi of his home city of Vienna, Moritz Gudemann, who had been close to Herzl. Gudemann wrote a pamphlet of his own to rebut *Der Judenstaat* in which he asserted that Jews did not constitute a nation, that the common thread linking them together was solely their belief in God, and that Zionism was incompatible with the teachings of Judaism. This same argument was to be raised continually against the cause of Zionism for many years into the future.

Despite such opposition, some of which was influential, Theodor Herzl was undaunted. He was a man with a mission, and he was steadfastly determined that his quest to achieve a Jewish nation would be accomplished.

What made Herzl's movement propel forward beyond the earlier efforts of Hess and Pinsker was the immediate establishment of an organizational framework within which Zionism's proponents could coalesce and the movement could effectively be nurtured.

The fledgling organization flexed its developing muscle in 1897, just one year after *Der Judenstaat* was published, with the convocation of the First Zionist Congress in Basel, Switzerland. The convention is noteworthy for two reasons. First, it constituted the initial meeting that brought Zionists together on an international level, marking the movement as an organizational force with which to be reckoned. Second, the convention revolved around the major policy concept embraced by the delegates. With Herzl supplying his support, a program was adopted that accepted the ideal of Palestine as the land of Jewish resurrection. The Congress spoke about "a legally secured Jewish home in Palestine."[8]

It is interesting to note that any language concerning the formula for creating a Jewish state was missing from the adopted agenda of the First Zionist Congress. Herzl could hardly be blamed for not wanting to touch off a debate on the subject of locating a new state in Palestine in view of the fact that few of the delegates in attendance had ever been there, and most were concerned principally about finding somewhere to relocate in order to rid themselves of the stigmata of anti-Semitism and pogroms. Despite his often displayed propensity for the grandiose, Herzl was also a shrewd political operator who wanted to keep all his options open. If land could be made available elsewhere for his purpose, he did not want to reject such a possibility out of hand but instead sought to explore the feasibility of the proposal.

With the result of the First Zionist Congress that of launching Political Zionism with resounding vigor, the duality of the Jewish ideological experience is exemplified by contrasting both the persona and the programs of Theodor Herzl with someone who listened to what Herzl had to say, disagreed, and went off in a different direction.

Ahad Ha'am attended that First Zionist Congress, leaving with disappointment after seeing that Herzl's projected destiny for the Jewish people was incompatible with his own.

Born in Russia under the name of Asher Zvi Ginzberg, this student of languages expressed a preference for and a fluency in Hebrew, in which he prolifically published articles from 1889 until his death in Tel Aviv in 1927. All of his Hebrew essays were published under his pseudonym, Ahad Ha'am, which means in Hebrew "one of the people."

Whereas Herzl saw Zionism's struggle in political terms, Ahad Ha'am became known as the father of Cultural Zionism for the distinctly different role he felt that the Jewish people should play. To Ahad Ha'am, leadership was symbolized not by a political force but as a spiritual entity in which the leader takes on the persona of a priest. He clearly saw the crossroads that Political and Cultural Zionism presented. Ahad Ha'am perceived that the struggle for and acquisition of a Jewish state would focus the attention and spirit of its people on political ends. The aim of Cultural Zionism was to promote the spiritual nature of the Jewish people, and Ahad Ha'am saw the pursuit of political ends as a distraction from that objective. The cornerstone of Ahad Ha'am's philosophy was a spiritual regeneration of the Jewish people. Rather than calling for the creation of a Jewish nation in Palestine as numerous Political Zionists were advocating, he instead called for the creation of a spiritual cultural center in the Holy Land. Such an entity would offer the kind of spiritual potential that would provide Jews with an opportunity to recapture their ancient roots, rekindle ancient ties with their great teacher Moses, and adopt a prayerful cohesive effort to realize an uplifting present and future.

The dual question of where one's focus should reside, that of achieving goals through Political Zionism or Cultural Zionism, resulted in greater numbers' embracing the pragmatic program of Herzl than embarking on the kind of spiritual mission advocated by Ahad Ha'am, though the father of Cultural Zionism retained a steadfastly dedicated following of his own.

Why would Herzl's message secure a larger audience than that propounded by Ahad Ha'am? The popularity of messages and causes are directly related to conditions at a given period of time. At the point in which the messages of Political and Cultural Zionism were vying for the attention of Jews, the focus was squarely on eradicating present conditions in the course of carving out a better existence. Zionism was a movement embraced largely by Eastern European Jews, and their motivations for doing so were in basic lockstep with the precepts of the man who became horrified by the Dreyfus Case and its aftermath, which promptly catalyzed him into action with a cause. Theodor Herzl's call for political action was in direct line with the aspirations of Jews beset by assimilation difficulties, by drab ghetto existences, and by painful pogroms. The vehicle for change, the instrument for upheaval to bring about comprehensive movement, lay in the political arena. Had Jews been in a more contemplative and less restless frame of mind at the time, the message of Cultural Zionism would doubtlessly have attracted greater attention. As things then stood, however, given the traumatic uncertainty of the times and the fervent desire for prompt and far-reaching change, Theodor Herzl was the man with the message around which the Jewish masses would rally.

Within Herzl, a burning urge abounded to be a kingly educator for the Jewish people and to lead them into a Promised Land in the manner of a present-day Moses. From the time of *Der Judenstaat*'s publication in 1896 until his death in 1904, this former bon vivant of comfortable means utilized every physical and mental resource to serve the Zionist cause. His incessant labors eventually broke his health, and when death finally came to him, observers were in accord that he was an "old" forty-four years of age, having pushed himself to the brink again and again until, despite the willingness of the spirit, his overwrought body gave out.

Along with his constant focus in the political arena, Herzl's flair for the mystical remained with him as well. As someone who perceived himself in the role of a Moses, entrusted with leading his people to their destiny, symbols assumed great importance to him.

A letter to Baron de Hirsch, an individual Herzl was seeking to enlist in the Zionist cause, illustrates his awareness of the power of symbolism and the important role that leaders play in connection with it:

"And then you would have asked in mockery, 'A flag, what is that? A stick with a cloth rag?' No, a flag, sir, is more than that. With a flag you can lead men where you will—even into the Promised Land. Men live and die for a flag; it is indeed the only thing for which they are willing to die in masses, provided one educates them to it."[9]

Herzl coined the phrase "If you will it, it is no dream" with respect to his pursuit, then set out to realize it as he moved with dispatch from his old profession of journalist and donned a new hat as a negotiator with world leaders on behalf of a people without a home of their own who were eager to build one.

Although Herzl had expressed an admiration for Argentina as a possibility in which to launch a Jewish nation, after examining potential options, he began concentrating on Palestine and the northern Sinai Desert. He spoke with the sultan of Turkey, because Turkey controlled Palestine and neighboring regions at the time, in Palestine. He met with representatives of the Ottoman Empire in Constantinople. While Kaiser Wilhelm of Germany was visiting the Holy Land, Herzl availed himself of the opportunity to plead his case before the head of a nation at the peak of its imperial powers, along with being the foremost ally of the Turks. Despite intensive efforts in which Herzl offered the assistance of world Jewry in helping to solve the Ottoman Empire's chronic financial problems, no deal was struck. His offer to the kaiser to help him establish a European community in Palestine as an outpost furthering German interests also failed to achieve fruition.

At that juncture, Herzl turned his attention to the principal colonial power of the world. Great Britain's crafty colonial secretary, Joseph Chamberlain, was favorably disposed toward Herzl's nation-building concept as a means of enhancing his own nation's self-interest. The power struggle that would culminate in World War One was under way; Chamberlain recognized the advantage of using a friendly Zionist nation as a means of solidifying a defense of the Suez Canal, and so the possibility was considered of creating a Jewish state in the northern Sinai region. This concept was by no means new, having been first advocated in 1840 as the brainchild of Lord Palmerston.

While Herzl was seeking unsuccessfully to achieve an agreement with Great Britain to obtain the opportunity of building a Zionist nation in the Holy Land, events of tragic urgency that occurred in Russia in 1903 prompted him to alter his course.

A series of vicious pogroms directed against Jews in Russia, which culminated in a ruthless Easter mass slaughter in Kishinev, created an urgent necessity within Herzl to cease his efforts toward achieving a state in the Holy Land in favor of a temporary exile for those in need. The Kishinev pogrom resulted in the deaths of forty-seven Jews and the wounding of approximately six hundred others. The Hebrew poet Hayim Nahman Bialik wrote movingly of the tragic events in "On the Massacre," in which he unveiled an impotent rage made helpless by an inability to do anything about the slaughter of innocent children, the brutal rape and murder of women, and the killing of men.

The abiding necessity to provide Jews with a safe haven, especially in the wake of the latest wave of pogrom tragedies, prompted Herzl to consider a tentative offer by the British government to settle in the territory of Kenya. Because the area under consideration was mistakenly called Uganda, Zionists referred to the proposal as the Uganda Plan. Elsewhere it was referred to as the East Africa Scheme.[10]

The new proposal to locate a temporary homeland for Jews in East

Africa was the focal point of the Sixth Zionist Congress, which proved to be the last under the direction of Theodor Herzl.

The importance of the issue under consideration was symbolized by the fact that the map of Palestine that had hung on the wall behind the president's chair was replaced by one of the territory where the proposed Jewish state would be situated in East Africa.

If Herzl needed any tangible evidence of the controversy surrounding the East Africa proposal, it came during the first session of the congress, when an incensed young woman ran up to the platform, reached out and grabbed the map of East Africa, and proceeded to rip it to shreds.

A resolution was later proposed to send an exploratory committee to East Africa to make a feasibility study of the proposal. The intense debate that followed revealed sharp division among the delegates, although when the vote was taken, the resolution passed by a 295 to 178 margin. The split among the delegates was further revealed by the 98 abstentions that were recorded.

Herzl was quickly given additional reason for chagrin when the same young woman who had earlier torn down the map of East Africa shouted in French with shrill fury: "Mr. President, you are a traitor!" Being called a traitor at a convention of the movement he had founded provided salt enough in Herzl's wounds over the controversy of the so-called Uganda Plan, but a final bitter note of irony surfaced when the majority of the Russian delegation also expressed opposition to his effort. This opposition was so deeply rooted that the Russian Zionist leading the protest convened in Kharkov in October of 1903 and passed a resolution challenging the Zionist leadership.

Even though Herzl had made it clear that a Jewish settlement in East Africa would not preclude the launching of a Zionist nation in Palestine, the stern opposition of so many Zionists, particularly among the Russian whose plight had motivated him so strongly, revealed that the proposal had struck a raw nerve in the psychical core of Zionists. Although the consensus opinion was that efforts needed to be made in the political arena, there was more than a residue of the cultural Zionist propounded by Ahad Ha'am influencing them. The objective was to settle in the land of Zion, in Palestine the Holy Land, and any substitute would be angrily and resoundingly rejected. This blunt reality was learned by Herzl not long before his overworked body expired after rendering unstinting duty to the Zionist cause.

Herzl died on July 3, 1904, and just three weeks later, the Seventh Zionist Congress opened in Basel, Switzerland, under the direction of

his colleague Max Nordau. After the report of the investigating committee was read the territory was found unsuitable for colonization.
The congress formally rejected the East Africa Scheme on July 27,
1905. It might well be that the investigating committee was influenced
by the practical reality that to issue a vote of approval on the feasibility
of the East Africa Scheme would have had the likely effect of bitterly
dividing the Zionist ranks at a time when forward momentum was
crucially needed.

With Herzl's death, a movement remained to be carried forward,
one he had nurtured like a baby during its gestation. While it is true
that the founder of political Zionism had not realized his goal of
establishing a Jewish nation in Palestine, he gave his movement its
initial impetus by creating a cohesive framework within which others
could carry on thereafter. The East Africa controversy to the contrary,
the Zionist ranks remained united in their burning urge to forge a
nation of their own in the land of their forebears.

The origin of Zionism resulted from a burning psychological need for
identity, of discovering then nurturing basic roots of Jews through the
acquisition of an entity of their own, the realization of Zion.

The legendary account of the wandering Jews along with critical
responses to them in nations where they had no identifiable roots,
notably in Eastern Europe, enhanced this longing to achieve an existence of their own, to find a place in the world they could call their
own while removing the all-too-frequent stigmata they felt in other
nations of being unwanted guests.

The vast Jewish migration that concluded with large numbers settling
in Eastern Europe produced a variety of responses. Some embraced
an assimilationist first posture, converting to Christianity and leaving
all vestiges of their hereditary roots behind. Certain Jews, in the wake
of criticisms directed at the non-Jewish population, often by intellectuals with formidable reputations, launched vehement criticism at
anything that bespoke of Jewish traditionalism. Those who sought to
maintain ties with their roots and secure at least a modicum of success
within their communities embraced a dual pattern of behaving in the
manner of the schlemiel as manifested in the stories of Jewish humorist
Sholom Aleichem amid the general public and as renowned and respected adherents of Judaism within the private sanctuary of Jewish
society.

Following a pattern of uncertainty and cultural rootlessness, the
already forlorn Jews then suffered the indignities of discriminatory

laws passed to minimize their monetary and professional effectiveness within the societies in which they lived, along with the physical and psychical traumas of pogroms.

The more harshly Jews were driven into isolation, the more frequently they received cultural denunciations regarding their origins and the stronger the urges became to prove that they and their cultural backgrounds were of intrinsic worth.

In that so much of the Jewish torment along with the criticism leveled at Jews in the nations where they lived related to their years spent wandering then settling in various nations, the natural reaction to squelch such attacks while proving their value as a people resided in establishing roots of their own.

Taking their desire to establish roots one step further, it was logical enough to envision the establishment of tangible roots through nationhood. And since the point of origin for Jews was the Holy Land, it was understandable that an urge to settle there would blossom on a major scale, resulting in the quest for Zion.

Theodor Herzl might not have known about the earlier writings of Hess and Pinsker staking out the same ground he covered in his famous work *Der Judenstaat*, which he used as the polemical framework from which to launch the Zionist movement, but the thoughts he enunciated struck a responsive and familiar chord in the minds and hearts of a people desperately seeking identity.

The thoughts of Herzl, Hess, and Pinsker were the thoughts of many; the organizational working framework established by Herzl gave them a vehicle for moving from expressions of incohesive frustrations to a structured organization striving mightily to bring a dream to reality.

# 3

# Arab Origins

Cultures bear indigenous personalities all their own, and to understand a particular culture along with the individuals who constitute it, it is essential to peel off all the current trappings and trace it back to the time and the land of its historic roots.

Any analysis of Arab origins must begin in the earliest stages of civilization in sandy desert regions baked by the harsh rays of a sharply insistent, always threatening golden sun. Despite its luminous intensity, the sun is far from the only savage intimidator confronting Arab desert inhabitants. Scourging the parched, dry desert earth and unleashing a devastating fury is a phenomenon constituting an Arabian version of the black plague. It descends like a great black wall, engulfing all who are unfortunate to be in its way. Arabs call it the *huboob*. It carries the potential to blind while stinging in the fashion of a swarm of bees tearing the skin like numerous pinpricks. The *huboob* is the merging of two forces, a ferocious wind and the assault force it generates through the swirling desert sand. Yet another harsh factor confronting Arab settlers was the geographical reality of the region's expansive desert makeup, affording little arable land.

It is believed on the basis of anthropological and archaeological findings that human life had its origins in the region known as the Middle East. Scattered fragments of ancient Arabia reveal occupation from the Old Stone Age, stemming from Paleolithic and Neolithic sites. Prehistoric skeletal remains can be traced to at least three racial stocks, Negroid, Armenoid, and Mediterranean.

47

The Arabs, like the Jews, are of Semitic origin. There are numerous biblical references to the Arabs, and both groups, Arabs and Jews, trace their lineage back to the same ancestral roots. Both groups regard Adam, Noah, and Abraham as their fathers.

The year 1255 B.C.E. plays an important role in the chronicling of world historical religious annals. That year the Hebrew tribes terminated their trek from Egypt to Palestine to stop for forty years in Sinai and the Nufud. Tradition recounts the marriage of Moses to an Arabian woman who worshiped an austere desert god named Yahu, later called Jehovah. This Arabian woman provided Moses with instruction about her god and may have launched a chain of events linking Christianity, Judaism, and Islam.

In attempting to analyze and explain both the roots and the development of Arab civilization, beginning with its embryonic origins some 3,500 years ago on the parched sand extending all the way to the present day, we would do well to view the overall question within the framework of the anthropological writings of Charles Darwin.

No matter how devoted or skeptical the reader might be concerning Darwin's evolutionary conclusions propounded in his lengendary work *The Origin of Species,* a study of Arab roots almost inevitably stimulates focus on the realm of the concept of survival of the fittest, a bedrock of Darwin's theory.

Throughout the annals or recorded history, the Arab has been equated with desert wandering, a nomad loath to spending lengthy periods of time in any one place.

Among the early societies that developed on the Arabian peninsula, a name was coined that for a long period of time was used as a synonym for Arab. The name was Bedouin, and much of the exotic mystery about Arab civilization that has generated interest and provided a springboard for the writings of Joseph Conrad and Rudyard Kipling, among numerous others, surrounds the evolution of this fascinating breed of nomad, who through the years has braved oppressive climatic obstacles in the pursuit of a most vigorous and triumphant survival.

The rationale for synonymously linking the names Bedouin and Arab was a common nomadic tribal existence. However, the name Bedouin also came to be identified with that of raider. Hence Bedouins could fall into the classification of being wanderers passing through a village or territory, and in accordance with the corollary meaning, they might also display a propensity for raiding.

The Arab people have, from ancient times, been divided into two distinct classes, those who dwell in cities and villages and those who wander from place to place with all their worldly possessions packed snugly into their camel bags. Both groups are classified as Arabs, but the wandering nomads are invested with the name Bedouin to differentiate between them and their sedentary kinsmen.

As one seeks to explore the role of the Bedouin in Arabian history an application of Darwin's survival-of-the-fittest concept is most instructive. Arabia is characterized as (1) containing seemingly endless miles of sandy desert terrain, (2) offering minimal potential for land cultivation, and (3) creating gigantic scarcities for the masses.

In accordance with Darwinian theory, those individuals who endure within a civilization possess characteristics most adaptable to survival. They in turn continue this process through procreation.

It is hard to imagine a situation in which this pattern of adaptability is given a sterner test than on the windswept sand dunes of Arabia.

What with so much of Arabia consisting of desert wasteland and sun-baked untillable soil and with so little of the barren region having access to major waterways, the potential for developing city life on a large commercial scale in the fashion that existed in European nations later on was negligible. Hence a prototype was born who became heroized and broadly mythicized by writers, composers, and poets alike: that of the rugged individualist capable of wandering from place to place, seeking to augment the meager belongings of a camel and the few possessions tucked within a camel bag.

Arabia was a land in which the harsh realities of nature were brutally undertaken on a daily basis. Removed from the sedentary underpinnings of a tightly woven city milieu, that special breed of warrior capable of confronting the brutal realities of nature known as the Bedouin became the focus of admiration.

Lacking the constraints of a tightly structured society, and existing in the wide-open expanses of desert terrain, the concept of freedom becomes paramount. The Bedouin therein became far more than an individual seeking to grapple with a hostile environment in the most positively adaptable Darwinian manner. He became a symbol of triumph, a glittering example for an entire society of free-spirited determination against the brutal obstacles of desert existence.

The Bedouin, the classic Darwinian example of human life battling aggressively against a hostile environment, disdained farming due to the futility of developing untillable soil. Seeking more promising outlets for his efforts, he understandably gravitated toward the more realizable pursuits of herdsman and trader.

Though it is true that the Bedouin led a nomadic existence, the popular misconception of the Bedouin as an aimless wanderer fails to grasp an essential point. The misconception becomes more understandable through an analysis of the perspective from whence the error arises. To individuals who are products of the type of structured, largely sedentary existences that constitute the leading modern industrial civilizations, such nomadic activity can be perceived as aimless wandering. The point that gets missed when reaching such a conclusion is that the entire sociological picture is inverted when one contrasts Arab roots with those of individuals of more traditional civilizations, particularly those who live in modern major cities. A highly industrialized civilization consists of numerous core cities that together make up a centralized, unified whole. Any outward activity flow in the nature of trade and commerce commences from a central core base, as represented by a multifaceted, highly industrialized city such as New York, Los Angeles, London, or Paris. The contrast between this type of energized central core in the form of a major city could scarcely be more pronounced than the example afforded by the social reality confronted by a Bedouin. Whereas the movement of an energized core city extends outward, the Bedouin began from a position firmly outside the vortex of any viable social movement and extended inward.

It is from that sociological genesis that the Bedouin concept of the raid, or *ghazw* in Arabic, came into being. This three-thousand-year tradition of the Bedouin was born out of simple necessity—the need for survival on the part of both this special breed of desert nomads and their omnipresent companion, the trusty camel.

What with the necessity of these desert warriors to travel countless miles in hot, sandy deserts in pursuit of sustenance, it was understandable that the camel would come to occupy a position of inestimable importance. The camel provided the Bedouin's staff of life. The animal was put to an astounding and varied series of uses. In that dates and milk were the main staples of the Bedouin's diet, the beast provided a source of food in addition to the necessary function of transportation. Its hair was used for making tents and clothes, and its urine produced medicine, hair dressing, and skin lotion, which provided protection from the piercing rays of the sun.

The desert was this unique warrior's preserve. Functioning in a habitat among the harshest in the history of civilization, with the omnipresent camel as the only permanent companion, Bedouins sowed seeds for a bedrock of rugged individualism in the most classic Darwinian sense. The basic life pattern of the Bedouin has changed remarkably little from the original domestication of the camel in the eleventh or twelfth century B.C.E. until the hot ground of Arabia was successfully explored by the ranks of modern technology through the discovery of oil.

In addition to cementing a pattern of bedrock individualism, the days, hours, and months spent combing arid expanses of sand astride a camel imprinted within the Bedouin a fierce pride in tradition, language, and blood, along with adaptive powers to a harsh environment. In the process, this sinewy, tenacious being developed a restless impatience for any outside authority, with loyalties confined to family and tribe. The harsh desert terrain and solitary existence developed within the Bedouin a contrasting duality of conduct and a quick-tempered bundle of nerves. The harsh conditions imposed the necessity of taking things slowly at least some of the time and of requiring respites from nomadic journeys under an insistent, piercing sun. This produced a lethargy within the Bedouin, which existed part of the time. These periods of relaxed activity would then be sharply interrupted by outbursts of frenzied activity, in which the desert warrior would recognize the necessity of productive activity to survive the rigors of the hostile environment.

Despite the natural propensity toward a ruggedly individualistic social pattern brought on by geographical factors, there remained within the Bedouin the natural adaptive element, which pervades humankind as well as all of the animal kingdom, that of seeking out common pursuits through a group pattern.

The functional social unit for the Bedouin was the wandering group, which consisted of a number of extended families, all of whom traced their common descent through a male ancestor. In addition to satisfying man's basic cohabitational urges, this rigorously male-dominated social entity derived another advantage in forming tribal bonds, that of increasing a Bedouin's effectiveness through traveling in numbers. The tribal units would camp together, wander together in search of pasture for their animals, engage in in-group marriages, and conduct raids together to secure camels, other animals, and assorted additional booty.

In Bedouin society, the basic element that has endured throughout the period of empire and exists until the present day is that of the clan, which consists of a number of tribes. An Arab tribal leader, the *sheikh*, is chosen by a council of clan chiefs and reigns at their discretion. The *sheikh* functions more as a mediator and peacemaker than as a ruler.

Despite the fundamentally individualistic nature of Bedouin society imposed by geographical factors, it is interesting to note that man's basic organizational nature was also exemplified through the creation of a quasi-governmental structure existing in layers. The pyramid embraced (1) the Bedouin as an individual, (2) the tribal unit, (3) the clan as an entity encompassing various tribal units, and (4) the *sheikh* as an overseeing representative of the clan.

Another widely held misconception about the Bedouins also needs to be confronted, which involves the concept of the *ghazw,* or raid. Due to the film industry's desire to dramatize, the depiction of Arab raids almost always unfailingly showcases an incident or series of incidents in which a marauding tribe plunders and brutalizes another, leaving behind devastation and lots of dead bodies. While such ferocious confrontations did occur in which the ultimate casualty rates were excessive, such were far from the rule. A restraining influence was exerted on raiding activities by tribal custom, which sought to benefit Bedouin society as a whole. A warrior had recourse to the sword in avenging injuries or deaths, with the prevailing custom being an eye for an eye. If, therefore, a member of one tribe suffered death or serious injury at the hands of another, the proper recourse lay in bringing to bear the same deed on the original perpetrator. In short, the personal attack initially brought would be met on an identical personal level.

Although the objective of achieving "an eye for an eye" often resulted in the perpetuation of lengthy blood feuds between conflicting tribes, the concept had a restraining effect as well, which served to prevent further bloodshed.

Bedouins recognized the difficulties arising out of prolonged battle with an opposing tribe or clan. Not only was there a measurable loss in human terms, but also the concentrated focus necessary for fighting battles of survival detracted from efforts to provide sustenance for oneself and one's family. Whereas the potential for death or serious bodily injury grew, the prospects for achieving a reasonable level of prosperity diminished.

The grim reality of existence permeated by the "eye-for-an-eye" axiom invested Bedouin raiders with a measure of caution, which they carried forth on their forays onto the turf of another tribe. The objective became that of carrying out painless raids in the form of quick, effective forays in which some animals and booty were spirited away without any physical attacks being launched. By functioning in such a fashion, they would not only remove the risk of getting bogged down in debilitating and prolonged battle with another tribe but would also not incur a bad name among the ranks of fellow Bedouins.

Another element also existed to limit Bedouin bloodshed, an outgrowth of code of machismo that evolved thousands of years before that current oft-used word was invented. As an outgrowth of the aforementioned tenacious individualism that developed as a natural concomitant of life in a harsh environment, the concept of manly pride was rigorously analyzed. A code of conduct emerged defining just how a man should behave. A basic precept of Bedouin unwritten law was that a strong tribe should never attack a weaker one. Strength was to be strictly equated with strength, and any deviation from that standard, such as attacking a weaker tribe, would result in scornful infamy against the perpetrating tribe.

On the other side of the coin, this harbinger of the macho code with the accompanying chauvinistic concept of women being seen and not heard and tending to family chores, rendered it paramount that an enemy attack be personally answered. If a member of a group were killed by a member of another group, the relatives of the victim have suffered because their group strength has been diminished. The honor of the group has suffered and the appropriate recourse is revenge. The responsibility for meting out revenge devolves upon the *khamsa,* the male members of the victim's kin group. The *khamsa* comprises all male members who are removed from the victim by no more than five links. The *khamsa* serves as the group on whose support a man can always count in any feud with an outsider. The *khamsa* seeks out the murderer. If the murderer cannot be found, however, any member of the murderer's *khamsa* is considered to be a legitimate target for revenge. With the aggressive members of the victim's *khamsa* taking charge, an effort is undertaken to avenge the murder in a manner prescribed by tribal law. At the same time, or following a respite, the peaceful members of the victim's family, generally the older men, launch a parallel effort to find a respected mediator or mediators to settle the tragic affair in a manner mutually acceptable to both sides.

The maxim "blood demands blood" has been a continuing concept within the fabric of Arab society to the present. It is equal to the concept of "strength against strength" in which revenge is the appropriate instrument for diminishing a tribe's numbers.

It is therefore understandable just how and why the most successful of the Bedouins developed adroitness in the art of stealing as many animals as possible in a raid of another group without clashing with the men who tended them.

What with the tribal bond being the solidifier of Bedouin society, unconditional loyalty was demanded. The worst fate that could befall a desert Arab was loss of tribal affiliation, which led to complete ostracism by his kin. Entry into another tribe became the only salvation, because hereditary rights and rank had no place among the Bedouins. Even from earliest times, however, the tribal structure devolved into aristocratic government.

Although it is estimated that today's Bedouins represent no more than 10 percent of the total Arab population, many of them can trace their roots to Bedouin stock. The impact of the Bedouin within the fabric of Arab society cannot be accurately measured solely in terms of ethnic lineage. The example of the Bedouin as a valiant warrior battling the ravages of a harsh desert environment is a story of tradition that is proudly nurtured by a historically conscious people aware of its triumphs of the past and seeking linkage to such glories of accomplishment in the wake of many present travails. The proud link to the Bedouin past has been absorbed through the intervening centuries so that, until quite recently, it was a customary practice among the best families of Damascus along with other Arab cities to reconsecrate this tradition in an interesting manner. These city-dwelling families, examples of Arabs who had made good and who were far from being sun-drenched warriors sitting astride camels that spirited them along dusty sand dunes, would send their sons for a year or two to one of the *asil* (noble) camel-breeding tribes of the Syrian Desert. Their objective was to expose their young to the experience, mentality, manners, and values of Bedouin existence in the same manner as a wealthy American family that sends a son to a military academy or prep school.

Another notable Arab tradition that has continued to the present and carries a direct linkage all the way back to the earliest Bedouin tribes is the propensity for flowery expression as definitively categorized in poetry.

The fiercely individualistic Bedouins of early times were a by-product of the desert and fashioned a physical life on their own, devoid of the rudiments of education. Hence they grew up illiterate. Books along with the accompanying trappings of the educated life played no role in shaping their destiny. A natural desire existed, all the same, for some measure of cultural expression, a universal phenomenon in humankind's pursuit of communicative fulfillment.

Such fulfillment was attained in the Arab tribe's poetic use of speech. If one is denied the opportunity of communicative interchange through books and newspapers, a natural medium for expressing the historical, as well as the romantic and dramatic, is that of poetry. As a result of the fact that poets were filling a vast communicative realm of expression resulting from vacuums that existed in other areas, they occupied a leading position of honor within the fabric of tribal society. The poet served the multiple functions of propagandist, satirist, oracle, and historian. The piercing verbiage of a skilled poet could bring to fruitful realization the Shakespearean adage "the pen is mightier than the sword." Advantage could be gained over a rival tribe without the costly expense of loss of life and blood while also raising the morale of the poet's own tribe. Should a tribe be actually immersed in battle with a bitter tribal rival, the proper use of timely invective could secure propaganda advantage.

Any sense of unity that existed among the pagan tribes can be attributable to the phrases of flowery praise conjured up by poets. Playing their chosen role to the hilt, Arab poets sang the praises of their tribe's hospitality. Even though competition for water and pasturage caused war, hospitality for the traveler was a necessity in this barren land. Poets traveled to numerous local fairs held in cities such as Amman, Hajar, and Ukaj, and the best poems were hung out there to be seen, though there were few who could read them. It was at these fairs that political differences among the tribes were accentuated.

While humankind's natural propensity toward collective expression was reflected in the works of the poet, there existed as well a desire to achieve a measure of religious expression both within and outside of the tribal structure during those early years of world civilization.

The prevalent mode of expression among early tribes was polytheism, stemming from various experiences the nomads had with nature, which in turn were classified as spirits and placed in the polytheistic lexicon of gods. The first spirits were perceived as inhabitants of trees and rocks and other such familiarly identifiable entities. When the nomads made contact with settled tribes, a cohesive effort resulted to classify and identify the various spirits, working them into the mosaic of a pantheon. Two of the more notable gods to whom the nomads made sacrifices were Mana, the spirit of doom, and Gadd, the bringer of good luck.

The well-nurtured spirit of rugged individualism springing from the Bedouin's independent existence in expansive desert regions was linked to nomadic and tribal propensities toward worship in the formation of a grand design, which held fast until the last third of the sixth century C.E.

Certain spirits became adopted as gods to be venerated and feared within certain tribes. The more strongly these spirits were seen to symbolize the unity of tribal identity, the more they became reflective of the cult itself. Worship of tribal spirits was a test of loyalty, and failure to accord the proper measure of deference was seen as treason.

Eventually the tribal pattern of spirit worship began to break down, but before the rupture occurred, this phenomenon reached its zenith in the place that became the heartland of early Arab desert civilization.

The city of Mecca became the great stopping place for the innumerable camel caravans that carried hot, dusty, thirsty riders looking for a place to relax and enjoy something of the good life before moving on, an important oasis situated along the spice route, where one could find good food and wine.

Because Mecca was situated geographically in a place that ensured it of receiving scores of visitors of varying beliefs from different locales, it became the ideal venue for developing new viewpoints.

Mecca achieved noteworthiness for being the home of the Kaaba, a word in Arabic meaning "cube" to define the building's shape. The Kaaba was a pantheon erected to worship more than 365 idols. A visit to the Kaaba was paramount in the minds and hearts of numerous visitors to Arabia's richest metropolis.

What with Mecca's becoming an international trading center, however, there was a good deal more than merely Roman gold and Indian spices that was exchanged: A developing interplay of religious ideas and concepts took shape in which elements of Christianity, Judaism, Magism, and the prevalent mode of worship of idolatry symbolized by the Kaaba were discussed.

During a period in which both Judaism and Christianity were being discussed with increasing frequency throughout civilized society, it seems inevitable that such contacts would be made and that such discussions would occur in Arabia's most cosmopolitan city.

Although idolatry was the prevailing mode of religious belief among early Arabs, careful study reveals a steady evolutionary progression toward the gradual embracing of monotheism, a concept adhered to by the burgeoning adherents of Christianity and Judaism.

The Magians believed in a good god, Ormuzd, and an evil god, Ahriman, who represented two competing forces vying for domination of the world. An easy transition that could be made by followers of this religion was to believe that Ahriman was the creature of Ormuzd and was in revolt against him. In fact, the duology appears closely comparable to the Christian concept of Almighty God battling against the fallen angel Lucifer, who assumes in common parlance the identity of Satan. A much closer symbiotic pattern exists regarding the Christian monotheistic God beset by the warring force of Satan on the one hand and the twin forces of Ormuzd and Ahriman on the other than the transition that had to be made toward Christianity by the idol-worshiping Greeks and Romans.

An outward generative thrust toward monotheism took place in Mecca with the belief in Allah, known as "the provider" and considered to be the most powerful of the local deities. He remained, however, a remote god up until the pivotal point of Arab history in the last third of the sixth century. By that time Allah had replaced the moon god as lord of the Kaaba, though still occupying an inferior position below various tribal idols along with three powerful goddesses: al-Manat, goddess of fate; al-Lat, mother of the gods; and al-Uzza, the planet Venus.

As Arabia moved into the final three decades of the sixth century, it is apparent that a basic lack existed, which prevented inhabitants of that region from developing a major civilization that would assume a prominent position on the world stage. The Arabs were in need of a cohesive unifier or major catalyst that could bring together previously disparate elements in the pursuit of a common goal. Throughout time, this kind of force has been presented through either a religious or secular vehicle or through a combination of both elements.

So often in the pages of history, one person has surfaced to fill a void, providing shape and definition for a nation and receiving support along the way from the prevailing religious leadership as well. The names of those who shaped national destinies and ultimately triumphed on a world scale are numerous, but Julius Caesar, Alexander the Great, and Napoleon Bonaparte are three names that frequently come to mind.

Those who believe that the destiny of a leader is inextricably linked to fate and an arrival at just the propitious moment in time en route to achieving noteworthy success on behalf of a people might take a look at the circumstances existing in Arabia at a pivotal moment in history, when a major event would occur to change its face forever.

At the advent of the seventh century, Arabian civilization revealed the crying need of a unifying force, a leader to bring together elements from a geographically large and essentially spread-out land. The task of bringing unity to Arabia on any major scale would not be an easy one, given the fact that its people either lived in small pockets, at least in the main, or existed as remote entities with miles upon miles of hot desert sand separating them. To be sure some measure of unity was established, groups bound themselves together through the institution of the tribe or clan. But examples of unity built upon such small numerical bases hardly constituted the kind of social cohesion that would lead to the development of a large civilization with worldwide impact. The great historical powers with dynamic sayings such as "All roads lead to Rome" or "The sun never sets on the British Empire" all began with both a strong and relatively united economic social core and strong and adventurous leadership. The numerous Arab tribes and clans contained individual elements that encouraged the status quo and discouraged the kind of centralizing effort that would be required to move Arabia into the ranks of a major world power. The adroit Bedouin tactic of conducting painless raids on other tribes, making off with their animals without harming those who tended them, was not the kind of conduct that cements unity. The concept of unity was every bit as lacking in the realm of religious worship as the same element of tribal cohesion prevailed. Gods were selected and worshiped on a vast scale by the numerous tribes spread out across Arabia.

A great watershed event finally occurred to unify Arabia and generate cohesiveness in a way that enabled that civilization of mostly nomads and few city dwellers to rally behind a common goal. Such common purpose arose in a manner that had not existed earlier, and the coordinating force extended across both religious and secular bounds.

The exact year in which this eventual prime mover of Arab civilization was born is uncertain, although historians place it at 571 A.D., which has been deemed to be a reasonable approximation if not totally accurate.

The boy who would some day shape the destiny of the entire world not only during his own time but also from that period forward was born in Mecca. As a youth he tended goats and sheep in the hills around the city where he was born and raised. In early adulthood he hired himself out as a camel driver to a rich widow in Mecca. He regularly drove her camel caravans to Syria to trade with rich merchants there. So this camel driver from Mecca, the most cosmopolitan city in Arabia, who had almost certainly had some contact with the newly developing concepts of monotheism inherent in Judaism and Christianity, was in a position to receive more of the same kind of contact in Syria. No doubt his youthfully curious mind began to make comparisons and contrasts between the polytheistic idol worship of his Arab brethren and the monotheistic God of Judaism and Christianity, along with the definitive figures of both of those movements: Adam, Abraham, Moses, and Christ.

The wealthy widow, Khadijah, who had placed this young man in her employ in his early twenties, grew fond of his sincere manner and reliability. Despite the fact that she was some twenty years his senior, the two were married. While Khadijah may not have been as properous as tradition has revealed, her wealth was sufficient enough to make her husband independent and provide him with much time for soulful contemplation. A sensitive young man given to introspection, his propensity toward solitary reflection was understandable in view of his youth. His father, Abdullah, died before he was born, and his mother passed away a few years after his birth. An orphan without brothers and sisters, he was raised first by his grandfather and then by an uncle, spending long hours alone in Mecca or in the surrounding countryside tending the herds.

With the comfort and love of a devoted wife, whose own prosperity ensured his own, and with sufficient time for the reflective solitude he valued, this quiet and unassuming man blended unobtrusively into Mecca life and may never have been known outside the tiny orbit of his existence had it not been for a series of events that occurred when he was forty years old, events that ultimately generated an upheaval that changed the face of the world.

This solitary man found a cave near Mecca, where he went regularly to meditate, and it was there that he is reputed to have had a vision and heard a voice command, "Recite thou in the name of thy Lord who created."[1] Following a brief respite, a second vision appeared.

Terrified, the man left the cave immediately and hurried home. Arrived with alarm, he asked his dutiful wife Khadijah to put some covers on him. Acording to his account, he heard the words, "O thou, enwrapped in thy mantle! Arise and warn."[2]

He returned to the cave, where he experienced more visitations, initially panic-stricken by the belief that the spirit tormenting him was none other than Satan. However, under the stout encouragement of Khadijah, he came to believe that these visions and the words that accompanied them came from Allah, and eventually, during those meditative sessions in the cave near Mecca, it was revealed that the emissary directly communicating Allah's message to him was the angel Gabriel.

From these beginnings, one of the world's great religions was ultimately founded, and the instrumental force behind it would accomplish an objective that nobody had before accomplished nor would even dare attempt, that of cementing a natural bond among the divergent tribal people of the Arabian desert.

Muhammad, who came to be known as the "messenger of God" would die in the knowledge that his efforts had achieved notable success, but it is doubtful that he envisioned the kind of historic grand sweep that eventuated, with the religion he founded serving, as the catalyst, the great unifier, which resulted in the achievement of one of history's greatest dynasties.

Perhaps the issues that cut through to the Arab masses more than any other and that made the herculean task of unification realizable were the simplicity of Muhammad's message and the ease with which that message could be followed and perpetuated by the masses.

To begin with, Muhammad did not claim to be a supernatural being or to have direct linkage to God. He instead defined himself as a communicator, a chosen vessel of God, whose sole function was to disseminate the message of truth as revealed in illuminative visions to God's children.

The religion that sprang from Muhammad's visions was called Islam and was based on the teachings revealed in the Koran, the recorded account of the concepts Muhammad maintained had been imparted to him by the angel Gabriel, concepts that had originated from Allah. "Islam" is a word derived from the Arabic *aslama,* which means to submit. The word "Islam" appears in several of the suras, or chapters, of the Koran, and followers of the religion are referred to as Muslims, a noun based on the verb Islam, which refers to "one who has submitted one to God and thereby found peace."

A basic tendency on the part of Westerners, which has been criticized by Muslims, is to refer to the belief of Islam as "Mohammedanism" and to those who follow it as "Mohammedans." Muslims are quick to point out that their prophet, Muhammad, did not claim to possess any supernatural powers, being instead a vessel for communicating the teachings of Allah. Hence, it is thoroughly inappropriate to use the term "Mohammedanism" in reference to Islam.

One element that sets Islam apart from most other religions and that has been cited as one reason for its success is that the figurehead of Islam is not deemed to be a spiritual being operating on another plane of existence but is considered a human being with the same basic characteristics as his followers. An empathy of experience and commitment thereby links Muhammad to his followers. Like them, he listened for the message, and the role for which he was enlisted was that of "messenger of God," a communicator of the teachings of

Allah, which he in turn shares with individuals such as himself. In addition, it was stated during Muhammad's life and has been repeated subsequently that the prophet could neither read nor write, an issue that has been used to buttress the belief that the concepts recorded in the Koran did indeed come from an outside source, Allah, and that the role Muhammad performed as a prophet was to have those divine messages recorded for posterity.

Islam derives a historical advantage over Christianity in that its roots are more manifestly verifiable from a recordation standpoint. A good deal more is known about Muhammad than was known about Jesus. Muhammad's historical existence is totally verifiable, and, what with the human events of his life having been recorded, there are no supernatural controversies presented as have surrounded God figures in religious history, such as the Christian claims of a virgin birth and a resurrection.

Interpretative controversy, which abounds within the ranks of Christendom regarding the New Testament, is missing from Islam. Much of the Koran was written before Muhammad's death, the suras having been dictated to faithful transcribers based on revelations from Allah to the Prophet, and the rest of it followed a few years later. There was and has remained only one Koran, whereas the New Testament contains four gospels and includes other additions.

In one basic respect, the early journey of Muhammad the mortal parallels that of Jesus Christ, the spiritual being Christians believe to be the son of God. The determined Prophet of Islam, infused with idealism, took his message to the masses. He was greeted with sarcasm and derision, as was Jesus, according to all recorded accounts, when the Christian message was initially disseminated. To those who rejected Muhammad's message during those early days in the history of Islam, the choice was simple. Why give up the long-held traditions of the Kaaba, a concept of polytheism structured around a multitude of gods, for an alien and untested monotheistic belief being propounded by a man who claims to be the messenger of the one true God Allah?

The message of Muhammad was a crystallization of many of the core beliefs of both Judaism and Christianity. The messages of the Hebrew prophets of the Old Testament that were later embraced by Christendom (with the basic addition being the inclusion of Christ)— of God's being one, of God's being all-powerful, and of God's being the creator of the universe—served as bedrock foundations of Islamic belief. The concept of a judgment day was also an embodiment of Old Testament belief. Rewards in paradise awaited those who heeded God's commands, and the scourging fires of hell were reserved for those who failed to heed them. Muhammad encouraged his followers to regard the leading figures of both Judaism and Christianity—Adam, Abraham, Moses, and Jesus—as prophets of Islam. The issue over which he broke ideological ranks with the two leading monotheistic religions was on the ultimate source of the one true God: God the sovereign was Allah; the contributions of the leading biblical figures, including Jesus, lay exclusively in perpetuating the message of Allah; and to the degree that God was seen to reside elsewhere, their teachings were in error.

When Muhammad's early preaching efforts were greeted with derision, he shifted his message from the God of love and the promise of paradise to a sterner one of the terrors of hell, which awaited those who ridiculed and failed to heed God's message.

Eventually his message began to take hold with the masses. As was the case also with Jesus, initial converts to the cause came not from the ranks of the prosperous and influential but from the poor and the humble. Muhammad's new converts were mainly slaves and the lower classes.

His chief opposition stemmed from those of the aristocratic and influential branch of Quraysh. Initially they were content to attack Muhammad through the verbal channels of sarcasm and ridicule, but as his message began to take hold with greater numbers of the masses, the alarmed Quraysh struck back more forcibly, turning from invective to active persecution as Meccan families who had been recently converted to Islam were forced to flee to Abyssinia in 615.

During this period of conflict, when Muhammad's message was under constant siege in his native Mecca, it was alleged that a dramatic nocturnal journey took place in which the Prophet was said to have been instantly transported from the Kaaba to Jerusalem prior to his ascent to the seventh heaven.

This memorable journey to Jerusalem would later attain great significance in the annals of comparative world religions in general and in the Middle East religious and political traditions in particular. Since Jerusalem was a way station on a memorable journey of Muhammad, the city therefore later assumed significance among Muslims as it became and continues to remain the third holiest city after Mecca and Medina in the Moslem world. The seeds were therein sown whereby Jerusalem assumed the elevated status of a holy city along with comparable beliefs on the part of Jews and Christians. Although Jerusalem ranks as the holiest city to followers of Judaism, whereas to Muslims it ranks third in significance behind Mecca and Medina, the memory of the journey remains a vital living force among Moslems. The Wailing Wall itself, which is considered sacred by followers of Judaism, is determined to be the halting place of the winged horse with a woman's face and peacock's tail on which Muhammad journeyed heavenward. These dual beliefs concerning an identical property prompted a serious disturbance in Palestine in August of 1929. The journey is considered by a Spanish scholar to be the original source of Dante's *Divine Comedy*.

Two years after the time of the nocturnal journey, an event of even greater significance to the Muslim world occurred in which Muhammad, at the behest of about seventy-five of his followers, moved to Medina, making it his home. Medina was a fertile ground for Muhammad's new monotheistic religion in that Jews there, asserting their expectation of a Messiah, helped to condition formerly polytheistic Arabs to accept the concept of a one-God religion.

Accompanying Muhammad to Medina were two hundred followers, through whose efforts they were able to slip past the watchful eyes of the Quraysh and reach their destination.

Once his cohorts had successfully entered Medina, Muhammad then joined them in what was his mother's native city, arriving there on September 24, 622, upon completion of what is termed the hegira, or flight. The name is misleading in that the journey, rather than being a flight, was carefully conceived over a period of two years. What with internal pressures becoming increasingly greater on the part of the Quraysh as the Islamic movement generated additional converts, the religion's leader recognized the importance of a safe haven where a future course of action could be plotted.

The hegira period marked the receding of the religious prophet Muhammad into the background and the emergence onto the Arabian scene of a skilled political and military pragmatist, who recognized that the ultimate route to success in perpetuating his religious concepts lay in achieving a foothold through concerted military effort.

The importance of the hegira in Islamic history was indelibly imprinted in 639, when the Caliph Umar designated the lunar year beginning July 16 of 1622 as the official starting point of the Moslem era. The Islamic calendar proceeded from that milestone event in Arabic history.

Recognizing that his ranks were outnumbered but desiring to strike a dramatic victory blow that would enhance his movement in a significant manner, Muhammad cagily took advantage of a "holy truce" period then in effect in which all forms of fighting were outlawed. The

leader instructed his loyal followers, the Medinese Moslems, to inter-
cept a summer caravan on its return from Syria to Mecca, striking at
the most vital point of the commercial metropolis in which his enemies
prevailed. The caravan leader, having heard about Muhammad's ploy,
contacted Mecca for aid. Despite being outnumbered by one thousand
to three hundred in terms of combat troops, the Moslems overcame
the reinforced Meccan caravan.

Though the Moslems had overcome great odds in registering the first
victory ever for Muhammad and his cause, the triumph would not have
assumed the major strategic significance it did without one overriding
factor. Islam itself was put on the military map and Muhammad had
manifested muscle in an entirely new realm, surfacing as a temporal
force in a continuing conflict he came to regard with increasing belief
as military and less as purely religious. If Islam was to acquire the kind
of broad base in which he and his followers believed, it was necessary
to achieve military victories. Also, with a victory now under his belt,
Muhammad and his followers could point to his success over the
Mecca caravan as divine sanction of the new faith.

The battlefield conduct on the part of Islam's warriors on that
occasion established a twofold precedent that has been pointed to
subsequently whenever Moslems engage in battle. The twin criteria
pridefully stressed are a relentless spirit of discipline tied to a greater
cause and a fearlessness toward if not contempt for death itself with
the accompanying recognition that the cause is greater than any one or
any number of individuals.

Even though the Meccans were able to avenge their defeat the
following year, actually wounding Muhammad in the process, the
forces of Islam had the triumph they needed in order to inject the
proper measure of optimism into their quest for recognition.

Islam recovered from its temporary setback, and as it gained greater
credence with the masses, it moved from a defensive to an offensive
posture, spiriting forward in Medina to become much more than a
religion within a state as it assumed a primacy equal to that of the state
itself.

Feeling the kind of confidence that accompanies the acquisition of
power, Muhammad, now that he had established a solid base in
Medina, began to Arabianize his steadily advancing movement. He
began with a campaign against the Jews for "siding with the confeder-
ates" as six hundred able-bodied men were killed while the rest were
expelled. Furthering his Arabianization efforts, the Prophet broke with
both Judaism and Christianity, with Friday being substituted for the

Sabbath, and the call from the minaret being decreed in place of trumpets and bells. Ramadan was fixed as a month of fasting. The direction to be observed during the ritual prayer was changed from Jerusalem to Mecca, the pilgrimage to Kaaba was authorized, and the kissing of the Black Stone, a pre-Islamic ritual, was sanctioned.

Now that a solid foothold had been gained, Muhammad sought to press on and achieve uncontested authority in his own Mecca, which he had abdicated under great pressure for Medina during the hegira, wherein he gained a foothold and looked ahead to achievements of the future. In 628, he led a body of fourteen hundred believers to Mecca and secured a peace treaty with his old enemies, the Quraysh, in which Meccans and Moslems were to be treated on equal terms. This diplomatic effort on Muhammad's part brought to a halt the fighting between his group and a dogged opposition. Not only did the treaty free Muhammad from the pressures of continuing conflict with the Quraysh, enabling him to concentrate on other objectives, but also he was able to utilize members of this proud tribe in future pursuits, two of whom, Khalid ibn-al-Walid and Amr ibn-al-As, became valuable warriors in future Islamic conflicts.

The Prophet's diplomatic efforts in Mecca realized ultimate fruition in January of 630. In a moment of supreme triumph, the now unchallenged leader of Mecca entered the sacred sanctuary of the Kaaba. No doubt many images were flashing through his mind during that climactic moment as he recalled the early days of the movement, when he preached with little success, converting a few of the poor masses but being ridiculed by the many, especially the powerful. The Quraysh, the very group with which he had exacted a rapprochement, had been bitterly opposed to his one-God concept. While he was issuing steadfast declarations to unite behind the singular spiritual force of Allah, classifying the memorable religious figures of the past as prophets, the Quraysh were ridiculing him with the rejoinder that they had numerous gods in their pantheon and saw no reason to cast them aside to follow the one God that Muhammad held to be preeminent. Now it was Muhammad who held the position of power, and he most certainly felt a surge as he recalled all the struggles of the past and prepared to establish the unchallenged acceptance of his doctrine of monotheism in the city where he was born; where he was married, worked, and lived most of his life; and where he had meditated in the silent solitude of a cave, receiving visitations from the angel Gabriel, which had changed his life. Now the moment was at hand, and Muhammad seized it with alacrity as he began smashing the many idols in his midst, said to have numbered three hundred and sixty in all. The last vestiges of the polytheism of old were destroyed with great conviction by the Prophet himself, making way for monotheistic Islam and its devotion to the precepts of Allah. As the destruction was accomplished, Muhammad exclaimed: "Truth hath come, and falsehood hath vanished!"[3]

The significance of keeping the Kaaba free from nonbelievers assumed tremendous importance during that crucial period when Muhammad destroyed the idols. The fervent degree of devotion of his adherents is underscored by the fact that a stricture written into the Koran at that time has remained in force during an intervening period of more than thirteen hundred years. The Koran passage declaring the territory around the Kaaba to be forbidden and sacred was later interpreted as prohibiting all non-Moslems from approaching it. While the verse was probably intended as a stricture against the polytheists, forbidding them from drawing near the Kaaba at the time of the annual pilgrimage, its thrust was continued and its injunctive force remained in effect. According to prominent Arab historian Philip K. Hitti, no more than fifteen Christian-born Europeans had succeeded in seeing the Holy Cities of Mecca and Medina and lived to tell about it, up to the time of the publication of the fifth edition of Hitti's *The Arabs: A Short History,* in 1968. The first to be chronicled was Ludovico di Varthema of Bologna in 1503; one of the most recent was the Englishman Eldon Rutter. The most notable of the ranks was the legendary British travel author and man of adventure Sir Richard Burton.

In 632, the tenth Moslem year under the new Islamic calendar, a triumphant Muhammad led the annual pilgrimage into his new religious capital of Mecca. This proved to be his last and has been characterized in Islamic history as the farewell pilgrimage. Three months after his return to Medina, the prophet began to complain about severe headaches. He died suddenly on June 8, 632, and although he had always claimed himself to be mortal, a man entrusted with spreading the message of Allah, many of his followers reputedly refused to believe him and expressed shock and dismay when he met death.

Many religious and social movements last no longer than the lifetime of a founder, but Islam's vitality was only beginning to be felt. While it is true that the fundamental groundwork laid by Muhammad prior to his death helped to enhance the force's momentum, there were several fundamental reasons why Islam achieved continuing success after its founder and leader had been laid to rest.

The fundamental irony regarding Islam's huge successes following Muhammad's death lay in the fact that what had started as a religion was transformed to a significant degree into a sociopolitical phenomenon, and it was under that banner that Islamic successes were to eventually magnify to the point where they would exceed the geographical dimensions of the Roman and Greek empires that preceded their world conquest.

In order to comprehend the social dynamics behind Islam's gigantic success on the world stage, it is necessary to harken back to the roots of early Arabia and the tradition of the Bedouin, the desert warrior whose impact has been indelibly felt in Arab civilization from inception.

In order to succeed, any religious or social movement requires the proper social climate, with both internal and external circumstances providing impetus. Such was certainly the case in Muhammad's Islamic movement, and the sturdy Bedouin played a major role in the sweeping transition from a fledgling religion to the position of the world's leading power. The Bedouin was a survivor in the fundamental Darwinian sense, a warrior who set out on his camel to conquer the ravages of a harsh desert environment through raids on tribes. Locked to arid desert regions, there was scant opportunity for the rugged Bedouin to break out beyond the constraining barriers put before him by nature. His life seemed destined to be nothing more than a series of battles over dry sandy turf. By banding together in tribes, Bedouins sought to gain advantage over competitors, but their circumference remained fixed, with any form of comprehensive social advancement being seemingly out of the question.

At that point, Islam as a sociological tool for advancement surfaced, and with it sturdy Bedouin warriors were able to fix their limited focus on new, previously undreamed-of horizons. While it is tenable to maintain that Muhammad's message of an enriching hereafter in paradise supplied motivation in generating enthusiasm for Islam, it would be inconceivable to dismiss the possibilities for Bedouin advancement in worldly potentials under the banner of rising Islam.

A perfect bargain was struck between Muhammad and his successors and the Bedouins. In order for the message of Islam to be spread within the confines of Arabia and beyond in the manner that the Prophet wished, it was necessary to organize an army of warriors who were strongly committed. The Bedouins possessed two admirable qualities that aided their potentials as soldiers, both of which sprang from their unique desert existence: an awesome power of endurance and remarkable mobility. As mentioned earlier, the harsh desert climate dictated that only the truly robust would survive, and the Bedouin's mobility sprang from his mastery of camel transport.

The Bedouin certainly possessed the raw tools to make a successful Islamic warrior, provided that one other all-important requisite was present, that of motivation. That requirement was substantially met as the Bedouin, previously victim of limited opportunities, suddenly realized that the opportunity to break free from his constraining geographical boundaries had arrived. Not only would he be receiving payment for services rendered as soldier in the ranks, but also golden opportunity had suddenly surfaced that enabled the Bedouin to look out far beyond the confining regions of sand dunes and small tribal entities to the comforts and luxuries of the civilized regions of the Fertile Crescent. Here at last was an opportunity to achieve the previously unrealized objective of acquiring luxuries in areas where circumstances were notably less harsh.

Most of Islam's conquering armies were recruited from the ranks of the Bedouins, and the expansion that followed marked the final stage in the lengthy process of gradual infiltration from barren desert regions to the adjacent Fertile Crescent, the last great Semitic migration.

The element of fortuitous historical circumstance manifested itself from the time of the earliest Muslim successes. Two factors commingled to provide the initial shot in the arm for what soon became a vast Islamic military machine: the unifying element of Islam and the inevitable result of momentum interlocking with success. In terms of unity, Islam brought a number of largely unruly, highly individualistic, often warring tribesmen into one camp. The old polytheistic gods of the individual tribes, along with their chauvinistic ways, were discarded as these previously discordant tribesmen coalesced under the unifying aegis of Islam. Once the Bedouin warriors had set out as an organized entity, their early objective was to stake out new territory for gain. These incessant raiders, who knew no other way of life and were now forbidden to engage in fratricidal warfare against Islamic brothers, sought new conquests. Booty was garnered and the successful process was carried forward. As the victories mounted, territorial aspirations increased.

The self-generating success pattern pushed along a tradition established by Muhammad, and much of the attraction of his Islamic message can be attributed to its universalism, making it attractive to large numbers of Arabs.

One of the major aspects behind the success of Muhammad's message was that he could easily be accepted by this disparate land of desert nomads and city dwellers because he loomed as "one of us" to people of varying walks of life. This phenomenon was particularly apparent among the Bedouins, who were to comprise the bulk of his Islamic army. Muhammad could be likened to an American politician who can draw votes equally from city and rural regions. Even though his roots were in the city of Mecca, Muhammad's gains from his initial preaching efforts came from the downtrodden segments of society, from the slave peoples. Despite the fact that he had married into money, Muhammad's beginnings were humble as he grew up without the benefit of a father or a mother and labored in the fields tending sheep when he was a young boy. His message was also humble, stressing his own human vulnerabilities and portraying himself as a communicative vessel of Allah. Once his message began to take hold among the masses, it was cognizable that the wealthier, more powerful segments of Arab society would observe common denominators with this new Prophet. He had, after all, used the springboard of a successful marriage to an older woman of means to develop into a prosperous businessman who assumed administrative supervision over many men who worked for him. Later, when he began to achieve success in the religious sphere, individuals of economic substance who had initially ridiculed his efforts began to perceive the blend of building confidence among the poor as a unifying religious healer along with the application of administrative leadership skills, which he had earlier demonstrated, as a way to achieve positive goals. In the early days of Arabia, as well as in the present, the universal rule holds that nothing impresses the movers and shakers of society more than succeeding, and once Muhammad began forging a foothold on the Arabian conscience with his new movement, his earlier ridiculers from society's wealthier echelons began to change their thinking about him.

This society was one in which the poor vastly outnumbered the rich, and one that was governed by highly individualistic activity, which frequently extended to the level of anarchy. In it, the overriding quality that enabled Muhammad to achieve the seemingly impossible role of unifier of the ranks of a disparate desert people was his ability to impress his followers that he was indeed one of them and that the course he was laying out for them as a messenger of Allah would meaningfully enhance their lives in a way they had not previously realized was possible. The successful identification of the masses through the one-of-us philosophy was no more apparent than in the manner in which the Prophet lived, even after having gained economic success. Even during the height of his glory he resided the same way he had during his earlier days of obscurity—in an old clay house consisting of a few rooms that opened into a courtyard. This same kind of old-fashioned house is used today by many Arabs. Muhammad could often be seen mending his own clothes. He was, and would remain, a man of the people, who was always within easy access of those desiring communion with him.

When Muhammad died, the little wealth he left he regarded as state property. He had taken about a dozen wives, some for love, others for political reasons, his favorite being Aishash, the young daughter of abu-Bakr. None of his children by Khadijah survived him with the exception of Fatima, who would later become the famous spouse of Ali. One of the Prophet's wives had a Christian background. She was Mary, a Christian Copt. One of the saddest events in Muhammad's life was the loss of his infant son Ibrahim, born to him by Mary and over whom he mourned bitterly.

To comprehend the dimensions of the Prophet's success as a unifier during his lifetime, one must recognize the sweeping changes he initiated through the supplanting of entrenched Arab beliefs. The basis for social organization in Arabian society, generated through the tribal concept, was that of blood kinship. The state of Islam gradually evolved from its root origins in the religious community of Medina. The new community of Emigrants and Supporters, the glue and fiber of the evolving movement, sprang from religious rather than tribal roots in forming the congregation of Allah. During his life, Muhammad fulfilled two functions: as spiritual leader and messenger of Allah and as temporal authority for the movement, existing in the same fashion as would a chief of state.

Muhammad emphatically expressed the central thrust of his burgeoning movement during his sermon at the "farewell pilgrimage," not long before his death:

"O ye men! harken unto my words and take ye them to heart! Know ye that every Moslem is a brother to every other Moslem, and that ye are now one brotherhood. It is not legitimate for any one of you, therefore, to appropriate unto himself anything that belongs to his brother unless it is willingly given him by that brother."[4]

Of all the statements attributed to Muhammad during his life, the one above could serve as the most meaningful and far-reaching in total import. With one exhortation delivered by the Prophet not long before his death, at a time when both his spiritual and temporal authorities stood at their towering zeniths, the previously vital bond of Arab relationship—the tribal kinship—was supplanted by the bond of faith.

A new type of brotherhood had emerged, that of faith with Islam as the bedrock of its foundation, replacing the tribal bond that had been the singular solidifying element of an otherwise disparate and highly individualized people. This new community of Islam would have no priesthood, no hierarchy, no central see. Its mosque would serve numerous functions as a public forum, military drill ground, and place of common worship. The leader in prayer, the *imam*, would also serve as commander in chief of the "army" of the faithful. Those in the army were solemnly compelled to protect one another against the outside world of those who did not follow the message of the Prophet. All Arabians who failed to heed this fundamental message were to be regarded as outcasts. Wine and gambling, which Arabs had thoroughly enjoyed, were abolished in one verse, and the previously popular activity of singing was frowned upon.

To comprehend the legacy of Muhammad the Prophet, referred to by his people as the "Messenger of Allah", it is vital to review the cental aspects of the book he left behind, the Koran, which is adhered to with unwavering devotion by Moslems. In the eyes of Islamic believers, the Koran represents the word of God as dictated through the angel Gabriel to Muhammad.

The fundamentals of Islam in the broadest sense can be basically understood by studying the five or six fundamental tenets of the religion. They are known as the pillars of Islam, the foundation upon which the religion rests.

They can be briefly categorized and analyzed accordingly.

1. *The profession of faith,* by which the first words uttered to a Moslem infant and the last to be spoken at the grave site are one and the same, that there is no God but Allah and that Muhammad is His messenger. This simple but profoundly meaningful statement is repeated over and over in prayer services.

2. *The ritual prayer,* which is recited five times a day, beginning at dawn and concluding at nightfall, and delivered by facing toward Mecca, is called the *fatihah,* or opening sura, and has been likened to the Lord's Prayer. It is recited by the faithful Moslem about twenty times a day. The basic element of Moslem prayer is the mention of Allah's name. The Friday noon prayer is the only public one. It is compulsory for all adult males. Certain mosques have been reserved for women.

3. *Legal almsgiving,* which operates in much the same manner as the Christian tithe, evolved into an obligatory tax on property and was collected through the early Islam state by regular officials and admin-

istered from a central treasury to support the poor, to build mosques, and to defray government expenses. Though the amount varied, it generally averaged about 2.5 percent. When the purely Islamic state ultimately disintegrated, almsgiving thereupon became a matter of conscience to devoted believers.

4. *The Ramadan* is a penitential fast in which all food and drink are prohibited from dawn until sunset for one month. Failure to adhere to this concept by so-called nonbelieving Moslems has resulted in violence perpetrated by certain Islamic governments seeking to enforce the Ramadan.

5. *The Pilgrimage* involves a commitment to be exercised by Islamic believers at least once during one's lifetime. All Moslems of both sexes who can afford to make such a trip are expected to journey to Mecca on a holy visit at a stated time of the year. It is essential also that Moslems be in the proper spiritual state, meaning that during this period, they are enjoined from sexual intercourse while observing fasting in accordance with the Ramadan. The concept of pilgrimages to holy places extends as a Semitic institution back to the time of the Old Testament. In that the Mecca Pilgrimage represents a hallmark of Moslem devotion that brings together innumerable believers from throughout the Arab world, many of whom have had to undergo great hardship to achieve it at least once during their life, it has achieved the effect of strengthening Islamic bonds of unity through faith. In addition to meeting fellow Arabs from different nations, the opportunity often presents to meet Islamic believers from other nations such as African states and China as well.

6. *The Jihad,* or holy war, was raised to the level of a sixth pillar by the Kharijites, the concept having been incorporated into Islam's earliest phases of expansion. The objective was emphasized that the geographical wall separating the "land of Islam" from the "territory of war" needed to be bridged. For a period of time following World War One, the Jihad fell out of use, but in recent years it has been embraced with fervent tenacity. The Shiite fundamentalist followers of Ayattolah Khomeini have used it as a rallying cry for the Hezballoh, the most militant Islamic sect, whose strategic cunning and ferocity befuddled Israeli troops during their most recent incursion into war-torn Beirut. The subsequent Israeli withdrawal in the face of tenacious pressure skillfully applied by outnumbered but highly motivated Hezballoh guerrilla forces prompted analysts to refer to the frustrated campaign as "Israel's Vietnam."

A careful analysis of the principles set forth in the Six Pillars of

Islam clarify for the non-Moslem just how effective a unifying catalyst their acceptance can be in the temporal realm when applied to the institution of war. The Prophet's message reverberates throughout Islamic ranks. The forces of the world boil down to two camps, Islamic and non-Islamic. Carried to its most militant heights, as exemplified by the current Islamic Jihad movement embodied by the Hezballoh Shiites, followers become infused with an all-consuming passion to overcome obstacles in the pursuit of achieving goals. The will of nonbelievers must be stamped out in the pursuit of an all-embracing commitment on behalf of Allah. Numerous current examples exist of suicide squadrons reminiscent of the kamikaze pilots of World War Two, who crash-dove planes into enemy ships, ensuring their own destruction in the process, on behalf of the Japanese Empire. Today's Islamic warriors plow automobiles containing explosives into strategic targets, generally containing Israeli soldiers, thus sacrificing their lives in the pursuit of carrying out Allah's will and ensuring themselves of a glorious life in the hereafter as described in detail in the Koran. Accounts are legion of Iranian troops whipped into an impassioned frenzy before going into battle with archenemy Iraq, with Allah's will mentioned again and again, sparking blind obedience.

The apparatus had been put into motion by Muhammad, but with his death the suddenly leaderless Islamic movement erupted in conflict as a successor was sought. A number of factions emerged, each asserting a claim and each putting forth a candidate to assume the mantle of power, available at the Prophet's death. One group favored Ali, Muhammad's son-in-law, to occupy the position of caliph. Its rationale was along the old Arab bloodline concept, with one additional twist: God in His wisdom must have arranged succession status through Muhammad's immediate family. A claim was also asserted by the Umayyad branch of the Quraysh tribe. These recent converts to Islam buttressed their claim by stating that the power and influence they exercised on the Prophet's behalf had aided the cause of Islam enormously at a pivotal point in its early history. Skeptics argued that what they were really interested in was a return to their previous position of influence before the Islamic ground swell and that their aid in the movement's development stemmed not so much from religious zeal as from an intelligent reading of the direction in which the political cultural winds were blowing. Another group of aspirants to the caliphate stressed the practice existing among Arab tribes of selecting for leadership the "oldest and wisest" among their ranks. It was this third group whose influence prevailed as Abu Bakr, Muhammad's father-in-law, was chosen as the prophet's successor.

The first task of Abu Bakr was to reunite the tribal chiefs of the Arabian peninsula, and once this objective had been accomplished he began to look elsewhere, seeking means of expanding Islam's borders.

In order for any great religious, political, or social movement to succeed on a broad international scale, two prerequisites must be met: the insurgent group must be properly prepared, and vulnerabilities must exist in the area or areas where expansion is sought, with the insurgent group's being tactically capable of exploiting such weaknesses.

Opportunities for Moslem expansion were enhanced in that the two leading empires that dominated the nations bordering Arabia in the seventh century were the Byzantine and Persian, whose influence had been overextended. Natives of these countries suffered under the oppressive tax systems and political corruption of their Greek and Persian masters, and when the highly motivated, well-trained Moslem forces under the generalship of Khalid ibn-al-Walid attacked, the Arabs encountered little resistance from the populace as they pushed their way toward Iraq and Syria. After winning a crucial victory at Ajnadyn on July 30, 634, all Palestine loomed invitingly, open for the taking. Six months later, the Syrian capital of Damascus was conquered.

With the Damascus victory complete, the Moslems demonstrated a concept that held them in good stead both in Syria and in other nations they would subsequently conquer. Considering themselves to be liberators as well as missionaries extending the influence of Allah, the Moslems, citing the Koran, chose not to pillage and plunder their area of conquest. Instead they sought no more than to exact tribute in the form of a poll tax from their subjects. In turn the subjects were promised security in their lives, property, and churches. As long as tribute was paid, they were free to continue to worship in any manner they desired.

The conquest of Syria came under the rule of Caliph Umar ibn-al-Khattab, who followed after the death of Abu Bakr. A man noted for simplicity and accessibility to his people in the manner of the Prophet himself, Umar, legend reveals, living a life as unpretentious as any Bedouin sheikh, owned only one shirt and one mantle, both liberally patched. It was said that he slept on a bed of palm leaves and had no concern other than maintaining the purity of the faith, upholding justice, and guiding Islamic destiny as its forward launch progressed.

It was revealed that Umar's character was so stern that he scourged his own son to death for drunkenness and immorality.

The Moslem legions pushed on during the caliphate of Umar, completing their conquest of Syria, then advancing to Iraq. At first, Moslem victories were numerous, but the Persian emperor eventually rallied his forces, and it took ten years before Islamic conquest was completed. Egypt was also conquered, and just as Umar's campaign into Persia was beginning to take shape, the caliph's life was ended by the poisoned dagger of a Christian Persian slave.

The productive reign of Umar, which lasted from 634 to 644, was followed by that of Othman, who continued the Persian assault until victory was complete. Othman's caliphate, which extended until his death, in 656, saw the Arab quest pushed west and south in search of treasure. Tribute was exacted from Carthage, and the Berbers of Tripoli were overcome. After the first Arab fleet was built, Cyprus was captured, Rhodes pillaged, and the Byzantine fleet destroyed off the Lycian coast.

While victories were being forged by Arab warriors on the battlefields and the onrushing tide of Islamic expansion continued, Othman's caliphate became enmeshed in internal conflict. Othman has appointed many of his kinsmen to prominent government positions, and a group spearheaded by Muhammad, the son of Abu Bakr, fought against the caliphate's nepotism and was responsible for Othman's death.

Ali was selected as caliph after Othman's execution, and the strife-ridden period that accompanied and followed his rule is important to note in terms of the present struggle in the Arab world between two contrasting elements of Islam.

The succession of Ali to the caliphate prompted immediate revolt on the part of one of Othman's relatives, Muawiyah, Governor of Syria. Through the strategic application of pressure, Muawiyah succeeded in having Ali's caliphate submitted to arbitration. The effort resulted in the deposing of Ali, which in turn alienated the Kharijites, a fanatical segment of Ali's followers. Ultimately the murder of Ali by a poisoned saber wielded by a Kharijite brought to a close what is termed the period of orthodoxy in Arab history, which was marked by battlefield successes on foreign soil and the subsequent enhancement of Islamic territory but was scarred by ultimate internal strife on the part of tribal factions vying for supremacy.

The bitter struggle surrounding the Ali caliphate engendered repercussions that markedly influence the composition of the Arab world today. The split in Islamic ranks stems from the belief on the part of

Ali's followers, who became even more militant following his death, in their leader's divinity. Despite Muhammad the Prophet's disavowal of any divine intermediary between Allah and his worldly subjects, the followers of Ali, designed as Shiites, felt the need for an incarnate manifestation of God, selecting Ali as that vessel. Ali became divine, as did his two sons, Hasan and Husain, to whom his wife, the Prophet's daughter Fatima, gave birth. Just as the assassination of Ali gave the Shiite movement additional impetus through martyrdom, this element was magnified when Husain, leading a military force against Caliph Yazid, Muawiyah's son, lost his life along with most of his badly outnumbered troops in a massacre.

The Shiites today constitute only some 10 percent of Moslem believers; the orthodox Sunnis are the remainder. The Sunnis acknowledge the first four caliphs as rightful successors of Muhammad but reject the Shiite claim regarding incarnation, treating Ali as a legitimate caliph in the tradition of the Prophet but nothing more.

The militant religious zeal of the seventh-century Shiites is every bit as graphically visible today as evident in the conduct surrounding Iran, the most devoted follower of that religious viewpoint. Just as Husain led a badly outnumbered military force against Caliph Yazid in the seventh century, which resulted in his own death as well as the slaughter of the vast majority of his cohorts, much media attention has been focused on the youthful suicide battalions of Iran in their bitter war with Iraq, which raged for almost ten years. Their faces frozen into expressions of intense hatred, they are pictured by television cameras while delivering incantations to Allah, prepared to have their own lives prematurely snuffed out by their enemies in the pursuit of achieving the ultimate goal of victory. No sacrifice is too great in the pursuit of carrying out the divine will of Allah, which they regard as a responsibility resting squarely in their hands.

This same Shiite zeal can be seen as the perpetuating catalyst behind the phenomenon of Ayattolah Khomeini, whose followers embraced him in a manner embodying divination, a characteristic absent in a traditional Sunni nation as represented by Egypt's President Mubarak. If Khomeini is perceived as divine or at least quasi-divine by his followers, the means to which they feel compelled to extend themselves in the pursuit of their goal becomes limitless. Spurred on by the putative godlike figure who sees himself in the same light, the natural bounds of rational ethical conduct, to which mere mortals find themselves bound, disappear in a wave of fanatical emotion, a swirling tide of activity that involves hostage taking, hijacking, skyjacking, bombing, and widespread killing of innocent victims far removed from the fray.

The second phase of Moslem expansion was highlighted by the conquest of Spain under the leadership of the freed Berber slave Tariq, whose forces, numbering twelve thousand, met and routed the twenty-five-thousand-man contingent of King Roderick on July 19, 711, near Gibraltar. The victory broke the main line of Visigoth opposition, and Tariq was able to move his troops with generally scant resistance all the way to Seville and Merida. Though opposition was strong in both these cities, it was ultimately overcome. From there it was on to Toledo, then to Zaragoza in the north.

With Zaragoza's constituting a Moslem foothold adjacent to neighboring France, and the rich treasures of its churches and convents looming appetizingly close, it was seemingly inevitable that this Islamic Empire flush with victories would turn its attention there. In 720, Septimania, a dependency of the defunct Visigothic kingdom, was captured. From there, Narbonne was secured, being eventually converted into a huge citadel and arms depot. An attempt the following year to conquer Toulouse was unsuccessful, however, as the Duke of Eudes overcame Moslem efforts in recording the first ever victory by a Germanic prince over Islamic forces. Subsequent movements by Arabs to penetrate beyond the Pyrenees Mountains were also unsuccessful.

In the early spring of 732, the forces of Abd-al-Rahman crossed the western Pyrenees, vanquishing the Duke of Eudes on the banks of the Garonne. From there they attacked Bordeaux, setting its churches on fire. Then Abd-al-Rahman pushed northward, where the objective became Tours, the resting place of the apostle of the Gauls, St. Martin, a monument of great importance to the Roman Catholic Church.

Seeking to preserve such a vital bastion of Christendom, the Duke of Eudes sought the intercession of Charles Martel, mayor of the palace at the Merovingian court and a formidable warrior with a string of victories to his credit, as exemplified by his surname of Martel, meaning "the hammer." For seven days, the Arab forces of Abd-al-Rahman and the Frankish forces of Charles Martel, mainly foot soldiers clad in wolfskins with long matted hair extending below their shoulders, engaged in light skirmishes. In the main, however, they stood facing each other with an air of anticipation, awaiting the moment that the major confrontation would begin. It finally happened on a fateful Saturday of 732. The Arabs forged to the attack but were repulsed by the shaggy-haired, determined Frankish warriors, who astonished their attackers by forming a hollow square during the heat of the battle. Shoulder to shoulder they stood, firm as a wall, as impenetrable as granite. The light infantry of the Moslems failed to surmount the resolute Franks, whose drawn swords viciously repulsed their attackers. One of the victims was Abd-al-Rahman himself. The fall of darkness stilled the battle, and when morning beckoned, Charles Martel found the silence of the enemy camp disquieting. He summoned some of his forces to spy on the enemy in an attempt to learn its intent. The scouts returned, revealing with elation that the Moslems had gone, deserting their tents and totally vacating the area.

Given the religious implications of the conflict at Tours, which pitted Christian forces seeking to hold on to their European terrain against the advancing wave of Islamic warriors, it was seemingly inevitable that historians would place great significance on it. Understandably, this has been true of Catholic historians, who regard the Battle of Tours as a milestone of their faith, when forces of the holy mother church rose to the occasion and turned back a strong and determined invader who threatened their existence. The major difficulty presented when one shapes historical circumstance to articles of faith is the embellishment of exaggeration that may occur in the process, often unwittingly. Given the magnitude of the victory in the minds of proponents, along with the religious overtones embodying matters of the soul, the tendency is for the enemy to appear stronger than it was in actuality, if not almost invincible. By focusing on the might of the overcome force the extension of such thinking leads its proponent to envision what would have occurred had the powerful invader not been repulsed. This theme was elucidated by the prominent British historian Gibbon, author of *The Decline and Fall of the Roman Empire,* who envisioned mosques rather than towering cathedrals making up the skylines of Paris and London, and the Koran rather than the King James Bible being extolled at Oxford and Cambridge had the Moslem forces triumphed on that Saturday afternoon in 732.

It is ironic that Gibbon, who wrote perhaps the definitive historical work on the subject of a major power's decline, focusing on the vicissitudes of change that cause a proud nation to achieve on a mighty upsweep of grandeur, pride, and idealism, then sink through a combination of overextension, headiness of power intoxication, and softening of resolve, would fail to perceive in the case of the Moslem Empire that these same universal elements contributing to decline were present that had been pervasive as well in the instance of the Roman Empire.

Another note of irony unfolds with the realization that the dramatic victory of the Frankish forces of Christianity over the warriors of Islam occurred in 732, exactly one century after the year of the great Prophet Muhammad's death in 632. The energetic ground swell of activity taking place within Islamic ranks during that century, which still constitutes only a grain of sand in an overall historical context, saw events proceed at a fervent gallop. At the time of the Prophet's death, Arabia was dominated by Bedouin tribes, which operated within their own restrictive spheres, having learned to prey upon other tribes as well as city folk, who had been traditionally regarded as inferior by these fiercely individualistic desert dwellers. The Prophet had devoted his life to building Islam as a bridge of unification for the Arab people, replacing the old tribal loyalties with a broader-based unity that all Moslems could uniformly embrace. Gradually this new spirit of unification took shape to the point where Moslems were able to join forces, advance under the star and crescent of Islam, and take advantage of the slothful decay within the ranks of the two major world powers, Byzantine and Persian, in order to achieve dramatic victories in what seemed to be an inexorable push toward global domination. By the time the dynamic Islamic military thrusts reached their zenith in 732, the followers of the Prophet controlled an empire extending from the Bay of Biscay to the Indus and the frontiers of China and from the Aral Sea to the upper Nile. Damascus, which Muhammad had refused to enter on the premise that he wanted to see Paradise only once, had become the capital of this vast empire. A triumphal march on such a huge scale conducted within the span of a century would be sufficient to exhaust the sharply channeled motivation necessary to sustain or further enhance the movement. Much had happened in such a relatively short span and against the backdrop of current internal strife at the political level, despite which the onslaught was able to advance until 732. Now it was the Moslems who found themselves in the same posture as the earlier powers they had conquered (Byzantium and Persia) had occupied. Battle weary, handicapped by internal strife, and seeing its direct control diminish as its legions pushed to ever more distant regions, Islam's mighty onslaught was quieted by the exhaustion of its momentum.

With the military phase of Islam virtually ended and with the exception of minor periodic forays, concentration became vested in cultural pursuits. Damascus became the fountainhead of this movement, the jeweled Moslem capital containing the glittering palace of the Umayyads in the heart of the city.

Another instance of Islamic internal strife, this time in the middle of the eighth century, resulted in another city of strength and influence emerging to rival the dominance of Damascus. Whereas the Umayyad dynasty was already weakened by a decaying of moral standards through the excesses of a harem system marked by a steady proliferation of slaves, an intensifying rivalry between the tribes of Northern and Southern Arabia generated additional impact. A racial tendency that had existed prior to Islamic days now erupted into open hostilities, with ancestral feuds abounding. In 747, a revolt undertaken by the Abbasids against their cousins, the Umayyads, led the way for a new city of wealth and influence, which was markedly influenced by Persia. This influence became so pronounced that Moslem culture dominated in but two major areas: Islam remained the religion of the state, and Arabic continued to function as the official language.

With the Islamic military thrust ended, Moslems were able to concentrate on achieving cultural advancement. As an embarkation point on their journey, they adopted the same pattern embraced by the Roman Empire of utilizing the best of Greek thought. The initial cultural impetus was accordingly derivative rather than original, but eventually many new routes were established and explored. After a launch into philosophy by translating and analyzing the works of Aristotle, progress was made through the efforts of Ibn Sina (Avicenna) (980–1037), considered the most famous of Muslim thinkers and scientists, who fashioned an important theory of creation and made significant contributions to logic and psychology; Ibn Hazm (994–1064), who was credited with four hundred volumes in philosophy, theology, history, poetry, and other areas; and al-Ghazali (1058–1111), one of Islam's most influential thinkers, who, after renouncing philosophy, turned to mysticism.

The Arabs are credited with inventing the alphabet, which is widely known, but they also achieved great progress in mathematics and medicine. The Muslims introduced Arabic numerals, the zero (known as *sifr*), and the decimal system in the ninth century. Omar Khayyám (1048–1122), famous for producing the legendary literary masterpiece *The Rubáiyát*, also excelled in the realm of mathematics, inventing an advanced algebra and preparing a calendar more accurate than the Gregorian. A significant mathematical contribution was also made by al-Khwarizmi (780–850), who invented a "modern" algebra, which transformed numbers into elements of relation.

Perhaps the most notable Arab advancements in knowledge came in the spheres of medicine and science. The Greeks supplied the intellectual impetus for Arab medicine as the works of Galen, Hippocrates, and others were translated by Hunayn ibn Ishaq (810–877), who also wrote original books on medicine. The highly versatile Ibn Sina (Avicenna), mentioned earlier for his contributions to Arab philosophy, authored the famous *Canon of Medicine,* in which he recognized the contagious character of disease. A major figure whose efforts embraced a number of scientific fields was al-Razi (865–925), known as one of the foremost doctors of all time. He gave the first clinical account of measles and smallpox and wrote the most comprehensive book on medicine ever done by an Arab. Also a leading alchemist, it was al-Razi who gave exact classification of substances and chemical processes. The first scientist to correct Ptolemy's erroneous optical doctrines was al Haytham (Alhazen) (965–1039), in the process laying the foundation of modern optics. His writings had a profound influence on medieval writers on optics such as Roger Bacon, Kepler, and Leonardo da Vinci.

In the literary world, the focus remained primarily on poetry, always of great interest to the Arabs, but major contributions were made in the artistic endeavors of architecture, pottery, textiles, metal and leather work, and bas-relief carving.

Moslem military advancement ended as early as 732, but economic and cultural advancements continued until they too terminated through exhaustion from their own momentum. The pursuit of materialistic ends precipitated a softening in the underbelly of Moslem culture, creating the same kind of vulnerability the Arab world had successfully exploited shortly after the death of the prophet and culminating in the rise of Islam.

Islam's rise came at the expense of the sated Byzantine and Persian cultures. The tired and overwrought had given way to the advancing tide of a religious movement whose impetus was bolstered by the desire for economic advancement.

Historical circumstances have a discernible way of repeating themselves, with only the principals and locations changing. Such was the case past the halfway mark of the eleventh century, as a rapidly fading Moslem world, which had capitalized earlier on Byzantine and Persian internal weaknesses, found itself vulnerably exposed to a poised, highly motivated threat enhanced by a religious fervor of its own.

Christian Europe had experienced waves of frustration for centuries over the success of Moslem military expeditions, which resulted in control of so much of the world, most notably in the Holy Land, which Christians construed as being the sorry dilemma of an infidel-con-

trolled territory sanctified by the historical developments and continuing spirit of true believers.

As early as 1071, Pope Gregory VII had been contemplating organizing an expedition to rescue the Eastern Empire from the Moslems, a
reaction to the capture of Jerusalem by the fanatical Seljukian Turks.

Though the Seljuk Empire demolished itself through civil war and
the Egyptians eventually succeeded in driving them out of Jerusalem,
the concept of the Roman Catholic Church's striking a blow against
Islam retained currency as the Byzantine emperior Alexius Comnenus
sent envoys to Pope Urban II in 1094 seeking mercenaries to help him
recapture Asia Minor from the Turks. In that the Saljuq Moslems
threatened Constantinople, Pope Urban could have seen the appeal as
providing an opportunity to reunite the Greek Church with Rome. The
schism then existing between the two churches had occurred as recently as 1054.

The fateful historic moment occurred on November 26, 1095, when
Pope Urban II, at Clermont-Ferrand in his native country of France, in
a memorable speech stirred the masses with his emotionally charged
rhetoric. Christendom was exhorted to "enter upon the road to the
Holy Sepulchre, wrest it from the wicked race and subject it"[5] to
themselves.

The rallying call of the faithful became "God wills it!" As its stirring
cry resounded throughout the land, response was swift and decisive.
By the spring of 1096, one hundred fifty thousand men, mostly Franks
and Normans, had answered the battle call as the first of the Crusades
was launched.

The activating force of religious militancy, which had stirred the
Moslem masses into action during the seventh century, was now being
turned against them, along with a familiar corollary motive, which had
played such a major role in priming the Moslem hordes into action.
Whereas the Moslems now occupied the position the Byzantine and
Persian empires had held in the seventh century of idealistically spent
entities whose power base had weakened due to internal disintegration,
the Christian forces were hungry for material gain. The great masses
of France, Lorraine, Italy, and Sicily jumped at the opportunity to
improve their depressed economic circumstances while simultaneously
striking a blow on behalf of Holy Mother Church. Feudal laws of
succession had produced a large class of landless and unemployable
younger sons eager to carve out estates of their own. The prospect of
realizing this ambition by achieving military successes in distant lands
filled them with the same type of keen-willed anxiety that had activated

the camel-bound Bedouins of the desert to great heights during Islam's seventh-century surge. These masses were in turn spurred on by merchants from Pisa, Venice, and Genoa seeking to enhance their commercial interests. As could be expected, the commercial forces exploited the propaganda tool of religious fervor among the masses as a motivator toward achieving personal enrichment.

The use of God's purported will as a rallying cry to battle carries with it tangible psychological advantages, as evidenced by the Moslems when used initially by them, along with the period in which they were victimized by the same cohesive fervor directed against them. The pursuit of what is termed to be God's will has a strong unifying effect, because the masses are concerned with perpetuating their spiritual well-being. What better way can one ensure being dealt with favorably by God than through risking one's physical being for a higher spiritual purpose? While achieving a spirit of unification among the masses, the level of tenacity of God's warriors tends to increase in that true believers feel that, should they be killed, their death serves a higher end, God's will, and that in dying for such a noble purpose, their eternal salvation has been realized. A notable example of this concept exists in the current Islamic Jihads taking place within extreme fundamentalist circles of the Arab world. While kidnappings, bombings, and other forms of terrorism are perpetrated against non-Arabs by militants, two Islamic nations, Iran and Iraq, have found themselves pitted in mortal struggle to determine who is properly interpreting the teachings of Allah. Squadrons of youthful Iranians, many of whom are preteens, march in lockstep to premature death in the name of Allah. Many of those who survive, their bodies burned beyond recognition by the effects of chemical warfare, envy the dead.

One pervasive manifestation resulting from holy wars is the grand paradox of interpreting God's word. While uniform agreement would exist that the end result of any religious faith would lie in promoting good will toward humanity, a visceral hatred and accompanying destructive impulse afflicts those locked in battle. Rather than practicing tolerance toward those who hold differing viewpoints, a seething cauldron of self-righteousness gradually builds until, ultimately, an all-consuming rage is directed toward the vipers and infidels of the world who stand in the way of achieving God's will. The result has been the infliction of much unnecessary torture and bloodshed, all of which is ostensibly carried out in the name of God. The Crusades at their worst typified this tendency at its extreme.

Though historians are prone toward classifying the number of Crusades as between seven and nine, prominent Arab historian Philip K. Hitti divides them into three periods: 1) an initial phase of Crusader triumphs extending to 1144; 2) a successful Moslem reaction culminating in the brilliant victories of Saladin; 3) the civil and petty wars ending in 1291 when the Crusaders lost their last foothold on the Syrian mainland.[6]

Anxious to capture Jerusalem from the Moslems, the advancing Crusaders achieved victories at Edessa, Tarsus, Antioch and Aleppo in 1098. The discovery of the "holy lance" which had pierced the side of Christ as He hung on the cross and had lain buried in a church in Antioch gave initial impetus to the advancing hordes of Christendom. Their forces, said to have numbered forty thousand, stood before the gates of Jerusalem on June 7, 1099. The Egyptian garrison was estimated as approximately one thousand. Mindful of the Old Testament account of the walls of Jericho toppling as a result of Almighty intercession, the Crusaders initially marched barefoot around Jerusalem, blowing their horns just as the biblical account records the Israelites had done at Jericho. When the walls failed to capitulate through spiritual intercession, the Crusaders opted for physical force, initiating a month's siege on the city. This effort culminated on July 15 with a full-scale invasion of the city followed by a massacre involving all ages and both sexes in which bodies were dismembered and their individual parts were observed throughout the streets and squares of Jerusalem.[7]

Spurred on by conquest, the Crusaders ultimately carved out states of their own in Palestine and Syria while making significant inroads in Egypt, at which time the Moslems then began to stage a successful counterreaction.

The spearheading force behind the Moslem assault was Saladin, a Syrian of Kurdish parentage, vizir of Egypt in 1169. His twin objectives were to banish Shiite doctrine in Egypt and to wage a successful holy war against the Franks.

On July 1, 1187, Saladin's troops captured Tiberias following a six-day siege, following which attention was turned toward neighboring Hittin, an area of strategic importance to the Moslems. Saladin launched his assault on a Friday, prayer day, a personal favorite for him. If the Franks could lay claim to having God on their side, Saladin could most certainly whip his troops into an equivalent passion of self-righteousness on behalf of Allah. The Franks were a highly vulnerable enemy, numbering twenty thousand but with many perilously close to dying from thirst and heat. Their army collapsed under the Moslem offensive. The most distinguished captive was Guy de Lusignan, King of Jerusalem, who was accorded a friendly reception by the conquering Saladin.

Reginald de Chatillon, one of the more flamboyant Frank leaders, incurred a tragic fate by provoking the wrath of Saladin in the crucial domain of Arabic etiquette. Reginald went into his captor's tent to secure a drink of water, seeking to take advantage of Arab hospitality. In this instance, however, the host had offered no drink. Accordingly, the rules of hospitality did not apply. Saladin used the opportunity to take the life of a man he did not care for to begin with as a result of attacks that Reginald had launched against peaceful caravans in violation of existing truce conditions. He also executed a number of Reginald's cohorts as well.

The crucial victory at Hittin supplied all the impetus that Saladin and his forces needed to capture Jerusalem, which fell on October 2, 1187. The capture of the capital of the Latin kingdom gave Saladin control of most of the towns in Frankish Syria-Palestine.

Once Jerusalem had been lost to the Christians, shock waves reverberated throughout Europe. The upshot was unification among once feuding rulers such as Frederick Barbarossa, Emperor of Germany; Richard Coeur de Lion (the lion-hearted), King of England; and Philip Augustus, King of France, who buried their old disagreements. Their sole objective became that of rescuing Christendom against the perceived Islamic infidels.

The united effort of the three European monarchs directed against Saladin's forces formed the basis for the most famous of the Crusades, the so-called Third Crusade, which involved the greatest numbers of warring participants and pitted in battle two of the most legendary figures of history—Richard Coeur de Lion and Saladin.

A determined King Richard captured Cyprus, then set his sights on Acre, which Christendom viewed as the pivotal point from which the Crusaders could conquer the Holy Land. Initially the attack was led by King Guy, who had been released by Saladin on the condition that he would never again do battle against him. Saladin arrived the next day to rescue the city. Warfare was waged both on land and at sea, and when King Richard arrived, the Crusader forces celebrated amidst bonfires. In what has been billed as one of the greatest military operations of medieval times, the siege of the Franks succeeded after two fierce years of battle, from August 27, 1189, to July 12, 1191. The conditions of the surrender were the release of the garrison on the payment of two hundred thousand gold pieces and the restoration of the Holy Cross. When the money had not been paid at the end of a month, Richard ordered the twenty-seven hundred captives to be slaughtered.

With Acre occupying the position of Holy Land leadership, which Jerusalem had formerly occupied, Richard continued to negotiate with Saladin to achieve peace. It was eventually concluded on November 2, 1192, with an agreement having been drawn that basically ceded the coast to the Latins and the interior to the Moslems. It was also stipulated that pilgrims to the Holy City should not be molested.

Saladin did not live long to enjoy the fruits of peace, being taken ill with fever on February 19, 1193, in Damascus and dying twelve days later at the age of fifty-five. His tomb close to the Umayyad Mosque remains one of the chief attractions in the Syrian capital even to this day. In addition to being a brilliant and courageous warrior and champion of Sunnite Islam, he was also a leader in education and architecture, founding numerous schools and mosques, and was responsible for the Citadel of Cairo.

Though the fighting continued for almost an entire century, the vigor of the Crusades had been essentially dissipated after the formidable figures of King Richard and Saladin departed from the scene. Christendom made one final thrust during the Sixth Crusade, led by King Louis IX of France. The Franks captured the Egyptian city of Dimyat, but they bogged down in the marshes of the Nile River when they sought to capture Cairo, resulting in the capture of most of them, including King Louis himself.

The last remnant of warring Crusaders was turned away from Syria and Egypt by elements of what turned out to be the last Arab dynasty, which would also have to be classified as the most extraordinary dynasty of all.

What made the Mamluks unique was their origin. The Mamluks constituted a dynasty of slaves. The word "Mamluk" means possessed and the body that comprised them consisted of varied races and nationalities forming a military oligarchy in an alien land.

History is replete with examples of groups' and individuals' rising due to the internal weaknesses exhibited by those above them. The rise of the Mamluks illustrates this principle, particularly as exemplified by the first and most distinguished in the line of Mamluk sultans, Baybars, who was originally a Turkish slave. Baybars was made leader of a section of the sultan's bodyguard. From that position he worked his way up to sultan, a quantum jump from slave status to the highest post in Egypt.

The petty dynasty ruling Egypt had followed the precedent of the caliphs of Baghdad with the same destructive result. By taking foreign slaves into their service as bodyguards, they invested the strong and the ambitious with a sterling opportunity to eventually overthrow their masters. At a period in history when Arab forces were sharply declining due to internal corruption and lethargy, the slaves rose through a combination of cunning and forceful brutality. With all other avenues of social advancement cut off in a regime marked by corruption and sloth, achievement was derived through bloodshed, and the rugged Mamluks proved more than capable of combining physical violence and cunning to their ultimate advantage.

Baybars achieved his first successes against the Mongols in Palestine, but he is known generally for destroying the Frankish opposition and bringing the Crusades to a close. A large, dusky man with a booming voice, Baybars may have used the physical realm to acquire power, but his tenure as sultan was noted for much more than military achievements. Not only did Baybars organize the army, rebuild the navy, and strengthen the fortresses of Syria, but he also dug canals, improved harbors, and connected Cairo and Damascus by a swift postal service requiring but four days in which relays of horses stood in position at each station. In addition, he fostered public works, beautified mosques, and was responsible for some enduring architectural monuments, including the great mosque and the school bearing his name. On the diplomatic front, he excelled by establishing a number of alliances that included European and Mongol powers.

Once Baybars, an enlightened dictator whose own prodigious abilities enabled the Mamluks to rise above a tradition predicated on blood and iron, had passed from the scene, the notable defects of an Arab society that had been gradually sliding downhill for centuries became more pronounced, as certain less skilled, frequently barbaric sultans accelerated a deterioration that would ultimately end medieval Arab rule by the early sixteenth century.

All the same, despite the unmistakable trend toward disintegration, aspects of Arab culture fought hard to buck the general overall thrust. Despite deterioration in the sciences, the Arabs managed after the middle of the thirteenth century to maintain their leadership in astronomy-mathematics, including trigonometry, and medicine, notably ophthalmology. The Mamluk period is also noted for architectural and artistic productivity on a scale and quality without parallel in Egyptian history since Ptolemaic and Pharaonic days.

By the end of the fourteenth century, the seeds of Arab destruction had been laid through the efforts of a series of corrupt and incompetent sultans, some of whom were bloodthirsty as well. From 1412 to 1421, the sultan was a drunkard who had been bought by a Circassian dealer. Another was not familiar with Arabic and had his two physicians beheaded when they were unable to provide him with relief from a fatal malady. The one who ruled in 1453 could neither read nor write, and a successor was not only illiterate but insane.

Although Mamluk leadership itself played a destructive role in undermining Arab civilization, the ravages of nature also contributed as locusts ravaged the land and famine became rife. Misfortune intensified with years of plague and drought caused by low water in the Nile River. It is estimated that during the Mamluk period, the population of Syria and Egypt was reduced by two thirds.

The final coup to the Arab Empire was administered by the Ottoman Turks on January 24, 1516, with the devastating victory by Salim, the Ottoman sultan, over a badly overmatched adversary. The triumph largely represented a victory of new concepts over old as the Turkish army was better equipped with new arms, which included artillery, muskets, and other long-range weapons. The Turks had been using powder for some time. The Mamluk army, consisting of Bedouin and Syrian contingents, stubbornly resisted utilizing such advanced concepts on the antiquated theory that personal valor is the decisive element in combat.

With the Ottoman Empire's having supplanted a long-standing Arab dynasty that had been in gradual disintegration for centuries, such prominent historical areas as Jerusalem, Egypt, and Syria sharply receded into the background as the Ottoman capital of Constantinople became the influential center of Islam as well as the seat of cultural and social existence.

The Arabs, their prideful past of military, cultural, and scientific dominance still foremost in their thoughts, saw themselves as embodying a part of the Ottoman Empire. The onetime rulers became the ruled for four centuries, and during that time, frustrations abounded and the passionate thirst for freedom and a restoration of the glories of old grew more evident.

It is instructive at this point not only to analyze where the Arabs stood but also to compare and contrast it with the posture of the Jews in what stands as a pivotal crossroads of history for both groups.

In the case of the Arabs, this proud people had stood at the apex of world power. As a result, the subservient position they held beneath their controlling masters of the Ottoman Empire for four hundred years was a particularly bitter pill to swallow. Certain among their restive numbers began to experience longings of independence, a return to those once proud days of old when, surging with a power and confidence instilled by the concepts of their Prophet Muhammad, they stood at the triumphant pinnacle of global achievement.

Equally proud, equally mindful of their early culture, the Jews also experienced a developing restiveness within their ranks. Whereas the Arabs longed to return to glories of old, however, the Jews, frustrated, angry, and weary of occupying minority status in nation after nation, sought to take the emerging forces of history by their roots and achieve a nation of their own. Rather than being a part of someone else's culture, consistently faced with the problem of blending into the social fabric of different European nations, many Jews were exceedingly tired of wandering and desired a nation of their own that they could develop and nurture themselves and that would stand as their own independent entity.

The religious and historical roots of both of these proud and determined peoples sprang from the same region, that of the Middle East, but yet, no matter how determined their resolve to achieve independence in that region, the controlling influence of the Ottoman Empire stood in their way: (1) Just how would this obstacle be overcome? both groups asked with increasing anxiety. (2) Next, should this initial hurdle be scaled, what should rightfully follow in these two scenarios that were being developed within the ranks of the Arabs and the Jews? Just how should the land be divided? Unfortunately, with the determined focus squarely on achieving independence and on dislodging the Ottoman Empire, too little attention was devoted to question number two as the emphasis was placed on both question number one and the supplanting of the controlling power in the area.

As World War One beckoned and the nations of the world began to coalesce into alliances, both Arabs and Jews began to sniff opportunity amidst the conflict that was taking shape. Through the fires of battle, a way was seen by each group to alter their subservient existence and attain the dreams that had sadly eluded them.

In that historical change is brought about by the combination of opportunity and the assertiveness of individuals and forces prevailing on such a potential for upheaval, attention must be focused on representative forces of change and the origins of their beliefs. Only by so doing is it possible to comprehend the ideological forces behind movements seeking to accomplish change.

By analyzing two specific individuals—one Arab, one Jew, one of international reputation, the other nameless—it is possible to better see the microcosmic forces at work within the two groups. Then one can more clearly perceive the dynamics that resulted in confrontation, a pattern of escalation that, should it go unchecked, could engulf the entire world in a nuclear confrontation.

In terms of worldwide name recognition, it could well be that the best-known Muslim of the twentieth century is a person operating independently of the world political power structure. His prowess as a fighter possessed of brilliant skills, in which speed of hand and foot were combined for successful results, was renowned in every continent of the world. As one of their own, Muslims took particular pride in his success.

The personality is former world heavyweight champion Muhammad Ali. To comprehend the psychological dynamics behind the man, which then translated into pronounced physical results, brings discerning individuals one step closer to understanding the roots of Arab Islamic thought.

Although it is true that Ali showed great promise as a fighter before he became a Muslim under his given family name of Cassius Clay and became an outstanding enough amateur fighter to win the light heavyweight championship at the 1960 Summer Olympics in Rome, it was after he converted to Islam and changed his name to Muhammad Ali after turning professional that he began to loom as a man with a mission, a seemingly indomitable force who spoke with great conviction about his dedication to Allah and his resolve not only to be the heavyweight champion of the world but also to become the greatest of all time, a symbol to be observed with reverence as a result of achievements accomplished. Whereas it may be true that many of his comments were structured in show business parlance to build bigger gates at the arenas and stadiums where he fought, it was every bit as clear that his determination to become "The Greatest" was the product of earnest resolve. When he was interviewed by the media after a great victory, Ali would unvaryingly give thanks and praise to Allah for making his triumph possible.

To listen to Ali in his sleek, well-conditioned prime speak about his achievements and give thanks to Allah for making them possible was to comprehend the thinking and determined attitude of a highly motivated, well-prepared Islamic warrior. It was Muhammad the Prophet who had invested Arabs with a spirit of pride and unity, which caused them to set aside tribal differences in the pursuit of victory in the name of Islam. Ali emerged as a modern-day descendant of this objective, achieving as a vessel of Allah, and it is no small wonder that the Ali mystique and enormous popularity that accompanied it was felt with particular significance in Muslim nations, where he constantly attracted huge throngs of people.

Ali was simultaneously imbued with another cultural tradition, which blended with that of Islamic zeal, that being the macho pride of the Bedouin. The tradition of the lonesome desert wanderer and warrior, overcoming the ravages of a hostile environment, was transmitted into a prideful code that became integrated into the mosaic of the Islamic spirit that had been inculcated into the Arabs by Muhammad the Prophet. Such a twofold impetus infused subsequent warriors of Islam with a fervent zeal to achieve victory. The more victories that Muhammad Ali the fighter achieved, the higher he projected his expectations. Author Norman Mailer commented on the pressure he generated unto himself by making increasingly bolder predictions about future successes and the defeats of opponents wherein, should he lose, the public humiliation would be vast. Yet he stood up under this pressure. In addition to his natural physical talents, the tremendous psychological impetus afforded him by the concepts of Islam along with Bedouin machismo handed down through generations provided Ali with an advantage over less committed rivals.

The Ali example could be accordingly enlarged and transferred to the status of scores of physically strong, religiously committed Arabs who, leading up to the pivotal period surrounding World War One, had lived under Turkish rule for four hundred years and who yearned to break free of the yoke of oppression that bound them. They sought to once more be free of any kind of foreign domination.

As for the determined spirit of the Jewish cause, a classic example is furnished by the case of a nameless young woman of the early twentieth century who sent shock waves through the 1903 Zionist Congress by way of two spontaneous acts of wild bravado, events that underscored the surge of restless discontent that hung over the collective body like a heavy fog that would not go away.

Here was Theodor Herzl, presiding over what would be his last Zionist Congress and hoping to provide at least a temporary healing balm for some of the pain being experienced by Jews victimized by pogroms. Even though this father of Zionism realized the depth of Jewish feeling to return to Palestine, which the Jews considered their natural homeland, he felt that a temporary remedy for the problems of discrimination that faced Jews in Eastern European cities could be the acquisition of a Zionist homeland away from Palestine. To Herzl, a homeland in East Africa could fulfill the immediacy of Jewish needs for a land of their own, where they could exist on their own, removed from the pain of pogroms along with the general social malaise of feeling unwelcome in so many in the cities where they resided.

Herzl's East Africa proposal sparked heated debate along with burning outward hostility. This seething resentment was demonstrated by the act of a young woman who rushed to the platform, grabbed the map of East Africa hanging on the wall behind the president's chair, and ripped it to shreds.

This same young woman, whose voiceless act of symbolic anger had thrown the proceedings into a tailspin, registered her intense feelings anew after debate had concluded and the vote had been taken on the resolution to conduct an exploratory study on the feasibility of the East Africa proposal. After the resolution passed by a 295 to 178 margin, amidst deep resentment on the part of many of the delegates, this same young woman shouted at Herzl in French, communicating a brief message of blunt intensity.

"Mr. President, you are a traitor!" she shrieked.

To Herzl, who was presiding over a gathering characterized by bitter division, this supreme insult no doubt constituted the final savage blow. Here was a man who had given everything to the Zionist cause he had founded, his health breaking in the process. He would soon be dead, and yet was presiding over the Zionist Congress. Even so, after accomplishing so much, after striving so mightily on behalf of the Zionist cause, he was called a traitor by some impudent young woman shouting at him in French!

Just what were the likely causes of this resentment that triggered such a volcanic response at none other than Theodor Herzl himself, the father of Zionism? Though we do not know the identity of the angry young woman who had hurled the "traitor" epithet at Herzl, it is possible to fill in the blanks and determine the young woman's likely background, along with defining the frustrations that resulted in two desperate acts' being perpetrated at Theodor Herzl's final Zionist Congress.

The prototype of a typical delegate at that Zionist Congress, as well as at those that preceded it and those that would follow, was that of an individual living in at least a reasonably large European city and feeling a strong measure of alienation. To understand the unique type of alienation felt by this young woman along with scores of other Jews is to revert back once more to the example of the schlemiel. The schlemiel feels left out, lacking indigenous roots in the society of which he or she is a part, and the tragic comedy perpetrated by the schlemiel is a twofold attempt to placate those in charge and those who construe Jews as strictly outsiders while easing at least some of the hurtful alienation through humor. By demonstrating a pattern of bumptiousness to the group in charge, which construes the Jews to be permanent outsiders, resentments can be diminished by essentially proving the low expectation level of the critics. Such conduct would never command respect, but it could and often did bring a level of relaxed tolerance from a haughty majority considering the minority to be markedly inferior.

Perhaps this angry young woman, like so many other Jewish youths, had seen her father or mother engage in schlemiel behavior at times in order to exact a certain level of tolerance from those convinced they were superior. Then later, in the privacy of home, removed from the dictates of a critical majority, these youths would see a different pattern emerge. They would learn about a period in time some two thousand years earlier when the Jews had a kingdom of their own. The names Moses, Abraham, David, and Isaiah would be enunciated amidst a recitation of accomplishments in a distant past. An identity began to emerge. With it came a feeling of cultural pride along with a deep longing, a surge of determination to one day experience a return to the land of Jewish roots. Palestine loomed as the culmination of a dream, a quest for identity and fulfillment.

Palestine loomed as the end of a tortuous two-thousand-year quest by Jews like the young woman who vented her frustration on none other than Zionism's founder, and subsequent events proved that she was not alone. Russian Zionists who opposed the East African plan convened in Kharkov in October 1903 and passed a resolution challenging Zionist leadership. This result came about despite the fact that it was the Russian Jews who elicited particularly strong concern over the harsh treatment to which they had been subjected in the waves of pogroms that swept through Russia. The way to get suffering Jews out of what represented a combat zone was to find a land to which they could emigrate. If Palestine was not available at the time for that kind of massive effort, then perhaps another land, such as East Africa, could be utilized at least temporarily, until such potential would be available in Palestine.

Despite the aforementioned pressures and problems that militated heavily on Theodor Herzl and played a dominant role in prompting him to sponsor the East Africa plan, why did this young woman along with the Russian dissidents and so many other ardent Zionists so emphatically oppose it? The answer lies in reverting back to those old Jewish roots, the accounts of an ancient heritage, and the swelling pride and hope they elicited during times of grief. Yes, the Jews felt, there was once a period of time when we had our own nation. They looked forward to someday returning to that same land, the land of their roots, and reconsecrating the nation that had been theirs. After two thousand years in the wilderness, they felt it was time to bring their wandering to an end and return to that land.

Symbols can be of great importance, and when a familiar and beloved symbol is discarded in place of a new one to which there is no bond of attachment, outrage can and often does result. Such was the case when the young woman rushed up to the speaker's platform and tore the map of East Africa from the wall, then angrily ripped it to shreds. During past Zionist Congresses, it had been the map of Palestine that was displayed on the wall behind the president's chair. Suddenly that one had been replaced by one of an alien land. This was intolerable to the young woman, who reacted with seething anger.

The Arabs and the Jews were two groups each with a past it sought to rekindle—and in the very same nation, Palestine, a land in which each held ancient roots of attachment.

Living directly under the yoke of Ottoman Empire control in the Middle East, the Arabs began to sniff opportunity amidst the conflagration that was taking shape with the imminent reality of World War One. Through the fires of conflict, a way was seen to alter their subservient existence.

Aiding the Arabs in their quest for freedom was an unlikely leader who had sprung not from their ranks but from a culture miles removed and decidedly different from their own.

This blend of the Arabs and the charismatic stranger they took into their midst provides one of the most fascinating accounts in the annals of history.

# 4

# Arabia's Mysterious Warrior

As the bright, warm Mideast sun shone down on the young American correspondent, his patience was being tried.

He was caught up in the legendary Middle Eastern practice of barter with a Turkish shopkeeper on a busy Jerusalem street. Whereas barter is a practice that has been handed down through the ages in the Middle East as well as throughout much of Asia, Americans are accustomed to less give-and-take, particularly over small transactions, seeking to name a price, then either meet it or move on. Haggling is as much sport as it is business to Middle Easterners, and in this instance the shopkeeper was trying to relieve the American correspondent, who was in Jerusalem covering the First World War, of twenty piasters for a handful of dates.

Suddenly, however, the American's attention was drawn away from the date negotiations and instead to a group of Arabs walking toward the Damascus Gate. What attracted his interest from the tirade he had been preparing to launch about the high cost of dates was the intriguing demeanor of one man, who stood in sharp contrast to his companions. He wore an agal, kuffieh, and aba as were worn only by Near Eastern potentates. The American's eyes then registered on the man's belt, into which was fastened the short curved sword of a prince of Mecca, the insignia worn by descendants of the Prophet.

The correspondent's finely honed reportorial instincts made him immediately recognize that the mysterious stranger was someone worth pursuing. Indeed, to captivate the American's curiosity to such a degree under prevailing circumstances was a feat unto itself, considering that the stall run by the Turkish shopkeeper by which he was standing was situated in the colorful bazaar section of Jerusalem, a winding labyrinth of shops and coffeehouses leading to the Church of the Sepulcher. The narrow lane, a colorful intersection of Eastern and Western cultures, brought together Russian Jews with their corkscrew curls, Greek priests in tall black hats with flowing robes, desert nomads in goatskin coats, and Turks in balloonlike trousers.

The correspondent quickly observed that he was not the only one on bustling Christian Street who was observing the stranger in the flowing royal robes. As the stranger passed through the crowds in front of the bazaars, people turned to observe him.

In addition to his attire, a number of other factors caused the American to take notice of the man's presence. Despite being small of stature, standing only five-foot-three, he had the bearing of a man totally in command, providing him with an inner stature that caused him to loom as a veritable giant. One was also struck by his complexion. Whereas Bedouins are noted for dark skin, scorched by persistent contact with an intense desert sun, the young man in the royal robes was as blond as a Scandinavian. Also, whereas the nomadic sons of Ishmael commonly wear beards, the youthful stranger was clean shaven. He walked rapidly, his arms folded, and his blue eyes appeared unaware of their immediate surroundings as he seemed to be immersed in total concentration on something else.

The first thought that flashed into the American's mind as he watched the young stranger pass by was that, rather than looming as a character who had stepped out of the pages of "The Arabian Nights," he came closer to representing one of the younger apostles of Christ returned to life. The thought became stronger as he observed the serenity of expression on the intriguing stranger's face.

"Who is he?" he asked the Turk, who was capable of speaking only a few words of English, drawing a shrug for a reply.

The American correspondent thought a moment about the stranger. Suddenly an answer flashed in his mind. The logical place to inquire about the fair-skinned young man in the royal robes was the headquarters of Colonel Ronald Storrs, governor of the Holy City, which were situated in a palace beyond the old wall, near Solomon's Quarries.

The American located Colonel Storrs in his office. He began to ask for the identity of this blue-eyed, fair-haired young man wandering about the bazaars wearing the curved sword of a prince, but before he could finish making his inquiry, the colonel opened the door of an adjoining room.

As the door flew open, the American found himself staring in the direction of the fair-skinned, blue-eyed stranger, who was deeply immersed in reading a book on archaeology.

Colonel Ronald Storrs made an immediate introduction: "I want you to meet Colonel Lawrence, the uncrowned king of Arabia."

As the American shook hands with this young man of mystery, he observed both his shyness and aloofness, concluding that he appeared more outwardly concerned over the pursuit of some sunken treasure than the pressing problems of the world during a period of international conflict, but the American correspondent had by then interviewed enough men of influence to know that some of the greatest and most fascinating of them defied analysis. Certainly this was true of the shy, blue-eyed man in his midst, as time and events would reveal as his knowledge of him increased.

That meeting in the headquarters of Colonel Ronald Storrs marked the beginning of a mutually beneficial association in which the fair-skinned Bedouin's fame would dramatically increase, largely through the efforts of the young American correspondent, whose own fame would catapult onto the world arena as a direct result of the energies he expended on one of the uniquely fascinating warriors in the annals of history.

T. E. Lawrence, about whom scores of books have been written and a major film starring Peter O'Toole has been made, is known as one of history's leading military folk heroes, but until the end of the First World War, not that many people were familiar with the man, his exploits, and what they represented on the world political scene.

As for the young American correspondent, his pursuit of Lawrence from the time of that first meeting in Colonel Ronald Storrs's headquarters to the time of the end of the war, when the desert warrior brought his military efforts on behalf of his adopted Arab brethren to a close, resulted in public attention that included a highly successful film and lecture series on Lawrence's contributions in the crucial Arab phase of World War One that began in London, then took him to many other cities and nations of the world. He then wrote a best seller entitled *With Lawrence in Arabia.*

It was no small feat to gain the confidence of the highly withdrawn, introspective Lawrence. No doubt the bond was cemented largely due to the adventurous spirit of both men.

The young American reporter, Lowell Thomas, enjoyed a life of widespread travel, which extended itself busily almost to the time of his death. In his almost ninety years of life, the noted commentator and author, whose concluding words of his nightly radio broadcast, "So long until tomorrow," became legendary, was synonymous with international travel, covering virtually every significant global locale in his radio and newspaper datelines along with numerous others known only to himself and a tiny handful. Perhaps the anecdote that Thomas often told, which he found the most humorous and which came closest to epitomizing his career, originated at a remote global outpost when an American tourist recognized him.

"Lowell Thomas!" a woman exclaimed. "Don't you ever stay home?"

Lowell Thomas took the wraps off the legend, and a paradoxical legend Lawrence proved to be. At times Lawrence appeared to disdain with unswerving tenacity success and all its trappings; on other occasions he courted it with the same zeal with which he had tried to avoid it. The one thing nobody could ever anticipate from Lawrence was predictability. The guesswork involved in trying to figure him out made him all the more fascinating.

As a skilled journalist, Lowell Thomas was undoubtedly intrigued by Lawrence's paradoxical behavior. Such a pattern enhances the aura of mystique about a man accomplishing incredible events in a frame of circumstances so unusual as to once more prove the validity of the adage that truth is stranger than fiction.

Despite the paradoxes, however, as one conscientiously ferrets out the facts concerning Lawrence, a pattern emerges that took him straight down the path to military greatness on behalf of a people who had been living under subjugation in their own land for four hundred years after having once been the premier world power. It was this unlikely figure who had been the catalyst in achieving this result. Perhaps the most notable paradox surrounding Lawrence's colorful life lay in the fact that the Arabs, a fiercely proud, highly parochialized people never noted for melting pot tendencies, would take into their hearts and minds and ultimately place their very existence in the hands of a foreigner from the faraway land of England. Not only was he a man from a strange land, but also his very appearance, that of a blue-eyed, fair-skinned blond, was the polar opposite of the dark-skinned people of the desert.

The best way to understand Lawrence and the movement he led is to examine the personal currents of him as a man in his early formative stages and to blend that information with the historical current he

helped to forge and then to nurture to fruition. The Lawrence phenomenon embodied the same merger of forces mentioned earlier as sociological precedents necessary to reach an accomplished conclusion: (1)
a compelling historical necessity and (2) a personal vehicle with the
necessary ability and popular identity to rally masses in the proper
direction.

Thomas Edward Lawrence was born in the peaceful Welsh village of
Tremadoc on August 16, 1888, the illegitimate son of a wealthy Anglo-
Irish landowner, Thomas Chapman, and a Scottish governess, Sarah
Madden, with whom Chapman had run away from his wife and daughters. To escape the censure of stern Victorian middle-class life, they
changed their names to Lawrence by deed-poll and made frequent
moves, so often that by the time young Ned, as his family called him,
had reached his eighth birthday, he had lived in Wales, Scotland, the
Isle of Man, Jersey, France, and Southern England. This early widely
traveled background on Lawrence's part might well explain the driving
inner restlessness he exhibited as a man, along with the kind of
rootlessness that, while making it seemingly impossible for him to
settle down, increased his adaptability to change. This type of marked
flexibility would loom as a solid asset for an individual roaming the
wide sandy expanses of desert land, devoid of any semblance of a
home base, and propelling himself and his men ever onward to the next
destination, which would come and go with the same rapidity as its
predecessors.

A brief tracing of the Lawrence family roots provides additional
clues regarding the fully developed desert warrior and what brought
him to that point. The Chapmans had originally come from Leicester-
shire and were cousins of the swashbuckling adventurer of old, Sir
Walter Raleigh. So often, eminent standouts in specific areas of endeavor are descended either directly or remotely from achievers in
those same areas, and such can be said regarding the linkage of the
colorful Elizabethan Raleigh, who along with Sir Francis Drake
emerged as a hero when the English triumphed over the presumably
invincible Spanish Armada, with "the uncrowned King of Arabia"—
to use the words of Ronald Storrs—who led his adopted dark-skinned
brethren to victory over their former rulers, the Turks, and the Turks'
German allies.

So often, individuals seemingly singled out by the fates to achieve a
celebrated destiny reveal themselves through precocious behavior.
Such was the case with Lawrence. On his first day at Oxford High
School, he was twitted by a classmate over the fact that the classmate

was one day older than Lawrence. Undaunted, and failing to be bowled over by the prevalent seniority oneupmanship in which children so often engage, Lawrence crisply retorted that the twist of fate about which the classmate was gloating was unfortunate in that, had he been born on the same day as Lawrence, he could then say that his birth was on the identical date as that of Napoleon. Such a response demonstrates a remarkable sense of history in such a young boy. The fact that the historical figure also happened to be one of the foremost tactical military geniuses in world annals makes the statement appear even more prescient in light of what Lawrence himself would later accomplish.

One of the numerous Lawrence paradoxes mentioned at great length by those who knew and studied him as an adult was his powerful penchant for solitariness. This tendency evidenced itself very early in his life. It is significant to note that contemporaries related that the young schoolboy known as Ned, while disdaining team activities such as cricket and football, participated avidly in gymnastics. Away from the schoolyard, he demonstrated a keen interest in tree climbing and hiking, notably individual pursuits.

As a man he would achieve a reputation for his ability to command men, but there was always a facet of T. E. Lawrence that would remain far removed from the crowds, away from personal contact.

Another of the Lawrence paradoxes embodied the subject of violence. The adult Lawrence would achieve a reputation as a fierce warrior capable of commanding the fearless Bedouins. Away from the battlefield, however, he was known to exhibit a pronounced distaste for violence.

The antiviolent strain in Lawrence revealed itself in his boyhood. It was combined with an equivalent sense of justice in an incident described later by his mother, Sarah. During playground activity one day at school, young Ned's attention was immediately seized by the sight of an older boy bullying a younger one. His sense of righteousness appropriately stiffened, Ned plunged posthaste into the fray, coming to the smaller boy's defense and becoming immediately engaged in a tenacious wrestling match with the bully. In the midst of the struggle, as the two boys tumbled to the ground, one of the bones in Ned's leg broke near the ankle. His mother added that her son did not grow much after that. Since he had, according to Sarah Lawrence, grown three inches during the preceding year and never grew much more following the ankle injury, it was her opinion that the subsequent growth decline was caused by the fact that the bones were not strong.

Although it is debatable that Lawrence's injury stunted his growth, it is a matter of record that he did not grow a great deal as evidenced by his adult height of five-three, and it is entirely possible that the savage tenacity he exhibited when he set his sights on a goal, particularly in the war arena, could have been prompted at least in part by the desire to overcompensate due to his lack of size.

Another area of interest—a piece of the total portrait of Lawrence through the sum of his often contradictory parts—is that of education. His family attested to his early precocity, and his intelligence was questioned by no one. Lawrence's major academic problem, manifested as he grew older, lay in the manner he applied himself. His older brother Bob recalled that when he was about five he was able to read a newspaper upside down, and that later in life he claimed that he could always read the newspaper of the man opposite him in the train. His mother recalled that he had always possessed a remarkable memory, that he was able to retain what he read after no more than a glance, and that he won prizes for his scholarship regularly. According to Sarah Lawrence, in the senior locals in 1906, her gifted son distinguished himself by placing first in English and literature and achieving an overall standing of thirteenth in the first class out of some 10,000 entrants.

His scholastic endeavors proceeding well, the bright young teenager was working diligently toward winning an Oxford University scholarship. His pleased and affluent father, sensitive to young Ned's need for peaceful solitude in his studies, built him a two-room bungalow in the garden of their Oxford home.

Just when Thomas Lawrence was inflating himself with pride as a result of the academic achievements on the part of his gifted young son, he was knocked back on his haunches by this man of paradox with a predilection for keeping people guessing—from opponents on a battlefield all the way to his own family members. Ned up and left home, enlisting in the Royal Artillery as an ordinary soldier. Though most Lawrence biographers, relying on Lawrence's own accounts, report that he spent somewhere between six and eight months in the Royal Artillery before his father bought him out and had him sent back home to Oxford, a recent Lawrence biographer, Britisher Michael Yardley, renders a different account.[1] Yardley, who spent three years traveling throughout the world in pursuit of the truth regarding Lawrence, contends that he could not have been in the Royal Artillery any longer than three months because there is no longer gap that can be accounted for after perusing the records. Whereas earlier biographical accounts have had great difficulty deciding just why Lawrence jumped on his bicycle and pedaled to Cornwall, where he enlisted in the Royal Artillery, Yardley states a plausible theory. He speculates that the birth certificate Lawrence was obliged to produce in 1906 for entrance to a qualifying examination for an Oxford University scholarship may well have been the means by which he learned about his illegitimacy. It is therefore conceivable that such a discovery, had it been made then by the means that Yardley suggested, could have sent traumatic shock waves reverberating through this sensitive young man. He had, after all, been brought up in stern Calvinistic teachings, and his older brother Bob would eventually go on to become a Christian medical missionary in China. There remains an equally plausible theory, however. This perpetual study in paradox may well have been seized with a desire for change, a wanderlust that could be satisfied by a new life in the military. In that the formal academic life had never suited him, young Ned might have simply decided that enough was enough and it was time for an abrupt change in his life.

As a result of losing precious school time, once Lawrence returned to Oxford he failed in his first attempt to win a scholarship. He had been granted an extra year to spend at Oxford High School following the brief army interlude. His father hired a tutor from the university, L. Cecil Jane, as Lawrence changed his major from mathematics to history. Jane, with a perceptive eye developed from dealing with many students, observed that Lawrence, although bright, was not a scholar by temperament and had to be coaxed into new areas of study by his own special interests.

The structured academic life, or virtually anything else that involved rigid formality, ran counter to Lawrence's basic grain. During his final two years prior to entering the university, he developed a keen interest in archaeology. During the summer of 1906, Lawrence set off by bicycle with a friend for a tour of the Normandy and Brittany coasts. The friend remained with him for two weeks before returning home. Lawrence stayed for another two weeks, making extensive notes on all the castles and historic buildings that he visited.

Artifacts became a major source of interest for the busy and thoroughly independent mind of young Ned Lawrence. On his bicycle excursions around the south of England, he made rubbings of monumental brasses. Adorning the walls of his bedroom in his bungalow at home were life-sized figures of knights and priests. Particularly ceremonial places were reserved for Sir John D'Abernon and Roger de Trumpington, a notable Crusader.

While still a small boy, Lawrence had bought two books on Layard's excavations of Nineveh, which he practically memorized. With his appetite for artifacts of antiquity having consistently developed, the inquisitive and acquisitive young Lawrence stumbled by chance on an opportunity to develop his collection. In autumn 1906, a good deal of rebuilding was going on in the heart of Oxford. Lawrence soon learned that the excavations were bringing to light quantities of early pottery and glass. A captivated Ned Lawrence bribed the workmen for a few pence apiece to deliver the specimens to him in good condition. When the construction operations were extended to other sites, Lawrence continued his offers, still collecting the best of what the workers secured amidst the rubble. His efforts yielded a fine series of vessels and pottery, glazed ware, blown and molded bottles, pipes, coins, and tokens, most of which were products of the fifteenth and seventeenth centuries. The cream of the collection was eventually presented to the Ashmolean Museum.

With Lawrence's increasing knowledge and interest in old pottery gradually expanding, he began spending a good deal of time at Ashmolean Museum. It was during one of his visits there that he met a man who was destined to play a pivotal role in his life, D. G. Hogarth, who served as keeper of the museum while also functioning as a Fellow of Magdalen College at Oxford University. Among other things, Hogarth must be credited with being the primary catalyst in steering the young Lawrence's interests in artifacts toward the Middle East.

During the summer vacations of 1906, 1907, and 1908, the energetic Lawrence, disdaining the sedentary pursuit of book learning, aggressively pursued his developing interest in ancient history and its numerous fascinating objects. His busy bicycle transported him all over France, where he visited many medieval castles, photographing, drawing, and planning them. During the spring of 1907, he visited the principal Welsh castles. He made a decision then to follow up these studies by traveling Syria to learn whether the castles built by the Crusaders had followed the models of Western Europe or those of Byzantine military architecture.

In October 1907, Lawrence went to Jesus College of Oxford University with a History Exhibition. His fiercely independent flair and disdain for conformity immediately rose to the surface in a number of different ways. He read history voraciously, but his appetite was self-induced rather than following along the prescribed lines of his instructors. His independent and original outlook motivated him to read widely about any subject that caught his fancy. His preference was for medieval sagas and romances, and he often indulged himself by reading until dawn. At times, armed with a book he found fascinating, he would wander for hours in the forests. The pattern he frequently followed of sleeping by day and studying by night fit into his quest for solitariness, the desire to be on his own and as removed as possible from any human contact. In any event, this young man with the unquenchable hunger for knowledge and keen air of independence spent only one term in residence at Oxford University, after which he was granted permission to return home to his bungalow, where he resumed his academic pursuits.

The embryonic pattern emerging within Lawrence at that time would lead to his eventual fascination for the desert and his achievements as a warrior on behalf of the Arabs. His preference for solitariness would make him far more adaptable to the lonely rigors of the Sahara Desert than someone without that attribute. There was also his steadily growing passion to acquire objects of antiquity and learn about their historical periods. Yet another trait also furthered Lawrence's potential for the desert life and the demanding self-induced physical tests he would impose upon himself. He would deprive himself of normal food and sleep, swim on frozen winter nights, and bicycle nonstop until he collapsed from exhaustion. Such a tough regimen would make him better able to endure the harsh conditions of desert existence.

The Lawrence Middle East mosaic that was gradually being woven took a sharp forward turn with the emergence of D. G. Hogarth as a shaping influence on his life. The Ashmolean Museum Curator had been asked by Canon Christopher, Rector of St. Aldate's Church at Oxford, which was regularly attended by the Lawrence family, to turn a watchful eye on T. E. in his university pursuits. The Oxford instructor Hogarth directed Lawrence's interests toward the Middle East, that ancient land whose archaeological findings have stirred the hearts of so many who have antiquarian propensities. Pursuing this interest, Lawrence decided that the subject of his thesis for his degree would be the military architecture of the Crusades. He boned up for the task at hand by taking lessons in simple Arabic and by conversing with Charles Doughty, famous traveler and author of what had then become Lawrence's favorite book, *Travels in Arabia Deserta*.

In the summer of 1909, having laid the preliminary groundwork, T. E. Lawrence set out for Syria. He put his stamina to the test once more by walking from Beirut to Haifa and from Acre to Aleppo, amassing material for his thesis while also experiencing for the first time what it was like to actually live like an Arab. So two more steps were taken in what, in retrospect, appeared to be one man's date with destiny: entering Syria for the first time and having the opportunity to live with the Arabs over a prolonged period of time.

Returning to Oxford, Lawrence went to work on his thesis. The effort was good enough to secure a first class in the Honours School of History in 1910.

It has been noted that Lawrence was fortunate to have attended a school with the generally liberal traditions of Oxford University in that he was accorded a freer reign to indulge his educational pursuits in his own way rather than being forced to follow a rigid pattern. As it was, his independent ways caused some of his instructors to look askance at his methods while recognizing his potentials. He was reminiscent of the brilliant eighteenth-century British philosopher and lexicographer Dr. Samuel Johnson for his dislike of formal academia in a spirited individualistic pursuit of knowledge. This reveals another of the many Lawrence paradoxes, that of ultimately excelling in the military field, in which the emphasis is on discipline, and individuality is sacrificed for the overall goal of cohesive unity. Despite his later accomplishments in rising to the rank of colonel with the opportunity to rise even higher had he wished to remain within the ranks, one can scarcely conceive of the free-spirited Lawrence of his Oxford University days succeeding as a student at Sandhurst, the military academy where Britain's future career officers were trained. In fact, Lawrence would have many clashes in the future with products of that academy whose ideas of military formality clashed resoundingly with the independent and highly informal manner of Lawrence.

Having earned his degree, Lawrence's destiny was set once more in the direction of the Middle East as his benefactor D. G. Hogarth once more entered the scene. Hogarth offered him an opportunity to participate in an expedition sponsored by the British Museum to uncover the ancient city of Carchemish on the bank of the Euphrates. He would be paid fifteen shillings a day for his efforts. Lawrence gladly accepted the opportunity but did not wait until the February 1911 starting date to travel with Hogarth to Carchemish to launch his efforts. The burning urges within him to see more of this land of exotic mystery, which held such fascination for him, prompted him to embark for Syria in the winter of 1910. He stopped en route in Constantinople, the heart of the Turkish Empire, where he admired the Roman walls and enjoyed the lively atmosphere. When he reached Lebanon, he spent a couple of months studying Arabic at the American Mission school at Jebail, near

Beirut, where his teacher was Farida el Akle, a young Syrian woman with whom he became good friends.

From the time that Lawrence left England in the winter of 1910 until June 1914, he remained in what was rapidly becoming his adopted land with the exceptions of Christmas 1912 and two weeks in July 1913, which he spent in England. He worked with Hogarth until April 1911, at which point his mentor returned to England. Lawrence stayed behind to sort out pottery, take photographs, and otherwise assist R. Campbell Thompson, who had replaced Hogarth.

Up to this point, Lawrence had demonstrated a marked aptitude for individualized study, with a preference for Middle Eastern antiquity. At that juncture of his life, this adopted son of the desert began to demonstrate a capacity for leadership among the Arabs, which would ultimately culminate with the title of "uncrowned king of Arabia." At the age of twenty-two, he was put in charge of the two hundred Arab workmen involved in the project.

On a visit to see Farida el Akle in Jebail, she asked the Arab accompanying Lawrence why he thought Lawrence was able to get along so well with Arabs.

"He is one of us," the Arab explained. "There is nothing he cannot do, and he even excels us in doing it."[2]

The Arab had described in a nutshell the fundamental basis on which this light-skinned Britisher had cemented a bond of trust and respect with a dark-skinned brethren. If an Arab were capable of performing a particular task, no matter how difficult, the irrepressible Britisher was willing to undertake the same responsibility. Generally his effort would equal or exceed that of his Arab brethren.

Later, Lawrence could look back on this period as one of the happiest and most contented of his life, and as he continued to joyously toil in a pursuit he loved and in a land that provided the type of solitude he enjoyed, political convictions began taking shape in his mind. The longer he remained in Syria, the more intense his dislike became of the Turks, the masters of Syria, who regarded the Arabs as their inferiors. His antipathy extended to the Germans as well, who were seeking to strengthen the grasp of the Ottoman Empire. He was also repelled by the obvious colonial ambitions of the French in the area.

Lawrence was a man who always combined a restless and inquisitive mind with a corresponding zeal for action, and a blueprint began germinating within him as he observed the political realities of Syria firsthand. During that restless period leading up to World War One, Lawrence concluded that Arabia should be free from the yoke of

Turkish rule. The Arabs could enjoy a great measure of freedom and self-government as a part of the British Empire.

In time Lawrence would play a major role in shaping the historical destiny of Arabia, but in order to have such an opportunity open itself to him, it was necessary for the appropriate circumstances to come about. Despite that Lawrence believed the Arabs were oppressed, the crucial question revolved around how the Arabs themselves felt about the circumstances they then endured. To answer that question it is necessary to go back to the period in which the great Islamic world dynasty had breathed its last gasp and the Arabs were supplanted in their own homeland by a triumphantly ascendant Ottoman Empire.

During four centuries of Ottoman domination, beginning with the triumph of the Turkish army over the Mamluks near Aleppo on January 24, 1516, the entire Arab East existed in a state of eclipse. The Ottoman Turks achieved one of the mightiest and lengthiest of Moslem states. They not only conquered the Arab lands but also extended their influence into the entire territory from the Caucasus to the gates of Vienna. They dominated the Mediterranean area from their capital of Constantinople. With the vortex of power emanating from the Turkish city, the once glamorous and influential Arab capitals of Medina, Damascus, Baghdad, and Cairo receded into the background. Those seats of culture and influence lay dormant while control flowed from the city on the Bosphorus River.

The Arabs were not the only group controlled by the Turkish sword. Dominion was exercised over a heterogeneous mass of alien nationalities, religious groupings, and linguistic units. These subjugated peoples shared the common fate of excessive taxation and oppressive rule. The vigorous creativity that had manifested during the height of Islamic political success fell into a dark decline during this period of Turkish domination.

Eventually, a restless stirring began to be felt within Arab ranks. Nationalistic aspirations started to surface. The locale from which these initial waves of activity occurred was Egypt as a result of the Napoleonic invasion in the closing years of the eighteenth century. Contact was established and maintained with the Western world. Soon representatives of Western institutions, such as missionaries, tourists, archaeologists, and traders flocked to the eastern shores of the Mediterranean.

The process resulted in the birth of the Arab national movement of the 1870s. A surge of Arab pride produced new widespread interest in the achievements of the glory days of the Islamic Empire. Classical

Arabic was revived and Arab literature and history were read and admired on an ever-expanding scale. The upheaval was accompanied by a political awakening and the desire for a reunited Arab world, the longings for which were most acutely expressed in Syria and Egypt.

These aspirations of the second half of the nineteenth century had a marked impact on a number of intellectuals as well as on Arab officers serving in the Ottoman army. At first the effort concentrated on political reform in the expectation that the Young Turks, who were vying for power, would effect meaningful change to better conditions for the Arabs.

The 1908 revolution of the Young Turks was successful. Their accession to power, rather than proving a springboard to a better future for the Arabs, resulted in just the opposite as the oppression continued while Arab frustrations increased.

The frustration of seeing their cherished hopes for improved relations with the Ottoman Empire dashed, many restless Arabs began looking for alternatives to following a pattern that appeared to offer only more of the same and all-too-familiar existence to which they and their forebears had been dispatched for four centuries. Their efforts were enhanced and their motivation accelerated when it became clear to Arab subjects just what kind of program the victorious Young Turks sought to implement. Many Arabs had heartily approved of their efforts to overthrow the Sultanate of Abdul Hamid, a sentiment they actively encouraged by leading the Arab subjects to believe that positive changes would accompany their rise to power. When the smoke cleared, however, and the Young Turks had triumphed, imprisoning Abdul Hamid in the process, the subject of their discontent was clearly revealed. The Young Turk movement, it had turned out, was a revolt against Abdul Hamid's concept of pan-Islam. Under the old sultan's theory, he was spiritual director of the Muslim world as well as its temporal leader. A surge of nationalism was undertaken. In their determined quest to achieve a "Turkey for the Turkish" in the words of their rallying cry, the Young Turks had to deal immediately with the Arabs, who constituted the largest alien component of Turkey. The Young Turks acted with dispatch. Arab deputies were scattered, Arab societies forbidden, and Arab notables proscribed.

The Arab desire for independence, which the Young Turks sought to squelch, increased rather than diminished with the restrictions and punishments their rulers imposed. The Arab societies went underground, and their basic nature was transformed from fraternal to conspiratorial. The Akhua, the Arab mother society, was dissolved, being replaced in Mesopotamia (Iraq) by the Ahad, a dangerous secret brotherhood whose membership was restricted almost entirely to Arab officers in the Turkish Army. Its objective was to acquire as much as possible in the way of military knowledge about their masters, then turn this prized information against them once the moment for active rebellion ripened.

An even more potent secret society existed in Syria in the form of the Fetah. This "society of freedom" consisted of landowners, writers, doctors, and public servants. Its goal was to ruin the Turkish Empire. The society received support within Syria, and the members put themselves in touch with sympathetic groups in locales as far apart as Egypt and Great Britain. Though the Fetah sought to operate secretively, the Turkish Government suspected its existence but was impeded from taking the kind of direct and decisive action it would have liked to have taken. Caution was promoted as long as English and French diplomats remained within Turkey, because those individuals encompassed modern public opinion within the country. As a result of the war, the agents were withdrawn in 1914. The Turkish Government then felt free to act.

The Young Turks moved with swift savagery. In Syria, Arabs were rounded up by the score and were punished, as were members of another group well represented within the Turkish populace, the Armenians. The Armenians had been armed and well organized, but their leadership deserted them, and as a consequence they were massacred. The men were routinely executed and the women and children were driven along the wintry roads into the desert, naked and hungry. It then became only a question of how they would die—as prey of passersby or through normal attrition. The Armenians were slaughtered not because they were Christians but because they were Armenians. Following the same line of reasoning, they herded Arab Moslems and Arab Christians in the same prison and hung them together on the same scaffold.

The Turks moved with trepidation against Arab officers and soldiers in the Army. When the concentration reached the danger point at which nearly one third of the Turkish army was Arab speaking in North Syria early in 1915, they broke up these divisions whenever possible, marching them off to fight in Europe or elsewhere so as to diminish the concentration level.

In the meantime, the Young Turks declared a Holy War to cement their Union and Progress banner with the traditional sanctity of a caliph's battle cry in the name of Allah. The big question that remained to be answered was whether those they sought to influence would be moved.

One highly important individual who was contacted by the Turks and whose support, if obtained, would be instrumental in helping to serve their ends, to head the long-reigning governmental apparatus in the Hejax, held sacred in Islamic circles because this was the region of the Prophet Muhammad. The Turks moved with a measure of discreet caution, knowing the consequences of gaining a foothold over the area and the influential man who controlled it.

The Sherif of Mecca, based in the birthplace and home city of the Prophet, obtained the title "Sherif" as a result of direct descent from Muhammad himself, the lineage being from the Prophet's daughter Fatima and Hassan, her elder son. The Emir of Mecca, the elected Sherif of Sherifs, represented the most senior and noble member of their ranks. The old Ottoman governments had treated the Emirs of Mecca with supreme caution. Though the Turks would have felt far more comfortable with a member of their own ranks ruling over the Hejaz, they recognized the strength of the Emirs and the difficulty of dislodging them from power. They would have been attacking the symbolism of the very religious persuasian they purported to practice, that of Islam. The Turks opted for a diplomatic solution. It was the Turkish Sultanate itself that confirmed the Emir in place.

The Hejaz was sought for important strategic reasons in concert with the Ottoman Empire's pan-Islamic design. The opening of the Suez Canal enabled them to garrison the Holy Cities. They envisioned the creation of a Hejaz Railway with increased monetary and military influence among the tribes.

Despite the fervent desire on the part of the newly constituted Turkish authority to fit the Hejaz into its grand design, the area loomed as a potential powder keg given recent experiences during the regime of the deposed Abdul Hamid. The earlier nervous tactical support given by the Sultanate to the Emirate in Hejaz had been dashed by Abdul Hamid, and an important additional question needed answering as to how those events might uiltimately influence history.

Abdul Hamid had seen the Mecca Emirate grow in importance and drift into a more independent course than the head of the Ottoman Empire wanted to see. As a result he began to depose a Sherif held in too high esteem by his people. Eventually he took away some of the family to Constantinople to be held under an "honorable captivity." Included in this group was Hussein ibn Ali, who was held prisoner by the Turks for eighteen years. During this period, he provided his four sons with modern education and experience, which proved to be solid dividends when their services were later needed to aid the Arab cause.

Once Abdul Hamid was overthrown, the victorious Young Turks reversed his policy and sent Sherif Hussein back to Mecca as Emir. No doubt they felt that Hussein's eighteen years under the Ottoman thumb in Constantinople had given him an appreciation of the discipline of the ruling system. It was hoped that that appreciation, coupled with his relocation back to Mecca and his people, would generate within Hussein a desire for cooperation and active promotion of the pan-Islamic program of the Young Turks. The question that remained was whether Sherif Hussein saw the situation in the manner that the new leadership of the Ottoman Empire desired.

The wily Hussein, operating quietly, immediately set out to restore the power of the Emirate. A shrewd political operative, he not only strengthened the position of the Emirate, but he also kept in close touch with the entire Ottoman Empire political scene through his sons Abdullah and Feisal, both of whom were in Constantinople. Abdullah served as vice chairman of the Turkish House, and Feisal was a member of Jidda. They served as their father's attentive eyes and ears regarding political happenings in the capital until war broke out, at which time they returned to Mecca.

With the outbreak of war, troubles abounded in the Hejaz. Sherif Hussein saw historical circumstances molded by external forces threatening to engulf his people in the process. Once the guns of war blazed onto the scene, the pilgrimage ended. As a result, revenues and commerce with the Holy Cities ground to a halt. Sherif Hussein had to endure the agonizing fear that Indian food ships would cease activity in the Hejaz because he was in the technical position of an enemy subject. Because the province produced scarcely any goods of its own, Hussein discerned with discomfort the eventuality that his people would then be at the mercy of the Turks for their very sustenance, and with it survival. As Hussein weighed his potential courses of action at a time when decision beckoned with increasing swiftness, he realized the horrible consequences that would ensue if the Turks decided to close the Hejaz Railway. The result would be the starvation of his people!

Never had Sherif Hussein felt himself to be at the mercy of the Turkish rulers as he did at that juncture, pushing upon him an immediacy that exceeded anything he had encountered during his earlier eighteen-year "honorable captivity." He knew the importance the Young Turks attached to receiving his support in advancing the cause of their Jihad, or Holy War, as they sought to ally the Muslim forces against Christianity. As temporal leader of the Hejaz, and with it the Holy Cities, the Ottoman Empire viewed the cooperation of the Sherif as vital for both spiritual and political reasons.

Should Hussein endorse this so-called Holy War on behalf of Mecca? With sharp division existing within the entire sphere of Ottoman dominance, he was aware of the bloodshed that stood to erupt if he enlisted his support. The Turks stood poised, waiting for an answer, and after a good deal of sober reflection Hussein reached his conclusion. This pious and meditative man felt that the concept of Jihad or Holy War was incompatible with aggressive warfare, while to purport to engage in such a conflict alongside a Christian ally, Germany, added to the illogical nature of the Turkish position. Hence Hussein rejected the Turkish demand. At the same time, he made a dignified appeal to the Allies not to starve his people for the dubious circumstance of being in a contested battle zone not of their own making. Now that he had made his decision, Hussein saw himself caught in the midst of the warring forces as the Turks greeted his refusal by instituting a partial blockade of the Hejaz and controlling the traffic on the pilgrim railway while the British left his coast open to specially regulated foods.

Sherif Hussein had turned a deaf ear to one request for support, but the next one he received came closer to home, evoking feelings of camaraderie. In January 1915, he received a concrete proposal for a military mutiny against the Turks. Making the appeal were Yisin, head of the Mesopotamian officers; Ali Riza, leader of the Damascus officers; and Abdl el Ghani el Areisa, representing the Syrian civilians.

As a political realist with both feet planted firmly on the ground, Hussein was aware of both the restless anxiety operating in the underground and the tenacious longings to escape from Ottoman Empire dominance. It had been four hundred years since the Arabs had been in unfettered control of their own Holy Cities. As memories of their past conquests drifted even further into the past, longings for freedom grew while their Constantinople-based oppressors tightened their grip in all areas. There were those within the Arab camp who saw the overthrow of Abdul Hamid and the rise of the Young Turks as an opportunity for advancement. Perhaps these new leaders would loosen the bonds of subservience and launch a productive phase of cooperation linking the Turks and the Arabs. Instead the bitterly disappointing response had been a quest for pan-Islam and a Holy War with one goal, that of making the Ottoman Empire more Turkish than ever.

Hussein realized the importance of cooperating with the underground operations seeking to redress old grievances against the Turks. Perhaps through the seeds of war, the potential was sown for a new Arab beginning, the achievement of independence. Hussein sent his son Feisal to Damascus to discuss the projects being analyzed, then to report back to him. He sent Ali, his eldest son, to Medina to quietly raise troops from villagers and tribesmen from the Hejaz. Ali was instructed to hold the troops in readiness pending favorable word from Feisal. Abdullah, his second son, was to sound out the British by letter and learn what their attitude might be concerning a possible Arab revolt against Turkey.

Feisal's report in January 1915 revealed not only favorable local conditions as far as summoning Arab troops for a revolt was concerned but also that the general war was not going well. The time was not ripe to turn the troops loose. In Damascus, there were three divisions of Arab troops ready for rebellion; in Aleppo there were two divisions prepared to join them once battle commenced. It then became a question of when, bearing on the crucial issue of improved British performance on the battlefield. A breakdown of Turkey on the fighting front was the signal that would send the Arabs into action.

The propitious turn of fate that Feisal was counting on occurred in the Dardanelles campaign, in which the Ottoman Army was decimated. The disaster was of a substantial enough magnitude that Feisal returned to Syria, preparing for the climactic moment to launch the Arab revolt, but just as the climate had become more favorable on the international front with the gigantic assist the Arabs had received from British forces, a chagrined Feisal found that the local situation had deteriorated. His Syrian supporters were either under arrest or in hiding, and many of their cohorts were being hanged on a variety of political charges. The battle-ready Arab divisions had been either exiled to distant fronts or distributed throughout Turkish units. Jemal Pasha, along with Enver Pasha, was the most ruthless enforcer of loyalty and executioner in the ranks of the Young Turks, and a saddened Feisal recognized that he had done his handiwork all too well in Syria. Under Jemal Pasha's control, the entire Arab peasantry lay in the grip of Turkish military service.

Feisal contacted Hussein, cautioning delay until Britain achieved an increasingly favorable posture. His hopes that the British could quickly capitalize on the losses that had befallen Turkey's forces in the Dardanelles were soon dashed, however, as Britain's forces, which had suffered decisive losses of their own in the Dardanelles, were in no immediate position to render the kind of assistance that Feisal was anticipating.

While Feisal agonized, hoping for a favorable change of conditions, he was forced to live as the guest of Jemal Pasha in Damascus. He knew that if any of the members of the secret society he had headed before the war revealed his activities, he would confront the same fate as scores of his Syrian friends, whose hangings he was forced to watch at the behest of Jemal Pasha. While Jemal gloated, Feisal was forced to witness the executions of friends whose ideals he shared, and who could have revealed them in an instant. On one occasion he dared to lash out at Jemal, informing him that such widespread bloodletting would prove to be his undoing. It took intercession on behalf of his Constantinople friends of influence to save him from paying the price for his harsh words.

Feisal risked his life by communicating with his father, a process that was achieved through the strategic use of intermediaries above suspicion who operated along the Hejaz Railway, concealing letters in cakes, in sword hilts, sewn between the soles of sandals, and in invisible writings on the wrappers of harmless packages. Feisal's reports were discouraging, cautioning delay until a more propitious occasion.

Despite Feisal's pessimism, Hussein decided that the moment for action was at hand. A devoutly religious man, he fervently believed that the hand of Allah would reside with his cause against the Young Turks, whose cause he despised. He regarded them as traitors to the cause of Islam, and the sixty-five-year-old Sherif was eager to do battle with this hated enemy in the Hejaz, determined to wrest control away from the hated Ottoman oppressor.

A letter was dispatched to Feisal from Hussein saying the troops were ready for inspection in Medina before starting for the front. Feisal sought permission from Jemal to leave for Medina from Jemal but was thwarted when he was told that Enver Pasha was on his way to the province and that they would accompany him to Medina to inspect the troops. Because Feisal had been operating under the false pretext of helping his brother Abdullah in his effort to raise forces to assist the Turks against the British in the Suez Canal, Feisal was obliged to continue on this pretext even longer than he had anticipated. He was being plagued by the dogged Enver Jemal and Enver Pasha right to the very end!

The review went as well as could be expected, but a note of irony was struck when some Arab chiefs engaged Feisal in private conversation. These same troops being reviewed by two Turkish leaders, believing them to be preparing for battle with the British in the Suez Canal, were engaging in a bogus drill for the benefit of the hated leadership they were primed to shortly rise up against. Feisal was asked by these chiefs about the advisability of killing both Enver Jemal and Enver Pasha on the spot. If this could be accomplished, they reasoned, the Turks would be divested of their principal leadership. Perhaps their rebellion could be won in a quick and decisive fashion, without shedding a single drop of Arab blood in the process. Feisal demurred, much to their dissatisfaction, explaining that both Jemal and Pasha were their guests. To kill them would constitute a serious breach of Arab etiquette. The chiefs attempted to persuade him further, and Feisal no doubt felt grave discomfort in disagreeing with them, considering the fact that he had been forced to endure a silent living hell while watching Jemal Pasha hang friend after friend of his from the scaffold. All the same he would not be dissuaded, refusing to kill the Turkish potentates. He escorted Jemal and Enver back to Damascus, saving them from death along the way. After heated discussion between Feisal and the Arab chiefs, even though they were unable to hear what was said, suspicions surfaced within them. They imposed a strict blockade on the Hejaz and ordered large numbers of Turkish reinforcements. Jemal and Enver sought to keep Feisal detained in Damascus, but when a telegram arrived seeking his return to Medina to prevent disorder, they reluctantly let him go on the condition that he leave his men behind.

Feisal had been through a traumatic period in which he had been forced to walk a tightrope with Jemal Pasha. Had he made a wrong move and revealed himself, his life would have been snuffed out as a traitor to the Ottoman Empire. Only through enduring the pain of watching his Arab brothers hanged could he await the opportunity of avenging their deaths and fighting for Arab independence. Yes, there had been that one occasion when he had lost his temper and told Jemal just how wrong his execution policy was, and yes, that time he had been fortunate enough to dodge a prospective bullet. Now he returned to Medina to survey the situation. A tense feeling of anticipation ran through him as he observed Medina overflowing with Turkish troops. The battle lay close at hand. His next stop was Damascus. From there he rode out into the desert to take refuge along with the Bedouin chieftain Nuri Shaalan. At the appropriate moment, he raised the Arab flag, filled with a surge of relief that the exasperating period of silence and underground communication was now over and a declaration had been made. The planting of the Arab flag in the desert sand provided the death knell to the pan-Islamic designs of a hated enemy. There would be no unity. There would be a savage battle for control of the land under which the Arabs had lived the past four hundred years as Ottoman subjects.

Little did Sherif Hussein or Feisal know it then, but their rebellion would be sparked by the presence of an outsider from a distant land. From the pastoral, scholarly setting of Oxford would be sent a young man into their midst who would embrace their cause with unencumbered zeal. They would take him under their collective wing as one of their own, rallying behind his leadership on the waves of determination he generated within them by his example. That man was T. E. Lawrence and it would not be long before their destiny-laden paths would cross.

When the First World War broke out in August of 1914, Lawrence was home in Oxford working on his part of a record of the Sinai trip he had made with colleague Dr. Leonard Woolley. The book was published in 1915 by the Palestine Exploration Fund under the title *The Wilderness of Zin*.

As Lawrence then turned his attention toward the war and serving his country, a pitfall surfaced. Though much myth surrounds the reasons why the future hero of the Arabian campaign was initially rejected for military service, the most plausible account appears to come from prominent historian Liddell Hart, whose biography *Colonel Lawrence* is considered to be one of the most insightful and detailed accounts of the great warrior's life. A good deal has been made of Lawrence's slight frame and five-foot-three height. Therefore it has been recorded that the British examiners got a look at him, chuckled to themselves, and sent him back home at least until such time as he "grew up." Hart reveals that with the glut of recruits seeking to aid the British cause, the height standard was raised to five-foot-five, two inches taller than Lawrence. The fundamental irony of this rejection was that, had the great militarist whose birthdate he shared, Napoleon Bonaparte, been attempting to enlist in the British Army in 1914, he also would have been rejected.

The determined Lawrence was not about to be deprived of service as a result of a failed height requirement, and so he wrote to an old acquaintance from his Carchemish campaign, Captain Newcombe, who during Lawrence's excavation had been spending his time updating British maps in the event that a future conflict would emerge with Turkey. Newcombe passed Lawrence's name on to the Intelligence

Department, explaining in the process about the long waiting list. Lawrence then decided to contact Dr. Hogarth, his old benefactor who had enlisted him for his Carchemish campaign, who was prominent in the Geographical Section of the General Staff. Aware of Lawrence's extensive knowledge of the Middle East, Hogarth concluded that the Geographical Section was the proper area to extract Lawrence's unique talents.

Word was passed on to Colonel Hedley at the War Office, while Newcombe spoke positively on Lawrence's behalf concerning his Sinai pursuits. He was put to work by Colonel Hedley to prepare maps connecting the Sinai Peninsula with Palestine. Hedley was impressed by Lawrence's knowledge and enthusiasm enough to recommend him for Egyptian intelligence work. In the meantime he leaned on his talented subordinate to finish the Sinai maps as soon as possible, realizing that he would not have his services for much longer.

In December, after Turkey entered the war, a decision was made to strengthen the Intelligence Service in Cairo. Lawrence was selected to serve there along with faces from his Middle East past such as Newcombe, who was recalled from France to participate in the new undertaking, and his old friend Leonard Woolley.

The irrepressible Lawrence served in the Cairo office, producing mixed results. Whereas he demonstrated a good deal of knowledge and exceptional tenacity, a number of his superiors regarded him as arrogant and not of the material of which officers are made. The knowledge that Lawrence had gleaned while living among the natives during his excavation surveys provided him with abundant information concerning the lower strata of the Turkish Empire and of the Arab secret societies. In that his knowledge of arcane Middle East facts and factors often far exceeded that of career military men many years his senior, and since he demonstrated not the faintest compunction to correct them whenever the situation arose, they began to look askance at what they viewed as the behavior of a young upstart. Nor was Lawrence's outspokenness confined to Middle East arcana. It extended as well to the punctuation and grammar used in written reports, raising more hackles in the process. There was also Lawrence's penchant for individuality, which continued to function even within the confines of military conformity. Veteran officers in particular were ruffled by Lawrence's failure to appear in proper military attire, and their sense of propriety was tweaked by his failure to salute. To career militarists, many of whom had rigid Sandhurst backgrounds, they saw this boyish stranger in their midst not as the definitive free spirit that he was, standing in contrast to military formality, but as an arrogant rebel who refused to see things within the context of the total picture.

When Lawrence heard about the Arab Revolt, he was jubilant. In a letter to his mother, he wrote that, in the event that it succeeded, it would be "the biggest thing in the Near East since 1550".[3] Once more his perspective was historical, and his central concern became that of being a participant in the history that would be made in the Arab Revolt. He sought to jettison his responsibilities with the Arab Bureau in Cairo and transport himself to the Arab desert to participate in the unfolding activities. As much expertise as he might have in the map department, he felt with a growing impatience that it was time for him to be where he believed the call of destiny had beckoned him. Even though he complained that his new chief did not like his manners, it has been speculated that the dislike he registered among his superiors regarding that same alleged shortcoming could have provided him with his ticket out of the Cairo office and into the unfolding military campaign in the Arabian desert. Lawrence's superiors, which included career militarists many years his senior, were growing increasingly exasperated by being constantly corrected and factually outflanked by someone who had the appearance of a boy. His meticulous knowledge of the microscopic details of Arab geography, gleaned from his archaeological expeditions and preserved by his phenomenal memory, rubbed too many egos the wrong way within the officers' ranks of the Cairo Bureau. It has accordingly been conjectured that many in the Cairo Bureau were delighted to see T. E.'s interests straying elsewhere and were not about to utter a discouraging word against his leaving their ranks.

T. E. requested leave from his Cairo activities to accompany Sir Ronald Storrs, the same man who would later serve as governor of Jerusalem and introduce Lawrence to Lowell Thomas, on an excursion to Jedda to talk with Hussein's second son, Abdullah. As a result of Lawrence's proven expertise in the field and his ability to deal with the Arabs in their quest to throw off the yoke of Turkish rule, the temporary leave soon became permanent. Lawrence's enemies in the Cairo Bureau were then able to breathe a collective sigh of relief.

After three days, Hussein had captured the small Turkish force in Mecca, and by September his forces had captured Jedda, Yenbo, Rabegh, Leath, Um Leij, Kanufdeh, and Taif. Buoyed by those successes, Lawrence looked forward to many Arab conquests in the future. After meeting with Abdullah in Jedda, he had the opportunity to converse with Ali in Rabegh. He was then provided with a camel and guide, journeying to the village of Hamra, where he met Feisal, who was stationed there with his troops.

The historic first meeting between the blue-eyed Englishman and the dark-skinned, chain-smoking Sherif, descended from the prophet himself, fostered mutual respect and the linking of two disparate cultures through which a common destiny was ultimately forged, which would ultimately bring to an end the four-hundred-year Turkish reign.

T. E. recalled the meeting accordingly: "Tafas [Lawrence's guide] said something to a slave who stood there with silver-hilted sword to hand. He led me to an inner court, on whose further side, framed between the uprights of a black doorway, stood a white figure waiting."[4]

Feisal projected an inspiring image. Tall and slender, wearing long white silk robes, his brown head cloth was bound with a brilliant scarlet and gold cord. Feisal revealed to Lawrence how Turkish superiority in heavy guns had made the capture of Medina impossible. He lamented that the English had given him only twenty-four-year-old Krupps, mountain guns with a range of three thousand yards. He expressed with burning conviction his desire to build up a mobile force with trained officers who would prove a match against Turkish regular troops. Lawrence pledged his best efforts to encourage his superiors to erect a base at Yenbo for stores, supplies, gun crews, and professional army advisers.

Any great leader possesses exceptional instincts, including the ability to determine in advance the propriety of making a particular move at the most opportune time. This applies particularly to the selection of an individual or individuals to assist a leader in future pursuits. As Lawrence assessed Feisal's abilities within the context of the turbulent struggle for Arab independence that was taking shape, his intuitive insight revealed to him that in the midst of this village containing eight thousand troops awaiting the call to battle was a man whose instincts and desires were akin to his own. In that Feisal was also a man of superior insight, he doubtlessly harbored the same impressions regarding T. E. Lawrence.

Lawrence revealed his feelings about Feisal within the context of the Arab Revolt and its early difficulties in the masterpiece that recounts his experiences in Arabia, *Seven Pillars of Wisdom*, renowned as much for its literary brilliance as its graphically revealing historical content:

I had believed these misfortunes of the Revolt to be due mainly to faulty leadership, or rather to the lack of leadership, Arab and English. So I

went down to Arabia to see and consider its great men. The first, the
Sherif of Mecca, we knew to be aged. I found Abdullah too clever, Ali
too clean, Zeid too cool.

Then I rode up-country to Feisal, and found in him the leader with the
necessary fire, and yet with reason to give effect to our science. His
tribesmen seemed sufficient instrument, and his hills to provide natural
advantage. So I returned pleased and confident to Egypt, and told my
chiefs how Mecca was defended not by the obstacle of Rabegh, but by
the flank threat of Feisal in Jebel Subh.[5]

Impressed with Feisal and determined to do all in his power to
render him with the assistance he needed to secure victory, T. E.
began his journey back to Cairo and the Arab Bureau. His last stop
was slated to be Khartoum, where he reported to Sir Reginald Wingate
and was dismayed to learn that Colonel Bremond, head of the French
Military Mission to Jedda, was urging an allied landing in the Hejaz
with himself as commander of a mixed brigade of French and English
troops. Knowing the Arab mind much better than virtually any other
non-Arab and recognizing the Arab distrust of foreign troops, he
dashed off a memorandum to Cairo stating his belief that the tribes
would scatter if foreigners landed in force. In that his expertise was
recognized within the Arab Bureau, the warning was heeded and
Bremond's plan was dropped.

As an apparent result of the success that Lawrence had enjoyed in
developing swift rapport with Feisal, his chief, General Clayton, told
T. E. to return to Arabia to act as liaison officer to Feisal.

This loomed as a golden opportunity for the energetic Lawrence to
make a direct mark on the Arab Revolt and to supervise from the
British viewpoint the activities of a man he deeply respected who was
striving mightily to free his people from Turkish servitude. As impressed as he was with Feisal and the Arab Revolt, however, Lawrence
then went into one of his paradoxical phases. This time he apparently
doubted his ability to handle the assignment in question. He reasoned
that his current position in Cairo was commensurate with his talents,
and he doubted his fitness for the other assignment due to a hatred of
responsibility, explaining, "and that in all my life objects had been
gladder to me than persons, and ideas than objects." Considering the
circumstances, Lawrence's position was a peculiar one. He had eagerly sought a leave from his Cairo post to look in on the Arab Revolt
firsthand. In so doing he made a positive impression on the revolt's
leading figure, who had articulated his needs, which were then reported
back to Lawrence's superiors. His own supervising chief, General

Clayton, as a result of what had transpired, had been convinced to believe that T. E. was appropriately qualified to handle the liaison post to Feisal. It was instead Lawrence himself who proved to be the doubter, and the reason he gave supporting his professional difficulties in assuming such a position appears decidedly specious. After all, he had been offered the position after making a favorable impression on a man he had expressed eagerness to assist. He had always related well to the Arabs, extending back to his excavation days, of which General Clayton was also well aware and which no doubt also had an influencing hand in his selection of Lawrence to serve as Feisal's liaison to British forces. On the opposite side of the issue, there was his own problem in dealing with a number of his superior officers in the Cairo Bureau, due in large measure to his contempt for formality. Therefore, to use his hatred of responsibilty would prove a far more salient argument for leaving Cairo rather than would turning down the liaison position. After all, who had the greater disposition toward formality— the Sandhurst products in Cairo with whom Lawrence clashed or the Arabs? It can be strongly argued that the Arab penchant for independence and Arab dislike of conventional responsibility, attitudes bred into them by years in the lonely expanses of the desert, were the reasons why Lawrence had always fit in well with Feisal and, conversely, why the Arabs in turn took to him. It might well be that Lawrence, now that destiny was staring intently at him, could have encountered a temporary lack of confidence. If such were the case it is understandable. After all, here was a young man still in his twenties whose primary interest had been archaeology and its broader connection within the scope of history. His first effort to enlist in the war had been turned down because of his height. Now, after a whirlwind of events had transpired, he stood at the core of the cause of a people who meant so much to him. With the movement of historical circumstance passing by in a blinding flash before his boggled eyes, one could expect even someone as uniquely outstanding as T. E. Lawrence to feel a few tugs of apprehension over the vastness of what lay ahead and his pivotal position as a molder of events. However, General Clayton proved to be an apt judge of Lawrence's talents. Despite T. E.'s expressed misgivings, Clayton held fast, and he was given the liaison position. By the first week of December 1916, Lawrence was back in Yenbo with the rank of captain, watching Arabs receive training in the art of demolition, given by Major Garland, one of the British Army's foremost experts in the field. It was hoped that such knowledge would prove helpful in short-circuiting Turkey's Hejaz Railway, its vital arms and personnel supplier throughout the area.

T. E. Lawrence had proved many times his extensive geographical knowledge of Arabia. Now he had an opportunity to display his creative expertise in the field of military tactics. Just as his archaeological flair was linked to a broad understanding of Arab history and culture, his military concepts were a response to the history he had read on the subject of warfare and were specifically geared to the area and the principals involved.

A quick study of the military prospects for the Arabs brought home some important points for Lawrence:

> I concluded that the tribesmen were good for defence only. Their acquisitive recklessness made them keen on booty, and whetted them to tear up railways, plunder caravans, and steal camels; but they were too free-minded to endure command, or to fight in team. A man who could fight well for himself made generally a bad soldier, and these champions seemed to me no material for our drilling; but if we strengthened them by light automatic guns of the Lewis type, to be handled by themselves, they might be capable of holding their hills and serving as an efficient screen behind which we could build up . . . an Arab regular mobile column . . .[6]

T. E. Lawrence as practical strategist immediately began to perceive the conflict both from the standpoint of geographical perspective and from the individualistic framework of Arab potential. He calculated the strengths and weaknesses of both the Turks and the Arabs, gradually beginning to develop a tactical strategy that he felt would produce a successful result for the Arab cause.

He perceived the Hejaz war as a conflict in which the Arabs could utilize natural talents to their advantage. Commenting on the mountainous terrain, he opined that such a geographical entity would serve the Arabs well against "an enemy so enriched in equipment by the Germans as almost to have lost virtue for rough-and-tumble war."[7]

Lawrence described the hill belt as a "paradise for snipers"[8] and maintained that Arabs were "artists in sniping."[9] The Arabs would be able to take advantage of steep slopes and take their adversary by surprise.

A discussion with Abdullah reminded Lawrence of the important role played by the Hejaz Railway on behalf of Turkish fighting forces. Due to failure on the part of the Arabs to cut the Hejaz Railway, the Turks had been able to collect transport and supplies for the reinforcement of Medina. As a result, Feisal and his forces had been driven back from the town.

The march of historical events that pointed Lawrence, step by step, on his road to destiny in Arabia fell into the realm of military knowledge. This information was eagerly digested by the young mind of T.E. without any correlative desire to embark on a military career. He began by reading books on military theory at about fifteen or sixteen. Eventually he tackled Clausewitz and Napoleon. His interest became sufficiently absorbed to "browse" through Napoleon's correspondence on his Italian campaign, which encompassed no less than thirty-two volumes!

In that Lawrence's chief interests were said to reside in medieval architecture and pottery, the question arises as to why he undertook as a schoolboy in his teens a reading pursuit of the theory of warfare that few veteran militarists would match during a lifetime. One reason was Lawrence's always abounding intellectual curiosity, coupled with the likely corollary that he found this type of reading stimulating to his mind. A more practical response is that by studying major warfare in depth, Lawrence was able to familiarize himself with a number of battlefields, which he could then re-create on maps. These efforts could not help but facilitate his antiquarian efforts. He began with sieges directly related to his pursuit of castles, then proceeded to bigger movements. One of his ambitious undertakings found him seeking to repeat the whole of Marlborough's wars by visiting all of the major battle sites. Later, when he visited Syria, Lawrence followed step by step the campaigns of the Crusaders.

One of the many books on the theory of warfare, which the young Lawrence absorbed with great interest, was Marshal Hermann-Maurice Saxe's *Reveries on the Art of War*. Published posthumously in 1757, the book was translated into English the same year of its publication and became a military classic of the eighteenth century. In that it had been written by the architect of victory over the English in Flanders, this one fact alone could have been enough to promote curiosity within Britain to read the book. But there was a great deal more to recommend it. The author expounded at length on his original concepts of warfare, which clashed with prevailing eighteenth-century conventional wisdom, concepts that had been put into actual practice by Saxe with successful results.

Now these lessons that had been poured into his fertile young mind through the pages of a military masterpiece resurfaced within Lawrence as he lay in his tent with a fever at a pivotal point in his burgeoning military career. He had been sent from Wejh to persuade Abdullah of the importance of destroying the Turkish garrison at Medina. The Turks had made Medina their stronghold in the Hejaz, and the obvious response on the part of the Arabs would be to attack and destroy it. This would appear to be no more than concluding the obvious. Or would it? Lawrence's initial response would have been a resounding yes, but as he lay there in his tent recovering from his fever, there were the principles of Marshal Saxe coming to mind and prompting him to reevaluate his thinking. Suddenly the seemingly obvious did not appear obvious at all anymore.

To comprehend the reshaping of thought that was taking place within Lawrence's mind on the subject of how best to do battle with the Turks, it is necessary to explore some of the fundamental concepts of Saxe's military philosophy, adapting their significance to Lawrence's efforts in the Hejaz campaign.

Despite Saxe's military successes and the intelligent insight into warfare theory that he described in *Reveries on the Art of War*, his public response was diminished due to the great victories achieved on the battlefield by Frederick the Great, which occurred shortly after Saxe's death. The strategy of Frederick the Great was far less sophisticated and considerably more basic than that propounded by Saxe. In today's parlance, Frederick the Great's battlefield philosophy would be classified as macho. The objective is to comfront an opponent directly, placing your might against that of the adversary. Through tenacious resolve and steady application of force, victory is ultimately secured. In marked contrast, Saxe coined the dictum that the "whole secret of war rests in the legs and not in the arms."[10] Saxe's concept of a superb fighting force was exemplified by the Roman Legion, which blended strength and flexibility. An army can function more adroitly according to Saxe if it exists at an "economic size," which enables it to assume greater powers of maneuverability. He developed this concept even further to embrace a divisional system of warfare. The divisional system organizes an army capable of moving and acting independently. Such a force could grip an enemy at certain points while it struck at others. Once Saxe had conceived of an army consisting of disparate branches capable of attacking an enemy in varying ways, he embellished his tactical evolution by revealing what he termed the "sublime branches of war." This was the facet of Saxe's theories that most likely appealed to the type of mind Lawrence possessed. The reason is that it allowed maximum room for creative thinking, on which Lawrence's perennially busy mind flourished. The objective of this kind of warfare is to constantly keep the opposing commander in a state of bewilderment, a concept that stands in marked contrast with the macho and increasingly-riskier-to-human-life posture advanced by Frederick the Great of going after an enemy directly with all the force in one's arsenal. If one can upset the enemy commander's balance, according to Saxe, the vulnerabilities of the opponent lie exposed. Rather than concentrating on its own strengths, this concept seeks to upend the enemy's equilibrium by forcing the adversary to concentrate on the opponent's tactics. Hence the enemy is put clearly on the defensive. In addition, bogus plans are perpetrated in the process in order to conceal the real nature of the army's tactical strategy.

Suddenly, as Lawrence lay there in his tent, having ruminated on all he had read on military theory with a particular focus on the concepts of Saxe, the answer came to him like a bolt of lightning from the sky. Up until that moment, his restless mind had focused on Medina. Now he saw the Arab struggle from a totally new perspective.

". . . as I thought about it, it dawned on me that we had won the Hejaz war," Lawrence revealed. "We were in occupation of 99 per cent of the Hejaz. The Turks were welcome to the other fraction till peace of doomsday showed them the futility of clinging to our window-pane."[11]

Up to the moment of Lawrence's revelation, Medina had assumed a position of supreme importance. Now he asked himself the question, "Why bother about Medina?" In the first place, given Arab limitations of manpower and deficiencies in sophisticated weapon skill, it was clearly impossible to capture Medina. After further reflection, Lawrence came to another fresh conclusion about Medina. It could actually be harmful to the Arab cause to capture it.

> It [Medina] was no base to us, like Rabegh, no threat to the Turks, like Wejh: just a blind alley for both. The Turks sat in it on the defensive, immobile, eating for food the transport animals which were to have moved them to Mecca . . . but for which there was no pasture in their now restricted lines. They were harmless sitting there; if we took them prisoners they would cost us food and guards in Egypt: if we drove them northward into Syria, they would join the main army blocking us in Sinai. On all counts they were best where they were, and they valued Medina and wanted to keep it. Let them![12]

By recounting his reading of military theory and focusing on the inventive mind of Marshal Saxe, Lawrence had fathomed a battle strategy in the Hejaz campaign as well as throughout the entire Arabian conflict. By shifting the focus away from capturing Medina and concentrating instead on holding the geographical entities that were not in Turkey's control, the enemy, rather than the Arabs, would assume the vulnerable posture. While the Turks held the advantage in weaponry as well as the capability of properly utilizing it, the Arabs had a decided edge in the important areas of mobility and familiarity with the terrain.

Lawrence saw the Arab objective in geographical terms, that of occupying all Arab-speaking lands in Asia. As much as the Arabs disliked the Turks, Lawrence did not see their objective as that of killing them. Their goal was to hold onto their land, and if the Turks were willing to go peaceably, so much the better as far as he was concerned. If, on the other hand, bloodshed was required, Lawrence would carry out his military objectives in the economical fashion described by Marshal Saxe. The Arabs were, after all, fighting for freedom, which is a pleasure to be tasted by a man alive.

Lawrence recollected in particular one key statement made by Saxe, which bore particular relevance to the Arab conflict with the Turks:

"I am not in favour of giving battle, especially at the outset of a war. I am even convinced that an able general can wage war his whole life without being compelled to do so."[13]

Concluding that within the Turkish Army, manpower was more plentiful than equipment, Lawrence decided that the road to victory for the Arabs resided in eliminating Turkish materials. The death of a Turkish bridge or rail, machine or gun, or high explosive was seen as more profitable than the death of a Turkish soldier. The war in which the Arabs would engage would be one of detachment. Attacks, which would be carried out with surprise, should be directed against the enemy's most accessible materials. Selective attacks against the railway, the enemy's means of transporting materials, would serve to gradually and systematically deprive the Turks of what they vitally needed. Without sufficient materials it would become impossible for the Turks to wage successful warfare. To exasperate the enemy, the Arabs would spread their forces out to take advantage of the vastness of a desert they knew so much better than their adversary. In addition to providing the enemy with a well-nigh impossible target, the Arabs would be on the offensive, deciding when and how to attack, leaving the Turks squarely on the defensive in seeking to cope with what to them were unpredictable attacks that had been calculated in advance by an elusive adversary.

The Arab War was seen as geographical rather than physical by Lawrence, and the strategy to keep the Turks pinned down in Medina in large numbers was vital to his twofold strategy of keeping the enemy bogged down in defending small land masses and controlling the largest land mass of Asia while sustaining the minimum number of casualties. Recognizing that the important factor of food would eventually confine the enemy to the railways, Lawrence's strategy became that of allowing the Turks to keep the railway system working, but just barely, and at a maximum level of discomfort.

Lawrence lucidly synthesized his analysis of this geographical struggle, in which he viewed the Turkish Army as an accident rather than a target in which its weakest link was attacked, in the following manner:

> Our success was certain, to be proved by paper and pencil as soon as the proportion of space and number had been learned. The contest was not physical, but mineral, and so battles were a mistake. All we won in battles was the ammunition the enemy fired off. Our victory lay not in battles, but in occupying square miles of country. Napoleon had said it was rare to find generals willing to fight battles. The contest of this war was that so few could do anything else. Napoleon had spoken in angry reaction against the excessive finesse of the eighteenth century, when men almost forgot that war gave licence to murder. We had been swinging out on his dictum for a hundred years, and it was time to go back a bit again. Battles are impositions on the side which believes itself weaker, made unavoidable either by lack of land-room, or by the need to defend a material property dearer than the lives of soldiers. We had nothing material to lose, so we were to defend nothing and to shoot nothing. The precious element of our forces were the Bedouin irregulars, and not the regulars whose role would only be to occupy places to which the irregulars had already given access. Our cards were speed and time, not hitting power, and these gave us strategical rather than tactical strength. Range is more to strategy than force. The invention of bully-beef had modified land-war more profoundly than the invention of gunpower.[14]

When Lawrence failed to find common cause with Abdullah on a plan of attack, he made contact with Feisal, determined to put into practice the concepts he developed as he lay recuperating. His efforts eventuated in a ride with Feisal's forces toward Syria. The ultimate objective was to occupy the Gulf of Aqaba. Strategists concurred that Aqaba would supply a needed launching pad for eventually breaking through to Damascus. Once that a foothold was accomplished in Damascus, the Holy Land of Palestine would become a feasible objective.

To recognize the magnitude of what was happening, one must compare and contrast the actual position given to Lawrence by his British Army superiors with that of the role in which he was functioning. Officially, Lawrence was no more than the liaison officer assigned to assist Feisal by the British Army. As was characteristic of T. E. Lawrence throughout his activities in the Arab campaign, however, the letter of the official portfolio was obscured by the comprehensiveness of his activities. From the outset, his influence was accepted by Feisal and his men. Not only was he a planner, but he was also a doer. Lawrence commanded respect because he was willing to undertake assignments shoulder to shoulder with the men on whose behalf he plotted strategy. Feisal recommended that Lawrence would find it easier to attain universal acceptance by his adopted Arab brethren if he wore their garb, and so he did. As a result, a number of the men believed for some time that he was a Syrian Army officer.

How did this British antiquarian interested in Syrian pottery and geography make such a swift and thorough transition so that Feisal and other Arabs would follow his recommendations with alacrity? The answer doubtlessly lies in a statement that Napolean once made on the subject of leadership. When asked how many men possessed the qualities necessary to lead men in combat, his reply was brisk and immediate:

"One in twenty," Napoleon responded.

"Approximately?" his questioner asked.

"Exactly," Napoleon declared.

In addition to the generally enumerated qualities of bravery and decisiveness that are most often associated with the ability to command, Napoleon focused on another basic requisite, without which courage and sincerity of purpose would prove insufficient. Napoleon referred to a basic quality of perception, a propensity for seeing and comprehending beyond the capacity of the average individual. This comprehension extends to the essential working instincts of the one in command. It was Lawrence himself who, in referring to his own developing theory of warfare, restated the Napoleonic one-in-twenty equation as he discussed the subject of battle tactics:

"Nine-tenths of tactics are certain, and taught in books: but the irrational tenth is like the kingfisher flashing across the pool, and that is the test of generals. It can only be ensued by instinct, sharpened by thought practising the stroke so often that at the crisis it is as natural as reflex."[15]

With Lawrence, the transitions and perceptions that it was necessary for him to embrace to achieve a successful command in spearheading the Arab Revolt were far more subtly acute than would have been the case in normal circumstances, with a leader commanding the forces of his own nation. Instead, Lawrence was saddled with the challenge of leading a cadre of free-spirited revolutionaries from a culture thoroughly disparate from that in which he had been brought up. While it was true that Lawrence, from the time he was a very young man traveling through Syria on archaeological pursuits, had felt a certain bond of kinship with the Arabs he encountered and had found a measure of tranquility in desert life that he savored beyond what he was acquainted with anywhere else, including his English homeland, it remained clear that there were enormous cultural differences that posed challenges for anyone who assumed the kind of position that he had. To wear Arab garb and fight side by side Arabs could gain for him a certain level of acceptance. To gain the kind of broader-based acceptance necessary to maintain a solid base of command over free-spirited warriors unaccustomed to discipline, particularly from a Britisher, required the highest measure of psychological adaptability. In that sphere, the Napoleonic one-in-twenty equation would have to be carried to its zenith.

Having traveled with Lawrence in his Arabian campaign and feeling a sense of awe over the adroit manner in which he acquitted himself as a leader, Lowell Thomas asked him how he had been able to handle such a difficult responsibility with such finesse. Lawrence explained:

The handling of Arabs might be termed an art, not a science, with many exceptions and no obvious rules. The Arab forms his judgment on externals that we ignore, and so it is vitally important that a stranger should watch every movement he makes and every word he says during his first weeks of association with a tribe. Nowhere in the world is it so difficult to atone for a bad start as with the Bedouins. However, if you once succeed in reaching the inner circle of a tribe and actually gain their confidence, you can do pretty much as you please with them and at the same time do many things yourself that would have caused them to regard you as an outcast had you been so forward at the start. The beginning and the end of the secret of handling Arabs is an unremitting study of them. Always keep on your guard; never speak an unnecessary word; watch yourself and your companions constantly; hear all that passes; search out what is going on beneath the surface; read the characters of the Arabs; discover their tastes and weaknesses, and keep everything you find out to yourself. Bury yourself in Arab circles; have no ideas and no interests except the work in hand, so that you master your part thoroughly

enough to avoid any of the little slips that would counteract the painful
work of weeks. Your success will be in proportion to your mental effort.[16]

Lawrence further illustrated the emphasis that Bedouins place on
externals by telling Thomas a story about a chief of the Shammar
Arabs, who was at the time riding a short distance behind Lawrence
and Thomas in the same caravan. Thomas had noticed a huge scar,
which spread itself in unsightly fashion across his face. Lawrence
unlocked the mystery of the scar for the benefit of his chronicler,
revealing an important point in the telling. While the chief was dining
with Ibn Rashid, the ruler of North-Central Arabia, he happened to
choke. Arabs consider choking on food a sign of bad breeding. Not
only does it indicate greed, but it is also thought that the devil has
caught the victim. The chief felt a wave of humiliation overcome him
after choking in the presence of Ibn Rashid. In his desperation, he
jerked out his knife and slit his mouth right up to the carotid artery in
his cheek, a painful deed meant to reveal to his host that a bit of meat
had actually stuck in his back teeth.

The systematic Lawrence incorporated his strategy for successfully
handling Arabs into a series of articles, known as the "Twenty-Seven
Articles." In addition to stressing the importance of studying the Arab
people closely and remaining constantly on guard, as Lawrence emphasized in his response to Lowell Thomas, he delineated the advisability of retaining close touch with Arab leaders. Another point mentioned was that of not mingling too closely with subordinates.
Lawrence also recognized the significance of Arab tribal customs and
the jealousies that frequently stemmed from the competition that
developed as an outgrowth of them. He felt that the best means of
working around the problems relating to tribal patterns was to magnify
and develop the growing conception of the Sherifs as the natural
aristocracy of the Arabs. As a result of intertribal jealousies, it is
impossible for any one sheikh to obtain a commanding position. Hence
the Sherifs form the basis for any unification of Arabs because their
reverence for pedigree and linkage of the individual to the Prophet
instill a sense of hopeful purpose.

Lawrence's understanding of the Arab mind together with his theory
of how the Arab Rebellion should be fought caused him to reject an
offer of British troops. When France later sought to be involved in the
Hejaz campaign, he vigorously opposed the idea. The French had
roots in Arabia stemming back to the days of the Crusaders and
continued to regard it as an area of natural national interest. Lawr-

ence's rejection of the imposition of foreign troops into what the Arabs saw as a natural indigenous uprising originated from both tactical warfare and political considerations. From a tactical standpoint, the desert terrain could be far more easily mastered by free-spirited Bedouins through surprise attacks. The use of regular troops would necessitate accommodating strategy so that the Turks would be fought in a more conventional manner. As stated earlier, T. E. believed that this type of warfare would prove a distinct disadvantage for the Allied cause while benefiting the Turks. The damage of fighting with foreign troops would be considerable from a political standpoint as well. The Arabs were filled with an idealistic fervor to take back what they felt was rightfully theirs—their natural homeland in which they had lived under the Turks in subjugation for four hundred years. To introduce them to the specter of fighting alongside British or French forces could, in Lawrence's mind, easily dampen this idealistic fervor while filling them with doubt as to what the future would hold even should their rebellion be successful.

A thorny point that existed throughout the period of Arab entrance on the side of the Allied cause and that extended into the Allied conferences following the war was the range of commitment that had been made to the Arabs to become involved in the military effort. The Arabs held the unmistakable view that they were fighting for freedom from Turkish domination of their land, but this position had never been unequivocally stated by representatives of either Great Britain or France. Sherif Hussein had sought a firm declaration acknowledging Arab independence within an area that stretched from the Taurus Mountains in the north to the Indian Ocean, excluding merely the Aden Protectorate, and from the Mediterranean to the Persian frontier. Sir Henry McMahon, High Commissioner of Egypt, finally provided Hussein with a direct response after much delay, realizing that some kind of favorable declaration need be given to encourage Arab participation in the conflict against Turkey and its German allies. McMahon was instructed in October 1915 to tell the Sherif that Britain pledged itself to recognize and support the independence of the Arabs within the boundaries he had proposed, subject to certain exceptions. These were the districts, not purely Arab, along the Syrian coast from the Taurus Mountains down to the west of Damascus. Another reservation was also imposed, however, providing a formidable obstacle, which loomed as a catch-22. The assurance was limited to those parts of Arab territories where Britain was free to act without detriment to French interests. In that France felt it had legitimate national interests there extending back to the Crusade period and, as an ally of Britain, would have to be contended with subsequent to any Allied victory in the war, the reservation could be used as a tactful dodge should the circumstances warrant it. The British imposed another reservation directly on their behalf by stating that the districts of Basra and Baghdad would be subjected to a measure of British control.

The wily Lawrence was only too well aware of the existing dichotomy between Arab expectations after entering the fray and the likely realization of them once the last shot had been fired and the air was clear of gunfire. The pain was all too evident in his somber words:

> For my work on the Arab front I had determined to accept nothing. The Cabinet raised the Arabs to fight for us by definite promises of self-government afterwards. Arabs believe in persons, not in institutions. They saw in me a free agent of the British Government, and demanded from me an endorsement of its written promises. So I had to join the conspiracy, and, for what my word was worth, assured the men of their reward. In our two years' partnership under fire they grew accustomed to believing me and to think my Government, like myself, sincere. In this hope they performed some fine things, but, of course, instead of being proud of what we did together, I was continually and bitterly ashamed.
>
> It was evident from the beginning that if we won the war these promises would be dead paper, and had I been an honest adviser of the Arabs I would have advised them to go home and not risk their lives fighting for such stuff, but I salved myself with the hope that, by leading these Arabs madly in the final victory I would establish them, with arms in their hands, in a position so assured (if not dominant) that expediency would counsel to the Great Powers a fair settlement of their claims. In other words, I presumed (seeing no other leader with the will and power) that I would survive the campaigns, and be able to defeat not merely the Turks on the battlefield, but my own country and its allies in the council-chamber. It was an immodest presumption; it is not yet clear if I succeeded, but it is clear that I had no shadow of leave to engage the Arabs, unknowing, in such hazard. I risked the fraud, on my conviction that Arab help was necessary to our cheap and speedy victory in the East, and that better we can win and break our word than lose.[16]

Lawrence's description of his activities regarding his response to Arab expectations of independence could best be defined as a perpetual juggling contest in which Arab morale was sought to be placed at its highest level by reassurances, while at the same time Britain held out its own options as to what the future of the territories held. A good example of how the British facilely played this same game was revealed when Lowell Thomas, shortly after meeting Lawrence and in the process of having lunch with General Sir Edmund Allenby and the Duke of Connaught, asked the renowned commander in chief and liberator of Palestine on behalf of the British Army he led just why Lawrence's efforts in Arabia had been kept such a secret from the public. General Allenby's response indicated the subtle level to which the British position had been formed. He explained that it was important to say as little as possible about Lawrence because Britain hoped that the large numbers of conscripted Arabs fighting in the Turkish Army might be persuaded to join Sherif Hussein in his fight for Arab independence. The British feared that the Arabs of Syria, Palestine, and Mesopotamia who had been conscripted by the Turks and who might be otherwise motivated to desert the Ottoman Empire to fight for Arab independence under Hussein might have misgivings in the event that the Britisher Lawrence and his role be revealed. They could then derive the impression that the Allies were inspiring the Hejaz Revolt, in which case its indigenously Arabian base, which the British sought to promote, could be compromised in the climate of Arab opinion. Allenby then added that, as a result of Lawrence's tremendous success and acclaim by the Arabs themselves, this fear was finally extirpated. He proved the point by personally inviting Thomas to join King Hussein's army and tell the world what the Arabs had been doing to win the Great War. Thomas immediately accepted and proceeded to do just that. The colloquy provides instructive insight into the fence-straddling effort the British had undertaken to convince the Arabs that their independence was the ultimate prize to be gained by joining the Allies while, after seeming to promise that independence on the one hand, carefully erecting sufficient semantical and tactical latitude to later ease away from such a commitment.

The British semantical posturing is much more easily understood when analyzing one key event, which took place on May 16, 1916, under a veil of secrecy and which would not become public knowledge until one year later. On that date, the Sykes-Picot Agreement was signed, unleashing a Pandora's box of eventual controversy. Under its terms, the old Ottoman Empire would be divided up into a Blue Zone, administered by the French, consisting of all of Syria north of Acre and West of Aleppo and extending well into Asia Minor, and British interests would be delineated in a Red Zone, consisting of the valley of the Tigris and the Euphrates from north of Baghdad to the Persian Gulf. Two further zones, "A" and "B," revealed the French and British spheres of influence wherein they would support an Arab state or confederation of states. These zones encompassed the desert and its fringes. Under the auspices of the agreement, provisions were also made to provide Russia with territory. This agreement was signed some three weeks prior to Hussein's formal announcement to launch the Arab revolt, which took place on June 5.

Hussein did not become aware of the Sykes-Picot Agreement until December 1917. By that time, the Russian czardom had been overthrown and a new government had been installed, that of the Communist Bolsheviks under Vladimir Lenin. Anxious to reveal to the world the alleged duplicities and hypocrisies they envisioned in the policies of capitalist governments, after combing the files of their vacated predecessors, the representatives of the newly installed revolutionary Russian Government decided to publish secret war agreements in December 1917, including Sykes-Picot. Sir Reginald Wingate, newly appointed High Commissioner of Egypt, sought to quickly reassure Hussein by asserting that Sykes-Picot did not constitute a formal treaty and that Russia's exit from the war had created an entirely different picture from that which had existed earlier.

Another period of diplomatic anxiety between Britain and the Arabs occurred on November 2, 1917, with the publication of the Balfour Declaration. The declaration and its ramifications on the world political scene will be examined at length later. For the moment it is sufficient to say that the Balfour Declaration was a communication from British Foreign Secretary Lord Balfour to Lord Rothschild, head of the British branch of the illustrious Jewish family. It declared that the British government viewed with favor the establishment in Palestine of a national home for the Jewish people. This time Britain sent Commander David George Hogarth to placate Hussein. Even though the declaration stated that "nothing shall be done which may prejudice the civil and religious rights" of the Palestine Arabs, Hogarth presented a stronger position regarding protection of Arab rights than his government had earlier taken. Hogarth told Hussein that the "Jewish settlements in Palestine would only be allowed insofar as would be consistent with the political and economic freedom of the Arab population."[18]

Despite the misgivings and inner doubts that Lawrence confessed to experiencing in reaction to the British policy of equivocation with respect to Arab rights, the free-spirited son of grassy British soil joined forces with the free-spirited sons of the desert in the common pursuit of overthrowing the yoke of the Ottoman Empire. Although later narratives would erroneously refer to this successful effort as a "mission entrusted to Colonel Lawrence," the undertaking was a private venture in which T. E. Lawrence used unique personnel in a crafty manner to achieve a desired result. No assistance had been provided by any British source as Emir Feisal furnished money, camels, stores, and explosives.

Tangible evidence of the consummate skill with which T. E. Lawrence wove himself into the fabric of Arab acceptance presented itself by the arrival of a welcome new addition to his forces, a dramatic Kiplingesque legend of his own time, a Robin Hood of the desert who was able to supply men of his own while commanding the respect of every other Bedouin among the forces.

The active participation by this legend, referred to by Lowell Thomas as "the greatest popular hero of modern Arabian history" and "the most celebrated fighting man the desert has produced in four generations,"[18] gave the movement a resounding shot in the arm. The diligent Englishman who had absorbed all of Arab custom of which he was capable joined forces with a Bedouin of commanding presence who would regard him as a blood brother.

In the tradition of this determined warrior, the genesis of his involvement in Lawrence's campaign resulted from a boldly emphatic proclamation addressed to the Sultan of Turkey; to Jemal Pasha, Viceroy of Syria, Palestine, and Arabia; and to the Mutesarif of Kerak, who was the Ottoman governor of the important district on the edge of the desert near the southern end of the Dead Sea where the warrior resided. The blunt message stated:

"By the grace of Allah, I, Auda Abu Tayi, warn you to quit Arabia before the end of Ramadan. We Arabs want this country to ourselves. Unless this is done, by the beard of the Prophet, I declare you proscribed, outlawed, and fair game for any one to kill."[19]

When Auda Abu Tayi, the Howeitat chieftain with the burning flames of nationalism stirring inwardly, heard about Hussein's declaration of revolt against the Turks, he and his Howeitat followers galloped across the desert to Feisal's headquarters and swore on the Koran at a banquet celebrating the occasion that they would make the Sherif's enemies their own. Suddenly the old warrior uttered a strong Muslim oath, reminding himself and his cohorts that he was wearing a set of Turkish false teeth. Frenziedly cursing the Turkish dentist who had made them, he rushed out of the tent and smashed them with resounding ferocity against a rock. For two months he was in agony and could eat only milk and boiled rice. Lawrence ultimately came to Auda's rescue, sending to Egypt for a set of acceptable Allied false teeth.

During the seventeen years prior to joining forces with Lawrence, Auda had killed about seventy-five men in hand-to-hand combat. All of the counted were fellow Arabs in that Turks did not register numbers in his fatality calculations. Among fellow Bedouins, notoriously acknowledged raiders as a group, he occupied a position second to none. The tall, ramrod straight, powerful Bedouin warrior with the heavily lined face maintained a catlike quickness at the age of sixty, and once he trained his efforts on the enemy, successful results obtained. The name "Auda" means "Father of Flying," a name commemorating his first ever flight, in which he implored his British pilot to soar higher and higher. The name served him well on one adventure in May of 1918 after the Turks had sent a large number of camels from Syria. They placed them in an impromptu corral at Maan Railway Station. Once Auda heard about this, he led a small party of twelve of his tribesmen on a bold dash into Maan. Thousands of Turkish soldiers were stationed in the area, but their presence proved to no avail as the element of surprise that Lawrence used in his military strategy for the Arab campaign was exercised with triumphant results. Before the soldiers were able to gain any bearing on what was happening, the "Father of Flying" had rounded up twenty-five of the camels and driven them off at a blistering twenty-five-mile-per-hour pace. This fearless warrior with twenty-eight wives possessed a scalding temper, but there remained as well a playful side, that of an impish child pulling off a prank and enjoying his efforts to the fullest. So extensive was his involvement in pranks that on one occasion, for the pure joy of it, he held up his intimate friend Emir Feisal.

This band of irregulars, honed by Lawrence into a solid fighting corps, produced results. In three days less than two months from the time that Lawrence's expedition left the seacoast at Wejh, the objective of capturing Aqaba had been accomplished. In typical Lawrence fashion, the triumph was not accomplished through direct strategic confrontations but by a series of intricate zigs and zags that left the enemy guessing in a dilemma of frustration. Lawrence's expeditionary force had covered a vast elliptical curve through the depths of Arabia before returning like a boomerang. Revealing a gradual increase of force, Lawrence struck the neighboring port of Wejh in the back. By pursuing the longest geographical route to his objective, Lawrence had taken the shortest path to military victory.

The capture of Aqaba proved a shot in the arm to British morale at a time when regular forces had been meeting with frustration after two separate attempts to secure Gaza had ended in setbacks. The victory also achieved the strategic effect of removing all danger of a Turkish raid through Sinai against the Suez Canal or the communications of the British Army in Palestine. A new line of operation had been opened up in which the Arabs could play a major role in a renewed British advance.

Perhaps the most impressive aspect of T. E. Lawrence's conquest of Aqaba was in the area of troop economy. Lawrence was the strategist who believed in taking the enemy by surprise and in launching hit-and-run raids in which the advantages were all on his side. By fighting in this manner, he was convinced that his own losses could be kept at a minimum, which indeed proved to be the case in the Aqaba operation. In it the Turks had sustained permanent losses of twelve hundred men, who had been killed or taken as prisoners. On the Arab side, only two men were lost! Compare those figures with the losses sustained by British troops in their March and April attempts to capture Gaza, and the accomplishment of Lawrence and his irregulars becomes even more compellingly staggering. The British succeeded in killing or capturing seventeen hundred Turks while losing three thousand men of their own. Whereas the British regular forces had sacrificed roughly two men to kill one Turk, Lawrence's irregular troops had sacrificed two of their number to kill twelve hundred Turks!

Through utilizing Aqaba as a strategic foothold, the Arabs were in a position to help Britain press on to victory in Palestine. The one thorn in the side of that strategy had been the failure of a top British military commander to rise to the surface. That factor also changed as a new face arrived in Egypt to assume command of British forces. It was Sir Edmund Allenby, who would join forces with Lawrence to push the Palestine campaign to a positive conclusion.

While the free-spirited Lawrence, whose lack of formality and whose disdain for conventionality had prompted dislike for him among the career military types with whom he had earlier dealt in the Arab Bureau, there were aspects of Allenby's makeup that enhanced prospects for a smoother relationship between the two men than had been the case in Lawrence's earlier dealings with other professional militarists. For almost three years during his tenure of service in France, Allenby had been the target of criticism. He was known as "The Bull," a name that described his relations with subordinates as well as his actions against the enemy. Allenby was an ardent cavalryman, and trench warfare seemed to irk his spirit. He seemed to also resent being subordinated in the command hierarchy. Allenby appeared to have been carved by destiny to assume an independent leadership role.

Command of the Egypt Bureau would give him that opportunity. His flair for independence and his propensity for rocking the boat, particularly where conventional military wisdom was concerned, gave Allenby some traits in common with the thoroughly unconventional T. E. Lawrence. While their undeniable differences would preclude the two men from reaching a perfect rapport, their similarities would enable them to understand one another better, making the formation of a joint effort easier to attain.

Lawrence recounted his first meeting with the tall, rangy commander with the stern expression and the dark mustache: ". . . he was hardly prepared for anything so odd as myself—a little bare-footed silk-skirted man offering to hobble the enemy by his preaching if given stores and arms and a fund of two hundred thousand sovereigns to convince and control his converts. Allenby could not make out how much was genuine performer and how much charlatan. The problem was working behind his eyes, and I left him unhelped to solve it."[20]

After Lawrence had given Allenby his ideas about eastern Syria and its people, as well as what he deemed to be a successful strategy to pursue, Allenby promised to do what he could. His input proved enormously beneficial in that the two hundred thousand pound figure Lawrence had sought was eventually increased to five hundred thousand pounds, of which Lawrence had a balance of ten thousand pounds to return when Damascus was reached.

To achieve control of Syria meant securing assistance from a fresh ladder of tribes, similar to his strategy of conquering Aqaba. Deraa and the Yarmuk Valley would provide the leverage to loosen the Turkish hold on the Hauran.

Lawrence's blueprint for victory sprang from a calculated goal to unify the Arabs against the Turks. Though his boyhood dream had been that of a united Arabia, the practical experience he gained by observing and living among Arabs made him recognize that such a result could be achieved only on a short-term basis, in the common pursuit of overthrowing a hated enemy. The tremendous fragmentation of Arab tribal bonds and the enormous diversities existing within these social groups would make it impossible to form any kind of uniform consensus among Arabs in the foreseeable future. Lawrence poured out his feelings on this subject to one of his biographers, Liddell Hart: "I have always been a realist and opportunist in tactics: and Arab unity is a madman's notion—for this century or next, probably. English-speaking unity is a fair parallel. I never dreamed of uniting even Hejaz and Syria. My conception was a number of states."[21]

Lawrence's successful Aqaba campaign instilled additional confidence within him that he had a winning tactical strategy to employ against the Ottoman Empire. The basis of that winning strategy stemmed from command of the desert. It was his tribal band of irregulars who were on familiar terrain, not the enemy with traditional roots in another land. Desert forays could be likened to sea warfare, with emphases placed on mobility and proper channeling of forces through an intricate series of communication bases.

Lawrence elucidated on the analogy between desert and sea warfare: "Camel-raiding parties, self-contained as ships, could cruise without danger along any part of the enemy's land-frontier, just out of sight of his posts along the edge of cultivation, and tap or raid into his lines where it seemed fittest or easiest and most profitable, with a sure retreat always behind them into an element which the Turks could not enter."[22]

The sure-footed sons of the desert could lose their pursuers in what constituted cumbersome, unfamiliar terrain for their Turkish pursuers. Lawrence had traversed much of Syria himself on foot before the war, in the course of which he traced the movements of the great Muslim warrior Saladin. He became aware of the value of this kind of geographical intuition in which the known was blended with the unknown contributes to the overall interest. This knowledge was evidenced in the following statement: "As our war-experience deepened we became adepts at that form of geographical intuition, described by Bourcet as wedding unknown land to known in a mental map."[23]

The winning tactical formula for Arab success against the Turks resided in never pushing an advantage, but engaging in what he called "tip and run: not pushes, but strokes," after which the objective became "to move off and strike again somewhere else."[24]

The distant war that Lawrence envisaged characterized by quick hit-and-run thrusts emphasized maximum use of that remarkably fleet animal, the camel, which makes hit-and-run tactics feasible on a wide scale. In that the camel-riding Arabs were free of the encumbering hardship of the kind of elaborate supply systems used in modern army warfare, their facility of movement must have made their frustrated opponents feel as if they were buried in quicksand as they desperately sought to catch an elusive foe.

The objective was to supply the enemy with targets, then frustrate the opportunity to strike at them in any kind of meaningful way. As Lawrence wrote: "We used the smallest force in the quickest time at the farthest place. If the action had continued till the enemy had changed his dispositions to resist it, we would have been breaking the spirit of our fundamental rule of denying him targets."[25]

The new strategy blended rather adroitly into the otherwise fractious infrastructure of tribal disharmony. Whereas it was impossible for Lawrence to mix or combine elements of various tribes due to strong mutual antagonisms, or to use men of one tribe in the territory of another for the same reason, the inability to concentrate forces in a centralized fashion enhanced the very concept Lawrence was seeking to implement. The nature of the Lawrence strategy was to spread out forces along the widest possible terrain of desert, making it impossible for the Turks to mount a successful overall campaign against them. Through spreading out his own forces, Lawrence in turn sought to isolate Turkish forces.

In seeking to limit the Turkish range of movement, an imperative element of Lawrence's overall strategy was the use of explosives, which he helped to elevate to the level of an art. In that the Turks had to cover wide expanses of desert through means other than the familiar Arab transportation vehicle of the camel, frequent use of the Arabian railway system became a necessity. Therefore, in the grand strategy of curtailing Turkish options while imposing isolation, the policy of blowing up trains and destroying tracks became a paramount objective. The act of placing explosives adjacent to a target was classified as "planting tulips."

T. E. Lawrence developed the kind of inward pride in his "tulip planting" that a horticulturist would be inclined to feel toward the realistic counterpart of the combative metaphor. He let his feelings be known during a conversation with Lowell Thomas: "Do you know, one of the most glorious sights I have ever seen is a train-load of Turkish soldiers ascending skyward after the explosion of a tulip!"[26]

Lawrence had dynamited so many trains along the Hejaz Railway that an adjustment in seat pricing was made in Damascus. Seats in the rear carriage sold for five and six times their normal value. Inevitably there would be a wild scramble for the rear location preceding train departures. The reason was that Lawrence nearly always touched off his "tulips" under the engine, the result being that the only carriages damaged were those in the front.

The "tulip planting" strategy employed by Lawrence varied in accordance with his objective. If he sought to merely derail the engine of a train, he would use only a pound of blasting gelatine. Should his desire be that of blowing up the train, he would use between forty and fifty pounds of blasting power.

It was Lawrence who executed this fine art of destruction. Even though his Bedouin warriors accompanied him on his mine-planting excursions, Lawrence preferred to handle the responsibility himself, after which the Bedouins were free to engage in their enjoyable pastime of looting. There were two reasons why Lawrence preferred not instructing the Arabs in the art of "tulip planting." First of all, the Bedouins were inclined to think of it as an enjoyable game, and it was Lawrence's fear that they would continue blowing up trains for sheer sport even after the war and enjoying the lucrative rewards to be derived from looting afterward. Second, it was dangerous to leave footprints along the railway line, so he preferred not delegating "tulip planting" to people who might be careless and jeopardize the interests of everyone.

A graphic illustration of effectively accomplished "tulip planting" and its aftermath was revealed through the firsthand observations of Lowell Thomas as he described one excursion on which he accompanied Lawrence and his Bedouin troops:

Many of the Turks dodged behind the embankment and began shooting through the carriage-wheels; but Lawrence, in anticipation of this, had posted two Lewis machine-guns just around a curve in the track, where they covered the opposite side of the railway embankment behind which the Turks had taken refuge. The gun-crews opened fire, and before the Turks knew what had happened their line was raked from end to end and every man behind the embankment either killed or wounded. The rest of the Turks who had remained on the train fled panic-stricken in all directions.

The Arabs, who were crouching behind all the rocks popping away with their rifles, charged down, tore open the carriages, and tossed out everything on board that was not nailed down. The loot consisted of sacks of Turkish silver coin and paper currency and many beautiful draperies which the Turks had taken from the private houses of wealthy Arabs in Medina. The Bedouins piled all the loot along the embankment, and with shouts of glee commenced dividing it among themselves, while Lawrence signed the duplicate way-bills and playfully returned one copy to a wounded Turkish guard whom he intended to leave behind. They were just like children around a Christmas tree. Occasionally two men would want the same silk Kermani rug and begin fighting over it. When that happened Lawrence would step between them and turn the rug over to some third man."[27]

Sherifs Ali and Abdullah played major roles in the raids on the Hejaz Railway and in the capture of great convoys of Turkish camels near

Medina. During 1917, Lawrence and his compatriots, with the able assistance of Feisal, Ali, Abdullah, and Zeid, the sons of Sherif Hussein, blew up twenty-five Turkish trains, tore up fifteen thousand rails, and destroyed fifty-seven bridges and culverts. During the eighteen-month period that Lawrence commanded the Arabs, they dynamited seventy-nine trains and bridges, prompting General Allenby to write in one of his reports that T. E. Lawrence had made train wrecking the national sport of Arabia.

It is easy to see how integral a role train and rail destruction played in turning the tide of battle in the Arabs' favor. Because the enemy lacked both the kind of mobility of warfare that the Arabs possessed and a familiarity with the seemingly endless desert terrain, the one necessary element to transport troop manpower along with the means of sustaining it—weapons, ammunition, and food—became the railway system. Once this vital transportation link was severely compromised, the Turkish posture became ultimately hopeless.

Another vital link in Lawrence's strategy of destroying Turkish mobility involved Medina. As essential element of the goal of spreading Arab tribal units so extensively that the Turks would be unable to cope with them revolved around keeping them bottled up in small areas through the deployment of large numbers of troops. Medina accordingly loomed as a master stroke for advancing Arab strategic interests as long as Lawrence could convince the adversary of its necessity. He was aided by the conventional wisdom, which had been passed along through many generations of warfare, that it is vital to have a major fortress to serve as chief artery for a fighting entity. It was thought that to abandon such a vital network or have it overrun by the enemy was to run the grave risk of losing a war. The ingenious Lawrence wanted Turkey to believe that concept, and to further encourage it he was willing to commit himself to obfuscation tactics. Though Medina provided the definitive example of Lawrence's clever ploy at work, it was utilized elsewhere as well whenever the Turks showed signs of amassing large numbers of troops to go after the Arabs. If Lawrence wished to avoid having the Turks attack Arab strengths, the shrewd measure to employ was to keep them bottled up where their forces would accomplish the least amount of good while providing the remotest source of difficulty for the Arabs. Hence the best way to keep large deployments of Turkish manpower committed to Medina and at other garrisons where the threat to the Arabs would be reduced was through convincing the enemy that those bastions of presumed enemy strength were valuable to them. Therefore, whenever the Turkish forces demonstrated restiveness, withdrawing troops from these bastions to deploy elsewhere, Lawrence would unleash forces of his own to convince the enemy that he intended to capture those outposts. By launching token assaults on Medina and convincing the enemy that his efforts were in earnest, Lawrence would accomplish a twofold purpose: (1) keeping the enemy bottled up in his own fortress in large numbers and (2) freeing his own forces to attack areas they deemed of vital interest, aided by the element of surprise over an enemy who had centralized manpower in another area.

Now that the deliverance of the Hejaz had become a virtually accomplished reality, the next goal on the agenda became the liberation of Syria from Turkish hands. Lawrence's previous accomplishments up to and including Aqaba had occurred almost entirely on desert land. As the focus shifted to Syria, the land to be contested was predominantly cultivated. Being a pragmatic realist, Lawrence was the first to realize that an effort directed toward a settled body as opposed to largely desert terrain required a fresh approach. Lawrence recognized that the Arab peoples in the north could be freed only through the aid of the British Army, whose northward advance was the necessary concomitant that would accompany the Arab effort. Although cooperation between the two forces was necessary, it need not be close, and that was the way Lawrence preferred. Allenby proved to be of a like mind.

As Lawrence explained it, "We agreed to keep the Dead Sea and Jordan between us—except when he gave me notice he was going to Amman, and I gave him notice I was recruiting in Sinai."[28]

With increased British involvement in the Arab effort, Lawrence became the beneficiary of a tactical enhancement to his own always burgeoning strategic repertoire. British air power was incorporated into Arab military assaults, providing the already bemused Turks with yet another worry.

Now Lawrence was able to fashion a four-pronged strategy, which ultimately broke the spirit and resistance of both the Turks and the German troops sent to Arabia to assist them, which included (1) using the familiar desert terrain of the Arabs and mobility attached to this knowledge coupled with a facility for handling the functionally speedy animal, the camel, to provide a basis for hit-and-run attacks in which the Turkish forces were at a keen disadvantage and were victimized by the element of surprise; (2) minimizing Turkish transportation of forces and supplies in what was to them a large and essentially unfamiliar land by demolishing trains and tracks and compromising the effectiveness of the railways; (3) keeping the enemy isolated defending garrisons, particularly the Medina fortress, and thus diminishing manpower in the overall Arabian pursuit; and (4) utilizing accompanying British airpower to consolidate attacks through the bombardment of enemy positions.

Another factor facilitating an Arab victory over the Turks was the natural attrition element militating against a major power that has extended itself too long and too far. This was what the Arabs themselves had experienced five hundred years earlier against the invading Christian Crusaders. Having endured for one hundred years of servitude under the Christians and an additional four hundred under the yoke of the Ottoman Empire, the Arabs were instilled with keen motivation to overthrow the Turkish regime. The Ottoman Empire had stretched itself to such extended lengths as to lose its elasticity and with that its functioning ability to control. With its principal roots in the distant city of Constantinople, the Ottoman Empire was forced to suffer the ultimate inconvenience of having its mode of transport in Arabia, its railway system, reduced to shambles.

Once the Arabs had seized control of Aqaba, it was necessary to mount a vigorous defense of their recently won objective. The Turks also recognized the strategic importance of Aqaba but were turned back in their attempt to reacquire it. From there Lawrence was free to focus on his ultimate objective of Damascus, and while he was initiating efforts in that sphere, General Allenby and his regular British forces trained their sights on Gaza. While Lawrence and his Arab warriors worked their way toward Damascus, they aided Allenby's objective by demolishing Turkish trains and segments of the railways, making it more difficult for the Turks to mount any kind of meaningful defense against Allenby's assaults. Deraa held a position of great importance in Lawrence's strategic calculations. Three separate railways emanated from that point, from which a direct strike into the heart of Damascus became a distinct reality.

During the course of Lawrence's otherwise successful pursuits, the dangerous uncertainties of war threatened him in a tangible way as he underwent three close calls on his life. The first two came about following a failure in the Yarmuk Valley. An attack directed at knocking out the first and biggest girder bridge in the valley, over which the railway from Palestine climbed on its way to Damascus, ran into unexpected difficulty when one of Lawrence's men dropped a rifle. A Turkish sentry heard the sound, and when he spotted machine gunners climbing to a new position, gunfire broke out. The Serahin porters within Lawrence's ranks, frightened of being blown to pieces, dumped their sacks of gelatine over the edge of the ravine and fled. As a result of the failure of their mission, the Arabs proposed that their effort should achieve at least one success before returning to their base at Azrak. It was proposed that they blow up a train. Even though Lawrence was opposed to the idea, realizing the meticulous preparation a successful mission required, the enthusiasm of his cohorts persuaded him to give the proposal a try. One train passed before the explosives could be put in place, and a second moved through the rain and mist before the man on watch could spot it. Finally, with rain drenching the landscape, Lawrence observed another train coming along, which was packed with troops. Although he would have liked to change his plans, it was too late to do so. When the engine reached him, he pushed down the handle of the exploder. Nothing happened! He realized that the troop transport train was passing some fifty yards away from him. Always resourceful, Lawrence saved his life sprawling out on his haunches in the manner of a casual Bedouin, someone not worth shooting. Mud and rain had diminished the splendor of his white and gold dress, aiding his mask of inconspicuousness. As soon as the train passed, he pushed the wires under the earth and bolted for cover. A few hundred yards up the grade, the train stuck. An officers' patrol used the opportunity to come back and have a look at the ground but observed nothing.

Despite the ill luck, the group decided to try anew the following morning. The train they sought to blow up was carring the Turkish commander destined to take over the defense of Jerusalem. Lawrence touched off the mine under the leading engine. So close was he to the explosion, however, that he was hurled violently backward. His toe was broken, his arms scratched, and his clothes torn. Seven of the Arabs were hit in a rush to bring Lawrence in. Turkish guns blazed as the huge escort of the designated commander of the Jerusalem campaign, numbering several hundred strong, began overwhelming the Arabs with their machine gun fire. Lawrence and his compatriots headed for the hilltop and jumped on their camels, wishing, for the moment, that they had had machine guns themselves to supply a better match. The only success, a limited one at that, which the Arabs could point to when they returned to Azrak were some sixty rifles they had seized in their first rush toward the train. For that they had been forced to endure the losses of several lives as well as the near loss of their commander, T. E. Lawrence.

The final incident that befell Lawrence appeared to have a profound negative impact on the rest of his life. It is also an incident that has been shrouded in controversy, particularly in recent years, among Lawrence biographers and students. This controversy will be considered at the close of this chapter, when it and other subjects of dispute concerning the always enigmatic T. E. Lawrence will be revealed and analyzed. The account presented here came about as a result of Lawrence's own revelations and were recorded devoid of speculation or doubt in early biographical accounts.

The account begins during the period after the close scrapes described above. When the bad weather sufficiently cleared, Lawrence, accompanied by three companions, decided to survey the Deraa area to gather information prior to launching an attack. He actually entered the city itself with Faris, an old peasant. Such an act involved great risk-taking in that the Turks had a price on Lawrence's head, and he assumed the prospect of being captured in an enemy stronghold. After walking past some groups of Turkish soldiers, who ignored him, he heard a sergeant call out to him in Turkish. Though Lawrence and Faris continued walking on, feigning ignorance, the soldier was not about to be dissuaded. He chased after Lawrence, grabbed him roughly by the arm, and exclaimed, "The Bey wants you."

Lawrence was conscripted immediately into the Turkish army, then told that his service could be terminated if he fulfilled the pleasure of the Bey that evening. Biographer Richard Graves stated his belief that the Bey was probably not the Governor of Deraa, but the garrison commander, Bimbashi Ismail Bey, or the militia commander, Ali Riza Bey. The Bey was said to be taken with Lawrence's blue eyes and fair skin. When he asked if he was a Circassian—a group of people from the Caucasus of Caucasian heritage but not of Indo-European speech— Lawrence responded that he was, hoping that his true identity would not be revealed. The Bey began making homosexual advances, kissing and pawing Lawrence. When Lawrence resisted, the Bey became infuriated and sent him out to be punished. Four men held him as he was whipped and beaten, after which, in his weakened condition, barely conscious, he was attacked by three men and raped. He escaped the next morning from the room he had been left in following the attack. An Arab gave him a ride on his camel to the nearest village, where he rejoined Faris.

Richard Graves wrote of the psychological scars the incident left on Lawrence both immediately following it and from a long-term standpoint: "That night he felt, not for the first time, that he wished to have no more to do with Arabia; but he had always tended to despise physical things, and his will told him that insults done to his body should not be treated seriously. On the way back to Azrak, his spirits were revived by the generosity of a raiding party, who let him and Faris pass unplundered, recognizing that Lawrence and his comrades deserved men's homage. Later, after the war and the Peace Conference, his experiences in Deraa played more horribly on his mind; and then he wrote that it was on that night in Deraa that the citadel of his integrity had been irrevocably lost."[29]

Shortly thereafter, Lawrence flew to Gaza for a meeting with Allenby, who indicated he was not greatly worried about the failure at Yarmuk. In that Lawrence had been responsible for the recent bombing of a train carrying none other than Jemal Pasha, the Turkish commander in chief in Syria, as a passenger, the Turks manifested a stiffening resolve to bring an end to the "tulip planting" and rebellion-leading Britisher in Arab clothing. They substantially increased the price on his head, leading both Lawrence and Allenby to conclude that action was needed to protect his safety. The question was resolved by assigning a crack ninety-man bodyguard detail to T. E. Lawrence's personal service.

Allenby's steady efforts also began bearing tangible results, and on the historic date of December 11, 1917, Lawrence took part in the official entry into Jerusalem after General Allenby's forces had vanquished the final enemy troops.

Allenby revealed to Lawrence that he could perform a useful role by moving north and capturing Tafileh, putting an end to the use of the Dead Sea to transport enemy food. A few days later, while seeking to accomplish that objective, as Lawrence was launching attacks along the railway line near Mudowwara, he had another close call. Sergeant Tom Beaumont, a British soldier who was present, remembered that one bridge that was destroyed crashed with a terrific roar. Beaumont then related the close call: "Fragments of masonry flew in all directions & a huge piece of metal only missed Lawrence by inches."[30]

The slender thread by which Lawrence's life precariously dangled was made even more evident by a Turkish poster he observed announcing a reward of twenty thousand pounds for Lawrence alive and ten thousand pounds dead.

The Arab onslaught continued as the renowned Bedouin warrior Auda abu Tayi and Sherif Nasir, Feisal's cousin, captured Tafileh with little bloodshed. Auda was soon paid off and sent back to the desert after his tribesmen began quarreling with their hated enemies, the Motalga, but Zeid and Jaafar Pasha had arrived from Petra to take control, and soon they were joined by Lawrence, who arrived from Guweira, and strategy began being planned for the anticipated Turkish counterattack.

When the hostilities ultimately concluded, Lawrence was recognized as having waged one of his most stirring battles of the war, summoning his men to greater efforts even after experiencing early adversities. The battle at Tafileh was significant because it constituted the one and only regular conflict in which the wily tactician of irregular warfare, T. E. Lawrence, would engage. With snow falling on the ground, and with weather so appalling that all the men and equipment could not reach Tafileh in time, hostilities began inauspiciously for the Arabs as the Turkish forces launched a furious counterattack on the village. The badly outnumbered Arab forces, consisting of some three hundred men to one thousand for the enemy, were initially repulsed, panicking and retreating from the village. Lawrence spoke earnestly to his rattled troops, asking them to keep the faith and promising a successful deployment of forces to surprise the enemy and seize the advantage. True to his word, Lawrence's tactical resourcefulness saw him order strategies that ran counter to the conventional wisdom espoused in prevalent military manuals. Conventional theory called for making either right- or left-flanking attacks on the enemy, followed by a frontal assault. On the Western Front, the extended trenches made flanking attacks almost impossible, while frontal charges were considered disastrous. There were no trenches, however, at Tafileh.

By the time that Lawrence made his move, a force of some four hundred and fifty had gathered in his reserve position, which he had ordered upon seeing the Turks move rapidly to outflank the advanced ridge. The Turks brought up their machine guns as they prepared for imminent action.

Lawrence sent eighty riders and five automatics to roll up the enemy's left wing. Another hundred men took three automatics and outflanked the Turkish right wing. With the enemy distracted by attacks on both its right and left flanks, Lawrence, ever the defiler of conventional wisdom, ordered an attack up the middle as he deployed his camel men and levies. Soon the enemy center collapsed under the swift surprise assault, and a major victory was secured. News of the victory was sent to Abdullah el Feir, who was ensconced beneath them near the southern shore of the Dead Sea. Three days later, he rode through the night with seventy horsemen to the lake port of Kerak, destroying the Turkish flotilla and stopping the flow of Dead Sea traffic as Allenby had requested. For Lawrence's efforts in that stirring victory of January 25, 1918, he was awarded the Distinguished Service Order. Turkish losses ran high, as some four hundred were killed and two hundred and fifty taken prisoners.

In the spring of 1918, Lawrence launched a new offensive against the Hejaz line. By the time early summer beckoned, it had become evident that the Turks were losing the war in both the Hejaz and Palestine. Concern began to grow among the Arabs, who had proved so vital in assisting the Allied cause, over proposed British and French plans for Syria and Lebanon. Of particular concern were the continual overtures that Turkish Syrian commander Jemal Pasha had been making in secret to Emir Feisal since the inception of the Arab Revolt. The Turkish leader had desired to keep options open for concluding a separate peace with Feisal and had made several specific overtures toward that end.

With the war effort now proceeding in their direction, the British Government had no desire to destabilize the military situation through encountering problems with the Arabs. On June 16, 1918, the government made a declaration of policy, which stemmed from a petition from seven prominent Syrian nationalists exiled in Cairo. The response, called the "Declaration to the Seven", pledged the British Government to recognizing "the complete and sovereign independence of all those Territories liberated from Turkish rule by the Arabs themselves."[31]

Hussein and Feisal saw this declaration as superseding the Sykes-Picot agreement. A few weeks earlier, Lawrence had written on an Army notepad, "We are calling them to fight for a lie and I can't stand it."[32]

In the manner of a hunting dog sniffing its prey, General Allenby could sense imminent victory. The groundwork was being laid for the final big push northward into Damascus. Lawrence was being used in a communicative capacity as he busily shifted his efforts between the Hejaz, Egypt, and Palestine. When he was not involved in those strategic consultations, he still found time to undertake raids on the Hejaz Railway.

As the war effort entered its final major phase, Lawrence was required to shift gears and assume a persona different from that which he had boldly embraced in his daring hit-and-run desert raids on Turkish forces. As the focus shifted to major population centers and away from Arabia's hot desert sands, with all roads and all efforts leading toward the ultimate goal of Damascus, the war became more orthodox when additional trained personnel arrived. Along with regular forces to strengthen the forthcoming major push toward Damascus, armored cars and airplanes were also provided. Though Lawrence had been previously accustomed to a different type of fighting and with other weapons, he proved to be a military leader of flexibility as he made successful adjustments.

T. E. Lawrence had been a man engaged in a gigantic balancing act from the very beginning as he juggled his British roots and his adopted role of Arabian Revolt catalyst and coordinator. He was also compelled to serve as mediator by keeping warring Arab tribes away from each other's throats in the interest of promoting at least a temporary piecemeal form of unity for the ultimate benefit of dislodging the hated Turks from their soil. His role often assumed an equivalent if not greater significance as a political consultant as opposed to his more publicized persona of military leader. The counseling facet of Lawrence was required as fatigue and dissatisfaction became factors among Feisal's men. Against this swelling backdrop of restlessness, a rift began developing between Feisal and his father. German agents were seeking to exploit this rift in a meaningful way in order to spread dissension among the Arab ranks. An opportunity arose when Feisal appointed Jaafar Pasha, the Mesopotamian officer in charge of Feisal's relatively small contingent of regulars, which consisted of less than one thousand men, to the post of Commander of the Arab Northern Army. All Feisal had done was to use the traditional military psychological ploy of providing a glossy title with an accompanying presumption of importance to an individual's role, thereby, it was hoped, making the individual feel better in the process. Since there was no evidence that Jaafar was taking on an expanded role, the maneuver appeared to be nothing more than a morale booster. The German agents, however, saw a chance to provoke a serious rupture between father and son. The agents succeeded in persuading an already embittered Hussein that Jaafar had declared himself Commander in Chief of the Arab armies with Feisal's blessing, with the correlative implication that the Mesopotamian officer was seeking to seize control of all Arab forces. Hussein denounced both Jaafar and Feisal, accepting the allegations of the German agents without while checking out the facts for himself. The already weary Feisal, rubbed raw from the strain of command in a long and arduous campaign, reacted to his father's criticism by resigning his post.

The resignation of Feisal hit Lawrence and Allenby like a blow to the solar plexus. Its timing could hardly have been worse because Feisal's forces were lined up parallel with Allenby's, pointed northward in preparation for the big push toward Damascus. Some of the troops of Feisal had actually started to move. In addition to the obvious leadership problems that Feisal's resignation would cause, there were also the adverse propaganda repercussions stemming from one of the Arab movement's leading figures' deserting the cause.

When Lawrence had an opportunity to observe the damage resulting from Feisal's resignation, he focused on some significant points. First of all, as anticipated, a great deal of Bedouin demoralization resulted from Feisal's departure. He was one of their own, a respected descendant of The Prophet himself. As a meticulous observer of Arab conduct who had fathomed a set of rules facilitating dealing with them, Lawrence observed a trouble sign over the fact that, since Feisal's departure, orders were being given directly to the Arabs instead of through their chiefs. Recognizing the sensitivity involved in bypassing the usual chain-of-command process, Lawrence predicted that the situation could last for only four more days.

Due to Lawrence's prompting, Allenby sent a message to Feisal in hopes of remedying a potentially highly damaging situation:

> It has been brought to my notice that you have tendered your resignation as King of the Hejaz. It is not for me to interfere in a personal question between your revered father and yourself, but I most strongly urge you to withdraw your resignation which at this junction threatens the destruction of Arab hopes. If your Highness resigns at this time all the work that you and your army have arduously performed will be rendered vain at the very moment when the chance of victory seems brightest. You owe it to the Arab cause and to those who so loyally fought with you to disregard every personal influence and complete the great task which you have so well begun.[33]

The calamity was averted as Hussein sent his son a half-apologetic telegram, which Lawrence intercepted and decoded. He exercised diplomatic tact by allowing Feisal to see only the first and less hostile half of the message. Students of history will observe a parallel between this event and the strategy of President John F. Kennedy during the Cuban Missile Crisis in 1962. After having received two telegrams from his adversary, Soviet Party Chairman Nikita S. Khrushchev, the first conciliatory and the second truculent in tone, President Kennedy chose to respond to the message in the first communiqué while ignoring the substantially harsher second telegram. In this instance, Lawrence saw the advisability in relaying only the positive, first half of Hussein's message to his son. Feisal agreed to resume command of his forces for the remainder of the war, even though old scars remained and an adequate degree of discipline was never completely restored.

As Allenby's advance was launched on September 19, the role assigned to Lawrence was that of coordinating the isolation of Deraa, the major rail terminus south of Damascus. Lawrence was given the familiar assignment of disrupting communication and his playing havoc with the rail system would prevent Turkish reinforcements from reaching Syria from the south. Lawrence responded with vigorous dispatch in an attack on the Nasib station two stops south of Deraa. Aiding him in the effort was a young officer in the Royal Engineers, Alec Kirkbride, who was destined to accompany him on his entry into Damascus.

One of the most controversial episodes of Lawrence's life occurred in the village of Tafas. Lawrence and Auda, with a body of irregulars, caught up with a retreating column of Turkish and German soldiers there. The enemy retreat was toward Damascus, and the resulting conflict has been termed "the massacre of Tafas" to describe its gruesomeness.

Lawrence did not deny that the Arab forces unleashed an avalanche of carnage. He described it in detail in *Seven Pillars of Wisdom*. He explained the grisly action as a response to the slaughter of Arab villagers, which included women and children. The direct catalyst of the attack was said by Lawrence to have been the reaction of Talal, the Sheik of Tafas, after observing a pregnant woman lying dead atop a bayonet onto which she had been forced. At that juncture, Talal, a skilled horseman and warrior for whom Lawrence and his men had the profoundest respect, uttered a horrible cry, put the spurs to his horse, and charged toward a retiring column. He expired, with his mare, riddled with machine gun bullets among their lance points.

The Arabs, exhorted by Lawrence and Auda, sought to exact immediate revenge on the enemy, as described tersely in *Seven Pillars*:

"In a madness born of the horror of Tafas we killed and killed, even blowing in the heads of the fallen and of the animals; as though their death and running blood could slake our agony."[34]

Lawrence's brutally graphic account next told what happened when one group of Arabs who had not received the "take no prisoners" order had taken some of the enemy captive:

Just one group of Arabs, who had not heard our news, took prisoner the last two hundred men of the central section. Their respite was short. I had gone up to learn why it was, not unwilling that this remnant be let live as witnesses of Tallal's price; but a man on the ground behind them screamed something to the Arabs, who with pale faces led me across to see. It was one of us—his thigh shattered. The blood had rushed out over the red soil, and left him dying; but even so he had not been spared. In the fashion of to-day's battle he had been further tormented by bayonets hammered through his shoulder and other leg into the ground, pinning him out like a collected insect.

He was fully conscious. When we said, "Hassan, who did it?" he drooped his eyes toward the prisoners, huddling together so hopelessly broken. They said nothing in the moments before we opened fire. At last their heap ceased moving; and Hassan was dead; and we mounted again and rode home slowly (home was my carpet three or four hours from us at Sheikh Saad) in the gloom, which felt so chill now that the sun had gone down.[35]

Once Allenby's forces had defeated the Turks in Northern Palestine, the occupation of Deraa and Damascus became only a question of time. As the final curtain was about to come down on the Middle East conflict, the emphasis was already beginning to shift from the battle-field to prospective dilemmas at the conference table. This is a natural enough phenomenon in the conduct of world affairs at the close of a major conflict, the act of posturing as the spoils of battle are about to be divided among involved nations. This time, given the realities of Middle East politics as related to the various involved parties in the Allied cause, the picture was particularly beclouded. Great Britain, in its rush to enhance its prospects in the region as part of a grand strategy for victory in World War One, had made numerous promises to various parties, some of which were blatantly contradictory. There had been the Sykes-Picot agreement, the Balfour Declaration, the Declaration to the Seven, and the various assurances and reassurances that had been given to Sherif Hussein by Sir Henry McMahon, David George Hogarth, and Sir Reginald Wingate. Now that victory appeared close at hand, the question arose about how the Arabs would be treated.

As for Lawrence and his Arab irregulars, as the campaign wound down to its conclusion—a triumphant sweep into Damascus—they began to assume a position in the background. The vast bulk of the Northern Palestine successes were achieved not through the efforts of Arab regulars or irregulars but by the Australian Mounted Division commanded by General Sir Harry Chauvel and the fourth and fifth Indian Cavalry Divisions commanded by Major-General Sir George Barrow and Major-General H. J. M. Macandrew.

The orders sent to General Chauvel by the British command were to approach Damascus and isolate it but not to enter the city unless forced to for tactical reasons. Giving such a restrictive order to a general hungry for final victory and beginning to inhale its satisfying aroma is no way to please him, and Chauvel was clearly disgruntled. The reason for the order was markedly political. If Chauvel's forces could be held off and Arab troops emerged first on the scene to occupy the capital of Syria and suffered considerable losses in doing so, then perhaps a satisfactory case could be made to the French that there was no sound alternative other than accepting the reality that Syria be handed over to Emir Feisal for services rendered on behalf of the Allied cause, up to and including the culminating act of liberating Damascus from Turkish hands.

Recognizing that Arab Postwar objectives could well hinge on a first-in-time, first-in-right race for possession, on September 27, Lawrence asked Alec Kirkbride to join a party riding to Deraa immediately after the Turks had retreated. Lawrence's urgent words were, "We must get there before the cavalry".[36] They did, hoisting the flag of the Hejaz.

As Lawrence was ensconced in General Barrow's camp in Deraa on September 30, word was received that General Chauvel's units were in the suburbs of Damascus. Some of his troops entered the city itself as a means of preventing a complete breakdown of law and order in a city reeling with uncertainty and dominated by conflicting emotions. Realizing that the race for control of Damascus, and with it Syria, was entering the home stretch, Lawrence secretly left the camp, jumped into the Rolls-Royce that had been made available earlier for his use, and headed for Damascus.

Outside Damascus, Lawrence met Nasir, Feisal's cousin, and Nuri Shalan, sending them into the city to raise the Hashemite flag. To their consternation, this had already been done by two Algerian brothers, Mohamed Said and Abd el Kadir. The Algerians were detested by Lawrence, who suspected them of pro-French tendencies. Mohamed Said had declared himself Civil Governor, a move made easier because Nasir was sick and in no position to assert himself. Lawrence took immediate charge when he entered Damascus with Auda, removing Mohamed Said and replacing him with Shukri Pasha.

By then the historic old city, the site of so many battles through the ages, had turned into a boiling cauldron of passions pent on immediate release. The burning frustrations of war had risen from the ashes like a gargoyle bearing its red fangs. Amidst the conflict, the Arab irregulars were hovering on the scene, intent upon receiving what they construed to be their just desserts for their efforts.

So here was Lawrence, the take-charge loner who sought to dominate events, frustrated by what he was observing. He was particularly concerned that, in the hate-filled chaos that had emerged, Turkish prisoners were being murdered in cold blood. Seeking to get a handle on events, Lawrence went out into the streets with Alec Kirkbride. An odd couple they must have appeared to be to anyone who saw them. There was Lawrence, short and wearing Arab robes with no arms but an ornamental dagger, striding alongside the tall, lanky Kirkbride, armed with a large service revolver. Whenever the pair encountered anyone butchering Turks, Lawrence would walk up to them and solicit them in a gentle voice to stop. Meanwhile Kirkbride stood nearby, brandishing his firearm and exerting not so gentle persuasion. Occasionally some would resent Lawrence's intrusion and would rebel, prompting Kirkbride to shoot them at once before the trouble could spread.

Kirkbride showed surprise at Lawrence's shock over the freedom with which he was using his revolver, going so far as to implore him to not be so "bloody minded." Once more Lawrence's paradoxical nature was brought to the surface. The same desert warrior who confided to Lowell Thomas the euphoria he felt when he saw Turkish soldiers being blown skyward by a "tulip" he had planted on other occasions felt a deeply rooted revulsion in the face of violence and bloodshed. Gradually his efforts began to bear fruit as a semblance of order was restored to the city. When General Chauvel entered the city, Lawrence was there to meet him, ruffling the Australian's feathers in the process. Chauvel wrote:

"Lawrence's excuse for his unceremonious departure from General Barrow (in Deraa) was that he thought I would like him to come in at once and find out what the situation was and tell me. He then proceeded to tell me that Shakuri was the Governor of Damascus."[37]

When Chauvel asked to see the former Turkish Governor of the city, Lawrence explained that he had left the day before, adding that Shakri had been elected by a majority of citizens. Chauvel had every reason to doubt the legitimacy of such a claim. Not only was it highly unlikely that sufficient organization could have been brought to bear during such a period of strife and uncertainty to hold an election, but also, in the event that such an election had been held, there would be tangible evidence indicating its reality. Chauvel did not appear to question Lawrence's highly suspicious claim. Perhaps he was shrewd enough to realize that, despite temporary gamesmanship, eventually that claim as well as others would be coolly and carefully analyzed at the conference table, which was what actually occurred.

Before any conference table was reached, however, Lawrence and Feisal were subjected to a rude awakening. It happened on October 3, when Allenby and Feisal arrived in Damascus. In that Allenby and Lawrence had been allies in what had proved to be a triumphant cause, the brilliant culmination of this effort would have been for them to celebrate as one, once the objective of capturing Damascus had been achieved. Instead, the brutally harsh realities of international politics entered the picture, preventing a happier result.

At a dramatic meeting, Allenby informed Feisal that France was to be the "protecting power" of Syria, declaring further that the Arabs had no claim to Lebanon at all. As could be fully expected, Feisal issued a strong objection. He declared that he was unaware of any French role in the matter, and that whereas he was prepared to have British assistance, it was his understanding that the Arabs were to have the whole of Syria including Lebanon but excluding Palestine. A country without a port was no good to him, he complained, stating his refusal to be guided by the French in any way.

Realizing both the delicate position he had been put in by conflicting British promises to various parties and the sobering reality of having to resolve such a dilemma, the resourceful Allenby enlisted a twofold strategy: using Lawrence as a scapegoat and pulling rank on Feisal. He asked Lawrence if he had not told Feisal that the French were to have "the protectorate" over Syria. Lawrence replied that he had not.

Allenby then pushed his inquiry further by asking, "But you knew definitely that he, Feisal, was to have nothing to do with the Lebanon?"

"No, sir, I did not," Lawrence replied.[38]

Allenby then informed Feisal that he was lieutenant-general under his command, and it was accordingly his obligation to follow his order and accept a French involvement, at least for the time being.

A thoroughly frustrated and dissatisfied Feisal then left the meeting. Lawrence stayed behind to register a complaint, informing Allenby that he could not serve with a liaison officer. He pointed out that since he was due for a leave anyway, he preferred taking it immediately. Lawrence's exasperation was double-barreled. He had hoped to see at least some measure of autonomy given to Feisal and his Arabs, who had fought so diligently in hopes of reacquiring their land from the hated Ottoman Empire. If another country were to be involved in the area, Lawrence hoped that it would be his own Great Britain in the role of a helpful overseer of Arab destiny. As a British intellectual brought up on Empire thought, Lawrence felt that a British guiding hand would be most acceptable under the circumstances. Also, in line with the same kind of British imperialistic thought, France was viewed with distrust. Allenby accepted Lawrence's request for a leave, and his dramatic role in the Arab Revolt ended on that sour note.

The passage of time has invested that meeting along with the subsequent Paris Conference meeting with a note of bitter irony. The question of what rightfully belongs to the Arabs has shifted from Syria to Israel, but the name Allenby continues to be present, long after the famed general left the world in body. It is the Allenby Bridge that separates Israel from Jordan, the point at which Palestinians shuttling between the two nations must be checked.

Lawrence was eager to return to England as soon as possible to participate in the debate over the future of the Middle East. Before he left for his trip home, Allenby conveyed the rank of an acting full colonel on him. Lawrence told Liddell Hart that the reason he had requested such a rank as a favor from his commander was to enable him to travel back to England in a private train compartment, along with allowing him to avoid as many bureaucratic formalities as possible.

The charismatic magnetism of T. E. Lawrence made its presence felt in Paris as he appeared with Feisal to plead the case for an independent Arab state in Syria. Feisal and Lawrence met with Zionist leader Chaim Weizmann. Feisal agreed to make room for four or five million Jews in Palestine, who would have a share in the government. In return for this, he would receive Jewish money and advisers to help him in Syria. When the official document was signed by the parties, Feisal added a proviso that he would not be bound by it unless the Arabs were given their promised freedom.

Some Arabs later blamed T. E. Lawrence for the creation of the State of Israel. Lawrence did hold a respect and reverence for the Jews stemming from their Semitic roots, the same as his Arab cohorts. Like Winston Churchill, he felt that a Zionist presence in Palestine would be helpful to all concerned because the immigrants would bring with them a good deal of business, technological, and professional expertise that could only serve to benefit the Arab populace as well. He always felt, however, that the area should be controlled by the Arabs themselves. It must also be remembered that neither Lawrence nor anyone else passing judgment on the impact of Jewish immigration to Palestine in the latter part of the second decade of the twentieth century could have foreseen the vast migratory problems that the Jewish populace would encounter as a result of the Nazi menace of World War Two.

Emir Feisal equally recognized the common heritage of Arabs and Jews, as evidenced by a statement he made in Paris:

> The Jews, like ourselves, are Semites. And instead of relying upon any of the great powers, we should like to have the cooperation of the Jewish people for assistance in building up a great Semitic state. I appreciate fully Zionist aspirations, even extreme Zionist aspirations. I understand the desire of Jews to acquire a home-land. But so far as Palestine is concerned, if they have made up their minds that it is Palestine or nothing, then it must be Palestine subject to the rights and aspirations of the present possessors of the land. Palestine is still in effect the land of the Arabs and must remain an integral part of the Arabian state.[39]

When one looks back to the less entrenched, hostile-free attitudes embraced by Feisal and Lawrence concerning the Jews as expressed by them in Paris, along with the collegiality with which they could discuss issues and reach common understanding with Chaim Weizmann, who would ultimately become the first President of Israel, the picture that sadly emerges is one of increasing hostility and tension developing between the parties in an atmosphere charged with emotion and bereft of discussion, eventually resulting in conflict. Succeeding chapters will delineate how productive goodwill was sucked out of the international political atmosphere in the manner of a seething vampire until war ultimately resulted, a sad consequence that could have been avoided.

As for the efforts of Feisal and Lawrence to achieve an Arab state in Syria, that effort was ultimately doomed to fail as the French, one of the leading Allied powers, stubbornly concluded that having lost a good many men in the war, they were entitled to some of the spoils of victory. Syria was remembered with relish dating back to French primacy there during the periods of the Crusades. Lawrence did his best to influence the American delegation at the Conference to intervene on the Arabs' behalf. An American presence in Syria was preferred by both Feisal and Lawrence to French hegemony, but the Americans were not eager to establish a presence there and backed away from a commitment. Conversely, French Prime Minister Clemenceau remained steadfast in his conviction that his perceived French interest in the area hold sway.

When the assertive combined lobbying efforts of Feisal and Lawrence had succeeded in achieving the creation of a Commission of Inqiury for Syria to find out from the people what kind of government they wanted, the French sabotaged the Commission's efforts by failing to appoint members of their own.

Some premature joy arose when a plan proposed by William Yale of the American Commission in Paris was considered. It called for the creation of two Arab states to be established in Mesopotamia under British protection. An Arab state ruled by Feisal in Syria under French protection would also be confirmed. Britain would hold a mandate over Palestine, where Zionists would be allowed to settle, and France would possess a mandate over Lebanon.

For a time it seemed that the British Cabinet would accept Yale's plan, but ultimately it fell through.

Sadly observing the handwriting on the wall, Feisal decided to make a separate peace with Clemenceau, which allowed him to keep Damascus and the interior of Syria. The following April, the Allies officially tendered the mandate for Syria to France.

The situation gradually deteriorated from that point, with the Arabs suffering misfortunes in the process. There was an Arab revolt against the government that the British had established in Iraq. In Syria, when details of the agreement reached between the British and French were revealed, an angry Arab populace reacted by rioting, some of them raiding French establishments as an act of reprisal for what they deemed to be a sellout to European interests. The French responded by marching on Damascus, eventually expelling Feisal.

Events in the Middle East left Lawrence deeply depressed. Even though he had become a national hero in his native England as a result of the exposure he received from the highly successful Lowell Thomas documentary lecture and slide presentation and had been elected to a Fellowship at All Souls College at Oxford University, he was crestfallen that Arab prospects in Syria and elsewhere had been rudely crushed. He had expressed misgivings before over having to live a lie in making the assurances that he had to the Arabs in order to ensure their continued cooperation in the fight against the Ottoman Empire, but now that the full weight of the fait accompli had come crushing down on his consciousness, he sank into a pit of gloom. He expressed dissatisfaction with life itself and wondered if he would ever finish his book *Seven Pillars of Wisdom*.

Eventually the book would not only be completed but also become an overwhelming international success. Fresh controversy was sparked over certain events described and claims made, which was hardly new. Controversy seemed to stick with gluelike tenacity to T. E. Lawrence.

Meanwhile, the enigmatic Lawrence began to withdraw from the very core of the society that had lionized him. Winston Churchill had at one point effectively prevailed upon him to assume a position in his Middle East Department of the Colonial Office. He remained there for awhile but eventually resigned, preferring anonymity. While functioning under Churchill, he helped persuade Feisal to accept the kingdom of Iraq. As participants at the Cairo Conference in March 1921, Lawrence and Churchill had defused an explosive situation after Abdullah had marched into Amman and announced that he would liberate Syria and restore Feisal. Churchill and Lawrence decided to allow Abdullah to establish an Arab government in Transjordan if he agreed to an overall settlement. Lawrence was sent to Amman to achieve Abdullah's acceptance. He lived with the son of Hussein and brother of Feisal for eight days, obtaining his agreement in the process. Later in the year Feisal was overwhelmingly elected King of Iraq. When the French protested that guerrilla attacks were being mounted against them from Jordan, demanding the surrender of some Arab nationalists, Abdullah at one point expressed a willingness to step down from his position in Transjordan. Lawrence implored him to remain firm, removing officers and using force where required, until he eventually restored tranquility. Churchill was eminently pleased with Lawrence's work, but even the wily master of persuasion, who had successfully persuaded T. E. to accept a position under him, was unable to prevail over this free spirit, who sought to resign. Eventually a disappointed Churchill agreed to let him go.

The next phase of Lawrence's life saw him plunge back into the same ascetic environment that had been such an intrinsic part of him in his Oxford undergraduate days. Some chroniclers explained his career turn as that of a monk without a religion seeking his own special kind of monastery. Under the name of John Hume Ross, he joined the Royal Air Force as an enlisted man. When his true identity was discovered, he was summarily discharged. Undaunted, his next move was to join the Army Tank Corps under another new name, T. E. Shaw, which was selected in deference to famous playwright George Bernard Shaw and his wife, Charlotte, with whom he had become good friends. Eventually he would officially become T. E. Shaw by having his named changed by deed-poll, the same official act that his father had used years before to alter his name from Chapman to Lawrence.

As a highly educated Oxford-trained intellectual, Lawrence soon found himself totally out of place in an atmosphere of brawling men with scarcely any formal education, who communicated in combative bursts of four-letter words. Life among these crude men largely devoid of purpose or hope depressed him greatly. He sought to gain a transfer back to the Royal Air Force, where he had been far happier. His close friend and father figure George Bernard Shaw successfully implored the powers that be to grant his request. All the while Shaw felt great ambivalence about the whole thing. Though he consented to help Lawrence, an angry Shaw wrote a letter castigating him for failing to utilize his enormous talents. Winston Churchill was also frustrated by Lawrence's decision. Lawrence defended it by stating that it was the only way to regain his peace of mind and prevent the onrush of insanity.

The constant irony of Lawrence's seeking anonymity clashing with the seemingly inevitable destiny he had with controversy of every description materialized when he successfully sought a transfer to the extreme solitude of Miranshah, the smallest Royal Air Force station in India. Just when it appeared that Lawrence had achieved the ideal state of tranquility, a rebellion broke out in nearby Afghanistan. Aware of T. E.'s presence there, journalists concocted an erroneous scenario in which the British Government was alleged to have instigated the revolt, using the famous "Lawrence of Arabia" to achieve its objective. Embarrassed by the incident, the government immediately recalled him back to England.

Lawrence was finally able to achieve solitude at Bovington Camp near Wool in Dorset. He lived comfortably in a nearby cottage called Clouds Hill, where he was visited by his friends from the British intellectual community. In addition to the Shaws, there were E. M. Forster, Robert Graves, and Thomas Hardy. As a lion of the literary world himself with the success of *Seven Pillars*, Lawrence had a natural affinity for eminences of the British book sphere.

With the exception of his books and classical music albums, Lawrence was a man to whom possessions meant little, but one passion of his life was his Brough motorbike, which he enjoyed driving at rapid speeds through the adjacent countryside to Clouds Hill. It was on one of these excursions that the life of this enigmatic man of contradiction would end. Also typically, there would be a storm of controversy surrounding the event that cost him his life, just as controversy had embodied so many acts of which he had earlier been a part.

Before the details surrounding his death and the ensuing controversy are discussed, it would be advantageous to describe some other events of Lawrence's life, concerning which there has also been great controversy.

The Lawrence revelation that has undergone the harshest scrutiny concerns the rape and severe beating to which he claimed to have been subjected in Deraa. The skepticism falls into two basic areas: (1) that the incident was blown out of proportion by Lawrence in the form of extensive exaggeration and (2) that the incident did not occur at all.

As to the charge of exaggeration, the record clearly reveals that Lawrence switched his stories saving his most dramatic account for *Seven Pillars of Wisdom*. Lawrence's original report to Intelligence General Headquarters, the original copy of which is located at the Humanities Research Center in Austin, Texas, stated the following:

> I went into Deraa disguised to spy out the defenses, was caught and identified by Hajim Bey, the Governor, by virtue of Abd el Kadir's decription of me. (I learnt all about his treachery from Hajim's conversation, and from my guards.) Hajim was an ardent pederast and took a fancy to me. So he kept me underground until night, and then tried to have me. I was unwilling and prevailed after some difficulty. Hajim sent me to the hospital, and I escaped before dawn, being not as hurt as he thought. He was so ashamed of the muddle he had made that he hushed the whole thing up and never reported my capture and escape. I got back to Azrak very annoyed with Abd el Kadir, and rode down to Aqaba.[40]

Lawrence gradually embroidered the terse account he provided for Cairo, culminating with the involved and highly descriptive account presented in *Seven Pillars*. After being approached by the man described as the Turkish Governor, known as the Bey, Lawrence claimed to have fought off his advances. After two sentries had subdued Lawrence, who resisted the Bey by kicking him in the groin, he revealed that the Bey had kissed and bit him, after which he then drew one of the sentries' bayonets "and pulled up a fold of flesh over my ribs." After the Bey had dabbed blood over Lawrence's stomach with his fingertips, he then ordered a corporal to preside over additional punishment to his already bloodied victim. Lawrence then revealed with lurid lucidity the flagellation to which he was subjected, describing vividly each cutting stroke of the whip. When the flagellation was completed, he claimed to have been taken back to the bey, who disgustedly rejected him "as a thing too torn and bloody for his bed."[41] Eventually, as described earlier, Lawrence made an escape and returned to his camp.

Before attacking some of the more notable pitfalls of his account as reported in *Seven Pillars*, disclosures by Richard Meinertzhagen, a friend who had served as an intelligence officer with General Allenby, bear serious reflection. When Meinertzhagen saw Lawrence at the Paris Peace Conference, he found him in low spirits and in need of confiding information to a trusted ally. He confessed to Meinertzhagen the two secrets that tortured him—his illegitimacy and the true account of what happened at Deraa. Lawrence expressed fear that the true account be revealed, that he was seized, stripped and bound, then sodomized first by the Bey, then by his servants, after which he had been flogged.[42]

Two noticeable flaws appear in the gruesome Lawrence accounts, concerning whether or not the sodomy is included and relating to two specific points that shred credibility. First of all, what with Lawrence's alleging that he had been stripped naked, it is virtually inconceivable that this blue-eyed blond would not have been correctly analyzed by the Turks as a European. The second point that raises severe doubts concerning Lawrence's veracity is the ease with which he allegedly escaped after being victimized by such repeated brutality. This point accordingly begs the question of why, upon his return to the camp, there were no visible signs reported of savage beating sustained by Lawrence. It will be recalled that, shortly after his return to camp, Lawrence journeyed to Cairo for a meeting with General Allenby, at which he acquitted himself without revealing any apparent physical or emotional traumas.

Recent Lawrence biographer Desmond Stewart is within the ranks of those who claim that Lawrence's purported Deraa affair never occurred at all. He cites the fact that Lawrence's movements at the time of the alleged attack were well-known to his British Army colleagues and were recorded in his own skeleton diary and letters. In addition, his account about the Bey of Deraa is at odds with recorded historical revelations, according to Stewart.[43]

Another basic revelation by Lawrence in *Seven Pillars*, whose authenticity has been challenged, is the basis for the slaughter of the Turks at Tafas. Whereas Lawrence cites atrocities on the part of the Turks as the motivator that propelled his Arab forces to such heights of rage, the respected Jordanian historian Suleiman Moussa contends that the initial massacre by the Turks may have been exaggerated by Lawrence to justify the carnage subsequently unleashed by his own forces against the Turks.

Lawrence remained a bundle of contradictions, even on the subject of how he spread stories. Although he related to Lowell Thomas that his distinguished ancestry included Richard Coeur de Lion (the Lionhearted), which was untrue, he wrote to his authorized biographer, Liddell Hart, requesting that he not mention his relationship to the legendary Sir Walter Raleigh, which was factual. He also exaggerated to Hart about the number of hours he had flown during the war as well as about the extent of injuries he suffered in a plane crash in France while he was attending the Paris Peace Conference in 1919.

T. E. Lawrence represented the definitive contradictory enigma, a man who could run the gamut from flamboyant prevaricator to introspective hermit; a man who expressed to Lowell Thomas supreme elation over watching a Turkish train explode, but who admitted to feeling pity over the tragedies befalling German troops fighting as allies of Turkey against his Arab forces.

Such contradictory multifacetedness, perhaps more than any other requisites, prepared Lawrence for the riddles and dilemmas that embody the Middle East. He expressed sympathy toward the German troops because they were fighting so valiantly, albeit for a then hopeless cause, so far from home. He too had journeyed far from home to do battle, though even in his native England, his conduct was often decidedly reclusive. Along with his inner contradictoriness, which enabled him to comprehend the Arab mind with its myriad nuances of thought and prolific tribal influences in a manner that few outsiders could ever hope to, he also had the ability to withdraw from what could be a potentially dangerous situation. His reverence for privacy enabled him to curl up with a book in his tent rather than to overly socialize in a setting replete with pitfalls. He established a set of rules on how to deal with the Arab mind, and he remained mindful of tribal disparities, knowing what to say to whom, and when not to speak.

If the Deraa affair never actually took place as an actual flesh and blood event, it nonetheless had roots within the psychic realm of Lawrence's complex mind. His repeated descriptive references to being whipped by Turkish captors becomes more comprehensible in view of the discovery by authorities at Clouds Hill, shortly after his death, of a series of letters he had written to one John Bruce, with whom he had become acquainted at Bovington Camp. The letters disclosed that Lawrence had paid money to his fellow Air Corpsman to flagellate him with a birch stick. They further revealed that Lawrence was being compelled to engage in such activity by an authority figure referred to only as "the Old Man." Though Bruce believed that such a person existed, no such person has ever been identified by biographical or other sources, leading to the inescapable conclusion that "the Old Man" was a creation of T. E. Lawrence's fertile psyche. Couple Lawrence's lurid descriptions of flagellation in *Seven Pillars* with his payment to John Bruce to perform that very same function and one observes a discernible masochistic pattern springing from a tormented individual immersed in waves of guilt originating early in his life.

Lawrence's stern Calvinistic mother projected guilt on him, which she herself felt as a result of luring his father away from his wife and family. His illegitimacy was a source of inner trauma for Lawrence during his entire life, interwoven with feelings of guilt catalyzed by his mother, and his father was reported to have whipped him often with switches. Such early patterns could help to precondition the sensitive Lawrence to follow a guilt-laden masochistic direction in adulthood. These feelings were significantly compounded by the dual role he was forced to play as a loyal British soldier and the man referred to as the uncrowned King of Arabia. At one point in the war, riddled with inner frustration, he was said to lament that the best thing he could do for the Arabs would be to tell them to stop fighting and go home. Yet he battled diligently until Damascus had been captured, and after the last battle had been fought, he moaned inwardly that turmoil lay ahead in the troubled region.

This acute sense of guilt flamed by his own dual loyalties plagued Lawrence through the rest of his life. It was appropriate that, during the final two years of his Air Force service, he was attached to civilian boatyards and attired in civilian clothes. He no doubt regarded this as the perfect balance, using the military as a sheltering personal vehicle while avoiding the dreaded formality that he hated in military life.

In that controversy and unending question marks of varying descriptions characterized T. E. Lawrence's life, it was symbolic that the same would govern his death. The official inquiry into the cause of Lawrence's demise concluded it to have been an accident prompted by a dip in the road, which prevented Lawrence, an expert cyclist, from observing two boys until he was practically on top of them. His resulting swerve to miss contact with them caused him to lose control. The motorcycle went into a skid, Lawrence was thrown over the handlebars, and the resulting impact caused a fractured skull.

At that same inquiry, which ruled the death of Lawrence to be an accident, however, one Corporal Catchpole, a noncommissioned officer at Bovington Camp, testified that he had been walking his dog by the side of the road at the time of the accident. Though he did not see the collision, he stoutly maintained that as he went to investigate the sight of the stricken Lawrence lying on the ground, he saw a black car pass by. The two young boys asserted with equal conviction that he had seen no such car. The mystery was exacerbated by the fact that military officials arrived immediately on the scene at Dorset and threw a blanket of secrecy around the entire proceedings under the Official Secrets Act. A question immediately surfaced. Just what was the need for military secrecy? After all, Lawrence had resigned from the military and was a civilian. Also, if the event were indeed no more than an accident, why was such secrecy dictated?

Many theories exist that Lawrence was murdered, most of them farfetched. Because his controversial life brought him into many direct and indirect dealings with various governments, some thought that he was killed by the French. Others opted for the Bolsheviks, while the Germans, the Zionists, the Irish Republican Army, and even the Arabs received mention. In none of these instances was there anything resembling tangible evidence to point to such a misdeed.

Another theory was that Lawrence, given to periods of brooding depression, engaged in at least a quasi-suicide act to take his life. Such an event would have seemed all too spontaneous, with the added element of missing the two young boys thrown in for good measure. The nature of the collision and its surrounding circumstances would render such a claim ludicrous on its face.

The theory that appears to have been taken most seriously was one involving the possibility of Lawrence's becoming involved in the British Fascist movement then being assiduously cultivated by an articulate former member of Parliament, Oswald Mosley. It is buttressed by the fact that Lawrence's final act prior to climbing back on his motorcycle for what turned out to be his last journey back to Dorset was to send a brief telegram to the British author Henry Williamson from a post office near Bovington Camp, confirming a luncheon date for the following day at Clouds Hill. Williamson was a staunch supporter of Mosley's Blackshirt movement, and Williamson's expressed purpose for wanting to visit Lawrence was to discuss Fascism and Anglo-German relations, the hopeful result being the enlistment of Lawrence's support in the cause.

Though Lawrence might have agreed to assume the position of willing listener, it is far from certain that he could be convinced to join Mosley's cause. In a conversation with Liddell Hart in June 1934, he revealed that the Fascists had been actively seeking his support, but that he had rejected their offer and "wouldn't help them to power."[44]

As earlier stated, Lawrence had a profound respect for Jews on the basis of their Semitic link to his beloved Arabs, but the type of Fascism being embraced by Mosley and his cohorts placed its emphasis on establishing cordial relations with Germany and preventing the outbreak of global war. The theory concerning Lawrence's being murdered in connection with links to the Blackshirts rests on the following hypothesis. Through the securing of a dynamic figure such as Lawrence to the Blackshirt cause, certain prominent members of the British Government, fearing the possible success of the Fascist movement with Lawrence as a leading spokesman, might seek to take his life. The two links enhancing this theory are the invoking of the Official Secrets Act following Lawrence's death, seen as a cover-up, and the mysterious black car reported by Corporal Catchpole.

As for invoking the Official Secrets Act, it was learned that the Air Ministry had undertaken plans to increase the British Air Force. It is distinctly possible that Lawrence had provided input that Air Ministry officials would understandably prefer to keep secret. As for the black car that Corporal Catchpole insisted he had seen, it remains as shrouded in mystery better than fifty-five years following Lawrence's death as when the original disclosure was made. The conflict between the two boys on the bicycles and Corporal Catchpole as to whether or not a black car was on the scene at the time of Lawrence's fatal accident has never been resolved.

In conclusion, a point can be made regarding the alleged desire on the part of certain prominent members of the British Government to silence Lawrence from becoming an anticipated spokesman for Mosley's Blackshirts. The fact, standing alone, that he had agreed to have lunch with Mosley admirer Henry Williamson affords proof of nothing more than what has been stated. Even if he agreed to discuss politics with him, it would be a far cry from available evidence to fathom a theory whereby Lawrence would emerge as a leading Blackshirt. Not only do we have respected Lawrence biographer and historian Liddell Hart's statement that Lawrence had been earlier solicited by British Fascists and had spurned each and every entreaty, but we also have the entire history of the man as part of the public record.

Any analysis of that record leads one to the inescapable conclusion that Lawrence looms as one of the most highly improbable candidates for a prominent position within Blackshirt leadership ranks. Here was a discernibly free spirit who yanked himself out of the public realm while holding an influential post under no less a personage than Winston Churchill. He left that position to labor in the obscurity of an enlisted man in the military. Even the redoubtable Churchill had been unable to convince him to change his mind. Then there was the political agenda of the Blackshirts. It would be stretching credulity to expansive heights to conceive of the free-spirited Lawrence's embracing such a regimented and dogmatized agenda, even if the anti-Semitic factor played no role. Assuming such a role in the Fascist ranks would be out of character for T. E. Lawrence.

In summation, just what are we to make of this man of controversy? He looms on the historical firmament as enigmatically as the mysterious black car that Corporal Catchpole insists he saw but that was never found.

From the standpoint of historical contribution—that essential function of clarifying present and future analytical perspectives by gleaning the lessons of the past—T. E. Lawrence provided meaningful insight into the Arab mind, affording tangible examples of how he could successfully make accomplishments, as a European outsider entering another world and in the face of widespread failure on the part of so many others. His most famous work, *The Seven Pillars of Wisdom*, along with his lesser known efforts and the many biographical accounts of his colorful life, reveal the numerous nuances of thought and social custom, often disparate, that exist within the Arab world. In seeking to resolve these disparities as an outsider attempting to understand the vast complexities of the overall picture, Lawrence provided a working base to increase understanding in the form of his Twenty-Six Rules for dealing with Arabs. One of the major mistakes made by individuals seeking to understand the current Middle East dilemma, particularly concerning the thorny issue of Palestinian rights, is to ask in befuddlement just why the Arab world, people linked by blood and the common religious heritage of Islam, cannot act cohesively to resolve the Palestinian question as well as others that confront them. The answer is that no broad base of unity exists, despite common religious and ethnic heritages. The truth of the statement is sharply underscored by a study of the various Arab nations and an analysis of the frequently disparate thinking of their leaders. The Arab world is an expansive enough ideological umbrella to simultaneously hold a King Hassan in Morocco, a Muammar Qaddafi in Libya, a Hosni Mubarak in Egypt, and a Hafjz al-Asad in Syria. The intrinsically complicated mind of Lawrence was able to sift through a sea of internal contradictions and disagreements to achieve at least a partial sense of fundamental unity in the pursuit of one major objective, the upheaval directed at overthrowing the hated Ottoman Empire. The illustrative historical example of Lawrence stands in present focus within the microcosm of current Middle East politics, a dangerous, burning crucible of discord that threatens to engulf the world in the kind of flaming Armageddon described by biblical prophercy. Here was a man who, through exercising consummate patience and creative imagination, was able to achieve a measure of unity. An equivalent level of understanding combined with analytical persuasion is currently needed to achieve peace and harmony in the bloodied, emotionally and politically volatile world of Middle East politics.

In seeking to unravel the steadily unfolding saga of the Middle East, we will next shift our focus back to the Zionist quest to achieve a homeland in biblical Palestine. Standing in the forefront of that effort was a man who displayed the same kind of tenacious resolve combined with innovative leadership skills that exemplified T. E. Lawrence. His story is no less revealing than Lawrence's in following the carefully woven fabric of pursuing a common goal through comprehending the universality of a muddled jigsaw puzzle and solving the puzzle through diligent application and mastery of detail.

# 5

# The Lion and the Fox

Day was just beginning to break in the Mediterranean seaport town of Jaffa, situated not far from Tel Aviv.

Inhaling the sea air, staring ahead at the port amidst the hazy glow of the beckoning dawn, was a young man of nineteen. If his stomach was churning nervously as his steady gaze fastened intently on the land toward which the small cargo ship on which he stood and which had transported him all the way from the Russian seaport town of Odessa, from which he had embarked on this climactic excursion, such a reaction was clearly understandable. Making contact with the land of Palestine marked the culmination of one dream and the beginning of another.

From his early youth, growing up in the town of Plonsk in East-Central Poland, not far from Warsaw, David Green had studied the Bible with an awestruck fascination. Whereas to many Jews the Bible and its teachings were explored as a religious testimony, a text to index where civilization had already gone as well as where it should proceed, this sober-minded young Jew from Plonsk saw the Bible as a historical chronicle revealing where humankind had been and providing concrete explanations for the interested observer as to where the future should lie. Through the rest of his long and productive life, he would continue to adhere to this same interpretation of the Bible as a historical guide. Despite numerous setbacks that would have destroyed the spirit and initiative of a less committed individual, the sustaining force of his beliefs as manifested by his historical guide to the future,

171

the Bible, pushed him forward toward the objective of a better tomorrow for himself and his Jewish brothers and sisters in the biblical land of Palestine.

Achieving his long-standing objective of traveling to and setting foot on Palestinian soil marked the culmination of one of David Green's dreams, but another broader goal, his ultimate dream, lay in the immediate future. He intended to play as instrumental a role as possible in making *Eretz Yisrael* a practical reality. The Zionist dream of erecting a homeland on the same soil that their forebears had occupied as long as two thousand years earlier had been resurrected and nurtured by Theodor Herzl, and young David Green had heard that message. Like other Zionists, he regarded Herzl as a messiah with the mission of leading his people to their ultimate destiny, one which Green deemed consistent with historical interpretation of the Bible.

So now, in the dawn of September 7, 1906, as the small cargo ship docked and his feet made their first contact with the soil of the land of his dreams and aspirations, David Green was prepared to embark on a great cause. Just two years after the death of his revered hero, Theodor Herzl, Green would put body and spirit into the effort to turn *Eretz Yisrael* from dream to reality, to help create a bedrock of human vitality of nationhood for his Jewish people.

In his native Plonsk, he had been filled with idealism, the kind of young man's idealism that is insufficiently tempered with the hard pragmatic realities, which any idealist promoting a cause must confront. The harsh pioneering conditions that immigrant Jews faced in the 1900s in Palestine were quickly manifested, and it took little time for David Green to become aware of them.

Green had actually received his first lesson on the brutal realities confronting him on his mission in Odessa, where he arrived after being transported in a horse-drawn carriage from his home in Plonsk. He and a like-minded idealist from Plonsk also planning to journey to Palestine, Shlomo Zemach, went to see Menachem Ussishkin, leader of the Love of Zion movement, at his office. Very much in awe of the prominent Zionist leader, who had replaced the deceased Herzl as his idol, an enthusiastic Green outlined an objective he hoped would gain the financial support of Ussishkin's organization. He sought financing for a newspaper that he and Zemach planned to publish in Palestine, its goal being the promotion of increased immigration to the Holy Land from other countries.

As Green faced Ussishkin, the heavyset Zionist leader trained his hard blue eyes with steely penetration on him. As he did, the etherealized awe in which Green had held him departed. The quick transition produced angry frustration and thorough exasperation at the nature of Ussishkin's expression, which wordlessly revealed his innermost thoughts. David Green observed that he was "looking at me as though I were crazy, and saying, 'Here's some idiot going to Palestine.' "[1]

Ussishkin's ensuing blunt words gave the young idealist and his colleague Shlomo Zemach additional grounds for exasperation. The Zionist leader emphatically declared that immigration to Palestine should be selective. Many hostile forces would need to be confronted. There were the Hassidim, the Turks, the entire Gentile world, and the Zionist fathers who had inspired David Green and Shlomo Zemach.

As the cargo ship completed its voyage, dozens of rowboats surrounded it. Emerging from the rowboats were crews of husky and bronzed Arab porters, either bare-chested or in soiled white robes. They attached ropes to the railing and hoisted themselves with catlike agility onto the cargo ship. They raced about madly, cursing in Arabic, Hebrew, and Yiddish as they grabbed bags and bundles, hurling them to companions in the rowboats.

The quick entry of the Arabs combined with their rapid physical activity in unloading the cargo ship's baggage caused a jolt to register within the psyche of the young Zionist idealist David Green. Perhaps the stern admonitions of hard-headed realist Ussishkin were reverberating in his brain. Why were Arab porters performing services that his own people should be carrying out in *Eretz Yisrael?*

The answer to that question would be supplied soon enough, and as the quick education of David Green continued, the veneer of idealistic naïveté he had carried with him onto the shores of Palestine would be peeled away layer by layer in the manner of plaster eroding through heat and age. Whereas certain passengers of the cargo ship would suffer disillusionment in the wake of discovering the brutal realities of life in Palestine, ultimately opting to return to their homes in Eastern Europe, the adversities would only serve to stiffen the resolve of Green. *Eretz Yisrael* was his destiny, and he was determined to see it through and realize his objective.

As he began to make his first contact with the Promised Land, which had dominated his dreams in his native Plonsk, he received another stiff jolt, which brought him into contact with the harsh realities he would encounter.

As he stood in joyous contemplation over his arrival in the land of his dreams, his ears were pierced by cries of gloom and doom. He, along with his fellow passengers, was being referred to as "new victims" by the shouters. Green cast his eyes in the direction of the communicators. He saw a contingent of broken men with despair in their eyes, their bodies shrunken and emaciated. They continued to speak to Green and the other arrivals. Had they not heard about conditions? Disease? Unemployment? Hunger?

He pushed on in the face of the brutal examples of what life had held for some in this new land. Soon he was filled with optimism once more.

"Waves of joy rose in me," he would later recall. "The signs in Hebrew on the shops, the Hebrew spoken in the streets, the stores and the restaurants. Now one cannot doubt; now one must believe! . . . A Jewish boy rides a horse . . . a little girl of eight passes on a donkey pulling a heavy load; images of our renaissance."[2]

Although young David was heartened by some of the images he observed, he sank back into a state of nervous awareness as an air of developing understanding about Palestine the reality as opposed to Palestine the dream came into sharper focus in the manner of a photographer seeing his own pictures reach a final stage of development. He observed Arabs squatting next to their carts, while in-between were situated the shops of poor Jews. Ragged idlers gathered around the carts and shops, seeking handouts. Customers scarcely better off eyed the displays, made their purchases of nuts, roots, seeds, cookies, lemons, or dates and went their independent ways.

Later, David, overcome by the conditions of despair and poverty he had discovered, would write his father and reveal that "The air smelled of charity and *bakshish* tips." The longer he surveyed the human drama unfolding in the dusty streets of Jaffa, the more brutally he felt the impact of one graphic fact. As he watched the swarms of Arabs congregating and going about their business, he realized just how overwhelmingly his own people were outnumbered by the Arabs. As of September 7, 1906, the day of David Green's arrival, the Jewish population in Palestine numbered about fifty-five thousand, whereas that of the Arabs was an astronomically vaster seven hundred thousand.

Despite the depressing disadvantage in numbers, irrespective of the acute poverty on the dusty streets of Jaffa, in spite of the gloomy warnings conveyed by the emaciated men with the broken spirits whom he had met on the waterfront, David Green would hold fast to his dream. Among those who quest for power and are fortunate enough to overcome the odds and achieve it, two basic categories are notable. There are the manipulators of power, typified by the Talleyrands and the Metternichs, who develop a pragmatic feel for the trappings of power and become ingenious brokers in the art of crafting empires through skillful dealings and manipulations. Then there are the power wielders who look at the shaping of history and its internal infrastructure from the focal point of one overriding destiny. Within the twentieth century, several examples of this basic type emerge. There were the Bolsheviks of Lenin, who sought to transform czarist Russia into a worker's utopia under the framework of a Marxist ideology. There was the Nazi movement of Adolf Hitler in Germany, a fiercely nationalistic phenomenon with the pronounced objective of establishing an Aryan superstate and superrace ordained by God's destiny to rule for one thousand years. In the post–World War Two era, amid the political chaos of French politics and a steady procession of governments representing a series of political parties emerged the solidifying image of Charles de Gaulle. The man who at the close of the war was saluted by his grateful countrymen as their most revered hero, the Commanding General of the Free French, who with the aid of American troops recaptured his country from a brutal and spirit-shattering Nazi occupation, accepted the call to service and assumed the presidency. The Gaullist movement was an appeal to French traditionalism, a nationalistic entity that drew on the nation's proud past in an effort to mold a prosperous present and future. The French nationalistic streak in de Gaulle reached its zenith in 1967, when he traveled to Quebec Province in Canada and urged a separate state for its French-speaking citizens.

In analyzing de Gaulle and understanding his fiercely proud nationalistic roots, it is interesting to note that, many years later, David Green would not only meet the distinguished warrior and statesman but would also classify him as the premier world leader in modern history. When one traces Green's ideological roots back to that momentous day in 1906 and before, to the formative stages of his youth in his native Plonsk, what emerges is a rock-solid foundation of biblical history—the recorded accounts of his Jewish people in their search for identity and meaning. His reverence for Theodor Herzl and the Zionist movement's continued quest to achieve nationhood in the revered Holy Land evoked the same kind of intensely nationalistic feelings as evidenced by Charles de Gaulle in his quest for French achievement in the political and economic spheres. Here were two proud men with a messianic zeal to achieve greatness on behalf of their respective peoples. Sharing such a common thread, Green's admiration for and understanding of de Gaulle and his objectives become readily discernible.

Even while he silently comprehended the disadvantage of being greatly outnumbered in this the land of the Zionist dream, Green's strong idealistic fervor, nurtured from early youth, caused him to see a joyous fulfillment of his goal at the end of a long and dedicated struggle. The Jewish numbers would increase. He would promote the cause of aliya, or immigration, through his writings. The message would get across, Jews would flock to the Holy Land, and the exciting concept of nation-building would be promoted on an idealistic and grand scale. As for the question of the role the Arabs would play, David Green had an answer. He hoped to cement a working partnership with the Arabs. Even though he was looking forward to the day when, through the outpouring of Jews into Palestine from the Diaspora, they would achieve a numerical majority, he felt that the Arabs would accept this reality once they realized the great benefits awaiting them. The Jews would make the Arabs their economic partners in forging prosperity for all.

After young David Green had been living in Palestine for about a year, enduring the hard life as he sought to help promote the Zionist goal articulated by his idol, Theodor Herzl, he embarked on a two-and-a-half-day hike from Jaffa through the gorge of Bab el Wad to behold the symbol of the cause to which he was dedicating his life, the walls of Jerusalem.

The experience he had caused him to react with alarm. What he discovered was a Tower of Babel existing at the spiritual center of Judaism, a sea of verbal confusion. He found Jews "speaking to each other in forty different languages, half of them unable to communicate with the other half."[3]

As a sad but wiser David Green left Jerusalem, one thought dominated his mind. Absent the bond of a common language, his Jewish people could not hope to achieve the Zionist objective of founding their own nation. From his early youth in Plonsk, he had been very much a practicalist in understanding the necessity of learning Hebrew. In fact, he had learned Hebrew and not bothered to learn Polish, because he deemed the Hebrew essential and the Polish irrelevant to his basic purposes. Not long after his first visit to Jerusalem, David Green returned. He assumed the post of editor of a Zionist trade union paper, which advocated revival of the Hebrew language. As he finished his first editorial, the young idealist stared at his own signature at the bottom of the page. A state of pensiveness overcame him as he continued peering at the name. Just what was it about the name Green that was identifiable with or linked to Hebrew? he asked himself. Nothing, came the quick inner response.

David Green reflected on his situation for a long moment. A flash came into his head. He picked up his pen and began scratching out the last name of Green. The new last name to replace the old was distinctly Hebrew, one he would carry for the rest of his life. He stared down at the new name, letting the change sink in fully.

David Ben-Gurion!

Not only was the last name decidedly Hebrew. It was one that characteristically matched the personality of the man bearing it. The name Ben-Gurion in Hebrew means "son of a lion cub." Henceforth David Green would be David Ben-Gurion, "the Lion." This man of unstinting tenacity, this purposeful innovator intent on pursuing one single cause with relentless vigor, would wear the mantle of "Lion" with self-assurance.

The Ben-Gurion of the early twentieth century was not likely to impress a casual observer with command of presence. A short, squat man with thick, bushy black hair and matching bushy eyebrows, his head was too large for his body. His face was decidedly not handsome. There were two distinct characteristics, however, that a perceptive judge of human behavior would observe and take careful note of, his strong jawline, which revealed a resolute inner conviction, and his eyes, the expression of which equaled the dogged determination of his jawline.

He stood a diminutive five-foot-three, making him the identical height as "the uncrowned King of Arabia" T. E. Lawrence. Though he lacked the Britisher's ideal physical proportions and smooth, even features, Ben-Gurion definitely possessed the same commanding presence as that exhibited by Lawrence. As in the case of Lawrence, David Ben-Gurion fell into that rare class of individuals embodied in Napoleon's one-in-twenty equation, a personality possessing the requisite degree of conviction blended with confidence to make strong and intelligent men eager to march under their command. Lawrence had been a dedicated antiquarian with a particular fascination for Arabian historical relics. Ben-Gurion's training had been in the labor union, journalistic, and political fields in pursuing the Zionist cause, but yet both men, when the critical moment appeared, were able to enter the military field and achieve great results, Lawrence in World War One and Ben-Gurion as Israel's commander in chief during its 1948 War of Independence. Both men were bitten hard and often by the scorching sting of malaria during their lives in the desert, yet each fought back stubbornly, doggedly refusing to yield to the fates of adversity. While the two were capable of eliciting fierce loyalty and confidence, they also were both loners, men who more frequently preferred the stimulation to be gained from reading a book than that afforded by socialization. Whereas Lawrence could and often did display mannerly grace and a distinctive British charm to prevail on a point of personal concern, the doggedly relentless, no-nonsense Ben-Gurion was more likely to succeed through a confident, often brusque presentation manifested by command of the facts. Whereas T. E. Lawrence was Oxford-educated and could speak the language of the cultural aristocracy with aplomb when it suited him, the self-educated Ben-Gurion would remain throughout his life a product of the middle-class laborer's quest for justice in the marketplace. One man could speak the tongue of the classics; the other communicated in working-man's basics.

An individual is composed of a series of life experiences that shape that person's development. The great French philosopher Voltaire placed particular emphasis on the first seven years of life as forming a sensitive core in overall development. When one carefully examines the early years of young David Green growing up in Plonsk, an impoverished shtetl, or small town, situated on the banks of the Plonka River not far from Warsaw, the character of Israel's first prime minis-ter, David Ben-Gurion, emerges in the manner of a sociological jigsaw puzzle in which the pieces are filled in one by one to completion.

The milieu in which David Green was born and raised was dominated by a strong sense of class consciousness. He grew up in the Pale of Settlement, the western zones of the Russian Empire, where some five million Russian and Polish Jews were confined. His father, Avigdor, was a lawyer, the Jewish equivalent of what in England would be termed a solicitor, but was not materially successful. The impoverished atmosphere of Plonsk was not conducive to great material achievement unless one was allied with the Hassidim, which Green was not. The Hassidim were the wealthy aristocrats and rabbis who ruled Plonsk. They strongly adhered to old-line Jewish traditionalism.

Avigdor Green's beliefs furnish an example of where his eventually successful son would emerge on the sociophilosophical landscape of Jewish thought. The elder Green disdained Hassidic concepts for the emerging doctrine of *Haskala*, or Enlightenment, which sought to merge Jewish tradition with modern secular thought. The ranks of the "enlightened" Jews generally broke down into three courses of action recommended for their people to take. These options were (1) remain where they were and help the Gentiles oust the hated czarist regime, (2) flee to the United States or some other free nation, or (3) sail for

*Eretz Yisrael* and become immersed in a bold experiment, which those advocating that course were confident would result eventually in statehood.

The elder Green favored option number three, thereby identifying himself, as would young David from a very early age, with the fledgling Zionist movement. This belief in aliya or returning to Zion, had been a fundamental belief in the case of Avigdor's father and David's grandfather, Zvi Aryeh Green, a notable scholar who taught Hebrew at the famous Kuchary school run by *Haskala* thinkers.

The belief embodying the return of Jews to the land of Zion ran afoul of two groups within the Jewish community, the Hassidim and the Bundists. The Hassidim awaited the arrival of the Messiah and believed that any talk concerning the creation of a Jewish state prior to then was premature and thoroughly inappropriate. The Hassidim saw God in pantheistic terms, the controlling force of every aspect of man and nature. The Hassidim spoke Yiddish and believed that Hebrew should be spoken only in prayer. In that the Zionists believed Hebrew should be the accepted language for Jews, a natural ideological clash resulted. The Hassidim aided police authorities, who demanded total adherence to Russian nationhood, thereby abhorring Zionist concepts, by turning in the names of leading Zionists. While the Hassidim were denouncing Zionists as heretics, the radical Bundists were excoriating Zionist thought as bourgeois and reactionary. The Bundists detested the Zionist preoccupation for a return to *Eretz Yisrael*, regarding such thinking as playing squarely into the hands of the hated czarist regime. The Bundists ardently pursued a socialist agenda with a heavy emphasis on Marxism, embracing revolutionary doctrine, which was becoming increasingly popular in pre-Bolshevik Russia. Bundists placed emphasis on class struggle. Jewish sufferings within the system were, in Marxist parlance, a calculated effort by the reactionary czarist regime to exploit the masses. As a result, the forces should be on uniting with all Russian workers in the common pursuit of overthrowing the forces of economic exploitation. Such a cohesive effort could then result in the overthrow of the system, of which all Russian workers would be direct beneficiaries.

Young David was a boy who manifested early precocity, as evidenced by the fact that he could speak fluent Hebrew as well as Yiddish before he began *heger*, Jewish elementary school. He astounded his first teacher by repeating an entire page from the Bible after hearing a classmate read it. His mother and father were excited to hear from a doctor that the abnormally large size of their son's head was indicative of a great mind. It was consolation to the Greens because his body was sickly and he contracted many childhood illnesses.

While young David Green opposed what he perceived to be the doctrinal harshness of Marxism and would engage its Jewish practitioners, the Bundists, frequently in personal and highly vituperative debate, he became drawn in early youth toward socialism. His strong identification with the plight of the working classes, which lasted throughout his life, was most assuredly linked to the poverty he witnessed in the Jewish community in which his body and soul were nurtured.

Green's rapidly developing, always active mind was influenced by two books that expanded his social consciousness, *Ahavat Zion (The Love of Zion)*, by Avraham Mapu, and *Uncle Tom's Cabin*, Harriet Beecher Stowe's graphic penetration into the evils of slavery in the pre–Civil War United States.

"These two books," Ben-Gurion revealed in adulthood, "more than anything else were responsible for my becoming a socialist."[4]

Another book with a pronounced impact on young David Green was *Resurrection*, by Leo Tolstoy, which fulfilled two purposes. It created within him a new awareness of Russia's social problems, which he saw unfolding in his very midst in Plonsk while also investing him with a reverence for life. So profound was this awareness that for a time he became a vegetarian to demonstrate his respect for all aspects of life.[5]

A shattering event occurred when David was eleven and filled him with a compelling sense of tragedy, which left scars for the remainder of his life. His mother, Sheindel, died at the age of forty-one while giving birth to a stillborn child. David was the sixth of seven children who would survive; four others died at birth or at a young age after he was born, and two had died preceding his birth. Many years later, Ben-Gurion revealed that he had seen Sheindel in his dreams regularly for two years following her death. As a very old man, he would, among his confidants, ruefully reflect on how traumatically he had suffered as a result of his mother's death, extolling her with teary-eyed praise. This tragedy was compounded by his father's remarriage and David's resentment of his stepmother.

David became aware of Theodor Herzl's Zionist movement when he was ten, and he greeted the leader's announced goal of establishing a Jewish nation in Zion, or *Eretz Yisrael*, with the spirited gusto of an idealist hurled by historic forces into the path of destiny. Not only was David responding to the strong Jewish heritage in his own family with its emphasis on Hebrew and its focus on the traditions of its people, but also this politically and historically oriented youth of acute sensitivities observed trends that were developing in his native land. Because Jews were in a numerical majority in Plonsk and did not suffer the devastation of anti-Semitism that affected Jews living in other areas, he was still acutely aware of what Jews were enduring in the wave of pogroms that rocked Russia in the early twentieth century. When Czar Nicholas II succeeded Alexander II in 1894, he was determined to root out what he termed to be revolutionaries opposed to his regime. Concerned by what he perceived to be a threat from Herzl's international Zionist concept, he cracked down ferociously through the institution of pogroms. One particularly brutal episode in Kishinev in 1903 claimed the lives of eighty-five Jewish men, women, and children, and hundreds more were beaten and raped.

David Green's response to this tragic ordeal was to call a meeting of all Plonsk Jews in the Great Synagogue. In front of hundreds of people who had come to mourn the victims of the Kishinev pogrom, David jolted his attentive listeners with a warning that if such an attack were to occur in Plonsk, they must not sit back and accept their fate. They must vigorously fight back! The audience could not help but be stunned, because such a course of action had not been recommended by anyone before.[6]

The idea of fighting back was a concept David was willing to embrace not only against enemies of the Jews but, if necessary, against Jews as well. In December of 1900, while he was announcing the formation of the Ezra Society youth group before some thirty of his colleagues, the meeting was rudely interrupted by an invasion of some twenty Hassidim. The lamps were blown out and a rousing battle commenced. The unflappability of young Green was demonstrated when, after the retreat of the Hassidim, the lamps were relit and he brushed back his hair, straightened his coat, and coolly announced that the meeting would resume.[7]

What form of Zionism did this young idealist, who equated Herzl and his message in the manner of the coming of a messiah, adhere to in his quest to make the aspirations of Herzl and the Zionist movement a vivid reality? Consistent with his concept of socialism and affinity for labor, David believed in Practical Zionism. Such a program was reminiscent of the concept in early American history of manifest destiny in that the emphasis was on cohesive effort on behalf of a vital cause to create a flourishing society. This could be done by conquering the soil through the spirited adventure of nation-building.

Years later, Ben-Gurion described the spirited idealism that molded this thinking in the realm of Practical Zionism:

> The more I imbibed the mood and talk in my father's house, and the more I read of Jewish history, the more convinced was I that only in the Jewish homeland would the Jew be rid of his bondage. It was the revolutionary spirit of the times that spurred me and my friends to do something about it. We would therefore argue with our fathers' friends and spend after-school hours preaching on Zionist platforms, that Zionism did not mean loving Zion from afar, but going there and building it ourselves.[8]

The quote from Ben-Gurion reveals his motivation in seeking to build *Eretz Yisrael* while shedding valuable light on an important element of his thinking from boyhood to death, the rejection of assimilationism as a solution to Jewish problems. The rousing debates he held with Bundists argued the basic question of whether Jews were better off in attempting to score breakthroughs in the nations in which they lived or whether a comprehensive change was needed such as the Zionists envisioned. Should one stay and fight in hopes of achieving a better Russia by joining forces with elements of change in a common cause? Or was it necessary to return to Palestine and forge a new society? The Ben-Gurion solution called for Jews to seek progressive change within society. In the final analysis, however, he was convinced that Jews would continue to suffer discrimination even should a new regime come to power:

> Even with a new regime the Jews would still be subject to discrimination and persecution—possibly not as bad as before, possibly not at all for a period, but always subject to majority whim or policy, always subject to restrictions if not downright maltreatment. It gives me no pleasure to note that what I and my friends thought and said about this in the early years of this century has unfortunately proved right. In Russia and other countries in eastern Europe where revolutionary regimes overthrew the previous administrations, it is the sad fact that Jews suffer discrimination. Many of the most vociferous Bundist leaders who gave energetic help to the revolutionary movements lost their lives in purges when the revolutionaries came to power.[9]

Ben-Gurion's commentary explains the Zionist position in a nutshell: the ultimate necessity of the Jewish people to establish a society of their own in the land of their initial roots as a people. So that no misunderstanding would occur, Ben-Gurion emphasized his steadfast belief that, even in the event it could be established that Jews would be able to function in other nations with the bonds of discrimination extirpated, the ultimate need to emigrate to *Eretz Yisrael* remained.

Ben-Gurion confronted that point head-on:

> Moreover, even if one could guarantee that Jews would be safe in a new liberal Russia or Poland, we Labour Zionists still insisted on rebuilding Zion. For we could achieve Jewish freedom, we felt, only if we could achieve national independence in our own land. We had the right of any other nation to develop our own language, our own culture, our own way of life, not on the sufferance of another people in another land administered by a government not of our own choosing, but as of right, by our own exertions with our own people in our own land where we could be our own masters.[10]

Ben-Gurion's explanation of Zionism's goal causes the student of history to reflect on the concept of Sholom Aleichem's schlemiel. Ben-Gurion and others of like mind saw the return to Zion as a spirited opportunity for the Jewish people to build a culture of their own. After some two thousand years of wandering from land to land and seeking to blend into the social, political, and economic tundra of many nations, the return to Zion would constitute a dramatic rebirth of the Jewish people. Herzl had reached that conclusion in the painful milieu of the Dreyfus trial, when he observed the city of Paris ablaze in an angry upheaval of anti-Semitism.

The Greens along with other committed Zionists were aware of the unique position Jews occupied in world history ever since their civilization had been uprooted by the Babylonians. During this long period, the dual purpose of Jews consisted of understanding and developing their Semitic roots and assimilating within the fabric of the given nation in which they lived. This unique sense of historical destiny on the part of the Jewish people was delineated by Jewish biblical scholar Yehezkel Kaufmann. In describing the entry of the Israelites into the land of Canaan, Kaufmann writes about the coming of Moses and places careful emphasis on Jewish monotheistic belief:

> It seems certain that this monotheistic view of human history is rooted in the historic sense of the Israelite nation, in its consciousness of itself as unique, elected—a feeling that it had from the time of the religious revolution in the days of Moses. There is no reason to defer the development of Israel's historic sense to the days of the monarchy. For, in the contrast to that of other nations, Israelite historiography was national,

not dynastic. Genesis relates the histories of the Patriarchs and of nations; kings are mentioned only incidentally. The goal of the story is the emergence of the people of Israel. And so the career of mankind is unfolded: the antediluvians and the annihilation of their line, the evolution of the nations from the sons of Noah, and the further emergence of new peoples through the generations until the last and youngest emerges— Israel. With Israel's birth the period of the formation of nations comes to an end. And it is this infant people that became the people of God . . .[11]

The Jews finally formed their own monarchy. The first three kings of Israel as related in the Jewish Scriptures were David, Solomon, and Samuel. During David's reign, the idea was conceived of a royal capital in the form of the Chosen City of Jerusalem. To this new capital was transferred the Ark of the Covenant, embodying the compact between God and the children of Israel. The biblical account in the scriptures describes the punishment visited on idolators, with an angry God seeking retribution in His name.

Yehezkel Kaufmann addressed this point in reference to punishment that God inflicted on the children of Israel as a result of pagan worship:

> The bitter wars with Aram deeply disturbed sensitive men in Israel, and gave rise to an anxious searching of soul. Why had God inflicted this terrible enemy on Israel? In the time of Ahab and Jezebel, God's wrath was ascribed to the worship of Baal and the wickedness of Ahab's house. For this Elijah predicts a harsh retribution. The sword of Hazael, king of Aram, will be unsheathed against Israel; only the "seven thousand" who "did not bow down to Baal" will remain . . .[12]

The destruction of Jerusalem occurred in 586 B.C.E. at the hands of the Babylonians. The Babylonian Exile prompted a scattering of the Jewish populace throughout Babylonia, Egypt, and the Mediterranean shore. The next major population upheaval occurred in 70 C.E. with the destruction of the second Temple by Titus. This triggered the great Diaspora, which resulted in the major portion of the Jewish world population settling in Central Europe. From the time of the Babylonian Exile, the Jews thereafter no longer engaged in idolatry as the rise of Judaism sprang into being during that period, accompanied by the unswerving belief in one God.

Ben-Gurion held a belief in God, but he scarcely ever attended synagogue, secretly ate ham for breakfast, and disdained wearing a hat in Jerusalem despite urgings by rabbis to do so. At the same time, he held a burning belief in biblical teachings and prophesies during his life. He regarded the Bible not so much as a religious but a historical instrument. The Bible was his principal source of inspiration, a guide in seeking Zionist goals and establishing moral standards. He believed in merging the ethical teachings of the biblical prophets with the discoveries of modern science. Ben-Gurion's concept of God was sketchy, certainly not a man with a head and ears, but an intangible spiritual source, which did exist.

David Ben-Gurion did not believe that the Jews constituted a "chosen people" of God. In his view, God did not choose Israel, but Israel chose God when all other peoples had rejected him. He substantiated this viewpoint with the quotation from Joshua (24:22):

"And Joshua said unto the people, 'Ye are witnesses against yourselves, that ye have yourselves chosen the Lord, to serve him.' "

When young David's idol, Theodor Herzl, died in 1904, it left the idealistic devotee crushed. But then, after the period of immediate mourning ended, adrenalin surged through David Green's body as he became filled with a new sense of commitment to the man who had triggered Jewish urgings toward a return to Zion. He declared his feelings in a letter to his friend Shlomo Zemach:

> There will never again arise such a marvelous man . . . But today more than ever I have faith in and am certain of our victory. It is clear to me that there is a day—a day that is not far off—when we shall return to that wondrous land, the land of song and truth, the land of flowers and of the visionaries' visions.[13]

The strong link to Jewish organized labor, which would parallel Ben-Gurion's Zionist goals throughout his entire career was forged in the middle of 1905, when he joined the Poalei Zion Party (Workers of Zion). Up to that point it had been his goal to enter a technical school with the intention of becoming an engineer, because such services would be needed in a developing Jewish society in Palestine. With great zeal he helped organize Jewish workers, seeking to instill the idea of Zionism in them. As always, the effort was focused on winning the minds and hearts of those he hoped would ultimately forge labor's inner core in the land of Zion. He also received the opportunity as a highly active member of Poalei Zion to work and become acquainted with many leaders of the future, people he would be later toiling alongside of in Palestine. He was not then considered a leading Zionist figure, accountably due to his teenage status, but in time he would be a force to be reckoned with by all. It is significant to note that just one year before joining Poalei Zion, David had gone to Warsaw in hopes of receiving a good education. He secured a job as a teacher at a heder, or religious school, and sought to gain admission to high school. The Russian authorities rejected his request because their "Jewish quotas" had already been filled, and a technical college turned him down because he did not have a high school diploma, exposing him to an educational catch-22, which he could not overcome. As a result, he disgustedly journeyed the forty miles back to Plonsk, where he then became immersed in labor activities.

It is always fascinating to look back with the advantage of hindsight and explore the critical moments that, while perhaps seemingly routine at the time, govern an entire course of conduct and, ultimately, the sweep of historic forces. This can be said about the rejections of young David Green in his efforts to enter the ranks of higher education. The quota system invoked by Russia and other European nations against Jews assuredly frustrated what would have been many successful professional careers had those barriers not been present. What proved doubly frustrating to David Green was that his application to attend technical school in Warsaw had been rejected despite the fact that his entrance examination marks were higher than those of all the non-Jews who had been accepted.

In the case of young David Green, this bitter pill of rejection through public administration due to a quota system, although painfully difficult to swallow at the time, might well have been the biggest positive break he ever received. It could well have been the stimulus that resulted in his major political triumphs and eventual assumption of a new nation's leadership mantle. Consider the following facts. Had Ben-Gurion gone on and become a successful engineer or lawyer, two options he considered pursuing, he might have been denied the type of powerful constituency he built up through assiduous cultivation and close identification that were achieved through his labor contacts. Although it is highly possible, if not likely, that Ben-Gurion, with his strong sense of commitment, would have been highly active politically from a professional position, it was his grass roots contacts that ultimately paid off and paved the way for him to assume the position of prime minister upon the creation of the nation of Israel. These same contacts, forged by years of intense effort in grass roots labor circles, enabled Ben-Gurion to govern for years and develop the strongest party in the nation. Out of this labor affinity developed leaders of the future, protégés who learned about politics from the master himself.

One of the major criticisms leveled against the leader David Ben-

Gurion from a protocol standpoint was what some saw as his irreverent casualness about attire and manner. He was frequently criticized by those offended by his methods of receiving heads of state or important diplomatic figures in wrinkled short sleeves. A derivative complaint was that when he spoke he was direct to the point of alleged crudity, his language bereft of the traditional diplomatic niceties. The afore-mentioned traits may have raised the hackles of certain persons in the diplomatic sphere, but they would be likely to achieve a different response among the Jewish masses. Here were the tillers of the soil seeking to forge a new nation under the harsh conditions of a land far from the Europe in which they grew up. Ben-Gurion in appearance and manner loomed as one of them, a man of the soil, a product of the labor ranks, who spoke and dressed plainly. Again, had Ben-Gurion been the recipient of a college degree and entered the professional ranks, he might well have blended into coat-and-tie society and exuded an altogether different image from the plain-talking labor leader who bore the same grass roots image as another man, the one who provided him with so much valuable support during a strategic crossroads in Jewish history, U.S. President Harry S Truman. Both Ben-Gurion and Truman could speak the language of the common man and woman, a propensity that can be exceedingly helpful in view of Abraham Lincoln's oft-repeated quote: "God must have loved the little people since he made so many of them."

During this critical period in David Green's life, when he was developing insight and maturity rapidly in pursuit of his Zionist objective, he achieved a memorable victory as a fledgling labor leader in Poalei Zion that taught him two valuable lessions: (1) he learned he was on the right track in the career he was pursuing, and (2) he became aware that political power can be amassed in the ranks of organized labor through cohesive effort. His social conscience sufficiently inflamed, young David decided to obtain justice for some of the most exploited workers in Plonsk, the seamstresses. Their ranks consisted largely of young girls in their teens who labored eighteen hours a day in dingy tailor shops. He visited the shops and urged the seamstresses to strike. Even though there had never been a strike in Plonsk before, they agreed. After a prolonged walkout consisting of pickets and goon squads, the frustrated employers capitulated, agreeing to pay the seamstresses the same amount for a reduced, twelve-hour-workday.

Being a man of vision, David recognized the consequences of his triumph in terms beyond the elation of the moment. He observed the troubled expressions of the employers as the pressures mounted. He saw the helpless authorities vexed by the diligent application of cohesive pressure. Finally, he observed the police intervening to end violence, with the ensuing delicious satisfaction of a Polish judge siding with the strikers. If such a result could be achieved in Plonsk, the visionary David concluded, then it was possible to score broadly based successes in Palestine using the same kind of cohesion.

During this same period, David Green undertook the challenge of winning the ideological battle in the Pale of Settlement against the challenge of the Bundists. A Bundist orator from Warsaw, sixteen-year-old Shmuel Segal, was recruited to debate Green in Plonsk's Great Synagogue. The verbal confrontation was so eagerly anticipated that shopkeepers shut down for the day. The drama was heightened by the fact that the speakers walked into the packed synagogue carrying pistols in their belts. Each was flanked by two bodyguards. They agreed to lay their pistols down on a table to avoid the possibility of a shootout that would desecrate the house of God. After hours of debate, David won the most disciples among the ranks of his hometown Plonsk audience. The debate then ended abruptly at the sound of a shout from someone in the rear of the building. The word "Police!" sent the audience scurrying immediately for the exits. All socialist organizations were under a ban, and the debate was an encounter between two of them. David Green disappeared from the synagogue, having concluded another heated encounter.

The moment of reckoning finally arrived for David when, following much planning, he decided it was time to travel to Palestine to begin his life's work of helping to build a Jewish nation. It would be insightful to analyze the forces shaping young David at the time he embarked for the land of his dreams on September 7, 1906. These same concepts that energized him as he approached his twentieth birthday would be pervasively interlinked to his goals and actions for the remainder of his life. They were as follows.

1. *Practical Zionism*—a pursuit of the goal of Jewish nationhood through cultivating and developing the desert land. Green never intended to function as a delegator but preferred instead to lead by example, undertaking all the hard work that he could endure. In addition to the instructions in Hebrew along with Jewish religion and tradition, which he had received from his father and grandfather at home, another factor loomed large among idealists such as David Green in motivating them toward Zionist statehood ambitions: The bleak and usually impoverished conditions of their social milieus made them increasingly eager to achieve something better in another land.

The drabness of Plonsk existence was sufficient to give David an extra push toward his goal.

2. *Labor socialism*—the integration of a large and dedicated labor force pooling its talents and efforts into a productive society. The socialist concept of Zionism that Ben-Gurion expounded is cognizable in view of the challenge that lay ahead, that of cultivating a desert land and achieving nationhood. He and other zealous Zionists felt the need of energetic cohesion toward a common cause to overcome the numerous obstacles in their path. Only by sticking together closely as a united force could they realize the transformation into nationhood. The Zionists did not anticipate receiving large chunks of money to aid their effort. Instead they accepted the challenge of achieving the goal of *Eretz Yisrael* by virtue of their determined hands and strong backs.

3. *Historical inevitability*—a bedrock belief that the prophecies of the Bible would come true and the Zionist goal would be realized through faith and assiduous effort. Ben-Gurion saw the Bible as an indispensable road map describing the course of the future. Scores of Jewish families living in European ghettos but dreaming of a better tomorrow would conclude their evenings with the memorable saying, "Next year in Jerusalem." As more Jews felt dissatisfied with conditions in nations in which they were becoming increasingly uncomfortable, the literature of the Bible assumed great importance. The prophesies registered a sense of inevitability. After two thousand years of wandering, the Jews would return to *Eretz Yisrael*. The harsh conditions of Diaspora life would be supplanted by a bold new adventure.

It took little time for David to become aware of the level of effort and degree of commitment necessary to survive the rigorous travails of Zionist pioneering in Palestine. His first job was spilling manure from tin cups in an orange grove. Though his squat body was never strong, David was able, through vigorous application of will, to compensate in some measure for the deficiencies of nature. It was a classic case of will and spirit triumphing over the limitations of flesh. In one characteristic example of Ben-Gurion's iron will, he made a wager with a fellow Jewish pioneer that he could stomp on more grapes than his colleague could. Some twenty-four hours later, he won his bet, almost collapsing in the aftermath in a stupor of exhaustion. Working in the fields in an era devoid of cheap and preventive drugs, coping with malaria became a painful way of life. Ben-Gurion was frequently afflicted:

> Oh we had malaria all right. I "malaria'd" quite often, and indeed the doctor told me, after several particularly heavy bouts, that I had better

leave the country and go back to Europe, for I obviously could not take it. Of course I just whistled at that kind of advice. But after all I was on my own. I was not yet married and I had no family responsibilities. But there in Hadera, three children died and still the parents wouldn't move. That takes a special kind of guts and dedication. Because of it, of course, Hadera flourishes today, and you need imagination to visualize its vines and orange groves and fields of wheat and barley and cotton, its factories and cottages and gardens, as one gigantic marsh . . .[14]

In a letter he wrote to his father, Avigdor, Ben-Gurion asserted that two kinds of workers would survive the ponderous obstacles of Palestine pioneering and remain: those with overriding will and those who have grown used to hard work. He urged against his own brothers' emigrating to Palestine, feeling that they lacked the requisite durability of commitment that he possessed.

What was it that instilled in young David the requisite commitment to remain in Palestine despite health obstacles? Omnipresent thoughts of Jewish revival and of the grand legacy of his recently deceased idol, Herzl, filled him with the zeal to overcome physical obstacles. In 1907, after moving from Jaffa to Sejera, he recorded the following impressions of his pioneering experience:

How sweet and easy is plowing! The handle of the plow in my left hand, the goad in my right, I effortlessly follow behind the oxen, my eyes fixed on the black earth as it surfaces, then breaks up beneath the plowshare. In slow-measured steps the oxen pace the field, as if they were prosperous landowners, with all the time in the world to think, to muse, to dream. When a Jew walks behind oxen plowing his ancestral soil and sees his fellow Jews nearby doing likewise, is it possible for him not to marvel?[15]

During the spring of 1908, the idealistic Ben-Gurion's pursuit of the Zionist dream working side by side with fellow Jewish immigrants was derailed when he received a letter from his father informing him of his obligation to serve in the czarist Army in his native Poland. It was an order David could not afford to ignore, because if he defaulted, his father would be fined three hundred rubles. In June, he sailed from Jaffa for Russia. He remained in Poland until the end of 1908, spending three months in the army. His father contacted a border smuggler to help his son desert both the army and the country. Avigdor Green gave the smuggler an advance payment, leaving the remainder of the transaction to be completed by his son. Young David, demonstrating reckless naïveté, asked the first man he encountered to take a message and the balance of the money to the smuggler. Fortunately for Ben-Gurion, the man did as told, and he was able to secure his escape. He returned to Palestine on a false passport, knowing he would never again be able to enter the Russian Empire under his own name.[16]

It was a happy Ben-Gurion who returned with eagerness, determined to see the *yishuv* (community) develop and flourish until nationhood became an accomplished reality. A tough task lay before his Zionist brothers and sisters. When David arrived in Palestine for the first time in 1906, the population consisted of an estimated seven hundred thousand Arabs and but fifty-five thousand Jews. The First Aliyah (immigration wave) had arrived in Palestine in 1878, just a little more than one generation before David set foot there for the first time. One major problem that immediately plagued the Jewish settlers and that was continuing to burden them at the time of David's arrival was the conduct of Jewish landowners, who preferred hiring Arabs and not Jews. The reasons were twofold: (1) Arab laborers would work for less money, and (2) the landowners felt that the Arabs were more adept in working the soil of their native land than were Jewish immigrants who had come from Europe.

The Jewish landowners soon found out that although this European wave of immigrants had significant adjustments to make in switching from an essentially city ghetto existence to becoming tillers of the Palestinian soil, their prideful determination caused them to overcome such deficiencies. One remarkable manifestation of zeal was the manner in which these immigrant settlers transformed themselves from their former positions as shopkeepers, salesmen, or even doctors and lawyers into laborers who toiled to the point of exhaustion. Like David Ben-Gurion, their commitment to Zionism was the invigorating element. The surging pride that dominated them actually reached the point at which, when they would work for a Jewish landowner and be offered extra money for their efforts, they would decline the extra compensation unless it was understood that the additional remuneration stemmed from their abilities rather than their common Jewish heritage.

While David Ben-Gurion was seeking to make history by helping to achieve a Jewish nation in Palestine, another man of equivalent idealistic commitment was making his own impact, but in a different manner from Ben-Gurion's.

Chaim Weizmann was born on November 27, 1874, in the town of Motol in western Russia, within the Pale of Settlement. His mother, Rachel Leah, would give birth to fifteen children within a twenty-five-year span beginning in 1871, which composed part of the Jewish population explosion of the nineteenth century. Weizmann was twelve years Ben-Gurion's senior, and it would be a fair assumption that, without the unyielding efforts of these two disparate individuals, despite their absence of esteem for one another, the nation of Israel could never have been born, at least at the time and in the manner that it attained realization. The two personalities could well be termed the "Odd Couple" of Zionism, two men who lobbied for the same ultimate goal and achieved it, but as markedly dissimilar entities with vastly different methods of operation. Not only were their methods different, but so were the constituencies they utilized in pursuit of their joint goal of the creation of a Zionist nation on Palestine soil.

Their low regard for each other's method of operation and personality probably stemmed from their notable dissimilarities. Although there exist certain examples of diametric personalities with broadly differing backgrounds who form otherwise compatible professional and personal relationships, a notable example being the plain-spoken, self-educated Harry Truman and his patrician, highly educated secretary of state, Dean Acheson, most relationships notable for their differences rather than similarities are inclined to produce more differences. As mentioned, David Ben-Gurion came from a background devoid of affluence and a poor Jewish town in which class consciousness and deprivation were rife. Although Motol and Pinsk, the Russian towns in which Chaim Weizmann spent his formative years were not models of affluent contentment, Weizmann was able to escape their drabber elements. His was a comfortable upbringing devoid of strife, and when it was time to move on in his successful academic career, it was to the cosmopolitan city of Berlin, where he had the opportunity to mingle with young intellectuals who were destined to go on to bigger and better things. Whereas Ben-Gurion in his teens became immersed in the grass roots labor movement first in his home town of Plonsk, then in Palestine, Weizmann traveled among the ranks of a young Jewish intellectual elite of future professional achievers.

The one basic area setting these two monumental achievers apart from one another from the standpoint of historical perspective is the vastly differing channels through which they operated to make their respective marks. As stated, Ben-Gurion was the quintessential grass roots operator, the labor leader who lobbied for the cause of the masses. Ben-Gurion was the pervasive insider, rallying the troops in crowded halls through exhortation and working with the masses side by side in the fields or for common political goals. The remarkable aspect of Chaim Weizmann's rise to greatness as a Zionist leader is that, contrary to Ben-Gurion, whose career success was directly related to his insider status, the Weizmann journey was facilitated by contact through channels other than the grass roots practitioners of Zionism. Weizmann's expertise was diplomacy. A widely traveled advocate of the Zionist cause, he would promote his case before heads of state, top administrators, and diplomats. Just as it is fair to say that Ben-Gurion was the quintessential insider, Weizmann was decidedly the outside man who used contacts and converted opportunities on the world scene to bring his Zionist goals to fruition. Weizmann's achievements stemmed from successfully cultivating intellectuals both within and far removed from the Jewish community. Though he never tilled Palestinian fields in the fashion of Ben-Gurion, Weizmann's entire life from the time of his initial involvement with the Zionist cause as a teenager saw him walk through numerous intellectual mine fields, his ultimate objective squarely focused in his mind. The experience he garnered in early conflicts within the Zionist movement trained him for the major battles that lay ahead, the successful resolution of which steered the course of Jewish statehood increasingly in the right direction. The efforts of the inside man and the outside man combined to achieve the objective of statehood.

If David Ben-Gurion was "the Lion" of the Zionist movement, Chaim Weizmann would have to be dubbed "the Fox" in that zealous crusade for nationhood. Just as Ben-Gurion was willing to take on all comers in debate to prove his point, Weizmann was a doggedly determined debater who, even as a very young man, was unafraid to tackle the venerable Theodor Herzl himself, Zionism's founder.

An examination of the early lives of Ben-Gurion and Weizmann brings to light two similarities between them: intellectual precocity and links to Zionist thought. Weizmann was linked ancestrally to a disciple of the Baal Shem Tov, the founder of Hasidism. Weizmann's father, Ozer, was a progressive Jew devoted to the *Haskala* (Enlightenment) movement. Young Chaim's early precocity surfaced when he recited a poem by Schiller in German to a rabbi one Sabbath afternoon. By the time he moved to Pinsk with his family in 1885, he knew the entire Bible, some of the Talmud, Hebrew grammar, some basic Hebrew, and a smattering of Hebrew literature.

Chaim's interest in the *Hibbat Zion* (Love of Zion) movement was implanted within him early by both his parents and the cultural milieu of Motol. Just prior to his move to Pinsk, he broadcast his commitment to *Hibbat Zion* not long after the organization's first conference in

November 1884. The letter to his teacher, Shlomo Tsvi Sokolovsky, had been often cited as evidence of the destiny that awaited Weizmann in Zionist ranks. It reflects the influences around him at home and in the Pale of Settlement. It is also possible that he was influenced by stories he had heard about the recent death of Moses Montefiore, the most famous Anglo-Jew of the nineteenth century, when he wrote:

> I am sending you one of my ideas for you to see, and that concerns Hevrat Hovevei Zion [the Society of Lovers of Zion] and Jerusalem which is in our land. How lofty and elevated the idea which inspired our brethren the sons of Israel to establish the Hovevei Zion Society. Because by this we can rescue our exiled, oppressed brethren who are scattered in all corners of the world. . . . In conclusion, we must support this society which understands what lies before it and sees the evil threatening us; therefore the obligation rests upon us to establish a place to which we can flee for help . . . Let us carry our banner to Zion and return to our first mother upon whose knee we were born, for why should we look to the Kings of Europe for compassion that they should take pity upon us and give us a resting place? In vain! All have decided: The Jew must die, but England will nevertheless have mercy upon us. In conclusion, to Zion! Let us go.[17]

Though Chaim Weizmann was by no means descended from a family of great wealth, his was a world of greater affluence than that of the young David Ben-Gurion. Ozer acquired a business from his father-in-law, a tree feller and a subcontractor of lumber. He employed seasonally sixty men, with whom he spent the better part of the year deciding which trees to choose, then cutting them down and hauling them away. The Weizmann home, probably acquired by Ozer Weizmann's father-in-law, Reb Michel, while not lavish, was well above the impoverished standards of Motol. It was exceptionally large for Motol, containing six or seven rooms, and was surrounded by a sizable flower and tree garden.

As for Chaim, he developed an early appreciation for the finer things in life, which would remain within him in adulthood. When he was two years old, he moved next door to live with his maternal grandparents. For the next two years up to the time of her death when Chaim was four, he was doted upon by both of them. Following his grandmother's death, his grandfather moved next door, along with Chaim, to the Ozer Weizmann household. His grandfather would travel all the way to Pinsk to buy him a special toy. His mother sought to satisfy Chaim's preference for silk shirts by sewing them for him.

Though Pinsk lay but some twenty miles from the village of Motol, the 1885 move by the Weizmann family to the provincial metropolis constituted a cultural quantum leap in the development of the precocious youngster Chaim. As evidenced by the letter Chaim wrote to his teacher not long before moving to Pinsk, he had already developed an active interest in the Zionist cause. In that Zionism sprang from an acute awareness of the Jewish role in world history, Chaim's already germinating curiosity could not help but be enhanced by a Jewish tradition in Pinsk that extended back to the early sixteenth century. The Pinsk Jewish community began in 1506. Seventy-five Jews coming from the West had established themselves in a "Judengasse" close by the prince's castle, obtaining permission to build a synagogue. By 1886, three hundred and eighty years later and one year after Chaim Weizmann and family had moved there, Jews constituted 19,017 out of a total population of 22,967, or 82.8 percent. This made Pinsk the second Russian city, after Berdichev, in terms of percentage of Jewish residents. Many Jewish-owned factories had their own synagogue. The factories and workshops would grind to a halt on the Sabbath. In addition to the Jewish community of Pinsk, to the east of Pinsk in Karlin a Jewish community was established in 1751. The Karlin community continued to steadily increase until it reached the boundaries of Pinsk. The result was that by the eighteenth century, two separate Jewish communities operated within Pinsk, the Karlin community and the Pinsk community. During the nineteenth century, the Jewish community of Pinsk became economically independent of the Gentile population. Jews then turned increasingly to wholesale and retail business, gaining ever greater control of the city's commerce.[18]

Once more an example is afforded of the early influence of an individual's playing a role on that person's later development. The lifelong concepts of Ben-Gurion were formed by the struggles of the laboring masses of Plonsk, which formed an indelible impact and shaped the role he would play in the Zionist movement as a labor leader. Weizmann grew up in a home atmosphere that was more bourgeois than that of Ben-Gurion. It was an atmosphere in which Jewish tradition was stressed, as in the Ben-Gurion household as well. What most certainly made an impact on the thinking and behavior of the adult Chaim Weizmann was this experience, during a formative period of development, of living in a community dominated by Jews in which their economy existed independently of any other influence. Through such an example, thoughts would understandably develop about a society on a broader scale and in a land far removed from Russia's Pale of Settlement, a Jewish nation in the land of Zion.

Perhaps the major cultural influence in Pinsk that shaped the ideological development of Weizmann, above and beyond all of the aforementioned, was the influence of the *Hibbat Zion* movement. The wave of pogroms within Russia touched the minds and hearts of the Pinsk Jewish community. Even though they themselves were personally untouched by the violence and oppression that was meted out by the czarist regime and unfortunately condoned by Russian radicals as well, the Jewish populace, which composed better than 80 percent of Pinsk, felt waves of sympathy toward the helpless victims. During the years between 1880 and 1914, almost two million Jews would leave Russia, with the United States receiving the largest number of immigrants. Almost two decades later, responding to the 1903 wave of pogroms that devastated the Jewish populace in Russia, David Ben-Gurion would jolt an attentive audience in Plonsk's Great Synagogue by advocating that Jews fight back if a pogrom were launched in their community. Plonsk, with its large Jewish population, was untouched by such activity. All the same, a strong identity bond existed between those affected and those untouched. The same held true in Pinsk, where the *Hibbat Zion* adherents concluded that anti-Semitism was an inevitable consequence of Diaspora life. The only solution to this continuing problem was through resurrecting, then strengthening, their traditionally Jewish cultural influences. Such had been Chaim Weizmann's thinking when he wrote his insightful letter to his teacher in Motol. Now, as he moved into his teens, the message of strengthening old cultural bonds in pursuit of Zionist goals became drummed into Weizmann's body and spirit with even greater intensity than before as part of Pinsk's Jewish community.

In his late teens, another significant development transpired that would affect sharply the course of Weizmann's entire life. While moving to Pinsk from Motol had constituted a prodigious cultural leap, Pinsk could by no stretch be equated with the cosmopolitan cities of Europe. In 1892, Weizmann would make an even larger cultural leap than he had in 1885 when he moved from Motol to Pinsk by continuing his education in the expansive cultural metropolis of Berlin.

The motivation for sending Chaim Weizmann to Berlin for schooling revolved around the same problem that would plague Ben-Gurion when he sought to enter the world of higher education. Strict quotas were imposed against Jewish students in Russia. In going to Berlin to circumvent this problem, Weizmann would meet many other Russian

Jews who had escaped to that city as a result of pogroms directed at the Jews.

Weizmann spent eight months attending a famous Jewish boarding school. In 1893, he made a pivotal move that would also advance him on his road to destiny in Zionist leadership ranks. Weizmann enrolled at Charlottenburg Polytechnik, one of the best scientific institutes in the West. In the culturally edifying atmosphere of a leading university, Chaim took yet another giant step toward increasing his knowledge and commitment to Zionism when he joined the *Verein* (Russian-Jewish Scientific Society). Considering the fact that Weizmann took to the subject of chemistry with early facility, the English version of *Verein* could create confusion. Despite the words "Scientific Society," the organization was founded in 1888, two years before the term "Zionism" became familiar, to further those very same ideals of increasing cultural knowledge about old Jewish tradition while applying those lessons of the past to concrete current aspirations. By joining the *Verein,* Weizmann became linked with some of the brightest young minds in the Jewish intellectual world. Many of these same individuals were destined to register significantly in the Zionist cause.

It was earlier revealed how David Ben-Gurion, through experiencing misfortunes as a result of the stringent quota system Russia imposed against Jews, failed to move into the ranks of higher education as he richly deserved to do on the basis of intellectual ability, only to see him carve a niche in the ranks of organized labor, the route that would lead to the creation of an impressive party machine and finally the crowning achievement of becoming Israel's first prime minister. A quirk of fate, which would serve to propel Weizmann into the inner councils of state, where he would labor with prodigious skill on Zionism's behalf, was the subject that he pursued and became a renowned international expert in, that of chemistry. It was through his efforts in that field that Weizmann would receive a coveted opportunity to enter the selective world of international diplomacy. When he shifted his focus to chemistry research in England, he gained the opportunity to deal with leading politicians of that nation at a strategic point in time. The contacts and experience derived from those efforts spurred both his entry into the high ranks of diplomacy and his momentum toward the achievement of his ultimate goal of a Zionist state in Palestine.

While Weizmann deprecated his studies in chemistry, pointing toward what he deemed the loftier studies that many of his Verein colleagues were pursuing, such as philosophy, economics, and law, it was through the very channel of chemistry that he would make a profound impact on Leo Motzkin, founder and leader of the Verein. A brilliant mathematician, Motzkin sought out Weizmann as a tutor to instruct him in the elementary principles of science, paying the younger student for the privilege.

For a time Weizmann was in awe of Motzkin, whose organizational and debating skills sparked admiration. Most assuredly the example afforded by Motzkin invested Chaim with a steadfast determination to develop those same skills, which he did with energetic tenacity.

During this same period of time, Motzkin introduced Weizmann to a leading Zionist intellectual figure who would help shape his thinking. Ahad Ha'am was the leader of Cultural Zionism. Even though Weizmann would always regard Ha'am as more of an aesthete than himself, with the latter's emphasis on studying and extolling the spiritual elements of Jewish tradition while considering political activity a frequent barrier toward attaining those spiritual objectives, Chaim Weizmann profited from their association in the manner expected of the pragmatic intellectual that he was. Weizmann regarded assiduous political negotiation and lobbying to be paramount elements in securing the Zionist destiny. In that regard he had nothing in common with Ahad Ha'am. On the other hand, he recognized both that the cause he advocated stood for something and that the destiny he sought to realize through political channels was interwoven with the spiritual and historical roots of the Jewish people. The young Weizmann and the young Ben-Gurion both had been imbued with the ancient cultural, historical, and religious roots of the Jewish people. Now Weizmann could constantly build on those roots through effective dialogue with Zionism's foremost spiritual thinker. Weizmann could profit from the association by enhancing his knowledge of Cultural Zionism. In the hard-nosed world of pragmatic politics, Leo Motzkin and others would serve as helpful advisers. The bonds between Weizmann and Ha'am would strengthen beyond those with Motzkin, a closer contemporary in age, and in the period leading up to World War One, Ahad Ha'am would be his foremost intellectual influence.

The cosmopolitan sophistication of Berlin made a favorable impression on Weizmann. His introduction to this major metropolis of world opinion set the tone for the course he would set as a Zionist diplomat traveling to major cities on an international scale. After completing his third semsester at Charlottenburg Polytechnic, he returned home to Pinsk at the end of the spring of 1895. He would remain there until early summer of 1896, when he returned to Berlin to resume his studies in the fall. Returning to Pinsk had a jarring effect on him as his analytical mind held the place in a harshly inferior light to worldly Berlin. A letter to his friend Leo Motzkin reveals the sharp disapproval he felt about a town that had earlier constituted a cultural step up the ladder from the village of Motol, where he had spent his earliest years. The deprecating tone in which he speaks of Pinsk reveals a side of Weizmann that surfaced recurringly throughout his life, that of snobbery. His level of impatience was that of the highly cultured, no-nonsense intellectual, and he would refer huffily to "riffraff" if he found what he deemed a requisite degree of sophistication lacking in an individual or individuals. An air of haughty disdain is present in his ruminations about Pinsk to Motzkin:

> . . . after Berlin, Pinsk had made such a vile, repulsive impression on me that I find it unpleasant, even distasteful, to share it, dear friend, with you. There is nothing here and no one: instead of a town—just an enormous rubbish-heap; instead of people, one comes across creatures devoid of a personality, with no interests, no desires, no demands . . . Hundreds of Jews push on and hurry about the streets of our town, with anxious faces marked by great suffering, but they seem to do it unconsciously, as if they were in a daze. As in any other well-organized society, there is a so-called intelligentsia here too . . . In point of fact, the male "intellectuals" are busy paying court to intellectual damsels, while the married men and women spend their time playing cards . . . All this is quite natural and understandable if one bears in mind . . . how few higher or even average interests they have. From all this you will understand that I am incredibly bored here. I have, of course, a host of acquaintances who would gladly spend their time with me—a student from Berlin . . . but I don't go anywhere and have not taken up at all with the jeunesse dorée of Pinsk . . .[19]

The scorn that the intense young intellectual heaps upon the citizenry of Pinsk bears heavily on a point he shared in common with Ben-Gurion. Early on, Weizmann learned to budget his time in a sternly efficient manner under the watchful eye of his sternest taskmaster—himself. He heaps scorn on conventional merrymaking among the masses due to his own dominant belief that far more important matters remained to be resolved. As a man with a mission, he had no tolerance for what he considered time wasting, namely, time spent away from one's goal. In cases when against his own better judgment he agreed to attend social functions, David Ben-Gurion was known to sit without saying anything during the entire evening. While maintaining warm relations with his staff as prime minister, Ben-Gurion found it difficult to communicate with visitors unless the individual had an informed working knowledge of the Bible, Zionism, or history. It is said that some individuals do not suffer fools gladly, and it would be apt to say that both Weizmann and Ben-Gurion would not suffer fools at all. Both men drove themselves at a frenzied pace, despite the fact that neither of them had a physically strong body. As a result, each suffered breakdowns at different points in their lives when they pushed themselves dangerously close to death's door. The history of the entire Zionist movement is characterized by dedicated individuals, often weak of body but sturdy of spirit, who pushed themselves to the brink. The human weaknesses were often attributable to having little money for sustenance, combined with overtaxing the body through excessive work.

A broader base of understanding about why Weizmann and Ben-Gurion demonstrated such noticeable intolerance for anything equatable with time squandering can be gained in connection with the examples revealed earlier in this book by the young girl who tore down the flag of East Africa and called Theodor Herzl "traitor" and by former world heavyweight boxing champion Muhammad Ali. The dominant aspect of both the young Zionist girl and the devoted Islamic follower Ali was that these individuals lived for a cause bigger than themselves. This trait was also strongly representative of both Chaim Weizmann and David Ben-Gurion. Both men profoundly felt that after some two thousand years in which Jews lived in a Diaspora, where they embodied only a part of some other nation's culture, it was time for them to return to their original land of Zion. This intensely central focus caused them to push themselves beyond what less committed individuals would endure.

The appearance of Herzl and the creation of the World Zionist Organization generated a tidal wave within the ranks of Jewish intellectuals. It came at a time when the *Hibbat Zion* movement, of which Ahad Ha'am was the spiritual leader and which advocated a spiritual center in Palestine, was foundering. Weizmann was impressed with Herzl's goal and his sense of commitment, but he questioned Herzl's methods in the process. It is significant to note that even though he was a young man of college age at the time, Weizmann refused to be caught up in a frenzy of idealism that would prompt him to back Herzl at all costs. The skillful critical faculty that would assist him in negotiations with world leaders later on was at work early.

It is interesting to note Weizmann's opinion of Herzl as stated in his autobiography written when he was in his mid-seventies and living in the nation he had helped to create as its first president. His portrait of Herzl was manifested within his own basic working conception of what Zionism should be and how it should be nurtured:

> To me Zionism was something organic, which had to grow like a plant, had to be watched, watered and nursed, if it was to reach maturity. I did not believe that things could be done in a hurry. The Russian Zionists had as their slogan a saying of the Jewish sages: "That which the intelligence cannot do, time (that is, work, application, worry) will do." There was no lack of Zionist sentiment in the Russian-Jewish masses; what they lacked was will, direction, organization, the feeling of realities. Herzl was an organizer; he was also an aspiring personality; but he was not of the people, and did not grasp the nature of the forces which it harbored.
>
> He had excessive respect for the Jewish clergy, born not of intimacy but of distance. He saw something rather occult and mysterious in the Rabbis, while he knew them and evaluated them as individuals, good, bad or indifferent. His leaning toward clericalism distressed us, and so did the touch of Byzantinism in his manner. Almost from the outset a kind of court sprang up about him, of worshipers who pretended to guard him from too close contact with the mob. I am compelled to say that certain elements in his bearing invited such an attitude.[20]

The frustrations felt by Weizmann over Herzl and the coterie of individuals surrounding him were shared by Leo Motzkin and other Russian Zionists. They believed that they were being frozen out of important activities. They yearned to inject the organization with fresh ideas, particularly in the cultural realm. Situated in the vanguard of the Zionist movement were the young Russian intellectuals—dedicated idealists such as Weizmann and Motzkin. When they felt their ideas were not being given a satisfactory degree of acceptance, they created their own offshoot of the Zionist World Organization known as the Democratic Faction. Both Weizmann and Motzkin played instrumental roles in the group's creation. Weizmann referred to its composition and purposes thus:

> . . . enough has been told here to indicate one set of reasons for the opposition to Herzl which took shape in the Democratic faction at the early Zionist Congresses. We were not revolutionaries; but it would have been even more inaccurate to call us reactionaries. We were a struggling group of young academicians, without power, and without outside support; but we had a definite outlook. We did not like the note of elegance and pseudo-worldliness which characterized official Zionism, the dress

suits and frock coats and fashionable dresses. On me the formalism of the Zionist Congresses made a painful impression, especially after one of my periodic visits to the wretched and oppressed Russian Jewish masses. Actually it was all very modest, but to us it smacked of artificiality, extravagance and the *haut monde*; it did not bespeak for us the democracy, simplicity and earnestness of the movement; and we were uncomfortable.[21]

The basic difference separating Weizmann and the Democratic Faction from Herzl and adherents concerned the burning question of just how Jewish immigration to Palestine should be approached. The First Aliyah into Palestine, which took place between 1882 and 1904, was small, but inroads were made through the creation of agricultural colonies. In 1882, Jews composed 5 percent of the total population. As mentioned earlier, by the time of Ben-Gurion's arrival in 1906, the Jewish population in Palestine had reached fifty-five thousand. Arabs constituted seven hundred thousand.

The Ottoman Empire vigorously opposed the creation of a modern Jewish settlement in Palestine and in 1882 imposed restrictions on Jews entering the nation. Baron Edmond James de Rothschild invested 5.6 million British pounds in Jewish colonization in Palestine, 1.6 million of which was spent between 1883 and 1889. He aroused great criticism in the ranks of the *Hibbat Zion* and later Zionist movements, however, due to the strings he attached to his efforts. Rothschild appointed directors who administered all affairs within the colonies. His gardeners supervised the farms. No less a figure than Ahad Ha'am sharply criticized Rothschild for creating in Palestine a servant class of Jewish colonists who depended on his handouts and on the labor of Arab workers. At one point, the spiritual leader of the *Hibbat Zion* led a contingent of his followers to Paris to speak with the youngest son of the legendary James Jacob Rothschild, the first head of the Paris branch of the family. The results proved highly disappointing because Rothschild scoffed at them, letting them know that his financial affairs and how they were run were his concern and not theirs. The meeting left the sensitive Ha'am deeply depressed, as Weizmann discovered when Ha'am later discussed the meeting with him.

Weizmann and his Democratic Faction cohorts found themselves at cross purposes with Herzl on the important objective of what should be done by Jews in advance of achieving statehood in Palestine. An optimistic Herzl believed that the breakthrough to a Jewish state lay close at hand. This objective, he believed, would be achieved by the

Jewish people soon acquiring by internationally guaranteed charter the legal right to settle in Palestine. At that point, efforts would be brought to bear to develop Jewish culture in Palestine. He therefore opposed any efforts by Jews in the Diaspora to enhance the cause of Cultural Zionism. Weizmann, along with Ahad Ha'am and another intellectual ally greatly admired by Chaim, Martin Buber, favored assiduous cultivation of cultural roots. Though Weizmann remained more of a political pragmatist than either Ha'am and Buber with their aesthetic focus, he regarded the cultural effort as indispensable to realizing Zionist goals. Such a grounding would serve as preparation for achieving nation status. Cultural Zionism could generate valuable impetus toward achieving the goal of a state in Palestine and at the same time provide the colonizing pioners with a road map of how to succeed and develop a successful nation once the appropriate political steps had been taken. Seeking to avoid a harmful split in the movement, Herzl astutely held Weizmann and his idealistic Russian cohorts at bay by tabling motions that would create a committee to undertake cultural endeavors. This left the young Russian idealists with bitter, unresolved frustrations.

As in the case of Ben-Gurion, Weizmann also invested significant time and effort doing battle with members of the Bund. Created in 1897, this organization, also known as the General Jewish Workers Union, which flourished in Lithuania, Poland, and Russia, was a much stronger and larger movement than Zionism before World War One. Considering the size of the Bund along with the fervent devotion of its members and its stern opposition to Zionism, conflict between the groups appeared inevitable. Zealous young intellectuals sought to influence the future course of action for Jews. In view of conditions existing within the Diaspora in Eastern Europe, the Bundist and Zionist viewpoints both loomed as discernible reactions to the past and blueprints for the future. The Bundist attachment to the communist doctrine of Karl Marx is understandable in view of the degree of isolationism and economic exploitation that Jews experienced in the Diaspora. In the case of the Zionists, their sensitivities were tapped by these same phenomena of Diaspora isolationism and economic exploitation, but the disparate responses of the two groups stemmed from differing historical viewpoints. The young idealists of both organizations, brought to a boil by Jewish frustrations of the past, reacted in the manner of the commentator figure prototyped by Peter Finch in the movie *Network*, who proclaimed with loud anger, "I'm mad as hell and I'm not going to take it anymore." In that both the young Zionists and Bundists were "mad as hell" and held strongly committed opposing viewpoints, it is no small wonder that angry invective dominated their heated debates. Bundists stressed the Marxist interpretation of history, which rested on a foundation of economic determinism and the amalgamation of workers under one international heading. Any discrimination or lack of opportunity with consequential economic deprivation suffered by Diaspora Jews was construed to be the result of exploitation by their oppressive masters. In short, Jewish difficulties were but one link in the massive chain that embraced workers of all nations and creeds. Therefore, the solution to Jewish social and economic difficulties in the Diaspora was to overthrow the capitalistic overlords, from whose policies such deprivation stemmed. Once the overlords were overthrown and workers had united, there would be no need for Jews to seek refuge elsewhere, such as Palestine. The Zionists, on the other hand, saw their plight in the Diaspora as reflective of the Jewish condition, that of not having a nation of their own. As a result, the Zionists believed, they were doomed to function in the role of outsiders, often unwelcome outsiders at that, in various nations of the world, primarily within Europe. The Bundists felt that a dramatic new assimilation would be achieved by Jews through joining a common cause with their fellow workers. Zionists, on the other hand, believed that assimilation would never work on a major scale because Jews would always represent only one small part of somebody else's culture, in the process depriving themselves of reestablishing their own ancient cultural roots in their own land of origin.

Chaim Weizmann's active involvement in Zionism would further blossom in a new setting. He had surrounded himself with the young student intellectuals of the *Verein* while in Berlin, and his next stop was to be another major international center of learning—Geneva, Switzerland. He moved there to join the organic chemistry department at the University of Geneva after earning his doctorate in Berlin with honors. His doctoral dissertation was on the action of electrolysis in the production of dyestuffs.

He plunged immediately into Zionist activities in Switzerland as he helped found the first Zionist society in that nation, called the Bern Academic Zionist Society. The Bundists figured importantly as a factor in Switzerland, and Weizmann was quick to jump into the intellectual fray. He engaged in some of his earliest public debates in Bern. One of the first was entitled "Marx vs. Zionism." After these rousing encounters, he would often seem to fortify his own ego and enhance his position in the minds of others with references to "routing" the opposition.

When a controversy broke out in Zionist ranks between Ahad Ha'am and Herzl associate Max Nordau, who would succeed Herzl as president of the World Zionist Organization after Herzl's death, Weizmann's posture was that of reconciliation between the two forces involved in the debate. At the same time, he defended Ahad Ha'am against what he viewed as a strident and unfair attack against him. The controvery came to a head in an article Nordau wrote as a response to a scathing review Ha'am had written about Herzl's utopian novel *Altneuland*, which described a futuristic Palestine twenty years after receipt of a charter from the sultan in 1903. Seeing nothing positive in *Altneuland*, Ahad Ha'am's central critical thrust was the contention that the type of society envisaged by Herzl involved imitating other nations in order to please non-Jews. He saw the society creatively described by the father of Zionism as being devoid of any national spirit.[22]

With Ahad Ha'am's critical response, the battle lines were clearly drawn between the two opposing Zionist schools of thought. Herzl requested that his close cohort Nordau answer points raised in Ahad Ha'am's review. As such he was calling upon the acknowledged leader of Political Zionism, Max Nordau, while the individual being singled out for criticism, Ahad Ha'am, was the acknowledged leader of Cultural Zionism.

Nordau's article, published initially in *Die Welt* and made available to Jewish newspapers throughout Europe, focused little attention on Ahad Ha'am's review. It was instead a free-swinging broadside in which Nordau used the review to scathingly accuse Zionism's spiritual leader of being deficient of intellectual substance. In Nordau's eyes, Ahad Ha'am was a bitter anti-Zionist and a pamphleteering troublemaker.

Weizmann entered the steamy intellectual climate by advancing a position he felt embodied the positive elements of both Cultural and Political Zionism. There were positive aspects to each view that he maintained should be included in Zionism's agenda, and he sought to articulate the specifics of his posture in such a way as to end the bickering and foster cohesive effort for the benefit of the movement as a whole. While defending his mentor Ahad Ha'am from Nordau's sharp criticisms and recognizing his spiritual contribution to Zionism, Chaim continued to feel that Political Zionism was also an important element in promoting the ideal of a Jewish state in Palestine. He accordingly felt that it was important to bridge the gap between what had appeared in the eyes of certain Zionists such as Nordau and Ahad

Ha'am to be irreconcilable viewpoints. The problem to be resolved was that of arriving at a balance between the two positions, which Weizmann sought to achieve through application of Synthetic Zionism. Though the term had been used before, it was Weizmann who, through dogged persistence, became most closely identified with the concept. Weizmann felt that the unfortunate gap existing between the two schools of thought could be bridged through two efforts he was ardently promoting: a Jewish university in Palestine and the creation of a periodical devoted to spotlighting Jewish culture. He also believed that the Democratic Faction could help dissipate the gap between East and West by merging East European Jewish "essence" with European civilization:

> What we regard as Jewish culture (Kultur) has till lately been confused with Jewish religious worship (Kultus), and when culture in the literal sense was discussed, the Zionists of West[ern] Europe thought that it referred to the improvement of educational facilities in East[ern] Europe. Perhaps it is now understood, because of the specific activities of Faction members, that the totality of Jewish national achievement is intended— particularly that literature, art, scientific research should all be synthe- sized with Europeanism, translated into modern creativity, and expressed in institutions bearing their own individual character.[23]

By the time that Chaim Weizmann asserted himself as an adherent of Synthetic Zionism, he had moved into the forefront of leadership in the Democratic Faction through a series of events that resulted in his catapulting ahead of the man he had faithfully followed from his days in the *Verein*. From then on, Weizmann would march to his own tune, and Leo Motzkin would never regain his top leadership position within Democratic Faction ranks.

The string of circumstances began when Weizmann met Sophia Getzova in Bern and became infatuated with her, which led to an engagement. Leo Motzkin heartily approved of the match because it would unite two prominent Zionist activists. During the period of engagement, he met Vera Khatzman on October 31, 1900, at the Jewish Club in Geneva after returning from the Fourth Zionist Conference. Later, the two met again, and he coached the attractive young medical student in French and chemistry. Eventually, once love blossomed, Weizmann felt compelled to break the engagement to Sophia Getzova, which drew the immediate ire of Motzkin along with Democratic Faction members. Motzkin was repulsed by the idea of Weizmann's spurning a loyal comrade of the Zionist cause. He was probably also troubled by the fact that whereas Sophia was from the ranks of Weizmann and himself, a product of the Pale of Settlement, Vera Khatzman was from outside the Pale, the daughter of a czarist army officer no less. A quiet and more retiring sort than the politically active Sophia, Vera spent her time concentrating on her studies, showing no interest in the Zionist movement up to the time of her meeting with Weizmann.

Leo Motzkin was convinced that a tragic wrongdoing had been perpetrated on Sophia Getzova, and he proposed a solution to the ordeal, which he recommended to Weizmann. Because Sophia had conducted herself with total propriety, the honorable solution would be for Chaim to marry her. Once the marriage had become an accomplished reality, he could then divorce Sophia and pursue his relationships with Vera Khatzman. Not surprisingly, Weizmann spurned his colleague's recommendation.

The romantic events in Weizmann's life were probably major factors in his forward thrust into the top ranks of Zionist politics among the young Russian intellectuals at the expense of Motzkin's diminished influence. Following the flap over the Weizmann-Getzova-Khatzman triangle, Motzkin refused to respond to communications from Chaim regarding the upcoming preparatory Zionist Youth Conference slated for Munich on April 1 and 2 of 1901. While it is impossible to state with any degree of certainty Motzkin's attitude toward Weizmann in the aftermath of Weizmann's decision to break his engagement with Sophia Getzova, he made no secret of his displeasure at the time, and his snubbing of Weizmann in the aftermath almost certainly had some bearing on Motzkin's perception of wrongful conduct on Weizmann's part. In the past, however, Motzkin had for no apparent reason periodically refused to respond to letters from Weizmann, but to do so at this stage of their relationship, with Weizmann playing an appreciably expanding role in Zionist intellectual circles, would be deemed less likely absent the appearance of an event to incur his displeasure.

When his former mentor in the *Verein* failed to attend the Munich conference, it was Chaim Weizmann himself who filled the power vacuum created at the top as a result of Leo Motzkin's absence. When the first Zionist Youth Conference convened in Basel, Switzerland, on December 18, it was Weizmann who delivered the inaugural address. Among the approximately forty delegates who represented universities in Germany, Switzerland, France, Vienna, Prague, and Russia was Sophia Getzova, who attended, it would seem, at Weizmann's suggestion. Though Motzkin appeared at the Basil conference and delivered a speech, he had done little to convene the meeting and had refused to prepare a paper for it. As for Sophia Getzova, despite being spurned by Weizmann for another woman, she remained active in Zionist activities, met Weizmann on future occasions at these functions, and apaprently harbored no ill will toward him.[24]

As Weizmann moved up the ladder of Zionist influence, he became more of an elitist as he immersed himself into the intellectual community to the exclusion of everyone else. The disdainful letter he wrote to Motzkin from his hometown of Pinsk while still a college undergraduate describing intellectual conditions there proved to be a harbinger of things to come. Whereas David Ben-Gurion would operate from a grass roots base, identifying and performing with the working classes, Chaim Weizmann, the university professor who was becoming an ever more pervasively cosmopolitan intellectual, would work within selective channels, seeking out an intellectual Zionist working elite within the major thought centers of Europe. Such systematic programming would soon thrust him into the power vortex of the British government. At the same time, as is characteristic of elitists, much of such behavior is a protective facade designed to shield the immersed individual from the trappings of society at large. Basic insecurity is the root cause for such demonstrably professed isolation. It appears that the inner complexities operating within Weizmann's psyche, riddled with fears and insecurities, were responsible for at least some of his elitist behavior. For one thing, the pressures of attempting to vigorously pursue two entirely different goals in the physically and emotionally draining fields of chemistry and Zionism pushed him to the point of exhaustion over and over again. He extended his health to the breaking point and would be forced to slow down long enough to recuperate, after which the cycle resumed.

A letter to Vera, the woman he would eventually marry, illustrates the painful experience of an overworked man in a state of great frustration.

To convene the Conference [World Zionist Congress] means to declare war on Herzlism as a whole, and not to hold it is quite impossible. You can only wage war successfully if you know who supports you; can we say confidently that such-and-such forces are backing us? No, certainly not . . . Where are the youthfulness, the freshness that are needed now? Though I was bright and cheerful until now, my heart is so heavy. The captain weeps. The man setting out to war weeps. We are nervy, unstrung, flabby, and we are unfit for the *Jewish cause*. All our lives we have been serving many gods, and now we cannot concentrate on the ideal of freedom, of our own freedom. How will it all end? I can see before me the faces of our best people. They are all helpless now, yet they are giants in comparison with me . . .[25]

The aforementioned example sheds light on the complexities and volatilities of Weizmann, who exhibited an expansive gap between resourceful leadership and emotional instability. Weizmann biographer Jehuda Reinharz stated, "His uneven disposition made for very frantic, sometimes hysterical outbursts. The smallest of incidents could cheer him, but it could also plunge him into depths of despair. It was during these moods of blackest depression that he longed for Vera more than ever."[26]

To comprehend the psychic frustrations of Weizmann at this pivotal stage of his life, it is necessary to examine all the factors at work. First, here was a man not yet thirty years of age being thrust by his own strong motives and the force of circumstances to a leading position in a major political movement. Second, he was also hurling himself exhaustively into the chemistry field, exerting much effort on experiments. As mentioned earlier, he was a man who had not been endowed with a strong body. Then there was yet another circumstance at work, that of his pronounced sensitivities. His revealing letter to Vera conveys the impression that the ongoing battles with Herzl and his colleagues on behalf of the Democratic Faction were exacting a major psychic toll. As is the case with highly sensitive intellectual types, confrontation can be distasteful. The distaste increases when the political warfare is against individuals one admires. Weizmann clearly respected Herzl and felt indebted to him for the contributions he had made to the Jewish cause. As a proud Jew, he was happy to be a member of the World Zionist Organization, and having felt a comradeship with its members, it was painful for him to do battle with individuals he would have allied himself with if the focus were on external rather than internal Zionist organizational mechanics.

On the subject of doing battle against opposing forces within Jewish ranks, Ben-Gurion did not seem to hold the same compunctions. Though it would be a mistake to say that he was a man devoid of sensitivities, it would be accurate to contend that his sensitivities were shaped differently from those of Weizmann. Weizmann was unquestionably a diplomat of the highest rank; Ben-Gurion, although emotional and capable of tirades, reacted to political phenomena in a different manner from Weizmann. Ben-Gurion had an instinctive political flair that Weizmann did not have. If Ben-Gurion blew up at a political opponent over an issue that was meaningful to him, rather than agonize internally following a confrontation as Weizmann was more likely to do, he was more apt to regard it as one of many inevitable differences of opinion that arise in the political world. Yet, at the same time, if Ben-Gurion regarded such an opponent as an enemy, he did not wish to have any discourse with him at all outside the realm of political combat. Probably Ben-Gurion's less sensitive posture had a good deal to do with the rough-and-tumble world of Zionist politics from whence he came. One man was the shirt-sleeved proletarian labor leader, and the other the silk-shirted diplomat-intellectual.

Another interesting contrast between Chaim Weizmann and David Ben-Gurion concerns the pursuit of their respective careers. While Weizmann was involving himself with two challenging careers, that of Zionism and chemistry, Ben-Gurion spent his life exclusively in the Zionist world. Weizmann felt that his efforts in chemistry could supply him with financial independence, thereby giving him the opportunity to pursue his Zionist cause. Ben-Gurion treated the Zionist cause like a jealous mistress—avoid other interests. Once again the conflicting life-styles of the two men were manifested. The Chaim Weizmann who, as a boy, had his grandmother dutifully sew silk shirts for him retained a penchant for elegance as an adult. He demonstrated a sartorial flair and lived in lavishly appointed homes when his chemistry career blossomed in both London and in Rehovot, Israel. On the other hand, Ben-Gurion raised more than a few eyebrows while prime minister by receiving heads of state in rumpled short-sleeved shirts. As for his residence, it was the most modest of any head of state of his day, the only exception to austerity being the twenty-thousand-volume library he maintained. It was a common occurrence during the chilly winter season for him to receive visitors at home while wrapped in blankets since he disdained the expense of central heating. Yet, once again, the distinctions served them well for the constituencies to which they appealed: the black-tie formality of the British diplomatic circles in which Weizmann traveled as opposed to the proletarian common folk who made up the natural constituency of the pragmatic socialist Ben-Gurion.

One of the paramount qualities required in any first-rate diplomat is the ability to see a cause or an issue in its most expansive framework. The structural composition of the forest is the sum total of its trees. The diplomat knows that a clear and unambiguous reading of the forest involves painstaking examination of the roots of every tree. Weizmann demonstrated this capacity early on. A classic example of his basic beliefs embodying what he hoped for Zionism to accomplish is contained in a letter he wrote to Theodor Herzl dated May 6, 1903. In it he delineates his concept of Synthetic Zionism, which he correlates with the raison d'être of the Democratic Faction:

> The Faction forms the connecting link between the older and the younger generation. It alone is capable of assuming the struggle against the revolutionaries, which indeed it does. It alone is freedom-loving and socially enlightened. It extracts the Jewish essence from among the masses and pours it into a European mold. But what the Jewish essence is, the European Zionists refuse to comprehend . . . Perhaps it is now understood, because of the specific activities of Faction members, that the totality of Jewish national achievement is intended—particularly that literature, art, scientific research should all be synthesized with Europeanism, translated into modern creativity, and expressed in institutions bearing their own individual character. We believe that this Jewish culture, being the most vital form of the people's self-expression, is more than a mere part of the national renaissance: next to the larger Palestine ideal of Zionism it represents its only remaining attribute, and can at least offer the modern Jew dissatisfied with a Shekel contribution an approach to a loftier view of life, with scope for enthusiastic action. Perhaps it is the only reply that we can make to our opponents, since the economic and political reply must be postponed to the future . . .[27]

The appeal by Weizmann to Herzl on behalf of the Democratic Faction is toward a broadly based consensus of Zionist effort. In the manner of the skilled diplomat straining to examine every root of every tree, Weizmann managed to embrace all of the varying groups to which Zionism was appealing. He hoped to eliminate internecine warfare among the ranks of the committed through the application of Synthetic Zionism. It is interesting to dissect his message and examine each of the groups targeted.

1. Bridging the age gap, using the Democratic Faction to connect young and old.

2. Extracting the Jewish message from the masses and pouring it into a European mold.

3. Embracing the totality of Jewish national achievement:
    a. Literature
    b. Art
    c. Scientific research.

4. Synthesizing the totality of Jewish national achievement as re-

vealed above with Europeanism, translated into modern creativity, and expressed in institutions bearing their own individual character.

5. Calling for a national renaissance as reflected in the aims of Spiritual Zionism's father, Ahad Ha'am.

6. Offering the modern Jew a loftier view of life with scope for enthusiastic action.

When one examines all that Weizmann accomplished in delineating in a letter to Zionism's father the meaningful objectives to be met through Synthetic Zionism, it becomes obvious just how and why he was able to achieve on such a wide scale later on in the diplomatic sphere with both the British and, late in his life on a most important mission for Zionism, U.S. President Harry Truman. His scientific mind enabled him to examine issues with microscopic logic, and his dignified diplomatic demeanor won him respect and attention.

As a dynamic young leader of the Zionist movement whose reputation was rapidly advancing, Weizmann naturally provided significant input into the spirited debate that Theodor Herzl's East Africa or Uganda proposal generated. Though he fails to cover the point in his autobiography, his first response was to endorse the proposal. However, less than one week later he came out swinging on behalf of the hard-liners who opposed the controversial measure, most of whom came from the ranks of his own Russian Zionists in the Democratic Faction, and delivered some of the harshest words against Herzl and his East Africa proposal of any delegate at the Sixth Zionist Congress. Jehuda Reinharz was quick to take note of Weizmann's inconsistency: "To put it mildly, Weizmann's remarks were disingenuous. Less than a week earlier he had backed the leader's stance on East Africa and had shown sympathy for his motivations. Yet he was now fully in the camp of the hard-liners. With his unerring political sense he understood that in his first public pronouncement on the subject after the congress he had to earn his right to be among them. An extreme position would help erase the memory of his erstwhile aberration."[28]

In Weizmann's own account, he emphasized his opposition as stemming from what he viewed as an aberration in policy from two planks adopted at the First Zionist Congress regarding Palestine. They came to be known as the Basel Program and consisted of both the promotion, along appropriate lines, of the colonization of Palestine by Jewish and agricultural workers and the strengthening and fostering of Jewish national settlement and consciousness.

The essence of Weizmann's powerful indictment of the East Africa proposal is contained in the following words:

The influence of Herzl on the people is very great. Even the opponents of Uganda cannot get away from it and they cannot make up their minds to state openly that this is a departure from the Basle [Basel] program. Herzl, who found the *Chibath Zion* movement already in existence, made a pact with it. But as time passed, and the idea of Palestine did not succeed, he regretted the pact. He reckoned only with external conditions, whereas the forces on which we base ourselves lie deep in the psychology of our people and in its living impulses. We knew that Palestine could not be obtained in short order, and that is why we do not despair if this or that particular attempt fails.[29]

Weizmann then placed particular emphasis on the last sentence of his speech, which he claimed was adopted by the anti-Ugandists as a rallying cry. He stated, "If the British Government and people are what I think they are, they will make us a better offer."[30]

Though Weizmann saw his statement about the British government at the close of his speech from the perspective of an anti-Ugandist rallying cry, in the overall course of Zionist history, it had a much broader impact. The reference to the British government in a speech by Weizmann was a harbinger of what was to come and of the role he was to skillfully perform on behalf of Zionists in quest of their homeland goal in Palestine. Weizmann's contribution rested in his negotiating skills in general, but in their usage in discussions with British government officials in particular.

In the aftermath of the controversy surrounding the East Africa proposal, Weizmann traveled to England to see if he could gain some insight into the overall question of assistance for the Zionist cause. While there, he held discussions with a member of Parliament held in anathema by the Jewish community in England and elsewhere. Sir William Evans-Gordon was sponsor of the Aliens Bill, which sharply restricted Jewish immigration to England. Responding to the pogroms, Jews had flocked to East London and Whitechapel in large numbers. When pressure was generated to hold back the immigration wave, the Aliens Bill was the result. Rather than rejecting Evans-Gordon out of hand as an obvious enemy, Weizmann scrutinized the totality of the man and the situation, opting for discussion. For one thing, Weizmann was quick to point out, he had met Evans-Gordon some years earlier when Evans-Gordon was on a tour of the Pale of Settlement in Russia. He felt that Evans-Gordon's position on the Jews, rather than being anti-Semitic as he was being charged by many, was sympathetic, an opinion Weizmann based on discussions between them in Russia. Weizmann saw Evans-Gordon as a politician caught in a tight situation in which legislation was being strongly advocated to correct a situation dominating the public's mind.

Weizmann demonstrated understanding for Evans-Gordon's position in the following manner:

> England had reached the point when she could or would absorb so many Jews and no more. English Jews were prepared to be absorbed in larger numbers. The reaction against this cannot be looked upon as anti-Semitism in the ordinary or vulgar sense of that word; it is a universal social and economic concomitant of Jewish immigration, and we cannot shake it off.''[31]

In Weizmann's estimation, Evans-Gordon had acted with the best interests of his country in mind. He had, according to Weizmann, been horrified by the oppression of Jews that he had witnessed in Russia but believed that it was physically impossible for England to make good the wrongs that Russia had inflicted on the Jewish population.

The incident with William Evans-Gordon is another manifestation of Weizmann's diplomatic prowess. Whereas many Jews would have eschewed discussion with the sponsor of a bill that sharply reduced Jewish immigration into England, Weizmann possessed the kind of expansive compass that stands as a constituent property of the successful diplomat. He possessed the vision to distinguish between what could superficially loom as anti-Semitism and the broad picture, in which national considerations, in this case those of England, were examined. Such insight into the thought processes and national objectives of another party enables a skilled diplomat to see the entire picture and respond accordingly, enhancing the prospects for fruitful discussion.

At this period the pivotal move that would form the linchpin of Weizmann's successes as an international diplomat for Zionism occurred. As is so often the case, its significance was not recognized until later.

It took a twist of circumstances in order for Chaim Weizmann to move to England in 1904. His interests in relocating there arose from a letter he received from William Henry Perkin Jr., a leading chemist and a professor of chemistry at the University of Manchester. Perkin invited Weizmann to work for him at his laboratory at Owens College, and the offer immediately intrigued Weizmann for two reasons. First, Perkin was a world-renowned chemist who worked in concert with other first-rank British chemists, including Nobel Prize winners. Second, Weizmann was aware that Manchester had a great dye industry, his principal area of expertise.

At that same time, a position became available at a teachers' training college in Jerusalem. Although the Manchester position involved a great deal more money, not to mention a coveted opportunity to work at a leading university with some of the greatest minds in the field, Weizmann decided instead to pursue the teaching post in Jerusalem. Here was a man deeply committed to the Zionist cause who was facing a possible opportunity to live and work in Jerusalem, the city of greatest historic significance to his people. Much to his chagrin, he was rejected. The reason given was that he was not sufficiently orthodox. No doubt this pursuit of a cultural agenda in the Zionist movement was a major contributing factor, if not the sole cause, if a candidate as highly qualified as he could be passed over for such a position.

After his rejection for the Jerusalem teaching position, and with the offer tendered by Perkin still available, Weizmann accepted, moving his base of operation to Manchester, England, in 1904. The year of his relocation from Geneva to Manchester was significant for yet another reason. It was the year of Theodor Herzl's death. No one knew it at the time, least of all Weizmann, but a new star would soon be rising in the constellations. Zionism's founder, international organizer, and negotiator was passing from the scene, to be replaced by a man of equal commitment but superior insight in the realm of international politics.

Weizmann's viewpoint as expressed in his autobiography concerning his move to England appears curious in the wake of what transpired there. It might well be that his feelings were jaundiced by battle fatigue highlighted by the East Africa proposal. He stated that the Zionist movement had reached an apparent "dead point" and that his struggles were destroying him. Weizmann contended he was "in danger of being eaten up by Zionism" and was also putting himself in the path of becoming an "eternal student."[32]

If Weizmann took any respite at all from Zionism, it was a very brief one, since he moved with gusto into a situation where a leadership vacuum existed in contrast to the situation in Europe that he had left. In England, Weizmann renewed acquaintances with William Evans-Gordon. He also made an excellent contact in Charles Dreyfus, who aided him in the two important areas of his life, Zionism and chemistry. He worked for Dreyfus at the latter's chemical factory in addition to his Owens College responsibilities and received Dreyfus's aid in gaining entry to political circles because Dreyfus was the leading Zionist exponent in Manchester.

Major politicians were eager to seek out the Zionist viewpoint. After all, there were twenty-five thousand Jews in Manchester, a significant number. They were part of the massive wave of immigrants from Russia that increased the number of Jews in England from sixty-five thousand in 1881 to three hundred fifty thousand by the beginning of World War One. The number had swelled following the infamous "Bloody Sunday" of January 9, 1905, when Russian police fired at innocent demonstrators, touching off pogroms and violent bloodbaths directed at Jews.

Early in 1906, a parliamentary election was being contested in Manchester. The Conservative Party candidate was Arthur James Balfour, formerly British prime minister. Charles Dreyfus, who also served as chairman of the Conservative Party in Manchester as well as chairman of the Manchester Zionist society, arranged a meeting between Balfour and Weizmann. Though Zionist allies in most matters, Weizmann and Dreyfus held opposing views on the East Africa question, and they engaged in frequent debates on the subject. It was Dreyfus's stated hope in arranging the meeting with Balfour that the former prime minister would demonstrate to Weizmann how wrong he had been in opposing the East African initiative.

The meeting took place in a room at the Queens Hotel, which served as his campaign headquarters. It was Weizmann's assumption that Balfour had agreed to see him for a brief period of time—fifteen minutes he was informed by Dreyfus—to break his routine because the corridors were filled with people waiting for a few words with the candidate. Much to the surprise of Weizmann and Dreyfus, however, the former prime minister talked with Weizmann for one hour. Balfour began by asking Weizmann why some Jews had opposed the East Africa proposal. Weizmann explained by launching into a monologue about the meaning of the Zionist movement. The central thrust of his message was the importance of Palestine, which he stated as the catalyst that had sparked the entire movement. Palestine was the sustaining force of Zionism. To illustrate his point, Weizmann asserted that, had Moses himself been at the Sixth Zionist Congress when the East Africa resolution was passed, he would have broken the tablets again. Weizmann credited the British government with good intentions but added that the Jewish people would never produce either the money or the energy to build up a wasteland and make it habitable unless the land were Palestine.

At that point in the discussion, fear began to overtake Weizmann. He was apprehensive that the apparent expression of interest on Balfour's face might be a mask. He felt self-conscious about his

English; he had been living in England only two years. He recalled "sweating blood" at that point as he looked for a less ponderous way of expressing himself. Just as he was attempting to make a graceful departure from the discussion, Weizmann was detoured by questions from Balfour, who now asked about the growth of the Zionist movement and about Theodor Herzl. Then an impulse finally seized Weizmann as he asked the former prime minister, "Mr. Balfour, supposing I were to offer you Paris instead of London, would you take it?"

A surprised Balfour sat up, stared at Weizmann, and replied, "But, Dr. Weizmann, we have London."

"That is true," Weizmann acknowledged. "But we had Jerusalem when London was a marsh."

Balfour leaned back and continued staring at Weizmann. He asked him if there were many Jews who thought like Weizmann. The Zionist leader's reply was that he believed he was speaking for millions of Jews who could not speak for themselves.

"If that is so, you will one day be a force," Balfour replied.

Shortly before Weizmann left the room, Balfour said, "It is curious. The Jews I meet are quite different."

"Mr. Balfour, you meet the wrong kind of Jews," Weizmann responded.[33]

The meeting with Arthur James Balfour was a turning point in Weizmann's life. Now he had met a prominent political figure of his new home, the political and financial capital of the world, and he had been able to state his case with his curious interlocutor listening attentively. As time passed, he would become better acquainted with Balfour, who would lose the 1906 election and go on to the House of Lords. As Lord Balfour, he would deliver the Balfour Declaration asserting the British government's belief in the Jewish right to a homeland in Palestine.

In addition to Balfour, Weizmann met another influential politician running for a seat in Parliament, who would emerge victorious running as a Liberal but who gained greater fame later as a Conservative. That man was Winston Churchill, who, at the time he met Weizmann, was and would later remain an ardent supporter of the Zionist cause. When the battle lines were drawn and energetic debate filled the House of Commons following World War Two over the question of Jewish statehood, Churchill was a forceful advocate of the Zionist position.

The painful separation that lasted until Vera completed her studies in Geneva ended in 1906 following her graduation. She and Weizmann were married in Zopott, near Danzig in Germany. From there it was on to Cologne and a meeting of the Actions Committee of the international Zionists. Chairing the proceedings was David Wolffsohn, presidential successor to Herzl.

Weizmann's comment on what happened to Vera during the course of the meeting is typical of what wives of busy international Zionist figures like Chaim Weizmann and David Ben-Gurion had to endure. During a period when a new husband and wife could be expected to be particularly close, as immediately following their wedding, Weizmann admitted, ". . . my young bride practically lost sight of me"[34] in the course of an eventful political week.

So by 1906, the year that David Ben-Gurion arrived in Palestine, Chaim Weizmann had newly launched a solid foundation for a Zionist career in a nation of pivotal international status, England; had made significant inroads into a successful career in chemistry; and had married the woman he loved. The future looked bright and the path leading toward accomplishments lay glitteringly before him.

It may be appropriate to enumerate here the concepts that energized Weizmann in his pursuit of helping his Jewish people to achieve a nation in Palestine. The major issues were:

1. *Synthetic Zionism*—consisting of the diplomatic skills of Weizmann the reconciler that were brought into play through a purposeful effort to merge the Practical Zionism advanced by David Ben-Gurion and the Spiritual Zionism advocated by Ahad Ha'am and Martin Buber with the forces of Political Zionism embraced by Max Nordau and the followers of Theodor Herzl. Through application of a united Zionist front, Weizmann envisioned a flexibility of movement in which Jews could both pursue the goal of a Zionist state through all meaningful negotiating channels and lay the cultural foundations for such a nation.

2. *Diplomatic initiative*—the forces of fate that found Weizmann in a nation of great influence and with the ears of many of its foremost political minds ready to listen to what he had to say. It was one thing to debate ardent Bundists and quite another to receive the undivided attention of a former prime minister of Great Britain such as Arthur James Balfour, a prominent figure who had the contacts and influence to assist Weizmann in his Zionist pursuit. Even though Weizmann's autobiography was written almost a full half century after his first meeting with Balfour, it is interesting to note how richly vivid the details of the conversation stayed in his mind. The reason is the psychological importance this pivotal meeting had for him. The astute Zionist emissary realized that he had found his niche, a facility for

communicating with the politically powerful to pursue his objective of a Jewish nation.

3. *Historical inevitability*—a fundamental point that Chaim Weizmann held in common with David Ben-Gurion: the tradition nurtured within them from childhood and instilled within them by fathers proud of the Jewish cultural roots flowing from their bloodlines. As the tradition developed, Zionism, embodied by a return to Palestine, became the natural vehicle to fulfill their expectations. Balfour, who had the finely tuned ear and active curiosity of a successful statesman, wanted to know why Weizmann had opposed the East Africa initiative advanced by England. Weizmann's response had been directly to the point; it was the spirit of Zion that energized the movement. The desire to return to the land of their Jewish roots was the solidifying bond that held Zionism together.

In the same way that Weizmann's meeting with Balfour proved a major catalyst in Weizmann's Zionist career, the first conference of the Poalei Zion, held in Jaffa in October 1906, made a major impact on the then David Green that would forever remain with him. The majority of the ninety members assembled to officially found the Palestine branch of the party consisted of a vocal, largely assimilated group of Russians from Rostov with an affinity for communist rather than Zionist thought. They knew little about Zionism and spoke only Russian, wore colorful Russian embroidered blouses, sang Russian songs, and danced Russian dances. When they ceased merrymaking and settled into the political business at hand, they struck with thunderous certainty, calling for strikes, class warfare, and an integrated community consisting of both Jews and Arabs. It appeared that they would dominate the proceedings for a while due to their advantage in sheer numbers and certainty of conviction. According to a colleague of David's, Israel Shochat, the future prime minister of Israel "came and saved the situation."[35]

The arguments he posed against the Rostovians became his working credo right up to that historic day in 1948 when he declared the creation of the nation of Israel. He urged a broad party base, just as Weizmann had advocated a broad base with his Synthetic Zionism agenda, stressing the importance of wooing the entire *Yishuv* and not just the workers. He made a plea for unity with non-Marxist groups, emphasizing the need for internal cohesion if the goal of a Jewish state were to be realized in Palestine. Alternatively, if it were not important to create a Jewish nation there, then why remain in Palestine in the first place?

It is through the fires of adversity that the strength of conviction is most sternly tested, and young David reached within himself to deliver the most persuasively cogent arguments he could muster in the face of being greatly outnumbered. As is so often the case during lengthy emotionally and intellectually heated confrontations, dedicated individuals more closely examine their own beliefs, which undergo at least some form of modification. Although David in his early days in Plonsk disagreed with the pronounced communist emphasis on Bundist thinking, his socialist inclinations left him respectful of Marxism. He believed that Marxism would be a workable tool in Palestine. Now that he was living there and toiling exhaustively in the fields, he had come to another conclusion. The Marxist doctrine of class consciousness and its response to social problems, highlighted by its emphasis on worker cohesion, was better adapted to industrially developed nations with large cities rather than the primitive land where he now resided. Marx's emphasis had been on communism's achieving realization in developed nations such as England, where he had lived when he wrote *Das Kapital*, and Germany. The supreme irony was that eleven years after David Green pondered these weighty questions at the Poalei Zion Conference, the first communist revolution was achieved in Russia, the land of David's birth, which was sorely lacking in industrial development and whose resources and spirit had been drained dry by a rapacious aristocracy. He would retain socialist beliefs, but they would be geared to the desert land of which he was a part. Lying at the heart of his socialist concepts was Practical Zionism, with the emphasis on manual work in a Zionist spirit of national purpose.

Despite being outnumbered, David argued nonstop with the Rostovians for three days. Moderate as well as radical members rebutted his views far into the night, and his and other loud voices penetrated the thin walls of the Chaim Baruch Hotel while sleepless guests in other rooms angrily protested.

"During those three days," Israel Shochat would write, "[David] revealed himself . . . as a dynamic force with an extraordinary ability to express himself, capable of bridging the gap between two distant worlds—nationalism and socialism."[36]

When, despite David's best efforts, the Rostovians adopted a platform akin to the Communist Manifesto, with Zionism receiving scarcely a mention, a crestfallen yet still stoutly determined David vowed that Palestine would never become a communist state. The marathon ideological confrontation moved him even more emphatically away from any vestige of Marxist thinking.[37]

Even in defeat, however, he still managed to push through a resolution calling for the creation of a Jewish state, even though the two companion planks he regarded as ultimately necessary to achieve that goal—union with non-Marxists and Hebrew as the national language—were rejected.

Before moving on to Jerusalem in 1910, the determined young David plunged into the labor ranks of Jaffa with the same gusto he had exhibited in Plonsk. Repeating a pattern he had launched in the city of his birth, he established a string of about a dozen miniunions in Jaffa embracing tailor, shoemaking, and carpenter shops. He also was a major participant in a strike at a winery touched off by the firing of workers.

When he entered Jerusalem in 1910 at the age of twenty-four, David's initial Practical Zion phase was over as he thrust himself with determination into labor activity, seeking to unite labor groups both young and old. It was during this phase that he renamed himself Ben-Gurion after Josef Ben-Gurion, the democratic leader of the revolt against the Romans in 66 A.D.

While he was settling into the full-time roles of labor leader, Zionist spokesman, and pamphleteer, Ben-Gurion retained his bedrock belief in the necessity of attachment to the soil. The vehicle for such attachment, of coalescing the efforts of Jews for a common purpose, was that of the kibbutz.

In order to trace the Jewish institution of the kibbutz to its origin, it is necessary to examine the interesting life of Aaron David Gordon, a utopian whose apoliticism was far removed from the highly political Ben-Gurion. Whereas Ben-Gurion sought to make the kibbutz an extension of the Zionist political agenda, Gordon embraced the concept from an ethereal viewpoint. Born in 1856, Gordon lived a mundane life in the Russian village of Trayance, where he worked as a cashier, until an abrupt departure from detail in 1903 altered his life irrevocably. After marrying, raising a family, and having established roots in his community, Gordon suddenly gathered his meager belongings and emigrated to Palestine. Initially he settled in Tel Aviv. When he did not find that city to his liking, he founded the first genuine kibbutz in Galilee. Known as Dagania, it is recognizable to Middle East historians as the birthplace of future Israeli military hero and defense minister Moshe Dayan. In Dagania, Gordon resumed his life as a worker and cashier, along with writing and teaching.

When one examines Gordon's beliefs, a marked similarity emerges between his thinking and that of the American transcendentalists of the mid-nineteenth century, Henry David Thoreau and Ralph Waldo

Emerson. The cornerstone of Gordon's belief was humankind's one-ness with nature, which appealed to Diaspora Jews emerging from crowded ghettos into a stimulating breath of fresh air. "Man cannot live without nature any more than a fish can live without water," Gordon wrote. "A fish out of water misses the burden of water, the challenge of the pressure."[38]

It was Gordon's devout belief that Jews had become historical pariahs because they had not been allowed to return to nature, whence they had originated. It was consequently necessary for Jews to curtail the city concept of the Diaspora in Palestine and fuse with nature. This belief was also expounded with conviction by Gordon's protégé Berl Katznelson, who would later meet and form a comradeship with Ben-Gurion. It is readily cognizable why Ben-Gurion was attracted to the thinking of Gordon and Katznelson, because it dovetailed with his Practical Zion concept of returning to the soil and carving out the seeds of a nation in the manner that their Jewish forebears had done two thousand years earlier.

As in the case of Ben-Gurion, Gordon's philosophy was anchored to the twin symbols of work and labor:

> We must emancipate the land and create a new [Jewish] culture. Our structure is founded on labor and work. Labor is our national task. . . .
> We must work with our hands, in the crafts, in the trades, from the most skilled to the coarsest. Labor is one of the most fundamental elements of life.[39]

Through working the land and developing new identities by creating with their hands in Palestine, Jews would forge a culture of their own. The cultural center through which such efforts emanated was the kibbutz, in which communal activity would further Jewish pride and stimulate creativity.

To Ben-Gurion, the sustaining force of Zionism was the pioneering efforts of its new settlers from the Diaspora. Contrasting emphases grew up between Ben-Gurion and political Zionists on the question of effectiveness: the issue of who was best symbolizing the Zionist movement. In referring to his spirited journeys of the 1920s in which he addressed Jewish citizens in England, Europe, and the United States, Ben-Gurion outlined his deep convictions on the subject of what Practical Zionism in general and kibbutz living in particular embodied:

During those years [1920], I also found myself as a representative of
Palestine labour . . . I do not say that Zionist leaders in the Diaspora were
opposed to use . . . They were positively proud of the work that was
being done in the country—most of which indeed was financed by the
funds they raised—and the kibbutz to them was something of a showcase
of Zionism, the symbol of idealism in which they could take vicarious
pride. But I felt that deep down they believed that whatever rights would
be secured in Palestine for the Jewish people would be gained less through
our practical pioneering work than through political negotiations with and
pressure on . . . governments. We . . . believed that they were secondary
to the task of development in Palestine. You may say this was just a
question of emphasis, of priorities; but I think it went deeper than that.
We on our side were convinced that unless we extended our physical
settlement of the land, the most eloquent and energetic political
aporoaches . . . would come to naught; and that in fact physical achievement was the weightiest political argument and the one to which . . .
governments would pay most heed.[40]

During the period just prior to the outbreak of World War One, Ben-
Gurion made one last attempt to undertake a formal college education
when he went to study law at the University of Constantinople. It was
there that he met a fellow Zionist with whom he developed a fondness
for debate. It was the beginning of a long association with Moshe
Shertok, who many years later would succeed Ben-Gurion as prime
minister and serve with distinction under him as one of his chief party
stalwarts. Though Ben-Gurion distinguished himself in his pursuit of
the law, which he felt would provide him with a beneficial reservoir of
knowledge in his labor work, his education was brought to a halt with
the outbreak of the war.

As the war broke out, Ben-Gurion stated his preference for a strong
Turkey as an alternative to Russia, with which the Ottoman Empire
was doing battle. He detested Russia for the czarist regime's hatred of
the Jews.

Up to then, the Jewish community had enjoyed a reasonable level of
tolerance by Turkish government officials, but the situation would
dramatically and cataclysmically change for Ben-Gurion and his people
with the Ottoman Empire's launching of a Jihad, or holy war, against
"infidels." The results of the Jihad and its impact on the Arab
community were described in detail in the previous chapter. Ben-
Gurion watched with mounting concern as Jews were victimized along
with Arabs.

Finally, an event occurred that infuriated Ben-Gurion to his very core. Five hundred Jews were expelled from Palestine. Ben-Gurion believed that he must speak out, irrespective of what the personal consequences might be. So did his colleague Yitzhak Ben-Zvi, with whom he edited a local Zionist newspaper, *Ahdut*. Ben-Gurion and Ben-Zvi protested the Turkish government's conduct against the five hundred deported Jews, which brought a swift response on the part of Ottoman authorities, who deported journalists Ben-Gurion and Ben-Zvi from Palestine on March 21, 1915.

Ben-Gurion and Ben-Zvi left together for New York, which would be the setting in another valuable phase in the development of Ben-Gurion in the Zionist movement and would see him take a major step in his personal life. Prior to his arrival in the United States, Ben-Gurion had operated to some extent in the shadow of his colleague Ben-Zvi, much like Weizmann had begun his early Zionist period in deference to Leo Motzkin. As Ben-Gurion toured the United States speaking out for the cause of Zionism, he began to come out from under Ben-Zvi's shadow and become his own man, a forceful advocate of a historic movement he stressed with the same sense of inevitability with which he had advanced it in Europe and Palestine.

On the personal level, Ben-Gurion found himself a wife, but before the events behind that story are told, it is imperative to dig deeper into his background, which gives clues to comprehending this highly complex man. The young woman he had seemed destined to marry from his boyhood in Plonsk was Rachel Nelkin. Though she was but nine years old when he first met her, Rachel was already regarded by many boys as "the prettiest girl in Plonsk."[41] A tall girl with striking dark eyes and black braided hair, she had a shy, gentle nature reminiscent of David's mother. In addition, Rachel Nelkin was a committed Zionist who had been on the boat that carried Ben-Gurion to Palestine. He was profoundly attracted to her, feelings that Rachel reciprocated, so it appeared strange, at least on the surface, that David would periodically withdraw and demonstrate diffident behavior just when it appeared that he was on the verge of winning the girl of his dreams. The erratic behavior was certainly recognized by Rachel, by no means a young woman devoid of other prospects, who eventually married another man.

Once Rachel had married and begun to raise a family, the logical conclusion to reach was that Ben-Gurion, realizing that he had lost his chance to marry her, would leave well enough alone. Instead, he periodically pined for her, to Rachel's chagrin. At a time when she was married with two children, Ben-Gurion wrote her a letter imploring her to leave her husband and join him with her two children. She refused to respond.

At another time, after he had returned from a national tour and had been pining for Rachel when he was alone, he met a young nurse named Paula Munweiss (originally Monbas) at the home of his friend and party colleague Dr. Samuel Ellsberg, at whose clinic the young lady was employed. In a Hollywood movie or a romantic novel one would expect Ben-Gurion to be swept off his feet and, having met the true woman of his dreams, cease his morose longings for Rachel, the married woman residing in Palestine. In actuality, another set of circumstances developed. Ben-Gurion found Paula to be reasonably desirable, but not in the all-consuming manner that Rachel had dominated his mind and emotions. The two had decidedly little in common. Ben-Gurion, apart from the fiery image stemming from his political confrontations, was an introspective intellectual with a passion for reading. Paula cared little for books and was emphatically extroverted, to the point of asking embarrassing questions and uttering outrageous comments.[42]

Meeting Ben-Gurion, while producing no hot romantic sparks within Paula, nonetheless generated impact to the point of historical prescience on the part of the gregarious nurse. Years later she would reveal to her elder daughter, Geula, her feelings about the man she married. Her first impression of him was that of a "refugee."[43] "No looks and no attractiveness, shabbily dressed, and his eyes watering badly," Paula related to her daughter about Ben-Gurion, "but when he proposed to me I knew I would be marrying a great man."[44]

Paula endeared herself to Ben-Gurion because she was a compassionate nurse who cared for mothers and children and had maternal instinct.[45] In such a lonely period, in a strange new country far from his home in Palestine, and at a time when he longed for security and attention and thought sadly about the woman of his dreams, who had married another man, it is understandable why and how he could become drawn to Paula.

The subject of far greater complexity was why Ben-Gurion, with an opportunity to marry the woman for whom he had passionately longed, had apparently withdrawn from that relationship, had pursued her after she had married, and then later married a woman with whom he seemed to have much less in common than with Rachel Nelkin. Although one could contend that such a riddle can be explained by the unpredictabilities of romance, in which passion and fortuity hold great sway and logic is often left far behind, another possibility emerges, one that fits within the framework of Ben-Gurion's lifelong commitment.

David Ben-Gurion believed that it was his responsibility as a man to marry and raise a family. At the same time, the specter of the "jealous mistress" in whose permanent shadow he would forever respectfully tread, that of Zionism, remained pervasive. The question was how to reconcile the two commitments. Knowing the tenacious durability of Ben-Gurion's commitment to Zionism, we might surmise that the jealous mistress syndrome frightened him off at a time when Rachel Nelkin was available for a commitment but that later, when he may have psychologically realized that his efforts would bear no fruit, he then made an effort to achieve a relationship. On the other hand, although Paula afforded desirable companionship and the prospect of being an attentive mother to his children, given her nursing instincts, at the same time he would not be driven to the same level of passion to which Rachel could lift him. On one occasion, long after he had married Paula, Ben-Gurion revealed his feelings to Rachel during an unguarded moment: "If I had married you, I would not leave home as often as I do now."[46] Although undeniably a testament to Rachel's permanent hold on David Ben-Gurion's emotions, the admission can also be seen as a possible reason why the Zionist leader married Paula instead of Rachel. The one thing that was necessary in order to further the Zionist cause was to spend less time at home and intensify his efforts to achieve his objective. Even as he proposed to Paula, he informed her that commitment to his life's goal must come first. He warned her that it would soon be necessary for them to move to Palestine, where they would be without electricity, gas, or motorized transport.[47]

At 11 A.M. on December 5, 1917, Ben-Gurion and Paula were married at the Municipal Building across from New York's City Hall. No sooner was the ceremony completed than he glanced at his watch, hastily excused himself, and left for a party meeting. Paula left to return to her job at the clinic. With characteristic Ben-Gurion brevity, and with his marked disdain for ceremony, that night he sat down at his desk and recorded the event in his diary: "At 11:30 A.M. I was married."[48]

The fervor of the Ben-Gurion commitment to Zionism caused guilt pangs to surface within the Jewish leader later as his son Amos was growing up. His sensitive awareness of his neglect of Amos, along with his favoritism toward Amos's sister, Renana, caused Ben-Gurion to state, "Amos, when I am old, the one thing I'll regret is that I didn't pay enough attention to you in your early life. But I have a mission to perform and I cannot divide my attention. So please, Amos, try to reduce the burden that I shall feel when I am old."

The son was deeply moved by his father's troubled revelation, to which he responded, "Don't worry, Father, I'll find my way. You go ahead with your mission."[49]

As war clouds gathered prior to World War One, Chaim Weizmann became an increasingly larger force in both the British and international Zionist movements. Eventually those efforts would bear fruit and propel Ben-Gurion and the rest of the Zionist movement into a state of euphoria. The achievement resulted, as is typical in the realm of diplomatic triumphs, from certain actions that were carefully calculated to combine with the fortuitous sweep of historic movement.

In addition to the valuable contact channel Charles Dreyfus afforded in assisting Weizmann's effort to meet top British political figures such as Balfour and Churchill, Weizmann received an inestimable additional boost by winning the friendship and support of one of Britain's most influential journalists. Charles Prestwich Scott served as editor of the prestigious political intellectual journal the *Manchester Guardian*. Scott believed devoutly in the Zionist cause. In addition to manifesting that conviction in print, he proved more than willing to promote the cause throughout Britain's leadership ranks while creating opportunities for Weizmann to do the same.

Not only was Weizmann etching a place for himself in the British social and intellectual firmament, but also he was pushing relentlessly forward in the World Zionist Organization. The Tenth Zionist Congress, held June 27–29, 1910, saw him score a dramatic breakthrough. He had been in opposition to the leadership of David Wolffsohn, spokesman for the old Zionist movement embodied by Herzl's supporters, who, opposing change, resisted the efforts of the Practical Zionists, on whose behalf Weizmann lobbied. When additional support for the Weizmann position was gained throughout the increasingly restless ranks, Wolffsohn observed which way the political winds were blowing and resigned, resulting in a vindication of Weizmann's position. This meant that for the first time, extending back to his earliest days in the movement when he assiduously lobbied on behalf of the Democratic Faction and when the Herzlians constituted a substantial majority, he was no longer in the role of the angry and assertive young man arguing for change from a minority position. With the resignation of Wolffsohn, he moved from the minority to the majority in the Zionist ranks.

The most important step that Weizmann made in advancing the international cause of Zionism during the World War One period was enabled not through his efforts on the political front but through his work in the field of chemistry. What with Britain immersed in war, a significant area of military focus was one concerning firepower—how to get the maximum result from gunpowder at the minimal cost. In this vital area, Weizmann shone like a beacon, to the gratitude of the British leadership.

The War Office of the British government was vitally concerned about the great expense involved in firepower, and the chemical fermentation process proposed by Weizmann would reduce the large quantities of acetone and butyl alcohol used in firing rounds of ammunition. The British situation had become dangerous in the military sphere due to an unprecedented shortage of acetone, an essential ingredient in the manufacture of cordite, the propellent explosive used by British forces. The Weizmann process aided the British war effort in two basic respects: (1) if used in the correct proportions, the chemicals in the fermentation process increased the smokeless quality of the gunpowder, and (2) the process had the effect of lowering the temperature of the explosion, thus reducing the erosion of gun barrels and making possible the firing of more rounds per barrel.

Weizmann's invention moved him to the front ranks of the British war effort. In the autumn of 1915, eleven years after he had moved from Geneva to Manchester, he moved to London to work in the War Department laboratories. By October, he was installed in an impressive leased residence on Addison Road, just west of Holland Park. Vera joined him along with their young son Benji, who had been born in 1907. Another son, Michael, was born in the Addison Road residence in 1916. During the period between his London arrival in September and the move to Addison Road, he shared a bachelor flat with Vladimir Jabotinsky, one of the most colorful figures of the Zionist movement, with whom both Weizmann and Ben-Gurion would engage in later clashes. Like Ben-Gurion, Jabotinsky had been deported by Ottoman authorities from Palestine. Relocating to London, the fiery, impassioned Jabotinsky had forcefully advocated the creation of a Jewish Legion to take up arms on behalf of Britain against the hated Turks in Palestine.

Despite the favorable opportunities potentially opening up to Weizmann through his work with the British War Office, where he was appointed honorary technical adviser on acetone supplies to the Admiralty, he moved with a measure of wariness at the outset, because he was traveling in new territory. Yes, he had met some prominent British politicians in the past and had distinguished himself in the Mayfair salon social circuit during his London excursions from Manchester, but now he was learning a new game, how to make your mark in the Whitehall circuit and comprehending the personalities forging the policies in those rows of gray buildings situated near the Thames in the shadows of the Houses of Parliament and Big Ben. His colleague Charles Prestwich Scott of the *Manchester Guardian* provided helpful assistance in that area.

Not only did Weizmann gain the advantage of visibility along with the opportunity to move in vital British power circles as a result of his valuable invention, but also he gained distinct advantage for himself and the Zionist cause by the results surrounding the period before and after the invention, which brought about certain changes in the British governmental hierarchy. The shell shortage, which Weizmann's fermentation process helped to eliminate, wrought changes in the government as Prime Minister Herbert Henry Asquith's Liberal administration toppled in May 1915. The Weizmann process ensured a cheap and plentiful supply of acetone, causing the acetone production figures in Britain to jump following implementation of Weizmann's invention, and events in government affairs resulted in the installation, as prime minister, of a staunch ally of Zionism who made Weizmann's efforts more fundamentally realizable. On December 6, 1916, King George V summoned David Lloyd George, asking him to form a new government because the wartime coalition government had reached a crisis stage. Lloyd George immediately assumed the mantle of power and would remain there until October 1922.

With Lloyd George occupying the office of prime minister, Weizmann had an ally in the highest position of authority in the leading commercial and military empire in the world at that time. His old friend Lord Balfour had provided beneficial assistance in the past, but it must be remembered that, whereas Balfour's efforts had begun after his days as prime minister were over and at a time when his influence had long passed its zenith, in Lloyd George, Weizmann had an ally at the very peak of his power and influence.

A quick examination of Lloyd George's roots can furnish understanding of his sympathies toward Zionism. Though born and raised in Manchester, Lloyd George was descended from an old Welsh family, and had early internalized the maxims of Welsh nationalism. As a nonconformist intrigued by the Jewish survivalist message of Zionism, he felt empathy toward the Zionist position as a result of coming from an element of British life removed from the major power vortex of London. Just as he had sought to put the cause of Wales on the political map of England, he could understand the efforts of Weizmann and his allies to seek a Jewish state in Palestine. His philosophical posture, despite original background differences, shares a basic similarity with other Zionist sympathizers of upper-class origin, such as Lord Balfour and Winston Churchill. Those prominent, establishment politicians of Christian Protestant beliefs felt that the Christian heritage of which they were a part owed a debt of gratitude to the Jewish tradition, from which Christianity had evolved, taking liberally from Judaism's literature and teachings. The cycle becomes complete when it is recognized that Islam has borrowed liberally from both the Judaic and Christian religious traditions, the difference being the tragic enmity that nonetheless transpired between Arabs and only the Jews.

Weizmann's newspaper ally Charles Prestwich Scott lobbied Lloyd George before Lloyd George succeeded to the prime minister's position. The future prime minister met Weizmann at one of his working breakfasts in January 1915. Also there was Herbert Samuel, the first practicing Jew ever to sit in a British cabinet, who would later play a major role in Middle East history as high commissioner of Palestine. Weizmann made a favorable impression on Lloyd George during the meeting, after which he prophesied to Samuel, "When you and I are forgotten, this man will have a monument to him in Palestine."[50]

With Lloyd Geroge favorably disposed toward Zionism and surrounded by cabinet ministers of similar mind, Weizmann had a glittering opportunity to rise to the surface as a major mover in British political circles. Not only did he continue to be consulted in scientific matters, but also he was even entrusted with diplomatic responsibilities. He was sent as chief British representative on a secret diplomatic mission to Gibraltar in July 1917.

On the international front, Lloyd George trained his sights on Palestine. His romantic instinct, honed by biblical study, merged with his political instinct to seize an advantage en route to winning a war as talk about a Jewish legion, the brain child of Vladimir Jabotinsky, became more prevalent.

It was in this climate that the Balfour Declaration became an accomplished reality. It came in the form of a November 2, 1917, letter sent from Foreign Minister Balfour to Lord Rothschild, head of the British branch of the celebrated Jewish family. The declaration, which Lord Balfour stated had been approved by the Cabinet, read as follows:

His Majesty's Government view with favour the establishment in Palestine of a National Home for the Jewish people, and will use their best endeavours to facilitate the achievement of this object, it being clearly understood that nothing shall be done which may prejudice the civil and religious rights of the existing non-Jewish communities in Palestine, or the rights and political status enjoyed by Jews in any other country.

In the period following presentation of the Balfour Declaration, a theory emerged that the action on the part of the British cabinet amounted to a quid pro quo in which Weizmann's great contribution to the British war effort through his acetone formula was rewarded by his grateful benefactors. When the Balfour Declaration is taken in concert with events that transpired before its disclosure, this theory must be dismissed as oversimplification. Weizmann rejected it with the assertion "History does not deal in Aladdin's lamps."[51] In fact, as will be discussed, Weizmann himself expressed dissatisfaction with the final wording of what amounted to the third basic draft, though he rejoiced in the overall import of the document.

The Balfour Declaration was the final product of heavy lobbying on the part of Weizmann and others not only with the British but also on an international scale. It constituted a historical mosaic pieced together through a combination of favorable historical circumstances and zealous cultivation of the end result. Without the existence of either of the components—historical circumstances and intensive internally directed activities—the Balfour Declaration would not have become an accomplished reality on November 2, 1917.

Weizmann summarized the effort as follows.

It was an extraordinary struggle that developed within English Jewry in the half-year which preceded the issuance of the Balfour Declaration—a struggle which probably had no historic parallel anywhere. Here was a people which had been divorced from its original homeland for eighteen centuries, putting in a claim for restitution. The world was willing to listen, the case was being sympathetically received, and one of the great Powers was prepared to lead in the act of restitution, while the others had indicated their benevolent interest. And a well-to-do, contented and self-satisfied minority, a tiny minority, of the people in question rose in rebellion against the proposal, and exerted itself with the utmost fury to prevent the act of restitution from being consummated.[52]

Dedicated as he was to the establishment of a Jewish nation in Palestine, Weizmann knew that a written declaration favoring a Jewish homeland in Palestine would carry little if any intrinsic significance unless it was accompanied by practical authority on the part of the nation making the declaration. He therefore sought to see to it that Britain was in a position to deliver on any promise it put into writing. Weizmann unleashed Zionist lobbying efforts designed to prevent a condominium between Great Britain and any other nation from occurring on the logical premise that having to appeal effectively to two masters was substantially more difficult than one, particularly since the one was a nation whose then governing leadership was sensitive to Zionist aspirations. The Zionists let their opposition be known to any condominium pairing Britain with either the United States or France.

The Zionist cause was aided during that period by the emergence of Weizmann's friend and confidante Lord Balfour, in his position as foreign secretary. Since Balfour had all along favored Zionist aims, he was lobbied once more on a trip to Washington, D.C., in April 1917, later in the same month that the United States entered the war. Louis D. Brandeis was the conduit to make contact with. The then head of Zionist efforts in the United States was asked by Weizmann to make the case for antiannexation regarding Palestine. In a letter written to Brandeis on April 23, three days after Balfour's arrival in Washington, Weizmann framed the issue accordingly: ". . . Whereas, in my opinion, Great Britain would not agree to a simple annexation of Palestine, and it does not desire any territorial expansion, it would certainly support and protect a Jewish Palestine. This is why American support for this scheme is so valuable at the present stage."[53]

Later, a clash would develop between Weizmann and Brandeis that would rock Zionist circles in the United States, but at that crucial pre–Balfour Declaration juncture the two men were united in purpose and commitment. Brandeis set out to make a favorable impression on Balfour and succeeded. A distinguished lawyer, Brandeis had the ear of President Woodrow Wilson, which Weizmann certainly recognized. It was Louis Brandeis who had drafted crucial antitrust legislation that President Wilson had sponsored, then shepherded through Congress to passage. Afterward, Brandeis was appointed an Associate Justice to the U.S. Supreme Court by Wilson. A decade earlier Chaim Weizmann had made a favorable impression on Balfour, and now it was Brandeis's turn to register a comparable impression. Balfour's niece and biographer Blanche Dugdale related that her uncle had confided to an associate that Brandeis, ". . . was in some ways the most remarkable man he had met in the United States."[54]

Also on the international front, Weizmann sent trusted emissary

Nahum Sokolow to France and Italy to state the Zionist case to representatives of the French Government, in the course of which he met with Georges Picot, who had been cosponsor with Sir Mark Sykes of the British Foreign Office of the Sykes-Picot Agreement, and to representatives of the Vatican in Rome. In the first case, the focus was on political concerns; in the case of the Vatican, the subject was Roman Catholic Church interests regarding holy sites in Jerusalem.

As president of the British Zionist Federation, Weizmann led the effort to secure a declaration of support vis-à-vis Palestine with a major push beginning in the spring of 1917. On May 20, at a special conference of delegates from the Zionist societies of Great Britain that was held in London, Weizmann delivered a warning that the Zionist initiative was about to be confronted with stern opposition. Four days later, on May 24, a long statement was published in the *London Times* as a joint effort by David L. Alexander and Claude G. Montefiore, both leaders of the Conjoint Committee, which opposed Zionist efforts in Palestine and adhered to an assimilationist position. The statement in turn triggered a sharply focused editorial debate involving prominent members of both camps and including a sharp rebuttal to the Alexander-Montefiore letter on May 28 by Weizmann himself. Weizmann and his allies were pleased that the editorial position of the *Times* was supportive of Zionism.

While Weizmann was away in Gibraltar on his earlier mentioned secret mission for the British war effort, the Zionist Political Committee prepared a draft declaration of support for its Palestine objective, which it contended was in harmony with the previously expressed sentiments of leading members of the British Government. Lord Rothschild made it available to Balfour. It read as follows:

His Majesty's Government, after considering the aims of the Zionist Organization, accept the principle of recognizing Palestine as the National Home of the Jewish people and the right of the Jewish people to build up its national life in Palestine under a protection to be established at the conclusion of peace, following upon the successful issue of the war.

His Majesty's Government regard as essential for the realization of this principle the grant of internal autonomy to the Jewish nationality in Palestine, freedom of immigration for Jews, and the establishment of a Jewish National Colonizing Corporation for the re-establishment and economic development of the country.

The conditions and forms of the internal autonomy and a Charter for the Jewish National Colonizing Corporation should, in the view of His

Majesty's Government, be elaborated in detail and determined with the representatives of the Zionist Organization.[55]

When the proposed Zionist formula was presented to the War Cabinet for consideration, strong opposition was mounted by Edwin Montagu. When he finished his presentation, Lloyd George and Balfour both suggested that Weizmann be called in for a response. The messengers sent to locate him were unsuccessful even though, as it turned out, he was at that moment in the office of War Cabinet member W. G. A. Ormsby-Gore only a few doors away. In retrospect, Weizmann deemed it a favorable fortunity that he had not been found, reasoning, "I might, in that setting, with Montagu in front of me, have said something harsh or inappropriate. I might have made matters worse instead of better."[56]

Despite the chagrin of Weizmann, who felt that the British Government was paying disproportionate attention to what he termed "a handful of assimilated Jews,"[57] the formula proposed by the Zionists was amended. Because the British Government was then involved in conducting a war, it is likely that, despite the pro-Zionist tendencies of most British Cabinet members, an attitude of compromise prevailed to prevent as much disharmony as possible under the circumstances. The leading government figures, most assuredly, remained mindful of the strong feelings on both sides of the Zionist issue.

The next version that was presented to Weizmann and his Zionist allies contained the following language.

His Majesty's Government view with favour the establishment in Palestine of a National Home for the Jewish race and will use their best endeavours to facilitate the achievement of this object, it being clearly understood that nothing shall be done which may prejudice the civil and religious rights of the existing non-Jewish communities in Palestine, or the rights and political status enjoyed in any other country by such Jews who are fully contented with their existing nationality and citizenship.[58]

Although Weizmann expressed disappointment over what he termed a "painful recession" from what the government was prepared to offer, he nonetheless deemed any favorable statement embodying the Jewish Palestine question to be superior to none at all. His disappointment stemmed from two parts of the revised statement. Whereas the initial version recommended by the Zionist leadership declared, "Palestine should be reconstituted as the National Home of the Jewish people," the revised statement spoke of "the establishment in Palestine of a National Home for the Jewish Race." Weizmann's second objection concerned the introduction of the subject of the "civic and religious rights of the existing non-Jewish communities" in a manner he felt imputed possible oppressive intentions to the Jews. Further, he believed that such wording could be interpreted as limiting Zionist work to the point of crippling it.

When the statement was considered by the War Cabinet on October 4, the anti-Zionists were given the exclusive opportunity to present their objections to a Palestine declaration. It was decided to send the text to eight Jews—four Zionists and four anti-Zionists—for comments and suggestions. Weizmann recommended two changes, stating a preference for the word "reestablishment" rather than "establishment" of a Jewish National Home out of deference to Jewish initial Holy Land roots. Also, by way of a suggestion from Louis Brandeis, Weizmann recommended that the term "Jewish people" should replace that of "Jewish race."

The version of the Balfour Declaration adopted on November 2 was only slightly modified from the second draft. The word "establishment" in connection with a National Home for the Jews in place of Weizmann's proposed "reestablishment" remained. The term "Jewish people" replaced "Jewish race." The final portion of the second draft was left out of the adopted declaration, deleting the words "by such Jews who are fully contented with their existing nationality and citizenship."

Once the final text of the Balfour Declaration had been approved by the cabinet, Sir Mark Sykes physically brought the document outside to Weizmann, where he was waiting.

"Dr. Weizmann, it's a boy!"[59] Sykes exclaimed.

Weizmann's initial response was, "Well, I did not like the boy at first. He was not the one I had expected. But I knew that this was a great departure."

The Balfour Declaration was greeted with triumphant acclaim by Jews throughout the world. The psychological fervor was understandable in that it marked the first official statement by a leading government of the world about Jewish rights to a Palestine homeland in the almost two thousand years since the destruction of the Jewish state in 70 A.D.

In the United States, a euphoric David Ben-Gurion saw the Balfour Declaration as grounds to alter his position on the war. He had opposed Vladimir Jabotinsky's call for a Jewish legion to fight for Great Britain due to his hatred of czarist Russia as well as his fear that doing battle with the Turks would result in repression by the Ottoman Empire against Jews in the Yishuv. Now conditions had changed, and Ben-Gurion saw himself come full circle to embrace Jabotinsky's position. The triumph of the Bolsheviks in Russia had supplanted the czarist regime in Russia, that dark symbol of pogroms and aggressive anti-Semitism that Ben-Gurion detested with every ounce of his conviction. The advent of the Young Turks brought repression against Jews and Arabs alike in Palestine. Then, with Britain's announcement of the Balfour Declaration, Ben-Gurion's mind was made up. The post-Balfour euphoria carried Ben-Gurion all the way to marriage, and the ceremony took place on December 5, just four weeks after the Balfour Declaration.

With the Balfour Declaration a fait accompli, two names became thrust into positions of acclaim. For Chaim Weizmann it meant recognition in international Jewish ranks as the preeminent figure in Zionist politics. It would not be long, just three years, before he would wear the mantle once held by the great Theodor Herzl as president of the World Zionist Organization. For Arthur James Balfour, who served only briefly as prime minister, his service as Britain's Foreign Secretary in the crucial World War One period brought him much distinction when Lloyd George utilized his expertise on the international scene to his best advantage. As for his association with the Balfour Declaration, the hotly debated historical document that bears his name, former Prime Minister Harold Wilson, who would grapple with Middle Eastern issues in the sixties and seventies, stated the following about Balfour and the declaration:

> By one Middle Eastern nation, and the Jewish community throughout the world, Balfour's name is still held in reverence. It was the Balfour Declaration of 1917 which designated Palestine as "a national home for the Jews." His successors as Foreign Secretary and Prime Minister, right up to this day, have been invited to Israel to make the annual speech at the Balfour Declaration commemoration dinner. When he signed the declaration—and some attributed it to Dr. Chaim Weizmann's contribution to the war effort in relation to the production of acetone—he might have thought of it as no more than the signature of a Foreign Office draft, though his friendship with Weizmann went back many years. Nevertheless, after he ceased to be an active politician, he looked back on the declaration as one of the most important events of his career.[60]

While the fait accompli of the Balfour Declaration embodied a great deal more than rewarding Weizmann for his acetone formula, which had enormously aided the British war effort, it was the Zionist leader's efforts in chemistry research, which provided accessibility to the British power structure. By leaving Manchester and going to London to continue his laboratory work, he developed access to Britain's most prominent leaders, from the prime minister on down. Weizmann's successes on the Whitehall ministerial circuit were in turn bolstered by the ascension of Prime Minister Lloyd George and Foreign Secretary Balfour into key positions of authority from which they could render meaningful assistance in helping to fulfill Weizmann's objective of a statement of support for a Jewish state in Palestine. One by one, the pieces fell into place, with the Balfour Declaration emerging as the finished product of Zionist efforts. Though Chaim Weizmann would have preferred a more emphatic statement of commitment, the Balfour Declaration nonetheless provided the Zionist leadership with a tangible document from a leading power in support of its principal goal.

Once Allenby's troops had finished their work in Palestine and the Ottoman Empire had been routed, it was Great Britain that would assume the key element in the Palestine picture as Weizmann, Ben-Gurion, and others from the ranks of the committed Zionists sought to use the Balfour Declaration as a launching pad to achieve their dream of a Jewish state.

When the euphoria of the Balfour Declaration and the triumphs of World War One faded, the thorny dilemma of resolving the Palestine issue became agonizingly felt by the British, on whose shoulders the oppressive mantle of responsibility devolved, as well as by the two groups affected by their decisions, the Jews and the Arabs.

# 6

# The Battle Lines Are Drawn

It was during the post–Balfour Declaration period of ebullience that David Ben-Gurion decided that World War One was indeed a cause worth fighting for and that a freshly esteemed Great Britain, which had taken a prodigious step in his eyes toward fulfilling his grandest Zionist dreams, could work hand in hand with himself and others to achieve Jewish statehood.

Ben-Gurion wished to play a role in shaping British and Jewish destinies as a member of the newly formed Jewish Legion. Feelings of optimism grew in him as he prepared to become a part of that grand effort. Vladimir Jabotinsky had been correct after all in urging cooperation with Great Britain, and with the Balfour Declaration an accomplished reality, the basis existed to forge a Jewish nation. Other Zionists reacted identically. To these individuals who toiled in the vineyards to achieve their goal of a Jewish state, the effort had shifted gears and accelerated forward with intensity. Whereas earlier the focus in the Zionist community had been on a goal set far into a future immersed in hazy uncertainty, the impetus provided by the Balfour Declaration moved the Zionist effort up from some amorphous period in the future to a phase in which the foggy uncertainty had lifted and land could be sighted. With Britain now having committed itself to the ultimate objective of a Jewish homeland in Palestine, in the minds of these heady idealists, of whom Ben-Gurion stood in the forefront, it was now only a question of time before their goal would be accomplished.

As is inevitably the case when support is rendered on behalf of a cause heavily immerse in idealistic expectations, the visceral response, dictated heavily by emotion, runs distances ahead of the analytical process. With the surging adrenalin charge and heady air of idealistic accomplishment, this period must pass before the true realities are closely examined. A portentous warning that the future may not beckon with the early luminosity envisioned by enthusiastic Zionist adherents was sounded by none other than Chaim Weizmann, who was more actively involved in pre-Balfour negotiations than any other leader in the Zionist movement. It will be recalled that, in response to Sir Mark Sykes's disclosure concerning the Balfour Declaration, Weizmann felt a mixture of disappointment and satisfaction. After Sykes had broken the news in humanistic terms by saying, "Dr. Weizmann, it's a boy!" the Zionist leader's response can be broken down distinctly into two parts: (1) "Well, I did not like the boy at first. He was not the one I had expected," (2) "But I knew that this was a great departure." As to the first part of Weizmann's response, that which indicated the absence of unbridled satisfaction, it was doubtlessly stimulated by the failure in the carefully crafted language of the declaration both to spell out any time frame in which a Jewish homeland would become an established entity and to make any reference to the mechanics involved in achieving such a result. Nonetheless, as an accomplished diplomat who realized the necessity of patience as a component in the achievement of an objective, Weizmann recognized a "great departure" from previous British policy, and that alone provided a broad measure of satisfaction. As a patient and pragmatic realist in the field of foreign affairs, Weizmann was also inevitably aware of the myriad forces at work in Palestine as well as the rest of the world during an international conflict. To that end, he must have felt a keen measure of satisfaction at having achieved such a commitment at all, which he recognized as something to build on following the war's conclusion.

On a more pessimistic note regarding the future of a Jewish state, Weizmann inevitably recognized as well the circumstances under which the Balfour Declaration was proclaimed. Given the uncertainties arising during a world conflict, a nation battling for its very survival on the battlefields is disposed toward forwarding attractive proposals to achieve military and diplomatic assistance while reducing as many prospects as possible of incurring the added enmity of nations and peoples with whom it is not already in conflict. This established rubric would become even more pronounced in the case of Great Britain, long renowned for its diplomatic skills and standing at a zenith in world affairs eminence.

While Jewish Zionist adherents were reacting enthusiastically world-wide in the aftermath of the Balfour Declaration, a careful analysis of the language revealed superbly constructed legalese that afforded Great Britain significant room to maneuver at a later point in time.

The opening words of the Balfour Declaration—"His Majesty's Government view with favour the establishment of a National Home for the Jewish people"—contain cautionary language. The words "view with favour" fall short of the type of unequivocal declaration of support that could have been made. In addition, the phrase "National Home for the Jewish people" falls short of sponsorship of the creation of a Jewish state. Continuing on, the words "will use their best endeavours to facilitate the achievement of this object" avoid committing the British to achieving the objective while referring instead to "best endeavours,"which, like beauty, ultimately reside in the eye of the beholder. The next words in the declaration could certainly be read as a cautionary caveat, "it being clearly understood that nothing shall be done which may prejudice the civil and religious rights and political status enjoyed by Jews in any other country." A careful analysis of the declaration reveals that the strongest words in the document are the emphatic "nothing shall be done" respecting the rights of not only the Arab populace of Palestine but those of Jews in other nations in the political or religious spheres. The emphatic "nothing shall be done" expression conveys a message of prudence that one might expect of a nation at war that, while desiring to please one group, Jewish Zionists, at the same time judiciously seeks to avoid ruffling the feathers of anyone else both in and outside Palestine, Jews and non-Jews alike.

To broaden the overall picture surrounding the Balfour Declaration, it would be advisable to refer to Chapter Four and the disclosures being made to Arab leaders, whose efforts were being sought to aid the British cause in Palestine against the then controlling Ottoman Empire, which was allied with Germany. The single most valuble asset in the British propaganda arsenal in terms of generating a commitment on the part of the Arabs to Great Britain was the dashing, always enigmatic, perpetually charismatic T. E. Lawrence, who was taken into the hearts and minds of Arabs by becoming one of them and by fighting side by side with them under the scorching desert sun. It should be remembered that Lawrence's warfare experiences, dramatic and intense as they were, along with his subsequent brief endeavor into international affairs, terminated in bitter disillusionment on his part. His stated reason for joining the Arabs in battle was to see them achieve political freedom. After word of the Sykes-Picot Agreement reached his ears beyond the veil of secrecy, he reacted with a burning inner rage, feeling that the people he was asking to fight on behalf of his country, Great Britain, in order to achieve a noble goal were being deceived in the slippery arena of world politics.

When one examines actions taken so as to placate Zionists on the one hand and Arabs on the other on the part of a nation at war seeking to perform a perilous juggling act in a section of the world noted for its internal volatility, the Middle East, the ponderous difficulties that would befall Britain in Palestine at the close of World War One become manifest. The desire to satisfy two forces, Arabs and Jews, who had markedly divergent agendas, along with protecting its own interests in the entire Middle East region and seeking to avoid offending either group, propelled Great Britain along a dangerous collision course in which it risked being damned by one or both groups no matter which direction it took.

To examine the Balfour Declaration from the standpoint of international politics, particularly vis-à-vis its relationship between Zionism and Great Britain, it is necessary to begin by stating what the declaration was and by proceeding from there to examine what it was not. In terms of what the declaration represented, it embodied a vigorous infusion into the Zionist cause in the form of support from what was then the world's leading empire. For the first time in the approximately two-thousand-year Diaspora, a declaration had been rendered by a major power pledging support for the ultimate creation of a Jewish homeland. This conclusion may be reached by examining the Balfour Declaration in the most positive light from the Zionist point of view and by placing the most optimistic spin on language that, as aforestated, was cautionary. In terms of being considered as binding international law, the Balfour Declaration had no force. It embodied a manifestation on the part of Great Britain to support the principle of a Jewish homeland in Palestine. It could in no way be considered a present agreement relative to Palestine, which was then a part of the Ottoman Empire, and Turkey had not indicated any support for the expressed British position. Arthur Koestler aptly summarized the Balfour Declaration as "one nation solemnly promising to a second nation the country of a third."[1] Turkey, the nation then in control of Palestine, was not involved in any way in the declaration, nor was the majority Palestinian population connected to the negotiating process leading to the declaration's finalization. The central issue of the Balfour Declaration's intrinsic weakness was taken up by Balfour himself in a letter to the prime minister dated February 19, 1919:

> The weak point of our position is that in the case of Palestine we deliberately and rightly decline to accept the principle of self-determination. If the present inhabitants were consulted they would unquestionably give an anti-Jewish verdict. Our justification for our policy is that we regard Palestine as being absolutely exceptional; that we consider the question of the Jews outside Palestine as one of world importance and that we conceive the Jews to have an historic claim to a home in their ancient land; providing that home can be given them without either dispossessing or oppressing the present inhabitants.[2]

A careful reading of both the Balfour Declaration as well as its author's above quoted letter to the British prime minister underscores the balancing act that those favorably disposed toward the Zionist cause within Great Britain were seeking to achieve in an attempt to assist Zionist efforts without penalizing Arabs by invading their interests. The earlier described pogroms unleashed against Jews in Russia and Poland had stimulated a fervent desire to return to what they considered a natural point of residence, that of their forebears. As the numbers of immigrants increased, concern was touched off within the Arab community that the new waves of Jewish settlers would jeopardize their own political and economic interests. Both groups looked with increasing concern to Great Britain to act on their behalf, the Jews to continue a settlement process they deemed essential, the Arabs to terminate or substantially curtail that process to protect their rights.

The British role in Palestine was enough to tax the keenest of minds as Zionists and Arabs sought to advance their respective causes. A situation that was inherently perplexing in the first place became mind-boggling when an additional force entered the scene, which generated global pressure and promoted widespread volatility with special emphasis on an already problem-burdened Palestine.

As is often the case with an international political problem, in this case the respective rights of Arabs and Jews in Palestine, the outcome is ultimately influenced by an entirely new factor springing from outside that nation or area, an element that imposes change and accelerates tensions to an all-time high, burying events in a burning quicksand of uncertainty.

A humble German foot soldier was injured during World War One, prompting little if any attention at the time. In the war's aftermath, he fell into a rage, one that eventually turned into an all-consuming quest to restore to a new level of greatness the once proud nation for which he had fought. Despite a conspicuous lack of formal education and a marked propensity for historical, political, economic, and sociological oversimplification, he compensated for his deficiencies by exploiting his frustration over Germany's postwar plight, which was shared by so many Germans. What this angry foot soldier, who had been born and raised in Austria near the German border, lacked in formal education and finesse he made up for by broadcasting a message that many of the German people hungered to hear. His shrill message of unbridled nationalism, delivered in an electrifying manner by a charismatic speaker capable of bringing thousands instantly to their feet and transforming them through his volcanic speaking powers into instruments of his political purpose, rang in their ears again and again. Through systematic repetition, he transformed them into loyal followers of his cause. His magnetic speech-making powers were pointed at his most formidable weapon, one to be rhetorically exploited in the fullest measure, the hated Treaty of Versailles, the terms of which had been forced onto Germany. In his exhortations for a stirring rebirth of German spirit, he heaped furious blame on those responsible for bringing the nation he loved to its sad plight, with archenemy France, Germany's long-standing foe, heading the list of international culprits. His lengthy speeches, which often began under the afternoon sun and ended in the glow of torchlights, were a clever mixture of vituperation in which passionate hatreds were whipped to a frenzy and an exhortative national purpose in which German virtues were extolled to the zenith, harkening the presences of Wagner and Bismarck.

Not only was this frustrated Bavarian a powerful speaker, but he was also a brilliant organizer. His first attempt to overthrow the German government in what came to be known as the Beer Hall Putsch resulted in his being sent to jail. Rather than becoming discouraged from continuing his fervent political efforts, his time under incarceration only stirred his passions to an even greater height, prompting him to write an angry warning to the entire world in general and Germany in particular outlining a future course of action. *Mein Kampf*, or "My Struggle," was ignored by a complacent world for too long, and by the time that it reacted, the megalomaniac was in power and carrying out the very misadventures that, when described prospectively, had generated little more than ridicule and disbelief.

It is impossible to conjecture just how the Palestine dilemma would have been resolved had the megalomaniacal Adolf Hitler not entered the world political scene, leaving a legacy steeped in destruction and blood, but one thing remains certain in the minds of all who have studied Middle East politics—the emergence of Hitler as a force to be reckoned with and his gory role in the global conflict that followed changed forever the Palestine landscape and rendered any form of compromise that may have been otherwise possible between Jewish Zionist and Arab forces virtually impossible.

The British position in seeking to reconcile the often conflicting demands of Jews and Arabs in Palestine was difficult enough, but once Hitler and his German command decided upon the "Final Solution" in 1942 as a means of resolving the "Jewish problem," which had enraged him from the beginning, his bitter hatred for Jews and his linkage of anything Jewish to equally hated Marxism, the posture of the Zionist command slumped from that of advancing a political agenda to that of survival. With the object of the "Final Solution" that of exterminating Jewry from the face of the earth, thereby launching the Holocaust, the various wings of the Zionist movement, from left to right as well as the center, concentrated on the objective of saving as many of their brothers and sisters as possible from the hideous finality of Nazi gas chambers in overcrowded concentration camps. The Zionists sought to bring as many Jews as possible to Palestine at the very time when the British, battling for their own survival against Hitler's crack Nazi troops, could least afford any diversion from their central focus on crushing the Third Reich machine.

In the destructive political rubble that followed World War Two, one thing became certain—the question of Jewish survival and the accompanying quest for a Jewish homeland in the land of their forebears were seen in a totally different fashion from the way those issues had been considered before. Any analysis of Palestine and the equities existing between Jews and Arabs had to include the additional gut-wrenching element of the Holocaust and widespread decimation of the Jewish population of Europe.

The only certainty in international politics is underlying unpredictability governed by the impact of unanticipated human forces. In the case of Palestine, the intruding element of uncertainty that overpowered all forces and prevented any measure of stability from being realized came in the form of Adolf Hitler.

The viability of any political movement, given the uncertainties of intervening events and forces in international politics, is sustained only by the flexibility of its leadership in responding to the changes foisted upon it.

In the cases of Zionist leaders such as Weizmann, Ben-Gurion, and Jabotinsky, whose followers basked in the afterglow of the Balfour Declaration and the perceived promise it held for Jews striving to achieve a homeland in Palestine, they spent the next three decades, beginning with the adoption of the Balfour Declaration in 1917 and extending to the event-filled post–World War Two period involved careful concentration of the traumatic changes brought about by global pressures and responses to them, remaining always mindful of the goal that was indelibly imprinted in their minds. That same concentration in the wake of continuing changes to the world scene needed to be maintained by the Arabs, who hoped to achieve successes of their own. Both of these proud peoples embraced civilizations extending back to the beginnings of recorded history and were fervently dedicated to achieving political freedom and progress amidst changes engendered by two world conflicts.

The forces erupting on the world scene and which impinged upon the Middle East resulted in three basic historical periods, each of which played a vital role in forging changes in the area, forces which through a historical ripple effect impacted well into the future, where they continue to be felt today.

To understand the basic forces at work during this momentous thirty-year period, it is instructive to break it down into three historical intervals, each helping to shape future events.

1. The post-Balfour period, encompassing World War One and extending to the onslaught of Hitler and World War Two, began with both Jews and Arabs having high hopes for the future of their people. Jews were encouraged by the adoption of the Balfour Declaration, and Arabs were optimistic about promises made to them by Britain if they cooperated with the British in the war. In that the Arabs had helped the British to overrun the Turks and dislodge the Ottoman Empire under T. E. Lawrence, as detailed in an earlier chapter, they looked forward to being treated with favor by a conquering Great Britain at the end of the conflict. The goal sought by both the Jewish and Arab interests, that of a preeminent Great Britain overseeing events in Palestine, ultimately eventuated. Each expected favorable treatment by Great Britain under the terms of the Mandate Britain had received under the provisions of the Versailles Treaty. The era was characterized by strife between the two sides along with a great deal of jockeying to incur the favor of Great Britain, frequently through the use of protest, which often reached the level of violence.

2. The World War Two period was dominated by two important

factors: (1) the efforts of Great Britain to proceed with its war effort without antagonizing either the Jews or the Arabs and (2) the overriding influence of the Holocaust culminating in the "Final Solution," Hitler's diabolical plan to eliminate the Jewish population of Europe. Inevitably the political as well as the human ramifications of the Holocaust affected Britain's desire to avoid any diversionary entanglements on the Palestine front as it concentrated on turning back Hitler's massive military machine. As the Holocaust factor mushroomed and the "Final Solution" began to be implemented, an element of desperation emerged in which Jewish refugees, spurred on by humankind's most basic instinct, that of survival, sought to reach a safe haven in the land of their forebears, Palestine. As more Jews were executed and Hitler's objective became increasingly apparent, efforts were intensified through underground channels to rescue as many Jews as possible by sending them on boats to Palestine. This policy conflicted with immigration quotas that Great Britain had been imposed on Palestine. The quotas, hotly contested by elements of Parliament at the time of their imposition, including Winston Churchill, were ignored by Jews hoping to rescue their own people from death. The debate within British circles concerning the quotas intensified once more, and the government found itself in the unenviable posture of either overturning its own edict, and thus sowing seeds of discord within Arab ranks in the process, or refusing entry to political refugees trapped in the bleak wilderness of alienation and despair, many of whom had seen their entire family suffer brutal deaths in Nazi concentration camps. Britain was trapped by the converging cruel realities of international politics and put in a box from which there was no escape, one in which scorn and bitter opposition would follow in the wake of any decision that was made.

3.  The post–World War Two period represented the crucial juncture at which a mounting crisis came to a head, the vexing components of which reverberated through the entire international community of nations. Resolution of the difficult Palestine problem became a major objective of the newly created United Nations and as such a form of testing mechanism for it. Amidst much debate, the nations of the world weighed a variety of options. Great Britain, exhausted by many years of commitment to a Mandate that had resulted in many headaches and frustrations, along with virtually incessant criticisms by both Jews and Arabs, voluntarily handed the vexing question over to the United Nations, hoping that its newly operating machinery could bring resolution and stability to an area immersed in conflict. Each side sought

to win as many allies as possible to its cause, and through it all, much attention was fixed on two nations, the United States and the Soviet Union. The United States had emerged from the war as a nation of increasing influence in world power centers, particularly in the community of democratic nations. The Soviet Union had fought valiantly, sustaining more combat losses than any other nation as it helped the forces allied against Hitler to dramatically turn the tide of battle against the Nazi machine. Due to its geographical proximity to the Middle East, it demonstrated understandable concern about political activities in that area. To the surprise of many observers of international politics, the Soviet Union decided to support the Jewish position on behalf of the creation of the nation of Israel. The United States took the same position, but not until after a lengthy process highlighted by heated debate, the interesting ebb and flow of which will be discussed. Once the vote had gone in Israel's favor, it was clear to any perceptive observer, particularly Israel's first prime minister, David Ben-Gurion, that the new nation conceived by a vote of the fledgling United Nations would endure only through battle against the Arab forces challenging its claim to statehood. The bloody conflict that followed was only the first of many to be waged between the two forces. As anyone who follows current events is aware, the fundamental bases of this same, enduring conflict remain unresolved as the battle for the hearts and minds of the people of the world continues unabated. The conflict that rages today in the West Bank and Gaza Strip, as well as in heavily ravaged Beirut and elsewhere, needs to be examined within the unfolding roots of conflict emanating in the Middle East. The present study has examined the historical development of the Middle East and its peoples from the dawn of recorded history to the issuing of the Balfour Declaration and has provided a basis for understanding the roots of the individuals as well as the backgrounds from which they came, but the three periods of Middle East history extending from the Balfour Declaration to the birth of the state of Israel and the 1948 War of Independence that followed saw the positions of the respective parties, as well as the posture of Great Britain, the pivotal nation regarding activities in Palestine governing Arabs and Jews until the end of World War Two, overwhelmed by the boiling cauldron of rapidly developing international events.

Before beginning scrutiny of the unfolding activities in the period immediately following the Balfour Declaration, we would be wise to draw a distinction between the significance of the period extending from biblical times and the dawn of recorded history to the Balfour

Declaration and the three crucial phases emerging in 1917 and continuing up to the creation of Israel and the War of Independence in 1948. The lengthy pre-Balfour phase can be regarded essentially as that of historical and sociological evolution in Palestine, though politics undeniably played a role as well, as is inevitably the case with people throughout the world. The reason for distinguishing therefore between the pre-1917 and post-1917 phases involves the degree to which politics became a predominant consideration in the affairs of Palestine as well as the rest of the Middle East.

In sharp contrast to the historical phase that governed Middle East activities in the pre-Balfour period, the lives of Jews and Arabs were influenced by the same phenomenon that inevitably altered the courses of other nations throughout the world. Onrushing technological advances caused the world to shrink and gave rise to the inevitable interlinking of nations with an intimacy that had not previously been possible. Hitherto distant nations turned into neighbors, becoming far more closely tied together economically and politically than before. George Washington, when he delivered his Farewell Address before leaving office after serving eight years as America's first president, cautioned his fellow citizens about the country's need to "avoid foreign entanglements," which seemed like a sensible enough posture in 1796 and in fact a course that many nations preferred to follow, but the intervening century and two decades between then and the World War One period had seen an entirely new world created through the advances of machinery. As technology galloped into the twentieth century, it became virtually impossible for any nation of size or influence to avoid the inevitable, that of involvement through the interplay of forces in the international sphere. The historic transformation is evidenced by the differing course being pursued by America's President Woodrow Wilson during the eventful Balfour Declaration period of World War One, as opposed to George Washington's call for isolationism. Wilson saw the conflict as one to "make the world safe for democracy" and sought to prevent future conflicts through the creation of a League of Nations, in clear recognition of the need for implemented international order in a shrinking world filled with diversity.

It is easily understandable why the Middle East would loom as an increasingly important area in world politics within the framework of this rapidly shrinking world dominated by technological advancements. The rich oil resources of the area represented one factor that generated attention; the area's strategic location near major water routes was another. Then there was the always pervasive emotional response based on the area's historical connections to events and individuals of three major religious faiths—Judaism, Christianity, and Islam.

Chaim Weizmann was a brilliant diplomatic tactician, who realized the sweeping changes taking place within the world political community during the volatile World War One period and who, by becoming a British insider, had managed to secure from Britain a declaration of intent concerning a Jewish homeland. His air of sophistication and bon vivant manner made him a natural to lobby effectively both in drawing rooms and at the formal ministerial levels of government. Hence the best strategy for Weizmann to follow both personally and politically, given the vastness of Great Britain's international influence, was to continue playing his British trump card. What with Britain locked in the throes of World War One, the most notable contribution to be rendered on its behalf was to enlist Jews in the war effort. Weizmann supported Vladimir Jabotinsky's call for the creation of a Jewish Legion, which became a delicate issue both inside and outside Jewish circles. An understanding of the situation then existing within Britain reveals the seeds of controversy.

During the summer of 1917, there were approximately twenty thousand Russian Jews residing in Britain who would have been ordinarily subject to military service. But because they were not British subjects, they were not liable for conscription. Legislation, never implemented, was placed before Parliament that would offer these Russian Jews residing on British soil a choice to either serve in the British army or be deported to Russia to fight there. The proposal generated much controversy in that it seemed to be questioning by implication the loyalty of the Jewish community as a whole.

Finally a compromise was reached, with raised additional eyebrows, causing Weizmann to become further immersed in the Zionism versus assimilation struggle being concurrently waged in the momentous period shortly prior to the adoption of the Balfour Declaration. The War Office announced the information that a Jewish Legion had been created from volunteers. This independent fighting unit would comprise an infantry regiment carrying the Star of David as an identifying badge and be earmarked for action on the Palestine front.

The War Office decision in late July 1917 elicited a polarization of discontent, which made Weizmann feel morosely isolated. The cacophony of reactions embraced virtually every viewpoint of Zionist and anti-Zionist thought. Some critics asserted that by placing Jews in a separate category from Christian groups such as Catholics or Methodists it was being implied that the Jewish contribution to the war effort had been theretofore negligible and that, furthermore, Jews had had to be bribed into service. Others alleged that yet another concession had been made to the Zionist lobby. The one criticism that stung Weizmann above all others, however, came from his idol in the Zionist movement, Ahad Ha'am, who took umbrage with him on the entire Jewish Legion issue.

The rationale behind Ahad Ha'am's disapproval of the Jewish Legion concept once again underscored the disparity of viewpoints that was pervasive in Zionist ranks. As mentioned in the previous chapter, Weizmann was a protégé of Ahad Ha'am, who represented a father figure image for him within the Zionist movement. As the acknowledged formulator of Spiritual Zionism, Weizmann found much of value in his mentor's intimate identification with Jewish tradition extending back to those proud years of early history prior to the Diaspora. On the subject of Political Zionism, however, the initiative lay with Weizmann in pursuing the concepts of Theodor Herzl.

The father of Spiritual Zionism, mincing no words, informed Weizmann that, whereas it was advisable to have Jewish soldiers at the Palestine front, they should not operate in a separate Jewish regiment. He termed such an event to embody "an empty demonstration, the result of which may prove disastrous both to Palestinian and, generally, Turkish Jewry and to our future work in Palestine, if, after all, it is not occupied."[3]

Weizmann received his old friend's stern rebuke on August 17. That same day he announced his retirement from Zionist circles. When his retirement decision was confirmed two weeks later in letters to both Sokolow and Ahad Ha'am, the latter replied immediately, taking issue with Weizmann's decision.

> We never elected you and we cannot accept your resignation. Your personal qualities and external conditions have made you the symbol of Zionism in the eyes of the public. You were chosen by the conditions of life, and these conditions will dismiss you when the time comes, when full victory or defeat will render the continuation of your work no longer necessary. [Resignation would be] an act of treason [and] from a personal point of view . . . would be moral suicide."[4]

Weizmann's resignation was classified by his biographer Norman Rose as no more than "a passing tantrum."[5] This also appeared to be one of those occasions when Weizmann felt he could get the attention of Ahad Ha'am and others in the movement by making such a declaration. Such a tactical move could accomplish the twofold purpose of reminding Weizmann's critics of his value to Zionism and of emphasizing his exasperation over criticisms being made. In any event, whether the resignation announcement was tactical or not, the lesson to be learned was that controversy remained in the Zionist movement over whether the ends were spiritual and cultural, as manifested by the teachings and writings of Ahad Ha'am, or whether they were political, as evidenced by the agenda of Theodor Herzl. Weizmann embraced both concepts, but the overriding question, even for Zionists seeking to advance both spiritual and political goals, was just which phase of Zionism should be preeminent? And to what degree as opposed to the other?

Apart from the debate raging within Zionist circles over which direction to take, there was the message being advanced by British assimilationists that the proper course for Jews to follow, in the same manner as Christians and those of other persuasions, was to integrate fully into the fabric of the society at large. The same issue being debated in the London press between Weizmann and prominent British assimilationists such as David Alexander and Claude Montefiore regarding a declaration of support for a Jewish homeland in Palestine, which came to fruition with the issuance of the Balfour Declaration, loomed in the Jewish Legion question as well. Assimilationist Jews and those who supported their position asserted that Jewish residents of Britain, be they from Russia or another country, should stand in the same position as anyone else, fighting in the traditional British uniform. The Jewish Legion was the brainchild of Jabotinsky rather than Weizmann, but Weizmann was certainly shrewd enough to recognize the propaganda value that attached to the formation of such an entity. At a time when Zionists were seeking to secure support from Britain in favor of a Jewish homeland in Palestine, many felt that the proper way to symbolize this desire, as well as to manifest their support for Britain's fight and at the same time broadcast their attachment to it, was by sending a regiment of Jewish soldiers to Palestine as a separate entity. It is also understandable why Great Britain would feel enriched by creating such a separate fighting force: By doing so, the British no doubt felt they were motivating Jews both in and outside Britain. Just as David Ben-Gurion was motivated to take up the call from his temporary residence in the United States, others could also be expected to come forward.

Great Britain had achieved its mighty empire in part because of astute reading of international phenomena and the accompanying ability to turn political events to advantage. The two-pronged approach that was used to still Zionist restiveness within Palestine during the war while encouraging Jews to fight on Britain's behalf was through the creation of the Jewish Legion and, some three months later, the issuance of the Balfour Declaration. Hence Jewish help was enlisted by a disclosure of support linked to a manifestation of future support, albeit cloaked in cautionary legalese in a document lacking real legal force but pledging assistance in the acquisition of a Jewish homeland. In response to questions that might be asked about the nature of the assistance that might be offered on Zionism's behalf, the British Government had a perfectly plausible escape mechanism. It was necessary to support the war effort during that critical period, and discussion concerning the specifics of the quest for a Jewish homeland would have to be deferred.

The Balfour–Jewish Legion strategy was part of an attempt to allay potential problems while solidifying the British war effort. When France made known its intentions to be a presence in the Middle East picture, the secret Sykes-Picot Agreement was reached. The Arabs were similarly provided with assurances that any battle undertaken against the Ottoman Empire would aid in their pursuit of freedom and removal of the yoke of control.

Having proceeded in so many directions at the same time in seeking to quell territorial disorder and pursue a united front, the period following the war would inevitably be one of sober reckoning in which all of the glossy objectives being discussed during the conflict could not hope to be realized after it concluded.

Another problem that had already surfaced during the war, which would register increasingly sharper impact within Britain in the years ahead, making Palestine a ponderous problem to manage, stemmed from the major differences dividing the leading figures of the British government on the one hand and the foreign dignitaries along with military officers on the other. When Lloyd George assumed the reins of Britain's coalition government during the war period, the event was correctly perceived as a triumph for Weizmann and the Zionist movement. Lloyd George clearly sympathized with Zionist goals, feeling an identification with their aims as he compared them to his own efforts on behalf of his native Welsh nationalism. He believed in a revival of Jewish nationalism in Palestine. Other leading figures sharing that view were Lord Balfour, Winston Churchill, Lord Alfred Milner, Jan Christian Smuts, and Robert Cecil, who had held these views even prior to the climactic year of 1917, when international exigencies brought the Palestinian question along with other issues to a head, and they would continue to adhere to pro-Zionist postures after the war ended.

This group headed by the prime minister contrasted sharply with the anti-Zionists. Edwin Montagu, Secretary of State for India, who asserted an anti-Zionist position in cabinet debates prior to the issuance of the Balfour Declaration, was one of a number of British foreign officers at odds with Lloyd George and his cohorts on the Jewish homeland issue. Chaim Weizmann received a stiff jolt when he was informed by Wyndham Deedes, Allenby's senior intelligence officer, of anti-Semitism on the part of British military officers in Palestine. He made his point by showing the Zionist leader extracts from the notorious anti-Semitic forgery *Protocols of the Wise Men of Zion*.

"What is this rubbish?" an astounded Weizmann asked.

"You will find it in the haversack of a great many British officers here—and they believe it!" Deedes replied.[6]

The *Protocols*, which Jews throughout the world from then on and up to the present would hear a good deal more about, proposed there was a Bolshevik-styled Jewish world conspiracy in which governments and their people would be slyly subverted to achieve the Jews' ultimate objective of international control. The *Protocols* were exploited to maximum advantage in World War Two by the astute Joseph Goebbels and his formidable Propaganda Ministry. Taking advantage of the revolutionary scare brought about in the immediate wake of Lenin's Bolshevik uprising in Russia, the Jewish world conspiracy theory was held by many people. It distressed Weizmann that so many of that number held positions in the British military administration in Palestine.

Standing at the forefront of criticism being leveled by Zionists at the British military administration in Palestine was Ronald Storrs, governor of Jerusalem, who was referred to in Chapter Four as the introducer of writer Lowell Thomas to T. E. Lawrence. Oddly enough, Storrs, despite the distrust in which he was held by Zionists, was in solid agreement with Weizmann on one basic point—the quality of his colleagues. Storrs referred to his men as consisting of "a cashier from a Bank in Rangoon, an actor-manager, two assistants from Thomas Cook, a picture dealer, an Army coach, a clown, a land valuer, a bo'sun from the Niger, a Glasgow distiller, an organist, an Alexandria cotton broker, an architect . . . a taxi driver from Egypt, two school masters and a missionary."[7]

Weizmann voiced criticism to his old friend Balfour on two fronts concerning the British military administration in Palestine. He complained bitterly about a local administration he felt was being run by "mediocre officials and second-rate juniors"[8] and revealed concern about a subject personally close to both him and Balfour: perceptions about the Balfour Declaration.

> All sorts of misinterpretations and misconceptions were put on the declaration [by British administration personnel in Palestine]. The English, they said, are going to hand over the poor Arabs to the wealthy Jews, who are all waiting in the wake of General Allenby, ready to swoop down like vultures on an easy prey and to oust everybody from the land. . . . You will therefore realize, dear Mr. Balfour, that we found ourselves in an atmosphere very unfavorable to our work."[9]

Weizmann's complaint to Balfour, coming at the time it did in 1918 after the Germans had been put on the run, demonstrated the anxieties of the waiting period that preceded the critical decision making that would take place at the end of the war. Weizmann was hoping to build upon the encouraging momentum he attached to the issuance of the Balfour Declaration. The attitude he observed within the ranks of the British military administration in Palestine, which included generous samplings of both anti-Zionism along with a good deal of outright anti-Semitism, could to some extent be connected to a natural rivalry that was gradually gathering momentum in Palestine. Two groups, Jews and Arabs, were hoping to benefit from the decisions made by the victorious Allies at the close of hostilities. Just as it was natural for Weizmann and his Zionist associates to formulate a position of their own, which they hoped would prove ultimately favorable, the same could also be said for the Palestinian Arabs, who comprised a substantial majority of the population. In that the British military administration had been working so closely with the Arabs, it was understandable that an empathy would be formed in which the British desired that their interests be properly served. When Weizmann saw that anti-Zionist opinion had mushroomed and that many British personnel were expressing fears of an attempted Jewish takeover, he sought to immediately dispel such thinking.

While Weizmann was wrestling with these weighty matters in the diplomatic sphere, David Ben-Gurion, swept into idealistic euphoria in the aftermath of the Balfour Declaration, joined the Jewish Legion. He was sent to Canada for training, where he spent one month, during which his initial fervor dampened, being replaced by boredom and ultimately disillusionment. He was astonished to discover that some of his fellow Legionnaires were "born criminals" and concluded that not since he was jailed in Warsaw in his youth had he met such "Jewish riffraff."[10] His disappointment stemmed from his belief that, as an army of liberators entrusted with leading the march toward an eventual Jewish state and universal redemption, the Jewish Legionnaires should represent the cream of Jewish culture. He agonized over the reality that some Jews did not qualify as potential redeemers, once more revealing his dominant belief in the Bible as a guiding historical and cultural force.

Eventually Ben-Gurion finished his training in Canada and was shipped with his battalion to England. He bemoaned army life with its rigid discipline and command, biding his time until he was sent to his destination. When he arrived in the Middle East, he lamented under a broiling desert sun east of Cairo that he had arrived too late. General Allenby had by then captured Jerusalem and was making his push north and east, applying the finishing touch to hostilities. Beset by keen disappointment, Ben-Gurion wrote in his diary, "I'm afraid that our battalion will not take part in the conquest of the Land."[11] On the positive side, he met two Zionist working colleagues, Ben-Zvi and Katznelson, but this bundle of energy and determination would once more see his physical limitations cut him short in a painful way. On his initial visit to Palestine in 1906, he had contracted malaria many times as his always iron will clashed with his physical limitations. This time, on his return to the area of the world he loved, Ben-Gurion contracted a bad case of dysentery, for which he was hospitalized in Cairo. While in the hospital, with his thoughts focused on America and his wife, Paula, who was expected to give birth any day, he became exultant on receiving word that she had given birth to their first child, a daughter named Geula.

On Ben-Gurion's first wedding anniversary, December 5, 1918, he received a gift that made him ecstatic, an assignment to Palestine. A surge of passion rushed through him as he arrived on the soil he was convinced held his destiny along with that of the Jewish people as a whole. As could be expected, he threw himself with vigorous conviction into political activity. By then he had formed a greater bond of kinship with Katznelson than with Ben-Zvi, regarding the former as an ideal alter ego. He had engaged Katznelson in lengthy discussions when they were in Egypt about Jewish labor unity. Now he was determined to put his ideas to work. A natural organizer in the same way that Weizmann had an affinity for diplomacy, Ben-Gurion would never fail to let a ready-made opportunity escape his tenacious clutches. He viewed the Jewish Legion as an ideal springboard from which to achieve his goal of an organized Jewish labor force. Such a unified force would be the natural catalyst for a Jewish workers' state, a means of overcoming cheap Arab labor. Through such unity great strength would result, the kind of collective energy that would make Jews a major force to be reckoned with in Palestine, a vital step on the way to achieving a state of their own.

The determined and independent ways of Ben-Gurion, which clashed with the rigidity of military discipline, caused him to run afoul of authority. Not long after he and his fellow Legionnaires had set up bivouac near Jaffa, he snuck out of camp in a driving rainstorm. He trudged through the mud, managing to sneak past British guards, then began to ardently campaign among political leaders, emphatically cajoling them to embrace his concept of uniting as Legionnaires for the greater cause of Palestine workers' solidarity.

Following a week of frantic campaigning, an exhausted Ben-Gurion returned to camp and was sternly punished for going AWOL. The demotion from corporal to private for leaving camp and going to Jaffa did not concern him as much as his transfer back to Egypt, where he would be out of contact with those he wished to be in contact in pursuing his goal. His Jewish colleagues in Palestine were not about to allow momentum to be wasted, however, as they sought to use this natural leader's talents in a common pursuit. Yishuv leaders exercised influence with British officials to secure frequent passes so that Ben-Gurion was able to regularly attend meetings. The crusade continued as he implored his fellow Legionnaires to remain in Palestine when their military service terminated.

Ben-Gurion's effort to secure the continuing help of Legionnaires in creating a unified workers' state eventuated in his initial clash with the leadership of the World Zionist Organization, a harbinger of the many battles that would occur in the future, often pitting him against the sagacious Weizmann.

The pioneering plans envisioned by Ben-Gurion hit a snag in the form of regulations. Any discharged soldier who stayed in Palestine needed a certificate issued by the Zionist Commission, which was representing the World Zionist Organization in Palestine. The issuance of the certificates was conditioned upon a job awaiting the applicant. The problem confronting prospective pioneers was the lack of availability of jobs.

Emboldened by his pioneering vision, which his iron will was deter-mined to convert into an accomplished reality, David Ben-Gurion began pressuring David Eder, British chairman of the Zionist Commis-sion, to create jobs. Should it be impossible to create a sufficient number of jobs to accommodate all of the prospective Palestine pio-neers, an alternative was recommended by Ben-Gurion, who de-manded that Eder issue false certificates to fulfill all needs.

Enraged by what he considered chutzpah, Eder contemptuously wondered what Ben-Gurion was doing steeping himself in internal Jewish politics while still wearing a British uniform. Why did he not at least secure a discharge first before plunging into political affairs?

The situation quickly and hotly escalated between Eder and Ben-Gurion. When more than fifty Legionnaires were court-martialed for refusing to leave Palestine, Eder indignantly refused Ben-Gurion's call for a World Zionist Organization protest. When the fate of the Legion-naires was being thrashed out at a meeting of Jewish leaders, the dispute came to a boiling head as Eder and Ben-Gurion clashed with the seeming inevitability of the irresistible force colliding with the immovable object. Eder asserted that the Legionnaires were not good soldiers anyway, asking Ben-Gurion rhetorically if he wanted their misbehavior to spark anti-Semitism in the British Army.

An apoplectic David Ben-Gurion leaped to his feet, shrieking "Lies!" in the wake of Eder's charge leveled against the soldiers. He ragingly threatened to sue Eder for slandering his brave fellow Jewish Legion soldiers.

The air became charged with nervous electricity as all eyes focused on the angry Ben-Gurion. The assemblage combined its anxiety of anticipation, in which it was wondered what Ben-Gurion would say next, with its air of shock over the gravity of the charge being leveled, analyzed alongside of the person making it. Just who was this David Ben-Gurion anyway? they could not help wondering. Here was a relatively minor politician boldly issuing a charge against a powerful World Zionist Organization figure. Making such a threat against Eder was tantamount to proposing to sue the revered Chaim Weizmann himself! Was this a classic example to Ben-Gurion of a battle between David and Goliath, the important exception being that this confronta-tion pit Jew against Jew rather than Jew against Philistine?

Despite his boldness and bluster, David Ben-Gurion was, in the final analysis, every bit as much a pragmatic realist as was the perceptibly smoother Chaim Weizmann. As the vitriol within him subsided and a cooler rationality emerged, Ben-Gurion ultimately backed off, but not without a good deal of snapping and growling. His bitter final shot as well as his message for the future was recorded on paper, and it pointed out the basic difference between him and Weizmann on how a Zionist organization should be run: The World Zionist Organization would, in his view, be covered with "the shameful stain of the mass departure of the thousands of Legionnaires."[12] In Ben-Gurion's view, he might have lost an initial skirmish in his battle with the organization's hierarchy, but he had at least been willing to emphatically register his disapproval of the way things were being run by what he deemed to be a powerful bourgeois establishment lacking the requisite sensitivity to understand and respond to the needs of workers. His iron will trained itself on the objective of forming a powerful workers' army and wresting control of Zionism from the bourgeois politicians. As leader of a strong and united proletarian force, he could then train his sights on Britain, insisting that the objective of a Jewish homeland as addressed in the Balfour Declaration be met.

With the objective of achieving worker unity in Palestine cemented in his mind, Ben-Gurion, aided by his cohorts Katznelson and Ben-Zvi, sought to merge his own party with other labor groups. No matter how hard he tried, however, Ben-Gurion was unable to succeed in getting the influential *Hapoel Hatzair* party to merge. Despite that setback, however, a major victory was achieved in February 1919, when the two groups agreed to unite to form one political party. If the labor efforts remained independent, at least a measure of political unity could be attained. In a banner-strewn hall to the exultant cheers of waiters, welders, farmers, and fishermen, the *Ahdut HaAvodah*, or Union of Labor, was formed. In a euphoric state, the members of the *Poalei Zion* and *Hapoel Hatzair* groups proclaimed in their spirit of unity that the prospects for a Jewish state were drawing near. Had they not been promised one by the British in the form of the Balfour Declaration?[13]

Chaim Weizmann knew that the creation of a Jewish homeland or state was far removed from the imminence expected by Ben-Gurion and other Zionist enthusiasts working within the ranks of labor. The Zionist rank and file, ablaze in triumphal optimism, had put the most positive spin on the cunningly worded Balfour Declaration. Weizmann's efforts had been concentrated in the diplomatic realm, and as the war drew to a close he primed his efforts toward exerting as much influence as possible at the crucial conference of the winning powers in Paris, France, where critical decisions would be reached affecting Palestine and the Middle East. Allies on the battlefield, these nations were now represented by skilled diplomats who met to negotiate their own country's self-interest politically and militarily. They hoped to protect their flanks while enjoying the fruits of victory. Sitting in the midst of the carving table were the spoils of the Ottoman Empire. For Great Britain, a momentous period of decision beckoned. Through diplomatic finesse, the British had managed to keep potentially adversary parties and interests temporarily quieted so that the broad objective of military victory could be achieved. Now these temporarily deferred problems had resurfaced, demanding proper attention. France was there to exert its influence in its host nation capacity. The Arabs had believed that they were fighting for their freedom from Ottoman Empire control, and their "uncrowned king," who had led the bold charge to seize the Gulf of Aqaba, T. E. Lawrence, had gone to Paris to assert his views on behalf of the Arabs he had led in battle. Chaim Weizmann went to Paris to see that what he deemed as constructive momentum stemming from the Balfour Declaration, albeit that the finished product was less than what he had desired, did not lose impetus. With Balfour as a starting base, a Jewish homeland could be achieved, hopefully sooner than later.

Weizmann's sharply honed diplomat's instincts made him aware of the nervous rumblings triggering within Arab ranks as a result of the issuance of the Balfour Declaration. He hoped to get a jump on the postwar peace conference by meeting King Feisal, the most prominent Arab leader, and outlining Zionist aims for him. They met in the spring of 1918 at Feisal's headquarters at Wadi Waheida on the Transjordanian plateau north of Aqaba during the period in which he was leading an Arab army east of the Jordan.

Weizmann stated the following about Feisal and his objectives.

He is the first Arab nationalist I have met. He is a leader! He's quite intelligent and a very honest man, handsome as a picture. He's not interested in Palestine, but on the other hand he wants Damascus and the whole of northern Syria. He talked with great animosity against the French, who want to get their hands on Syria. He expects a great deal from collaboration with the Jews! He is contemptuous of the Palestinian Arabs, whom he doesn't even regard as Arabs.[14]

When one reflects on the above statement, the old adage "The more things change, the more they remain the same" comes immediately to mind. Presidents Hussein and Assad of Iraq and Syria can be at loggerheads, with Assad's even committing an Arab heresy for a time by supporting the cause of Persian Islamic nation Iran against fellow Arab state Iraq during that bloody conflict. Following the end of hostilities in that war, Iraq then supplied help in the Beirut conflict to the native Lebanese Christian forces doing battle against Shiite militants representing the Hezballoh faction allied with Syria and Iran. It can also be recalled that not so many years ago, after Palestine Liberation Organization (PLO) forces had moved from the occupied West Bank to Jordan, they ended up in battle against the Jordanian army of King Hussein. Not only was the Jordanian ruler Hussein eager to push the PLO forces out of his own nation, but he was also willing to accept the help of the Israeli army, which assisted in the dislodging effort. Those PLO elements then moved into Beirut and areas adjacent to it, which caused Israel to launch an invasion designed to uproot such forces from Lebanon. Eventually, Israel would become stymied in Lebanon, withdrawing its forces. The United States then became part of a United Nations peacekeeping force, ultimately withdrawing as well. The pattern that emerges from this inchoate crazy quilt of international political activity involving nations both in and outside the region is that Arabs can by no means be expected to ally themselves with other Arabs and that, given the fundamental instability of the region, the pushing of a single button at a given moment in time can produce surprise, quick responses, and ultimate confusion. Given the substantial number of subgroups linked to umbrella organizations such as the PLO and the *Hezballoh*, or Party of God, it is readily understandable why so much internecine warfare has occurred within Arab ranks, as have the difficulties of reaching unity in decision making pertaining to issues involving the Arab cause.

Whereas wide disparities of viewpoint also exist within Israeli ranks within Israel's multiparty parliamentary structure—disparities profoundly felt throughout the history of the Zionist movement—one basic difference separates Israeli disagreements from those arising within Arab ranks: On matters relating to basic Israeli security, a consensus can swiftly and broadly be achieved, from the Labor Party forces on the left to the Likud bloc on the right, with the disparate splinter groups on both the right and the left thrown in for good measure. Despite the mutual enmity between David Ben-Gurion and Menachem Begin, both were quick to forget about Ben-Gurion's having referred to Begin as a "fascist" when a conflict with Nasser's Egypt was drawing closer. Expressing supreme deference and reverence toward Israel's elder statesman, Begin implored the then retired leader to return to government on his nation's behalf.

So while King Feisal spoke dismissingly about the Palestinian Arabs, he informed Weizmann about his own agenda in the Middle East, expressing his distrust of France. In that France had been allied with Britain in the war, it remained a force with which to be reckoned at the conference table as negotiating lines began to be drawn.

As for Weizmann, he would continue playing his British trump card, which he felt had benefited him well to that point. Given the reality of the Balfour Declaration and the support of Great Britain's Prime Minister Lloyd George, who would lead his country's delegation at the Paris Peace Conference, Weizmann believed that the Zionist objective of statehood could be most effectively advanced by continuing to identify with the world's leading empire. As such he advocated that Britain be invested with a Mandate over Palestine.

The one thing that the cautious Weizmann wished to avoid was rocking the boat by placing pressure on Great Britain at that time by betraying impatience. When in Palestine, he had been confronted by Ben-Gurion, who had asked him pointedly, "Why don't you demand a state in Palestine?"

"We didn't ask for one because they wouldn't have given us one," Weizmann explained. "We asked only for the conditions which would allow us to create a Jewish state in the future. It is simply a matter of tactics."[15]

Weizmann biographer Norman Rose credits Ben-Gurion for understanding the validity of Weizmann's argument for the strategy of patient gradualism at that time, but he faults Weizmann for imperiousness. Rose cites the rebuke as evidence of an underlying tension between the two men over a different problem, Weizmann's perception of political strength within the Yishuv, particularly in the area of labor, where Ben-Gurion's power resided.

> Weizmann consistently underestimated the political strength of the Yishuv, in particular that of its labour groups. He refused them representation on the Zionist Commission, favouring his own hangers-on. Criticism mounted that he was weak and compromising in his relations with the British, a theme that haunted him for the rest of his political life. He eventually reached an accommodation with his Palestine labour critics, but they remained uneasy associates.[16]

No doubt a major reason for Weizmann's imperiousness in disposing of questions from Ben-Gurion and other labor sources about the imminence of declaring a state stemmed in part from his autocratic intellectuality and his superior insight into where things stood based on the proximity of his perspective near the corridors of power. An urbane intellectual such as Weizmann unquestionably was often displays an impatience or even a petulance that embodies condescension when asked about issues of importance with which he deems himself highly informed. Such an autocratic intellectuality would in this case be coupled with the undeniable fact that he did indeed possess greater insight into the issue of Jewish nationhood as seen in the power vortex of Great Britain and elsewhere. The temptation then looms on the part of an autocratic intellectual such as Weizmann to say, in effect, to his questioner, "I know a good deal more about this issue than you do, so kindly run along and tend to your own matters."

There are obvious pitfalls in pursuing the kind of autocratic pattern that the urbane, no-nonsense intellectual Weizmann displayed toward the labor faction in Palestine headed by Ben-Gurion. While Weizmann was concentrating on molding favorable action from major power centers in Great Britain and elsewhere, emphasizing the importance of reaching positive agreements on behalf of Zionism, he failed to comprehend the immense contribution being forged by Ben-Gurion and those of equal commitment. The master diplomat, who felt at home in his own circle, saw the importance of his efforts but minimized the vital role being pursued on the Zionist front by Ben-Gurion and his foot soldiers. While Wiezmann pursued the cause of Zionism on the diplomatic front, Ben-Gurion and his labor forces were seeking to change the entire geopolitical landscape of Palestine. Without the existence of dedicated pioneers tilling the soil and establishing an economic infrastructure within Palestine, the most fruitful achievements in the diplomatic sphere would be rendered meaningless. On the other side of the same coin, without success on the diplomatic front in the nature of favorable impetus from Great Britain and others, Ben-Gurion and his forces would have little if any land to till and would lack sufficient numbers and strength to achieve any kind of infrastructure in Palestine.

In that both successful diplomatic results and dedicated pioneering of the land were essential ingredients in achieving Jewish statehood in Palestine, the lamentable element in Zionist politics pertaining to Weizmann and Ben-Gurion was that they were not able to form a closer working rapport through better understanding of the role that each other was carrying out. If Ben-Gurion was guilty of impulsiveness in terms of unrealistic timing expectations regarding the accomplishment of Jewish nationhood, Weizmann was culpable for practicing elitism to the exclusion of labor. Perhaps such a result was inevitable, however, when considering that Weizmann and Ben-Gurion had come from disparate backgrounds, were dealing with dissimilar constituencies, and each pursued their objectives with a single-mindedness that, if carried beyond a certain point, inevitably produces a certain degree of tunnel vision.

In the previous chapter it was noted that Ben-Gurion apologized to his son for not being a more devoted father, citing his pervasive commitment to Zionism and his asking for and receiving his son's forgiveness. In the case of Weizmann, the matchless zeal of his own commitment to Zionism was also felt within his family. Abba Eban, destined to become Israel's foreign minister as well as its first United Nations ambassador, asked Weizmann's son Michael when both were undergraduates at Cambridge if he would like to join the University Zionist Society. He received the following response from the son of the great Zionist leader: "We have enough Zionism at home."[17]

The alienation extended as well to Weizmann's son Benji, who, during a period of strife with his mother, attempted to enlist in the cause of the Spanish Republic in Spain's civil war, calling it "the only cause I know worth fighting for"[18] but was eventually turned back at the Spanish border, barely avoiding imprisonment. It no doubt tortured Weizmann that both of his sons failed to identify with and participate in his all-encompassing lifework. The alienation between father and offspring in the cases of both Ben-Gurion and Weizmann clarifies why each man was not better able to empathize with the other's role more closely. Here were two unique and distinctly dissimilar men marching to the tune of their own respective drummers.

His objective squarely focused on making the best possible case for the Zionist cause in the aftermath of the great war, Chaim Weizmann sought a meeting with Emir Feisal once hostilities had concluded and Armistice Day was celebrated on November 11, 1918. The Jewish and Arab leaders met at the Carlton Hotel exactly one month following Armistice Day, on December 11, for a preliminary discussion, which Weizmann found satisfactory. On January 3, 1919, they signed an agreement specifying the "closest possible collaboration" between Arabs and Jews in the development of "the Arab state and Palestine" while envisaging the implementation of the Balfour Declaration. The agreement also made allowance for "large-scale" Jewish immigration while protecting the rights of the Arab peasants and tenant farmers. It also provided for Jewish economic assistance to the Arabs and a united Jewish-Arab front at the Peace Conference.

Feisal shrewdly included a cautionary proviso to the agreement, which stated the following:

"If the Arabs are established as I have asked . . . I will carry out what is in this agreement. If changes are made, I cannot be answerable for failing to carry out this agreement."[19]

T. E. Lawrence served as an adviser to Feisal during his London meeting with Weizmann, as well as at the later Paris Peace Conference. Weizmann biographer Norman Rose stated that Lawrence may then have been acting as a British intelligence operative and that the charismatic and always enigmatic desert warrior was suspected of being less than frank with Feisal about the full extent of Zionist aspirations or the true purpose of British objectives.[20]

To understand the motivation of Feisal in his London conference with Weizmann and what he hoped to gain from the accord signed by the two men, it is important to remember what the Arab revealed to Weizmann during their earlier meeting. He had demonstrated a greater concern for France's objectives in the Middle East, particularly respecting Syria, than he did about Zionist aspirations in the area. He hoped that, through cementing good relations with Weizmann, he could obtain Zionist assistance against the designs of the French.

Noted Middle East expert Fred J. Khouri, in his definitive work *The Arab-Israeli Dilemma*, makes the following observation regarding Feisal's posture with respect to his meeting with Weizmann and the agreement which followed.

> . . . by this time Feisal had lost touch with Arab nationalist feeling, especially in Palestine. These factors helped induce him to sign an agreement with Weizmann . . . welcoming Jewish immigration to Palestine. However, he specifically made this agreement dependent upon the fulfillment of the wartime pledges of the British regarding Arab independence. When Britain did not fulfill her promises, the Arab contended that this agreement had no further validity . . .[21]

As a follow-up to his accord with Weizmann, Emir Feisal wrote a letter to prominent American Zionist Felix Frankfurter, who would later become a distinguished Associate Justice of the U.S. Supreme Court, in which he referred to Arabs and Jews as "cousins" and asserted that there was room for both groups in "Syria." At the same time, Feisal made clear that the Arabs would not accept a Jewish state as such but only a possible Jewish province in a larger Arab state.[22]

Despite the sincere intentions of both parties, it is plain to see that neither Feisal nor Weizmann could achieve the kind of diplomatic wherewithal by meeting with each other and securing an accord for which they had striven. Feisal's objective in meeting with Weizmann was to secure cooperation from the Zionist leader in aiding his efforts in thwarting French designs in Syria and elsewhere in the Middle East, where Weizmann would be of little or no influence. Weizmann, on the other hand, hoped that reaching an accord with Feisal would serve as a springboard toward achieving consensus cooperation with Arabs, particularly in Palestine, an area where Feisal could provide little assistance.

The position embraced by Weizmann and the Zionist delegation at the Paris Peace Conference was built around two basic objectives: the inclusion of the Balfour Declaration in the peace treaty and the establishment of a British Mandate for Palestine. Out of these two basic points stemmed other objectives to be pursued. In connection with seeking implementation of the Balfour Declaration in the final treaty, the Zionists, with the objective of ultimately securing a Jewish state in Palestine, wanted the major powers to disregard the concept of self-determination in Palestine until such time that the Jewish population there, which represented only 10 percent then, had reached majority status. To bring such majority status into being, the Zionists sought unlimited Jewish immigration into Palestine and "close settlement" by Jews on the land there. Last, the Zionists sought the establishment of a Jewish Council for Palestine, representing the Jews in Palestine and elsewhere, with legal status and considerable powers. The Zionists continued to use the term "national home" rather than "state."[23]

With the war now over and the status of Arabs and Zionists to be decided at the Paris Peace Conference, not to mention the designs of France in the Middle East as well, the British diplomatic juggling act that went on during the war as a means of defusing any sources of conflict to interfere with the crucial military effort would necessarily be peeled off piece by piece. The question was at whose ultimate expense?

As mentioned earlier, the Arabs were disturbed by the contradictory posture taken by Britain as a result of assurances given by Sir Henry McMahon, British High Commissioner of Egypt, to Sherif Hussein of the Hejaz, Feisal's father, concerning British recognition of Arab independence on the one hand and the secret Sykes-Picot Agreement with France on the other. The Arabs believed that the assurances given by McMahon at a time when he was seeking Hussein's cooperation in the war extended to all the regions lying within the frontiers proposed by the Sherif. Exceptions were cited by the British, but it was the belief of the Arabs that the Palestine area was covered within the ambit of inclusion. The British excluded the "districts of Mersin and Alexandretta and portions of Syria lying to the west of the districts of Damascus, Homs, Hama and Aleppo," all of which "lie well to the north of Palestine."[24] Britain's position was that careful consideration had to be given respecting the districts of Aleppo and Beirut because of ally France. Britain also stressed the need for special administrative arrangements for the Baghdad and Basra vilayets. Hussein accepted the exclusion of the Mersin-Adana districts along with a temporary occupation by Britain of the vilayets of Baghdad and Basra. He rejected other modifications but agreed not to press his case until after the war out of deference to Britain's preoccupation with the conflict. He believed that Britain would not betray the Arabs once the war ended, and he was no doubt particularly encouraged by the unambiguous promise included in McMahon's assurances not "to conclude any peace whatsoever of which the freedom of the Arab peoples . . . does not form an essential condition."[25]

As discussed in Chapter Four, the McMahon assurances were instrumental in achieving Sherif Hussein's vital cooperation in the war effort. The Arab revolt was launched on June 5, 1916, spurring strong reaction against the Ottoman Empire throughout the Hejaz and northward as the whole countryside began to rise against the Turks. The revolt was also helpful to Britain and its allies in that, by being forced to concentrate such energies on the Arabs, the Ottoman Empire became limited in its ability to provide assistance for champions of its cause elsewhere.

Out of that backdrop of events came the Sykes-Picot Agreement, which, as mentioned earlier, was made public by the Russian revolutionary government when discovered among the papers left behind by the uprooted czarist regime. The May 16, 1916, agreement clearly conflicted with the McMahon assurances. Sykes-Picot provided for the dividing up of many Arab-inhabited territories into French and British areas of administration along with zones of influence and provided for the internationalization of Palestine. Once Hussein learned about this agreement, which conflicted dramatically with the McMahon assurances, Sir Reginald Wingate, Britain's new high commissioner for Egypt, sent Hussein two telegrams that reaffirmed former British pledges to the Arabs while stressing that the Sykes-Picot Agreement had not taken on the binding formality associated with a treaty. One can rest assured that the nonbinding aspect of Sykes-Picot had not been emphasized to the French in the manner that it had to the Arabs. The McMahon-Sykes-Picot dichotomy signified the most glaring example of Britain's wartime policy of plugging the dike to prevent a diplomatic floodtide from gushing into the Middle East so that the war effort could continue to be explored in as unimpeded a manner as possible.

Hussein's confidence in Britain remained unshaken even in the wake of the publication of the Balfour Declaration as Britain sent David George Hogarth, T. E. Lawrence's old archaeological mentor who had sparked his interest in Syria, to serve as troubleshooter to Hussein. Although the wording of the Balfour Declaration had been studiously ambiguous by stating that "nothing shall be done which may prejudice the civil and religious rights" of the Palestine Arabs, Hogarth assumed the dexterity of the diplomatic contortionist in twisting the document's factual reality for Hussein in order to serve a purpose.

Hogarth gave assurance to Hussein that the "Jewish settlements in Palestine would only be allowed insofar as would be consistent with the political and economic freedom of the Arab population." Hogarth's substituted wording of "political and economic freedom" carried a far more compellingly favorable ring to Arab ears than "civil and religious rights," the actual words in the declaration itself. Hussein was not only willing to accept Hogarth's explanation but also went on to assert his own freedom from any form of religious prejudice, welcoming Jews who wished to settle in Palestine or in any other Arab territory just as long as those areas remained under Arab control. A doubtlessly relieved Hogarth had succeeded in enabling Great Britain to dodge yet another potential diplomatic bullet.[26]

Despite Hussein's acceptance of British assurances, in June of 1918, at a time when active recruiting was being carried out in Palestine for the Sherifian Army, an assurance was conveyed that "the recruits were being given to understand that they were fighting in a national cause to liberate their country from the Turks."[27] In response to a formal inquiry on the part of seven Arab spokesmen from various parts of the Ottoman Empire, who were then living in Cairo, the British government on June 16, 1918, formally reassured the Arabs that it would abide by its pledges. With respect to the Arab territories, including Palestine, that had already been liberated by the allies, the government's policy was "that the future government of those territories should be based upon the principles of the consent of the governed."[28] The declaration made to the seven Arabs maintained a stony silence on the subject of territorial reservations or any other limitations that might conceivably eventuate from the Sykes-Picot Agreement or the Balfour Declaration. No effort was made to refute the conclusion drawn by the seven Arabs that Britain was "not free to dispose of Palestine without regard for the wishes and interests of the inhabitants of Palestine."[29]

Arab concerns became manifest once more in October 1918. Their restiveness produced an official communiqué on November 8, which outlined the intentions of the British and French governments in the liberated areas. The communiqué was circulated to the press and posted on village bulletin boards throughout the Levant, including the Palestine area. It stated:

> The goal envisaged by France and Great Britain in prosecuting in the East the war . . . is the complete and final liberation of the peoples who have for so long been oppressed by the Turks, and the setting up of national governments and administrations that shall derive their authority from the free exercise of the initiative and choice of the indigenous populations.[29]

A pledge had been given to the Arabs committing Great Britain and France to assist in establishing "indigenous governments and administrations in Syria and Mesopotamia."[30] The communiqué did much to assuage Arab doubts about Allied postwar intentions in that France as well as Britain was a party to it and since the Arabs considered Palestine to be an integral part of Syria.

The Zionist delegation, which arrived in Paris for the Peace Conference, was broadly based in composition, including prominent individuals from various nations. The chief characteristic of the assemblage, which was particularly evidenced by the erudite Chaim Weizmann, was its familiarity with Western diplomacy and psychology. This gave the Zionists a decided advantage over the Arabs, who had no one to match a Chaim Weizmann, who lived in London, had been throughout Europe and elsewhere making his case on behalf of the Zionist cause, and possessed a background of experience in dealing with Western diplomats.

Professor Khouri emphasizes the Arab delegation's shortcomings in Western diplomatic experience along with the accompanying disadvantage they inevitably suffered as a consequence. He summarized the situation as follows.

> T. E. Lawrence, British leader of the Arab revolt, helped the Arab delegation which was led by Amir Feisal, son of Sharif Hussein, but the

delegation was at a serious disadvantage because it lacked men of world stature with experience in Western affairs, diplomacy, and psychology. As a result, the Arab case was not presented effectively at the Peace Conference.[31]

For the Zionists, the crucial phase of the Peace Conference consisted in their February 27 appearance before its Supreme Council, also known as the Council of Ten. The meeting would reinforce the fact that the Zionism versus assimilationism argument was far from dead. Nahum Sokolow opened the Zionist case, acting, in Weizmann's view, "as if two thousand years of suffering rested on his shoulders."[32]

An unanticipated bombshell then shook Sokolow, Weizmann, and others when delegate Sylvain Levi spoke. Levi began by praising the Zionism of the pre-1914 era, but he roundly attacked the proposals being advanced by the Zionists at the conference. He contended that such proposals, should they be accepted, would exacerbate the Arab question. He saw Russian Jews as an "explosive element," which would introduce "dangerous" ideas into Palestine. Levi also showed a nervous concern that the Zionist concept of a National Home would sharpen the question of dual loyalties.

Weizmann and his allies, although rocked by Levi's vigorous on-slaught against their proposals, received a break in the form of good timing as U.S. Secretary of State Robert Lansing turned to Weizmann, asking him to define the Zionist conception of a National Home.

Weizmann promptly seized his opportunity to go well beyond reply-ing to Lansing's inquiry. He made a swift and forceful reply designed to demolish the arguments advanced by Levi.

"I replied briefly and forcefully," Weizmann recalled, "and the general opinion was that Levi had been demolished. It was a marvelous moment, the most triumphant of my life!"

Lord Balfour likened the speech to "the swish of a sword" and congratulated him afterward, as did Baron Giorgio Sonnino, the Italian foreign minister. The French remained silent but later issued a state-ment indicating that they would not object to Britain's assumption of responsibility for Palestine.

When the delegates filed out of the chamber, Sylvain Levi offered his hand to Weizmann, who rejected the gesture with the terse com-ment, "All is over with us. You have betrayed us."[33]

To Chaim Weizmann, who doggedly pursued Zionism with the ultimate objective of a National Home for the Jewish people in Pales-tine, a difference of opinion with those who held assimilationist or deviationist beliefs resulted in irreparable conflict. Zionism and the ultimate goal of a Jewish homeland in Palestine were the glue and the cement that held his life together, the passion that directed his energies to the brink of exhaustion and beyond. His verbal confrontation with Levi might well have taken him back in time to the heated debates in which he had engaged with his hated Bundist rivals during early manhood in his native Russia. Just as he would find no common ground with the Bundists, the same definitely applied to Sylvain Levi. For a Jew to betray Weizmann's vision of Zionism amounted to a betrayal of everything he deemed beneficial and necessary for his people. When it came to deviation from his grand goal of Zionism on the part of those within the Jewish ranks, there would be no forgiveness. His view held fast whether it was the Bundists, the British assimilationists such as Montefiore and Alexander, or Levi.

Concern about the Middle East and Palestine constituted only a portion of a much larger geographical picture that preoccupied the Allied nations at the Peace Conference. U.S. President Woodrow Wilson hoped to make the Paris Conference the first chapter of a grand design for international peace in which appropriate safeguards would be applied so that, in retrospect, World War One would be truly seen as "the war to end all wars." The linchpin of President Wilson's focus was a newly created League of Nations. With this organization serving as a centerpiece, the rule of international law could be followed and international tensions could be settled short of war.

The central element to be embodied as a living covenant in the League of Nations would be the right of self-determination of individual nations without outside interference, an objective springing from the "Fourteen Points" comprising Wilson's working program.

Wilson's League of Nations objective was one that could not be established without great cost. To obtain the necessary support to realize his goal, he needed the cooperation of Premier Georges Clemenceau of France. France's enmity toward defeated Germany was intense and long-standing, and Clemenceau was every bit as determined to see Germany severely punished as was Wilson to see his "Fourteen Points" and the creation of a League of Nations become accomplished realities.

Woodrow Wilson was far too shrewd to be unaware of the glaring inconsistency confronting him. His peace objective, buttressed by the creation of an international body, stood in glaring contradiction to the determined design on Georges Clemenceau's part to punish his old antagonist Germany. Yet, without agreeing to Clemenceau's proposal,

Wilson realized that his League of Nations would become an unfulfilled ideal. Wilson's approach was accordingly pragmatic, a concurrence in the harsh terms regarding Germany in order to achieve the formation of the League of Nations.

At the outset of the Peace Conference, Chaim Weizmann had been skeptical about the ability of the allied nations to achieve a lasting world peace,[34] but it is doubtful that his correctly dubious mind could have then envisioned the inferno of international turmoil that would ultimately spring from the harsh decisions being taken by the allied nations to the detriment of Germany and, extending the point further, the broad impact that these ultimate actions would have on the Zionist movement and the overall cause of Jewry worldwide.

The ultimate impact of the Treaty of Versailles on Germany and eventually on the entire world political structure at the outbreak of World War Two will be analyzed eventually in detail. This part of the study would be incomplete, however, without revealing the final blows to President Wilson's quest to achieve peace through the vehicle of the League of Nations.

When President Wilson returned to the United States, the subject of the League of Nations was hotly debated before the U.S. Senate, the ratification body for treaties negotiated by a president. Senator Henry Cabot Lodge of Massachusetts, a Republican, who chaired the powerful Senate Foreign Relations Committee, led the opposition, and the proposal for U.S. participation in the League of Nations was defeated.

The rejection was a savage blow to Woodrow Wilson, who had campaigned tirelessly by train around the country, speaking from rear platforms in an attempt to rally public opinion on behalf of U.S. participation in the League of Nations. While delivering a speech in Pueblo, Colorado, the exhausted leader, whose fragile health had been pushed to the limit, suffered a stroke, which largely incapacitated him for the remainder of his term of office.

In the presidential election of 1920, the subject of League of Nations participation became a major issue as Democratic Party nominee James Cox carried the banner of fellow Democrat Wilson in favor of participation in the League, while Republican nominee Warren Harding promised a "Return to Normalcy" a withdrawal from the idealistic pursuits of Wilson, particularly in the international sphere, in favor of more mundane domestic pursuits.

The national temperament of 1920 favored Harding's approach, and he was elected in a landslide. Thereafter, the League of Nations proposal faded from the scene. His health irrevocably broken, Woodrow Wilson died not long afterward, his bold vision of U.S. international leadership in a League of Nations unrealized.

The irony that grew out of the 1920 U.S. presidential race was that Cox's running mate, a young and ambitious assistant secretary of the Navy in Wilson's administration named Franklin Delano Roosevelt would some two decades later emerge as a leading player on the world scene when an aggressive and revitalized Germany spearheaded by Adolf Hitler sought to rule the world in the turmoil that arose from the volcanic ashes of the Versailles Treaty. As an element of that struggle, the diabolical policies pursued by Hitler's Third Reich threatened the existence of the Jewish people, who had been singled out for extermination under the plan known as the "Final Solution."

While those were storm clouds that would not surface for some time, the seeds of future conflict were being sown at the Paris Peace Conference. Other seeds were being sown as well with respect to Palestine and the Middle East in that the conference failed to dash contradictory expectations on the part of both Jewish Zionists and Arabs.

While the strategy on the part of Weizmann and his colleagues in the Zionist delegation called for a British Mandate for Palestine as part of a continuation of the promise of support they felt had been rendered in the form of the Balfour Declaration, the Arabs similarly believed that a British Mandate for Palestine would be a basic step toward providing the freedom and independence they have been promised in the McMahon Assurances and communiqués that had been issued right up to the convening of the conference itself.

The Arabs held understandably optimistic hopes in view of the adoption of Articles 20 and 22 of the League of Nations Covenant, which formed an intrinsic part of Wilson's "Fourteen Points" in embracing a natural transition from subservience to national independence.

Article 22 was specifically in point in that it related to certain communities taken from the Ottoman Empire that had "reached a stage of development where their existence as independent nations can be provisionally recognized, subject to the rendering of administrative advice and assistance by a Mandatory until such time as they are able to stand alone. The wishes of these communities must be a principal consideration in the selection of the Mandatory."[35]

The Arabs envisioned the mandate system as an effort to fulfill promises made to them at various times during the war along with the Wilsonian vision underlying an allied victory, which was seen as promoting principles of independence, self-determination, and democracy based on popular consent. The Arab interpretation was that these principles embodied the cause of majority will within Palestine, which indisputably meant independence.

The Arab position was further fortified by language in Article 20 stating that League of Nations members agreed "that this covenant is accepted as abrogating all obligations and understandings *inter se* which are inconsistent with the terms thereof."[36] The Arabs believed that Article 20 therefore rendered null and void both the Sykes-Picot Agreement and the Balfour Declaration because both documents were inconsistent with the League Covenant.

The assumptions on the part of the Arabs relating to the impact of the League Covenant on previous obligations of a contradictory nature appear highly understandable in view of the facts. In fact, none other than Lord Balfour himself acknowledged the point in August 1919 by conceding that "the contradiction between the letter of the Covenant and the policy of the Allies is even more flagrant in the case of the 'independent nation' of Palestine than in that of the 'independent nation' of Syria. For in Palestine we do not propose even to go through the form of consulting the wishes of the present inhabitants of the country."[37]

Already, long before Palestine erupted into a battlefield pitting Arabs against Jews, danger signs pointing toward future conflict were present. While the Zionists were hoping to use a British Mandate as a prelude to establishing a Jewish nation or homeland—using the interim period to spur immigration from other nations until a majority status could be achieved—the Arabs conversely believed that by relying on principles enunciated in the League of Nations Covenant along with previous assurances offered to them by both the British and the French, they would enjoy freedom and nationhood now that the grip of the Ottoman Empire had been finally broken.

The extent of the disparity between what the Arabs anticipated in obtaining from a British Mandate and what the Zionists envisioned becomes graphically clear in Weizmann's response to U.S. Secretary of State Robert Lansing's questioning of Chaim Weizmann when the Zionist delegation appeared before the Supreme Allied Council of the Peace Conference at the earlier alluded to February 27,1919, meeting marked by Weizmann's clash with Sylvain Levi over the future of Zionism. Walter Laqueur records in his definitive volume *A History of Zionism* his response to Lansing's question of what was meant by the phrase "a Jewish national home" :

Weizmann replied that for the moment an autonomous Jewish government was not wanted, but that he expected that seventy to eighty thousand Jews would emigrate to Palestine annually. Gradually a nation would emerge which would be as Jewish as the French nation was French and the British nation British. Later, when the Jews formed the large majority, they would establish such a government as would answer to the state of the development of the country and to their ideals.[38]

So there we have it, two groups convinced that they were ultimately moving toward nationhood in Palestine while nothing was being done by the leading powers to reconcile these sharply disparate views of the future of Palestine. The most auspicious time to head off potential conflict is in early stages, before antagonisms have become maximally sharpened, but the question of Palestine's future and what it held for Arabs and Jews was only one of many questions being faced by the allied powers. A large part of the world and how to deal with it in the wake of a divisive world conflict were paramount issues on the minds of delegates representing the leading powers. The central focus was on the League of Nations question and the role that internationalism could play in preventing future wars. The League afforded a diplomatic framework; the tenacious Georges Clemenceau approached the same issue by applying political force to conquered Germany in the punitive sphere, hoping to prevent a subsequent German military renaissance, in the final analysis precipitating the very result he hoped to avoid.

One step was taken in the correct direction at the Peace Conference by President Wilson, who, with the approval of the conference's Supreme Council, sent Henry C. King, president of Oberlin College, and Charles Crane, an American businessman, to the Middle East to furnish an on-the-scene report of the situation there.

The King-Crane Commission found that an overwhelming number of Palestinian Arabs wanted Palestine to remain part of Syria with Feisal as head of state. The Arabs insisted that, should a Mandate be established, it include Palestine as well as Syria and that it be temporary, with either the United States or Great Britain assuming the role of mandatory power. The commission issued a solemn warning against "the extreme Zionist programme for Palestine of unlimited immigration of Jews, looking finally to making Palestine a Jewish state."[39]

Although the King-Crane Commission believed that some of the aspirations and plans of the Zionists were praiseworthy, it concluded that the Zionist proposals as a whole would be unfair to the Arab majority and would require the implementation of military force. In conclusion, the commission recommended that Palestine be kept as part of Syria and that only a limited part of the Zionist program be carried out.

The net result of the King-Crane Commission's efforts was that they were ignored by the Peace Conference. The report was not even made public until 1922, leading Middle East expert Fred Khouri to reach the following conclusion:

> Since this document gave more support to the Arab case than to the Zionist one, the conference's failure to consider the report or to publish it before the Palestine Mandate was set up by the League of Nations had the practical effect of aiding the Zionist cause and depriving the Arabs of favorable documentary evidence.[40]

The sad conclusion one must reach after studying the Paris Conference was that, in their precoccupation with the overall world picture, the allied powers failed to take the opportunity to properly address the Palestine picture with its widespread ramifications, particularly regarding the stated objectives of both Jews and Arabs in Palestine.

The unmistakable message to be drawn from the Conference was its underlying failure to properly address the Palestine question respecting the contrasting positions being advanced by Arabs and Israelis, but on the diplomatic front it was apparent that the Zionist delegation had achieved success. The gain made by Weizmann and his able associates did not stem from concrete policy but due to the fact that the Zionist case for a National Home had been articulately conveyed by Chaim Weizmann and Nahum Sokolow as well as others. The adroit performance by the Zionist delegation left a favorable impression on delegates of the allied nations. As a result, those nations, particularly Great Britain and the United States, would be inclined to view favorably efforts by Zionists in the future to achieve their objectives. It is to the wily diplomat Weizmann's credit that he chose not to risk rocking the boat by overreaching. Instead he opted to follow a course he believed to be safe, steady, and practical, ever mindful of his past diplomatic successes with Britain and confident that his relations with them would continue to be fruitful. The British trump card had resulted in the Balfour Declaration, he reasoned, and if a British Mandatory could be established in Palestine, he could constructively build on his strong diplomatic ties with the British Government.

Colonel Richard Meinertzhagen, a committed Zionist and friend and confidante of T. E. Lawrence during the war, was a member of the

British delegation to the Conference. He urged Weizmann to strike at once and demand Jewish sovereignty in Palestine.

Weizmann biographer Norman Rose recorded the Zionist leader's response to Meinertzhagen's recommendation:

"Weizmann refused, believing the time was inopportune for such an extravagant demand, calculating that it would wreck the concept of 'Mandatory Zionism' which he considered the only practical course."[41]

Whereas Weizmann saw the implementation of a British Mandatory as serving his objective of helping to facilitate the ultimate creation of a Jewish homeland, Emir Feisal made the following statement to the Conference.

> In Palestine the enormous majority of the people are Arabs. The Jews are very close to the Arabs in blood and there is no conflict of character between the two races. In principles we are absolutely at one. Nevertheless, the Arabs cannot risk the responsibility of holding level the scales in the clash of races and religions that have, in this one province, so often involved the world in difficulties. They would wish for the effective superposition of a great trustee, so long as a representative local administration commended itself by actively promoting the material prosperity of the country.[42]

While remaining outwardly hopeful, Feisal implied in his statement a cautionary apprehension over the potential of future conflict in Palestine. The same apprehension can also be gleaned from the report of the King-Crane Commission. It is regrettable that the commission's report was not a subject of serious study at the Peace Conference.

Author John Davis, former Commissioner-General of the United Nations Relief and Works Agency for Palestine Refugees in the Near East, has provided a reason why the King-Crane Commission's report was so widely overlooked. The effort was undertaken at a time when there was a possibility that the United States could assume the Palestine mandate. Davis related that "Balfour indeed was anxious to avoid British responsibility for Palestine and favoured American supervision. The United States, however, was not prepared to take on the task and the King-Crane findings remained disregarded."[43]

Because the Palestinian views revealed in the King-Crane Commission never received an airing at the conference, the Arabs left Paris without making the kind of impression on Britain and the other nations that the Zionist delegation had in its presentation. As a consequence, Great Britain, soon to become the Mandatory Power over Palestine, came away from the Peace Conference with a keen awareness of

Zionist objectives in the Middle East but without an equivalent perception of the Arab position.

In addition to the aforementioned reason given for Zionist success at the Paris Conference in terms of Weizmann's contigent's being more experienced than the Arab delegation, yet another reason looms large as to why the Zionists made a more enduring impression than did the Arabs. Zionism was an international entity with active proponents present in leading nations of Europe and the United States. The same decidedly held true in Great Britain, where Weizmann himself made his case consistently to leading representatives of the British Government as well as to leading diplomats and representatives of the press. As also indicated, Weizmann, Sokolow, and other significant figures in the Zionist movement visited other nations and had contact with government figures as well as individuals within the movement. Ben-Gurion and Ben-Zvi passionately argued the case for Zionism in the United States, while Zionism was being actively embraced by influential Americans such as U.S. Supreme Court justice Louis Brandeis and prominent Harvard University Law School professor Felix Frankfurter, who would later become a U.S. Supreme Court justice as well. The World Zionist Organization attracted many prominent Jews from nations around the world to its ranks, and the members often carried weight far beyond their actual numbers due to the degree of commitment they exhibited along with the influence they held within their own communities and nations. On the other hand, the Arab cause was held in high esteem by many within British ranks, but Arab sympathies resided mainly with foreign diplomats and among members of the military, the most illustrious of whom, T. E. Lawrence, served as a delegate for the Arabs at Paris. This could not be regarded as a successful trade-off, however, in view of the Zionists' decided edge in gaining the ears of such leading British government figures as Balfour, Churchill, and Smuts. Whereas the Zionists had achieved a favorable listening post at the highest levels of the British Government while establishing a broad international network through which to air their views, the Arabs, on the other hand, occupied a posture of relative insularity. On the issue of Palestine, they held the position that it was theirs by right, and with a wide population advantage over the Jews, they beleived that independence and statehood would be theirs. Therefore they did not exert the same concerted effort on an international scale so as to mold opinion in their favor as did the advocates of Zionism such as Weizmann, Ben-Gurion, and Sokolow.

Because British officials in London were more familiar with the

Zionist case, which was being so effectively presented by Weizmann to sympathetic individuals such as Lord Balfour, it is understandable that these individuals would be disposed toward underestimating the degree of Arab nationalism that existed in Palestine. Later this situation would change as the Arab position was advanced and listened to with deference by British policymakers in the Whitehall Ministries, but during the crucial post–World War One era, when broader communication with both sides would have been advantageous in understanding the Palestine situation in all its facets, Britain's awareness was restricted by a shortfall of input from the Arab side. Once the British Mandate was implemented, the intentions of the Arabs would become clearer, but the lessons would be learned from examining conflicts steeped in bitterness and blood rather than through the forum of reasoned discussion. Once more the bitter lesson of humanity would emerge that knowledge is generally derived after painful experience.

Through a morass of conflicting promises delivered during the pressure of wartime, when ensuring tranquility was the hallmark consideration in the Middle East, the seeds for misunderstanding and conflict were sown.

The Zionist case hinged on a return to Palestine as a fulfillment of biblical prophecy, an opportunity to regain the land of their forebears following a period of some two thousand years of Diaspora. For their part, the Arabs contended they had a more valid claim to Palestine than did the Jews: Their continuous occupation of Palestine from the seventh century to the twentieth century provided a stronger historical claim than one based on a considerably shorter occupation that had ended some two thousand years earlier. The world would be thrown into chaos if both groups were permitted to lay claim to an area that their ancestors had claimed at one point in history.

With respect to religious claims in the area, it can be said that Christians and Moslems also have historical cases to make concerning the importance of Palestine within the frameworks of their religious creeds.

Debate continues to the present among religious scholars regarding the contention that the land of Palestine had been exclusively promised to the Jews by virtue of their religion.

Fred Khouri addressed the argument against the exclusivity belief, which has been propounded by fundamentalist Jews along with Christian fundamentalists:

> . . . the Old Testament promise of a return was fulfilled by the return of the Jews from Babylon when the Second Temple was built; and in any

case, the return was to come by divine guidance and intervention, not by human, political action. Furthermore, one group could not be legally or morally bound by the religious beliefs of or by the promises made to another group. As for humanitarian considerations, the Christian world was attempting to right an unhappy situation created by Christian intolerance—at Arab expense alone . . .[44]

Arab scholars along with others who dispute Zionist objectives in the Middle East argue emphatically against using the Bible as supportive evidence to advance Zionist aims. Henry Cattan, a Palestinian legal scholar who in 1947 presented the Palestine Arab case at the second speical session of the General Assembly of the United Nations on behalf of the Arab Higher Committee, contended that "The Zionist exploitation of the Bible has generated support not only for the Balfour Declaration, but also for the UN partition resolution and the creation of a Jewish state. Nowadays the Bible is also relied upon for the annexation of the West Bank and Gaza which the Israeli authorities like to describe by their biblical names of Judea and Samaria."[45] He then went on to discuss the overall historical impact of Hebrew or Israelite occupation of Palestine.

> The Hebrew or Israelite occupation of Palestine was a biblical episode which came to an end centuries ago, as did other invasions. It is evident that the Zionist claim to a "historical right" to Palestine is based on false historical premises and lacks any juridicial basis. The addition of religious considerations derived from the Bible does not improve its quality. The claim was designed to justify the Zionist plan to usurp the land of Palestine from its original inhabitants. . .[46]

In the midst of the great Jewish Diaspora, a burning desire existed among many to reclaim what they believed to be their natural right to the biblical land of Palestine. In other cases, where assimilation had been accomplished and Jews had fit comfortably into the fabric of their particular societies, the Zionist message was challenged. Whether or not Zionism flourished or was a disregarded entity depended on the degree to which the Bible was embraced as either a religious or a historical guide. Hence natural ideological confrontations would emerge between Zionist adherents such as Weizmann and Ben-Gurion with the Bundists, who embraced a Marxist agenda and regarded Jews as just one group in the international proletariat seeking a uniform goal, and, on the other hand, the successful assimilationists such as Montefiore, Alexander, and Levi, who looked upon Jews as one group representing part of a given nation, such as England or France, of which they construed themselves to be an inherent part. To these assimilationists, Jewish culture had a place, but only with regard to their historical roots in the same way that proud Americans talk about their forebears on the old Irish or Italian sod.

The Diaspora consciousness relating to Jews and the pursuit of national status was recognized by Dana Adams Schmidt as he described Israel at its twenty-five year mark, the period prior to the October War, the last Israeli-Arab conflict. Schmidt saw Israeli heritage accordingly:

> The state of Israel was twenty-five years old in 1973—a child among nations. Israel at twenty-five is a difficult child, the product of a complex past. Her fathers were prisoners in Egypt and had conquered the Promised Land. They were exiles in Babylon, scattered from Jersalem across the face of the earth, harried through the ghettos of Warsaw and Kiev, Casablanca and Baghdad. Israel's fathers were merchants in Leipzig, bankers in London, professors in Vienna. And six million of her people were killed in the Nazi gas chambers.[47]

While certain Zionists were making the case for a Jewish homeland in Palestine on the basis of religious prophesy and others, notably Ben-Gurion, saw such a promise to the Jewish people by interpreting the Bible as a historical document, the universal concept embraced by all Zionists and those who sympathized with their cause was linked to the search for a national identity, a need to lay claim to a state of their own after years of wandering and of being part of some other nation's heritage. In the cases of individuals who had successfully made their way into other nations, the degree of Jewish consciousness was inclined to diminish and, in certain instances, be extirpated. Often the embracing of Jewish biblical history was, at least to a degree, the result of the feelings of alienation encountered in particularly problematic nations such as those in Eastern Europe, where anti-Semitism was more pronounced, ghettos often existed, quotas were invoked against Jews, and economic and social assimilation were attainable to a lesser extent than in Western nations such as England, France, and the United States. It is notable that, even when Zionism was embraced in a nation such as the United States, leading adherents such as Louis Brandeis and Felix Frankfurter would clash with Chaim Weizmann principally because of the differing natures of the societies from which they had come. When the sharp break came between Weizmann and Brandeis, which will be discussed, it concerned a broad difference of opinion in the role of international Zionism, and differing perceptions resulting from substantially different experiences derived from their backgrounds in disparate nations.

A link can be established pertaining to the leading Zionist and the national experiences from which they evolved. Theodor Herzl, Zionism's founder, came from Vienna. Although he had not been victimized by anti-Semitism to the degree that many other Jews of Vienna had, a sensitivity was nonetheless present. As discussed earlier, what heightened Herzl's sensitivity and ultimately galvanized him into action, a position from which he wrote Der Judenstaat, was the Dreyfus Case. The degree of shock that sprang Herzl into action was the realization that strong anti-Semitic sentiments existed even in a city as cosmopolitan as Paris. All the same, his roots were in Vienna, a city where anti-Semitism was a marked reality. Chaim Weizmann, destined to become Israel's first president, lived most of his life in London, but his Zionist roots had been shaped in Czarist Russia, notorious for its pogroms. David Ben-Gurion, Israel's first prime minister, although growing up in Plonsk, a predominantly Jewish town but unaffected by the pogroms, nonetheless was touched by so many of his Jewish brothers and sisters in Poland who had incurred such tragedy. Also, he experienced quota discrimination firsthand in his quest for higher education in nearby Warsaw.

The ideological cofrontation between Arabs and Jews, which would sharpen appreciably as it led up to the creation of the nation of Israel and the wars that would follow, resulted from several basic viewpoint differences, which can be separated into two categories.

2. *Religious and historical*—Did the Jews enjoy a special status resulting from religious prophecy? Zionists and Christian fundamentalists have frequently cited the words of Genesis 12:7 concerning God's promise to Abraham relative to the land of Canaan: "To your descendants I will give this land." Zionists have used this passage to justify the reacquisition of Palestine. Arabs and others of their similar viewpoint contend that the term "descendants" is not restricted to Jews but includes Arabs, both Moslems and Christians as well, who claim descent from Abraham's son Ishmael, and that all are children of Abraham. The historical argument carries God's promise to Abraham historically forward to embrace the years of wandering and the absence of an independent national indentity for international Jewry.

2. *Political*—This line of argument was established for the first time on a wide international scale by Theodor Herzl, who began with the religious and historical arguments, extending them one step beyond to

encompass a blueprint for action in the world political arena. The major element stressed in the political argument was the cruel impact of the Diaspora on Jews internationally, the suffering that resulted from having no national identity of their own, and the bruises from the ravages of anti-Semitism. The solution to this tragic continuing problem in the eyes of Herzl and his followers was a Jewish homeland. The Arabs, understandably, cited their own long history in Palestine, which encompassed a continuous occupation of Palestine from the seventh to the twentieth centuries. Now that the iron grip of the Ottoman Empire, under which they had been subjugated for centuries, had been broken, it was time for them to achieve an independent status that was long overdue. While many Palestinians openly sympathized with the suffering that Jews had endured in Eastern Europe and elsewhere, the Arabs were quick to add that it had come about through no fault of the Arabs. As such, and constituting a substantial majority in Palestine, they should be able to rule through the principle of self-determination and should be penalized for an unfortunate problem suffered by Jews that was not of their making. Jews would argue in turn that Palestininans could stand to benefit financially from the economic and technological input into Palestinian society that Jews would generate. Arabs would then respond by saying they did not wish to acquire such benefits by surrendering their independence in the process. Jews would also cite a greater need for nationhood, pointing out that whereas Arabs had a number of nations to themselves, the Jews had no nation at all. Palestinians would reply that this is true, but that they retained an identity of their own as Palestinians, which they sought to assert through the concept of majority rule. Realizing that Jews made up a small number of the post–World War One population in Palestine, Weizmann and Ben-Gurion accordingly hoped to increase the Jewish population until Jews constituted a majority.

The arguments continued to be raised on both sides, but in the main they were made apart from one another rather than in a conference setting where a broad interplay of ideas could be exchanged. Also, rather than recognizing the divisions that existed and seeking to reconcile them through discussion, no leading nation such as Britain or the United States was willing to come forward and provide leadership impetus for fruitful discussion. As so often happens in world politics, crises result from seeking to sweep thorny problems with myriad complications under the rug.

One compromise proposal was discussed during that critical period before open hostilities flared with such frequent rage. At a time when

Jews represented 10 percent of the population of Palestine, and at a time when the official Zionist position called for a national home rather than statehood, it was suggested that one large Jewish federation could be established in Palestine with a Jewish national home created within this federation. Had this proposal been effectively pressed by Britain during a period before major problems that would later surface could take root, it might well have proved acceptable to a number of Zionists as well as to Arabs.[48]

While the quest to achieve Zionist homeland status in Palestine was being pursued through diplomatic channels, with emphasis on Great Britain, by Chaim Weizmann and through pioneering efforts in the Yishuv by David Ben-Gurion, who concentrated on organizing Jewish labor into a cohesively effective force, admonitions given by Middle East specialists, including Zionists as well as pro-Zionists, tended to be ignored. This group emphasized the importance of communication and understanding between Jews and Arabs. One such warning was delivered by the director of the Palestine Office of the Zionist Organization:

> We have before us the task, which in no wise can be evaded, of creating peaceful and friendly relations between the Jews and the Arabs. In this respect we have to catch up a great deal that we have neglected, and to rectify errors that we have committed. It is, of course, quite useless to content ourselves with merely assuring the Arabs we are coming into the country as friends. We must probe this by our deeds.[49]

Zionist sympathizers within the British ranks such as Mark Sykes and Richard Meinertzhagen also stated the belief that the success of the Jewish cause hinged on developing an understanding and reconciling Arab national aspirations with their own. The objective to be met according to these concerned analysts was that of breaking down Arab hostility. If patience and moderation could be exercised by the Jews in this pursuit of understanding, then Arab opposition "may possibly be averted . . . through a policy of peaceful penetration, without the blaring of trumpets and special privileges such as Dr. Weizmann and other official Zionists desire."[50]

The Jews were counseled to seek a position of supremacy in the land through their own merits. Instead, however, the efforts continued on the diplomatic front and on encouraging settlement in Palestine. The shortcomings of the Zionist effort lay in the failure to pursue the diplomatic front to a greater extent with Arab representatives themselves.

It must certainly be recognized that communication is a two-way street and that it was important for the Arabs to exert some effort as well in an attempt to understand the Jews and their motives. The problem was the position the Arabs then occupied. When the final shot of World War One was fired, the Arabs found themselves emerging from the stifling shadow of the Ottoman Empire, under which they had languished for so many centuries. That blazing drive and determination, accompanied by Islamic pride, which had catapulted the Arabs at one time toward leading-power status in world civilization was but a memory of a bygone period. It remained, however, enough of a memory to invoke Arab nationalistic pride and to nurture a zest for freedom. Nonetheless, with a civilization that had been languishing rather than flourishing during the centuries of Ottoman dominance, the Arabs were in a very disadvantageous position in competing with Zionists on the diplomatic and political fronts. The elite of the Zionist leadership had been trained on European soil and had been forced to compete for achievement against non-Jews, often under disadvantaged conditions, such as being forced to battle quota systems, in some of the major cities of Europe. Many had received their education in some of the world's leading universities and gone on to distinguish themselves in professional life. A good example of such an achiever was Weizmann. Then there were those such as Ben-Gurion, who, although lacking the same level of formal education as Weizmann and others achieved, had still managed to acquire valuable training on the city streets of Europe, often under difficult circumstances. By being pitted in confrontations with anti-Zionist groups such as the Bundists and by seeking to organize workers in the manner that Ben-Gurion had, Jews learned valuable lessons that served them well, whether they were university trained or self-educated, as they labored on the diplomatic and organizational fronts. The Arabs as a group did not possess a comparable level of skill at that pivotal moment in history, when decisions were being made that would influence events in Palestine and elsewhere for years to come.

Fred Khouri summarized that critical period accordingly:

In short, the conflicting pledges and indecision of the British, the impatience of the Zionists to achieve their goals in complete disregard for the feelings and interests of the Palestine Arabs, and the political immaturity of the Arabs themselves at this critical stage in the history of Palestine helped to launch the chain of events which produced the Arab-Israeli dilemma confronting the world today.[51]

Although Weizmann and his Zionist colleagues had acquitted themselves favorably at the Paris Conference, the issue of whether Great Britain would receive a mandate for Palestine would not be decided until the allied powers met at San Remo in April 1920 to work out a treaty with Turkey and rule on the disposition of territories that composed the deposed Ottoman Empire. The thin veneer that had adhered during the war via contradictory promises delivered to Jews and Arabs was already beginning to wear off in the power jockeying that was commencing. Advisers of King Feisal, against his better judgment, had convinced him to proclaim the autonomy of Syria, including Palestine, with himself as king. This constituted an illegal act in the eyes of the allied powers. The Arab Middle East had been thrown into turmoil as Iraqi and Egyptian nationalists demonstrated against foreign rule. Palestine flared into violence. When Weizmann arrived in Egypt after leaving Palestine, he was deluged "by a torrent of depressing news. Killings in Upper Galilee; more attacks by armed bands on Metullah: the Jews defended themselves, six were killed, among them Trumpeldor . . . demonstrations in Jerusalem; the administration frightened and therefore crawling to the Arabs; a desire to dissolve the Jewish Battalion; a desire to get rid of Meinertzhagen; in a word nothing but bad news all along the line."[52]

The same Weizmann who had argued persuasively at Paris for a British Mandate, an opportunity in his view to carry forward on the impetus of the Balfour Declaration, swiftly turned on the nation with which he had labored so painstakingly to develop a constructive rapport. Such was the volatile nature of Middle East politics. Great Britain continued to be split on how to resolve the ponderous problems pertaining to Palestine and the Zionist quest for a homeland.

The bad news that greeted Weizmann's arrival in Egypt worsened even more before he left the Middle East on April 10. More violence had been directed against Jews, this time predominantly in the Old City of Jerusalem. Six Jews were dead, many others were wounded, and much property was destroyed, including synagogues. Weizmann's response was to fire off two indignant telegrams demanding a commission of inquiry. He now felt that the overwhelming majority of British officials regarded the Balfour Declaration as a catastrophic policy mistake and that these individuals were now doing their utmost to undermine it. Their protégé Feisal was, in his view, no more than "a broken reed." He lamented that there were "so few Meinertzhagens and Deedeses." These were "the only Englishmen who have come up to the mark; the rest are wolves and jackals!" It has been speculated by Weizmann biographer Norman Rose that one individual Weizmann had in mind in his bitter "wolves and jackals" denunciation was General Louis Bols, senior British officer in Palestine, who was convinced that the Zionist Commission "should be broken." When Weizmann met Edmund Allenby in Cairo, the famous general described the Zionist leader's mood: "He was in a state of great nervous excitement, shedding tears, accusing the administration of being anti-Zionist and describing recent events as a pogrom."[53]

Weizmann was outraged over the arrest of Vladimir Jabotinsky during this period. It will be recalled that, during the interim period between setting up a new home in London, and while Vera remained behind in Manchester during that pre–Balfour Declaration phase, he had shared quarters with Jabotinsky in a Chelsea flat. The charismatic but explosive Jabotinsky was, from the standpoint of temperament and policies, antithetical to the more cautiously pragmatic Weizmann. Jabotinsky was also perceived by Ben-Gurion, ever critical of Weizmann for overcaution, as highly volatile and extreme. Despite urging a more confrontational stance against Britain than Weizmann was willing to pursue, Ben-Gurion was apprehensive, as was Weizmann, that Jabotinsky's stance was so aggressive that Zionists could suffer a backlash at the hands of Britain should he be allowed to prevail. Despite his differences with Jabotinsky, who from his prison cell was conducting an anti-Weizmann campaign, the pragmatic Weizmann still regarded the arrest as a blow directed against the entire Zionist organization. At the time of his arrest, Jabotinsky was serving as director of the political department of the Zionist Commission. The reason for his arrest was the accusation that he was organizing Jewish self-defense in Jerusalem, where violence had erupted.

"They could just as well convict me," was Weizmann's angry response.

Contrary to the wishes of many in the Yishuv, Weizmann, despite angry protest against the arrest, refused to take any precipitous action to secure Jabotinsky's release. Remaining the diplomat, and doubtlessly ever mindful of the importance of the upcoming San Remo Conference, he relied on patient negotiations. While he might fulminate to Jewish authorities and send terse wires protesting the treatment his fellow Jews were receiving in Palestine, particularly in Jerusalem, his diplomat's instincts kept him realistically focused on San Remo and what it might hold for Zionism should favorable decisions be rendered.

As of 1920, Weizmann held an opinion of Jabotinsky that could be

likened to a matador with a grudging admiration for a particularly
fierce and brave bull. He admired Jabotinsky's assertiveness in pursuing the cause of Zionism, but he believed that, just as in the case of the
bull who throws caution to the winds in pursuing his adversary the
matador, such strategy can be ultimately disastrous.

"Anyone meeting a lion on the other side of the street would run
away, except Jabo, who would beckon it with his finger," Weizmann
said of his political adversary. At the same time he distrusted his
judgment, delivering the harsh view that "J. is not normal. I regret it
deeply . . . something is eating him up all the time and he is becoming
impossible."[54]

The controversy over Vladimir Jabotinsky's efforts on behalf of
organizing a Jewish defense capability in Palestine provided one more
harbinger of a major battle to come. As tensions increased between
Jews and Arabs and as pressure was applied by Palestinian Arabs over
recent Jewish settlers and the impact of increasing Jewish strength by
numbers as against the Arab majority in Palestine, problems would
emerge as to how Jews should defend themselves. The issue of whether
Jewish actions should be primarily reactive and defensive in nature, or
whether they should launch more aggressive tactics of their own,
would bitterly divide the Yishuv and generate pressure in Jewish
dealings with the British.

During this period, following Paris and shortly prior to San Remo,
Chaim Weizmann believed that it was time to develop a clear-cut policy
for Palestine. He lamented what he saw as an unsatisfactory military
administration there, remaining mindful of anti-Zionist sentiment that
existed in certain quarters of the British military. He hoped that power
would be shortly transferred from military to political administrative
hands. Should such a power shift materialize under the British Mandate
that he hoped would be created, he would be able from his London
base to keep a close watch over activities. Weizmann was a familiar
figure in Whitehall circles. In addition, whereas he was apprehensive
about the political leanings of various personalities in the British
military, he had fared well in the main in his dealings with prominent
political figures. So it was on to San Remo with the objective of helping
to bring into being a civil administration in Palestine that would view
Zionist objectives with favor. He wished to see continued the momentum generated by the Balfour Declaration.

On April 25, 1920, Weizmann and the Zionist cause achieved a
significant diplomatic victory at San Remo. The two-pronged approach
of Weizmann called for the installation of a British Mandate over

Palestine and a correlative acceptance of the terms of the Balfour Declaration.

The Supreme Allied Council of the Peace Conference allocated the Mandate to Great Britain on April 25 while adding an important rider investing the Mandatory with responsibility for giving force and effect to the Balfour Declaration.

Agreement regarding the actual terms of the Palestine mandate gave rise to protracted controversy. The final draft was approved on September 29, 1923. The key provision, Article 2, asserted the following.

> The Mandatory shall be responsible for placing the country under such political, administrative and economic conditions as will secure the establishment of the Jewish National Home, as laid down in the preamble, and the development of self-governing institutions and also for safeguarding the civil and religious rights of all inhabitants of Palestine, irrespective of race and religion.[55]

The second paragraph of the preamble reproduced the text of the Balfour Declaration, and the third paragraph began:

> Whereas recognition has thereby been given (through the Balfour Declaration) to the historical connection of the Jewish people with Palestine and to the grounds for reconstituting their National Home in that country . . .[56]

The United States became a party to the Balfour Declaration through its signature at the Anglo-American Convention of 1924, which set forth in its preamble the entire text of the League of Nations Mandate.

The actions of 1923 and 1924 regarding the embracing of the Balfour Declaration within the framework of the League of Nations and by the United States, a nonmember, carried forth the impetus that Weizmann had helped to establish with his painstaking diplomacy, most of which had been carefully concentrated on the British.

The language remained to be worked out, but the constructive breakthrough was achieved at San Remo. While Weizmann's principal focus had been on Great Britain, he had sought to achieve a snowball effect wherein pro-Balfour sentiments would redound throughout the international community through the League of Nations and elsewhere.

John Davis saw San Remo and its successful aftermath in the following manner: "World Zionism has thus scored one of its most notable triumphs. Moreover, as Weizmann foresaw, the value of the

Mandate to the Zionists lay above all in the fact that it provided them with a basis for seeking international recognition of the concept of the Jewish people."[57]

While Weizmann had scored a major triumph, the San Remo Conference evidenced much of the confusion that had become such an indelible part of Middle East politics and that continues to plague the area to this day. The Mandatory for Palestine, which included Transjordan by inference, along with Iraq was assigned to Britain. Syria along with Lebanon was assigned to a French Mandatory. The precise terms of the Palestine Mandate remained to be submitted to and ratified by the League of Nations. The question of border allocations dragged on for two full years of wrangling between the British and the French. Norman Rose summarized the border problems accordingly: "In the final analysis, the borders of mandatory Palestine reflected the interest of the two Great Powers [Britain and France], not the ambitions of the Zionist movement."[58]

If the Middle East had been mired in a quicksand of uncertainty prior to Versailles and San Remo, this dilemma was only enhanced by events growing out of decisions made at the Peace Conference and in its aftermath. Promises had been made to both the Arabs and the Zionists, and more nimble diplomatic toe dancing was performed by Great Britain in concert with the allied powers in an attempt to please as many parties as possible. As a result of the San Remo decisions, the French felt free to oust Feisal from power in Damascus and impose their own rule in Syria. One year later, in August 1921, the British repaid their old war debt to the Hashemites by installing Feisal as king of Iraq. In the wake of Feisal's tragedy in Syria, where he had expressed an unflinching desire to rule, Palestinian Nationalism was recharged, as evidenced by the violence of March and April.

In the wake of Weizmann's San Remo triumph, Lloyd George left him with the words, "Now you have got a start; it all depends on you." Weizmann encapsulated events at Paris and San Remo by stating that "a new era" had begun. The outcome of events at San Remo seemed to vindicate his policy of persistent and cool negotiations with his eyes ever focused on the future, no doubt feeling he had earned a breather from complaints on the part of critics such as Ben-Gurion and Jabotinsky that he lacked tactical aggressiveness.

As mentioned in an earlier chapter, Emir Abdullah, son of King Hussein, was made ruler of the newly created territory of Transjordan as a reward for his efforts on behalf of Britain against the Turks.

Winston Churchill with assistance from T. E. Lawrence handled the negotiations on behalf of Great Britain.

Despite the boundless optimism Weizmann felt in the aftermath of the San Remo Conference, perceptive analysts observed trouble on the horizon as the great juggling act continued to please Arabs and Jews in a situation in which doctrinal disparities were growing. Consider the commitment on the one hand by Britain and the allies to put into effect the Balfour Declaration, which called for the creation of a Jewish homeland in Palestine. Such a commitment contravened Article 22 of the League of Nations Covenant, which carried forth the principle of self-determination on the part of peoples inhabiting territories that have ceased to be under the sovereignty of states formerly governing them. In specific reference to communities detached from the Ottoman Empire, which included Palestine as well as Syria, Lebanon, and Iraq, Article 22 stated that "their existence as independent nations can be provisionally recognized subject to the rendering of administrative advice and assistance by a mandatory until such time as they were able to stand alone."[59]

The Covenant of the League of Nations, which included Article 22, was approved by the Peace Conference and incorporated into the Treaty of Versailles. Whereas Article 22 addressed the question of self-determination for the territories, San Remo called for putting the Balfour Declaration into effect. The important question that remained was how these two objectives could be reconciled. If Article 22 were carried forth, then the Arab majority would hold sway over Palestine. Any commitment to granting a Jewish homeland in Palestine would reside with the Arabs if self-determination were achieved. Meanwhile the same powers who had devised Article 22 were committing themselves to the concept of a Jewish homeland by carrying forward the impetus generated by the Balfour Declaration. Clearly these powers could not commit the Arabs to such a policy no matter what their desires may have been while at the same time adhering to Article 22 and the objective of independence on the part of those living in Palestine, which then consisted of a large Arab majority. When one examines the reality of the then substantial Arab majority, Weizmann's posture of declining to seek a Jewish homeland at the Peace Conference looms as tactically intelligent. His twofold objective lay in (1) creating a favorable climate for immigration by having Great Britain, the nation he trusted most and with whom he had a close working rapport, assume a Mandate and (2) pursuing immigration aggressively so that the Jewish minority would have an opportunity to eventually achieve majority status. As tensions increased within Palestine as time elapsed, Arabs cited Jewish immigration as the catalyst for the conflicts. Jews contended that they should be allowed to emigrate to the land they had once ruled some two thousand years earlier. These parallel arguments continue to be debated some seventy years later as the conflict rages amidst shrill voices.

Arabs contend that the international status of Palestine at the close of the war, under the guidelines of Article 22, called for independence. This argument was concurred by international legal scholar the Earl of Birkenhead, who wrote:

> The position of Palestine and Syria is that they were integral portions of the Turkish Empire (which has renounced all right or title to them: Article 16 of the Treaty of Lausanne, 1923), they have become administratively, partially dependent now upon an appointed mandatory state, but they are acknowledged—in the terms of Article 22 of the Covenant—to be entitled to provisional recognition of independence . . . The status of Palestine and Syria resembles very closely that of states under suzerainty.[60]

Military administration over Palestine ended on June 30, 1920. Assuming the reins of authority was Sir Herbert Samuel, who became Britain's first high commissioner. Weizmann had lobbied diligently and for some time for Samuel's appointment. Though Samuel's attitude during the March disturbances was more cautious than what Weizmann would have liked, he was heartened by the idea of a Jew sympathetic to Zionism and prominent in British political affairs who would serve as the first civilian Governor of Palestine. In his view, this was a forward step toward the goal of a Jewish homeland. He was delighted further upon hearing that trusted Zionist ally Wyndham Deedes would be serving as Samuel's chief secretary.

While much has been written in terms of the past and present regarding Arab disunity, the Zionist movement has also been rocked by its share of controversy. At a time when Weizmann's position had reached its zenith within Zionist circles, when he was basking in the afterglow of victories such as the Balfour Declaration cemented by successes at Paris and San Remo, a major controversy loomed on the Zionist front, which commanded a good deal of his attention.

Louis Brandeis had made an excellent impression on Weizmann when they met for the first time in London in June 1919. Yet, even while Weizmann was conceding in a comment to Vera that the American "makes an excellent impression," he also added, "It's a pity that he's sixty-three years old already and came to us after he had given his strength to others, *to strangers*."[61] (Emphasis added.)

The comment concerning giving strength to "strangers" was darkly fortuitous in anticipating future difficulties that would emerge between these two men of intellect, both committed to Zionism, but individuals from disparate cultural backgrounds.

The Weizmann-Brandeis differences, which ultimately escalated into internecine warfare, exemplified one of the basic difficulties of Zionism as an international entity. It was exceedingly hard to hold together elements representing varying cultures on an international scale. Despite their differences in other areas, Weizmann and Ben-Gurion were alike in that their Zionism was rooted in strong biblical tradition as an outgrowth of Eastern Europe's Diaspora. Chaim Weizmann, no matter how many miles he would put between his hometown of Motol and his adopted home in London, would always retain the unencumbered zeal of traditional Zionism in its European form. Louis Brandeis was a classic example of the Horatio Alger rags-to-riches success story that grew out of the American experience. He became a leading attorney in Boston, a respected legal scholar, a trusted friend and subordinate of President Woodrow Wilson, and finally a member of the leading judicial tribunal in the nation, the U.S. Supreme Court. Brandeis, who embraced Zionism at the age of fifty-six, was reared in the American tradition and its concepts of British-style jurisprudence. No doubt he saw the British Mandate in Palestine as an opportunity for the Yishuv to evolve in the same manner as America had learned from the example of the British. He once remarked, "We must develop Palestine in the spirit of Anglo-Saxon manhood." Weizmann's view was totally different. He regarded the Mandate as an opportunity to mold Palestine into a classic example of traditional Zionism as manifested in the European experience of which he was a part.

As a pragmatist who understood the origins of power, Weizmann had instincts that told him that Brandeis was his most formidable power competitor in the Zionist ranks at that time. Weizmann, sensing that a power struggle lay ahead, sought to illustrate the basic difference between Brandeis and himself as he coined the slogan "Washington versus Pinsk," symbolically illustrating the choice to be made by Zionists between his own Russian brand of European Zionism and the American variety propounded by Brandeis. He labeled Brandeis's concepts with the prejorative term "Yankee Doodle Zionism."

Weizmann had emerged from the World Zionist Organization's London Greater Actions Committee meeting in the summer of 1919 in an angry frame of mind following a confrontation with Brandeis and the American delegation. The disagreement had resulted from a resolution proposed by Brandeis's delegation that the Zionist Organization be recognized as the Jewish Council. It would be free of any non-Zionist elements since the act of mixing believers and nonbelievers was seen by Brandeis and his followers as detrimental to the development of Palestine. Weizmann, representing the London leadership, believed that all Jewish bodies interested in furthering the concept of the National Home should be included within Zionist ranks, even the Jewish minority councils in Eastern Europe.

Brandeis lieutenant Julius Simon drafted and proposed a resolution stating that the Zionist Organization should be recognized as the Jewish Agency and that "the co-operation of all Jews" should be secured. Weizmann proposed adding the words "and Jewish organizations," to which Brandeis objected. When Simon's resolution reached the floor, Weizmann argued furiously against it, following which a vote was taken. The result was a hung vote. A vexed Brandeis then ordered that Jacob de Haas, a revered Zionist figure, be summoned to the floor to cast the deciding vote. Not a single voice was raised in protest, indicating the authority wielded by Brandeis in Greater Actions Committee circles. The entire body waited in silence until de Haas was located and he appeared on the floor to cast his vote.

Brandeis's tactic succeeded. The Zionist Organization was duly recognized as the Jewish Agency while Weizmann fulminated over what even the resolution's sponsor, Simon, called "totally unparliamentary procedure."

As the meeting ended in confusion, an irate Weizmann confronted Felix Frankfurter. Weizmann, renowned for his elephantine memory, assured Frankfurter, "We shall not forget this vote." His bitter parting shot revealed the enormous differences between the Zionism he embraced and that espoused by Brandeis and Frankfurter.

"Brandeis could have been a prophet in Israel. You have in you the making of a Lassalle," Weizmann exclaimed. "Instead, you are choosing to be only a professor in Harvard and Brandeis only a judge in the Supreme Court."[63]

By trivializing the significance of a Harvard professorship and membership on the U.S. Supreme Court, Weizmann demonstrated an absence of awareness concerning the reverence in which Frankfurter and Brandeis were held in American Jewish society for their achievements. To Jews seeking to climb the American success ladder, both men served as beacons of hope, role models for up-and-coming ambitious Jewish Americans. Brandeis embraced Zionism at the age of fifty-six, an act of rediscovery of his Jewish roots, following a long and distinguished career in which he forged his way to the top of the legal profession. Trained in British Common Law, the foundation of American jurisprudence, Louis Brandeis once remarked, "We must develop Palestine in the spirit of Anglo-Saxon manhood."[64] This view was far removed from that of Weizmann, whose childhood was rooted in a Jewish Eastern European tradition in Motol. Zionism was his life's work. His profession, chemistry, through which he made his fortune, always played only a subordinate role. He accordingly failed to recognize appropriate distinction between one who had achieved a position on the highest judicial tribunal in America and a friend who would eventually become a Supreme Court justice as well.

When Julius Simon proposed to Weizmann that he resign and turn over Zionist leadership to Brandeis, Weizmann began preparing for battle. He recognized that the battleground would be the Zionist Organization of America on Brandeis's home soil.

In preparation for that ultimate conflict, Weizmann scored an impressive victory at the World Zionist Conference in London in 1920, being elected president.

Relations between Weizmann and Brandeis plummeted to a new low after Brandeis suggested to Lord Reading, the lord chief justice of England, that Zionist congresses be suspended for a number of years to allow time for a new executive to conduct the affairs of the National Home free from political rivalry. The posture marked a reversal from Brandeis's position in the summer of 1919 in that he was proposing an executive comprising both Zionists and non-Zionists. The eminent American jurist assumed that Weizmann would support him. Instead Weizmann destroyed the proposal before it could gather needed momentum. Brandeis fumed, "Dr. Weizmann, you are not a man with whom I can work."[65]

Another clash developed between the two over the administration of the *Keren Hayesod* (Palestine Foundation Fund), the intended financial instrument for the development of Palestine. Brandeis believed that the *Keren Hayesod* should be staffed by investment corporation experts. Previously, fund business had been conducted sloppily by officials of the Zionist Organization. Under the Brandeis concept, authority over the investment bodies would reside with the national Zionist federations. With American Jews expected to make the most substantial contributions, effective control would reside with Brandeis's group.

Although aware of shortcomings of the World Zionist Organization,

Weizmann regarded the Brandeis move as a power play that, if carried out, would result in suicide for the organization. He believed that what was needed in the World Zionist Organization was an infusion of his ideas under the aegis of his leadership. Weizmann believed that Brandeis's tactics were being motivated by Jacob de Haas, Brandeis's chief adviser and formerly private secretary to the venerable Theodor Herzl. Jacob de Haas had never concealed his dislike of Weizmann or his resentment of his newly acquired status.[66]

Weizmann's triumph at the London Conference included the establishment of the *Keren Hayesod* on his terms. When the Zionist Organization of America convened in Buffalo, New York, in November 1920, however, a number of resolutions were passed that overturned London decisions pertaining to the *Keren Hayesod* and regulated their activity along lines foreseen by Brandeis.

The battle lines were clearly drawn between the two as Weizmann arrived in America on April 2, 1921. Although the criticism has been leveled that Weizmann was a leader lacking the common touch, he possessed sufficient pragmatic skill to know when the common touch was needed. His American foray was one such occasion.

Envisioning himself as a "Jewish Columbus" with the goal of rediscovering Jewish America, Weizmann's arrival at New York's Battery resembled an old-fashioned political rally. Cars drove in from the Bronx and Brooklyn with flags flying and horns blowing. A motorcade awaited his party, transporting them along the streets of the Lower East Side, lined with proud and excited Jews, to his destination, the Commodore Hotel. He was a guest of honor at a reception at City Hall. The local pro-Weizmann committee that orchestrated the response was seen as a rebel group in the eyes of the powers of American Zionism, headed by Brandeis.

To solidify the impression he would register on American Jews, Weizmann brought with him an impressive retinue, headed by Albert Einstein, there for the twofold purpose of awakening American interest in the Hebrew University and providing a symbol of world Jewry working amicably with Weizmann.

The crucial test of Weizmann's leadership came at the Zionist Organization of America convention in Cleveland. He attended meetings but did not directly participate in activities, seeking to influence events through his presence.

When the votes were counted, Weizmann had scored an impressive triumph, winning by a count of 153–71 and emerging in unchallenged control of the world Zionist movement through his London base.

Despite achieving impressive numbers while turning back the challenge to his leadership, Weizmann's victory was pyrrhic as applied to the important American Zionist scene. Brandeis immediately resigned, taking with him trusted colleagues who comprised the giants of American Zionism. They included Felix Frankfurter, Judge Mack, Stephen Wise, and Abba Hillel Silver. The group that replaced them, while more representative of American rank-and-file Zionists and unquestionably loyal to Weizmann, lacked the power, prestige, and influence of the Brandeis contingent.

Weizmann, who regarded his victory as an essential step toward consolidating his international leadership, scoffingly referred to Brandeis as a "straw man" since he was absent from the Cleveland proceedings due to his U.S. Supreme Court responsibilities in Washington, D.C. Once more Weizmann revealed his disparate conception of Zionism from that embraced by Brandeis. To Weizmann, Brandeis represented a man who had deserted his minions, letting them do battle on their own rather than fighting side by side with them. While Brandeis believed that his participation in U.S. Supreme Court sessions involved a bond of sacred trust with the American Government and its people, in Weizmann's view, that responsibility could never excuse an absence from a convention dealing with crucial elements of Zionism. Zionism would always be the compelling force in Chaim Weizmann's life.

Brandeis did not even attempt to hide his displeasure in his resignation letter:

"We who believe in those principles and policies cannot properly take part in any administration of Jewish affairs which repudiates them."[68]

The disenchantment felt by Brandeis and his followers manifested in frequent complaints against Weizmann. Despite his conspicuous organizational and administrative skills, he was frequently criticized for his "imperious manner" and "haughtiness" as he crisscrossed the world speaking for Zionism.

David Ben-Gurion, with a commitment to Zionism unsurpassed even by Weizmann, had his chance to appraise the potent leader for the first time at the 1920 London Conference, his first since 1913. He considered Weizmann's attitude toward Ben-Gurion's people, the workers in the Yishuv, to be patronizing.

The longer Ben-Gurion listened to the words of Weizmann in the setting of Albert Hall, the more incensed he became over his steady message of gradualism. The delegates were instructed to move slowly and not ruffle the British. The gradualist philosophy rankled Ben-Gurion. This impetuous man of the soil believed the only way to build a state was by rolling up one's sleeves and going to work. His bedrock conviction was that only through the purposeful dedication and selfless energies of those in the Yishuv could statehood be realized in Palestine.

One by one, Weizmann and his similarly impeccably dressed colleagues mounted the Albert Hall platform to decry the lack of funds to spark immigration and development of *Eretz Yisrael*. While patience was emphasized as the order of the day, an angry impatience swelled within Ben-Gurion. His nervous energies mushroomed as he squirmed in his seat until finally rising to speak. The blunt Ben-Gurion heaped verbal abuse on Weizmann and his followers. To proceed with patience, as those in the Yishuv were being implored to do, would only snuff out the zeal of the pioneers. If the workers were willing to make such enormous sacrifices, then the World Zionist Organization should at least supply the means to enable them to succeed. On the other hand, he wondered why private Jewish farmers who hired Arab workers should receive Zionist aid.

"Because you are useless!" a member of the assemblage shouted.

Ben-Gurion, seized by the same torrent of angry self-righteousness as when he defended his fellow Jewish Legionnaires from the identical charge of uselessness, accused the speaker of slander. Unless he retracted his words, Ben-Gurion warned, "we'll throw him out of the hall."[69] The man then apologized.

Weizmann mounted the rostrum, in no mood for apologies, sharply attacking the Palestine delegates with blistering sarcasm. After finishing to a tumultuous round of applause, Weizmann had gained the support of the delegates for his views, and Ben-Gurion's ideas had been rejected.

Ben-Gurion's frustration then crested with the cries of "Papa! Papa!" from his infant daughter, Geula, who sat in her mother's lap. The presiding officer promptly ordered the little girl out of the hall.

Though outvoted at the 1920 London Conference, Ben-Gurion was determined to fight another day when the odds were in his favor. The battle lines were emerging between the shirt-sleeved man of the soil, Ben-Gurion, who believed that the future of Zionism rested with the spirited pioneers of the Yishuv, and Weizmann, the neatly attired executive who headed the London school then in power and who believed that Zionism's future success was linked to negotiation and a patient gradualism.

While Ben-Gurion and Weizmann sized each other up with the anxiety of two athletes prior to competition, the very nation over which they sought to exert control, Palestine, began to bristle with the restless energies of conflict.

# 7

# Mandate and Conflict

The blood motif that has marked Middle East history for so many generations resurfaced in the wake of the Versailles Treaty.

The sunbaked sand of the Palestine desert became covered with the blood of Arabs and Jews as fighting broke out in March 1920 in the Jewish settlements in Northern Palestine as Arabs opposed the adding of more Jews to those communities. By May, anti-Jewish riots had erupted, leaving 47 Jews dead and 146 wounded. A total of 48 Arabs met death, and 173 were wounded, mainly by British troops seeking to quell the violence.[1]

In the wake of this stern harbinger of future events in the region, the British Government appointed a Commission of Inquiry to determine the cause of the rioting. There would be subsequent uprisings in 1921, 1929, and 1936 with each commission reaching the same conclusion— Palestine opposition to Jewish immigration amidst fears of Jewish intent to establish a National Home contrasted with Arab desires to achieve independence.[2]

The Palestine mandate envisioned by Weizmann and his followers as a necessary step toward realizing a Jewish National Home and eventual state became a reality in 1922 but under circumstances that left the region muddled in controversy.

The clouds of uncertainty had been gathering over Palestine since the end of the war. Great Britain, wishing to avoid conflict with Arabs and Jews, had made public pronouncements that led each side to believe it had legitimate expectations. The Zionists considered the

Balfour Declaration to be controlling policy in the region, and the Arabs believed that the "Fourteen Points" advanced by President Wilson supported their right to self-determination and nationhood. Bleak memories remained of the Sykes-Picot Agreement and the mission of reassurance to the Arabs by David George Hogarth that their interests and aspirations would be served by continuing to fight against Turkey.

The Arabs viewed the mandate as unjust and undemocratic, as well as a violation of promises made to them. Its validity was challenged as a breach of the League of Nations Covenant in that Palestine was not "provisionally recognized" as independent, and the wishes of the inhabitants were not the "principal consideration in the selection of the mandatory" power as recognized by the Covenant.

Fred Khouri cited the following basis for Arab discontent: "The Arabs were especially aroused because, whereas numerous articles of the mandatory agreement referred to the Jewish community by name, the Arabs, 90 per cent of the population, were referred to merely as 'the other sections' of the population."[3]

Sir Herbert Samuel, a well-known Jewish Englishman and former cabinet minister, was appointed the first high commissioner in Palestine. The initial Jewish reaction was tumultuous. Menachem Begin, who would become prime minister of Israel in 1977, recalled reaction within the Jewish community over the appointment: "When Herbert Samuel was made the first High Commissioner, his picture was in all the shops in Eastern Europe and he was considered to be our prince, the first Jewish prince in the Land of Israel."[4]

The exultation proved short-lived as Samuel, in response to the May 1920 riots, suspended Jewish immigration to pacify Arab feeling. An anguished cry surfaced in Jewish ranks from Chaim Weizmann on down. Samuel had been placed in an impossible situation. He sought to pacify conflicting groups with a hazy policy mandate focused on two irreconcilable entities—the Balfour Declaration and the League of Nations Covenant.

A policy move made by Samuel in 1921 that impacted negatively upon Jews for years was the appointment of Haj Amin Al-Husseini as Mufti of Jerusalem and president of the Supreme Moslem Council, the most powerful Arab office in Palestine. A hostile anti-Zionist, Haj Amin had been tried in absentia for his part in the 1920 riots and sentenced to fifteen years' imprisonment. He had fled Palestine, only to return in a blaze of glory to accept a position that carried impressive spiritual as well as financial and political authority. During the Second World War, he actively supported Nazi Germany.

Years later, when asked about Samuel's performance as High Commissioner of Palestine, David Ben-Gurion gave the following explanation.

> . . . arriving as High Commissioner in a country with two rival communities, he was most concerned to show no favouritism between Arab and Jew, the more so because he was himself a Jew. I understood his difficulties. Granted his background, he must have felt a psychological need to show the Arabs that he was not biased. Maybe his very friendliness to the Zionist cause may have prompted him to lean over and even more backwards to demonstrate that he was being "fair." And I am afraid that this led him to pursue policies, and to recommend policies to the British Government, which were not in keeping with the specific injunctions of the Balfour Declaration and the League of Nations Mandate, by virtue of which the British ruled, which were to promote the establishment of the Jewish National Home.[5]

The appointment of Haj Amin al-Husseini caused consternation not only in the Zionist ranks but in those of the Arabs as well. A bitter struggle had arisen in Jerusalem's Muslim ranks between the Husseini faction and moderates led by Raghib Nashashibi, the mayor of Jerusalem, who opposed the Husseini policy of noncooperation with the mandate authorities. The two groups cooperated on occasion, notably the Arab general strike of 1936–37, but genuine Arab unity was difficult to obtain and was generally short-lived even on those occasions when it was reached.

Arab frustrations became increasingly pronounced as they considered themselves political outcasts on their own soil. The perceived injustice on the part of the Mandate was articulated on behalf of the Arabs by Professor John Garstang.

> For more than a thousand years, almost as long as English folks have inhabited this country [England], an Arab people has dwelt in undisputed possession of the soil of Palestine. Gentle by nature, hospitable and courteous in bearing, they form an ordered society, with their own doctors, lawyers, judges, government officials, landed gentry, small owners, agriculturists and peasants . . . The Arabs gave a cordial welcome to Lord Allenby's Proclamation of November 1918, with its definite promise to the peoples of Syria and Palestine of "National Governments and Administrations deriving their authority from the initiative and free choice of the indigenous populations." . . . What has clouded the horizon for

Palestine—and for Palestine alone of all the mandated territories—has been the imposition . . . of a difficult and hazardous experiment. "The Jewish National Home," as a Jewish writer recognizes, "is quite novel and finds no counterpart in international law . . . It is being created in a territory largely occupied by another race." . . . It is on record that in 1921 Mr. Winston Churchill affirmed to a deputation at Jerusalem: "We cannot tolerate the expropriation of one set of people by another, or the violent trampling down of one set of national ideals for the sake of erecting another."

The Arabs found that, though constituting more than 90 percent of the population, their status was not recognized in the mandate, which omits all mention of their name. They found that their request in 1922 for the creation of a national independent Government was dismissed as incompatible with the pledges made to the Jews. . . . This meant in so many words that the pledge given in 1918 to the "indigenous populations" must be broken. This was the first blow to British good faith, whereon the Arabs had relied.[6]

The Arab claim was rooted in the belief that, as occupants of Palestine for more than a thousand years, and constituting a substantial majority, they deserved to be accorded the self-determination and nationhood consistent with Woodrow Wilson's "Fourteen Points" that had been adopted into Article 22 of the Covenant of the League of Nations. The yoke of the Ottoman Empire under which they had lived for four centuries had finally been broken by British conquest in World War One, so the Arabs believed that the time had come to assert themselves and achieve independent of Palestinian soil.

The Jewish claim to Palestine was rooted in a combination of historical inevitability based on biblical beliefs coupled with the conviction that the descendants of their forebears deserved to return to the soil their forebears had occupied some two thousand years earlier before they settled in other nations. Returning to the promised land had been a sustaining life force for many Jews living in Eastern European ghettos, who deemed the realization of the goal of Theodor Herzl, the establishment of *Eretz Yisrael*, to be the culmination of a great mystical experience.

A pervading mysticism embracing arrivals in the Second Aliyah during the first decade of the twentieth century, one of whom was Ben-Gurion himself, is described by Israeli author Amos Elon.

Some pioneers of the second wave (aliya) have described their decision to emigrate to Palestine in almost mystical terms. "Everything was suddenly crystal clear; the fog parted, my entire body shook with excitement. . . . It was as if I had suddenly awakened from a bad dream. I knew what I had to do. Nothing else mattered."

Others claimed that at the very moment they set foot in Palestine they had been "reborn." Ben-Gurion started to count his years afresh from that date on, considering everything that preceded it a waste of time. "I wish that the remaining years shall not go up in smoke," Berl Katznelson, the labor leader, wrote shortly after his arrival, "and that the *real* life will soon begin."

The poet Bialik wrote to the pioneers: "The very dust will come alive under your bare and sacred feet." This indeed was how they felt in the ecstasy of the first months or years, even before the barren fields they had sown turned green, or the virgin hills they had cleared of boulders were covered by forests . . ."[7]

The dichotomy of the Zionist quest to return to the promised land of Palestine and the nationalistic aspiration of Arabs to regain independence over their own soil was recognized by David Ben-Gurion at a dramatic point. While he was being detained by Turkish authorities as an agitator, in a military compound in Jerusalem he made a young Arab's acquaintance. The Arab, son of a wealthy Jerusalem family, had been a fellow law student of Ben-Gurion's a few months earlier at the University of Istanbul.

The meeting came about as Ben-Gurion paced in the courtyard, awaiting a last-minute appeal to Djemel Ahmed Pasha, the Turkish Governor-General, as he faced the prospect of "expulsion in perpetuity" from the country where he felt his destiny lay. The Arab asked if he could be of any help to Ben-Gurion. The conversation that ensued would remain with the Jewish leader always due to the import of the lesson he derived.

"I told him I was under arrest as a Zionist, that the Turks wanted to expel me from the country," Ben-Gurion explained. "He looked me up and down silently. 'As your friend,' he said, 'I am deeply sorry. But as an Arab I am pleased.'

"It came down on me like a blow. I said to myself, 'So there is an Arab national movement here' (and not just Lebanon and Syria). It hit me like a bomb. I was completely confounded."[8]

The meeting with the young Arab was recounted by Ben-Gurion more than a half century later. Though the realization he derived from the meeting—that the Arabs also had a national movement—may have registered a profound impact on Ben-Gurion at the time, the discovery was apparently kept in the back of his mind. His goal continued to be the settlement of *Eretz Yisrael* into a national entity. Ben-Gurion was deported from Palestine by Turkish authorities with his colleague Ben Zvi, but any benefit that the young Arab felt would result from the young Zionist's expulsion from Palestine was short-lived at best. Events moved swiftly for Ben-Gurion in the seven years between his expulsion by the Turks in 1915 and the starting point of the British Mandate in 1922. Besides his prolific Zionist activities in his temporary home base in America, he found a wife, became a father, fought in the Jewish Legion, and returned to work and organize in the Yishuv.

Ben-Gurion's roots were planted in the labor movement. It was from that organizational core that he would ultimately forge a nation. The tool to accomplish this objective was the *Histadrut*, a labor army he believed had been born in his native Plonsk when he called the seamstresses and bath attendants out on strike.

The major problem impeding the development of the *Histadrut* into a major economic force in Palestine was its expansive composition in which room was made for the many Zionist workers' groups within Palestine. Ben-Gurion biographer Dan Kurzman likened the *Histadrut* to a mother of the workers' group with all of them yelling "Mama" and pulling her apron strings at once. Ben-Gurion decided that his party, *Ahdut HaAvodah*, must control the strings. The *Ahdut Ha-Avodah* had its strife to contend with, although the situation improved after a hectic Vienna convention in which the *Poalei Zion*, an umbrella component of *Ahdut HaAvodah*, split when its more radical members demanded it join the Comintern of the Communist Third International immediately. Ben-Gurion and his allies remained steadfast, and in the ensuing conflict they rose and stalked angrily out of the hall. A long-anticipated rupture within the ranks had occurred, but after thinking events through, Ben-Gurion was certainly gratified that the split had finally occurred, since now the moderates in *Poalei Zion* would no longer have to compromise with extremists. Almost everyone now remaining in the party, as well as in the umbrella *Ahdut HaAvodah*, was a real Zionist.

Conflicts nonetheless remained within the Zionist ranks, even after the dissolution of extreme elements from the organization. Some members asserted that the *Histadrut* should constitute an end in itself, a collection of socialist trade unions seeking fatter paychecks and greater benefits while preaching the class struggle. They argued that they did not want the *Histadrut* corrupted into a political tool.

Ben-Gurion emphatically contended that the *Histadrut* was not an end in itself but constituted a means to an end, the creation of a Jewish state. Socialism assumed great importance as a potential tool to build the state. In Ben-Gurion's design, the party must become a "labor army" under military discipline. Ultimately the Yishuv would become one giant Soviet-style commune, or kibbutz, the pioneer collective settlement system that had taken hold in the countryside. The difference between the Ben-Gurion kibbutz concept and the goals sought by rabid Soviet communists would be the absence of terror and force.

When Ben-Gurion's comrades of both the left and right shouted him down during his remarks concerning his commune concept, he resigned from the party's central committee. This marked another of numerous occasions when he would use resignation as a ploy to achieve political gain in the way that Chaim Weizmann periodically threatened to resign from Zionist positions of responsibility. When the call to return did not come, Ben-Gurion returned to the fold minus his commune design.

The important thing to the pragmatic Ben-Gurion was that he had control of the *Histadrut*, the apparatus through which he devoutly believed he would forge a nation. He saw the ranks swell during the course of the Third Aliyah, which began after World War One, in which some thirty-five thousand Jews flooded Palestine. Encouraged by the Balfour Declaration and seeking to escape Russia, where Jews were attacked by troops and peasant mobs in the bloodiest pogroms to date resulting from the anarchy of the Russian Revolution, the numbers flocking into Palestine encouraged Ben-Gurion to believe that the *Histadrut* could flourish. Shortly it would serve 80 percent of the Jews in Palestine as an entity embodying a work-creating force with its own industries, companies, cooperatives, mines, banks, and socialized medicine system.[9]

Ben-Gurion and his cohorts had fought vigorously against local Palestinian Jewish communists, and he hoped he would achieve success in dealing with the new Russian regime that he uprooted the hated czarists and their Jewish pogroms. He had encountered numerous frustrations in trying to secure money from the World Zionist Organization to help finance the *Histadrut*. It rankled him that many of the organization's leaders wallowed in wealth but did not want to contribute to his socialist designs. He hoped to open branches of the *Histadrut* Workers' Bank and a joint commercial bank in Moscow, convinced that many wealthy Jews resided in the Russian capital even under the communist system, and hoped they would contribute to his venture.

His opportunity to visit Moscow transpired in the summer of 1923 following an invitation for the *Histadrut* to display Palestinian fruit, grain, farm machinery, and other rural products at Moscow's International Agricultural Exhibition. Ben-Gurion led the delegation into the Soviet capital with hopes of building bridges to the three million Jews still living in Russia.

Hopeful of developing a bond with Vladimir Lenin, leader of the fledgling Bolshevik state, Ben-Gurion's initial impression of the Russian leader was complimentary: "Lenin is a great man. He possesses the essential quality of looking life in the face . . . His eye looks afar at the forces dominating the future. Nevertheless he follows a single path, one that leads to his goal, while taking various detours according to circumstances."[10]

It took little time for Ben-Gurion's rosy optimism toward Russia and Lenin to dissipate. The few but powerful Jewish communists in Russia abhorred Zionism. Ben-Gurion discovered that the Jewish Section of the government had even attempted to bar the *Histadrut* from the fair. Ben-Gurion's frustrations mounted further upon reading an article apparently inspired by the Jewish Section and alleging that the *Histadrut*s wares were grown and processed by exploited Arabs and that Ben-Gurion himself belonged to the group that had seized the *Histadrut* to make it its private property.[11]

The bitter Moscow experience caused Ben-Gurion to recognize the difference between the pragmatic socialism he embraced, more closely exemplified by Scandinavian European nations today, and the fierce Marxist dogmatism heavily influenced by the idea of working-class struggle to which Russian Jewish communists adhered. These Russian Jewish communists dismissed Palestinian Zionism as a poor bourgeois substitute for the international class struggle they envisioned as a viable world revolutionary movement. Marxism was propounded universally by Russian Jewish communists, who saw Palestinian Zionism as a regional entity removed from the international class struggle of which they felt themselves to be an inherent part.

A somber David Ben-Gurion reflected on his Russian experience as he sailed back to Palestine across the Aegean Sea: "We discovered Russia, a Russia that calls for class struggle to give power to the international proletariat and that deprives its workers of all the rights of man and citizen . . . One does not know what remains from the past and what forebodes the future."[12]

From his chilling Orwellian view of Soviet Russia, Ben-Gurion drew a fresh portrait of Lenin minus the rosy optimism of his initial opinion.

There is a man with a will of iron who worried little about human life and the blood of innocent victims of the revolution. An incurable sickness has struck this giant of thought, this great captain, and the ship struggles in the storm to reach the distant bank of a magic land that no man has yet contemplated. And in the uncontrollable sea amid the ruins of the cruelest struggle in human history float the remains of Russian Judaism.[13]

During the critical 1919–36 period, Palestine Arabs and Jews found themselves at cross purposes on the all-important topic of Jewish immigration into the country. Zionist leaders wanted the mandate to be used as a holding pattern, in the course of which, through encouraging widespread immigration, Jews could steadily alter their minority status in Palestine until they forged a numerical majority. The effort would then shift from immigration to the creation of an independent Palestine, the objective the Arabs had been pursuing since British troops liberated Palestine from Turkish rule. To Jews, immigration was the key to establishing the Zionist state they dreamed about; to Arabs, immigration represented the holding action preventing Jews from obtaining a majority.

During 1919–36, $400 million was invested by Jews in Palestine. New industries were established, and Arab land was purchased by the Jewish National Fund. The total amount of Jewish-owned land increased from 594,000 dunums (one dunum equals one-quarter acre) in 1922 to 1,533,000 dunums in 1939. Some of this acreage had been what Britain considered state-owned land for nominal sums under ninety-nine-year leases. Other land was purchased from absentee owners living in Syria and Lebanon who had been isolated from their properties by British and French mandate boundaries. Arab tenants and workers were evicted from this land. The land bought by the Jewish National Fund became the inalienable property of the Jewish people. It could not be resold to Arabs, nor could any Arab be employed on it.[14]

The subject of Jewish immigration as a condition precedent to erecting a Jewish state became such a thorny topic that in June 1922, Winston Churchill, long a Zionist supporter, and at the time secretary of state for the colonies, issued a policy statement that not only reaffirmed the Balfour Declaration but also proclaimed that the British Government had no intention for Palestine to become "as Jewish as England is English." Churchill then went on to say that the British Government did not contemplate the subordination of the Arab population, language, or culture, that immigration would not exceed the economic absorptive capacity of the country, and that the special position of the Zionist Executive did not entitle it to share in any degree in the government of the country.[15]

With friction increasing on both sides over immigration, the military arm of the *Histadrut* assumed increasing importance. That *Hagana* would form the military impetus during the Civil War, which occurred when the British Mandate ended and the War of Independence of 1948 was fought.

During the Mandate period, the Jews in Palestine enjoyed many advantages over the Arabs. Since the Mandate provided for a Jewish agency empowered to serve as official spokesperson of world Jewry on immigration, agriculture, education, and other interests within Palestine, Jews developed their own communal organization comprising elected officials and an administrative apparatus, which eventually assumed expanding quasi-governmental functions. This experience proved invaluable to the Jews when it came time for them to establish their own government. The advantage was further enhanced because Jewish immigrants during this period came from advanced European nations, affording them greater educational opportunities along with broader political and economic experiences than those of their Arab neighbors. In addition, despite conflict within Zionist organizations such as the World Zionist Organization, Palestine Jews achieved a greater degree of unity in developing a new territory than did the Arabs, who often became immersed in class division and conflicts resulting from centuries of tradition. The goal of Zion moved Jews throughout the world to pool their often considerable talents and resources. Their extensive influence reached into the highest echelons of nations throughout the world and into the League of Nations itself in their pursuit of the goal of aiding the Zionist cause in Palestine.

While supporters of Zionism were turning their attention to the goal of statehoood in Palestine, the Arab world fragmented into many political units consisting of mandates, protectorates, and independent states. As the spoils of war were divided by the conquering powers, France acquired Syria and Lebanon as mandates, and Britain became mandatory power for Iraq, Transjordan, and Palestine. The British retained colonies and protectorates along the southern and eastern edges of the Arabian Peninsula and maintained special relations with Egypt. Only the Hejaz and the Nejd (later to become Saudi Arabia) and Yemen were allowed to become independent states as a result of World War One.

Economic disparity and its resulting inequities plagued the Arabs enormously during this period. By 1936, the Arab population had increased 67 percent during the previous two decades, due largely to a high birth rate. A small group of Muslims constituted the wealthy landowning families, with a growing number joining an evolving middle class that lived chiefly in the towns. Though the Mandatory Government introduced government services, it provided little money for public education. School registration steadily increased, but facilities never equaled the ever-growing demand. The 1931 census revealed literacy rates of 57.7 percent for Arab Christians and 14.5 percent for Muslims. Literacy rates consistently rose, but performance levels were insubstantial as opposed to the decidedly higher Jewish literacy rate.[16]

As both Jewish immigration into Palestine and land purchases increased, incensed Arabs reacted with acts of violence. Such an outbreak in 1929 resulted in the creations of the Shaw and Hope-Simpson Royal Commissions in 1929 and 1930. These commissions expressed the same sentiments as others that would follow them in asserting that the basic cause of the violence was the intensifying conflict between the nationalist aspirations of Arabs and Zionists in Palestine. The commissions listed the following factors as contributing to Arab unrest.

1. The Arabs feared that continued Jewish immigration coupled with land purchases would eventually render them a minority in what they considered to be their own country. The Arabs resented what they construed to be the superior attitude of Jewish immigrants entering Palestine and what they viewed as an absence of concern for the Arabs and their interests. They saw Zionist demands growing at their expense and did not know where such demands would end.

2. The Arabs were fearful about becoming dominated economically and politically by the Jews. The more the Zionists stressed their economic, financial, and technical superiority over the Arabs, the greater Arab apprehension became. The Arabs lamented that, although the Zionists were claiming to bring great material benefits to the Arabs, not only did Zionists exclude Arabs from their farmlands forever, but also Zionist industries frowned on the hiring of Arab workers. The Arabs believed that whatever benefits they may have been deriving from the Jewish presence were incidental and at the ultimate expense of displacement from their land. They also felt that continuing widespread Jewish immigration would create future unemployment among Arabs.

3. The Arabs believed they suffered a great disadvantage whenever the political battlefield shifted from Palestine to London, where the Zionists could always present their case with maximal effect to both the British Government and in the sphere of public opinion. They complained that, time and again, when a royal commission made a recommendation favorable to the Arabs, Zionist influence in Parlia-

ment and the press forced the government to modify the recommendation in the Zionists' favor. Lacking confidence in the British Government and questioning their ability to influence events by peaceful means, many Palestinian Arabs began to believe that force was the only viable option left to them. Since violence had sometimes led to more favorable British statements, if not actions, the Arabs were encouraged to continue such violence.[17]

The Shaw and Hope-Simpson commissions served as catalysts in a policy decision that infuriated Jews. The bombshell that rocked the Zionist community occurred in October 1930, when Colonial Secretary Lord Passfield, responding to Arab immigration concern, issued a White Paper limiting the number of Jews that could set foot on Palestine soil and restricting land purchases. Nine years later, Lord Passfield would issue a second White Paper far more restricting to Jewish immigration, which touched off an even bigger firestorm in Zionist ranks.

The reply from the Yishuv to the 1930 White Paper was swift and devastating, as David Ben-Gurion, referring to population figures showing that Arabs outnumbered Jews eight hundred thousand to one hundred fifty thousand, wondered if his people were forever destined to be a persecuted minority in what he considered their land. He launched an angry response to the British Labor Party's "betrayal" with "White Paper" of his own, sending pamphlets to all groups affiliated with the *Histadrut* and the Jewish labor movement throughout the world. He encouraged rebellion against the British, declaring that the Jews were being threatened with extinction. He took his message to the street as well: Late one night, he stood on a corner surrounded by sweepers with long brooms, waiters from nearby cafés, street vendors, and an assortment of other people, delivering the following strident message: "No White Papers or papers of any other color will decide our fate. We will determine our own destiny. We must resist!"

"But we are only a handful," someone countered. "How can we resist the British Army?"

"Numbers are not important!" Ben-Gurion responded. "Only the will is, the will of the people!"[18]

Though Ben-Gurion's Zionist colleagues admired his resolve, they were skeptical about his line of attack. They asked if the Jews were being asked to battle the entire British Empire.

Eventually Ben-Gurion calmed down. In the estimation of his biographer Dan Kurzman, his explosive verbal extremism was just another example of his tactical artillery at work, the objective being that of frightening the enemy. Kurzman explained further:

> When one avenue of advance was blocked, as it was now, he would simply ram down another. Few of his colleagues really comprehended the subtleties of his political guerrilla strategy—when to feint, when to retreat, when to thrust ahead, with the mind never deviating from the central goal. His new Mapai Party would have to conquer the whole Zionist movement and then, with himself at the helm, no Zionist would dare challenge destiny.[19]

Always the pragmatist, despite the tone of his rhetoric, Ben-Gurion believed that British actions such as the Passfield White Paper enhanced his position in his ongoing battle for Zionist leadership against Chaim Weizmann and the World Zionist Organization he headed. Weizmann's success stemmed from patient diplomacy with the British. His two biggest successes had been the Balfour Declaration, in which he played the major Zionist role, and his assiduous lobbying, particularly at the Paris Peace Conference, toward achieving a British Mandate for Palestine. The second objective resulted in no small part from the favorable impression Weizmann made on leaders and diplomats representing the allied powers. As long as the British trump card worked, Weizmann's primacy within the Zionist movement was virtually assured. With unrest swelling within Jewish ranks moving into the 1930s after the turbulent conflicts with the Arabs in the 1920s, along with increasing impatience to see the Balfour Declaration fulfilled, the sharp rhetoric of Ben-Gurion was beginning to influence many more Jews, as opposed to the policy of patient gradualism followed by Weizmann.

Sensing that Weizmann was ripe to be toppled, but doubtful he could be overthrown within his own World Zionist Organization, Ben-Gurion attempted a backdoor approach to accomplish his aim as he launched the founding conference of the World Congress of Labor Eretz Yisrael in Berlin on September 27, 1930. The intention was to establish an international organization of his own in order to drain delegates away from the World Zionist Organization until control resided within his own group. However, Ben-Gurion's Mapai colleagues refused to leave the Zionist Executive to join his group, and he had little choice other than accepting their decision. All the same, the objective of toppling Weizmann from power remained in his mind.

While Ben-Gurion and his Yishuv colleagues were demonstrating their impatience, Weizmann was using his influence with the British in an attempt to nullify the document. Given his prodigious diplomatic skills, he almost assuredly used the opportunity to draw a distinction between himself and Ben-Gurion, stressing the problems that would ensue if his leadership suffered a decline in confidence and he was replaced by the tenacious labor leader. At a dramatic moment, one could hear him ask British representatives if they would rather deal with a trusted old friend such as himself or with the mercurial Ben-Gurion.

The Weizmann initiative bore fruit as British Prime Minister Ramsay MacDonald, in February 1931, wrote Weizmann a letter partly rescinding the Passfield White Paper. MacDonald agreed to reduce the restrictions on Jewish immigration, settlement, and land purchases. The letter denied that the mandatory was considering the prohibition of either Jewish immigration or land acquistion.

Just as the Passfield White Paper had angered the Jews, the MacDonald letter to Weizmann was seen by Arabs as a further British betrayal of Arab interests. Within Arab circles, it was called the "black letter."

While Weizmann was hoping that the MacDonald letter would enable him to regain lost prestige, the situation remained critical for him as the World Zionist Organization convention scheduled for Basel on June 30, 1931, loomed closer. Would Ben-Gurion use the opportunity to make his long-awaited move to wrest power from Chaim Weizmann's hands? As much as he wanted to gain control of the Zionist power apparatus, the pragmatic Ben-Gurion decided to support Weizmann at the Basel convention. Why was he supporting a man he had called "ridiculous and wretched"[20] in his diary? The strategy revolved around a phrase oft-quoted in democratic nations about preferring "the lesser of two evils," which in this instance meant stopping a mounting force of persuasion in Zionist circles.

The man Ben-Gurion perceived as a danger to his Mapai Party was Vladimir Jabotinsky, whose right-wing Revisionist Party loomed for many as the wave of the future. As a firebrand, Jabotinsky, who gave the deceptive appearance of a mild-mannered professor, could make Ben-Gurion appear dispassionate. To Ben-Gurion, he was a man to be both feared and envied. It was Jabotinsky who had backed the formation of a Jewish Legion in World War One, while Ben-Gurion had initially supported Turkey out of his hatred for czarist Russia. He was a man of many skills, a poet, playwright, philosopher, and linguist. No doubt there was a certain self-consciousness in Ben-Gurion due to Jabotinsky's magnetism and because he had had a formal education that Ben-Gurion had dreamed about but never received.

Ben-Gurion viewed Jabotinsky's Zionism as one-dimensional and fascistic, and the ideological struggle raging in Europe at that time between social democracy and fascism only deepened his distrust. Jabotinsky demanded a state immediately. His proposed state would embrace not only all of Palestine but Transjordan as well on the rationale that Transjordan had been a part of Palestine until 1922, when the British turned it into a separate country under the rule of the Hashemite dynasty. Despite Ben-Gurion's often expressed impatience toward Weizmann's gradualism, he was patient when it came to waiting for the kind of Jewish nation he envisioned, one that would lead to universal redemption.

A marked contrast exists between the two men as evidenced by patterns of early development that militated on their adult lives. Ben-Gurion was the product of a Zionist Jewish background with a heavy emphasis on biblical tradition. Jabotinsky was born and raised in cosmopolitan Odessa in a non-Jewish environment. Jabotinsky seethed with impatience, seeking immediate results. Once they were achieved, he would concentrate on matters such as quality of life and purity of ethos embodying the fundamental concerns of Ben-Gurion. If the state to Ben-Gurion represented a biblical mandate, to Jabotinsky it was primarily an assertion of national honor.[21]

Ideologial disparities immediately surfaced at the Seventeenth Zionist Congress. Ben-Gurion led off, dressed in a dark suit and sport shirt, ripping not into old antagonist Weizmann but into the Revisionists of Jabotinsky. With scowling frenzy, he branded Jabotinsky and his followers as "chauvinists" filled with hatred for the workers and the Arabs. Jabotinsky stuck to his rhetorical guns in demanding a tougher policy toward the British. Weizmann asked for more restraint and moderation: "The Arabs must be made to feel, must be convinced, by deed as well as by word, that whatever the future numerical relationship of the two nations in Palestine, we on our part contemplate no political domination. Provided that the Mandate is both recognized and respected, we would welcome an agreement between the two kindred races on the basis of political parity."[22]

Weizmann stressed that only steady progress in land settlement, education, and immigration would create the necessary conditions for achieving political progress.

The walls of Jericho fell to the sound of shouts and trumpets. I never heard of any walls being raised by such means.

I have heard other critics of the Jewish Agency sneer at what they call the old *Hibbat Zion* policy of "another dunam and another dunam, another Jew and another Jew, another cow and another goat and two more houses in Gederah." If there is another way of building up a country, save dunam by dunam and man by man, and farmstead by farmstead, again I do not know it.[23]

Ben-Gurion's colleagues were rocked by Weizmann's acknowledgment that the basic precondition of achieving a Jewish majority before establishing a state was not necessary, a heretical view in the eyes of Mapai adherents. They began questioning whether Weizmann truly was, as Ben-Gurion claimed, "the best of the bourgeoisie."[24]

In his rapidly weakening state, Weizmann turned to his British allies once more. He decided that his best prospect for averting defeat lay in having his old enemy Ben-Gurion save him. He urged Ben-Gurion to fly to England immediately to see Prime Minister Ramsay MacDonald. He showed Ben-Gurion a letter from MacDonald indicating the prime minister's willingness to establish an Arab-Jewish legislative assembly in Palestine based on parity—equal representation—despite the fact that Arabs substantially outnumbered Jews. If an agreement could be negotiated, a great victory for Zionism would be achieved and Weizmann would be spared the humiliating defeat he seemed on the threshold of suffering.

Ben-Gurion, relishing his first meeting with a head of state, a function previously reserved for Weizmann, flew to England in the company of Zionist leader Lewis Namier to meet MacDonald at his country home in Chequers. After breakfasting with MacDonald and his family, the men moved into the prime minister's elegant office, sank into soft leather chairs, and discussed business. Ben-Gurion was startled by MacDonald's remarks as he began to sound like a Zionist himself. Ben-Gurion could not help noticing the contrast between his remarks and his support of the Passfield White Paper, which he later partially abrogated. The prime minister was dominated by one thought—upheaval in Zionist circles as well as in Palestine itself should Weizmann be brought down at the Zionist Congress. No doubt the nervous specter of Jabotinsky was hovering over MacDonald's shoulder as well. MacDonald's concern for Weizmann's fate prompted him to recommend sending his son Malcolm, his aide, to Basel to intercede on Weizmann's behalf. Realizing that such a move would boomerang considering the impatience and discontent felt in the Yishuv concerning Britain, Ben-Gurion and Namier tactfully dissented, after which they left for Basel.

Ben-Gurion and Namier, hoping to get back to Basel as soon as possible to render whatever assistance they could to Weizmann, missed their plane. They were told that for fifty pounds they could hire a private aircraft. Ben-Gurion and Namier explained that they were forced to travel by train.

"What about the time factor?" they were asked.

"How could a couple of poor workers afford a private plane?" they replied.[25]

The act of frugality might have helped to doom Weizmann. The British excursion was a failure because Britain never followed up on the Arab-Jewish legislature concept. When the tired travelers arrived back in Basel, they learned that Weizmann had been defeated by a 123 to 106 count, with Mapai and a sprinkling of General Zionists supporting him.[26]

It appears that Weizmann ultimately "hung himself on his own petard" by arranging a meeting with a British prime minister to save himself from censure. A major thrust of Jabotinsky's Revisionists along with others critical of Weizmann's leadership was Weizmann's close connection to Britain. Another complaint was Weizmann's manner as the words "haughty" and "imperious" continued to be used by his critics.

While Weizmann's defeat was mortal in that he would never regain the level of influence he once held in Zionist circles, it was cushioned by the selection of Nahum Sokolow, his longtime colleague and associate, as president of the World Zionist Organization. Sokolow's election ensured that Weizmann's influence on the organization and on Zionism in general would continue.[27]

Weizmann and Ben-Gurion found satisfaction on one point, the failure of Vladimir Jabotinsky to conquer the Zionist Executive. The tempermental Jabotinsky, true to his reputation, reacted to his defeat by tearing up his delegate's card and storming out of the conference hall, taking his equally frustrated Revisionist colleagues with him.[28]

Just when it appeared that many Zionists might be satisfied with parity concerning the Arabs rather than face an uncertain future anticipating a numerical majority, events unfolding far from the Middle East would generate great influence. Jews had been emigrating to Palestine in considerably smaller numbers than expected by the Zionist leadership. Zionist leaders by the early 1930s therefore altered their earlier demand for a Jewish-dominated Palestine. Instead they opted for a system providing parity between Arabs and Jews, regardless of either group's numerical strength, but these perceptions changed as storm clouds surfaced from Central Europe. The wave of anti-Semitism was gathering frightening momentum, and its tangible result was a steady increase in immigration into Palestine.[29]

During the historically pivotal year of 1933, 30,000 Jews entered Palestine, breaking the record. A total of 13,000 of the new immigrants came from Poland; another 5,000 were from Germany. The new entrants accounted for 15 percent of the Jewish population at the level at which it stood at the beginning of the year. In 1934, another 42,000 Jews entered Palestine; in 1935, the figure burgeoned to 61,000. The 1933–35 immigration period represented a figure equaling two-thirds of the Jewish Palestine population as of January 1933.[30]

The Palestine Arabs became alarmed by the sizable Jewish population increase coupled with a corresponding expansion in land purchases. Arabs began to close ranks, and in April 1936, all major groups, including Muslims and Christians, formed a Supreme Arab Committee, later known as the Arab Higher Committee. A widely supported general strike was called to put pressure on Britain to follow policies in support of the perceived rights of the Arab population. Tension and hostility swiftly mounted between the Arab and Jewish communities, with many acts of violence perpetrated on both sides.

With increasing frequency since the early 1920s, violence had been an unfortunate reaction to Arab and Jewish differences in Palestine, but the formation of the Arab Higher Committee along with the accompanying strike activity added another dimension to a struggle that had been theretofore restricted to Palestinian Arabs and Jews. Local committees for the defense of Palestine along with parliamentary defense committees were organized in various Arab countries, and international conferences were held to muster support for the Palestine Arabs. In 1936, the monarchs of Saudi Arabia, Iraq, Transjordan, and Yemen jointly intervened to end the Palestine strike, the first ever Palestine involvement by Arab states from outside the area.

Reactions to European political events added new dimensions to a struggle previously restricted to the triangle of the interested parties— Arabs, Jews, and the British mandatory authority. While Arab leaders outside the area were becoming actively involved for the first time, the Germans and Italians also initiated propaganda efforts to generate Arab ill will against Britain. With Palestine being an area rife with discord, it was seen as an appropriate Achilles heel to exploit to advantage.[31]

The confounding triangle continued to exist, with Britain seeking to achieve equity and stability after the internal confusion that had been generated by earlier conflicting promises made to Arabs and Jews. The one element that was not needed was severe external pressure from outside forces. As European storm clouds gathered, an already prickly dilemma became even thornier.

# 8

# War and Holocaust

The power to move minds can be a great blessing or a great curse on society, depending upon the messenger.

The messenger of the 1930s had honed his technique in a prison cell following World War One, during which war he had served Germany as a humble infantry corporal. Out of his deep frustrations a corrosive philosophy emerged, one steeped in violent hatred, and his stream of vitriol was launched against Jews. This frustrated messenger with a blueprint for action began his broadside by attacking Jews on hygienic grounds.

> The cleanliness of this people, moral and otherwise, I must say, is a point in itself. By their very exterior you could tell that these were no lovers of water, and, to your distress, you often knew it with your eyes closed. Later I often grew sick to my stomach from the smell of these caftan-wearers. Added to this, there was their unclean dress and their generally unheroic appearance.[1]

From his stinging hygiene indictment the messenger expanded his venomous assault.

> Was there any form of filth or profligacy, particularly in cultural life, without at least one Jew involved in it?
>
> If you cut even cautiously into such an abscess, you found, like a maggot in a rotting body, often dazzled by the sudden light—a kike!
>
> What had to be reckoned heavily against the Jews in my eyes was when

I became acquainted with their activity in the press, art, literature, and the theater. All the unctuous reassurances helped little or nothing. It sufficed to look at a billboard, to study the names of the men behind the horrible trash they advertised, to make you hard for a long time to come. This was pestilence, spiritual pestilence, worse than the Black Death of olden times, and the people was being infected with it! It goes without saying that the lower the intellectual level of one of these art manufacturers, the more unlimited his fertility will be, and the scoundrel ends up like a garbage separator, splashing his filth in the face of humanity. And bear in mind that there is no limit to their number; bear in mind that for one Goethe, Nature easily can foist on the world ten thousand of these scribblers who poison men's souls like germ-carriers of the worse sort, on their fellow men.

It was terrible, but not to be overlooked, that precisely the Jew, in tremendous numbers, seemed chosen by Nature for this shameful calling.

Is this why the Jews are called the "chosen people"?[2]

Written in the privacy of a prison cell, *Mein Kampf* represented a hate-filled view of the world in which its megalomaniacal author, Adolf Hitler, revealed a blueprint for conquest in the form of a Third Reich destined to endure for one thousand years. It ruled Germany for twelve years, falling far short of its architect's bold expectation, but it etched an indelible blueprint of turmoil and suffering. When the smoke cleared following the cataclysm of World War Two, the result was fifty million lost lives. In his hateful quest to eradicate the people he deemed least fit for life, the Jews, Hitler snuffed out six million lives in an unrelenting campaign known as the Final Solution. The Holocaust that resulted dramatically altered the course of Zionism by generating a desire born of survival for Jews to emigrate to Palestine.

Walter Laqueur, author of *A History of Zionism*, makes the case that "only a catastrophe of unprecedented extent . . . enabled Zionism to achieve its aim of a Jewish state . . ."[3]

Both Weizmann and Ben-Gurion met with resistance from many Jews as they argued the merits of Zionism. In England, during his diligent lobbying on behalf of Jews in Palestine, which crystallized in the Balfour Declaration, Weizmann engaged in fierce essay debates with anti-Zionists Claude Montefiore and David Alexander. At the Paris Peace Conference, Weizmann clashed with delegate Sylvain Levi, whose assimilationist views were antithetical to Weizmann's Zionist designs. These were far from isolated incidents. Laqueur cited the rationales of Zionist opposition.

1. As a secularist movement, it was incompatible with the religious character of Judaism.

2. As a political movement, it was inconsistent with the spiritual emphasis of Judaism.

3. As a nationalist movement, it was out of keeping with the universalist character of Judaism.

4. It was a threat to the welfare of Jews, because it confused Gentiles in their thinking about Jews and thus imperiled Jewish status.[4]

Zionism had been under steady ideological assault by liberal critics who emphasized the achievements of Jews had been made by assimilation in Europe. Although discrimination existed, in extreme cases taking the form of pogroms, assimilation had made great strides in Central and Western Europe, and many Jews in those countries felt rooted to them. The point was made that Jews who had grown up in those countries had much more in common with their non-Jewish fellow citizens than with East European Jews, not to mention Jews in Morocco or Yemen. In addition to the natural affinity many Jews felt toward their native land, when thinking about their Jewishness as being linked to a particular nation and not an idealistic Zionist concept, another factor emerged. Even among Jewish intellectuals who might otherwise be drawn toward Zionism as a fascinating concept, the majority were moving into fields such as science or medicine, which were much less subject to ideological exploration and wherein ethnic origin did not greatly matter.

The dilemma confronted by Weizmann and Ben-Gurion in seeking to draw European intellectuals to their cause—individuals they knew could achieve positions of influence in the Yishuv—was the twofold argument of natural attachment to the nation of birth and residence and a level of achievement within that nation that stimulated continuing involvement there.

Laqueur summarized the case for liberalism and assimilation.

It was only a catastrophe of unprecedented extent which enabled Zionism to achieve its aim of a Jewish state. It could not have saved east European Jewry. It had a blueprint for a solution but the conditions for the transfer of millions of Jews simply did not exist. The debate between Zionism and assimilation is, in a sense, over; few now advocate assimilation as the liberals and the protest rabbis did at the turn of the century. But as the majority of the Jews have not chosen to become citizens of the Jewish state, the dilemma persists and Zionism has not won the battle. Since a national or even a cultural revival in the diaspora is unlikely, assimilation is bound to take its course in the years to come with or without the benefit of ideological justification.[5]

The intellectual battle persists over the fundamental question of Zionism's role in international Jewry as opposed to assimilation, but as the turbulent period beginning with Hitler's assumption of Germany's chancellorship commenced, the overriding consideration of survival surmounted all other issues in the minds of European Jews facing an increasing threat of extinction.

The seeds of the bloody conflict of World War Two are traceable to the same Paris Peace Conference that muddled the Palestine picture by producing conflicting promises to Arabs and Jews. In his transcendent objective of achieving a League of Nations he hoped would provide the internal working machinery to prevent future global conflicts, President Woodrow Wilson made numerous concessions to France's Premier Georges Clemenceau, which ensured the continuation of a political-military grudge match with hated rival Germany.

The resulting Treaty of Versailles, through its harsh imposition of terms on Germany, generated hate and mistrust in the minds of many, but none more virulent than with one disgruntled German foot soldier whose rage profoundly altered the course of history. Memories of Treaty of Versailles humiliations smoldered within Adolf Hitler when, in June 1940, his chance to exact revenge on a now humbled France surfaced. He insisted following Germany's conquest that the French sign the armistice agreement in the same railroad car where Marshal Ferdinand Foch had forced the Germans to sign the armistice in 1918. The site was marked by a stone tablet bearing an inscription revealing the hatred between the two nations in which the world conflict was blamed on "the criminal pride of the German empire."

William L. Shirer, then a CBS correspondent, who would later write the powerful chronicle of the Hitler years, *The Rise and Fall of the Third Reich*, stood nearby during the armistice ceremony. He reported that Hitler's face was "afire with scorn, anger, hate, revenge, triumph." After the appropriate documents had been signed and the armistice was in place, Hitler had the stone blown up and the train shipped to Germany. Symbols meant a great deal to Adolf Hitler, as exemplified by his formidable propaganda ministry headed by Joseph Goebbels.[6]

The Goebbels ministry exercised adroit insidiousness in fostering hatred against Jews through the earlier-mentioned tract *The Protocols of the Wise Men of Zion*. The work was published in Brussels in 1864 as an illegal propaganda pamphlet satirizing Napoleon III, then emperor of France. The author was Maurice Joly, a French lawyer, who spent fifteen months in prison when the emperor discovered the satirist's identity. By the advent of the twentieth century, *The Protocols* were resuscitated for propaganda use by General Ratchkovsky, leader of the French division of the Ochrana, the Russian czar's secret police. By selective editing, the tenor of Joly's message was left intact, but a fundamental change was made: the conspirators were Zionists meeting secretly in Basel in 1897. Since it was well-known that the Zionist movement had been founded at a Basel congress in 1897, the incorporation of that publicly known fact gave the work an additional appearance of credence. By the time that the Goebbels machine retrieved the document, the Jews were being subjected to infamy for the second time in a nation where virulent anti-Semitism exceeded that in czarist Russia with its pogroms. The same Joseph Goebbels who thought that people would not believe a small lie but would a large one took a page from Russian anti-Semitics to drive home the impact of Jewish conspiratorial aims as evidenced by *The Protocols of the Wise Men of Zion*.[7]

*The Protocols* demonstrate the will to believe the worst in a people, in this case the Jews, irrespective of the truth. The process of injecting large doses of hate into masses willing to believe the worst lay at the cornerstone of Hitler's campaign against the Jews as well as against other people, such as the Slavs, who were deemed unfit to occupy the same soil as the proud sons and daughters of Germany. This dangerously infantile thinking eventuated in the Holocaust. The destruction of innocent victims in gas chambers had its tragic roots in what psychiatrists and psychologists call arrested development, because the salient difference between the arrested development of Adolf Hitler and that of other individuals was that Hitler was in a position to wreak havoc on an entire world.

Harry Overstreet likens Hitler's approach to proselytizing German youth to that of Russian physiologist Ivan Pavlov in his experiments with his dog.

> By effective stimuli we can build far more enlightened and capable human beings; but by equally effective stimuli, we can build creatures in whom human powers are dangerously distorted. In the schools that Hitler designed for German youth . . . the "meat and bell" technique conditioned a whole generation of boys and girls to contempt for non-Aryans, to cruelty to Jews, to spying upon parents and neighbors, to unquestioning

obedience to the Fuehrer. The Nazi youth—male and female—who poured like a scourge over Europe, had been conditioned into creatures unrecognizable as human by common standards of decency.[8]

In order for a megalomaniac like Hitler to rise to power in a highly sophisticated European nation such as Germany, extreme conditions were a necessity. One vital factor was the long-standing enmity between Germany and France. Spearheaded by France's Georges Clemenceau, harsh Allied terms were imposed upon Germany at Paris. France regained the iron-rich provinces of Alsace and Lorraine, which the Germans had annexed in 1870 when Otto von Bismarck defeated Napoleon III, as well as a trusteeship over the rich coal mines of the Saar. The Austro-Hungarian and Turkish empires were chopped up into a goulash of new nations such as Czechoslovakia and Yugoslavia. A newly independent Poland acquired parts of the German industrial area of Upper Silesia, Posen, and West Prussia, investing Poland with a corridor to the Baltic Sea. Germany alone would be disarmed, forbidden to maintain more than a hundred thousand troops or to possess any major warships, submarines, warplanes, or tanks. Germany was compelled to formally admit that it was guilty of aggression, and it was forced to pay all war damages, a sum estimated at more than $100 billion, which translates to approximately $600 billion today. Until the Germans accepted these harsh terms, the Allies would continue the strangling naval blockade that had been imposed in 1915. Confronted by a grim and haunting reality, Germany succumbed and accepted the terms of the Treaty of Versailles.

Germany was a nation in ruins in the aftermath of war, riddled with turmoil and mass hunger. It had lost nearly two million men, and its mutinous army had disintegrated; its leader, Kaiser Wilhelm III, had fled into exile in Holland. Out of the chaotic political anarchy of the times, the Social Democrats proclaimed a republic with themselves in charge but were being challenged by the Communists for control of the streets.

Lying in a hospital bed northeast of Berlin at this time was a twenty-nine-year-old corporal, partially blinded by mustard gas, who lusted for vengeance in the wake of the defeat and humiliation of Germany. The forces of vengeance that had motivated Georges Clemenceau would now be unleashed by Adolf Hitler but in a bid for global supremacy. The Middle East principle of "an eye for an eye" was alive and well in Europe.[9]

Two leading powers that could have given stability to the global scene in that period of uncertainty, the United States and Great Britain, instead went on hiatus from global responsibilities while attempting to assure themselves that all was well.

In America, where the "return to normalcy" slogan of President Harding was playing well, it was believed by many that the threat of war could be terminated by fiat. Bolstered by French cosponsorship, the Kellogg-Briand Pact was signed. It was immediately hailed as a harbinger of a new epoch because a number of governments had simply declared that war was abolished.

Sumner Welles, assistant secretary of state during 1937–43, regarded the Kellogg-Briand Pact as highly destructive due to its delusionary impact in America and throughout the world.

> I doubt whether, during the years which have elapsed since the Senate rejected the covenant of the League, any aspect of American foreign policy has proved to be more truly harmful in its effect upon the vital interests of the United States. The Kellogg-Briand Pact stimulated the delusion of a great body of the American people that the mere formulation of a wish is equivalent to positive action. It was regarded by many millions of American citizens as a complete justification for the refusal of their government to take part in the League of Nations or to participate actively in any other practical form of international co-operation which would have required action and sacrifice. To them it represented a happy and decorous means of evading rather than accepting responsibility. It lulled to sleep any still lurking feeling of national obligation. It blinded the American people to the danger to their own security inherent in any increasingly unstable world. It greatly accentuated the demands of ultra-pacifist organizations for total disarmament by this country, whatever else other nations might be doing. For a time at least, a majority of the American people were convinced that with such an ironclad guarantee of safety, they need no longer concern themselves about the kind of world they lived in. They could be confident that war was a thing of the past.[10]

While America basked in the false glow of complacency engendered by Kellogg-Briand's abolition of war by fiat—what Sumner Welles regarded as the high watermark for isolationist thought in America—Great Britain was mired in what Winston Churchill later called "the years the locusts had eaten" in which, lulled to sleep by a complacency of their own, Prime Minister Stanley Baldwin would be followed by Neville Chamberlain, coarchitect, with Adolf Hitler, of the Munich Agreement, wherein the Sudetenland was handed over to Germany in exchange for what Chamberlain asserted was "peace in our time."

In Britain, Churchill's grim warnings were ignored until the beast had virtually arrived on the doorstep, while in America, even after the mantle of leadership had passed to Churchill, President Franklin D. Roosevelt, despite his distrust of Hitler and his sympathy for the British cause, was hamstrung by a strong isolationist tide. Ultimately, the situation reached the point where Roosevelt, concluding that imperiling events from abroad could not be ignored, risked impeachment by secretly opening the Office of Strategic Services (OSS) in a Washington office building. Forerunner of the Central Intelligence Agency, the OSS was headed by William Donovan, who maintained close contact with the British.

The powerful Committee to Defend America First, whose membership comprised many influential Americans, resisted efforts to aid Britain. Pursuing an isolationist view, the organization's most influential speaker was legendary American aviator Charles Lindbergh. The isolationist ranks also included rabid anti-Semites such as Father Charles Coughlin and Gerald L. K. Smith, who sought to link any aid-Britain movement to a Jewish effort to draw the world into war. Opposition to Hitler's Third Reich was viewed as a smokescreen designed to cover up international Jewish monetary designs.

Post-Versailles Germany was a nation reeling with economic uncertainty. Crippled by extreme inflation, which produced economic hardship on a vast scale, a sophisticated nation riddled with doubt and fear for the future proved vulnerable to the strident nationalistic tones of Adolf Hitler, himself a creature of severe frustration. Born in Bavaria, a region known for anti-Semitism, Hitler contracted a lung ailment at sixteen that necessitated a long recovery period, in which he was doted upon by his mother. Given to fits of moodiness and withdrawal, the headstrong young Austrian rejected his father's suggestion that his son follow him into the civil service. Hitler had grandiose plans to become an artist, scoffing at the idea of a regular job with only the prospect of a steady paycheck after every week. His father retired from his civil service position and died when Hitler was thirteen. He was considerably older than Hitler's mother. This death did not profoundly move Hitler, but when his mother died from breast cancer, he was inconsolable. This cruelest psychological blow of his life, one from which he would never recover, occurred when he was nineteen.

Besides his passionate desire to become an artist, another strong urge germinated during his formative teen years. By the age of sixteen he had already developed his obsession with politics. William L. Shirer wrote:

By then [when Hitler was sixteen] he had developed a violent hatred for the Hapsburg monarchy and all the non-German races in the multinational Austro-Hungarian Empire over which it ruled, and an equally violent love for everything German. At sixteen he had become what he was to remain to his dying breath: a fanatical German nationalist.[11]

Hitler's Vienna period was marked by failure to achieve as an artist, hunger, and intense introspection. It was not surprising that this maladjusted, previously sheltered individual, having been thrust into the real world and failing in the area where he had predestined himself for greatness, would withdraw into a realm of hatred intermingled with fantasy. Throughout his description of his gloomy Vienna phase in *Mein Kampf*, Hitler's venomous prose was directed at the Jews in his belief that his own failure as an artist was related to a perceived conspiratorial apparatus of the Jews, who were said to control the arts in the city, along with the newspapers.

The historical, political, and sociological concepts developed in *Mein Kampf* and practiced by Hitler were a half-baked smorgasbord gleaned from a series of authors who had had an impact on Germans to one extent or another beginning in the early nineteenth century. An analysis of these authors and their impact on Hitler, who lacked the trained social scientist's skills to logically develop ideas from a cohesive perspective, put the lie to his claim in *Mein Kampf* to having formulated his ideas about the Jews and German history on his own during his formative Vienna period.

The master race concept so shrilly and forcefully advanced by Hitler had also been strongly advocated by Johann Gottlieb Fichte at the University of Berlin, where he held the chair of philosophy, in 1807 as he confronted a Germany crushed and humiliated by defeat against Napoleon at Jena. The powerful words of Fichte were meant to rally Germans in the wake of a bitter military defeat, just as Hitler would advance the same arguments to stir up hatred and instill nationalistic pride in a Germany reeling from its World War One setback. To Fichte the Jews along with the Latins, especially the French, constituted inferior races, and only Germans held the potential for regeneration.

With Fichte's death in 1814 surfaced a towering figure of world philosophy who would wield thematic influence among proponents of the "isms" of the far left and the far right, Communism and Nazism. Assuming the philosophy chair vacated by Fichte's demise was Georg Friedrich Hegel. Hegel's dialectical theory heavily influenced Marx, who saw history as a pattern of evolving events, culminating in a

Communist state. Hitler derived from Hegel the concept of the State as the highest order of society, the possessor of supreme rights against the individual, existing above all special privileges. Hegel foresaw such a State for Germany once it recovered its God-given genius.

Heinrich von Treitschke was a professor of history at the University of Berlin between 1874 to his death in 1896. He glorified the state in the manner of Hegel but going one step beyond by declaring subjects of the state as little more than slaves. He was noted for the saying, "It does not matter what you think so long as you obey."[12] Von Treitschke also deemed war to constitute the highest expression of man.

Friedrich Wilhelm Nietzsche, like Goethe, held no high opinion of the German people and regarded most German philosophers, including Fichte and Hegel, as "unconscious swindlers."[13] Insanity eventually overtook him, yet even before his breakdown his work was short on balance and long on diatribes. What was it about this man, no German nationalist or enthusiast about things Germanic, that so impressed the ultranationalist Hitler? The reason was Nietzsche's extolling of the Superman in history and his view of how a ruler race could sweep civilization, led by a daring leader surrounded by an elite that would become "lords of the earth." Such language excited Hitler, as did Nietzsche's resounding excoriations of liberal thinkers like John Stuart Mill, who dared to see humanity in compassionate terms.

The French diplomat Count Joseph Arthur de Gobineau's racial concepts had a pronounced influence on Hitler's favorite composer, Richard Wagner, during that eccentric musical genius's last six years before his death. The leading contribution by Gobineau was a four-volume work published in Paris between 1853 and 1855 entitled *Essay on the Inequality of the Human Races*. The white race was deemed superior to all others, and the jewel of the white race was the Aryan. The French author lamented that the contemporary Aryan suffered from intermixture with inferior races, which he found to be evidenced by the Southern European of his time.

On any scale of Hitlerian influence, the person invested with the title of spiritual father of the Third Reich was not a German but an Englishman, Houston Stewart Chamberlain, son of an English admiral, nephew of a British field marshal and two British generals, and eventual son-in-law of fellow anti-Semite Richard Wagner. Coming from a distinguished military family, Chamberlain was believed to be destined for a career in the British Army or Navy, but his delicate health ruled out such a career. He was educated in France and Geneva, where French became his first language. From the time of his involvement with Germany between the ages of fifteen and nineteen, he was irresistibly drawn to that nation. Eventually he became a German citizen as well as one of the nation's foremost thinkers. A neurotic who was subject to frequent nervous breakdowns, Chamberlain claimed that he saw demons. It was during an alleged nineteen-month siege of demon possession that Chamberlain penned his most enduring work. *Foundations of the Nineteenth Century* spanned 1,200 pages. It was published in 1899, achieved an impressive sales record over many editions and years, and influenced the anti-Semitic mind-set of Hitler and the Third Reich.

Chamberlain arrived at the same conclusion as Gobineau, whom he admired, that the key to history and civilization was embodied in race. After extolling the Teutons and evaluating the importance of every nation based on the proportion of genuine Teutonic blood in its population, Chamberlain reserved the longest chapter of his book for the Jews. After asserting that the Jews and the Teutons constituted the only pure races left in the West, he proceeded to launch into traditional anti-Semitic verbiage, later used to good advantage by Hitler's propagandists.

Chamberlain found himself on tenuous ground in his strong declarations about Christ alongside his statements concerning Jewish inferiority. According to Chamberlain, the contemporary world had received three great bequests from ancient times: Greek philosophy and art, Roman Law, and the personality of Christ. So how did Chamberlain reconcile his tremendous respect for the influence of the personality of Christ on the contemporary world with Christ's Jewish roots? Chamberlain denied that Christ was a Jew, and he set out to prove his point by citing Christ's Galilean origins and his inability to pronounce correctly the Aramaic gutturals, which Chamberlain regarded as clear signs that Jesus had a large amount of non-Semitic blood. If Jesus Christ were not a Jew, then what was his origin? Chamberlain concluded that Christ was probably an Aryan, if not entirely by blood, then due to his moral and religious teaching in contrast to the perceived materialism and abstract formalism that he felt characterized the Jewish religion.

Hitler was the only public figure to attend Chamberlain's funeral on January 11, 1927. Kaiser Wilhelm II, who had been influenced by Chamberlain's writings, was barred from returning to German soil due to Treaty of Versailles restrictions and was represented by a prince. During the strategically vital period of the 1920s, when Hitler was seeking support, he was shunned as a rabble-rouser by many. Chamberlain, however, had been an early and enthusiastic supporter of the Third Reich, and Hitler felt he owed the eccentric Englishman a debt of gratitude, so Chamberlain's works became standard Nazi gospel.

Hitler's paranoia took on two basic components: (1) a messianic complex with the dominant belief that he had been singled out to lead Germany to greatness and (2) a series of hate objects composing an enemy list, which fed his lust for power and justified the extreme ends he embraced toward his power objective.

Hitler put his blueprint for revolutionary upheaval, delineated in *Mein Kampf*, to work in a troubled nation tortured by a painful war defeat and an economic apocalypse. After becoming chancellor in 1933, he attacked his enemies, specifically anyone whom he could not count on for blind fealty. A book-burning at the University of Berlin highlighted destruction of works by Jewish authors such as Einstein and Freud but also included German non-Jews such as Thomas and Heinrich Mann as well. A huge exodus out of the country got under way and consisted of Jews and non-Jews alike. The fearsome knock on the door, a concomitant of the most brutal dictatorships, had become increasingly commonplace.

Pastor Martin Neimöller, a celebrated German clergyman, had been a decorated World War One U-boat commander who briefly supported the Nazis. His penalty for changing his course was a four-year internment at Dachau. His statement regarding the Nazi pattern of operation ranks among the most memorable:

> They came first for the Communists, and I didn't speak up because I wasn't a Communist. Then they came for the Jews, and I didn't speak up because I wasn't a Jew. Then they came for the Catholics, and I didn't speak up because I was a Protestant. Then they came for me, and by that time there was no one left to speak up.[14]

Christopher Isherwood lived during the turbulent period of Nazism's rise in Berlin. His observations triggered a popular work, *The Berlin Stories*, which in turn spawned the eminently successful stage musical drama and Academy Award–winning film *Cabaret*.

"Hate exploded suddenly, without warning, out of nowhere, at street corners, in restaurants, cinemas, dance halls," Isherwood wrote. "Knives were whipped out, blows were dealt with spiked rings, beer-mugs, chair-legs or leaded clubs."[15]

Isherwood's graphic words illustrate the culmination of phenomena that, taken together, represent a theorem as precise as any in the laws of physics: Two elements—political uncertainty (generally with strong economic overtones) merging with an emergent political force reacting to fearful uncertainty (in this case Hitler and his Third Reich)—combine to form a terrifying third force, which emerges as a seething gargoyle. The masses of a troubled nation, in this case Germany, constituted a third force, dominated by angry intolerance and seeking vengeance on the rest of the world. Sown by seeds of despair and uncertainty, molded by wounded national pride and economic crisis, this third force takes on a personality all its own, in the manner of an angry mob seeking revenge against a helpless individual caught up in the vortex of rage.

The pattern becomes clear when examining Hitler's tormented inner rage and his response to deeply rooted psychological traumas exending back to early boyhood. When articulated in a political framework, these unhealed psychological wounds connected cohesively with the intense frustrations of the German people's reaction to sociopolitical events. Hilter, uniting with the distraught elements of German society, formed a third force, a fire-breathing gargoyle determined to exterminate all in its path.

An examination of the roots of German frustrations exploited by Hilter makes it easier to observe the crucial role played by hate objects. Anger and frustration sweep away logical discourse. Half-baked would-be solutions are tendered to angry masses that devour them. The hate objects, paramount among which were the Jews, were necessary objects to satiate the hungry appetite of the all-devouring gargoyle, which demanded flesh and blood. Burning vengeance knows neither bounds nor logic. Simple answers are sought for complex problems. Hated enemies afford convenient targets for hate and easy solutions to problems. To Hitler his failure to achieve success as a young man in Vienna was inextricably tied to the influence wielded by Jews. Later, in *Mein Kampf*, he extended the same notion to the entire German nation. To restore itself to greatness, Germany must crush the Jews.

The assiduous hate campaign that Hitler launched against Jews fit into both a psychological pattern in which a thoroughly troubled individual fed from his neuroses and an insidious pragmatic political program that, given the confusing uncertainties of the period, bore fruit.

The anti-Semitic pattern can be categorized as follows.

1. *Psychological*—The severely troubled Hitler, beset by insecurities, needed hate victims to justify his past failures and afford him a

badly needed veneer of superiority. This phenomenon can be symbolized by the past hatred felt by poor white dirt farmers of the Southern United States against blacks. As a downtrodden group, poor whites, who had much in common with blacks in terms of poverty and alienated victimization, instead turned their rage upon them because it felt so good to abuse someone conceived of as occupying an even lower station than yourself.

2. *Mass psychology*—The rallying cry for a revolutionary political party seeking to achieve an upheaval among troubled masses is that of hate, of calculated revenge. The best means of dramatically symbolizing such hate and revenge is through a victim. In this case, the Jews of Germany made up about 1 percent of the population, which rendered them a small enough group to be successfully bullied by Hitler's Nazi goon squads.

3. *Pragmatic politics*—Hitler greatly admired the popular mayor of Vienna, Karl Luger, who appealed to anti-Semitic feelings of many Viennese in order to enhance his popularity. As mentioned earlier, anti-Semitism was also a pervasive force in the Bavaria in which young Adolf Hitler grew up. Once more an analogy can be drawn to U.S. politics as exemplified by Southern politicians who curried favor with voters by lacing speeches with heavily antiblack invective in the days before blacks were allowed to vote in the region.

4. *Panacea*—This element is linked to Hitler's grand design of a master race incorporated into a regime destined to endure for one thousand years. In order to achieve such a superstate, a Plato's *Republic* of modern times, it was necessary to drive out all those deemed by the regime's Nietzschean Superman, Adolf Hitler, as unfit, and to Hitler, Jews bore that indelible mark of inferiority. They and other perceived inferiors such as the much-maligned Slavs needed to be cleared away so that the master race could function unimpededly.

In *Mein Kampf*, Hitler likened the subjugation of lower human species to humanity's the taming of wild beasts. The first stirrings of culture, according to Hitler, occurred when Aryan conquerors bent the vanquished to their will. As long as the Aryan retained the whip hand the evolution of culture continued, and when the subjugated peoples arose and assumed the level of conqueror, the world experienced cultural disintegration.[16]

Culture constituted one word of supreme importance to Adolf Hitler—purity. As other cultures began establishing themselves, that purity was lost, with grave consequences ensuing. Hitler spells out in

*Mein Kampf* what he perceives as the grievous consequences of Aryan purity lost.

> As soon as the subjected people began to raise themselves up and probably approached the conqueror in language, the sharp dividing wall between master and servant fell. The Aryan gave up the purity of his blood and, therefore, lost his sojourn in the paradise which he had made for himself. He became submerged in the racial mixture, and gradually, more and more, lost his cultural capacity, until at last, not only mentally but also physically, he began to resemble the subjected aborigines more than his own ancestors. For a time he could live on the existing cultural benefits, but then petrification set in and he fell prey to oblivion.
>
> Blood mixture and the resultant drop in the racial level is the sole cause of the dying out of old cultures; for men do not perish as a result of lost wars, but by the loss of that force of resistance which is contained only in pure blood.[17]

Hitler's dichotomy is clear. The world is broken down into those with racially pure bloodlines and all other less fortunates, who are described as "chaff." Jews and Slavs were the foremost examples of chaff, and when Hitler assumed power, he forbade marriages between Germans and members of those groups, disregarding the fact that a good deal of Slavic blood was intermixed in the German people, especially among those in the Eastern Provinces. Such anthropological evidence, however, was ignored by the determined historical march of the Third Reich, whose successful goal fell into the same pattern of inevitability as the classless society Marx envisioned as the ultimate result of Communism's historical triumph.

As Hitler's consolidation of power became more pronounced in the wake of economic recovery, his popularity rising to 90 percent among the voting electorate, he began to carry out his programs more boldly. As Jews became more affected in Germany, pressures within Palestine appreciably heightened because of increased immigration and growing resistance on the part of the Arabs, which in turn enlarged pressures on the British.

On April 28, 1935, an important announcement was delivered by German Minister of the Interior Wilhelm Frick giving advanced notice of the Nuremberg Laws, which would be passed in September. The time had come, Frick revealed, to deprive all Jews of their German citizenship. The march to leave Germany was on, and the Jews who remained awaited harsh fates, as events would confirm.

On October 28, the Germans launched an assault against thousands of Polish Jews, who had lived for many years in the Reich. Children were snatched from the streets without parental notification, jammed into trains and trucks with thousands of others including the aged and infirm, and taken to the Polish border. They were allowed to take only ten marks and the clothes on their backs. In the biting cold, they sought refuge in empty railroad cars and abandoned heatless barracks in a no-man's land between the German and Polish borders.

As world attention became increasingly focused on this cruel perpetration of misery and suffering wrought by a callous political regime, the plot thickened with the emergence of the Zindel Grynszpan family of Hanover. One of the Grynszpan sons, seventeen-year-old Herschel, had fled to Paris earlier. Herschel read a letter from his father describing the family's torment as victims dumped in the cold at the Polish border. The longer he read the letter, the more painfully young Herschel's heart ached for his family. He had been in an overwrought state since leaving Poland, and the letter pushed him over the brink. On November 7, Herschel Grynszpan visited the German Embassy in Paris with the intention of assassinating Ambassador Johannes von Welczeck. He demanded to see the ambassador but was received instead by a minor official, Ernst vom Rath, shooting him instead.

A tragic note of irony surrounds the assassination of Ernst vom Rath as the target of misplaced aggression by a distraught, embittered young Polish Jew. The target of the bullets intended for Ambassador von Welczeck was under investigation by the Gestapo at the very time the shots were fired. Ernst vom Rath was the subject of an inquiry due to his opposition to anti-Semitism!

Given the propagandistic propensities of Hitler and Goebbels, along with their successful use of symbols, the vom Rath assassination was seized upon with alacrity. Vom Rath, under suspicion of heresy, assumed the fresh identity of martyr to the Fatherland. Even before his death, as he lay unconscious in Paris, the Nazi machinery was moving into gear as the press instigated a massive reprisal against the Jews.

Overlooked by the German press, the conduct and statements of Herschel Grynszpan in the custody of the Paris police revealed a pattern of sorrowful confusion. He broke down and sobbed, "Being a Jew is not a crime. I am not a dog. I have a right to exist on this earth. Wherever I have been I have been chased like an animal."[19]

Ernst vom Rath died on November 9. A "spontaneous" demonstration was organized by Reinhard Heydrich, who commanded the Security Service organization under Heinrich Himmler. At two o'clock in the morning the day after vom Rath's death, the Nazis launched a wave of arson, looting, murder, and arrests that left world opinion quivering in response. In the ensuing wave of destruction, some 195 synagogues were burned and more than 800 shops were destroyed and 7,500 looted. A total of 20,000 Jews were arrested and delivered to concentration camps. Official German figures listed 36 deaths, which was disputed by newsmen and diplomatic observers on the scene. The widespread devastation unleashed by German authorities left the streets covered by glass from the thousands of shop windows that were shattered in the onslaught. As a result, the disaster became known as *Kristallnacht*, or the "night of broken glass."[19]

Events in Germany had an inevitable impact on life in the Yishuv. Just as the "night of broken glass" would hold momentous historical impact for Jews, an event that took place on Palestine soil two years earlier, June 16, 1933, compounded the dilemma confronting Jews seeking an appropriate response to events affecting their brothers and sisters in Germany.

With emotions rising sharply in the Yishuv as the subject of German treatment of Jews was debated, the Jewish Agency sent its political secretary, Chaim Arlosoroff, to Berlin to negotiate the transfer of German Jews to Palestine. The agency's rationale was that, should Germany be willing to cooperate, Berlin would respond by throwing open the door to Palestine to these refugees.

The Jewish Agency initiative was vehemently condemned by Revisionists and David Ben-Gurion for different reasons. The Revisionists believed that such activity constituted "trafficking with the enemy." Ben-Gurion's opposition related to the question of priority. He opposed any pattern of conduct that, in his view, would have the net effect of placing German refugees from Hitler on a higher plateau than other Jews who should also comprise a functional part of the Yishuv. On July 9, 1933, Ben-Gurion made his position clear in a communication to his party.

> If the situation in Germany offers us new groups of volunteers, fine, but I view Zionism in its totality: The Jews of [Eastern Europe], and especially the youth, are as important as the German youth. They must be saved no less rapidly than the young Jews of Germany.[20]

That same summer of 1933, Ben-Gurion campaigned in Eastern Europe to encourage Jewish immigration to Palestine as he visited Poland, Lithuania, Estonia, and Latvia. He felt that Chaim Arlosoroff and the

Jewish Agency would be better served emulating his example and appealing to Zionism "in its totality."

The all-consuming quest by Ben-Gurion to perceive Zionism "In its totality" led to a fatal tunnel vision in which, due to his focus on achieving his paramount objective as most of these German Jews would be ultimately exterminated in death camp gas chambers during World War Two. Arlosoroff and the Jewish Agency were perceptive in recognizing the imminent dangers confronting German Jews in view of a Nazi leadership dedicated to their ultimate destruction.

As for Chaim Arlosoroff, the future looked bright for the thirty-four-year-old Zionist leader, but at the same time it also held cause for apprehension. He believed that his German excursion would bring results as the Nazis agreed in principle to allow Jews to emigrate to Palestine in exchange for their property. He had also been excoriated upon his return from Germany as the "criminal Arlosoroff" and "Mapai's Red diplomat crawling on all fours before Hitler" in *Bir-yonim*, the newspaper of the extreme Revisionist wing. He knew that many disapproved of the Berlin initiative, including Ben-Gurion, but the ascetic young man who had been born in the Ukraine and had received a doctorate in Berlin at twenty-three, saw the future with a clarity that Ben-Gurion and others could not match. He foresaw the makings of a Holocaust and felt that if he could save even one Jewish life, the trip was a success.

On the evening of June 16, 1933, just three days after his return from Berlin, Arlosoroff and his wife, Sima, dined on the veranda of Tel Aviv's seaside Kaete Dan Hotel, then went for a stroll on the beach. The night was oppressively warm, and a few people were in the area because it was a Friday and most Jews were at home savoring their Sabbath meals with their families. As the two walked along the beach in the moonlight, two men approached. One of them thrust a flashlight into Arlosoroff's face and asked:

"What time is it?" When Arlosoroff reached for his pocket watch, the other man pulled out a pistol and fired at him. The strangers sprinted away. Shortly after, Sima managed to stop a car, which sped the victim to the hospital, but to no avail, as Arlosoroff died.

The killing of the brilliant young Zionist leader touched off a tumult of controversy in a Yishuv that was already a tinderbox of explosive political emotion. On his deathbed, Arlosoroff told a visiting colleague that the men were not Jews. His widow told Jewish officers working for the British police that the killer and his companion were Arabs. Earlier she had assured the two men who had driven her and her dying husband to the hospital that she was "one hundred percent sure that the attackers were Arabs."[21]

Initially, the unchallenged conclusion in the Yishuv was that the murderers were Arabs, but in time, the shadow of suspicion gravitated toward the Revisionists. Meticulous attention was focused on the *Biryonim*, which had excoriated Arlosoroff for meeting with German authorities. Its viewpoint was considered by conventional Zionists of Mapai as decidedly fascistic; Mussolini had received praise in the publication. Additional suspicion resulted from a statement in *Biryonim* that the Jewish people "will know how to act appropriately" to Arlosoroff's "crime." That chilling warning, interpreted in the wake of the murder and coupled with the known Revisionist propensity for violence, pointed a finger of suspicion in the direction of the Revisionists.

To Ben-Gurion and his colleagues the Arlosoroff murder provided a golden opportunity to cultivate goodwill with the British in the mutual interest of both parties. The Hagana had been formed by essentially moderate Zionists to protect themselves against a perceived Arab terrorist threat, and its mandate was that of self-defense. Since the objective on the part of leading Zionists such as Ben-Gurion and Katznelson was to cultivate the best relations possible with mandatory power Great Britain, their eyes focused on the future and the objective of statehood. One of their greatest fears, which could hurl a serious roadblock in their path, was an outgrowth of extremism within Jewish ranks. They feared the volatility of Jabotinsky as well as some of the more extreme Revisionists such as those who belonged to *Biryonim*. Accordingly, they were happy to aid the British in attempting to solve the Arlosoroff murder. As for the British, who sought to preserve order in troubled Palestine, they were more than happy to accept the cooperation of the Hagana, hoping it would make their job easier to perform.

Ensuing events called to mind Franz Kafka's "The Trial." Avraham Stavsky, who belonged to *Biryonim* and was reportedly planning to leave Palestine urgently, was fingered by a Jewish employee in the immigration department. The *Hagana* secured a copy of Stavsky's photograph and showed it to Sima Arlosoroff, who identified Stavsky as the man with the flashlight. Police later showed her photographs of ten people. Again she identified Stavsky as the man with the flashlight. The widow retracted her initial statement that her husband's attackers were Arab. Her original testimony also mysteriously disappeared from police files. Abba Achimer, a *Biryonim* leader, was charged with perpetrating the crime since he had written an inflammatory article a few months earlier that appeared to justify political murder under certain circumstances. Revisionist cell leader Zvi Rosenblatt was arrested as the accused trigger man after being fingered by Rivka Feigin, a woman of dubious reputation, who had earlier been thrown out of the same cell that Rosenblatt led.

With Stavsky, Achimeir, and Rosenblatt in hand, the prosecution set out to prove its case. Authorities were then rocked, on their heels as an Arab being held in prison on an unrelated murder charge confessed that he and another Arab were the two men who had accosted Arlosoroff on the beach and that his friend had fired the fatal shot at the Zionist leader by accident. He explained that he and his friend were playing a prank and had wanted to "have some fun" with Arlosoroff's wife. "Do you know that you could be hanged for this crime?" he was asked. The prisoner then withdrew his story. No further investigation occurred regarding this extraordinary confession, but the matter did not end there. Two years later, the same Arab again insisted that he and his friend had been responsible for the Zionist leader's death. The prisoner's account went uninvestigated.

The most damaging evidence concerning efforts to convict the three Revisionists surfaced years later from Yehuda Arazi, a *Hagana* member and police inspector who conducted the original investigation for the British and, after World War Two, headed the secret *Hagana* network that transported illegal immigrants and arms into Palestine. His published allegiations revealed that the British, aided and abetted by Mapai and the *Hagana*, had deliberately sought to place the blame on the Revisionists. Arazi wrote the following in a report to the British intelligence chief on August 28, 1933: "It is my impression that all the witnesses, beginning with Mrs. Arlosoroff, have wanted to incriminate the suspects at any cost."[22]

Arazi was abruptly removed from the case after this disclosure. Considering his lifetime of service to the Zionist cause and his links to both Mapai and the *Hagana*, Arazi's disclosures do not appear to have been motivated by ill will.

In the trial that followed, Rosenblatt and Achimeir were acquitted, and Stavsky was found guilty and sentenced to hang. He was later freed for lack of sufficient evidence as the explosive and politically embarrassing Arlosoroff affair ended.

Political duress frequently results in classic cases or injustice. Such examples are legion among dictatorships, but even in democratic societies, the pressures generated by instability and uncertainty can project the worst about individuals and situations. A classic example in U.S. history is the My Lai Massacre perpetrated during a controversial U.S. military involvement in Vietnam. British authorities as well as the *Hagana* feared the impact of the Revisionists on an already divided Palestine, in which tensions were rapidly accelerating between Jews and Arabs. Frustration over the explosive Revisionist connection in the perpetual mine field of Palestine had driven the British and the *Hagana* to excessive levels in which three innocent men could have been easily hanged for a murder in which none had been involved.

The pragmatic David Ben-Gurion, a politican with a penchant for draining every drop from a potentially favorable situation, saw the Arlosoroff incident as a successful opportunity, despite its absence of legal resolution. The affair had created an unfavorable climate for the Revisionists, and Ben-Gurion was determined to apply all available pressure on his feared enemy.

The determination of Ben-Gurion to oust Jabotinsky and his supporters from the Zionist movement became clear at the Zionist Congress in Basel two years earlier, in 1931, when he did something virtually unthinkable for Ben-Gurion—he supported his long-standing enemy Weizmann to thwart a leadership challenge from Jabotinsky's Revisionists.

In a letter to party leaders on July 9, he wrote, "This is the moment when I find myself steeped in bitterness before . . . the profanation that surrounds us. Still drenched with Arlosoroff's blood, impure forces raise their heads and try to make us serve them . . . The coming [Zionist World] Congress will be decisive. It will be our last chance."[23]

The Ben-Gurion strategy is obvious to the politically astute. Whether or not the Revisionists were responsible for the death of Chaim Arlosoroff, out of the controversy surrounding his murder a climate emerged in which Revisionists were linked to violence. Ben-Gurion sought to perpetuate this connection, hanging it around Revisionist necks like an albatross. The ploy of linking the Revisionists to violence and discord bore fruit when Eastern European crowds taunted and hurled stones at Ben-Gurion, unwittingly helping him make his case through their own violent conduct.

The campaign paid off handsomely, as evidenced by world returns for convention delegates. The results were exultantly received by Ben-Gurion in his hotel room as Labor registered a total of 44 percent of the world vote, for an impressive gain of 15 percent; the Revisionists received 16 percent, for a net loss of 5 percent.

At the World Zionist Congress that convened on August 25, 1933,

Ben-Gurion stood in a position of unrivaled power. Labor was now securely in command, and he would leave the convention as Zionism's most powerful leader. All the same, he remained fearful of the opposition that the Revisionists, with Jabotinsky in the forefront, could still present. He even wrote to a colleague that he feared Jabotinsky might destroy the parliament, in this case the Zionist Congress, in the same way that Hitler and Mussolini had crushed the parliaments in Germany and Italy.

A resolution sponsored by Ben-Gurion and his colleagues to eradicate from the Zionist movement elements constituting a danger to the rebuilding of *Eretz Yisrael* wreaked havoc in the convention hall. Ben-Gurion had hoped that Revisionist power would simply wither away, but now the movement was dangerously split.

Despite major differences, Labor and Revisionist delegates alike did not want to see the Zionist movement dangerously split, and so an agreement was reached to which Ben-Gurion acceded. He was asked to join the Zionist Executive. Much to his surprise, Revisionists urged the move along with his own Laborities in a unified gesture. His labor union roots remained strong as he sought to retain control of his *Histadrut* post while simultaneously serving as chairman of the Zionist Executive. He was allowed to do so, emerging from Prague as Zionism's most powerful leader.

Volatility within Zionist ranks persisted, however, even in the wake of the Prague accord. Once the air of good feeling pervading the Prague Congress faded away, the Revisionists threatened Ben-Gurion's power anew by breaking up strikes called by the *Histadrut*. The streets erupted with stone throwing amidst loud and angry cursing. At a time when Ben-Gurion felt that Jewish unity was paramount in view of disconcerting events occurring in Germany, disharmony was rife.

While in the midst of despair over current circumstances, a letter arrived at Mapai headquarters from the Revisionists suggesting direct talks between the two sides with the prospect of achieving a modus vivendi. Ben-Gurion would have undoubtedly refused to meet with Jabotinsky and his Revisionists had he felt they lacked a necessary power base. Following the humiliation the Revisionists had suffered in Prague, he hoped they were finished as a viable entity within the Yishuv; however, instead of fading from the scene, they had staged a dramatic comeback. Now that he was the most powerful Zionist leader in the world, a position he had dreamed of from his earliest days in the movement, Ben-Gurion did not want to risk being undone by conflict within his own Jewish ranks when he wanted to keep his energies free to deal with British authorities in pursuit of his ultimate goal of a Jewish state. He remained painfully aware of Jabotinsky's demand for the immediate creation of a Jewish state, and there had once been a time when a younger Ben-Gurion had posed the same question to Chaim Weizmann. But now he agreed with his bitter rival Weizmann that such a demand would only increase pressures within the ranks of the Arabs and upon the British when tensions within Palestine were already at a boiling point. As bitter a pill as it was for him to swallow, Ben-Gurion recognized only too painfully that the determined Jabotinsky was not about to abandon the political scene. The street battles served as painful reminders to Ben-Gurion that the Revisionists remained a viable political force.

Delegates of the two parties met in London in early October 1934, with Ben-Gurion and Jabotinsky contemplating their first ever face-to-face meeting. Ben-Gurion had referred to Jabotinsky as "Vladimir Hitler" in describing what he perceived as intransigent and unreasonable behavior. At the same time, however, he had always harbored a secret admiration for Jabotinsky, a man of many parts—political leader, historian, playwright, poet, orator. He also believed that Jabotinsky held a deep hatred for him.

When the men finally met, Ben-Gurion was surprised to learn that Jabotinsky admired him as well, an equivalent respect for a talented adversary. Initially, they were astonished to learn that their views were not as contradictory as they had imagined, but when they began to consider joint action, their disagreements surfaced. Jabotinsky, who placed great value on political pressure, urged that two million European Jews petition their governments and Great Britain to let them enter Palestine. Ben-Gurion held fast to his own formula: underground pioneer action as the means by which to achieve a state.

Ben-Gurion and Jabotinsky met almost daily and engaged in long sessions of bickering and bargaining. Finally, after one harrowing all-night session, on October 26, they emerged with an agreement and staggered exultantly into the early morning London fog. The agreement forbade all "acts of terror or violence in any shape or form" as well as "libel, slander, insult to individuals or groups."[24]

The two continued to work industriously to achieve other agreements. Ben-Gurion signed a labor truce that would, it was hoped, result in peace between the *Histadrut* and the Revisionist trade union movement. Further accords were anticipated as well when, all of a sudden, a deep and abiding frustration welling up from deep within him, Ben-Gurion broke off all negotiations and returned home to Palestine.

What had brought the negotiations to a halt?

The joy Ben-Gurion exuded as a result of his negotiating efforts was not being shared by his Labor comrades in the Yishuv. The first indication of where he stood occurred the day following his pact with Jabotinsky renouncing terror and violence between the two groups. Berl Katznelson read about the accord in the Palestine press and immediately telephoned Ben-Gurion, issuing a warning that "The comrades take a negative view of the agreement."[25]

Ben-Gurion brushed off the warning but was rocked by a series of cables from Palestine sharply denouncing his accord with Jabotinsky and his efforts to achieve others. Moshe Shertok, who had replaced Chaim Arlosoroff as head of the Jewish Agency's political department, asked, "What is the meaning of the panic and excitement?"[26]

The pragmatic realist Ben-Gurion believed that a rapprochement with the Revisionists served the best interests of Labor, but the bitter clashes with Revisionists had been too numerous for the rank and file. A cable finally arrived from Katznelson stating it was urgent that Ben-Gurion return home.

While Ben-Gurion would return to turmoil admist his ranks, Jabotinsky had problems keeping his own allies in line as bitter memories remained over efforts by Mapai in concert with British authorities to hang three of their members for the murder of Chaim Arlosoroff.

One young firebrand who idolized Jabotinsky but disagreed strongly with him on the subject of cooperation with Labor replied to his leader's support for approval of the pact of the Sixth Revisionist World Conference in Cracow, Poland, in January of 1935 with the following stern words: "You may have forgotten that Ben-Gurion once called you 'Vladimir Hitler,' but we have a better memory."[27]

The firebrand, Menachem Begin, would eventually become prime minister of Israel after many clashes with Ben-Gurion and his protégés. His Likud Party bloc would eventually supplant the Labor Party founded by Ben-Gurion, which would rule the nation until Begin's historic breakthrough in 1977. Though Begin and other delegates were disturbed by the prospect of an agreement with the hated Mapai forces, Jabotinsky exerted enough control over the Revisionists to gain overwhelming endorsement of the agreement.

Ben-Gurion did not uphold a comparable measure of control over Mapai. In a highly charged atmosphere replete with stone throwing and fisticuffs, Ben-Gurion was thwarted by his own organization as the measure was defeated by a vote of sixteen thousand to eleven thousand. An infuriated Ben-Gurion castigated his troops for "sinning" against the *Histadrut*, but painfully accepted the results. No political figure could survive a lifetime, as Ben-Gurion did, without being a realist. This reality involved an acumen for letting well enough alone and not pressing a losing point.

Despite Ben-Gurion's words of consolation, Jabotinsky had no choice but to leave the World Zionist Organization and found a separate Revisionist Zionist movement, which he promptly did.

Meanwhile Jews and Arabs continued moving on a collision course. George Antonius, historian and leading theoretician of Arabism in his time, was a moderate Arab leader. Following discussions with other Arab leaders that had provided no results, Ben-Gurion met with Antonius in April 1936 in a final effort at meaningful dialogue. Antonius said that he understood the Zionist arguments but that the Arabs had no alternative but to oppose the "flooding" of the country by the Jews, which in turn would undermine the Arab position in Palestine. He concluded that an impasse had been reached and there was no way to reconcile conflicting claims of Arabs and Jews.

Ben-Gurion disputed Antonius's conclusion, stating his belief that Arab culture could develop and Arab independence was still a tangible goal elsewhere in the vast Arab world, even if Palestine became "predominantly" Jewish. He stated his position the following way:

> It is not by caprice that we return to this country. For us it is a question of existence, of life and death. We have come here and shall come here whether there will or will not be Arab-Jewish understanding. Riots will not stop us. If we have the choice between riots in Germany, Poland or in any other country, and riots in Palestine, we prefer riots in Palestine. Still, I ask what is better for both our sides—to fight or to help one another?

Ben-Gurion suggested that a Jewish autonomous area within the Arab federation could render a large measure of assistance to its neighbors. Antonius, with some reluctance, consented to explore this possibility. The record is unclear whether he agreed to a politically autonomous Jewish area in Palestine. More than likely he envisaged a small Jewish canton along the coastal plain. He insisted, however, that even in that location Jewish immigration must be controlled, a point passionately rejected by Ben-Gurion. Jewish immigration could not be limited beforehand, he insisted in turn. The scope of immigration, Ben-

Gurion asserted, was beyond the control of the Zionist movement and depended largely on the degree of suffering and persecution to which Jews were subjected. Ben-Gurion was prepared to accept only one limitation, that of the territory open to Jewish settlement.

According to Ben-Gurion, the following conversation then occurred.

"What is the territory?" Antonius asked.

"The territory is *Eretz Israel*," I answered.

"What are the borders of *Eretz Israel*," Antonius asked.

"The borders of *Eretz Israel* are known from history," I answered.

"Borders are artificial things," Antonius remarked. "They are here today and there tomorrow. . . ." He asked again what the territory was.

I answered, "It is the country between the Mediterranean in the west, and the desert in the east, between Sinai in the south and the source of the Jordan in the north."

"You are including Transjordan?" Antonius asked with more surprise.

"Of course," I answered. "Is the Jordan river the border of *Eretz Israel*? Is it an *Eretz Israel* river . . . ?"

"Well," said Antonius, "you suggest that what England has not granted you, you will get from us? This is an Arab country and we have a right to full sovereignty."

"In Syria, yes," I said. "In *Eretz Israel*, we have seen before you. We return to our own country."[28]

Ben-Gurion published the above dialogue more than thirty years later without comment. Israeli writer Amos Elon presented it as a classic example of the dual-sided Ben-Gurion, whose fierce temperament carried him to flights of rhetoric that represented a more dogmatic stance embracing more than what, in final circumstances, he would agree to accept. In the internal political discussions of the Zionist movement, he remained a moderate well removed from the excesses of the Revisionists and Vladimir Jabotinsky.

Elon made the following observation concerning Ben-Gurion's views in 1936, when he held his dialogue with Antonius: "If at this stage the Jews had been offered a tiny independent state (comprising the coastal plain and parts of Galilee—smaller even than Antonius's canton), Ben-Gurion would have agreed, though reluctantly."[29]

The suspicion held by Arabs was that Ben-Gurion, in supporting partition, was anticipating future expansion in Palestine once a firm power base were established in one part of the country. Years later, in 1949, after Israel had achieved statehood, Ben-Gurion rejected all offers of expansion and declared himself to be fully content with a state of Israel in only one part of the country. After the 1967 war, he expressed a willingness to return the occupied area won by his troops on the battlefield in exchange for a peace treaty.

The Ben-Gurion of the late 1930s was reluctant to accept what he deemed an unacceptably small part of Palestine, yet hinted at the same time that he would nonetheless agree to such a proposal. The wily pragmatist stated that such an acceptance was likely "to be a decisive stage *on the road toward the realization of Great Zionism* [Ben-Gurion's italics]. It will establish within the shortest time the real Jewish force which will lead us to our historic destination."[30]

Amos Elon believed that the estrangement between Ben-Gurion and Weizmann could be measured by comparing the reasoning of the two men in supporting partition then. Weizmann stated his position accordingly:

> I know that God promised all of Palestine to the children of Israel. But I do not know what borders He set. I believe that they were wider than the ones proposed. If God will keep His promise to His people in His own time, our business as poor humans who live in a difficult age is to save as much as we can of the remnants of [the people of] Israel. By adopting this project we can save more [Jews].[31]

The British Government, seeking to redress grievances on both sides, invested the Peel Commission with a mandate to study the Palestine situation and make a recommendation. After much study and deliberation, the Peel Commission released its report on July 7, 1937. The solution it proposed was the partition of Palestine into an Arab state and a Jewish state. The latter would be small, encompassing a strip of coastline running from south of Tel Aviv and then widening south of Haifa to include Nazareth and the west shore of Lake Tiberias. Britain was to retain under permanent mandate the holy places—Jerusalem, Bethlehem, and a corridor to the sea at Jaffa—and the Arabs would take the rest.

The Peel Commission report, consisting of some four hundred pages, is a classic work examining in microscopic detail the history of Palestine along with the goals and objectives of both Jews and Arabs. It pointed out that through partition the Jews would obtain the state they desired and could control their immigration since they would shed their centuries-old albatross of always being a minority in someone else's nation. Under the proposal advanced, they could bring in as many refugees from Nazi Germany as they wished, the only limit being the country's capacity to absorb them, a criterion over which they would be the judge. The Arabs were perceived by implementation of the Peel prescription as achieving their long-stated goal of independence. Although the independence would extend to only one part of Palestine, the report pointed out that it would be in the larger area of the country. Was it also not in the interest of the Arabs, the report further pointed out, to make this sacrifice and rid themselves of the fear of being swamped by continuing Jewish immigration?[32]

Lord Peel and his colleagues admitted that the British had made mistakes in Palestine and did not fully realize the difficulties afforded by the mandate. Though the partition package proposed was realistically seen by commission members as imperfect, compromise of the "half-a-loaf-is-better-than-none" variety as proposed by the commission's recommendation was seen as the only solution that offered the prospect of peace.

The proposal of the Peel Commission was stoutly opposed by Vladimir Jabotinsky and his Revisionist movement. In that the Revisionists were on record as favoring a revision of Zionist policy and development of a Jewish National Home over the entire land of Israel, including Transjordan, such opposition was to be anticipated. Jabotinsky communicated his opposition directly to the Commission asserting: "A corner of Palestine, a canton—how can we promise to be satisfied with it? We cannot. We never can. Should we swear to you that we should be satisfied? It would be a lie."[33]

The Revisionist posture is particularly understandable since most of its membership came from Eastern Europe. Jabotinsky was from Odessa, Russia and many others, including Menachem Begin, were from Poland, where the Jewish community consisted of three million people, or about 10 percent of the population. Jabotinsky's objective for Jewry was stated with blunt urgency to the Peel Commission. "We have got to save millions, many millions."[34]

To Jabotinsky a Jewish majority in Palestine constituted a minimum demand. He did not think such an objective was unreasonable in the eyes of the Arabs, his rationale being that the Arabs had many states while the Jews had none. The Jewish establishment as well as the British and the Arabs all questioned the wisdom of such thinking. Massive immigration was deemed wholly unrealistic in view of the barriers of survival involved in so many pioneers' surfacing in rapid order. A few years later, Jabotinsky's ideas would be seen in a different light as the gruesome statistics from Europe became known. Vladimir

Jabotinsky seemed to understand the pervasive sweep of Hitler's destructive objective toward the Jews in a way that Ben-Gurion did not.

Although initially considering partition as falling short of fulfilling even minimal objectives, after a period of reflection, the Zionist leadership began to see the Peel Commission proposal as providing future hope.

Josiah Wedgwood, a pro-Zionist member of the House of Commons, stated, "If partition is accepted and goes through, I hope that the Jews will treat it merely as a stepping-off ground for further advance."[35]

This sentiment was embraced at the Twentieth World Zionist Congress in Zurich that August. Weizmann believed that the Negev Desert was unsuitable for colonization but felt that anyhow "it would not run away." Ben-Gurion stated that the Zionists would give up no part of the land of Israel but also that it was possible that the overall Zionist objective could be achieved most quickly by accepting the Peel prescription. A majority of the Congress agreed to negotiate for frontiers favorable to a possible partition.

The Zionist response to the Peel Commission's formula was a stepping-stone posture in which the idea of exploring partition was linked to a future goal of extending beyond what was initially acquired. The Arabs studied the Jewish response carefully, mindful that acceptance of partition could represent a first step toward seeking additional territory later.

At the same time that the Zionist Congress was taking place in Zurich, four hundred Arab delegates were meeting at Bludan in Syria to review the Peel Commission's report. Their response was swift, as they declared fundamental opposition to partition of any kind. The Arab delegates asserted that independence would benefit them little if, in the nature of acquiring it, they would lose Jerusalem, Jaffa, Haifa, and Northern Palestine forever. The entire question involved one fundamental issue—possession. The Arabs contended that Palestine belonged to them and any abdication on their part of what they deemed to be legitimate land claims constituted a violation of principle rather than a compromise.

With Arabs and Jews sharply divided on Palestine's future—a division accented rather than diminished by the Peel Commission report—another force cast its presence, with the net result a further exacerbation of tensions.

Until the middle of 1937, Nazi Germany had willingly let Jews emigrate. The same Third Reich that would later attempt to exterminate Jewry from the world pursued a vicious yet still more passive form of anti-Semitism than what would be later practiced in concentration camps, where the stench of death hung chillingly in the air. At that point, though, the Hitler philosophy called for "dumping" as many Jews as possible on other countries. The Nuremberg Laws had induced about one hundred twenty thousand Jews to leave Germany forever. One third emigrated to Palestine, where under a system known as Haavara they could export part of their property.

Rumors of partition in Palestine reached Berlin in early June, prompting immediate reevaluation of Third Reich policy. Foreign Minister Konstantin von Neurath warned in a telegram to London, Baghdad, and Jerusalem that the prospect of a Jewish state might inspire a change of German policy.

Middle East scholar Lord Nicholas Bethell eludicated the reasons for German concern.

The proposed state gave Germany the worst of both worlds. It would be too small to "dump" more Jews in. On the other hand, it would become a consolidating point for Jewish political influence, as the Vatican was for Catholics or Moscow for communists. The time had come to support the Arab cause as a counterbalance to world Jewry and as a means of embarrassing Britain.[36]

It is understandable why Palestinian Arabs would at that point favor an alliance with the Third Reich. Whereas the Jews had solid access to the top echelons of the British Government through the Weizmann connection and had an influential Zionist network in the United States, the Arabs lacked comparable influence in important world cities such as Washington, London, or Paris. The World Zionist Organization had been an important umbrella in extending international influence among the ranks of influential Jews and sympathetic non-Jews. The Arabs also sought to develop influence in a major world sector, and Germany afforded such an opening.

However, not only were the Palestinian Arabs entering dangerous territory in dealing with Hitler's Germany. The messenger making the overture was the Mufti, who on July 15 called on Consul General W. Dohle, the German representative in Jerusalem, to tell him that the Palestine Arabs were united in their rejection of partition and in "sympathy for the new Germany."[37]

The irony surrounding the Peel Commission report was that the objective had been to achieve compromise and defuse passions and hostilities pitting Arabs against Jews in Palestine. While the British Government was proclaiming its acceptance of the report and demonstrating its resolve "to give effect to a scheme of partition," the Arab delegates in Bludan were rallying around the concept of Arab nationalism—a unifying principle—and asserting united conviction that partition as embodied in the Peel report would never be accomplished.

The major element that concerned the British Foreign Office as an outgrowth of the Bludan meeting was that now the Arabs were acting as a unified group. With steadfast purpose, this newly unified body was issuing a challenge to Britain's mandatory hold on Palestine. The Royal Commission, created with the best of intentions by Britain to reduce tensions in Palestine through finding bases for compromise between Arabs and Jews, had instead generated a tactical boomerang in which Arab unity had risen to the surface. Now the British posture in Palestine was even more tenuous than it had been before the Peel Commission report was released.

Not only had Arab unity become a freshly pervasive entity, but also the movement was being led by a force noted for combative volatility. Agents of the Mufti controlled the movement from a headquarters in Damascus. Men were sent to the towns in Syria and Lebanon. They purchased arms from the population with funds earmarked for exclusively religious purposes. Pamphlets were disseminated through the Arab world denouncing British imperialism, injustice, and cruelty. An active assassination list was maintained on British officials. Periodically, details of the list would be leaked into Palestine, producing squeamish reactions as British personnel sought to protect themselves from attack.

On June 13, the situation moved from a threatening posture to one of overt action when an attempt was made on the life of Roy Spicer, Inspector-General of the Palestine Police.

Yelland Andrews, District Commissioner for Galilee, was a British civil servant stationed in Palestine who had every reason to feel apprehensive. He held a place on the assassination list for having organized the Peel Commission's program and was believed to have influenced it toward partition, making him a hate object in the eyes of the Mufti and his colleagues. He realized he was a marked man and took precautions. On September 26, Andrews felt like celebrating. He had heard that the rebel command in Damascus had removed his name from the assassination list. In gratitude he decided to go to church in Nazareth to celebrate his altered status. As Andrews and his bodyguard entered a narrow lane near the Anglican church, both men were shot dead by Arab gunmen.

British opinion was outraged. The fires of revolution were burning more intensely than one year earlier, when the 1936 disorders had plagued authorities. Stung by accusations in London of weakness and timidity, the authorities moved swiftly against the Mufti and his troops. Five members of the Arab Higher Committee were arrested and deported to the Seychelles. The Mufti was dismissed from the presidency of the Supreme Moslem Council, the source of his large funds. He sought refuge in the most holy shrine in Jerusalem, *haram esh-sharif*, where no British soldier or policeman would enter, in order to escape apprehension. From there the Mufti escaped overland and by boat to Lebanon. In all, some fifty suspects were arrested and detained in a camp at Acre, which already held one hundred fifty political prisoners.

For a time it appeared as if the disturbance had been quelled and order restored. Instead there was only a lull before another storm as the Mufti's terrorists struck again. On the night of October 14, Jewish colonies and buses were attacked, the oil pipeline was set aflame, a train was derailed, and two British policemen were killed in an ambush.

Palestine was ablaze with terrorism as rebels lurked in the hills in areas where there were few roads, launching search and destroy missions as they descended on Jewish settlements and British posts and then scurried back into the hills. Arabs were often victims as well. Arab policemen and other personnel of the government were kidnapped, tried by kangaroo courts, and executed.

A practice that Israeli soldiers have used against suspected Palestinian terrorists was utilized by British authorities. When a village was suspected of harboring rebels, one large house was selected. If an incident was later attributed to that village, the house would be demolished.

Collective punishment, mainly through fines and curfews, became commonplace. The British would apply pressure to a community, seeking to impose order through collective punishment. Often after sufficient collective punishment had been meted out, the community would turn in the terrorists handcuffed.

Orde Wingate, a British officer of strong pro-Zionist views, countered Arab terrorism with ruthless doses of his own as he led "special night squads" of mixed Jewish and British units against the rebels. His methods prompted Hugh Foot, a young administrator who later became governor of Cyprus and other British colonies, to assert that Wingate "forfeited our reputation for fair fighting."[38]

British activities to restore order precipitated stories in the Arab community about brutality, which hardened resistance all the more and increased resentment against the authorities. The pattern was consistent and depressing to the British. Telephone lines were cut, bridges were damaged, trains were derailed, convoys were ambushed, and fighting persisted in the hills.

The Mufti called for a holy war and the troops responded, but at a great cost as the Arabs lost men at a ten-to-one ratio. In 1938, 69 British and 292 Jews lost their lives in the conflict. Some 1,600 Arabs, rebels, and others were killed.

Meanwhile, on the European front, Hitler invaded Austria on March 12, absorbing it into the Third Reich. All the while, his propaganda forces focused on the Palestine dilemma as the Nazi newspaper *Volkisher Beobachter* continued denouncing the British for brutality while praising the Arab rebels as freedom fighters.

To understand the political situation in Palestine required analyzing the shifting tides of change across a wide landscape. First there was the triangle of interests—the Jews, the Arabs, and the British Mandatory that sought to balance conflicting objectives. The Peel Commission report brought a strong reaction. The Arabs made their opposition to partition tangibly felt. What about the Jews? The answer required looking to Chaim Weizmann, the man who had been Britain's leading Zionist contact for years. In that atmosphere of uncertainty of 1938, marked by Arab protest in Palestine and the rise of Hitler in Europe, Weizmann was a committed partitionist. His pragmatism had always had a more cautious nature than that of his rival Ben-Gurion. Weizmann's partition posture was part of his policy of "maximum pressure for minimum demands." He viewed the situation as twofold: fulfill the Balfour Declaration in part of Palestine—an admittedly piecemeal solution, or watch the entire Palestinian scene stagnate under the manifold pressures of a clash of competing interests. Whereas certain Zionists saw partition as a vital first step toward obtaining the rest of the country, Weizmann's first priority was a Jewish state. Even a small entity would exert control over immigration and facilitate relief for European Jewry.

Weizmann was pinched between two forces. On one side there were the British; on the other his old nemesis Ben-Gurion and his equally impatient Mapai colleagues. Despite major tactical differences over Palestine, Ben-Gurion would withhold criticism as long as the British

354 WAR AND HOLOCAUST

trump card, which Weizmann had been playing since pre–World War One days, accomplished results. The hint of stagnation brought immediate pressures. While Ben-Gurion was questioning the efficacy of continued dealings with Britain, a more militant presence surfaced to challenge Weizmann with increasing vigor. That force was the Revisionist Party of Vladimir Jabotinsky.

An event occurred on March 15, 1938, to undercut Weizmann's position even more than before within the Yishuv. Just three days following Hitler's occupation of Austria, the British announced a six-month immigration quota of only three thousand, the smallest figure in years. The timing could hardly have been worse from the British standpoint, coming when the sizable Jewish community of Vienna stood in mortal peril. An increasing number of Jews within the Yishuv were convinced that diplomacy and evolutionary expectation through conventional political processes would be insufficient to accomplish the twofold purpose of achieving a Jewish state and saving the Jews of Europe. Increasing numbers of Jews within the Yishuv were concluding that to achieve these objectives it would be necessary to fight.

The principle of *havlaga,* or self-restraint, had been preached within the Yishuv during the turbulent period when tensions between Jews and Arabs dramatically escalated. David Ben-Gurion championed *havlaga* in his belief that Jews would benefit in their relations with the British if they practiced restraint and fought only in self-defense. Ben-Gurion believed that by pursuing moderation the Jewish negotiating posture would improve among British authorities.

Vladimir Jabotinsky felt the same degree of increasing frustration as evidenced by Jews in Palestine who felt that the conventional negotiating process, along with patience and a tacit assumption that things would work out eventually, was insufficient. The military arm of the Revisionists, *Irgun Zvai Leumi* (National Military Organization), was provided with a new mandate by Jabotinsky starting in August 1937. The message was circulated to retaliate against the Arab community. In November, under the command of Moshe Rosenberg, the *Irgun* killed ten Arabs in an act of outright reprisal. The Jewish Agency, always bitterly opposed to the Revisionists, immediately condemned the *Irgun* for "marring the record of Palestine Jewry."[39]

Controversy seemed to follow Vladimir Jabotinsky, and as the *Irgun* sprang into action within the Yishuv, the Revisionists became involved in yet another controversial incident, the case of Shlomo Ben-Yosef, which provoked wide controversy. Ben-Yosef was hanged in the Acre fortess on June 29 for an unsuccessful reprisal attack on an Arab bus.

Fellow *Irgun* members saw the execution as a cynical manifestation of policy extending from the British practice of hanging rebellious Arabs. Now these same authorities hanged a Jew to demonstrate their impartiality. The killing inflamed passions within the *Irgun*, and furious activity followed. A series of bomb attacks on Arab-populated areas was launched. Five Arabs were killed in Jerusalem and Tel Aviv, followed by 23 in Haifa, 10 in Jerusalem, and another 39 in Haifa.[40]

The *Irgun* was well organized in Poland, the nation where most of them had been born. The rightist Polish government provided arms and training facilities for the Irgunists based on the mutual objective of furthering Jewish emigration. Two schools of thought emerge on the motivation behind the Polish government's assistance. One theory elucidated by Irgunist Yitzhak Shamir, who with fellow Polish-born Irgun member Menachem Begin would later become an Israeli prime minister from the *Likud* bloc, adheres to a "strange bedfellows" rationale. Shamir explains: "It was a political agreement. They helped us for anti-semitic reasons. We explained to them, 'If you want to get rid of the Jews, you must help the Zionist movement.' " A less harsh view of the Polish government's motivation has been asserted by Irgunist Nathan Yalin-Mor: "They saw us as fighters for the freedom of our people. And they thought that Zionism would bring an end to Polish anti-semitism. They believed that there would always be anti-semitism, as long as there were three million Jews in Poland. They were very helpful in issuing passports to Jews who intended to enter Palestine illegally."[41]

Although Begin and Shamir would later become prime ministers of Israel, one man actively involved in Irgunist activities then became a more prominent topic of dicussion when events of that period are addressed. A handsome young revolutionary linguist and poet who had been born in the small Polish town of Suwalki became a link between the Irgunists and the Polish government, traveling extensively between the two countries. The young man, Abraham Stern, would later become disenchanted with the *Irgun* and form a revolutionary militaristic organization of his own, *Lehi*, which would gain notoriety under the ominous label of the Stern Gang.

Analysis of the critical period of the middle and late 1930s illustrates another vicious circle of violence that precipitated hard feelings and postures on both the Arab and Jewish sides, making it more difficult for moderates to hold sway. Jewish immigration becomes a thorny issue, because Arabs feel threatened and resort to violence. In turn, Jews react to violence with violence of their own as each side accuses the other of being responsible for the pattern of conflict as well as the ultimate reason behind it. The subject of partition led to a violent response by Arabs, opening a Pandora's box of conflict in which acts of terrorism became increasingly pervasive on both the Jewish and Arab fronts. Chaim Weizmann, mindful that his cautious pragmatism wedded to a solid working foundation with Britain would be supported by Ben-Gurion and Labor only so long as measurable progess could be seen, became concerned about *Irgun* activities. In conversation with Malcolm MacDonald, Palestine's colonial secretary and son of former Prime Minister Ramsay MacDonald, Weizmann not only indicated that he was disturbed by the July attacks on Arab areas but also told MacDonald he had heard that illegal shipments of Revisionists to Palestine were being financed by Nazis.

Malcolm MacDonald, in the unenviable position of being caught in the middle between Arab and Jewish objectives that were being pursued with increasing violence, saw the enormous cost resulting from the injection of the concept of partition into Palestine politics through the Peel Commission prescription. He warned Weizmann in August 1938 that the British Government was moving toward abandoning partition as a viable concept. Although partition remained official stated policy, MacDonald was being encouraged to explore other possible avenues of agreement between Arabs and Jews.

MacDonald was enough of a political realist to perceive the problems raised by partition. Nazism was on the rise and uncertainty throughout Europe was dramatically increasing. Neither MacDonald nor his government could afford a full-scale battle raging in Palestine between Arabs and Jews. If Britain pushed partition earnestly, political temperatures would inevitably rise in Palestine because of Arab opposition.

Muhammad Mahmoud, Prime Minister of Egypt, informed MacDonald that the Arabs would never agree to the Jews' achieving 40 percent of the Palestine population and might not agree to 35 percent either. Mahmoud presented a bleak picture, declaring that, should partition be imposed, Britain would never have peace and would lose its valuable friends in the Arab world and in India.

Izzat Tannous, head of the Palestinian Office in London, made the following statement to MacDonald that proved chillingly prescient in light of later events:

"The Arabs would never consent, except if they were forced to, to the surrender of part of their country to an immigrant race. And if a Jewish state were established, the Arabs would only await the day when they could attack the state and drive the Jews out."[42]

MacDonald and his allies in Whitehall felt the cumulative pressures of Palestine tugging at them on all sides as they became enmeshed in an ever-tightening web. The Mufti's propaganda was blackening Britain's reputation throughout the Moslem world while Jews begged Britain to help relieve their sufferings in the wake of an expanding Nazi floodtide. Both sides kept reminding Britain of past promises made that they expected to be fulfilled.

Years after his service in Palestine, MacDonald reflected on the volatile 1938 period:

> I was advised that unless we reduced Jewish immigration there was a real risk of the Arabs' joining Germany and Italy. In 1938 it looked as if there was going to be another war and it was vital that we won it. If war came, we knew that the Jews would be on our side anyway. They had no alternative. But the Arabs were doubtful. If they turned against us, we could lose our position in the Middle East, including the Suez Canal, and a large part of our war potential. Britain was my main consideration, but I also thought that our winning the war was equally vital for the Jews, because if we lost there probably wouldn't be a national home at all. I put this to them and begged them to make a temporary sacrifice, on the ground that Britain's interest was also the interest of the national home.[43]

Enormous political pressure was being generated by both sides on Great Britain on behalf of two groups who felt threatened. Among the Jews, paramount urgency was attached to emigration and saving their brothers and sisters in a rapidly deteriorating Europe in which they were victimized. Arabs attached equal importance to ending Jewish immigration, fearful they would otherwise be outnumbered in Palestine and lose it.

A conference was scheduled at St. James Palace in London on February 7, 1939, in hopes of resolving ever-widening differences between Arabs and Jews. Representatives of the Arab Higher Committee and the Jewish Agency agreed to attend. The Arab Higher Committee had issued a document at a Cairo meeting demanding the end of the Jewish National Home, Jewish immigration, and land transfer to Jews; the end of the Palestine Mandate; and an independent Arab Palestine linked to Britain by treaty. The elected Assembly of the Yishuv met two weeks after the Cairo conference and called for the fulfillment of the Balfour Declaration. The Jewish proclamation asserted their entitlement to extend the Jewish National Home, which the Arabs demanded that Britain terminate. They further declared their right to buy land freely and bring in as many immigrants as the country's economy could absorb, contrasting squarely with the stated Arab resolve to end all Jewish immigration.

The areas of disagreement separating the two sides were so vast that storm clouds loomed over the proceedings from the beginning. Jamal Husseini, leader of the Palestinian delegation, was the Mufti's cousin, immediately arousing Jewish mistrust. Weizmann complained that the conference was in reality being run by Husseini rather than the British.

"We had terrible trouble," Malcolm MacDonald said, "because for days neither side would sit round the same table in the same room. We had to talk to the Arabs in the morning, the Jews in the afternoon."[44]

MacDonald recognized that the two sides were too far apart to hope for any accommodation. He decided that the conference could serve a constructive purpose, however, in providing him with an opportunity to sound out thinking and hopefully facilitate a plan of action.

During the first week of the conference, MacDonald met with several non-Palestinian Arab leaders in private and submitted his plan for three hundred thousand Jewish immigrants over ten years. The hostility in the swift Arab response prompted realization on his part that immigration remained the key Arab concern, bringing home clearly the Foreign Office's advice that to keep the "moderating influence" of the Arab states he would have to scale down his immigration figure.

Chaim Weizmann delivered a formal reply to MacDonald's outline of the Arab case, focusing on the contention that the Jews had entered Palestine without Arab consent. A skilled diplomat with a lengthy background of negotiating with the British, Weizmann fastened his focus on the Balfour Declaration. Such a position was hardly surprising. Not only had he been Balfour's catalyst, but he knew as well that it had served as the linchpin of support for the National Home concept. Weizmann told MacDonald it was time to decide some major points regarding the Balfour Declaration, the resolution of which would determine the rights of Jews in Palestine.

The question of whether the Jews had entered Palestine by consent should rest on the following points, according to Weizmann:

1. Was the Balfour Declaration an act of restitution or *not*?

2. If it was not, Britain could tell the Jews that they had no business in Palestine.

3. If it was, then Britain should tell the Arabs that the Jews had entered Palestine by right.

The Weizmann position posed a fundamental question in such a way as to ensure a favorable response unless Britain was willing to concede that it had not been serious about the Balfour Declaration in the first place, which would be an admission that the government had not meant what it was saying at the time. Weizmann was forcing the issue by asking, Were you providing us with a meaningful pledge or behaving in a brazenly cynical manner? If you meant what you were saying then how can you renege on such a commitment now, after so many Jews had emigrated to Palestine in expectation of fulifllment of Balfour?

The Arab position remained the same as it had been since the Paris Peace Conference. The issue had always been self-determination, which they proclaimed as a right under the Treaty of Versailles. They had fought with the British to drive mutual enemy Turkey from Palestine and were entitled to self-determination. Heavy Jewish immigration was perceived as a barrier to that objective, so they felt an abiding necessity to oppose it.

Operating in the manner of a man treading on thin ice, MacDonald spoke with moderate Arabs, seeking an answer to the immigration dilemma by trying to determine what would be tolerated. Achieving a tolerable level in the eyes of moderate Arabs loomed as the best result MacDonald could obtain, given the steadfastness of conviction that opposed immigration. MacDonald hoped to secure an immigration figure that would also be acceptable to moderate Zionists as well, realizing that the issue was every bit as important to Jews as to Arabs, with each clinging to disparate agendas.

He returned to the bargaining table with moderate Arab delegates Fuad Hamza, Ali Maher, and Tawfiq as-Suwaydi from Saudi Arabia, Egypt, and Iraq, respectively. After some discussion, the Arabs agreed to urge their Palestinian colleagues to accept an immigration figure of 75,000 Jews over a period of five years.

Years later, looking back on the dilemma that he faced during one of the pivotal moments of history for his country as well as the entire world, MacDonald spoke with the pain of the statesman trying to make the most of what was ultimately destined to be seen as a bad deal by both sides:

"Our impression was that this [the 75,000 immigration figure] would offend the Arabs grossly, but we would get by with it. So we fixed the quota of Jewish immigration and the spread of years at the maximum we thought the Arabs would swallow."[45]

Having sought to blend Jewish immigration with Arab tolerance, the question then arose as to the reaction of the Zionists, who, like the British, had their eyes trained on events in Europe. On March 15, 1939, Hitler reduced the "peace in our time" belief of Neville Chamberlain to a sad shambles as his armies invaded Prague and annexed Bohemia and Moravia to Germany. Weizmann and Ben-Gurion were sensitively attuned to the impact of the aggressive Third Reich march on Jews throughout the European continent. At a time when immigration would be sought with even greater urgency as an escape vehicle from Nazi tyranny and, in many cases, to avoid death itself, MacDonald and his government were proposing a sharp reduction from the 300,000 figure previously quoted by MacDonald to Weizmann down to 75,000. The 300,000 figure had been scaled down from an earlier number of 450,000, with each allocated over a ten-year period. Possibilities of immigration in numbers of 45,000 and 30,000 Jews per year had been whittled down to an average of 15,000 Jews per year over a five-year period. Considering the apprehensions the Jewish leadership felt regarding the Third Reich and its impact on European Jewry, it is not surprising that the reaction from the Yishuv was swift and decisively negative.

On March 16, the day after Hitler's invasion of Czechoslovakia, influential American Zionist Rabbi Stephen Wise addressed the current immigration proposal within the wide ambit of British-Jewish relations. Speaking at the Roosevelt Hotel in London, Wise began by warmly praising Britain as a defender of democracy in the world and pledged full Jewish support in Britain's struggle against fascism. He then turned to the immigration proposal and the prospect of British abdication of what he saw as a solemn pledge to appease Hitler, Mussolini, and the Mufti. Wise then discussed the broad import of Palestine immigration and what it meant to Jews.

> Do you know what permanent minority status means? It means that for 1,900 years we have prayed and dreamed, and for sixty years we have worked hard and toiled and our best have put their most into the upbuilding of Eretz Israel, and after all that, and the promise of the Mandate and the [Balfour] Declaration, Palestine would become nothing more than another Jewish ghetto.[46]

Weizmann declared himself in "irrevocable opposition"[47] to the immigration proposal, reserving the brunt of his fury for Malcolm MacDonald, now seen as a traitor to Zionism. He made a final attempt to change MacDonald's mind at a meeting on May 13 at MacDonald's country home in Great Waltham in Essex. Weizmann would understandably feel a greater sensitivity to the immigration proposal than would other Jewish leaders, such as Ben-Gurion, Katznelson, and even Jabotinsky, in view of his close relationship with Britain and increasing criticism by impatient Zionists. At one point, MacDonald stated that

Jews had made mistakes in the past, to which Weizmann testily replied, "Oh yes, we have made mistakes, our chief mistake is that we exist at all." He added with ironic bitterness that in Hitler he at least found the virtue of absolutely frank brutality, whereas MacDonald was betraying Jews and handing them over to their assassins under a semblance of legality. MacDonald said he was aware that Jews were calling him a hypocrite and a coward. Weizmann answered with the iciness he sometimes evidenced, "I have never called you a coward." The meeting a disaster, Weizmann left for London, adding that he would be returning to Palestine to help the Yishuv bear the shock.[48]

The controversial proposal took shape in the finalized document known as the White Paper of 1939, announcing the intention to establish an independent Palestinian state following a transition period. The document encompassed three sections. The first part asserted that the British Government had lived up to its obligation to the Jewish people and the National Home as evidenced by the population rise to 450,000, or almost a third of the population of Palestine. When peace and order were restored, the transition period, during which Palestine would remain under British rule, would begin. After five years, "an appropriate body representative of the people of Palestine and of His Majesty's Government will be set up to . . . consider and make recommendations regarding the Constitution of the independent Palestine State," which would safeguard holy places, the rights of the Jewish minority, and Britain's foreign relations and strategic interests. The British Government would "do everything in their power to create conditions which will enable the independent Palestine State to come into being within ten years."[49]

Part two of the White Paper involved immigration during the transitional period. The Yishuv would be permitted to increase the Jewish third of the total population with 75,000 Jews being permitted entry. For each of the first five years, 10,000 immigrants would be allowed. Therefore the previously discussed 15,000 average over a five-year period was altered by insertion of the proviso that an additional 25,000 Jews would be admitted above the yearly totals, which resulted in the same final figure. The warning was also issued that if any Jewish immigrants entered the country "illegally," their number would be deducted from the yearly quotas. The totals were to be subjected to the criterion of economic absorptive capacity, the determination of which rested with the high commissioner. After the period of five years, no additional Jewish immigration would be permitted unless the Arabs of Palestine were prepared to "acquiesce in it."

The third part of the document dealt with land, decreeing, "There is now in certain areas no room for further transfers of Arab land [to Jews]."[50] The high commissioner would be invested with "general powers to prohibit and regulate transfers of land. These powers will date from the publication of this Statement of Policy and the High Commissioner will retain them throughout the transitional period."[51]

Parliamentary debate was heated and cut across party lines. Much criticism of the document concerned what White Paper opponents discerned as the government's new pro-Arab policy. Laborite Philip Noel-Baker, foreign policy authority and internationalist who had won the Nobel Peace Prize, was keenly aware of the problems inherent in British immigration enforcement in the wake of the unfolding tragedy occurring in Europe. If Jews were excluded from Palestine legally, then Noel-Baker was convinced that they would enter illegally. The problem in his view then revolved around enforcing the law, with the only way of stopping the immigrants "to tell those kindly British soldiers to shoot them down."[52]

Winston Churchill delivered a strongly pro-Zionist speech declaring that the land restrictions and proposed Arab veto on Jewish immigration were contrary to Article Six of the Mandate, which bound Britain to "facilitate Jewish immigration under suitable conditions" and to encourage "close settlement by Jews on the land." Churchill believed that the Jews had made the desert bloom, had started thriving industires, and had founded a great city on a barren shore. Far from being persecuted, the Arabs had prospered, Churchill contended, under Jewish immigration. Now the House of Commons was about to decree that it all should end. "What is that but the destruction of the Balfour Declaration? What is there but a breach of faith?" Churchill asked.

The issue of whether the White Paper of 1939 constituted a breach of promise by the British Government registered profound concern on House members. The government held a majority of 248 votes over other parties in Commons, but when the White Paper was submitted for a vote, the 268 to 179 figure by which the measure passed involved a shrinkage to 89 of the majority.

President Roosevelt did not agree with his state department's view that the new policy was legal. "Frankly, I do not see how the British government reads into the original Mandate or into the White Paper of 1922 any policy that would limit Jewish immigration," he wrote on May 17, 1939. He believed that the white paper was "something that we cannot give approval to by the United States."[54]

Roosevelt did not concur with the British view that it would be illegal to convert Palestine into a Jewish state against Arab wishes. To Roosevelt the reference to maintaining "the civil and religious rights of the existing non-Jewish community" meant only that the Arabs could not be deprived of citizenship or of the right to take part in government. It did not mean that they could not lose their majority status. Roosevelt's impression, which he felt was conveyed to the world at the time of the Mandate, was that Palestine would be converted into a Jewish Home, "Which might very possibly become predominantly Jewish within a comparatively short time."[55]

Although the White Paper received approval in the House of Commons, the British were squeamishly aware that the Council of the League of Nations, which had entrusted the Palestine Mandate to Great Britain under specified conditions, could decide that Britain was in violation of terms of the mandate and declare the White Paper invalid under international law.

The Permanent Mandates Commission, a League of Nations advisory body, evalutated the White Paper and issued a report in mid-August. Weizmann had visited all the commissioners excepting Lord Hankey, Britain's representative. Only the French and Portuguese commissioners supported Hankey. The other four, representing Belgium, Holland, Norway, and Switzerland, stated that the new immigration and land purchase proposals violated Article Six and that the plan to hand Palestine over to Arab majority rule contravened Britain's duty to establish the Jewish National Home.[56]

Britain continued pressing its case, arguing that it was not bound to continue Jewish immigration indefinitely while asserting that Arab rights would be prejudiced by unlimited Jewish land purchases. British spokesmen hoped that when the Council of the League considered the question on September 8 that a broader and less legalistic view would be embraced.

The times were indeed explosive. The September 8 meeting never occurred. Hitler's plans to invade Poland were afoot, and on August 23, they advanced a quantum leap as Hitler signed a nonaggression pact with Stalin, freeing him to move. On September 1, the invasion of Poland was launched. Two days later, Britain and France declared war on Germany.

At a dark point in British history, the White Paper was seen in London as one of the few positive incidents on the international scene. Though the Arabs rejected it publicly, in private the mood differed considerably. It drove a wedge between the Mufti and the rebels on one side and the moderate Palestinians and the Arab states on the other. George Antonius, while stating his disappointment that Britain still recognized the validity of the Balfour Declaration and the Mandate, called the White Paper "a substantial advance towards the recognition of Arab rights."[57]

Although opposed to what he saw as the annulment of the Balfour Declaration with the issuance of the White Paper, political realist Ben-Gurion was "absolutely certain that this policy cannot be carried out for long" and that the British would not use bayonets to force the policy down Jewish throats.[58]

Following Hitler's invasion of Poland, Ben-Gurion issued a statement that once more delineated his pragmatism: "We must help the British in their war against Hitler as if there were no White Paper; we must resist the White Paper as if there were no war."[59]

Ben-Gurion's attitude abruptly changed when the British administered new land regulations on February 28, 1940. Jews were allowed to settle only in a narrow "Pale" embracing 5 percent of Palestine. The territory, situated west of Jordan, was mostly urbanized. Ben-Gurion called an immediate meeting of his colleagues, stating that "war on the White Paper now takes precedence over anything else!"[60] He suggested to break off relations with the "hostile administration in Palestine and not let Jews be mobilized as hewers of wood and drawers of water."[61] His comrades wondered if he could be serious, considering the high stakes of Britain's battle against Hitler. Ben-Gurion acknowledged the importance of the struggle, but as a Jew he felt that any problems of the Jewish people took precedence. He believed that once Britain became convinced of the seriousness of his intentions, the undesirable policy would change. When his associates were unmoved, he resigned huffily, only to be called back immediately. Ben-Gurion announced that he would lead a protest against the British, but only in Palestine. In the ensuing demonstrations, Jews clashed with police, resulting in deaths and injuries, after which Ben-Gurion's colleagues prevailed on him to halt his activities. Peace prevailed, but Ben-Gurion remained enraged. The protest, while more than likely one of his pragmatic eruptions by which he sought to get Britain's attention, also sadly demonstrated his lack of awareness, compared to others in his ranks, of the gravity of Hitler's challenge to the world and the enormous impact it generated within Jewish ranks. Insightful Jewish analysts recognized the dark and foreboding clouds gathering in Europe as an enraged Hitler gained momentum, intent upon crushing the one group of people he considered most odious—the Jews.

Jews were immersed in a battle for survival, hoping to prevail against a sinister force intent upon their destruction. Deportations commenced in which Jews were taken to camps where they were told they would perform work. Many did, and under the most beastly circumstances, but the ultimate objective was death, by either work, experimentation, or execution.

The first deportation of Jews from Cracow, Poland, was described as movingly by Tadeusc Pankiewicz, the only known non-Jew to witness it. His pharmacy lay within the perimeter of the Cracow ghetto, and from it he had a view of Harmony Square, where the deportees were assembled. He related his story in a book published in Cracow in 1947 about the events occurring on June 1 and 2, when the first deportation occurred.

The march of the deportees has started. The first rows appear at the Square; people are pushed, stamped on, hit; like ghosts, they keep moving on at a slow pace, quietly, gravely, but with dignity. A few run in clusters, some run singly, others look as if they had lost their minds. They are all surrounded by German police, each one with his rifle in his hands, the finger on the trigger ready to shoot. . . . All this is taking place amid constant screaming of the Germans, merciless beating, kicking, and shooting. Many were killed, many wounded during these very first moments of the deportation. . . .

The shots are echoing all over the ghetto. There are dead bodies; wounded people are carried on stretchers; blood leaves marks of German crimes on the sidewalks and streets . . . The SS men are continuously loading valises filled with valuables they took from the deportees during the searches. Everything they see is taken: rings, wedding bands, watches, cigarette cases, even cigarette lighters. Some deportees look at each other; others wait for their turn; indifference and apathy show on their faces. . . .

When will all this end? This disturbing question is on everybody's mind. I look out of the pharmacy window, standing far back so as not to be seen from the outside. The Germans don't like witnesses to their crimes. Each time during such actions the streetcar traffic was discontinued and even German cars were stopped.[62]

Pankiewicz then describes the actual deportation.

The deportation has started. The Square slowly becomes empty of people. Some are transported in cars, others walk on foot, rushed on by the shouting Germans, pushed around, trampled on, beaten, They run along the . . . streets in the direction of Plaszow. On the way, guards of the German Special Service fire at those who cannot catch up with the others. The road of the deportees is marked by dead bodies.

At the railroad station. . . . they were loaded into cattle cars with quicklime sprinkled over the floors and small grilled windows up on the ceilings. They packed 120 persons to a car. The doors tightly closed, a German guard was posted at each car. No water or bread was allowed, and the scorching heat was unbearable. Some people had brought along their locksmith tools and managed to escape by breaking loose the windowgrill and jumping out of the train. They endangered their lives by hitting themselves against the railroad poles or by falling under the wheels of the moving train; but mostly death awaited them from the bullets of the escorting policemen.[63]

Auschwitz, located over 50 miles west of Cracow in an unhealthy, malaria-infested swamp area, became a grim symbol as the definitive Nazi death camp. Transports were examined by SS doctors upon their arrival. Some were singled out for work, and an estimated 60–90 percent were driven directly to the gas chambers, situated adjacent to the crematoria. The signs at the entrances said BATHS. The unsuspecting Jews believed that they would be deloused, a custom at all camps. As they entered, light music was played, such as tunes from *The Merry Widow* and *Tales of Hoffmann,* by an inmate orchestra of "young and pretty girls all dressed in white blouses and navy-blue skirts," as one survivor recalls. To the strains of the melodic sounds the inmates were taken to the "shower." Sometimes they were even given towels. As many as two thousand of them were packed into the chambers like sardines, after which the massive door was shut, locked, and sealed. While the executioners watched through heavy glass portholes, the naked prisoners would look up at the showers from which no water sprouted, wondering what was happening. It took a while for the gas to have an effect, and when it did, coming through the perforations in the vents, the prisoners usually panicked, crowding away from the pipes and moving toward the door, clawing and mauling each other. Twenty or thirty minutes later, a crew of Jewish inmates who had been promised their lives took over, preparing to take the dead to the crematoria. They searched for gold and removed teeth and hair, which were considered strategic materials by the Germans.[64]

Besides serving the purpose of an efficiently run killing factory, in which the soldiers were expected to maintain a brisk execution quota in the manner of industrial factories vying for maximum productivity, Auschwitz and the other camps served as laboratories in which Jews were ruthlessly utilized in so-called medical experimentation.

A summation of the experiments was included in the book *Doctors of Infamy*, a report in which prominent American medical professionals, including some who took part in the U.S. Military Tribunal in Nuremberg after the war, were participants.

Among the experiments were:

1. High altitude rescue experiments conducted in decompression chambers on ground level. Unfailingly, as the pressure dropped and a vacuum was created, the prisoner's lungs ruptured after intense pain and suffering.
2. Rewarming persons after subjecting them to extreme cold in icy water or exposing them completely naked in zero or subzero weather. No one survived.
3. Testing the effectiveness of poisoned bullets.
4. Testing the effects of drinking different solutions of sea water.
5. Injecting typhus and other viruses into the body, and gasoline into the veins, to study the resistance of individuals and racial or ethnic groups.
6. Performing surgical experiments involving bone, muscle, and nerve grafting; measuring the effects of electric shocks.
7. Testing the effects of inhaling mustard gas and being inflicted with phosphorous burns.
8. Performing castrations, sterilizations, and abortions to determine the most economical and effective methods of eliminating "inferior" races.
9. Making an intensive study of the characteristics of twins and the effects of bodily damage on them (presumably to increase the Aryan birth rate and produce the "superior" race).
10. Performing complicated operations on sensitive parts of the body, and diverse experiments, equally lurid.[65]

Elie Wiesel, Nobel Peace Prize recipient and survivor of the Holocaust, writes movingly about the ignorance of the prisoners in the face of the grave tragedies that awaited them.

The names change, and the places too, but the story remains the same. In my little town, too, there were rabbis who opposed the Zionists; young people who tried to leave for Palestine illegally; assimilated Jews who came to the synagogue only once or twice a year; Hasidim and emancipated Jews . . . And all were to meet at the edge of the yawning abyss.

In our town, too, we should have taken steps. Rumors had reached us: the enemy was ruthless. We could have gone into hiding. We didn't. As elsewhere, the Jews in my town refused to believe that men—even Germans, even Nazis—could commit crimes so odious, so monstrous.

The consequence: we too were in the streets that spring of 1944 to see the Germans on their motorcycles. We too found them rather polite.

The trap, everywhere the same, was closing in on our illusions and smothering them. . . .

I myself remember a little shamos (beadle) who had returned from Galicia in 1942, alone, without his family. He told stories that made us shudder: he had seen Jews forced by the Germans to dig their own graves; he had witnessed mass executions, massacres . . . We thought: "It's not true. Such things can't be."

And I also remember a police inspector who just before we moved into the ghetto had promised my father: "If something happens, I'll warn you in time." One night we heard a knocking at the window. By the time we opened it, nobody was there. The liquidation of the ghetto began the next day.[66]

Wiesel then examines the second step of the tragic Holocaust equation, the first being the obliviousness of the Jews as to what was happening to them, along with the disbelief and indifference on the part of world leaders and governments that could have prevented or minimized so much of the bloodshed. Considering the unique perspective of Wiesel to write about these events logically combined with his powers of advocacy, his words register compellingly.

The blindness of the Jews was equaled only by the indifference of the Allied leaders to their plight. Because yes; on an individual level surely, on a collective level perhaps, the tragedy could have been avoided, or at least limited. If only Washington had been more understanding, if Switzerland had been more welcoming and London less hostile toward illegal refugees . . . And yet, with money, with a little luck, it was possible to cross into Switzerland, to hide in an Italian village, or to obtain false papers . . . If only one had known! But we didn't know. If the leaders of the Free World had taken the trouble to warn Hungarian Jews, to inform them, to advise them not to obey the evacuation orders, to flee the transports—how many might have managed to save themselves?

But we didn't know. Perhaps we didn't want to know. It was easier that way. For example, Marika Frank Abrams continued to live—to live?—in ignorance of the gas chambers even when she was already in Auschwitz! How then can we be surprised that Greek Jews changed drachmas for German marks in order to buy land in Poland? Or in order to pay for the trip? . . .

It was not until the war was over that the survivors recognized their error: the world had known and had remained silent. How was one to re-

enter that world? How was one to trust a humanity that was simultaneously betrayed and betraying? . . . How can we not admire all those
orphans, those lonely women, those outcasts, those strays, who were
able to overcome despair and hate and assert their right to life and even
to happiness?

The danger lies in forgetting. Forgetting, however, will not affect only
the dead. Should it triumph, the ashes of yesterday will cover our hopes
for tomorrow.[67]

Elie Wiesel's words ring with sobering clarity and truth. The message of Hitler's atrocities in the wake of his 1938 conquest of Austria
and its impact on the nation's 200,000 Jews, 180,000 of whom lived in
Vienna, was duly reported in *New York Times* accounts.

On March 16, the following appeared.

Adolf Hitler had left behind him in Austria an anti-Semitism that is
blossoming far more rapidly than ever it did in Germany. This afternoon
the Jewish quarter of Leopoldstadt was invaded by triumphant crowds
that called families from their houses and forced them to kneel and try to
scrub from the pavements slogans such as "Hail Schuschnigg" which
were part of the former Chancellor's plebiscite campaign. This humiliation was carried out under the supervision of Storm Troopers wearing
swastika armlets. The crowds were composed . . . of some of the worst
elements of the population, assembled to jeer at the Jews, and shouting,
"Perish Jewry!" 'Out with the Jews.' "[68]

As the Nazi hate campaign generated momentum, the sense of
tragedy among Austrian Jews accelerated. A March 20 *New York Times*
report focused on the grim response of the victims.

The death carts of the Anatomical Institution are busy daily collecting
the bodies of those poisoned by their own hands or by those nearest and
dearest to them. Death seems to them the kindest gifts to those, well-
favored or humble, for whom once smiling Austria has become a vast
prison from which there is no outlet and within which all chance of a
livelihood is dead . . . Is this Vienna . . . with its truckloads of palefaced
citizens being hurried through the streets to vanish through the great
gates of the central prison—for many of them the first stage of the journey
to the concentration camp?[69]

On March 22, ten days after the first German troops had marched
into Austria, President Roosevelt initiated an international conference
involving thirty-two governments in a cooperative effort to assist the

emigration of political refugees from Germany and Austria. The idea had been spawned by Sumner Welles. The conference was convened in Evian, France, on July 6 and adjourned July 15. The only constructive outcome following ten days of tedious deliberations was the agreement by tiny Santo Domingo to accept 100,000 refugees. The United States did not alter its racial quota policy for immigrants, and British fears focused on the numbers of refugees from the medical profession.

This apprehension was described in an editorial in Lord Beaverbrook's *Sunday Express*. The charge was made that "just now there is a big influx of foreign Jews into Britain. They are overrunning the country. They are trying to enter the medical profession in great numbers. They wish to practice as dentists. Worst of all, many of them are holding themselves out to the public as psychoanalysts. A psychoanalyst needs no medical training but arrogates to himself functions of a doctor. And he often obtains an ascendancy over a patient of which he makes base use if he is a bad man."[70]

The *Express* editorial reeked destruction in two pernicious respects: Jews in dire need of escape from a regime dedicated to their annihilation were being turned aside due to professional fears, and the blanket assault on psychiatrists painfully resembled Third Reich propaganda pertaining to corrupt Jewish professionals exerting unsavory influence on Gentiles in the purported practice of medicine.

With the slaughter of Jews continuing apace, efforts were made to escape by any means possible. Due to British restrictions on emigration into Palestine and confronted by a world turning a deaf ear to the ongoing tragedy, some sought escape by boat under perilous circumstances.

One boat tragedy takes precedence over all others because of its timing and circumstances—that of the *Struma*. The tragedy occupied such significance in the mind of Menachem Begin that in his first speech as prime minister, delivered to the Knesset in May 1977, the *Struma* received careful mention. The fate of the *Struma* is depicted in Yad Vashem, Jerusalem's permanent memorial to the six million Jews exterminated during the war, and is officially labeled as a crime against Jews comparable to those perpetrated by Nazi Germany.[71]

The journey began on December 12, 1941, from the Black Sea port of Constanza with a cargo of 769 Jewish-Romanian refugees. Half the passengers were women and children. An amount of 200,000 Romanian lei, or more than $1000, had been spent for each place on a ship designed for no more than a hundred people. Before the *Struma* left

Constanza, Romanian officials came aboard and confiscated all the passengers' valuables and most of the ship's provisions for the journey. The engines, which had been specially fitted, broke down shortly after departure. The *Struma* huffed and puffed along the coastline, stopping several times for improvised repairs, and finally reached Istanbul. When British authorities announced that the 769 passengers would not be permitted to land in Palestine, the Turkish Government decided to turn the ship back. It was torpedoed in the Black Sea and sunk, losing all but one or two of its passengers.[72]

The *Struma* was one of many "Little Death Ships" packed with refugees from the European conflict seeking safety in Palestine from the Nazi boot. Colonial Secretary Lord Moyne, determined to carry out the White Paper policy, showed no willingness to adjust it even in the wake of the unrelenting tragedy suffered by European Jewry. In the case of the *Struma,* Moyne cited three reasons for denying its passengers entry into Palestine: (1) troublesome immigration pressures on High Commissioner Harold MacMichael, (2) the influence of encouraging more Jews to embark, and (3) the traffic was encouraged by the Gestapo and might be used to infiltrate Nazi agents. The claim that Jewish refugees were potential infiltrators of Nazi agents, totally unjustified by the facts, parallels an identical one made by Assistant Secretary of State Breckinridge Long in his opposition to immigration of Jewish refugees to the United States. Such policies resulted in one million places on U.S. immigrant quotas remaining unfilled between 1933 and 1943, when a brutal regime was seeking to exterminate an entire group of people from the face of the earth.[73]

During the first six months after the outbreak of war, when immigration became paramount, no permits at all were granted. The Land Transfer regulation of 1940, against which Ben-Gurion fumed, confined the Jews to a pale of settlement embracing 5 percent of the total area of Western Palestine. Not even land classified as "uncultivable" was exempt from prohibition, prompting the Jewish Agency to protest that "such discrimination (was) . . . explicitly forbidden by the mandate."[74]

While violent antigovernment demonstrations were erupting throughout Palestine opposing Britain's unrelenting struggle against illegal immigration, the "Little Death Ships" packed with refugees sailed toward the shores of Palestine. In November 1940, 1,770 Jews arrived in Haifa on two vessels, but whereas British policy in the past had been to detain immigrants in Palestine, it was now decided to deport the new arrivals to the island of Mauritius in the Indian Ocean. Eventually, following bloody clashes, the *Hagana* decided to precipitate sabotage on the *Patria*, which was to take the refugees to Mauritius. Due to a calculation error on the amount of explosives used, and an insufficient number of lifeboats aboard, more than 250 immigrants were killed. The British Government intervened at that point and permitted those rescued from the *Patria* to remain, but the refugees from the *Atlantic*, some 1,700, who had arrived at the same time, were to be exiled, never to be allowed to return to Palestine. The *Salvador* sank in early 1941 in the Sea of Marmora, losing 200 lives.[75]

A clear-cut conflict of wills had surfaced in which British immigration policy as embodied by the White Paper clashed with the survival aims of Jewish refugees seeking to escape the ongoing carnage in Europe. As the confrontation continued, an inevitable day of reckoning loomed in which the objectives of the mandatory power and the emergent refugees fleeing the Holocaust would have to be addressed. Weizmann biographer Norman Rose framed the picture as follows.

> No administrative statute could prevent the boats from running the British blockage—*Patria, Darien, Struma, Mekfure, Nyasa, Salvador, Exodus*— names of vessels engraved on the Jewish conscience as bearing martyrs to the Jewish state. The sinkings, the drownings, the internments, the expulsions served as a permanent reminder to Zionist leaders that after the war a political solution would have to be found for the survivors. Weizmann was now talking freely of two or three million Jews who would enter the Jewish state once hostilities had ceased.[76]

The crucial issue of Jewish homelessness resulting from Hitler's campaign against Jews was discussed at the Biltmore Conference, held at New York's Biltmore Hotel in May 1942. Called by the American Emergency Committee for Zionist Affairs, with six hundred delegates participating, the Biltmore Program was adopted, concluding with the following.

> The Conference declares that the new world order that will follow victory cannot be established on foundations of peace, justice, and equality, unless the problem of Jewish homelessness is finally solved. The Conference urges that the gates of Palestine be opened, that the Jewish Agency be vested with control of immigration into Palestine and with the necessary authority for upbuilding the country, including the development of its unoccupied and uncultivated lands; and that Palestine be established as a Jewish Commonwealth integrated in the structure of the new democratic world. Then and only then will the age-old wrong to the Jewish people be righted.[77]

A clash resulted between Weizmann and Ben-Gurion following the Biltmore Conference regarding the policy statement calling for a Jewish State in Palestine. According to Weizmann biographer Norman Rose, the program was drafted by Meyer Weisgal and Louis Lipsky, trusted Weizmann aides, and embraced the basic points of an article written by Weizmann that appeared in the February 12, 1942, issue of *Foreign Affairs*.[78]

When Ben-Gurion barnstormed the Yishuv in the fall of 1942 passionately advocating the Biltmore program in Palestine, Weizmann sourly noted that Ben-Gurion had conveyed "the idea that it is the triumph of his policy as against my moderate formulation of the same aims."[79]

Rose regarded the clash as stemming from personality rather than policy differences. The disparate operating patterns of the two leaders, as well as the differing constituencies to which they appealed, provide significant credibility for Rose's belief. The younger Ben-Gurion, the shirt-sleeved labor leader and spokesman for the Yishuv, plainly wanted the senior statesman of Zionism, who was in declining health, to step aside.

The two men openly clashed in the study of Rabbi Stephen Wise's New York home on June 27, 1942, six weeks after the Biltmore Conference. When the meeting ended that evening, the sympathies of the eight people present were with the witty and urbane Weizmann; Ben-Gurion had attacked with the ferocity of a pit bull, harshly and heartlessly hurling charges, chief of which were faulty reporting and keeping his contacts to himself. If Weizmann could be cold and impersonal, Ben-Gurion had a predilection for volcanic explosions and volatility. Rather than being manifestations of lack of control, the temper eruptions appeared more reminiscent of what then Vice President Richard Nixon said of Soviet Premier Nikita Khrushchev: "He doesn't lose his temper, he uses it." All the same, whether this occasion represented loss of control on Ben-Gurion's part or dramatic posturing, it elicited a negative reaction from the group. Even Ben-Gurion confidante Miriam Cohen, who attended the meeting and took the minutes, stated that his remarks fell on her "like a bombshell. . . . I wished that the earth would open and swallow me . . . None of us thought he was capable of such behavior; no one had ever seen him in so belligerent a mood or heard him speak so harshly."[80]

Ben-Gurion biographer Shabtai Teveth regarded the 1942 meeting in Rabbi Wise's study as a failure in the short term but an ultimate success in the strategic sense of laying down a long-term strategy. He points to the fact that Weizmann was not elected president at the Zionist Congress of 1946. The 1942 strategy of openly confronting Weizmann is perceived as recognition on Ben-Gurion's part that his unchallenged leadership was necessary to accomplish the ultimate goal of a Jewish state in Palestine.

History was certainly moving in Ben-Gurion's direction during those war years. If he received disproportionate credit at Weizmann's expense, as the older leader complained, for the ideas embraced in the Biltmore Program, this can be attributed to a greater visibility on Ben-Gurion's part at the grass roots level of the Zionist movement. His energies were put to perpetual use both in the Yishuv and internationally. The Zionist movement in America, somewhat quiescent until World War Two, came alive in the wake of tragedy. New interest was sparked as reports of tragedy and suffering filtered in from Europe. What with Ben-Gurion's making purposeful strides in cultivating fresh American support, the older Weizmann, who was rapidly losing his sight and declining in energy, was perceived as the diplomat with the close alliance to Britain. With bitter policy conflicts abounding in the Yishuv between British enforcers of the White Paper's restrictive immigration policy amidst the onrush of Jewish refugees seeking to escape from European tragedies, the old trump card of Weizmann ceased to carry its once vital ring. Despite the link of a common objective—the defeat of the Third Reich—sentiment in Zionist circles, especially in the Yishuv, was militating against Britain as attitudes hardened with the enforcement of White Paper policy.

Weizmann initially believed that history might repeat itself in the form of a gigantic personal contribution to the British war effort. His World War One invention had generated enormous goodwill. The Balfour Declaration and Britain's Palestine Mandate followed. At the Weizmann Institute in Rehovot, a process called aromatization, a catalytic cracking of heavy oil leading to higher yields of benzine and toluene, was proffered but rejected. The aging leader was also forced to endure the loss of his son Michael, who gave his life fighting for the Royal Air Force. While the British trump card diminished in value for Weizmann, the position of Ben-Gurion grew stronger with his control over Yishuv residents. Weizmann would remain a diplomat to serve Zionist ends at strategic moments, but it would take a political pragmatist such as Ben-Gurion, a man of the soil who empathized with the Yishuv's pioneers, to take the ultimate final step in the creation of a Jewish State.

By early 1944, the Zionists had helped the British induct some 43,000

Jews into military service. Screened by the Jewish Agency, many already belonged to the Hagana. Responding to pressures in Britain and the United States, the British finally agreed in late 1944 to establish a separate Jewish Brigade Group as part of its army. The smuggling of arms into Palestine had begun before 1939 and continued through the war, intensifying after 1943. Realizing that a future conflict could take place with the Arabs, the Jews sought to prepare themselves for that eventuality. Between 1939 and 1943, close to 20,000 illegal immigrants were added to the 19,000 legal ones.[81] At the same time, when the transitional period specified by the White Paper ended in 1944, only about two-thirds of the 75,000 permits set aside had been utilized.[82] New villages were quickly created in sections never previously inhabited by Jews, so as to represent a basis for making claims should partition proposals be revived. Other villages were created for strategic reasons.

With Yishuv Jews aware of the dangers befalling their brothers and sisters in Europe, tension surfaced in June 1942 with the onrush of Field Marshal Erwin Rommel, known as "the Desert Fox" for his mastery of such terrain. On June 30, Rommel's troops reached El Alamein, situated 150 miles from Cairo and 60 miles from Alexandria. At this juncture, the Germans were only 500 miles from Tel Aviv by road. As German forces converged on Palestine from the Sahara and the Ukraine in a giant pincer movement, Abba Eban, a liaison officer between the *Hagana* and British forces, recalled with sad foreboding the historical account of Jewish destiny at Masada 1,839 years earlier.

Eban described Jewish contingency plans in the event of a Nazi triumph at Alamein.

If disaster had occurred in Alamein, we would have gone into various caves and hide-outs near the Dead Sea and near Haifa. A scheme was prepared by Professor Ratner of the Techneion. Those who spoke Arabic would have mingled with the population. The idea would have been to make the occupation as expensive and unprofitable as possible. As for what the Germans would have done with the Jewish population, we could only believe the worst, although the news of the Wannsee Conference had not yet percolated. We would live as the guerrillas did in Yugoslavia, but we assumed that our existence would not be very prolonged.[83]

A meeting occurred in the Berlin suburb of Wannsee on January 20, 1942, with Reinhard Heydrich presiding over a small group of Nazi elite that included Adolf Eichmann. In the course of a one-hour meeting that included lunch and drinks, the Final Solution was revealed, along with its means of implementation.

Heydrich delineated his plan for implementing the directive of Hermann Göring. Jews would be brought to the East for use as labor. They would be used in road building, and a large number would perish. The survivors would inevitably be put to death under the terms of the Final Solution, because by surviving such an ordeal, under laws of natural selection they would have to be regarded as ". . . the germ cell of a new Jewish development, should they be allowed to go free." Accordingly, in the interest of preserving Hitler's conception of "racial purity," they must be destroyed.[84]

The precise means of destruction would not be decided until the spring of 1942, when gas chambers were built in the Polish camps. This information passed into the hands of Gerhart Riegner—a refugee from Nazi Germany—through a leading German industrialist. Riegner relayed the information in Lausanne, Switzerland, as a representative of the World Jewish Congress, even specifying the instrument of murder: prussic acid, the lethal ingredient of Zyklon B gas. According to Arthur Morse, the U.S. State Department attempted to suppress the Riegner message.[85]

The threat to the Holy Land posed by Rommel's desert legions was extirpated by early November 1942. Hitler's lack of tactical insight caused him to undervalue the vast gains to be derived by conquering Egypt and sweeping northeast to capture the valuable oil fields of the Middle East then proceed to the Caucasus to meet the German armies in Russia, which already were beginning an advance toward that region from the north. Hitler did not initially send Rommel the necessary supplies and reinforcements. When he finally did, he failed to count on the tactical significance of the island of Malta, which was successfully used by the British to decimate Rommel's supplies and enforcements. General Bernard Montgomery, Britain's "Desert Fox," was then able to subdue Rommel, making Palestine and its Yishuv safe from Nazi onslaught.[86]

On July 1, 1942, a document was published by the Polish Government in London revealing that an estimated 700,000 Jews had been killed in various Polish cities.[87]

A tumultuous response to the carnage was made by the "Stop Hitler Now" rally at Madison Square Garden on March 1, 1943. Organized by Rabbi Stephen Wise, the Garden's 21,000 seats were filled. Police estimated that 75,000 persons had attempted to enter the building while 10,000 remained in the streets throughout the meeting, listening to the proceedings as amplifiers carried the passionate appeals for government action.

Chaim Weizmann, known for cool diplomacy rather than blazing rhetoric, aroused the packed Garden audience with a moving exhortation.

> The world can no longer plead that the ghastly facts are unknown and unconfirmed. At this moment expressions of sympathy without accompanying attempts to launch acts of rescue become a hollow mockery in the ears of the dying. The democracies have a clear duty before them. Let them negotiate with Germany through the neutral countries concerning the possible release of the Jews in the occupied countries. Let havens be designated in the vast territories of the United Nations which will give sanctuary to those fleeing from imminent murder. Let the gates of Palestine be opened . . . The Jewish community of Palestine will welcome with joy and thanksgiving all delivered from Nazi hands.[88]

The response from the United States and Britain was to call a conference on refugees. The April 1943 Bermuda Conference was, like the earlier Evian Conference, notable not for what was accomplished but for what was left undone. The only concrete action taken by the Bermuda Conference was to remove 21,000 refugees in Spain to North Africa. Of that number, 14,000 were French nationals, mostly of military age, who had escaped the German occupation. Some 3,000 were Poles and Czechs of military age, while 4,000–5,000 were Jews regarded as stateless or of enemy nationality.[89]

Arthur Morse passed judgment on this bleak period of U.S. History and the inaction of the government, which did nothing to help individuals seeking to avoid a date with death in a Nazi gas chamber by stating:

> Riegner's information was greeted with incredulity by men who had read an endless series of messages detailing the Nazis' inexorable degradation of the Jews. Programs of rescue suggested to the United States government had been obstructed, thwarted and delayed long after recognition by the highest authorities that the Germans were indeed carrying out a planned massacre of the Jews of Europe. Finally, after the direct presentation of evidence by the Treasury Department, Franklin Roosevelt had been shocked into action. In early 1944 he announced the formation of the War Refugee Board for the "rescue, transportation, maintenance and relief of the victims of enemy oppression and . . . the establishment of havens of temporary refuge for such victims."[90]

When the war finally ended in 1945 and the carnage was calculated, numbering some eleven million Nazi concentration camp victims, six million of whom were Jews, the dimensions of the Jewish quest for statehood in Palestine were permanently altered. When the dust cleared, Arab resistance had a new factor to contend with—the steadfastness of survivors without identities, of individuals too crushed to return to their previous European homes in the wake of cataclysmic destruction. This quest for identity reenergized the pursuit of statehood. Recognizing this reality, the Arabs reacted, fearful of losing their freedom aspirations, which they had believed would be realized after the hated Ottoman Empire was repulsed in World War One.

As usual, in the unpredictable pattern of Middle East politics, many surprises would occur in the decisive post–World War Two period. During the intervening eventful three years between the end of the war and the creation of the State of Israel, two veteran political leaders would play major roles in the forces of historical movement. One would generate influence as a perceived villain, affecting results outside the ambit of his intentions. The other, thought to be through as a leading political figure, was recruited for one last major mission that produced salutary results for the cause he represented. Both individuals were in poor health and would not live many years beyond their final appearances on the world stage, but history remembers them as major figures in the dramatic Middle East saga of which they were a part.

# 9

# The Tortuous Road to Statehood

Time and circumstances often generate alliances and friendships, a notable example being the close working relationship between Franklin D. Roosevelt and Winston Churchill during the Second World War. Roosevelt and Churchill were drawn together by parallel goals and interests. Had their objectives been disparate, close alliance would have been impossible, no matter how promising the prospect for cooperation based on respective life patterns.

In a different set of circumstances, one could easily conceive of a close relationship developing between two men whose entire lives had been connected to the labor movement and tirelessly and energetically devoted to workers who had placed their trust in them. Each had a hard-crusted veneer, a no-nonsense demeanor that workers admired. Both exemplified a steadfastness, a charisma born not of fluid speaking tones or good looks, but of the rock hardness of determined men concentrating on a central objective.

Ernest Bevin, based on the evolutionary patterns of his eventful life, could have been classified as a British David Ben-Gurion, or Ben-Gurion a Middle Eastern Ernest Bevin, but events during the turbulent post–World War Two period cast them on opposite sides, where they squared off as enemies rather than allies.

The route of Bevin's ultimate rise to power as British Foreign Secretary proves as fascinating as any Horatio Alger story. His father died before he was born and his mother before he was seven. Mrs. Bevin was intensely religious, a Methodist dissenter against the established Church of England. She fell ill when young Ernest was only six, and his last recollections of her were reporting to her bedside Sunday evenings to relate highlights of the minister's sermons. No doubt influenced by his mother, Bevin later became a lay preacher for a time during his twenties. Ben-Gurion, it will be recalled, had been profoundly affected by the death of his own mother in his boyhood and in later years would tearfully reminisce about her in conversations with close friends.

A second striking similarity between Bevin and Ben-Gurion is that both were largely self-educated, although the Jewish leader received a good deal more schooling than Bevin, whose formal education ended when he was eleven.

Bevin worked many odd jobs before finding a permanent position at the age of eighteen. He was a kitchen boy in a restaurant, a grocery errand boy, a hotel porter, a streetcar conductor, and a dray-horse driver. At eighteen he found employment in the mineral water business, and for the next eleven years made regular rounds in his hometown of Bristol, a port city in the west of England, with a horse and cart for a wage of eighteen shillings a week, plus small commissions on sales.

His wages gradually crept up to two pounds a week. He married, and his wife, Florence, bore him with a daughter, the only child from their marriage.

"It sounds hard when you look back on it, but you've got to remember that conditions were very different then," Bevin told a friend in later years. "I hadn't anything to complain about. They were good people I worked for and they treated me well. You had to take what was going. You got a job and you lost it and you picked up something else and made do with whatever came along."[1]

Times were difficult, and Bevin, the teetotaler and lay preacher, saw his interests shift to a political and economic horizon as he traded his pulpit for active membership in the Bristol Socialist Society. By 1908, while still in his twenties, Bevin emerged as one of the organization's leaders during a time of great depression, when at least 20,000 men, women, and children subsisted on paupers' handouts. He raised community eyebrows by organizing a protest to generate action by the Bristol City Council for relief as a large crowd of unemployed assembled at Bevin's behest and marched quietly to morning church service at Bristol Cathedral. They silently filled empty pews alongside the city's wealthy, sang and prayed, then silently filed out when the service concluded. In the ensuing uproar over the incident, Bevin's mineral water service was boycotted by some of his regular customers, but his employer stood by him. The incident bears a similar ring to the kind of social protest David Ben-Gurion would generate under comparable circumstances.

On August 27, 1910, a pivotal event occurred in Bevin's life. He became a founding member of the Bristol Carmen's Branch of the Dock, Wharf, Riverside and General Laborers' Union. Six months later, the union organizers decided that a full-time secretary was needed. Bevin was selected, exchanging his two pounds per week plus commissions position with the mineral water company for a two pounds per week post as a union official. His work captured the attention of the national Dock Workers Union. Bevin was brought to London and made assistant national organizer. When his boss died, he became national organizer for the British Dock Workers Union at the age of thirty-four.

David Ben-Gurion had achieved a great victory in his native Plonsk when he championed the cause of the seamstresses, pressing a strike until favorable terms were reached. Ernest Bevin catapulted from the ranks of a labor leader known only on labor-management turf into a nationally known figure when he fought the shipowners before a Labor Ministry court of inquiry into a dockworkers' claim for a new minimum wage of sixteen shillings a day, which represented approximately four dollars at that time. He shocked experts by deciding to argue the case for the dockworkers himself rather than hiring a battery of lawyers to confront the skilled team of advocates employed by the shipowners. Bevin argued skillfully and prevailed before the special tribunal.

It was a logical progression for Bevin to move into the political arena, using his union leadership position to good advantage in the Labor Party. In the manner of Ben-Gurion as a Yishuv political leader, union solidarity came first. Both men embraced a nondoctrinaire pragmatic socialism with unionism as the linchpin. The motivating factor for opposing the rise of fascism in the 1930s was, in Bevin's estimation, the destruction of the trade union movements in Italy and Germany prior to the assumption of power of Mussolini and Hitler. When war came and Churchill was named prime minister in a coalition between Labor and the Conservatives, he appointed Bevin Minister of Labor, where he served during the entire conflict.

When the wartime coalition was dissolved and Britons went to the polls for the first general election in ten years, Ernest Bevin became a man of destiny. Clement Attlee achieved one of the major upsets in the history of democratic politics as Labor swamped Churchill and his Conservatives. Attlee was the closest working confidante of the new prime minister, so it was axiomatic that Attlee would invest Bevin with a major leadership role. It came in the form of the Foreign Minister's post during a period of upheaval and transition of unique significance in world annals.[2]

To Ben-Gurion, fellow labor leader and fellow socialist, the appointment of Ernest Bevin as Foreign Minister had every reason to loom as eminently promising. On one previous occasion, during his labor union days, Ben-Gurion ally Dov Hos asked for Bevin's support in annulling a recommendation of Colonial Minister Lord Passfield concerning Jewish immigration restrictions. After listening to Dov Hos's arguments, Bevin promised "to instruct my boys" to vote against the government if the restrictions against the Jews were not withdrawn. Bevin's "boys" were the roughly fifteen members of Parliament who were nominees of his union. Ben-Gurion credited Bevin's pressure as generating a major impact on British Prime Minister Ramsay MacDonald.[3]

Future prime minister Harold Wilson grimly summarized the postwar Middle East situation: "There cannot have been in twentieth-century British history a greater contrast between promise and performance than was shown by the incoming (Labor) Government over Middle East issues."[4]

The Labor landslide victory of 1945 brought to Parliament in leadership positions many members of the winning party who had vigorously manifested pro-Zionist views from the 1930s. Many had joined the party or become activists in the fight against Nazism and Hitler's persecution of the Jews.[5]

The Labor Party's National Executive Committee published a statement, *The International Post-War Settlement*, which received overwhelming support at the December 1944 Labor Party annual conference. The document was specific on two subjects, Germany and Palestine. Just as Germans who were not prepared to become loyal citizens of other states had to return to Germany, in Palestine there was a case "on human grounds" and to facilitate a stable settlement for "transfer of population."[6] The document conceded conflicting previous British policies regarding Palestine, coming out emphatically for a Jewish National Home and permitting Jews, ". . . if they wish, [to] enter this tiny land in such numbers as to become a majority."[7]

The National Executive Committee statement then made the following points.

> Let the Arabs be encouraged to move out as the Jews move in: let them be compensated handsomely for their land and let their settlement else-

where be carefully organized and generously financed. The Arabs have many wide territories of their own; they must not claim to exclude the Jews from this small area of Palestine, less than the size of Wales. Indeed, we should re-examine also the possiblity of extending the present Palestinian boundaries, by agreement with Egypt, Syria or Transjordan. Moreover, we should seek to win the full sympathy and support both of the American and Russian Governments for the execution of this Palestine policy.[8]

In one sweeping paragraph, the Labor Party statement had committed the party to encourage the Arabs to move out of Palestine for generous compensation, to consider extending Palestinian boundaries by agreement with Egypt, Syria, and Transjordan, and to seek the full support of the American and Russian governments in pursuing the earlier-stated objectives.

In view of Arab opposition to Jewish immigration, and accompanying determination to remain on their land, the Labor Party statement looms as high on ambition and lacking practicality, particularly as applied to the objective of Arab cooperation both within and beyond Palestine. Written and presented to the party at a period during which Jews were being executed in the gas chambers of Nazi concentration camps, both sympathy for the victims of the Holocaust and recognition of the necessity to right such grievous wrongs motivated Labor to seek to obtain the strongest measure of security for Jewish survivors.

Largely forgotten in the determination of Laborites at the 1944 party conference to provide a Jewish Homeland for the survivors of Hitler's Final Solution was the tense period of the 1930s when a besieged Malcolm MacDonald, serving as Colonial Secretary, attempted to balance the interests of Arabs and Jews while Britain was being confronted by the challenge of Hitler. MacDonald ended up severely castigated by both sides. Now that the war with Hitler was won, euphoric Laborites might be inclined to believe that the responsibility of Ernest Bevin as Foreign Secretary had been lightened and that he could concentrate with a diligence unavailable to MacDonald during the trying prewar period and resolve the Palestine dilemma; however, basic conflicts that had previously existed continued between the two sides. In addition, now that the war was over, Britain was part of a world order in transition. Much of that awesome responsibility of determining Britain's response to the shifting tides of world politics resided with Bevin, the most trusted ally of incoming Prime Minister Clement Attlee.

Harold Wilson refers to Bevin as ". . . the only man to whom Attlee ever deferred."[9] Bevin was perceived by intimate Labor insider Wilson as filling a gap that was missing in Attlee's life. Attlee lacked Bevin's experience with workers as a trade unionist. As leader of a party solidly linked to unionism, Attlee, while esteemed by Labor's rank and file, seemed to stand at a distance. Bevin, a man of scant formal education and Horatio Alger–like achievements, rose to the ranks of leadership due to the respect he commanded from the men with whom he dealt. Recognition of his abilities prompted Churchill to name him Minister of Labor in 1940 despite an earlier conflict between the two men during the General Strike of 1926. Bevin believed that his background of experience in the economic sphere at the center of numerous clashes between labor and management made him an ideal candidate for Chancellor of the Exchequer in a Labor Government. At one point it appears that Attlee was prepared to name him to that position, with Hugh Dalton to receive the Foreign Secretary post. Instead, a reversal of roles occurred, with King George VI being the presumed catalyst as Attlee was said to have deferred to the monarch.

Confirming evidence of King George's role in Bevin's selection as Foreign Secretary is derived from Sir John Wheeler-Bennett's *Life of King George VI* in a quote from the king's diary.

> I then saw Mr. Attlee and asked him to form a government. He accepted and became my new Prime Minister. I told him he would have to appoint a Foreign Secy. and take him to Berlin. I found he was very surprised his Party had won, and had had no time to meet or discuss with his colleagues any of the Offices of State. I asked him whom he would make Foreign Secy. and he suggested Dr. Hugh Dalton. I disagreed with him and said that Foreign Affairs was the most important subject at the moment and I hoped he would make Mr. Bevin take it. He said he would but he could not return to Berlin till Saturday at the earliest. I told him I could hold a Council on Saturday to swear in the new Secy. of State. I hoped our relations would be cordial and said that I would always be ready to do my best to help him.[10]

The king's perception was accurate as foreign policy played a major role in British considerations with the conclusion of a long and painful war. A realist, Bevin recognized the overextension of Britain in foreign affairs. On February 20, 1947, he sent a message to Washington informing the United States that Britain could no longer carry the burden of military and economic support for Greece and Turkey. That same day, Attlee announced in the House of Commons that Britain would be withdrawing from India in one year and would grant full independence to the subcontinent whether the India-Pakistan problem was resolved by then or not.[11]

The plight of Great Britain as the new Labor government took power was summarized by foreign affairs analyst Don Cook.

> . . . the new Labour government, with its economic back to the wall, sent John Maynard Keynes to Washington to extract, in arduous and difficult negotiations, a postwar American loan of $3.75 billion, which Britain will be repaying until the end of this century. Under these conditions, Britain was desperately holding the world's pressure points in 1945, 1946, and 1947—Greece, Turkey, Trieste, Iran, Iraq, Syria, Lebanon, Palestine, Transjordan, Egypt, the Suez Canal, Ethiopia and the horn of Africa, India, Burma, Ceylon, the forward occupation zone in Austria, the major occupation zone of West Germany—the major navy in the Atlantic. There was no lack of realization in London that the nation was weakened and historically overstrained. The desperate problem was what to do about it—how to pull back without leaving a vacuum everywhere.[12]

In order to understand the ramifications of Britain's postwar policy in the Middle East and elsewhere, it is essential to understand the core of the citizenry's thinking during that great period of transition. The massive Labor victory in 1945 was over a Conservative Party led by the redoubtable Winston Churchill, the voice in the wilderness warning of Nazi Germany's intentions, who was eventually listened to and selected as Prime Minister of Britain's coalition government during the war, wherein he spearheaded his country's response to Germany's formidable challenge. The shock element related not only to the fact that had Labor won, but by an astounding 146-seat margin over all parties, constituting one of the greatest landslides in British electoral history. As earlier noted, Attlee was taken by such great surprise by Labor's astounding triumph that he had not even devoted much time to the selection of government ministries to serve under him. What had caused this shocking upset to occur? Perhaps a clue was provided when Bevin, with Churchill, took a tour of the English Channel ports on the eve of D day. The troops, prepared for their Normandy landing, cheered their commander Churchill as he thrust his right hand triumphantly in the air, making the V-for-Victory sign. Some men in uniform, drafted from the Transport Workers Union, recognized Bevin standing on the dock and called out that June evening of 1944: "See they don't let us down when we come back this time, Ernie."[13]

The transport workers already had their minds focused on the Britain to which they would return after the war. Promoting domestic order was on their minds as well as those of many other British citizens. John Maynard Keynes saw Britain as ". . . facing a financial Dunkirk,"[14] as it sought to rebound from the war as the world's leading debtor. Great sacrifices had been made on the international front, and now that Hitler and the Axis powers had been subdued, thoughts turned inward toward rebuilding the nation internally. At that pivotal moment, the British people, spurred on by a swelling labor-class tide, opted for the agenda of Clement Attlee and his Labor Party. Responding to its solid mandate from the voters, the Labor Party engineered an ambitious domestic agenda that saw the creation of a National Health Service, National Insurance, the nationalization of the British Railway system, and a partial nationalization of the steel industry.

In order for Britain to concentrate on its domestic agenda, it was necessary to dispose of significant international questions that would affect it and the rest of the world. Therefore the election of a Foreign Secretary assumed fundamental importance. British interests were sought to be protected when an abdication of power had become historically inevitable. Little more than a decade later, following the Suez Crisis, Harold MacMillan would communicate the words "Over to you" to President Dwight D. Eisenhower in what was seen as the final step toward abdicating British international responsibilities by transferring such authority to the United States. The pivotal period after World War Two marked the beginning of that phase that concluded with the MacMillan communiqué to Eisenhower. It was historically symmetrical that Great Britain, which had grappled intensively with the issue of Palestine and the overriding issue of balancing Arab and Jewish aspirations, would see its historical position in world affairs largely terminate in a Middle East crisis in response to the nationalization of the Suez Canal by Egypt's President Nasser. For Britain, the Middle East was an albatross it could not seem to shed, no matter how fervent its desire to do so.

When Ernest Bevin assumed the post of Foreign Secretary in the Attlee Labor Government, his objective was clear—work in close concert with the Americans to achieve a harmonious world order during a period of transitional upheaval. World War Two ended after introduction of the awesome weapon of destruction that had been discussed with such apprehension, the atomic bomb, which was unleashed with devastating ferocity on the Japanese cities of Hiroshima and Nagasaki. A wary eye was focused eastward on the Soviet Union and the global acquisitiveness of its ruthless dictator Josef Stalin.

Amidst the rumblings, a new world body was created the same year the war ended, 1945, with a mandate to achieve peace through discussion and implementation. The fledgling United Nations, created in San Francisco, was the anticipated antidote to the tragedy that befell the world following World War One, when the combination of the vengeful Treaty of Versailles coupled with the ineffectivness of the League of Nations, sorely absent U.S. participation, produced a momentum culminating with the rise of Hitler and a bloody world conflict marked by the loss of fifty million lives.

It was Bevin's intention to help promote international order as a viable working partner with the United States. In that he deemed it imperative to work toward a revitalized Europe in the wake of war destruction, it was only natural that the former union leader, along with Prime Minister Attlee, would see Palestine as a problem of ever-heightening dimension. At a time when Attlee and Bevin were concerned with confronting Britain's internal needs and promoting tranquility in Europe amidst the threat of Soviet expansion, the Palestine dilemma remained. Attlee and Bevin did not wish to dissipate energies in the Middle East when the focus of British interests lay much closer to home.

Whereas Attlee could send Lord Louis Mountbatten to India to successfully negotiate the cession of that British colonial state to the Indians, enacting a partition and the creation of Pakistan to mollify conflicting religious elements of Hindus and Muslims, Palestine was a thorn of much pricklier composition. The Palestinian dilemma was magnified by the existence of so many, often diverse, viewpoints among both Jews and Arabs, which gained expression through the various groups and their competing interests. Pre-partition India involved two tenaciously competing groups, but with identifiable goals, giving Mountbatten a greater opportunity to achieve a settlement than was presented to Bevin and Attlee with the diffusion of thought and action embodied in Palestine. In addition, Palestine presented another problem that did not exist in India, that of the Holocaust's survivors and what to do with them. They had fled Europe to preserve their lives from Hitler's onslaught. Now that the war was over, a debate erupted over where they should go. The British Government was caught up squarely in that dilemma as well, a corollary of the total question of Palestine and whether a Jewish state should be created.

Once hostilities had concluded, analysis began into just how and why an event of the destructive impact of World War Two occurred. The grim statistic of the destruction of six million Jews, the figure quoted by the prosecution at the Nuremberg war crimes trial, prompted grim concern. While it is true that fifty million lives were lost in the conflict, the Jews had been a group singled out for total destruction under the plan known as the Final Solution. Although no verifiable records are available due to the destruction of same by German authorities, the calculation deemed most reliable in the international community, and accepted by the prosecutors at Nuremberg, is that some six million European Jews were executed in the Holocaust out of an estimated Jewish population in Europe of between nine to ten million. The decimation therefore resulted in the loss of 60–66 percent of the Jewish population of Europe.

With the war over, recriminations flew concerning the question of how a megalomaniac like Hitler, hungry for world conquest, could come as perilously close as he did to succeeding without being stopped in his tracks at an earlier point. Also examined was the companion issue of the Holocaust and why more Jewish lives were not spared through joint international cooperation.

An initial catalyst was the Treaty of Versailles and the animosities engendered within Germany because of the harshness of terms imposed largely through the efforts of an embittered Premier Clemenceau of France against a then helpless nation he passionately hated. There was the tragic specter of Hitler recording in *Mein Kampf* his grandiose design for a new international order achieved by military conquest while a world of dozing disbelievers failed to take him seriously. At a time in the late 1930s, when Europe and Britain were under siege, a large and influential segment of America was fastened to isolationism. The impassioned exhortation to "Avoid foreign wars!" redounded in editorials in the isolationist Colonel Robert McCormick's *Chicago Tribune*. Aviator Charles Lindbergh, a national hero, vigorously advocated a noninterventionist posture before large throngs throughout the nation, at which German salutes were observed from certain fervent audience members.

At U.S. Government levels, isolationist sentiments were so strong that Franklin D. Roosevelt, in the triumphant blush of the greatest presidential victory in U.S. history, in 1936, saw fit to sign rather than veto the Neutrality Act passed by Congress despite his personal misgivings of being hamstrung in the wake of crucial international developments.

Another international sore point related to the willingness to sell military weaponry and materials to Nazi Germany, a crass instance of the desire for economic gain outstripping morality.

Drew Pearson and Robert S. Allen detailed in *Look* magazine how American airplane builders helped Germany erect its unlawful air force, forbidden under the terms of the Versailles Treaty, in secrecy. The article, which appeared in the May 23, 1939, edition, made the following disclosures.

> [The] most prosperous industry in the United States today is aviation. And the reason is that the airplane builders have cut into the juiciest racket in the world—munitions. They make big money out of war!
>
> Massed in Germany today are rows of military airplanes—bombers, fighters—more than 10,000 of them. They constitute Hitler's most effective threat against France and Great Britain. They won his victories at Munich, in Czechoslovakia, in Austria.
>
> And on almost every one of Hitler's planes, American plane builders reaped a profit.
>
> [The] key company in rearming Germany was Pratt and Whitney of Hartford, Conn. In 1934 the Senate Munitions Committee reported that "Pratt and Whitney shipped (airplane) engines to Germany in great quantities," aiding Hitler to break the German-American peace treaty in defiance of appeals from Secretary of State Cordell Hull.
>
> Pratt and Whitney also granted patents to a German subsidiary and helped the Nazis to conceal from France and England how fast they were building up their forbidden fleet.[15]

The article goes on to detail massive sales figures realized by Douglas, Glenn Martin, and Lockheed from Germany and other nations, including China and Japan, as of early 1939 compared with 1932, prior to the massive war buildups. In 1932, Douglas had realized sales of $2.3 million. The figure burgeoned to $28.3 million in 1938. The U.S. Army withheld figures on 1939 orders on hand. For Glenn Martin, the 1932 figure of $1.78 million catapulted to $12.4 million in 1938, while orders were on hand as of February 28 for $30.3 million. For Lockheed, the 1932 figure over the seven-month period calculated in the report came to $23.3 million, and in 1938, sales of $10.3 million were recorded. As of January 1, 1939, Lockheed had reported orders of $33.3 million.[16]

While American industry was immersed in the international profiteering realized from the buildup that led to war, the American Zionist movement, as reported, was becoming increasingly vocal and active amid reports of the perils encountered by Jews in Europe. While the years passed and death tolls mounted, frustrated by failure of the U.S. and British governments to establish a viable program to rescue and repatriate refugees fleeing the Nazi boot, the Jewish movement in America, from whose ranks Zionism had realized but lukewarm success in the past, rallied to assist their brothers and sisters immersed in the life-and-death struggle in Europe.

The major American Jewish thrust toward aiding in the creation of a Jewish state in Palestine following the war, which was to enhance Ben-Gurion and his followers in the Yishuv both politically and economically, resulted from the commitment on the part of American Jews to help save Jewish lives during World War Two. Standing in the front of American Zionist ranks were two prominent rabbis, both veterans of Zionism in America and internationally. Each came from a major city, where he headed an influential congregation. And both rabbis held powerful political connections.

Rabbi Stephen Wise, based in New York, had long been a friend and confidante of leading Democratic Party figures, notably President Roosevelt. Wise's politics were decidedly liberal and he had headed the Zionist Organization of America since 1935, providing it with visibility and prestige that it had lost since the departure of Louis Brandeis. Rabbi Abba Hillel Silver, from Cleveland, was a conservative Republican with strong links to Ohio's Senator Robert Taft, leader of the conservative wing of the Republican Party. Besides holding disparate political views, Wise and Silver clashed on the philosophy and direction of Zionism in a world context. While having clashed with Weizmann earlier as a member of the Brandeis group, Wise ultimately forged close working ties with Zionism's leading diplomat. Silver, on the other hand, found himself in harmony with the leader of Palestine's Yishuv, David Ben-Gurion, heading the "maximalists," the group opposing Wise's more moderate stance in favor of scuttling the gradualist approach of initially seeking a Jewish community in Palestine under a U.S. or British protectorate and militantly pressing for the immediate creation of a sovereign Jewish State.

Silver, a former colleague of Wise's during the Brandeis days, made his position emphatically known in an impassioned speech at a January 1941 fund-raiser promoting the creation of a Jewish state quoting the words of the Irish rebel Daniel O'Connell, hero of the Irish struggle for national liberation: "Agitate! Agitate! Agitate!" along with revolutionary Frenchman Georges-Jacques Danton's "*L'audace, encore l'audace, toujours l'audace!*"[17]

While Silver and the maximalists were calling for greater pressure to be exerted on the British on behalf of Zionist statehood, Weizmann and his followers, notably Stephen Wise, believed that such persuasion should be abandoned in deference to the world conflict in progress. With Jews suffering death and persecution at the hands of Hitler, it was thought appropriate to cooperate with Britain and not provide additional pressure to its awesome war responsibilities.

Regrettably, David Ben-Gurion was among those who underestimated the degree of persecution to which Jews were being subjected and who placed a disproportionate amount of his wartime emphasis on Jewish statehood objectives in the face of the overriding necessity of saving Jewish lives.

Ben-Gurion biographer Dan Kurzman ruefully notes, "While Ben-Gurion and the other politicians intrigued in the name of saving their people, they appeared to take little note of events in Germany that were daily demolishing this cause."[18]

One glaring case in point was the November 15, 1942, issue of the Ben-Gurion–Jewish Agency–controlled journal *Haaretz*, which editorialized, "The reader should be reminded that all the information from the occupied areas comes from doubtful and unreliable sources and should be treated with caution and suspicion."[19]

The following day, November 16, the Mapai daily *Davar*, edited by Ben-Gurion stalwart Berl Katznelson and strongly influenced by Ben-Gurion himself, published an article on cultural life in the Warsaw ghetto, at a time when 90 percent of its inhabitants had already been liquidated![20]

The same day that the story ran about the Warsaw ghetto, a group of 69 British and Palestinian Jews, who had been exchanged for German prisoners of war, arrived in Palestine from occupied Europe. After giving testimony about the tragic fate befalling Jews in Europe in an interview with members of the Jewish Agency, one of the survivors wrote:

> They did not believe me! They said I exaggerated! They asked me questions and subjected me to an interrogation as if I were a criminal inventing a story in order to cause someone harm, in order to deceive people deliberately and for ulterior motives . . . They tried hard to weaken my certainty, so I should doubt the veracity of my information.[21]

The focus on Ben-Gurion's awareness of the Holocaust takes the form of the question U.S. Senate and House investigators perennially raised about Richard M. Nixon during the Watergate Hearings of the 1970s: "What did the president know and when did he know it?" As to what Ben-Gurion knew and when, biographer Kurzman reveals:

Ehud Avriel, who helped to form a Rescue Committee, would say that his mentor, Ben-Gurion, knew as early as summer 1942. But Ben-Gurion would never admit that he knew what he did when he did, claiming after the war that news of the Holocaust "reached us late, and then [the people] wouldn't believe us for a long time." In 1942, however, the Nazis were in an *early* stage of their extermination program, and there is no evidence that Ben-Gurion seriously tried to inform his people about the catastrophe at any time during the war.[22]

As leader of the Jewish Agency, the shadow Jewish government, Ben-Gurion could have used his influence to stir world opinion concerning the Jewish tragedies occurring in Europe. Although he eventually formed and operated a small Rescue Committee, which operated mainly out of Istanbul in neutral Turkey, he failed to generate the kind of zealous, single-minded commitment that was needed in response to a Final Solution dedicated to the proposition of Jewry's annihilation. Regrettably, when he focused on the Holocaust later in the war, it was from the perspective of the impact the destruction of European Jewry would generate on the Zionist cause.

Ben-Gurion's objective appeared to be making the most of a post-Holocaust Jewish order rather than mounting a spirited crusade against the atrocities themselves, as evidenced by the following: "It is possible to convert the great disaster of our people in exile into a powerful lever of redemption. A catastrophe of millions is also capable of redeeming millions. And Zionism's message . . . is to cast the great Jewish catastrophe in mighty molds of redemption."[23]

Ben-Gurion, who as a young man had spiritedly rallied the seamstresses of Plonsk in pursuit of economic justice and had devoted his entire adult life to the cause of Zionism, had failed to unleash his volcanic energies during a period of urgency when Jews were threatened with extinction. Why was he so reluctant to perceive the inevitable and act upon it with his typical zealous conviction? Dan Kurzman sees the situation in the following context. While acknowledging that Ben-Gurion was surely as horrified as anyone else about the destruction of his people, if not more so, Kurzman opines that in the tough-minded world of Ben-Gurion there was no room for sentiment and the sense of guilt it would breed. His priorities needed to be focused on his "messianic" pursuit of the singular mission of his life, the achievement of a Jewish State in Palestine.[24]

As war events began to turn decisively against Hitler, elements within the Zionist movement started jockeying for control in the post–

World War Two era. Having emerged from the Biltmore Conference in a formidable posture along with Ben-Gurion, Rabbi Abba Hillel Silver sensed that the time was ripe to wrest the leadership reins from the rapidly aging, rapidly tiring elder statesman of Zionism, Chaim Weizmann, and place it in maximalist hands. A major opportunity surfaced in January 1943 as delegates from thirty-two national Jewish organizations met in Pittsburgh to decide the role the American Jewish community would play after the war in helping to build Jewish Palestine.

A vigorous clash erupted at the Pittsburgh Conference between the maximalists, led by Silver, and the moderates, spearheaded by Rabbi Stephen Wise. As the delegates were well aware, the two groups representing Silver and Wise constituted intrinsic parts of the broader picture, into which both Weizmann and Ben-Gurion fit. The result of the Conference was the creation of an American Jewish Conference embodying sixty-four Jewish groups, including the American Jewish Committee, representing 1.5 million American Jews, the most representative convocation of its kind ever to take place. The objective of the conference was to promote the Zionist enterprise while isolating the anti-Zionist American Jewish Committee.

With the organizational machinery hammered into preliminary workable shape, the first meeting took place in August with moderate Zionists eager to control the "maximalist" objective of a "Jewish commonwealth" and emphasize the support of Zionism through philanthropy. Silver seized the initiative by attacking Wise and calling for the delegates to endorse the Biltmore program. The incensed delegates of the American Jewish Committee walked out, but the conference sided with Silver, who emerged from the meeting as the new leader of American Zionism, committing himself to a program featuring "loud diplomacy."

The upshot of Silver's effort was the creation of an American Jewish lobby. That same year of 1943, the ambitious Cleveland rabbi gave the Zionist Organization of America's one-man lobbying operation in Washington a swift infusion of energy. He renamed it the American Zionist Emergency Council and began mobilizing American Jewry into a mass movement. The project was highlighted by the establishment of local committees on a national scale. Activists were tutored in the art of making direct contact with local congressmen and senators via telegrams and letters. Form letters were sent out that required only a signature before being mailed to the president or federal legislators. The glue was in place to launch a major maximalist effort opposing the gradualist objectives of Weizmann, whose emphasis was on patient negotiation. Silver's efforts have borne fruit even to the present, in which a well-organized Jewish lobby promotes the cause of Israel. Over the short term, the pivotal period of the 1940s, the effort invested American Zionism with the shot in the arm it needed to bolster the cause of a Jewish state after the war.[25]

The power shift in American Zionism from Stephen Wise to Abba Hillel Silver provided David Ben-Gurion with major support to drive Chaim Weizmann from international leadership. Ben-Gurion watched the passing of two influential Zionists from the scene during the 1940s. The death of his old nemesis Vladimir Jabotinsky, in 1940, failed to release him from militancy pressures on the political right because Jabotinsky's leadership successor, Menachem Begin, would forge the *Irgun* into a formidable military machine that Ben-Gurion felt compelled to oppose. In August 1944, Ben-Gurion's friend and reliable Zionist confidant Berl Katznelson died. While grieving deeply over the loss of his friend, Ben-Gurion nonetheless kept his objectives in clear focus, pushing for a Jewish state and seeing the war effort to its conclusion. Once the Axis powers had been beaten, he concentrated on grabbing sole control of the international Zionist machinery by toppling his old foe Weizmann.

The militancy of Silver, despite his ideological agreement with Ben-Gurion on the subject of toppling Weizmann from Zionist leadership ranks, was part of a broader subject that put Ben-Gurion in a delicate position. The effect of a brutal world conflict in which European Jewry found itself facing extinction, coupled with a beleaguered British Government seeking to enforce the White Paper and diminish problems within the Yishuv while battling for survival against Hitler's onslaught, generated turmoil in Palestine.

Abraham Stern, founder of *Lohamei Herut Israel*, or *Lehi* (Fighters for the Freedom of Israel), embraced a policy of personal terror and assassination as an effective means of achieving political results. The *Lehi*, or Stern Gang, as the group was also called, engendered fear and hatred within the Jewish community as well as among British personnel in Palestine due to the ruthless indiscriminateness of the attacks waged. On January 9, 1942, two Lehi men robbed a bank and gunned down two Jewish cashiers. On January 20, a Lehi bomb killed two Jewish policemen. On January 30, the pro–Jewish Agency *Palestine Post* called on "the whole population to put a stop to such unprecedented crimes,"[26] while British authorities posted a reward of one thousand pounds on Stern's head.

The eventual capture of Stern and the events that followed formed a backdrop of controversy from which many saw him as a cornered criminal who panicked, while others saw him as a hero. The British police tracked him down in an episode resembling a James Bond adventure film. British police cleverly obtained notes smuggled out of Jaffa Hospital by two wounded members of the gang. One of the men, Moshe Svorai, persuaded a British policeman to deliver to his wife, Tova, a letter, which indicated there was someone else in the apartment. The actual whispered address of the apartment where Moshe and Tova Svorai lived was overheard by a guard at the door of the hospital room. As police suspected, one individual then occupying the attic apartment in Tel Aviv was none other than the notorious Abraham Stern.

A party of British and Jewish policemen descended on the apartment, finding and arresting Tova Svorai. As they searched the premises, the officers found Stern hiding in a cupboard. Two of the officers left at that point, while the remaining three held Stern captive in the room.

Ensuing events touched off controversies that included several lawsuits. Geoffrey Morton, one of the policemen, writes:

> He (Stern) was taken out and, while he was bending down to tie his shoelaces prior to being taken to headquarters, he suddenly dived under the gun of the policeman who was covering him and made a mad rush towards the open window leading on to the flat roof . . . Stern could not possibly have got away, for the house was surrounded and he had some infernal machine rigged up and he was making a desperate attempt to reach it. None of the police in the room could get to the window before him. So, in order to prevent another shambles, I shot him dead.[27]

An inquest returned verdicts of justifiable homicide in the cases of Stern and the two men shot at the 30 Dizengoff Street address. The British record states that Stern was "shot dead whilst attempting to escape."[28] Morton disputed the term "shot trying to escape" due to its inaccuracy and the unsavory connotations relating to the specter of tracking down Stern during a period in which Nazi officialdom was capturing and punishing Jews regularly. He maintains that Stern had in the past threatened, if ever faced with capture, to blow up himself and the police.

"So when he dived he dived for the window, I shot him. Full stop,"[29] Morton stated.

Morton subsequently won three libel suits in England against publishers of books questioning his actions. What he must have realized was that he was trapped in the circumstances of the times that, coupled with the conditions of Stern's death, created a climate of sympathy for the deceased, even among many Jews who had previously condemned him. The Stern episode fueled earlier complaints about high-handed behavior on the part of the British police. A myth generated around Stern that he was a hero killed fighting for Jewish rights in Palestine, which retains a certain measure of currency even today. Former *Irgun* and *Lehi* members, many of whom joined the Israeli Government in 1977, see Stern as a martyr killed in the act of helping his Jewish people to achieve statehood in Palestine.

Efraim Dekel, then head of *Haqana* intelligence, is one of the Israelis holding a different view of Stern: "It was not a very good way for a leader of a guerrilla group to die, being dragged out of a cupboard. He could at least have shot his way out, taken one of the policemen with him, died like a hero. He was more of a poet than a fighter."[30]

*Lehi* vowed to avenge its leader's death. Morton was provided with a team of three police bodyguards. On May 1, 1942, when he was driving with his wife from his home in Sarona to Jaffa, a land mine exploded near the car.

Morton explains:

"They must have set it off a second or two early. My wife and I were not badly hurt. They were so sure that they were going to kill us that they had two more landmines buried at the cemetery on Mount Zion, ready for our funeral, which I expect would have been quite a posh affair, with a lot of senior British officials."[31]

While many *Lehi* members were rounded up, arrested, and placed in detention camps, the organization continued to generate influence and engage in terrorist acts. On November 6, 1944, two *Lehi* members perpetrated an act that threatened to nullify the patient negotiations of Weizmann and the lobbying of Ben-Gurion on behalf of the Zionist cause in Palestine.

During a period in which Chaim Weizmann was engaged in discussion with Winston Churchill at his country home in Chequers, an event was being formulated that would seriously jeopardize his efforts, put the Zionists on the defensive, and diminish much of Churchill's enthusiasm for their cause.

On November 4, one week before Weizmann was slated to leave for Palestine, he drove to Chequers for a discussion with Churchill. It was a productive interview that lasted two hours.

Weizmann discussed the meeting in his autobiography.

He [Churchill] spoke of partition, and declared himself in favor of including the Negev in the Jewish territory. And while he made it clear that no active steps would be taken until the war with Germany was over, he was in close touch with America on the matter of the Jewish National Home. Hearing that I was going to Palestine shortly, he recommended that I stop off in Cairo, and see Lord Moyne who, he said, had changed and developed in the past two years . . . .[32]

Weizmann would never have the opportunity to discuss the issue of a Jewish state with Colonial Secretary Moyne. Just two days following his meeting with Churchill, November 6, Lord Walter Moyne, a close friend of Churchill, was gunned down along with his driver in Ghezira, a pleasant suburb of Cairo.

Moyne had upset many Zionists with a June 1942 observation in the House of Lords that large-scale immigration into Palestine was "a dream."[33] He had also been colonial secretary during the ill-fated *Struma* episode. Though they could not be certain, Zionist militants blamed Moyne for urging the Turks to turn the ship back from Istanbul into the Black Sea. According to Churchill, Moyne's thinking had altered, but Weizmann along with the rest of the world would be deprived of knowing what he might have said had the meeting suggested by Churchill taken place.

Did the June 1942 House of Lords statement combined with the alleged order to turn back the *Struma* provide the twin catalysts precipitating Lord Moyne's assassination? According to Irgunist Nathan Yalin-Mor, they had no bearing at all.

Really these acts by Lord Moyne were without meaning for us. They were useful only as propaganda, because they allowed us to explain to the people why we had killed him. What was important to us was that he symbolized the British Empire in Cairo. We weren't yet in a position to hit Churchill in London, so the logical second best was to hit Lord Moyne in Cairo.[34]

The two young Stern Gang gunmen, Eliahu Hakim and Eliahu Bet-Tsouri, had witnessed the *Patria* tragedy and were devoted to carrying out extremist acts against British authorities. The "Little Death Ship" *Patria* had blown up November 25, 1940, as it lay at anchor off Haifa. The death toll was 267. Stories began circulating that the bombing was a mass suicide, a reaction to what the Yishuv saw as an act of despair generated by Britain's inhumane policies. In reality, the tragedy stemmed from an unforeseen error on the part of the *Hagana*. In an effort to immobilize the ship's engines and keep the refugees in Haifa, exerting pressure on the British to allow the refugees to remain in Palestine, the *Hagana* overcalculated the amount of explosives required. The result was a tragic loss of lives.[35]

The day after Lord Moyne's assassination, Chaim Weizmann sent a letter to Prime Minister Churchill expressing the following.

> I can hardly find words adequate to express the deep moral indignation and horror which I feel at the murder of Lord Moyne. I know that those feelings are shared by Jewry throughout the world. Whether or not the criminals prove to be Palestinian Jews, their act illumines the abyss to which terrorism leads. Political crimes of this kind are an especial abomination in that they make it possible to implicate whole communities in the guilt of a few. I can assure you that Palestine Jewry will, as its representative bodies have declared, go to the utmost limit of its power to cut out, root and branch, this evil from its midst.[36]

The death of his close friend Moyne had a profound impact on Churchill that he disclosed in a somber warning to Zionists, expressed in remarks delivered in the House of Commons on November 17. In the course of eulogizing Moyne, Churchill stated:

> If our dreams for Zionism should be dissolved in the smoke of the revolvers of assassins and if our efforts for its future should provoke a new wave of banditry worthy of the Nazi Germans, many persons like myself will have to reconsider the position that we have maintained so firmly for such a long time.[37]

Churchill's warning had an immediate impact on the Yishuv as moderate Zionists realized the dangers of alienating a supporter of Zionism such as the prime minister and others within the British policy hierarchy. The *saison*, or "hunting season," was launched, in which Ben-Gurion's Jewish Agency committed itself to ferreting out extremists in the Zionist movement. The *Hagana*, which had provoked the ire of British authorities for stealing weaponry and ammunition targeted for England's war effort, focused on the *Lehi* and the *Irgun* as targets of opposition. The *Hagana* insisted that the weaponry and ammunition were needed as protection against Palestinian Arabs who followed the Mufti, drawing a distinction between their own aims of peacefully achieving statehood and the methods of those who practiced terrorism.

The major historic significance of Lord Moyne's death, according to

British historian Lord Bethell, who served briefly as a junior Conservative Party member of the British Parliament and went on to become a member of the European Parliament, was its effect on Churchill personally. Herbert Morrison, chairman of the Cabinet Committee on Palestine, stated that Churchill had originally requested a discussion of October 16 proposals concerning Palestine in Parliament. Churchill's earlier discussions with Roosevelt and other Allied leaders had raised the promise of a Jewish state after the war. Weizmann knew that a partition scheme already existed, and Churchill's productive November 4 meeting with Weizmann perceptibly raised the Jewish leader's hopes of achieving Zionist objectives in Palestine. However, at the very moment when the future loomed promising and it appeared that his gradualist approach of patient negotiation with the British was bearing fruit, the Moyne assassination brought threatening storm clouds to replace the bright sunshine of political expectations of Weizmann.

In addition to killing a British statesman who was a close friend of longtime Zionist ally Churchill, the murder by the *Lehi* operatives underscored the widespread division existing within Zionist ranks. Bethell pointed out that four months passed following the Moyne assassination without action being taken on the October 16 proposals. Finally, on February 26, 1945, Morrison reminded Churchill, "You felt that it was impossible to discuss future plans for Palestine while these outrages were going on and gave instructions that the discussion of the report should stand over."[38]

Lord Bethell regards the period following the Lord Moyne assassination as critical according to Churchill as well as that of general Zionist momentum with the British Government. He states, "It was during these crucial months that the fire went out of Churchill's Zionism, that the partition scheme lost its momentum, allowing its opponents in the Foreign Office and the British Army to gather their strength for a counterattack."[39]

Former members of *Irgun* and *Lehi* deny that any momentum was lost, firmly believing that Britain was never about to support the concept of Jewish statehood. To militant Jewish underground members, the assassination of Lord Moyne was necessary to make known their intentions to prevail at all costs. In addition, it was deemed necessary to drive their British enemies, seen as the obstacle preventing realization of their goal, out of Palestine. Though the *Irgun* knew nothing in advance about the plot to kill Lord Moyne, its members adopted the view that the assassination embodied an act of heroism and patriotism in furtherance of the Zionist cause.

Eliahu Hakim, one of the killers, expressed self-righteousness in a letter to his parents from Cairo's central prison: "I am absolutely calm and my conscience is settled, because I have the feeling that I have done my duty. Our deed stemmed from our motives and our motives stemmed from our ideals. And if we prove our ideals were right and just, then our deed was right and just."[40]

The ensuing struggle between the Jewish Agency and forces of *Irgun* and *Lehi* during the *saison* represented one of many historic milestones symbolizing aspects of a much broader picture, an unfolding sociopolitical scenario continuing to the present. Ben-Gurion found himself locking horns with an equally determined, equally committed adversary, Menachem Begin. Ben-Gurion would become Israel's first prime minister. His Mapai, or Labor Party, would retain control of the Knesset (Israeli Parliament) for four years beyond his death, until 1977, the year that Begin assumed the prime ministership as leader of the *Likud* Party, a coalition representing the Sephardic elements of Israel. Although Begin and Yitzhak Shamir, who would eventually become a *Likud* prime minister, both came from Poland and hence were a geographical part of the Ashkenazic Eastern European element that, under the Polish Ben-Gurion, had forged a working majority until the historic 1977 breakthrough, their similarities ended with geography. Begin and Shamir held fundamental beliefs rooted strongly in biblical tradition, and it was Begin who referred to West Bank territory by its biblical names of Judea and Samaria. Whereas traditional Labor Party origins stemmed from Eastern Europe, the *Likud* followers of Europeans Begin and Shamir were the Sephardim, with roots in Asia and Africa. They were more traditionally religious, less educated, and less worldly than the Ashkenazim who embraced the Labor Party under Ben-Gurion.

Those two elements, both of which would eventually assume power in Israel, clashed sharply on the meaning of the Lord Moyne assassination. Irgunist Yalin-Mor regarded the Moyne assassination as a vehicle that had brought the Zionist cause to the attention of the world. He justified the killing of Moyne's unarmed driver, Lance Corporal Arthur Fuller, as also necessary: "Bet-Tsouri shot him because he was walking towards Hakim. He was putting the operation in danger."[41]

A distinctly opposite view was expressed by Rabbi Stephen Wise, who told a British official in Washington that "it was better to destroy the assassins and have done with it."[42]

Weizmann worried about the destruction of his negotiating efforts in a letter intercepted by British censorship: "I warn you that I shall not be able to continue with my political work if terrorism is not suppressed. It must be, to prove to Mr. Churchill that we earn what is given to us."[43]

Assassination turmoil figured further in the disposition of Hakim and Bet-Tsouri. For a few weeks, it appeared that Lord Moyne's killers might be saved by the indecision of Egyptian Prime Minister Ahmed Maher, but on February 24, 1945, he was assassinated after declaring war on Germany. Soon after that, his successor, Nokrashi Pasha, signed the death warrant. On March 22, Lord Moyne's killers were hanged. While the executions went unmourned by most of the Yishuv, where their deed and methods were largely rejected, time and circumstances altered perceptions concerning the Lord Moyne assassination.

In Israel, admiration eventually grew for Hakim and Bet-Tsouri. In June 1975, some two years before the *Likud* came to power, the men were reburied with full military honors on Mount Herzl in the presence of Israeli ministers. Lord Bethell identifies Shamir as one of the three *Lehi* leaders who had ordered the killing,[44] stating that the two murders, especially that of the innocent and unarmed Arthur Fuller, ". . . discredited the Zionist cause morally, alienated Churchill and blocked the progress of the partition scheme."[45] Bethell projects what might have otherwise transpired.

This [partition] scheme . . . might well have gained the support of the Jewish Agency, in which case it could have been imposed by force of British arms as part of the rough-and-ready settlement of various similar disputes at the end of the war. In such circumstances the Arabs might well eventually have acquiesced, in which case Israel would now be smaller in size, but at peace with her neighbours.[46]

Irgunist leader Begin considered the *saison* a shameful betrayal of the Jewish war of liberation. Harkening back to his biblical roots, he likened the *Haqana*, the Jewish Agency, and other participating groups to the legendary Cain, who slew his brother Abel in the Book of Genesis.

Begin unleashed the following vitriolic invective on his enemies at the end of 1944.

You are raging mad, Cain. Thousands of your agents throng the streets of Jerusalem and Tel Aviv, the towns and the settlements, brought there to denounce, not to protect, to spy, not to work, for fratricidal war, not for any war of liberation. . . .

You have chosen your ally, Cain. The oppressive government of the homeland and the Nazi-British secret police are your allies. You are serving them day and night, delivering men into hands which are stained with the blood of millions thrown back from the homeland's shore into the foundries of Majdanked, your own brothers . . . Sometimes by deceit, sometimes by stealth, but always brutally you drag suspects off to unknown destinations, subject them to Gestapo-like tortures in orange groves, then hand the victims over to the Nazi-British secret police, your ally, for further tortures and for deportation to Eritrea . . .[47]

British authorities complained for the opposite reason to Begin's, maintaining that the value of the information supplied against Jewish underground operations had been scant. The complaint was also raised that the Jewish Agency was feeding them names of men they had quarreled with who had no connection with terrorism.[48]

The dispute between Weizmann and Ben-Gurion and supporters of each of them would continue in the explosive postwar atmosphere of the Yishuv and elsewhere, such as the aforementioned American Zionist dispute pitting Stephen Wise against Abba Hillel Silver, while Begin's *Irgun* and the *Lehi* comprised incendiary alternatives beyond the militancy of Ben-Gurion. The wily Ben-Gurion realized the position in which he was immersed. As a moderate, he stood on disparate ground from Weizmann the diplomat but did not wish to see potential Zionist gains jeopardized by the terrorist activities of those he felt would tilt the balance away from the cause he espoused.

Before focusing on the ongoing leadership battle between the Ben-Gurion and Weizmann forces, however, with the role played by the *Irgun* and *Lehi* in forcing the issue of Jewish statehood, it is essential to return to the response of the incoming Labor Government by Attlee and Bevin to the challenge presented by Palestine of reconciling two seemingly irreconcilable groups, the Jews and Arabs.

On July 26, 1945, when Clement Attlee assumed the prime minister's post, he found waiting for him a memorandum addressed to his predecessor and expressing "the hope that the British Government may find it possible without delay to take steps to lift the restrictions of the White Paper on Jewish immigration to Palestine."[49]

The Truman letter was written before the British election results were known. The expectations expressed were the concern of a new prime minister. Churchill's last letter about Palestine before leaving office was written to his Colonial Secretary and Chiefs of Staff on July 6, the day after the voting. It bore the mark of a tired and disillusioned man. Churchill stated, "perhaps the Americans should take the problem [Palestine] over."[50]

Truman wrote to Attlee on August 31, enclosing a report by his special envoy Earl G. Harrison about the problems of Jewish refugees, particularly displaced persons. Truman called Attlee's attention to the fact that the available certificates for immigration to Palestine would soon be exhausted, suggesting that "the granting of an additional 100,000 of such certificates would contribute greatly to a sound solution for the future of Jews still in Germany and Austria, and for other Jewish refugees who do not wish to remain where they are or who for understandable reasons do not desire to return to their countries of origin . . ."[51]

Attlee's September 16 reply focused on the universal level of suffering as a result of the war, concluding that the Jews should not be placed in a special category.

> One must remember that within these camps were people from almost every race in Europe and there appears to have been very little difference in the amount of torture and treatment they had to undergo. Now if our offices had placed the Jews in a special racial category at the head of the queue, my strong view is that the effect of this would have been disastrous for the Jews.[52]

The recommendation of the Labor Cabinet Committee on Palestine, headed by Herbert Morrison which included Bevin, was that the highest number of immigrants that could be admitted to Palestine after exhaustion of the White Paper's quota without prejudice to future policy would be a temporary continuation of immigration at the current rate of 1,500 beyond the 75,000 limit. Consultation with Arabs from Palestine and other Arab League states was deemed imperative. The Morrison Committee recommended that the White Paper policy be maintained and that no further immigration should be allowed for the time being without Arab acquiescence.[53]

British caution regarding Palestine was part of a broader geopolitical picture in which Middle East interests were carefully evaluated. Attlee biographer Trevor Burridge explains the picture as follows.

> The Middle East was a region of vital consequence for Britain and the British Empire. With the exception of Cyprus, all other territories in the

area either had or would shortly obtain full independence; protection of Britain's vital interests depended on the collaboration of those states . . .[54]

The wide disparity that developed between the emphatic declaration of support of Jewish statehood expressed at the Labor Party's 1944 annual conference and the posture embraced by Attlee and Bevin as prime minister and foreign secretary, respectively, of a Labor Government that assumed power just one year later demonstrated once more the substantial gap between policy pronouncements by a party out of power contrasted with the reality of crafting a policy while in office. The 1944 party conference's statement represented a declaration of sympathetic support for a people targeted for extinction by a ruthless regime. Party idealists held sway in the report that was drafted. Now that Labor was in power, the pragmatic technocrat Attlee was seeking to achieve the proper balance to walk through coals without being thrown off course. The foreign policy juggling act involved keeping Britain's interests in perspective during a time of great transition. Britain could not allow Palestine to erupt like a volcano when so many other problems needed to be resolved.

Ernest Bevin was determined not to be overcome by Palestine. As an assertive former labor leader who took on management and political opposition, including Churchill, from the position of neither giving nor asking for quarter, this rugged self-made man, in his anxiety about taking charge of the thorny Palestine dilemma, upset Zionist leadership of all stripes, from Weizmann to Ben-Gurion, extending to the radical elements of the *Irgun* and *Lehi* as well. The mercurial temper of the fiery ex–labor leader tended to polarize the issue of Palestine, antagonizing Zionists and generating sympathy for the children of the Holocaust while Bevin was perceived by many as a villain kicking a helpless people.

Much has been written about the Palestine Triangle, the tripartite interests of Britain, as mandatory power, and the Jews and Arabs occupying the area. At the close of the war, a reevaluation of those interests was necessary, with a fundamental party being added to the picture. When this amended picture was analyzed, the otherwise seemingly contradictory impact of Ernest Bevin on foreign affairs in the key postwar period can be understood. Otherwise, he stands as a contradiction, condemned by many for his Palestine policy and statements, while praised by eniment statesmen such as Churchill and Dean Acheson.

The assessment of Palestine interests following World War Two necessitates converting the Palestine Triangle to a Palestine Quartet of interests, which break down accordingly:

1. *Great Britain*—Rebounding from the devastation of the war, in which the country was riddled by punishing attacks from the *Luftwaffe*, endured the humiliating defeat of Dunkirk, and was pressed to its limits by rationing, Britain was spared bankruptcy by a U.S. loan. Bevin, a tenacious anticommunist, was determined to help thwart Stalinist aggression. His recognition of the dangers in Greece and Italy helped spark the Truman Doctrine, which revitalized those besieged nations and prevented communist successes from being realized in those countries. He also emphatically endorsed and aided in the implementation of the Marshall Plan, which provided ravaged noncommunist Europe with a vital economic transfusion, diminishing its vulnerability to Stalinist aggression. Bevin's tenacious resistance to Zionist aims in Palestine also stemmed from concern over communist Middle East aspirations. He knew that the Communists wanted the British out of Palestine. His conclusion was that Stalin desired to establish a fulcrum of interest that could be extended to the entire area of the Middle East.

2. *The Arabs*—Concern mounted as news of the displaced persons flooded international news channels. Arab leaders realized only too well the impact that the sympathy that was generated on behalf of homeless people—cut off from family and country and decimated by the toll of war—could have on public opinion, thereby generating a reaction on the part of political leaders. They were concerned that the arrival of large numbers of Jews would jeopardize their position in Palestine, which they saw as their own country, and which they felt should be governed by them as a result of promises they believed had been made to them prior to and following their cooperation with the Allied Powers in uprooting the Ottoman Empire from the area in World War One.

3. *The Jews*—With the extermination of an estimated 60–66 percent or better of the Jewish European population in the Holocaust, the survivors, often minus their entire families, were rescued by Allied troops to languish in hellish Displaced Persons camps without a country, thoroughly uncertain of the future. The Jewish Agency in Palestine, with Zionists throughout the world, lobbied forcefully for the admission of homeless Jews into the Yishuv. The Displaced Persons tragedy, resulting from the Holocaust, was seen by Zionists as the ultimate catalyst necessitating the immediate creation of a Jewish state.

4. *The United States*—The new player in the Palestine equation was

the United States, which emerged from World War Two unscathed by the physical devastation visited upon Great Britain and European nations. With Britain both physically and economically wounded from the game fight it was required to wage to survive Nazi assaults, America stepped into the leadership vacuum created by Britain's decline. It was America that possessed the economic might to assist war-torn European nations whose vulnerability presented an inviting target to the rapacious designs of Stalinist Russia. Ernest Bevin recognized the reality of the situation. His strong anticommunist convictions prompted him to act with vigorous dispatch in prompting U.S. assistance to the troubled region, which came in the form of the Truman Doctrine and the Marshall Plan.

A pronounced area of disagreement with America arose, however, in the Middle East, in marked contrast to the level of cooperation that existed between Bevin and America on European policy.

The dichotomy represented by Bevin's performance and policy posture regarding Europe vis-à-vis his Middle East stance resulted in a wide disparity of opinion pertaining to the man and his impact on foreign affairs during the momentous postwar period, when the world was in a state of great volatility. Foreign affairs analyst Don Cook, a European correspondent for the *Los Angeles Times*, wrote glowingly of Bevin and his tenure as Foreign Secretary.

> For the last five years of a prodigious life, in the decisive period immediately following World War II, Bevin shaped and directed British foreign policy—and by extension the policies of Europe and the Atlantic Community—with a strength and personality unmatched by any foreign secretary in this century. Anthony Eden was at the Foreign Office longer than Bevin (ten years with two interruptions) but left less of a stamp on the institution or on history. Nor do any notable foreign secretaries of the century come near to Bevin's stature or achievements: Lord Lansdowne, Sir Edward Grey, Lord Curzon. Many have held the office. Bevin filled it.[55]

Cook concedes that Bevin's handling of the Palestine question remains "a botch and a blot that obscures his greatness," adding that if Bevin were less than adroit and frequently insensitive and inept over Palestine, "at least he was not devious." He points to the insolubility of the Arab-Jewish dilemma in subsequent decades, concluding that "it cannot be said that he (Bevin) failed where somebody else might have succeeded."[56]

Cook credits Bevin with three major initiatives that thwarted Communist designs in war-ravaged Europe: (1) when he informed Washington that Britain could no longer afford the burden of economic and military support for the tottering Greek regime in its civil war against the Communists, providing the impetus for the Truman Doctrine; (2) responding vigorously to Secretary of State George Marshall's pledge of assistance to Europe in what ultimately took shape as the Marshall Plan; and (3) initiating through secret diplomacy the question of an American security guarantee for Europe, which served as the springboard for the creation of the North Atlantic Treaty Organization.[57]

Two months after Stalin's death, Prime Minister Churchill paid tribute to Bevin's accomplishments during a House of Commons foreign affairs debate: "Stalin found himself resisted from a very early stage by the firmness and tenacity of the late Ernest Bevin, who marshalled and rallied democratic sentiment strongly against this new movement of Russian Soviet ambitions. . ."[58]

While Churchill heartily approved of Bevin's accomplishments relating to European affairs, he took great umbrage to his Palestine policies in a 1949 House of Commons debate, which will be discussed later.

Zionists were so incensed with Bevin's perceived insensitivities to the plight of Jews after the war that Bevin emerged as the great enemy. Whereas policy analysts such as Cook, heads of state such as Churchill, and foreign policy shapers such as Dean Acheson would balance Bevin's shortcomings in Palestine with accomplishments over the broad sweep of European terrain, helping check Communist aggression in the process, to Zionists and their supporters the need to aid the Displaced Persons was linked to the creation of a Jewish state, with Bevin seen as an intransigent stumbling block. Zionist ire was further exacerbated by statements of Bevin regarded as tactless and insensitive at best and anti-Semitic as well as highly insulting at worst.

At a November 13, 1945, press conference at the Foreign Office following a speech in the House of Commons, Bevin made a remark that infuriated Jewish elements. Referring to the refugee problem, the Foreign Secretary stated, "I am very anxious that Jews shall not in Europe overemphasize their racial position . . . I want the suppression of racial warfare, and therefore if the Jews, with all their sufferings, want to get too much to the head of the queue, you have the danger of another anti-Semitic reaction through it all."[59]

The comment, which related to an earlier sentiment expressed by Attlee in a cable to Truman concerning feared violent reaction by other concentration camp victims should Jews be placed in a separate category,[60] touched off a furious reaction from Jewish elements. The reference to wanting "to get too much to the head of the queue" was seen as a stereotypical perception of Jews as pushy. Some of the fury also related to a perceived insensitivity on Bevin's part over the level of suffering Jews had endured at the Nazi concentration camps and continued to experience at Displaced Persons camps.

At a Foreign Office meeting in early 1947, as the lights went out from electricity cuts plaguing economically devastated Britain, Bevin joked with his brutish trade unionist humor that there was no need for candles since the Israelites were present. Following the meeting, both Ben-Gurion and Moshe Shertok complained about Bevin's tasteless-ness and lack of sensitivity.[61]

Later that same year, at the Labor Party Conference in Bourne-mouth, Bevin, with reference to the Truman recommendation that 100,000 Displaced Persons be accepted in Palestine, asserted that the reason the Americans were so intent on dumping Jews into Palestine was that they did not want "to have too many of them in New York."[62]

Such comments, made during an emotional period following the Holocaust, prompted Zionists to label Bevin as an anti-Semite. There is little question that he operated contrary to the aims of Zionists. Both Attlee and Bevin believed that Jews would be better off returning to their former countries and attempting to help rebuild them. Attlee referred to German Jews and the role they could play in that regard. Considering the suffering accorded Jews in those nations, and that many had neither home nor family to return to, such thinking reveals Attlee's lack of understanding of the tragic dimensions facing Jews, particularly the plight of Displaced Persons, in the postwar period.

The catalyst for Truman's recommendation that 100,000 Jews be sent to Palestine was special envoy Earl G. Harrison's conclusion that emigration to Palestine constituted the only feasible solution to the Displaced Persons problem. Although Attlee shared Bevin's basic convictions, it was Bevin with whom Jewish leaders such as Weiz-mann, Ben-Gurion, and Shertok dealt. Also, it was Bevin and not Attlee who poured forth combative invective.

Was Bevin actually anti-Semitic? As Weizmann biographer Norman Rose points out, a man of sixty-five of known strong prejudices was not likely to become anti-Semitic overnight. Rose reveals that when he entered the Foreign Office, Bevin was already suffering from a serious heart condition that subjected him to periodic blackouts.[63] Bevin's American working colleague, Secretary of State Dean Acheson, who Bevin affectionately called "me lad," recollects an evening in New York when the foreign secretary collapsed. Acheson referred to Bevin as being in "failing health"[64] in 1949 and recounts that he died one month after his resignation on March 9, 1951.[65] Clearly a man who was operating under the strain of confronting the major problems of the world in a state of rapidly declining health would be far more inclined toward outbursts of combativeness. Had he been in more robust health, it is likely that much of the friction occurring in the tense atmosphere of Middle East discussion could have been avoided. With such avoidance the anti-Semitic charges may never have been made.

Another aspect of the unfolding confrontation between Bevin and the Zionist leadership concerned the response to pressures generated by Yishuv forces that both Weizmann and Ben-Gurion sought to control—the *Irgun* and *Lehi*. A vicious cycle was set into motion that eventuated in hardened resistance by Bevin. The problem of Palestine remained before Bevin, a dilemma of contrasting pressures and interests between Arabs and Jews. When no quick resolution was reached on the issue of the Displaced Persons, pressures were stepped up against British military and police personnel in the Yishuv. These pressures focused on violence from *Irgun* and *Lehi* forces, which angered the already physically overwrought Bevin, who was determined not to be bullied on the Palestine question, and who had a variety of problems to consider in places such as India and Europe when the world political power structure was dramatically changing, particularly as applied to British interests.

Bevin was not the only party immersed in frustration over increased resistance activity in the Yishuv. Chaim Weizmann, the apostle of moderation, had been advocating mass immigration of Displaced Persons into Palestine. He feared that if he failed to accomplish his objective, violence might ensue. Six months after the war, having failed to achieve results, Weizmann watched with trepidation as Ben-Gurion's *Hagana* forces began coordinating efforts with the *Irgun* and *Lehi* in the Jewish Resistance Movement. He anticipated action from Britain eventually and believed, whereas most of the Jewish Agency and *Hagana* leadership did not, that the present conflict with British leadership was only temporary. Ben-Gurion, despite his cooperation in the *saison*, was becoming increasingly restless about the Displaced Persons problem. Weizmann believed that Ben-Gurion was deliberately keeping him uninformed about what he termed "aggressive" policies directed against British military forces. He frequently learned from the newspapers about spectacular actions by the resistance movement. His astute political instincts, honed through a lifetime in Zionist politics, must have alerted him that his days of effective leadership in the Zionist movement were diminishing. The moderate who had played the British trump card repeatedly was seeing his power slip away as resistance increased against British mandatory authority.

It was during this period that Weizmann met Bevin for the first time. The former labor leader was in a combative mood. Bevin was incensed by the refusal of Zionist leadership to cooperate in the continuation of White Paper policy on a limited basis of 1,500 immigrants a month. "What do you mean by refusing the white paper certificates?" Bevin asked Weizmann tartly. "Are you trying to force my hand? If you want a fight you can have it." The British foreign secretary closed the door on any possibility of admitting 100,000 refugees.

The men met five days later on October 10, but the impasse remained. By the time they met again on November 1, the *Palmach*, the elite corps of the *Hagana*, had broken into an internment camp at Athlit and freed 200 immigrants. In a smoothly coordinated effort the resistance movement simultaneously attacked British installations throughout Palestine. Understandably, the atmosphere could not have been chillier when Weizmann arrived for his meeting with the feisty foreign secretary. A muscle twitched at the side of Bevin's mouth as he accused the Yishuv of declaring war against Britain. No doubt Weizmann, who had had no hand in the strategy resulting in the events that infuriated Bevin, saw his leadership role in the Zionist movement dissipating fast. He was caught in a helpless vise. Weizmann had not been informed of policy measures he heartily disapproved of, after which he listened to a harangue about them from Bevin, who represented the nation he had worked with for so many years. The Foreign Secretary's message was clear and blunt. He would not negotiate under threat of violence.

> I cannot bear English Tommies being killed. They are innocent . . . I do not want any Jews killed either, but I love the British soldiers. They belong to my class. They are working people . . . The problem is intolerably difficult . . . but we are honestly trying to find a way out.[66]

A lengthy career in any area results in concepts and methods that harden as the years pass. Bevin's impassioned statement to Weizmann indicates that the self-educated Horatio Alger–like figure saw events from the perspective of a highly committed labor leader. His loving reference to British soldiers as working people belonging to his own class explains the challenge to Weizmann of getting a fight if he wanted one. The diligent labor leader was there to protect his "boys" from harm. As the Jewish Resistance Movement increased its level of aggressiveness against British soldiers, with death and injuries resulting on both sides, Bevin wanted all to know that he stood squarely with "his boys."

Weizmann was saddened by what he regarded as a fundamental error to recognize the nationalist forces at work in Palestine within the Jewish movement. He saw his British trump card dissipate even more when his old ally Churchill, profoundly altered by the Lord Moyne assassination, announced in a House of Commons speech in August 1946 that he did not believe that the Jewish problem could be resolved by "a vast dumping of the Jews of Europe into Palestine." He disappointed Weizmann further by suggesting an idea embraced by both Attlee and Bevin: "I am not absolutely sure that we should be in too great a hurry to give up the idea that European Jews may live in the countries where they belong."[67]

Try as valiantly as he might, Chaim Weizmann saw his dream of peaceful evolution toward a Jewish state forged through British cooperation collapsing. Those counterforces were in full swing in Palestine, with Jews demanding implementation of the Biltmore program while Arabs prepared for a "new crusade" to hang onto their land. With British authorities under constant siege by *Irgun* and *Lehi* forces, who were receiving increased cooperation from *Hagana* and *Palmach* elements, Field Marshal Bernard Montgomery, Chief of the Imperial General Staff and the man who thwarted Germany's Middle East advance at El Alamein, returning from a trip to Palestine, implored the Cabinet to take immediate action against Jewish forces in Palestine. The Cabinet concurred, authorizing Palestine High Commissioner Sir Alan Cunningham to crush the "more extreme elements" in the Jewish Agency, who were believed to be controlling terrorism through the *Hagana*. British authorities understood that a level of cooperation now existed between the *Irgun* and *Lehi* forces and the *Hagana*, and they were determined to restore order in the Yishuv.

The action the British termed "Operation Agatha" and that Jews termed "Black Saturday" began at dawn on June 29, 1946. Every available soldier and policeman was mobilized for the concerted action concentrated on Jewish Agency headquarters and other offices in Jerusalem, along with twenty-five settlements elsewhere in Palestine. A total of 2,718 Jews were detained. A *Hagana* arsenal was discovered at Kibbutz Yagur, southeast of Haifa. A curfew was declared throughout Jewish Palestine. While the massive raid resulted in the capture and detainment of certain leading figures—notably Moshe Shertok—

Ben-Gurion was in Paris, escaping apprehension. The *Irgun* and *Lehi* were untouched. They lacked rural bases of operation, and the British did not know where to find them. All the same, the Yishuv was shaken by the action, and Golda Meir, one of the handful of political leaders remaining at large, proposed a campaign of civil disobedience.[68]

Menachem Begin had a more forceful response in mind. His focus was the King David Hotel, whose southern wing housed the headquarters of the British Administration, with the military police and special investigations branch operating in an annex. Begin reasoned that by bombing the King David, the seat of British administrative authority in Palestine, he would be making a statement concerning the determination of Jews like himself to resist British efforts in stemming what he viewed as the inevitable tide leading to Jewish statehood. The Polish-born Begin, who had seen his family perish in the Holocaust, had sought *Hagana* cooperation for the venture in the spring of 1946. The *Hagana* vetoed the plan as too provocative, but when Begin resubmitted it two days after Black Saturday, approval was given.[69]

Chaim Weizmann became aware of the plan, promptly summoning thirty of the Jewish leaders still at liberty to his Palestine home in Rehovot. He asked them to arrange for the suspension of all *Haqana* activity until the August meeting of the Jewish Agency in Paris. The aging apostle of moderation then argued forcefully, "In all states it is the custom for the President to be the supreme commander of the armed forces. I have never needed this authority and have never considered interfering in your affairs. But this time, for the one and only time, I use this right and demand that you cease all activities."[70]

According to Golda Meir, Weizmann agreed to support her proposal for a campaign of civil disobedience. It was in the realm of violence that the veteran leader clearly drew the line.[71]

Communication between the *Hagana* and *Irgun* following Weizmann's Rehovot statement is blurry, but those who have carefully studied the King David episode are apparently in general agreement that the *Haqana* then pulled out of the operation. Begin, maintaining his steadfastness, decided to see it through to completion.

While planning continued for the King David operation, on the political front rivals Attlee and Churchill agreed that Palestine could clearly embody a burden beyond Britain's resources to carry alone. They felt that perhaps partition would be the inevitable result. Their thinking was motivated by a cable from British Ambassador Stonehewer Bird from Baghdad stating that, should Britain agree to accept 100,000 Jewish refugees from Europe, extreme violence would result in which British and American nationals would have to be evacuated and Britain would be forced to intervene militarily.[72] Experts predicted that the Jews would not cease their rebellion, prompting the possibility of a two-pronged British military involvement. John Glubb, the British leader of the Transjordan-based Arab Legion, which had fought with Britain against the Nazis in Iraq, issued a glum warning that if 100,000 Jews were admitted into Palestine, Syria and Iraq would make treaties with Russia, threatening the spinal cord of the Empire.[73] Concern was also raised over a report by Britain's chiefs of staff that, should the 100,000 refugees be admitted, a general Arab uprising would result surpassing those of 1936 and 1938–39 and necessitating massive reinforcements.[74]

Despite the concurrence between Attlee and Churchill regarding partition, the British Government was resolved, for the time being, to retain, if possible, with American agreement a large part of its mandatory responsibility. U.S. Ambassador Henry F. Grady, along with his deputies, arrived in London on July 11, 1946. Over the next two weeks, they and the British team, led by Herbert Morrison, reached agreement on the idea of a federal Palestine with provincial autonomy. It would be divided into Zionist, Arab, and central government districts. The proposal was a variation of the 1944 partition plan. The 100,000 would be allowed to enter the Zionist area, but it would encompass only 1,500 square miles. The proposed state would remain, in the last resort, under British control. The United States agreed to grant $50 million to develop the Arab area.[75]

Unaware of these political developments, Begin went ahead with his preparations for the assault on the King David Hotel. Begin contended that, despite Weizmann's intervention and withdrawal of *Hagana* support, the operation was being conducted on behalf of the *Hagana's* desire to destroy documents taken from the Jewish Agency. Begin stated, "The British found documents which proved that the Jewish Agency knew about the operations of the Hagana. They found a report by Mr. Shertok, who was then chief of the Political Department, which proved that he knew about the destruction of the railways. They were frightened that the British would declare the Jewish Agency illegal."[76]

Typical of the sharp disparity existing between *Irgun* and *Hagana* accounts of the King David episode, Israel Galili, who was privy to the *Hagana's* role, contends that even though Black Saturday triggered the operation, the decision in principle to destroy the hotel had been taken weeks earlier for political reasons. He labels "nonsensical" that the explosion would destroy specific documents and "nonsensical" that such documents existed only in one copy.[77]

The operation took place, adding one more violent episode to the bloody saga of the Middle East. Begin biographer Eric Silver graphically depicted the King David Hotel tragedy in one compelling paragraph.

At 12:37 p.m. on Monday, 22 July 1946, six minutes ahead of schedule, 350 kilograms of TNT exploded in the empty Regence restaurant, blowing the central piles from under the southern wing of the King David Hotel. Fifty offices of the British civil and military administration collapsed in a roar of smoke and cement dust, masonry was hurled into the main road outside, killing and maiming passers-by. One British official was flung against the wall of the YMCA opposite the hotel, leaving a silhouette of blood and a severed head behind him. Rescue workers were still finding bodies a week later. The final casualty figures were announced on 31 July. Of the ninety-one dead, twenty-eight were British, forty-one Arabs, seventeen Jews, two Armenians, one Russian, one Greek and one Egyptian. There were forty-six wounded. More than half the dead were clerks, typists, messengers and other junior staff of the secretariat and the hotel. Menachem Begin was shocked by the casualties, but sprang to the defense of his men. Four decades later he still held the British responsible. They did not heed the warning given by telephone to the hotel switchboard. The Irgun's clandestine radio announced with typical Begin selectivity that it mourned the Jewish victims. It would not mourn the British dead, since Britain had not mourned the six million Jews who died in the Nazi Holocaust. "And with this mourning and with this anger over the deep Jewish tragedy, we shall continue going our way, the way of suffering, the way of struggle." The Irgun seemed not to have noticed that most of the dead were neither Jewish nor British, but Arab. In the words of Thurston Clarke, "For the Irgun, the Arabs were invisible."[78]

Begin contends that, "We did not want to hurt one living soul. The ethics of the Irgun demanded every possible precaution to prevent civilian casualties."[79] Begin took great pains to deal with this question for two reasons, one being the loss of life and injuries incurred in the explosion, the other relating to his steadfast contention that the *Irgun* was always careful to restrict attacks to British authorities, the mandatory power against which he was at war. He draws a distinction between the *Irgun* strategy of restricting attacks to British authorities and the Stern Gang's assaults against the British as well as civilians.

A warning was transmitted to the King David Hotel in advance by Adina Hai, a sixteen-year-old Jerusalem schoolgirl and *Irgun* courier, who telephoned the switchboard rather than the number of the secretariat. The *Irgun*'s Jerusalem commander, Yitzhak Avinoam, who gave young Adina Hai her orders, thought that an alarm had been installed at the switchboard that, at the touch of a button, would relay his message to the management and the British authorities. Unknown to the *Irgun*, the switchboard operators apparently did not have the authority to sound the alarm on their initiative. Hence the message was not received by the British in time to take action and avert tragedy.[80]

As recently as 1976, Begin was laying the blame for the tragedy on Chief Secretary Sir John Shaw, having allegedly been told by Israel Galili of the *Hagana* that, after receiving the warning, Shaw exclaimed, "I am here to give orders to the Jews, not to take orders from them." Galili cited as his source a now deceased American reporter. Shaw sued a small London Jewish newspaper for libel in 1948 when it published the story. The newspaper withdrew the allegation rather than defend the action in that it could locate no witnesses to corroborate the claim. Both Shaw and his secretary, Marjorie King, swore under oath that he had received no warning.[81]

The King David Hotel incident would remain a thorn in Begin's side throughout his long political career. Despite his emphatic assurance that warning had been provided to vacate the premises, as Begin biographer Eric Silver points out, such actions are fraught with danger of error, and neither the *Irgun* nor its commander Begin can be absolved of responsibility for what transpired. The King David tragedy had been cited as evidence of Menachem Begin's terrorist bent. In referring to Begin's omission to mention Arab casualties in the bombing, Silver's comment can be explored in the light of President Jimmy Carter's recent statement that he believed Begin thought of Palestinian Arabs as subhuman.

Much of the initial sympathy generated by the tragedy in favor of the British was dissipated when a letter the new British General Officer Commanding for Palestine General Sir Evelyn Barker issued to his troops reached the press and the Zionists. Though written in a state of great anger following the King David Hotel tragedy and later regretted by Barker, his harsh words were construed as a representation of British motives at their worst.

No British soldier is to have any social intercourse with any Jew and any intercourse in the way of duty should be as brief as possible and kept strictly to business at hand. I appreciate that these measures will inflict some hardship on the troops, but I am certain that if my reasons are fully explained to them they will understand their propriety and will be punishing the Jews in a way the race dislikes as much as any by striking at their pockets and showing our contempt for them.[82]

The King David affair revealed to the British the need of finding a way to extricate themselves from the quicksand of Palestine. The awakening was akin to American reaction following the Viet Cong's "Tet Offensive" of 1968 regarding the impasse of Vietnam. The King David incident had a major impact on Ben-Gurion and the *Hagana* as well. The principle of *havlaga*, or restraint, needed to be reestablished in the wake of the tragic deaths of innocent victims. Ben-Gurion saw a momentum toward the ultimate realization of a Jewish state and did not wish to see progress threatened by rash conduct. The *Hagana* withdrew from the coordinated Jewish Resistance Movement, with which it had engaged in joint actions with the *Irgun* and *Lehi* forces.

The sagacious moderate Weizmann had warned that the "hot ice" of violence could reap tragic consequences for Zionism. Ben-Gurion recognized the need for melting the "hot ice." Such an opportunity arose at a meeting of the Zionist Executive in Paris on August 2, 1946. The majority voted against any armed struggle until the next Zionist Congress. Ben-Gurion concurred, but as the quintessential pragmatist, he knew he needed the continuing support of the militant American Zionist Abba Hillel Silver, who had captured the leadership reins from the moderate Weizmann ally Stephen Wise. The bloc of delegate votes Silver could deliver at the upcoming World Zionist Organization Conference at Basel in December was crucial. At the same time, Ben-Gurion recognized the prudence of calming the troubled Zionist seas at a time when terrorism threatened future efforts. When the Zionist Executive voted to approve partition, the assiduous fighter for the Biltmore program abstained, thereby tacitly approving of the action while refraining from putting such an endorsement on record in deference to Silver and his supporters.[83]

When the World Zionist Congress convened in Basel that December, the decimation of European Jewry was reflected in the composition of the delegates. The familiar faces of the numerically dominant European nations had been replaced by fresh American faces, the backers of their militant leader, Abba Hillel Silver.

Chaim Weizmann recognized that the Congress's composition was not kindly disposed toward him. The strength of Silver's delegation augured well for Ben-Gurion and poorly for Weizmann. Weizmann recounted the experience ruefully.

> It was a dreadful experience to stand before that assembly and to run one's eye along row after row of delegates, finding among them hardly any of the friendly faces which had adorned past Congresses. Polish Jewry was missing; Central and Southeast European Jewry was missing; German Jewry was missing. The two main groups represented were the

Palestinians and the Americans; between them sat the representatives of the fragments of European Jewry, together with some small delegations from England, the Dominions, and South America.

The American group, led by Dr. Abba Hillel Silver, was from the outset the strongest, not so much because of enlarged numbers, or by virtue of the inherent strength of the delegates, but because of the weakness of the rest. The twenty-second Congress therefore had a special character, differing in at least one respect from previous Congresses: The absence—among very many delegates—of faith, or even hope, in the British Government, and a tendency to rely on methods never known or encouraged among Zionists before the war.[84]

The ailing veteran leader shed his mediator's mantle and launched fiery rhetoric more characteristic of his opponent Ben-Gurion, who was seeking to ease Zionism's elder statesman from his leadership position by making him "honorary president"[85] of the World Zionist Organization. Weizmann refused to accept the position, concentrating his firepower on the dangers of "resistance" and urging agreement by the Zionist congress to attend a London conference. He spoke glowingly of eleven new settlements in the Negev that had been established the evening after Yom Kippur in 1946, stating that they would ". . . have greater political significance than a hundred speeches about resistance, especially when the speeches are made in Washington and New York, while it is intended that the resistance shall take place in Jerusalem or Tel Aviv. We must stop being intoxicated by our own words."[86]

Weizmann's thundering words against "resistance" prompted Emanuel Neumann, a Silverite, to shout angrily, "This is demagoguery."

Weizmann paused, stunned by the rebuke, then lashed out with spontaneous fury: "Somebody has called me a demagogue. I do not know who. I hope I never learn the man's name. I—a demagogue! I who have borne all the ills and travails of this movement! The person who flung this word in my face should know that in every house and every stable in Nahalal, in every workshop in Tel Aviv or Haifa there is a drop of my blood."

The delegates rose to their feet in applause, following which Weizmann issued a stern warning: "You know that I am telling you the truth. Some people don't like to hear it—but you will hear me. I warn you against false prophets, against facile generalization, against distortion of historical facts."[87]

The half-blind Weizmann made his way from the hall following what supporter Baffy Dugdale called "the greatest speech of his life,"[88] but the delegates voted against him 171–154 on the question of attending the London Conference while reiterating the Jews' claim for all Western Palestine as their Jewish state. No president was selected to replace Weizmann, nor was he elected to the Jewish Agency Executive. Though it then appeared that Chaim Weizmann had been reduced to a figure of the past, within two years he would be called upon to engage in a diplomatic initiative in which the realization of the Zionist dream of a Jewish state in Palestine hung in the balance.

As 1947 dawned, Palestine raged with increasing violence. On January 31, the British Government evacuated from the strife-torn country all British women, children, and male civilians in nonessential jobs. British journalists, businessmen, and clergy were permitted to stay behind at their own risk. Following the evacuation of the British civilians, Palestine was gradually transformed into an armored camp. Jews were evicted from the residential quarters of Haifa, Jerusalem, and Tel Aviv without being provided alternative accommodation.

A new term was added to the lexicon of the bloody Palestine saga. "Bevingrads" referred to the blocks thus freed by the evictions, which were transformed into British Security Zones. "Bevingrads" were also known as "British ghettos" and consisted of small, fortified enclaves surrounded by barbed wire and sandbagged barricades. Despite such elaborate precautions, the tide of terrorism was not thwarted.[89]

All the while more refugees continued arriving on Palestine's shores. Referred to by Arthur Koestler as "little hell-ships," they would be spotted at sea by Royal Air Force patrols, then escorted to Haifa by units of the Royal Navy. The passengers were forcibly transferred to deportation ships by marines and airborne troops. Resistance would be overcome by tear gas, oil jets, and baton charges. Women would scream, babies would cry, and deaths would result from the trampling and commotion that ensued.

Eventually a decision was made by the British Government to deport "illegal immigrants" to Germany rather than Cyprus. Arthur Koestler cited the reasoning that Cyprus, being closer to Palestine, might provide encouragement to detainees to continue their efforts to reach Palestine. Another rationale is the belief of Attlee and Bevin that Jewish refugees should return to their former European nations and assist in rebuilding them rather than emigrate to Palestine.[90]

In July 1947, the Attlee-Bevin policy suffered a severe propaganda defeat in the case of the refugee ship bearing the symbolic name of *Exodus 1947*. Jammed with 4,500 European immigrants, it was towed into the port of Haifa. After a fierce struggle in which three Jews were killed, control had been wrested from the ship's *Hagana* defenders. The refugees were forcibly disembarked for transfer back to Europe. Barely twelve hours after their arrival, following their forty-six-day journey, the passengers were shipped back to West Germany. Eventually they were confined in internment camps near Lübeck. The journey was monitored carefully at each stage by the world's newsreels, press, and radio, and resulted in a great outpouring of sympathy for the Jews and scorn for the British leadership.[91]

The treatment accorded homeless Jewish refugees aboard ships, along with the reported beatings and misconduct suffered by Jews in refugee camps and following forced European repatriation, provoked additional impetus toward resolution of the Palestine question and accelerated pressures on the British Government to surrender its reins of authority.

Several months prior to the *Exodus* incident, Bevin had made a major move. On February 18, 1947, he revealed to the House of Commons his decision to submit the Palestine question to the United Nations. The move came on the heels of a ruling by legal advisers to the Foreign Office that, under the terms of the Palestine Mandate, the British Government had no authority to "award" the country to either the Jews or the Arabs, or to partition it.

Although the decision to surrender the Mandate was welcomed, the speech outlining it was badly received. Historians Jon and David Kimche referred to Bevin's oration as "one of his more insensitive performances."[92] The outspoken foreign secretary denounced Truman's interventions as unhelpful meddling, a reference to the president's urging that 100,000 Displaced Persons be allowed to emigrate to Palestine. Bevin also cautioned against excessive haste in reaching a decision, telling Parliament, "After 2,000 years of conflict, another twelve months will not be considered a long delay."[93] Truman later described it as noteworthy for "the callousness" of "its disregard for human misery," which, not surprisingly, paralleled the general Jewish reaction.[94]

While the British Cabinet had been happy to clutch at the legal straws afforded by the Foreign Office ruling, Bevin was angry and frustrated by the decision to submit the Palestine question directly to the United Nations. Influenced by the many veteran Arab hands in the Foreign Office, Bevin believed that Britain could not afford to withdraw from the Middle East. In addition to his earlier-mentioned concern about the area's falling under Soviet influence or, worse yet, dominion,

Bevin was also influenced by pocketbook considerations. He felt that "the wage-packets of the workers," to use his terminology, were too deeply involved in the area to lightly abandon it.[95] A distinction must accordingly be drawn between Bevin and Attlee on the question of referring the Palestine question to the United Nations. In Bevin's case, he saw the move as a means of gaining a needed breathing spell for Britain at a time when the controversy was at a boiling point and when international criticism of his handling of the Palestine issue abounded. Given Britain's years of experience in the Middle East, climaxed by a Mandate authority extending beyond a generation, Bevin believed that British expertise would be required to resolve the bitter impasse that existed.

Prime Minister Attlee, in sharp contrast to Bevin, was more disposed toward viewing Palestine along the lines of India, Greece, and other nations from which Britain had been forced to withdraw give its precarious economic posture. The nation that had filled the power vacuum relinquished by Britain with respect to other areas of influence, the United States, was seen by Attlee as the logical party to help resolve the Palestine dilemma. While recognizing the importance of Middle East oil resources, Attlee believed that they could no longer be ensured by military power. The area's political stability had to be achieved, and an agreement with the U.S. was deemed vital.

While Attlee and Bevin were encouraged by sympathetic expressions of U.S. State Department experts, their opinions were not influenced by the most vital consideration confronting President Truman—that of domestic political pressures.

Shortly after the King David Hotel tragedy, the partition proposal recommended by the American contingent led by Ambassador Grady and the British counterparts was slated to be debated in the House of Commons. Though the established date for discussion was July 31, the outline of the plan, modeled along the Swiss canton system, became known beforehand. It was rejected by Weizmann as worse than Lord Peel's 1937 plan, while Abba Hillel Silver denounced it as "a conscienceless act of treachery." By July 30, one day before the scheduled Parliament debate, it was attacked in the U.S. Senate as a betrayal of the Jewish homeland, an attempt to strangle the Yishuv by confining its residents inside an economically nonviable ghetto.

On the same day that the partition formula was denounced in the U.S. Senate, Truman decided to reject it, despite the fact that it had been proposed by his own nominees. State Department official Loy Henderson explained to the British Ambassador to the United States

Lord Inverchapel that even though there was nothing in the plan that would have been unacceptable to the United States, it had been abandoned by Truman for domestic political considerations. Two prominent Jewish-American figures were once more locked in bitter opposition, with each refusing to permit the other the opportunity for advantage.[97]

Stephen Wise and Abba Hillel Silver, in addition to seeing the Zionist picture from different perspectives, represented varying viewpoints in American politics. Wise represented the liberal tradition of the Democratic Party of New York City. The Manhattan rabbi held strong ties with both Franklin D. Roosevelt and Harry S Truman. Silver, on the other hand, headed a synagogue in an affluent section of Cleveland, with roots in the conservative Republican Party tradition that exemplifies a significant part of politics in what is termed America's Midwest heartland. The Cleveland rabbi was a close friend of the prominent conservative Senator Robert Taft, who was known as "Mr. Republican." Silver also had close ties to Thomas E. Dewey, the Republican Governor of New York, who challenged Wise's candidate, Truman, for the presidency in 1948. Understandably, these two giants of the American and world Zionist movements loomed like two figures standing face to face, daring the other to blink. Each strove mightily to convince Jewish voters that his side best represented their interests.

In addition to vying for Jewish votes in New York, where more Jewish Americans lived than in any other city and the largest city of the nation's most populous state, New York, there were also significant numbers of Jews living in such pivotal presidential electoral vote states as Ohio, Pennsylvania, Illinois, and California. Another important factor not lost on either Wise or Silver was the significant roles prominent Jews played in American politics, with an influence that exceeded their actual numbers. American Jews tended to be politically active. The most affluent of their number could be counted on to support their party and candidate preferences with substantial contributions. They often also participated openly in the process, along with less affluent Jews, assisting in the nuts-and-bolts of democracy through making speeches, serving on committees, or knocking on doors to urge large voter turnouts on behalf of preferred candidates.

American Jews tended to be liberal in persuasion and to vote Democratic. Silver certainly knew this. His most realistic strategy, therefore, going into the 1948 presidential election, was to entice enough traditional Jewish Democratic voters into the Republican camp to swing the balance toward his party in key states. The closer the election, the greater the importance of the swing voters he hoped to entice away from the Democrats. Wise's strategy was the reverse of Silver's, that of influencing traditional Jewish Democratic Party voters to stay the course.

Henderson's explanation to Inverchapel was that Truman could not afford to support the Grady-Morrison initiative, because the two main American Zionist leaders, Silver and Wise, belonged to the Republican and Democratic parties, respectively, and that neither could afford to approve the plan and give advantage to the other party in the November 1946 congressional elections.[98]

In that other Jews, notably Weizmann, opposed the Grady-Morrison plan for not going far enough, while Arabs denounced it for going too far, it would most likely have been defeated within the political climate of 1946. All the same, the domestic political issue was one that would be hotly debated on both sides of the Atlantic regarding Grady-Morrison as well as a broad range of strategy questions relating to Palestine.

On the eve of October 4, 1946, which was Yom Kippur (the Jewish Day of Atonement), one month before the congressional elections, President Truman once more publicly advocated that 100,000 Jews should be admitted into Palestine immediately. He offered to pay the expense of transporting them to that country and aid them to make the new land productive.[99]

The Truman statement, coming at a time when British authorities were seeking in separate Paris and London conferences with Arab and Zionist leaders to achieve a mutually acceptable agreement, provoked a firestorm on the other side of the Atlantic. Later, Bevin would contend, in the House of Commons on February 25, 1947, that he might have succeeded in getting the Arabs and Zionists to confer with each other had Truman not issued his Yom Kippur statement. He also alleged that, in response to his exhortations to Secretary of State James Byrnes to dissuade the president from his position, Byrnes told him that if Truman did not speak out in this manner, his rival Dewey would.[100]

Dean Acheson, who helped prepare the Yom Kippur statement, saw it in the following context.

> We joined forces again at Yom Kippur in a move which, as one looks back, seems to have been of doubtful wisdom. At the time I did not think so, and agreeing with the President that the situation called for restatement of his views, helped him prepare them. The statement was attacked

then and has been since as a blatant ploy for the Jewish vote in Illinois, Ohio, Pennsylvania, and New York in the congressional elections only a month away and an attempt to anticipate an expected similar play by Governor Dewey. Plainly it could be so interpreted, but I do not believe that it had any such purpose.[101]

Herbert Feis, a former State Department colleague of Acheson's during the Roosevelt years and Pulitzer Prize–winning historian, places the Yom Kippur statement in a different framework, citing that "It was the autumn of 1946, and the American election campaign for Congress was under way. The Democrats and their opponents rivaled each other in their advocacy of admission of Jews into Palestine. . ."[102]

The charges and responses would continue throughout the anguished search by American and British authorities for a solution to the Palestine question, and persist to this day through biographies of participants and additional viewpoints of historians. Each allegation from Britain of domestic political motivation to curry favor with Jewish voters would be met by heated American denials.

An intense debate occurred in the House of Commons on January 26, 1949, in which opposition leader Winston Churchill, after praising Bevin's policies as Foreign Secretary in helping thwart Soviet expansionism, sharply attacked his Palestine posture, alleging that he could have made an agreement with the Americans had he sought one. During the lengthy debate, Bevin made the following observation relative to Truman and the American position.

His Majesty's Government were at this stage faced with a problem which had never faced Governments before the war. The United States had long been interested in Palestine, but it was not until 1945 that American interests in Palestine and pledges made in America became one of the determining factors. I have to be very careful what I say here, or I shall be accused of disturbing relations with America; but in defence of His Majesty's Government I ask the House to realize that at this point the whole question of who should be elected to certain offices in the United States turned on this problem, and the United Kingdom had very little latitude after that time. We had to consider the matter on an entirely different footing . . .[103]

Relations between President Truman and Prime Minister Attlee had never been cordial. Frostiness existed between the American president and Bevin as well. From Potsdam, in a letter to his daughter, Margaret, Truman contrasted his feelings about Churchill with those of Attlee and Bevin: ". . . he [Churchill] is a likeable person, and these two [Attlee and Bevin] are sourpusses."[104] Had the dividing issue of Palestine, about which Truman as well as Attlee and Bevin held strong and often conflicting views, not been present, relations between the men may well have been much warmer despite Truman's initial impression. Truman's Secretary of State in his second administration, Dean Acheson, got along well with Bevin. Though disparate personalities could explain the coolness of Truman toward both Attlee and Bevin, it should be noted that Acheson dealt with Bevin and Attlee on a largely European agenda in which a consensus existed.

If Truman looked upon Attlee as a "sourpuss," the British Prime Minister saw the American president and his Palestine policy as "irresponsible." Attlee did not agree with his military advisers that full control of Palestine was essential to vital British interests, nor did he share Bevin's fears concerning the dangers of Soviet dominance of the Middle East. Attlee believed that the only questions that needed settling were those of the method and timing of a British withdrawal. He saw in Palestine the existence of a problem that did not exist with India, from which Britain was withdrawing. Attlee saw a vacuum in Palestine, what he termed "the conflict of two imperialisms, Jewish and Arab."[105] He did not see the two imperialisms as existing at equal strength. Should the Arabs feel provoked, as in the case of 100,000 refugees suddenly arriving in Palestine, Attlee feared that a massacre might result. He believed that premature British withdrawal without a negotiated settlement or American involvement also threatened to precipitate disaster.

Attlee biographer Trevor Burridge summarized the British prime minister's view of Truman vis-à-vis Palestine with these grim words:

> Both Attlee and Bevin had hoped that the US could be persuaded to step in, and both came to feel . . . that the US "had been thoroughly dishonest." The Jews had indeed suffered terribly, and this had thrown up a number of problems which President Truman and others had exploited for their own purposes. Attlee's feelings went deeper: to him, the Americans had committed the cardinal political sin—they had run away from responsibility.[106]

Domestic political considerations were as unavoidable for Harry Truman respecting Palestine politics in the postwar world as they had been for British authorities when the Balfour Declaration was considered. In the context of World War One, British policy considerations had been more international, while Truman, as president of a nation with a key Jewish voting bloc, was influenced to a greater degree by domestic factors than the British had been when the Balfour Declaration was adopted. The American chief executive was also influenced by the broader national and international pictures, however, and remained sympathetic to the suffering Jews had experienced during the Holocaust and the consequent tragedies encountered in the Displaced Persons camps.

On April 20, 1945, eight days following his predecessor Roosevelt's death and his assumption of office, Truman met at the White House with Stephen Wise, chairman of the American Zionist Emergency Council, who discussed with the new president the persecution of Jews at the hands of the Nazis and the problems of resettlement for Holocaust survivors.

Truman recounted in his memoirs the State Department communication that had been provided for him two days earlier relative to Palestine. The communication warned the new president that Zionist leaders would be likely to seek a commitment at an early date ". . . in favor of the Zionist program which is pressing for unlimited Jewish immigration into Palestine and the establishment there of a Jewish state. As you are aware, the Government and people of the United States have every sympathy for the persecuted Jews of Europe . . . The question of Palestine is, however, a highly complex one and involves questions which go far beyond the plight of the Jews in Europe." The communication concluded with cautionary phraseology: "There is continual tenseness in the situation in the Near East largely as a result of the Palestine question, and as we have interests in that area which are vital to the United States, we feel this this whole subject is one that should be handled with the greatest care and with a view to the long-range interests of the country."[107]

Truman then expressed his own beliefs.

Since I was in agreement with the expressed policy of the Roosevelt administration on Palestine, I told Rabbi Wise that I would do everything possible to carry out that policy. I had carefully read the Balfour Declaration, in which Great Britain was committed to a homeland in Palestine for the Jews. I had familiarized myself with the history of the question of a Jewish homeland and the position of the British and the Arabs. I was skeptical, as I read over the whole record up to date, about some of the views and attitudes assumed by the "striped-pants boys" in the State Department. It seemed to me that they didn't care enough about what happened to the thousands of displaced persons who were involved. It was my feeling that it would be possible for us to watch out for the long-range interests of our country while at the same time helping these unfortunate victims of persecution to find a home. And before Rabbi Wise left, I believe I made this clear to him.[108]

The Truman position, enunciated little more than a week into his presidency, demonstrates a heartfelt concern for the Displaced Persons and a desire to assist them. While the Yom Kippur statement would be delivered the following year in the charged political atmosphere of a congressional election, the policy expressed coincides with Truman's stated posture when he assumed office, along with statements advocating the receipt of 100,000 Displaced Persons into Palestine following the mission of special envoy Earl Harrison and the recommendation of the joint British-American Committee of Inquiry, which in each case advocated the acceptance of that same 100,000 immigration figure. Truman's sympathy for the Displaced Persons would continue, but other issues, highlighted by the question of the creation of a Jewish state, resulted in a crisscross of factors embodying international and domestic political considerations and, ultimately, reconciling disparate viewpoints within his own administration.

Foreign policy analyst Herbert Feis was almost assuredly accurate in his assessment of Ernest Bevin's expectations upon handing the Palestine problem over to the United Nations. Feis believed that Bevin hoped Britain would retain the Mandate, focusing on the fact that the British Foreign Secretary had asked the UN to decide how its Mandate "can be administered . . . or amended."[109] While Bevin and his Foreign Office colleagues, in contrast with Prime Minister Attlee, relished the prospect of the Mandate's being sent back across the Atlantic, Harry Truman had other ideas, in sharp contrast with those of Bevin, about the role of the United Nations in resolving the Palestine question.

As a Democratic president, Harry S Truman had particularly strong feelings about the fledgling United Nations. Created in San Francisco immediately after the war, it made its temporary headquarters during that period in buildings left over from the 1939 World's Fair at Flushing Meadows on Long Island. It was significant that Truman appointed Eleanor Roosevelt as a special-committee delegate to serve under the head of the delegation, former Republican Senator Warren H. Austin of Vermont. Mrs. Roosevelt's deceased husband, who was also Truman's predecessor, had been a major figure in the League of Nations debate as running mate to James Cox, the Democratic nominee for president against the triumphant Warren G. Harding, who had campaigned on an anti-League platform manifested by the slogan "Return to Normalcy." Earlier, Franklin D. Roosevelt had served as Undersecretary of the Navy under President Woodrow Wilson, who had unsuccessfully championed the cause of American participation in the League.

A turbulent generation had passed in which two world wars had been fought. Harry Truman, as a staunch Democrat and successor to a president who had been immersed in the League of Nations fight, was determined to see that the fledgling United Nations succeed where its predecessor organization, denied important U.S. participation, had failed. Rather than using the organization as a pretext for giving Britain a breathing respite and fresh input before asking it to resume its Mandate, Truman saw the organization being handed a solid test to prove its mettle. In Truman's view, the UN had been created to handle delicate international problems, which its machinery could resolve short of war. It is significant to note that, at a time when the special committee appointed to tackle the Palestine problem had made its recommendation, the internationalist Eleanor Roosevelt had told Truman to "help the U.N. by supporting the majority report."[110] While Mrs. Roosevelt was and would remain a supporter of a Jewish state, she used the argument of United Nations unity on Truman at a time when the new organization was being sternly tested.

Responding to Bevin's request, the Unted Nations prepared for a special session of the General Assembly to provide recommendations on the Palestine question, which would be considered by the General Assembly in its September 1947 session. The special session commenced on April 28. On May 16, the United States proposed to the special session the appointment of a committee to study the problem, which consisted of neutral nations. They were Australia, Canada, Czechoslovakia, Guatemala, India, Iran, the Netherlands, Peru, Sweden, Uruguay, and Yugoslavia. The committee was empowered to seek testimony on a broad scale, from which recommendations for Palestine would be based. The General Assembly issued an appeal to all factions in Palestine to refrain from hostilities while the study was conducted.[111]

Despite pleas for peace, violence escalated during July in a Palestine in which passions exploded on all sides. Jews battled Arabs, Jewish terrorists fought the British, and British troops tried to preserve order while defending themselves. One thorny incident that prompted concern on all sides was the hanging of two British sergeants by Jewish terrorists, which was condemned by Weizmann and Ben-Gurion. When the British reacted by killing five Jews and arresting Jewish leaders in

Palestine, the moderate Zionists abandoned their anti-terrorist posture. A perfect illustration of the "eye for an eye" syndrome was exemplified by *Irgun* chief of staff Haim Landau concerning the hangings of the British soldiers: "We had nothing against them personally. We just wanted to stop the hangings."[12] This same vicious cycle exists today in the Middle East. It is particularly noticeable in Israel's occupied territories, where Israeli authorities and the Palestine Liberation Organization justify attacks of various types as retaliatory, registering the belief that responses in kind will terminate the basic causes of physical aggression. The "eye for an eye" syndrome, as exemplified by Middle East history, was by no means new during those turbulent days following World War Two, when British authorities occupied the position of enforcement now held by Israelis and Jews rather than Palestinians and fought against what they considered unjust circumstances.

During that same period when UNSCOP (United Nations Special Committee on Palestine) was studying the Palestine question, Bevin sought cooperation from American Secretary of State George Marshall to bar the support and cooperation by Americans of illegal departures of Palestine-bound immigrants, particularly from European ports, a phenomenon discussed earlier. Bevin asked that a close watch be maintained on certain charitable organizations. He observed that many funds encouraging illegal immigration had come from donors in the United States.[113]

An unexpected turn in UNSCOP deliberations occurred when Jorge García-Granados, Guatemala's ambassador in Washington, representing the smallest nation on the committee, assumed a leading role both in committee discussions and in the General Assembly's ultimate receipt of the committee's report. During UNSCOP's visit to Palestine, García-Granados assiduously advanced a militantly anti-British posture, maintaining that UN authority must not be hindered by the British administration. He emphatically opposed British restrictive regulations. In UNSCOP discussions, he was generally supported by committee members Enrique Rodríguez Fabregat of Uruguay and José Brilej of Yugoslavia.[114]

García-Granados expressed movingly his urgent desires for freedom in Guatemala, detailing in his book *The Birth of Israel* his arrests in 1920 and 1922 for political activities. He manifested the profound impression President Wilson and his Fourteen Points had made upon him as a teenager.[115] As a freedom fighter from a small nation, García-Granados had a built-in sensitivity to anything he perceived as a large power attempting to enforce its authority by what he deemed un-democratic means on a smaller group. This was how he envisioned the Palestine picture.

Herbert Feis reveals the following:

> García-Granados was harshly critical of Britain's emergency regulations in Palestine, which enabled the High Commissioner to suspend basic personal rights and liberties at his discretion. Consequently he was rather sympathetic with the underground Irgun movement, whose terrorist activity he considered as political and not criminal in nature. Having failed to induce UNSCOP to hear the testimony of underground leaders, he went (accompanied by Fabregat) to meet them personally. The UNSCOP chairman himself had already seen the Irgun leaders, but kept it secret from his colleagues.[116]

The Guatemalan also figured in a debate over whether UNSCOP representatives should visit Displaced Persons Camps in Germany. Moslem committee members representing India and Iran opposed such a visit on the implied ground that it had nothing to do with the Palestine question. García-Granados argued emphatically on behalf of the visit. When it was ultimately decided to send alternates to the camps, García-Granados visited them personally, as did Fabregat of Uruguay and the Australian delegate.[117]

A final diplomatic thorn pierced Britain's side in the form of the international reaction to the *Exodus* incident. Not only did it alienate friends in the United States, France, and elsewhere concerning British policies, but also it provided the Soviet Union with an opportunity to pose as a befriender of Jews. The timing could hardly have been worse from Britain's viewpoint, either, considering that the *Exodus* incident occurred when UNSCOP's deliberations were taking place.

UNSCOP made its report to the General Assembly in September. All members agreed that the mandate should be terminated and that, under UN auspices, some form of independence be granted to Palestine. A majority report, recommended by Canada, Czechoslovakia, Guatemala, the Netherlands, Peru, Sweden, and Uruguay, proposed the partition of Palestine into a Jewish and an Arab state. Independence would take effect following a two-year transitional period beginning September 1, 1947. The British government would administer the interim government under UN supervision, while 150,000 Jews would be admitted. The minority plan, favored by India, Iran, and Yugoslavia, called for a federal state that would become independent in no less than three years. Until that point it would be under an authority designed by the UN. Australia abstained.[118]

On September 12, an ad hoc committee consisting of one representative from each country in the General Assembly was recommended by UN Secretary General Trygve Lie to consider the proposal of UNSCOP. That committee convened on September 25. Committee Chairman Herbert Evatt of Australia requested the Arab Higher Committee and the Jewish Agency to send representatives to its meetings.[119]

The General Assembly session beginning in September 1947 signified the second year of the fledgling international body and the first in which Truman's new Secretary of State George Marshall would participate. He soon found himself sitting in the middle of a potential powder keg in an arbiter's position as the conflicting viewpoints bombarded him from his own U.S. representatives.

As mentioned earlier, Eleanor Roosevelt ardently supported the creation of the Jewish state, emphasizing that the UN position should be sustained. Her opinion differed from that of Loy Henderson, expert in the State Department's Office of Near Eastern and African Affairs. Henderson registered a fear also held by Ernest Bevin: that of the specter of Soviet influence pervading Palestine. Henderson expressed the belief that partition could be imposed on the Arabs only by force and that they would rally to the Soviet Union if it promised support. Another member of the delegation, General Hilldring, replied that the Russians had already made a stand in favor of a federalized Palestine and that the U.S. should support the partition plan and be willing to amend it.[120]

Ambassador Warren Austin reflected pessimism regarding the feasibility of partition. He doubted that a small state could be carved out of such a small area. Such a state "would have to defend itself with bayonets forever, until extinguished in blood. The Arabs would never be willing to have such a small state so near to their heart." Austin agreed with Marshall that if the United States supported UNSCOP's majority report, it must be prepared for the possibility of using force to support that posture.

On September 17, Marshall made a statement to the General Assembly, which his biographer Forrest C. Pogue evaluates accordingly.

Marshall's final pronouncement (on UNSCOP's majority report) partly met the desire to favor the majority plan but without unequivocally endorsing it. In attempting to give voice to both groups in the U.S. delegation, Marshall avoided finality. He praised the U.N. Special Committee on Palestine for the great progress it had made in reaching a unanimous decision on eleven of the recommendations relating to Palestine. He recognized that neither party to the controversy would be satisfied with the final recommendations for partition. As for the United States, it gave great weight "not only to the recommendations which have met with the unanimous approval of the Special Committee, but also to those which have been approved by the majority of the Committee."[121]

Despite Marshall's attempt to straddle the fence on partition, supporting the basic concept yet falling short of definitive acceptance, Arab reactions were nonetheless swift and decisively negative. Representatives of Iraq, Syria, Lebanon, Egypt, and Saudi Arabia declared that the Secretary of State had committed the U.S. to the majority report. Prince Feisal, tersely summarizing the Arab position, asserted that "the United States had embarked on a dangerous course for the United States and the Arab world."[122] No more than a week after Feisal's grim warning, the Arab Higher Committee called for a general strike in Palestine as a protest against the majority report. The Arabs demanded immediate termination of the Mandate, the establishment of an Arab democratic state, and withdrawal of the British.

The same day that the Arab Higher Committee was calling for a strike, the new U.S. Ambassador to Iraq George Wadsworth was informed by representatives of two Arab states that they had been approached by the Soviets with the suggestion that the Russians would support the Arab position on Palestine if the Arabs backed membership of the Ukraine on the Security Council. A Polish delegate had also mentioned the proposal.

Although the Arabs had not responded to the prospective Soviet-Arab deal said to be in the works, the United States once more was confronted by the Soviet influence factor, which cast a giant shadow over Marshall and his entire State Department. The Soviet-Arab speculation came at a time when Marshall was informing the U.S. delegation that, while the United States supported the majority plan in principle, it would want to amend the proposal regarding boundaries and economic plans. If two-thirds of the General Assembly supported the majority plan, the U.S. would be willing to aid in its enforcement but not provide military units. Marshall added that the United States should make no effort to persuade members to adopt the majority plan while indicating he was considering legislation providing for increased immigration of Displaced Persons.[123]

A bombshell was dropped on October 13 when the Russians, to the astonishment of most of the General Assembly, announced their support of partition. Naturally this had the impact of fueling more apprehensive speculation on the part of the cautious Near East Division of the State Department about the motivations of the Soviets as well as possible long-term implications arising from their action. At a time when the U.S. and Britain sought to check expansionist initiatives by the rapacious Stalin, who was also reneging on promises made to the Allies at Yalta, such concerns were understandable.

As the General Assembly vote on UNSCOP's recommendations loomed closer, Secretary Marshall was confronted by conflicting directions being pursued by the U.S. delegation to the UN and the Near East Division of the State Department. Working-level members of both groups attempted to achieve some measure of harmony in October and early November. Henderson and his staff charged that some pro-Jewish members of the delegations were emphatically urging partition and ignoring strong British disagreement. It was further contended that the pro-Jewish delegates were urging quick decisions that could only be effectuated if the United States took on most of the responsibility for enforcing a settlement.[124]

While tension and disagreement was accelerating within U.S. State Department circles, the British in late October registered strenuous disapproval over illegal immigration into Palestine from the Black Sea area. The British particularly protested against private American groups' running loads of immigrants southward by using U.S. military vehicles still marked with U.S. Army signs and by dressing operators in U.S. Army uniforms.[125]

One point being sharply debated before the General Assembly vote concerned the disposition of the Negev. The Jewish Agency insisted that this area must be Jewish, but the Near East Division of the State Department believed the area should go to the Arabs because it was overwhelmingly Arab in population and had been so historically. Secretary Marshall on November 12 said the decision to include the Negev in the proposed Arab state had been made by the State Department "by full delegation under the chairmanship of the Secretary."[126]

In order to comprehend the forces at work shaping policy, it is essential to go back and review the entire Palestine picture from the end of World War Two, examining it from the perspectives of the individuals involved. In the forefront of the picture was President Truman, whose sympathy for the Displaced Persons has been discussed. Also mentioned was his first meeting with a Jewish representative after assuming office—the April 20, 1945, White House visit from Stephen Wise, in which Truman reiterated his concern for the Displaced Persons. He asserted himself on this point several times, to the consternation of Attlee and Bevin, affirming his conviction that 100,000 Jewish immigrants should be immediately accepted into Palestine.

While his sympathy for Hitler's Holocaust victims remained consistent, Harry Truman, referred to by Chaim Weizmann as "the most powerful man in the world," reflected the traumatic volatility of this ever-ticking time bomb known as Palestine, a Mount Vesuvius of international affairs with periodic eruptions. He sought the counsel of those in his government seeking a judicious resolution to a problem immersed in conflict. Truman's problem realm fell into three basic categories.

1. Addressing conflicting viewpoints within the ranks of his advisers, notably those who favored the prompt creation of a Jewish state contrasted with the voices of restraint led by Loy Henderson and the Near East Division of the State Department.

2. Weighing viewpoints of those outside his administration, from the British to the Arabs, as well as Zionists lobbying within America for the creation of a Jewish state.

3. Evaluating the human argument of Jewish immigration needs predicated on the tragedies befalling the Displaced Persons, with whose plight he sympathized.

Each area of concern brought with it contrasting arguments and pressures, such as those raised by Truman's advisers concerning partition, the international impact of the creation of a Jewish state in terms of U.S. relations with Arab countries, and the emotional issues of Displaced Persons and the counterargument by Arabs that they should not become innocent victims because of the misconduct of Nazi Germany.

In addition to the foregoing considerations, there was that of inevitable domestic political considerations. The Yom Kippur statement was delivered in an atmosphere in which a new president, who had succeeded the only chief executive in U.S. history to win four successive elections, battled an onrushing Republican tide that threatened to overwhelm Democratic candidates in the 1946 congressional elections. In addition, his strongest Republican rival for the 1948 presidential election, New York Governor Thomas E. Dewey, was seeking reelection with the determination of running up a large winning majority, which would generate momentum for his presumed upcoming bid.

Dewey was determined to turn up the political heat on Truman. One issue he could utilize was the fate of world Jewry, for which he sought broad support by New York City's Jewish voters. Truman issued his Yom Kippur statement on October 4. At a Jewish dinner in New York two days later, Dewey said, "It must be an immigration of not one hundred thousand but of several hundreds of thousands."[127]

While Dewey was doing his utmost to surpass Truman in political oneupmanship, the president had through his Yom Kippur statement embraced the Jewish Agency's resolution adopted in Paris in August expressing willingness to negotiate on the basis of a viable Jewish state in an adequate area of Palestine, meaning partition, rather than of the whole of Mandatory Palestine. By concurring that the U.S. Government "could give its support" to partition, he had delivered the most pro-Zionist statement ever offered by an American chief executive.[128]

Despite such an emphatic declaration of support, Truman recognized the political mine field in which he walked, referring to the Palestine situation in October 22 correspondence, little more than two weeks after the Yom Kippur statement, as "insoluble," and adding that besides problems posed by the British, ". . . the Jews themselves are making it almost impossible to do anything for them." He concluded his correspondence with an expression of resolve: "I am going to spend the rest of my time here at this place working for the best interest of the whole country and let the chips fall where they may."[129]

Two individuals, one within Truman's administration, the other a long-standing friend and former business partner, diligently labored to keep Harry Truman's mind focused on furthering the Zionist cause. The Zionist case was fervently pled within the White House by David K. Niles; the friend and partner from his Kansas City harberdashery days was Edward Jacobson.

Niles, born Neyhus, was the son of Russian Jewish immigrants who grew up in a poor section of North Boston. He had been appointed an administrative assistant to Franklin D. Roosevelt specializing in minority problems. Truman, who liked Niles very much, retained him in the same capacity. Given his Eastern European Jewish heritage and position, it was only natural that Niles would become involved in Truman's dealings with American Jews over Palestine. An old-line progressive with links to Robert LaFollette and Al Smith and a crusader in his native Boston to save Sacco and Vanzetti from execution, Niles maintained close ties with leading members of the executive of the Jewish Agency. His sensitivities on the subject of Zionism were reportedly so pronounced that he would break into tears on the subject of Palestine.[130]

Jacobson also had Russian roots. He was born on the East Side of Manhattan of immigrant parents from Russian Lithuania and had been raised in the Orthodox Jewish tradition. At the turn of the century, the Jacobsons moved first to Leavenworth, Kansas, then to Kansas City, where young Eddie, then a stock boy for a dry goods firm, met a youthful bank clerk named Harry Truman. Their relationship developed when they served together in World War One, with Jacobson serving as assistant to regimental canteen officer Truman. After the war, their partnership continued as they established a haberdashery business, which ultimately failed in the recession of 1921. Truman left the business world for a career in politics that took him to the highest office in the land, while his old friend drifted back into the haberdashery business, ultimately prospering with his own store in Kansas City. The two men remained in touch, with Jacobson becoming a frequent visitor to the White House. Jacobson brought Jewish leaders with him to meet Truman. Eventually the Kansas City haberdasher would visit his former business partner at the White House in the position of quasi-ambassador to the new state of Israel.[131]

While Niles and Jacobson were respected confidants of Truman, Abba Hillel Silver emerged at the bête noire of the American Zionist movement where the president was concerned. On the one occasion that Truman received the Cleveland rabbi at the White House, the head of American Zionism reportedly stirred Truman to pound on his desk.[132]

Whereas Silver's longtime adversary Stephen Wise had been a prominent Democratic supporter of both Roosevelt and Truman, Silver had close ties with Ohio's Senator Robert Taft, his party's minority leader. Truman saw the hand of Silver in three instances when Democrats were sought to be outmaneuvered in the area of Zionist support. The militant rabbi was credited with influencing Taft in favor of unrestricted Jewish immigration as a prelude to a Jewish homeland. Silver had also worked with Taft to secure a pro-Zionist plank in the 1944 Republican Party Platform. The point that brought an angry response from Truman was the strong attack by Robert Taft in the Senate of the Morrison-Grady Plan, which carried over to a large body of both houses of Congress. Truman despised the Cleveland rabbi so much that one year later, he wrote to Niles: "We could have settled this Palestine thing if U.S. politics had been kept out of it. Terror and Silver are the contributing causes of *some*, if not all, of our troubles."[133]

Zionist pressures began to sorely rankle Truman. His anger and

frustration were vented at Jews in general rather than Silver in particular at an emotionally charged cabinet meeting on July 30, 1946. Henry
Wallace warned the president that the Morrison-Grady Plan was
"loaded with political dynamite," which set the notable Truman temper in motion. He replied that he was "put out" with the Jews.
According to Wallace he then snapped, "Jesus Christ couldn't please
them when he was here on earth, so how could anyone expect that I
would have any luck?" Wallace recounted further that "Truman said
he had no use for them and didn't care what happened to them."

Wallace pointed out to Truman that it was easy for Jews to reach an
agitated state of mind in an environment in which so many of their
numbers had perished in the Holocaust, while James Forrestal worried
aloud that if another war occurred, the United States would need oil
from Saudi Arabia. Truman replied to Forrestal that he wished to
handle the problem not in the light of oil but of justice.[134]

The inflammatory words of Truman expressed to his own cabinet far
surpass anything attributed to Ernest Bevin concerning disrespect
toward Jews. In another context uttered by some other speaker they
would reflect virulent anti-Semitism, but Harry Truman was a man
who gave vent to his spleen by hurling angry invective. Fortunately
the remarks were not made in a public forum. The angry words reflect
a growing frustration within Truman regarding a tense issue shrouded
in controversy that was looming closer to a resolution. Whatever that
resolution may be, it seemed destined to trigger dissatisfaction on one
side or another, if not both.

Despite the successes of Abba Hillel Silver and David Ben-Gurion
at the World Zionist Congress in 1946, the man who had been rudely
rebuked and displaced from leadership, Chaim Weizmann, returned to
the position of Zionism's top diplomat. For years he had been the
inside man in negotiations with the British. Now that the power
pendulum had swung to the United States he would work with that
government. His health continually breaking, his blindness worsening,
Weizmann remained a man with a mission. Now that he could see his
objective nearing realization the veteran Zionist spokesman summoned
up every bit of energy left in him for one last major effort. He had seen
Truman in 1945, just after the president had assumed office through
succession and before Weizmann incurred the humiliation of the 1946
World Zionist Congress. Now his diplomatic expertise was needed on
a matter of great importance to the Jewish cause in Palestine.

The urgent issue was the Negev. David Niles and Lord Inverchapel,
the British Ambassador to Washington, set up a secret meeting for

Weizmann with Truman on November 19, 1947. Unknown to the U.S. UN delegation or the State Department, Weizmann was seeing Truman to plead the case for a boundary change in the partition proposal being favored by the United States.

It is understandable that Weizmann would be considered a desirable spokesman by Truman adviser and Zionist supporter David Niles. America's most powerful Zionist leader and Ben-Gurion ally Abba Hillel Silver was anathema and unwelcome in the Truman White House. Weizmann, an ally of prominent Democratic supporter Stephen Wise, had a lifetime of impressive Zionist credentials—his promotion of the Balfour Declaration, his successful advocacy at the Paris Peace Conference of a British Mandate for Palestine, and his prominent role in the founding of the Hebrew University on Mount Scopus. The meeting was recounted by Truman biographer Robert J. Donovan.

> The president gave him [Weizmann] a friendly reception. Weizmann was a chemist and lost no time spreading before Truman a vision of what the Jews would do to make the desert bloom with desalted brackish water. In his eloquence he said almost exactly the opposite of what Marshall had told the delegation. As maps were laid on the president's desk, Weizmann recounted the successful experiments the Jews already had conducted on desalination in Palestine and told how they were producing carrots, bananas, and potatoes in places where not a blade of grass had grown for thousands of years. Truman, the erstwhile farmer, had an imagination that responded to such a vision. Unless the Jews had access to the waters of the Gulf of Aqaba, however, Weizmann said, the desert would remain a desert. Furthermore, he continued, if the gulf were dredged, it could accomodate sizable ships and thus provide the Jewish state with an outlet to the seas, particularly vital if Egypt were to become hostile and close the Suez Canal to Jewish shipping. The Gulf of Aqaba is an arm of the Red Sea. Again Weizmann was contradicting Marshall, whose message to the delegation Truman would not have seen.[135]

The cordial meeting ended with Truman promising Weizmann to get in touch with the U.S. delegation immediately. At one o'clock, about the same time that a buoyant Weizmann was leaving Truman's office, acting Secretary of State Robert Lovett sent a message from the State Department to the delegation with final instructions not to yield to demands of the Jewish Agency, but to vote for transfer of the lower Negev to the Arabs.[136]

The situation was then hurled into a state of chaotic uncertainty when, at three o'clock, just as Herschel Johnson was to enter the meeting of Subcommittee No. 1, Truman called the delegation and spoke to General Hilldring. Hilldring informed the president of Lovett's instructions, indicating displeasure about them. Truman said he agreed with Weizmann's views. While not issuing direct instructions, Hilldring believed that the president was conveying his wish that Johnson support the majority report granting the Negev to the Jews. "Nothing should be done to upset the apple cart," Truman related.[137]

In those days, before the permanent United Nations headquarters had been built in Manhattan, its committees met in the remodeled plant of the Sperry Gyroscope Company at Lake Success on Long Island. Robert Donovan observed that the cluttered disorganization of the plant-turned-headquarters symbolized the chaotic state of affairs unfolding there on the Palestine question.[138]

Caught in a perplexing middle ground between the president's expression of support for the Jewish position and Lovett's instructions favoring the Arabs, a dilemma that surfaced just before the committee meeting, Hilldring and Johnson decided that the only prudent position to embrace for the moment regarding the Negev question was no position at all. A flurry of telephone calls followed, after which, at six o'clock, Lovett called Truman. The president said that he had not sought to change Lovett's instructions. He merely had expressed concern lest the United States stand out as a minority on the question.[139]

Lovett canceled his earlier instructions and told Johnson and Hilldring to act independently but not to allow the United States to be placed in the position of lone dissenter on the Negev issue or sacrifice any gains that may have been made with the Arabs, if this could be avoided. Events were happening fast as the partition vote drew closer.[140]

On November 22, Johnson withdrew his proposal to award the Negev to the Arabs. He sought to compensate the Arabs, however, by sponsoring a resolution providing that Beersheba and a strip of land along the border with Egypt be assigned to the Arab state. This was a proposed compromise previously suggested by the Jewish Agency.

After the flurry of indecision involving Truman, the State Department and the UN delegation Subcommittee No. 1 awarded the Negev to the Jews. Aware of Truman's call to Lake Success but unaware of the flurry of indecision and confusion, which exended to the president as well, Weizmann credited Truman with influencing the favorable committee vote: "Obviously the President had been as good as his word, and a few short hours after I had seen him had given the necessary instructions to the American delegation."[141]

Now the Palestine partition plan reached the General Assembly. The activities that transpired prior to the vote were more representative of a freewheeling partisan political convention beset by unyielding pressures from competing interests than an international political body that, in its idealized form, was meant to deliberate questions with diplomatic expertise, removed from backroom arm-twisting.

The pressureful atmosphere pervading the General Assembly vote prompted Truman to write to Robert Lovett:

> "I have a report from Haiti, in which it is stated that our Consul in Haiti (Robert H. McBride) aproached the President of that country and suggested to him that for his own good he should order the vote of his country changed, claiming that he had instructions from me to make such a statement to the President of Haiti. As you very well know, I refused to make any statements to any country on the subject of its vote in the United Nations.
>
> "It is perfectly apparent that pressure groups will succeed in putting the United Nations out of business if this sort of thing is continued and I am very anxious that it be stopped."[142]

Another pressure focus was the Philippine Republic. During the closing debate its delegate, Ambassador Carlos P. Romulo, indicated that his government would oppose partition. Robert Donovan recounts the ensuing events.

> A United States "representative"—evidently Clark Clifford—thereupon told Joaquin M. Elizalde, the Philippine ambassador to Washington, that such a vote would impair United States–Philippines relations. Ten United States senators cabled President Manuel Roxas of the Philippines, putting pressure on him, he later complained, to reverse his decision on Palestine. In distress, because of the effect such an action would have on the Mohammedan (Muslim) population of the islands, he instructed Romulo—lest the Philippines' relations with the United States suffer—to vote for partition, which Romulo did. Indeed, according to Loy Henderson, Romulo's vote also had been solicited by two justices of the United States Supreme Court, Felix Frankfurter and Frank Murphy.[143]

At a meeting with Lovett on November 24, Truman issued instructions that the U.S. delegation was not to use threats or improper pressure to influence other delegations. While Lovett passed the order on, many events occurred behind the scenes. In Robert Donovan's opinion the president was probably unaware of these activities.[144]

David Niles maneuvered busily behind the scenes. According to Herbert Feis, Niles imparted telephone instructions to "use any and all sorts of persuasion and inducement to win votes for the Resolution."[145]

Niles communicated his message to Herschel Johnson concerning the use of persuasion during the same period that Lovett was passing Truman's order along instructing the U.S. delegation to refrain from pressuring other delegates. In that he was communicating messages in his role of presidential assistant, Niles's statements concerning the exercise of pressure on behalf of Jewish interests further confused an already thoroughly muddled picture. Niles also persuaded some Greek-American businessmen to cable an appeal to the government in Athens to support partition, which failed to influence the Greek Government away from its antipartition posture.[146]

Confusion on the partition issue extended well beyond the levels of the U.S. UN delegation, the State Department, and David Niles. It included Harry Truman as well. While instructing Lovett against the use of pressure on the partition question and informing him by letter of what he saw as the impropriety of American diplomatic intervention in Haiti, some notes were later found among the president's papers. They were undated and unsigned and appeared to be in the handwriting of Charles Ross, a fellow Missourian who served as Truman's Presidential Press Secretary. They were attached to a memorandum dated November 20, 1947, and referred to the cabinet meeting held November 11, eighteen days before the final General Assembly vote. The notes said:

> 1. We have been in touch with Liberian minister to try to get the Government's instructions changed to support us.
> 2. I think we have Haiti.
> 3. We may get Philippines out of No into abstention or, with luck, yes.
> 4. Cuba still won't play.
> 5. Greece is uncertain but has the excuse of the Balkan Commission vote trade with Moslems.[147]

Rather than conveying the diplomatic aloofness Truman had requested in his communications with Robert Lovett, the cabinet notes read more like those of a delegate chairman at a party convention seeking support through aggressive arm-twisting.

Truman biographer Robert Donovan recounts a scenario dominated by intense pressure on behalf of partition.

On November 27 [Congressman Emmanuel] Celler telegraphed Truman that he had been spending considerable time at Lake Success and feared that partition might fail by one or two votes. He asked that the United States delegation be allowed to put pressure on recalcitrants like Haiti, China, Ecuador, Liberia, Honduras, Paraguay, and especially Greece, "which is immeasurably indebted to us" (because of the Truman Doctrine). In fact, Celler said, it might be necessary to have Lovett put pressure on Greece.

Fearful of a Jewish boycott of his firm's products, Harvey S. Firestone, Jr., of the Firestone Tire and Rubber Company, which had a concession in Liberia, brought pressure on the president of that country, William Tubman. Liberia voted for partition. Intrigue was rife.

Former Ambassador William Bullitt was a leading advocate of American aid to China. According to an official memorandum by George Kennan, Baruch admonished Bullitt to tell his Chinese friends that unless China voted for partition the Chinese would not get a penny of American assistance. Bullitt passed this warning on to Dr. V. K. Wellington Koo, the Chinese ambassador in Washington. China, however, decided to abstain from voting. Koo explained to Bullitt that the large Moslem element among the Chinese necessitated such a course.

On November 25 Matt Connelly had informed Truman in a memorandum that Lovett had called to say "that our case is being seriously impeded by high pressure being exerted by Jewish agencies. There have been indications of bribes and threats by these groups." The memorandum added: in the case of Liberia, certain groups have informed the Liberian delegation that if they do not go along, the Stettinius pact with Liberia will be cancelled. In the case of Nicaragua, the delegate was told by some of these groups that if he went along these groups would see to it that they were recognized by the United States.[148]

During this same period Chaim Weizmann wrote Truman from the Plaza Hotel in New York to indicate disturbance over "unwarranted rumors" circulating concerning pressures being employed on behalf of partition. He denied that his representation had "gone beyond the limits of legitimate and moderate persuasion."[149]

Dr. Nahum Goldmann, a leading Weizmann associate, called on Adolf A. Berle, former assistant secretary of state, seeking his assistance in securing Haiti's vote. Berle cabled Haiti's president, Dumrais Estime, receiving assurance by return cable that the desired instructions were en route to the Haitian delegation.[150]

The reference by Truman's secretary, Matthew J. Connelly, to bribes offered on behalf of partition support was echoed in a memorandum from Llewelyn E. Thompson Jr., head of the State Department Division of Eastern European Affairs, to Loy Henderson. Reporting on a conversation with Guillermo Belt, the Cuban Ambassador, Thompson related that Belt had stated, "that one Latin American delegate had changed his vote to support partition in return for $75,000 in cash and that another Latin American delegate, I believe the Costa Rican, had refused a forty thousand dollar offer but that subsequently had been ordered by his Government to support partition. It was Mr. Belt's belief that some members of the delegate's government had accepted the bribe."[151]

The Arabs engaged in activity of their own to thwart partition. Greece, the object of much American concern, ultimately voted against partition. Greek support arose from a secret agreement with the Muslim nations in which, in return for the Greek vote, the Muslims agreed to back Greece in all future matters of interest to Athens arising before any United Nations organ.[152]

The long and arduous prevote ordeal finally concluded on November 29, 1947, when the General Assembly acted on the partition recommendation of the United Nations special committee. A two-thirds majority was required for the resolution to be adopted. The partition measure prevailed by slightly more than that figure as 33 nations voted in its favor, 13 voted against, and 10 abstained.

Under the terms of the partition plan Palestine would be split into two states linked economically. The population figure of that period was 1,200,000 Arabs and 568,000 Jews. The United Nations would rule Jerusalem under a trusteeship. The Jewish flag would fly over the Negev, Eastern Galilee, and the coastal strip from just north of Haifa to the Gaza Strip border. The Jews would control 55 percent of the land with a 58 percent Jewish citizenry. The Arab flag would be seen over the West Bank of the Jordan River, Western Galilee, the Gaza Strip, and an Egyptian-Sinai border zone. Under the partition plan, the Arabs received 45 percent of the land with a population 99 percent Arab. A five-member United Nations Palestine Commission would join Britain in administering Palestine to prepare for partition.[153]

As a result of discussion in the General Assembly, certain details of the partition resolution adopted by UNSCOP had been changed. The size of the Jewish state had been somewhat reduced as Jaffa was transferred to the Arab state as well as a sizable part of the Negev near the Mediterranean and Egyptian frontiers. This territory would become a scene of conflict during the 1956 Suez campaign and the 1967 Israeli-Arab war.[154]

It was one thing for the United Nations General Assembly to propose by a better than two-thirds majority that Palestine be partitioned into separate states for Arabs and Jews and another for the Arabs to abide by that vote. The Arab states immediately asserted that they would not be bound by the United Nations vote. Overnight violence erupted in the Middle East in the wake of the UN vote, just a prelude to the bloody conflict that would follow up to the present, better than forty years later, with no prospect of cessation in sight.

The dangerous prospect for continued Middle East strife as a result of partition was not lost on Secretary of Defense James Forrestal. He voiced his apprehensions at a cabinet luncheon on December 1, just two days after the General Assembly vote. Truman sought to placate his concern by reiterating his position that U.S. military personnel would not be used to enforce peace in Palestine. Forrestal reminded Truman of the prospect of the U.S. being asked to contribute its share of an international peacekeeping force in Palestine. Truman had acknowledged to Robert Lovett on October 9 the possibility of U.S. troops being used in such a UN peacekeeping capacity.

Finally the specter of the Soviet Union was raised at the December 1 cabinet meeting. As one of the Big Five members serving on the Security Council, the Soviet Union might also be requested to supply personnel in a joint UN Middle East action. With concern at an optimum level over Soviet expansion efforts in Europe, participation on its part in the administrative, policing, or military operations in Palestine was viewed with concern. The Truman Administration did not want the great Russian Bear to reach out with its gigantic claws at the Middle East. As Robert Donovan said, "The worst of the Palestine problem was still ahead for Truman."[155]

Britain, which had limped through the winter of 1946–47 with Marshall Plan assistance, was gearing up for another winter ordeal as the partition plan was debated in the House of Commons on December 11 and 12. Besides being preoccupied with domestic considerations, Britain resented other Western countries for refusing to open their gates widely to Jewish immigration. The British had focused attention on the development of a new policy complemented by provisions for enforcement, but the United Nations majority had instead proceeded with the partition program. Clearly smarting over what it deemed a failure of responsible cooperation, the British Government believed it had been forced to endure a no-win situation while bearing a villain's mantle as well.

Considering the bitterness of Attlee and Bevin, it was understandable when the foreign secretary announced, "We have no intention of opposing that decision (for partition) but we cannot ourselves undertake, either individually or collectively in association with others, to impose the decision by force."[156]

The message was clear. The British, custodians of a Mandate that extended for more than a generation, created after one world war and terminating following a second, wanted out. The statement was correctly construed that the British Government would not cooperate even in the creation of a United Nations police force in Palestine. The Mandate would be surrendered by the British on May 15.

The fighting that erupted on November 29, 1947, was localized and limited. It gradually increased in scope until, with the withdrawal of British troops on May 15, 1948, when the Jewish state was declared, the first of many bloody Israeli-Arab conflicts commenced. As British troops and administrative facilities were withdrawn in preparation for the Mandate's termination, a series of military and political vacuums were created which each side hoped to fill first.

This method of evacuation put the Arabs at a disadvantage. The Jewish Agency, the labor machinery of the *Histadrut*, the development of the kibbutz concept and other quasi-governmental institutions established through the years in the Yishuv by the industrious Ben-Gurion and others gave the Zionists the necessary machinery to transfer into a Jewish state. Great inroads had been made in establishing health, social and other essential public services in contrast to the Arabs. While the Jews were prepared to step into such a vacuum in the creation of a state, the Arabs, in sharp contrast, had failed to set up their own quasi-government organizations.

Another area that worked to the distinct advantage of the Jews and corresponding disadvantage of the Arabs was that of leadership. Whereas Ben-Gurion already had an entrenched administrative bureaucracy in place directed by trusted subordinates, many of the Arabs' ablest leaders had been prevented from returning to Palestine from forced exile abroad. Observing the conflict at hand and fearing future instabilities, many local Arab business and political leaders began to flee Palestine with the inception of fighting. As the termination of the Mandate loomed near, a sense of desperation gripped Palestinian Arabs concerning the future. As Fred Khouri explains, "By April, as a result of these developments [failures to establish quasi-government entities], plus a partial breakdown in many essential services, a number of Jewish military victories, real and imagined atrocity stories, and Jewish psychological warfare aimed at encouraging the Arabs either to surrender or flee, large numbers of Arabs lost their self-confidence and were gripped with fear about their future. Consequently, by May 15, about 200,000 Arabs fled their homes in panic.''[157]

As the British evacuation from Palestine continued, the headaches suffered by Attlee, Bevin, and the Whitehall Ministries were transferred to Truman, Marshall, and the State Department offices at Foggy Bottom. Paramount in the thinking of State Department policymakers was the concern that partition would upset an already delicate international balance of power. The foremost practitioner of this view was Loy Henderson of the Near East Division. Although he became known by Zionists as an enemy due to his cautionary concern over the establishment of a Jewish state, his position had been shaped by pragmatic policy considerations rather than any anti-Jewish propensity, and although he would never enter the field of rhetorical combat with Jewish forces in the manner of Ernest Bevin, Henderson shared one point in common with the British Foreign Secretary—a strong concern over the role the Soviet Union would play in any altered Middle East political and territorial composition. This concern prompted him to urge a cautionary approach in implementing the partition agreement. This caution was transferred to secretary Marshall as well and came to influence President Truman.

Ben-Gurion and Weizmann no doubt felt frustration over the Soviet Union factor, which cut both ways in terms of their statehood designs. The support advanced by Russia for partition, coupled with concurrent U.S. backing, tilted the General Assembly balance in the Jewish direction. At the same time, with the United States concerned about Soviet expansion interests in the Middle East, the Russian factor weighed against Jewish interests as U.S. diplomats pursued alternatives other than partition, which they feared would immerse the region in great conflict, generating a scenario wherein the Soviet Union could profit from an influential international area ridden with strife.

While the Soviets initially supported Jewish aspirations, ultimately the concerns of Henderson and others became realized when, after a bloodless coup in Egypt in 1952 deposed King Farouk, General Gamal Abdel Nasser assumed power. With steady Soviet military support Egypt became a Soviet client state until the 1970s, when Anwar Sadat assumed power after Nasser's death. Even with loosened ties between the two countries, the Soviet Union continued to support Egypt and other Arab states. During the 1973 Arab-Israeli war, tensions between the United States, which backed Israel, and the Soviet Union, which supported the Arab states, brought the superpowers to the point of a possible nuclear conflict.

The Jewish forces had less than a week to celebrate their General Assembly success before U.S. caution began to take root. Even before the vote, Loy Henderson had recommended—with Marshall's approval—an embargo on the export of U.S. arms to the Middle East. The policy did not seek to restrain Britain from continuing to sell arms to the Arabs, although the British had limited such sales. The embargo action was announced on December 5, provoking dismay on the part of the Zionists.[158]

The position that began to evolve in the State Department shortly following the partition vote, supported strongly by Loy Henderson, was that the United States recommend that Palestine be placed in trusteeship. Because of the fear of additional fighting, the concern that prompted the Middle East embargo, and the prospect of the Soviet Union's profiting from instability in the region, a trusteeship was seen as an insurance policy for the troubled area. A trusteeship, unlike partition, would not consist of separate Arab and Jewish states. Palestine would instead be a ward of the United Nations rather than the League of Nations. The trustee possibility was discussed in secrecy during the period following the General Assembly vote.

Early in 1948, the Arab League tentatively decided to deny U.S. companies pipeline rights until the United States changed its policy. On January 15, it was announced that the armies of its members, consisting of Egypt, Iraq, Lebanon, Saudi Arabia, Syria, Transjordan, and Yemen, would occupy all of Palestine when the British withdrew. On the same day, the Jewish Agency informed the United Nations Commission on Palestine that either an international police force would have to impose partition or the Jews would have to be allowed to import arms and organize their own militia. The UN had no armed force, and the British refused to allow the Jews to organize and train a militia while their forces were still present. The forces of the *Irgun* and *Lehi* continued to function in the area, however, with effectiveness.[159]

The Palestine crisis had materialized at a time when the United States was concentrating major attention on Europe, where tensions loomed in Berlin, Czechoslovakia, and Greece. The possibility of a communist breakthrough in Greece was viewed with such grave concern that, at a National Security Council meeting on February 12, a question was raised concerning sending American ground troops to that beleaguered nation. Five weeks later, as the Czechoslovakia crisis worsened, President Truman asked Congress to restore the draft because of events there. Faced with the prospect of juggling available forces in the midst of potential military crises in Czechoslovakia, Greece, and Berlin, Secretary Marshall said, "the United States was playing with fire while having nothing with which to put it out."[160]

The gravity of European developments begged the question of just what the U.S. posture should be in Palestine, another world powder keg, which State Department policymakers such as Loy Henderson believed was eminently exploitable by the Soviets. State Department thinking during this period broke down in the following manner, according to Truman biographer Robert Donovan.

> A school within the Department of State and the Pentagon, the views of which were more or less reflected by Forrestal, Marshall, Lovett, and Henderson, believed that war in the Middle East and loss of Arab friendship would be too high a price to pay for a Jewish state. Forrestal particularly advanced the view that American military reserves might be completely drained in the dispatch of forces to the Middle East as part of a United Nations contingent to enforce partition. The opposing viewpoint, reflected by Truman's advisers, was that a Jewish homeland might be secured instead by lifting the arms embargo so that the Jews could get the weapons to defend their own state, perhaps aided by some United Nations action to deter other Arab nations from invading Palestine. Truman was plainly worried by the argument that troops would be needed, and he insisted that American troops would not be sent to Palestine, except possibly as a part of a United Nations force.[161]

George Kennan and Deak Rusk of the State Department shared the concerns of Henderson and Forrestal about the dangers of enforcing partition in Palestine. Kennan felt that the United States had accepted "intolerable commitments from which it should remove itself as rapidly as possible." He stated further that the Palestine situation "defied solution" at that point in time, concluding with the warning that the United States should not "attempt to be our brother's keeper or to offer moral advice to other powers" when the United States was unable to bear its own full share of responsibility for the consequences.[162] Rusk cited the UN Commission on Palestine's words that partition was unworkable without force. He warned about the prospect of a war in Palestine involving the Arabs against the Jewish state and UN representatives, or war by the UN against the Arabs in Palestine and the Arab states. Rusk reminded Robert Lovett that the UN Charter authorized the United Nations to resist aggression and maintain peace but did not authorize force to compel a political settlement. He stated, "The purpose of the United Nations is to keep peace, not to make war."[163]

While leading State Department functionaries viewed partition with increasing reluctance, Ralph Bunche of the UN staff warned Warren Austin that if the United States gave up on partition it would constitute a deathblow to the prestige of the United Nations.[164] With each passing day, Harry Truman began to feel more like a man caught in a firestorm. He wanted the fledgling United Nations to succeed, but there were other important considerations as well. There was the possible economic impact of alienating the Arabs when oil was vitally needed for Europe in concert with Marshall Plan objectives. There was also the potential military impact of Palestine.

Attention was stirred in the Pentagon over rumors that U.S. armed forces might be needed to enforce partition in Palestine. This concern emanated from the UN Commission on Palestine report of February 16, to which Dean Rusk alluded in his earlier assessment. The report forced the issue of whether the partition resolution would be enforced or whether another alternative would be considered. Major General Alfred Gruenther of the Joint Chiefs of Staff had already reported to Secretary of Defense Forrestal that current strategic planning had been significantly altered by the contingency of U.S. troops being sent to the Middle East. Gruenther met with Truman as well as State and Defense Department officials on February 19 to suggest that U.S. participation in Palestine would require a force of between 89,000 and 120,000.[165]

As he prepared to leave for a Caribbean vacation, President Truman was informed about the growing fears that partition was unworkable. He was also made aware that support existed within the General Assembly to reconsider the resolution that had been passed by a better than two-thirds margin on November 29. Just before Truman left on his vacation he was apprised by Marshall that Lovett was working on a statement for Austin to make in the Security Council, the text of which would be sent for presidential approval.[166]

On February 21, the State Department sent a working draft of the paper Austin would present to the Security Council the following Tuesday. It was communicated while the president was cruising aboard the *Williamsburg* in the Virgin Islands. Austin's speech would enunciate the U.S. interpretation of the legal status of the Security Council, which was perceived as possessing authority to deal with internal or external threats to the peace of Palestine, but not to enforce a recommendation by the General Assembly, meaning that it did not have the power to enforce partition. The message also clearly stated that if, in the face of Arab intransigence the Security Council could not develop an alternative to partition, the issue should be referred to a special session of the General Assembly.[167]

The message contained the following significant words:

"The Department of State considers that it would then be clear that Palestine is not yet ready for self-government and that some form of United Nations trusteeship for an additional period of time will be necessary."[168]

Truman sent a cable to Marshall on February 22 approving in principle the basic position advanced in the State Department message, indicating that nothing presented to the Security Council should be interpreted as a recession of the U.S. position advocated in the General Assembly. The State Department then sent Truman a text of Austin's speech, assuring the president that it did not constitute a recession from the position taken by the United States in the General Assembly. Predicated on the information the president received, he should have been aware of the State Department shift from partition to the creation of a trusteeship in Palestine. Much seemed to hang on the semantical interpretation of the word "recession" and whether such a change fit that definition. The question of what the president was or was not aware of in the realm of the shift from a policy of partition to that of the creation of a trusteeship would later stir up a tempest in diplomatic circles within the Truman Administration.

While American Jewish groups were unaware of the backstage State Department maneuvering away from partition and toward trusteeship, they began lobbying President Truman heavily during the presidential election year of 1948. They sought his support to push along partition, which they saw as a cause dangerously stagnating. The pressure began to annoy Truman, who refused to see any Zionist leaders. As the euphoria following the partition vote gave way to anxiety among American Jewish leaders, Chaim Weizmann was urged to return to the United States and seek another appointment with Truman. Matt Connelly replied to Weizmann by letter of February 12, relating that such a meeting was "out of the question."[169]

The Jewish leaders remained determined to inject the diplomat of Zionism back into the discussion process despite Truman's refusal to meet with any of their people. On February 20, Eddie Jacobson was awakened in the middle of the night in his Kansas City home by a telephone call from Frank Goldman, president of B'nai B'rith, in New York. Goldman was in despair over Truman's imposed isolation. If anyone could help the cause as a Truman contact man, Goldman reasoned, it would be the president's old friend Jacobson. The call to Jacobson came just as Truman was planning to depart for his vacation in the Virgin Islands and Key West. An anxious Goldman asked Jacobson to charter a plane in the darkness of night to catch the president before he left the White House, then urge him to meet with Weizmann. This approach was not feasible since Truman was on his way south while Jacobson was in Kansas City. Jacobson instead wired Matt Connelly for an appointment.

Truman sent Jacobson a reply by letter from Key West on February 27, informing his former business partner that Weizmann could not tell him anything he did not already know. The tone of the letter revealed the frustration of a chief executive caught in the throes of a ponderous dilemma:

"The Jews are so emotional, and the Arabs are so difficult to talk with that it is almost impossible to get anything done. The British have, of course, been exceedingly noncooperative. . . . The Zionists, of course, have expected a big stick approach on our part, and naturally have been disappointed when we can't do that."

Truman then added a comment that indicated he had been listening carefully to the State Department view being propounded by Henderson, Kennan, and Rusk, along with Secretary Marshall, on the subject of partition:

"I have about come to the conclusion that the situation is not solvable as presently set up."[170]

When Truman's vacation ended Jacobson flew to Washington. He went to the White House on March 13 without an appointment. Connelly received him and, in the normal course of events, arranged for him to see Truman. Connelly requested, however, that Jacobson not bring up the sensitive topic of Palestine.

Jacobson entered the Oval Office, finding his old friend looking tanned and fit from the days in the tropical sun. Jacobson initially engaged the president in small talk about their families and events of common interest, after which, despite the Connelly admonition, the Kansas City businessman introduced the subject of Palestine. The sensitive topic provoked an immediate emotional reaction on Truman's part.

"He immediately became tense in appearance, abrupt in speech, and very bitter in the words he was throwing my way," Jacobson recalled in his account of the episode. "In all the years of our friendship he never talked to me in this manner or anything approaching it."[171]

Truman told Jacobson he did not want to discuss Palestine, the Jews, the Arabs, or the British. He was satisfied to let the issue take its course in the United Nations. Jacobson continued to press the Palestine issue, reminding Truman of the admiration he had previously expressed for Chaim Weizmann. He related that Weizmann was old and ill, and that he had made a long trip to the United States to see the president. Truman continued to seethe, however, to the consternation of his old friend.

"He replied how disrespectful and how mean certain Jewish leaders had been to him," Jacobson recalled. Truman named individuals, but Jacobson omitted them from his account of the meeting. Almost assuredly, one of the perceived offenders of the president's sensibilities had been Rabbi Abba Hillel Silver. The longer the conversation continued, the more crushed Jacobson became over the harsh tenor and content of Truman's words.

"I suddenly found myself thinking that my dear friend . . . was at that moment as close to being an anti-Semite as a man could possibly be," Jacobson reflected, "and I was shocked that some of our own Jewish leaders should be responsible for Mr. Truman's attitude."

Jacobson had difficulty gaining Truman's acceptance for a meeting with Weizmann "because, after all, he had been slandered and libeled by some of the leaders of my own people whom he had tried to help while he was in the Senate and from the moment he stepped into the White House." The realization that a reaction to what Truman regarded as offensive and mean-spirited tactics by Jewish leaders had made the president adamant against seeing anyone else, even Weizmann, caused Jacobson to feel despair. Suddenly Jacobson's eyes focused on the model of an equestrian statue of Andrew Jackson atop a table on the west side of the room. Soon he found himself pointing at that statue as he pled his case once more. Andrew Jackson was the president's hero. Well, he had a hero too. Eddie Jacobson's hero was Chaim Weizmann.

"Now you refuse to see him [Weizmann] because you were insulted by some of our American Jewish leaders," Jacobson said, "even though you know that Weizmann had absolutely nothing to do with these insults and would be the last man to be a party to them. It doesn't sound like you, Harry, because I thought you could take this stuff they have been handing out to you."[172]

Truman recounted the pivotal meeting with Eddie Jacobson to Merle Miller. Truman recalled receiving a call from Jacobson late on the morning of March 13 from his room at the Statler Hotel revealing his wish to see the president at the White House.

"Eddie, I'm always glad to see old friends, but there's one thing you've got to promise me," Truman recalled. "I don't want you to say a word about what's going on over there in the Middle East. Do you promise?"

When Jacobson, who had promised Truman he would not discuss the forbidden topic of Palestine, brought it up anyway, an emotional scene followed, which was recounted by Truman:

"Great tears were running down his cheeks, and I took one look at him, and I said, 'Eddie, you son of a bitch, you promised me you wouldn't say a word about what's going on over there.' And he said, 'Mr. President, I haven't said a word, but every time I think of the homeless Jews, homeless for thousands of years, and I think about Dr. Weizmann, I start crying. I can't help it. He's an old man, and he's spent his whole life working for a homeland for the Jews, and now he's sick, and he's in New York and wants to see you. And every time I think about it I can't help crying.' "[173]

Jacobson noticed that Truman had begun drumming on his desk. He then swung around in his swivel chair, gazed out at the Rose Garden in contemplation, then finally whirled back and looked his old friend in the eye.

"You win, you bald-headed son of a bitch," Truman said. "I will see him."[174]

Five days after Truman's meeting with Jacobson, the elder statesman of Zionism—the man who had been rejected by the forces of Ben-Gurion and Silver at the Zionist Congress of 1946—would play his final key role on behalf of the movement he had served his entire life as its leading diplomat. Once the Israeli nation came into being with Ben-Gurion as its prime minister he would be named the country's first president, which was a ceremonial position in which there was little contact between Ben-Gurion and Weizmann, who became increasingly frail and would die in 1952.

Summoning up every last bit of energy in his frail body, Weizmann prepared to make his case.

The meeting with Truman, according to overall significance regarding his final goal and its prospect of early accomplishment, exceeded in importance Weizmann's original meeting with Balfour, his exhortations at Whitehall that resulted in the Balfour Declaration, and his effective role at the Paris Peace Conference, which had helped to achieve his goal of a British Mandate for Palestine. He saw the prospect of a Jewish state as imminent and was determined to do all in his power to persuade the president to support partition. He considered Harry Truman to be the most powerful man on earth and saw the international power pendulum swing from Britain to the United States. Although he had spent most of his life in diplomatic contact with Britain, for which he was often condemned by Ben-Gurion and others, his final overture was toward the then reigning international power, the United States.

Truman recognized the possible explosive repercussions a meeting with Weizmann would have should the media be alerted, and so the strictest precautions were taken to ensure secrecy. Weizmann slipped through the East Gate of the White House for the meeting, exiting just as unobtrusively. The men conversed cordially for forty-five minutes. Weizmann did most of the talking, pressing Truman to lift the arms embargo, and to support partition and Palestine immigration.

The president responded that the State Department was considering lifting the embargo, and he reasserted his long-standing support of immigration. The question of partition was the focus of Weizmann's major effort, as well as that on which success would be realized. The emotional plea of the sick, half-blind Zionist leader had an impact on Truman. When the veteran diplomat left Truman's office an agreement was understood to exist between the men regarding the president's support of partition.[175]

The next chapter in the unfolding saga of Palestine would produce another conflict. The issue was destined to be awash in controversy and misunderstanding to the last moment. On the afternoon of March 19, less than twenty-four hours after Chaim Weizmann left the White House believing he had been given an assurance on partition, Warren Austin rose to address the Security Council of the United Nations. The U.S. delegate delivered the speech drafted by Loy Henderson advocating the trustee plan toward which the State Department had been recently gravitating.

Arabs were jubilant and Zionists felt they had been betrayed. Harry Truman was livid, scribbling on his calendar that the State Department had pulled the rug out from under him and that he had been put "in the position of a liar and a doublecrosser."[176]

The State Department had done no such thing. With Truman's mind preoccupied with a crisis in Czechoslovakia and one looming in Berlin, the best explanation for the contradiction in his own mind was forgetfulness. He probably either did not recall that he had been apprised by

Marshall and the State Department when he was in Caribbean waters on the *Williamsburg* concerning Austin's proposed speech or had forgotten substantive details of those communications. The handwritten notes of Clark Clifford, Special Counsel to the President, verify that Truman was informed about developing policy within the State Department on trusteeship:

> 5. Marshall & Lovett left no word that President was to be informed when Austin was to speak.
> 6. Text of Austin's speech was not submitted to President for his approval.
> (a) It was the same substance as the draft previously submitted to President.[177]

In that the president had previously approved the text of Austin's speech aboard the *Williamsburg*, and no substantive changes had been added in the interim, Marshall and his colleagues had every reason to believe that Truman was fully aware of the content of Austin's speech and its trusteeship recommendation. The difference in interpretation lies in the belief that the trustee question involved only a postponement of the objectives elucidated in the General Assembly's partition vote and not an abandonment. Marshall, Austin, Henderson, and others believed that, in the present climate of violence, any attempt to carry out the UN partition resolution was premature and would be fraught with dangers. Truman's response sent from the *Williamsburg* about the working draft sent by Marshall contained concern that the position to be advanced by Austin not be seen as a recession of the view taken by the United States in the General Assembly. When the text of the speech was sent to Truman, it contained an assurance that trusteeship would not constitute such a recession. To Weizmann and others in the Zionist movement, such a move constituted abandonment of the General Assembly resolution on partition, but the State Department considered the shift to a trusteeship to be a cautionary step taken at a dangerous point. In the State Department's view, the final objective remained the same. As a result the trustee issue was not seen as a step backward as the Zionists perceived it, while Truman, prior to the Weizmann visit, appeared to agree.

The State Department had every reason to believe that Truman was not opposed to the recommendation of a UN trusteeship, because the president had done nothing to register his disapproval of a position concerning which he had been informed. It must also be remembered that neither Secretary Marshall, Ambassador Austin, or anyone else in the State Department or U.S. UN delegation knew about Chaim Weizmann's visit to the White House, much less the deep impression that the Zionist leader made.

At his March 15 press conference, Truman sought to calm the troubled waters of controversy over trusteeship. He said that despite U.S. support for partition, it could not be carried out peacefully under current circumstances. He sought to reassure Weizmann and the Jews by asserting that trusteeship "is not proposed as a substitute for the partition plan but as an effort to fill the vacuum soon to be created by the termination of the mandate . . . Trusteeship does not prejudice the character of the final settlement."[178]

Truman biographer Robert Donovan poses another possibility regarding the president's angry reaction to a State Department toward which he conveyed every impression of agreement. Donovan concludes that perhaps the major element that caused Truman to erupt in the face of circumstances of which he was apprised was a failure to discern the devastating opposition by Jews over trusteeship. The president, sailing the Caribbean waters on vacation while simultaneously remaining immersed in European problems, may have been inclined to accept his State Department's analysis that Austin's speech represented no major departure from the U.S. pro-partition posture in the UN while, had he been aware of the potential Jewish response, he could well have taken a closer look at the direction in which Secretary Marshall and colleagues were proceeding. Once the eruption occurred it is plausible if not likely that Truman, not recalling the precise details of the State Department viewpoint, believed that there was great disparity between what he advocated and the position Marshall and his men were advancing. Then after he had an opportunity to review the facts, he sought to squelch the controversy at his March 25 press conference.

One fact was unmistakable. Truman was now in major political difficulty with the American Jewish movement. Jacobson recalled how almost immediately after Austin's speech he began receiving calls and wires from all over America "telling me what a terrible traitor my friend, Harry Truman, turned out to be and how he betrayed the Jewish people and how he had violated his promise . . . There wasn't one human being in Kansas City or anywhere else during those terrible days who expressed faith and confidence in the word of the President of the United States."[179]

Not only did the president's reputation with American Jewish leaders suffer preciptiously, but also he found himself confronting the problem in a presidential election year in which he was a decided underdog to the well-financed, highly organized campaign of Governor Thomas E. Dewey of New York. Truman's political posture had eroded in 1946 when the Republican Party, for the first time since the 1920s, won control of both houses of Congress. Truman faced a decidedly uphill battle.

Clark Clifford, Special Counsel to the President, held tremendous power within the Truman White House. Not only did he have the president's ear on any question he deemed significant, but also he served during 1948 as chairman of Truman's campaign. While Marshall was the articulator of going slow on partition and on the creation of a Jewish state his main adversary was Clifford, who argued that Truman abandon truce efforts and declare his intention to recognize the new nation as soon as it was proclaimed. Robert Lovett immediately criticized the Clifford recommendation, declaring that it would damage the U.S. position in the United Nations, where a U.S. resolution for a truce was still being considered. Lovett felt that the United States should first know the nature of the proposed state and its boundaries, and he believed that the Clifford move would be so politically transparent as to defeat its purpose.[180]

While U.S. efforts toward generating interest in trusteeship continued, increasing impatience generated among Jews in the Yishuv. David Ben-Gurion spoke for the Jewish Agency he headed by stating bluntly, "It is we who will decide the fate of Palestine. We cannot agree to any sort of trusteeship, permanent or temporary—the Jewish state exists because we defend it." Rabbi Silver, Truman's nemesis and Ben-Gurion's U.S. ally, had some terse words for the trustee concept. He saw the Austin proposal as "a shocking reversal" and "a fatal capitulation" to Arab threats. Silver warned that any change in the partition plan "will have to be imposed upon the Jewish community of Palestine by force."[181]

The steadfast Jewish posture was further exemplified by an April 12 statement issued by the General Zionist Council in Tel Aviv: "We have decided, relying on the authority of the Zionist movment and the support of the entire Jewish people, that upon termination of the mandatory regime there shall be an end of foreign rule in Palestine, and that the governing body of the Jewish state shall come into being."[182]

Events moved rapidly toward May 15, when the British Mandate would effectively terminate in Palestine. Fighting raged on in the Holy

Land despite the adoption of a Security Council resolution calling for a cease-fire and the creation of a Truce Commission to supervise an end to hostilities. The Jews would not accept a truce while, they charged, Arab troops from Syria, Lebanon, Transjordan, and Iraq were concentrated in Palestine. The Jews feared that the Arabs would manipulate a truce to strengthen their military position while the Arabs, according to Robert B. Macatee, the U.S. Counsul General in Jerusalem, were determined to continue the fight "until Zionism [is] eradicated."[183]

The Security Council called a special session of the General Assembly, which convened April 16. The United States continued to push for trusteeship, which the Jews rejected as a barrier to statehood. The Arabs, despite their earlier euphoria over what was interpreted as a shying away from partition by the United States, opposed trusteeship on the fear that it constituted a subterfuge for partition. Most member nations recoiled from trusteeship because it was thought to be unenforceable.[184]

Clark Clifford continued advocating partition. He raised the argument that recognition was consistent with U.S. policy from the beginning. Clifford also believed that a Jewish state was inevitable, and therefore the United States should recognize this truism sooner rather than later.

Clifford, the inside political man in the Truman Administration who was running the 1948 presidential campaign, was, in the words of Robert Donovan, "both a source and a conduit" in generating pressure from Democratic leaders on Truman to recognize the Jewish state. In a race that was decidedly uphill for Truman, Jewish votes were considered indispensable to prevent losses in crucial states such as New York, Ohio, Illinois, Pennsylvania, and California. While Clifford helped orchestrate pressures from leading Democrats, he joined David Niles in preparing draft statements that Truman might make in concert with recognition.[185]

Secretary of State Marshall adhered to a trusteeship posture, and in a conversation with Moshe Shertok, who as Moshe Sharett was destined to become Israel's first foreign minister, he emphasized the pitfalls that could be inherent in the prompt establishment of a Jewish state.

I . . . stressed that it was extremely dangerous to base long-range policy on temporary military success. There was no doubt but that the Jewish army had gained such temporary success but there was no assurance whatever that in the long-range the tide might not turn against them. I told Mr. Shertok that they were taking a gamble. If the tide did turn adversely and they came running to us for help they should be placed clearly on notice now that there was no warrant to expect help from the United States, which had warned them of the grave risk they were running.[186]

General Marshall, a distinguished military man who had mapped Allied strategy from Washington in World War Two, saw the Jewish situation vis-à-vis Palestine with a career military officer's eye. He warned Shertok of being misled by early military successes, stressing the importance of not being guided by military advisers. Marshall used an example fresh in his mind, the collapse of Chiang Kai-shek in China, where early successes were followed by bitter losses and eventual defeat at the hands of the communist forces led by Mao Tse-tung.[187] Marshall's conversation with Shertok manifested the secretary's basic concern that the Jews not rush into a military situation destined to eventuate in tragedy. His approach to the Palestine situation was in no way comparable to the grudge match that evolved between Ernest Bevin and the Jews.

The disparate viewpoints of the Truman Administration on the Palestine issue came to a thundering collision just forty-eight hours before the Mandate was due to expire at a strategy conference called by Truman. In the opening round of statements at the May 12 meeting, Secretary Marshall referred to his warning to Moshe Shertok four days earlier.

Truman gave Clifford the floor, having instructed him before the meeting to present the case for recognition of a Jewish state. He recommended that the president get the jump on the Soviets and restore Truman's position in the eyes of the Jews prior to the contretemps arising from the Austin speech advocating a trusteeship in Palestine. Clifford advocated that Truman announce his intention to recognize the Jewish state the following day, May 14, one full day before it was slated to come into existence.

The first participant to rebut Clifford's recommendation of recognition was Under Secretary of State Robert Lovett, who emphasized that the issue was still before the UN Security Council and that the United States was a member of the Truce Commission. Lovett argued that the United States could not unilaterally discharge the Security Council of the issue and that any effort to do so would be improper in light of U.S. efforts to promote a truce. He then observed that the special session of the General Assembly had been called at the request of the United States and that it was still considering the question of the future government of Palestine. On that ground alone he opposed premature recognition. He saw the effort as a transparent attempt to win Jewish votes that he believed would cost more than would be gained. Lovett concluded his presentation by resurrecting State Department fears that a state of Israel might be vulnerable to Communism or even become a lair of the Soviets. He read from a file of intelligence telegrams and reports concerning Soviet activity in sending Jews and communist agents from Black Sea areas to Palestine. Lovett, unlike Clifford, saw no urgency in granting U.S. recognition to Israel ahead of Russia.[188]

A bombshell was then dropped by Secretary Marshall. He had resented the very presence of Clifford at the meeting in that he found the special counsel's participation unseemly since he felt it imposed political considerations on an issue the secretary believed should be devoid of such factors. Marshall saw honestly in Lovett's charge that Clifford's approach was political, and he believed that it would damage the presidential office.[189]

The fire seething within Marshall was then unleashed.

> I remarked to the President that, speaking objectively, I could not help but think that the suggestions made by Mr. Clifford were wrong. I thought that to adopt these suggestions would have precisely the opposite effect from that intended by Mr. Clifford. The transparent dodge to win a few more votes would not in fact achieve this purpose. The great dignity of the office of the President would be seriously diminished. The counsel offered by Mr. Clifford was based on domestic political considerations, while the problem that confronted us was international.
>
> I said bluntly that if the President were to follow Mr. Clifford's advice and if in the elections I were to vote, I would vote against the President.[190]

Marshall concluded that they should take a fresh look at the Palestine situation on May 16. President Truman, seeing that the meeting was spinning out of control, brought it to a close, stating that he was "inclined to agree with Marshall but that they should sleep on the matter."[191]

Marshall's words undoubtedly jolted the president, coming as they did from a man he considered one of the leading Americans of the century, a man of presidential stature himself. As a career Army officer, Marshall was probably more rankled than someone with a civilian political background would have been over Clifford's presence at the meeting. To Marshall, accustomed to living by a chain of command, the international nature of the Palestine question fell strictly within his purview. Since Palestine fell within his domain, someone outside that ambit, notably Clifford, with what Marshal viewed as an exclusively domestic agenda, should not be attending such a meeting, not to mention seeking to prevail on the president with his own solution to the Palestine issue.

The team of Marshall and Lovett might have temporarily dissuaded the president from acting in the direction that Clifford sought regarding Palestine, but his momentum continued in the same direction. Jewish leaders soon became aware of the substance of the May 12 White House meeting. David Ginsberg, a prominent Washington attorney who was advising the Jewish Agency, telephoned Weizmann in New York on the afternoon of the thirteenth to request that he write a personal appeal to Truman for recognition and rush it to Washington by messenger on an overnight train.[192]

Lovett sent Clifford a copy of an opinion by Ernest A. Gross, legal adviser to the State Department, which held that although there was no legal bar to recognizing the Jewish state, the United States "probably should not recognize the existence of any new state" while the General Assembly was in special session. This view represented the one taken by Lovett at the May 12 meeting, the essential point being emphasized that the United States maintain a posture consistent with that advanced by the U.S. delegation while seeking a truce in Palestine. The U.S. delegation had stressed to other nations that no action of a political nature should be taken during those deliberations to alter the status quo or prejudice the claims of either Arabs or Jews. It was seen as incongruous by Lovett and others for the United States to promote the establishment of a Jewish state while the special session continued to confront the issue of achieving a final solution.[193]

In the midst of the eleventh hour premandate termination-wrangling, Truman received Weizmann's letter, in which Zionism's leading diplomat and elder statesman made the following points.

The leadership which the American Government took under your inspiration made possible the establishment of a Jewish State, which I am convinced will contribute markedly toward a solution of the world Jewish problem, and which I am equally convinced is a necessary preliminary to the development of lasting peace among the peoples of the Near East. . . .

Considering all the difficulties, the chances for an equitable adjustment of Arab and Jewish relationships are not unfavorable. What is required now is an end to the seeking of new solutions which invariably have retarded rather than encouaged a final settlement. . . .

I deeply hope that the United States, which under your leadership has done so much to find a just solution, will promptly recognize the Provisional Government of the new Jewish State. The world, I think, will regard it as especially appropriate that the greatest living democracy should be the first to welcome the newest into the family of nations.[194]

Weizmann received his wish. The United States was the first nation to recognize the new State of Israel, while the circumstances bore an air of volatility that climaxed the tide of combative uncertainty underlying the Palestine question from the World War One years onward. Aware of Truman's feelings about recognition, Robert Lovett dropped his opposition, pleading with Clifford at 5:30 p.m. to at least delay the announcement until the General Assembly session ended, which he estimated would be about 10 o'clock. Clifford agreed to consult Truman but stressed that time was of the essence and that he doubted the president would delay his recognition announcement.

At 6:15, a vote loomed before the General Assembly on the trusteeship question, a cause the State Department had championed. Just as the vote was about to be taken on the resolution the United States had proposed, a rumor began spreading through the General Assembly chamber that caused the delegates to burst into laughter. The *New York Times* had allegedly reported that the United States had recognized the new Jewish state of Israel. U.S. delegates Philip Jessup and Francis Sayre had been among those laughing at the obviously erroneous report. After all, had such a step been taken, they would have been notified. Or would they? Alternate U.S. delegate John Ross hurried over to them, nervously informing Jessup and Sayre of the commotion erupting over the bulletin and of the demands for an answer.

An embarrassed Jessup, unable to supply an immediate answer, sent for the news ticker copy to learn what had occurred. To his astonishment, Charles Ross had announced at 6:11 from the White House:

The Government has been informed that a Jewish state has been proclaimed in Palestine, and recognition has been requested by the provisional government thereof.

The United States recognizes the provisional government as the *de facto* authority of the new State of Israel.[195]

The reason why the United States conferred de facto (in fact) rather than de jure (in law) recognition to the new state was due to its provisional nature. Despite the formal distinction, the de facto recognition was full and unconditional.

With the confirmation of the recognition report, the General Assembly disintegrated into pandemonium. Among the most angry and frustrated of the body was Ambassador Guillermo Belt of Cuba. Only three hours before the U.S. announcement recognizing Israel the Cuban ambassador had helped the United States steer the trusteeship resolution through committee. In the midst of the postannouncement confusion Ambassador Belt proclaimed his intention to rise and announce Cuba's withdrawal from the United Nations. Belt reasoned that he preferred withdrawal to membership in an organization in which a leading member was guilty of duplicity. Porter McKeever, press officer of the U.S. delegation, restrained Belt from going to the podium by sitting on him.[196]

Robert Lovett expressed his view of the tumultuous events culminating in recognition three days after the vote.

My protests against the precipitate action and warnings as to consequences with the Arab world appear to have been outweighed by considerations unknown to me, but I can only conclude that the President's political advisers, having failed last Wednesday afternoon (at the May 12 meeting) to make the President a father of the new state, have determined at least to make him the mid-wife.[197]

Besides devastating verbal blasts from Andrei Gromyko of the Soviet Union and from spokesmen from other nations, notably the Arab states, criticism was also leveled by U.S. Ambassador Warren Austin and Eleanor Roosevelt in letters to Secretary Marshall as a result of the inept handling of the recognition question respecting the General Assembly. Austin lamented, "Nobody trusts us anymore." Mrs. Roosevelt quoted several delegates as having "stated quite frankly that they don't see how they could ever follow the United States' lead because the United States changed so often without any consultation." Austin believed that Arab anger was understandable, but pointed out that other nations felt they had been double-crossed.[198]

Far away from the scene of controversy in New York an event of great significance was occurring. A smartly attired Scot, wearing the freshly pressed uniform of a general of the British Royal Artillery, stepped out of the entrance of his Jerusalem residence and took one last look at the sweeping historical panorama at his feet. There it was, the Old Walled City, the scene of so many dramatic events throughout the annals of history. It stood there ancient and unchanging, spread upon its barren hilltop.

Sir Alan Cunningham, the British high commissioner, was presiding over his final ceremony marking the end of British rule in Palestine. A British Mandate that had begun with a post–World War One wave of hopeful expectation was ending with the painful knowledge of imminent warfare. There below the garden wall where Cunningham stood some 160,000 people awaited his departure before commencing deadly combat for land each felt entitled to by the will of God.

On the balcony of the high commissioner's residence at seven o'clock of May 14, 1948 five soldiers of the Highland Light infantry stood at attention. A bugle sound in the crisp morning air drew General Cunningham to attention as well. As bagpipes began to play the Union Jack descended from its proud perch. With that final symbolic act, the thirty-year British Mandate ended. Rather than resolving problems, as was hopefully anticipated at the outset, difficulties and tragedies compounded until, by the Mandate's end, Britishers felt the same shell-shocked bewilderment that Americans would experience after the final U.S. troops were withdrawn from Vietnam and Russians felt regarding the Afghanistan conflict. Incidents and problems grew until, by the end, British soldiers and policemen in Palestine reeled under the painful ordeal of trying to maintain order in a hostile setting where each warring group detested their presence.

The ceremony concluded, Sir Alan Cunningham climbed into the black limousine that would take him on his final Palestine journey to the airport. It was a four-ton armored Daimler built for King George VI to transport him through the streets of blitz-ridden London during the war. The very act of Attlee's sending it to his High Commissioner of Palestine to enhance his safety provided silent commentary of the gravity pervading Britain over the climate of 1948 Palestine. In the past Cunningham had refused to ride in the Daimler, but for his final journey across Jerusalem he would, in response to formal orders from his security officer.

Before he stepped into the automobile, Sir Alan took one last stroll along the paths of the garden of his residence. He pondered the many occasions when he had amidst the scent of his roses, contemplated the fate of a condemned Jewish prisoner or struggled to forget the sight of British bodies mangled by terrorist bombs.

Thirty years had passed and the lines were clearly drawn for battle. The impasse remained between Arabs and Jews. Just as Ben-Gurion and Antonius had failed to reach agreement, the conflicting parties in the 1948 environment prepared for the first of many Arab-Israeli wars.

Today, following much warfare and bloodshed, the influence of Ben-Gurion continues to be felt through the presence of protégé Shimon Peres, who as Israeli Foreign Minister has guided a peace process leading to the once unthinkable, an agreement with PLO chief Yassir Arafat, and the highly improbable, an accord with Jordan's King Hussein. Israeli Prime Minister Yitzhak Rabin reflected on the painful bloodshed of Middle East conflict during White House ceremonies announcing both agreements. The former Israeli general and hero of the 1967 Six Day War referred to the loss of life on both sides, as well as the burning desire felt by so many Israelis for peace. He emphasized this point in his dramatic meeting with Hussein by bringing some of these individuals to Washington for the event.

While Rabin and Peres have staked the Labor Party's future to a policy of negotiation and an ongoing peace initiative with the Arab world, they remain mindful of voices of discord from the more fundamentally based Israeli right, many of whom are West Bank settlers and recent arrivals in Israel. Arafat and King Hussein have their own bitter critics, as evidenced by terrorist activity in the immediate wake of both accords.

Bold new ground is being staked out by Jews and Arabs. Warring rivals have examined the harsh reality of "an eye for an eye leaves both sides blind," and now seek to forge a peaceful future.

# Notes

## Chapter One

1. Otto Nathan and Heinz Norden, editors, *Einstein on Peace* (New York: Schocken Books, 1968), p. 467–468.
2. Nathan and Norden, *Einstein on Peace*, p. 529.
3. *New York Times*, June 12, 1953.
4. Nathan and Norden, *Einstein on Peace*, p. 3–4.
5. Nathan and Norden, *Einstein on Peace*, p. 4–7.
6. Ronald W. Clark, *Einstein: The Life and Times* (New York: World Publishing, 1971), p. 376–377.
7. Clark, *Einstein*, p. 378.
8. Clark, *Einstein*, p. 379.
9. Clark, *Einstein*, p. 379–380.
10. Clark, *Einstein*, p. 381.
11. Clark, *Einstein*, p. 402.
12. Clark, *Einstein*, p. 550–556.
13. Clark, *Einstein*, p. 558.
14. Clark, *Einstein*, p. 554.
15. Clark, *Einstein*, p. 619.
16. Nathan and Norden, *Einstein on Peace*, p. 637.
17. Nathan and Norden, *Einstein on Peace*, p. 639.
18. Nathan and Norden, *Einstein on Peace*, p. 639–640.

## Chapter Two

1. Walter Laqueur, *A History of Zionism* (New York: Shocken Books, 1976), p. 84.

2. Jay Y. Gonen, *A Psychohistory of Zionism* (New York: New American Library, 1975), p. 29–31.

3. Gonen, *A Psychohistory*, p. 31.

4. Laqueur, *A History of Zionism*, p. 72.

5. Laqueur, *A History of Zionism*, p. 74.

6. Laqueur, *A History of Zionism*, p. 92–94.

7. Uri Avnery, *Israel Without Zionists* (New York: MacMillan, 1968), p. 41.

8. Avnery, *Israel Without Zionists*, p. 42.

9. Gonen, *A Psychohistory*, p. 53.

10. Gonen, *A Pshchohistory*, p. 78.

## Chapter Three

1. Koran 96:1.

2. Koran 74:1.

3. Philip K. Hitti, *The Arabs: A Short History for Americans* (New York, St. Martin's Press, 1968), p. 28.

4. Hitti, *The Arabs: A Short History*, p. 30.

5. Hitti, *The Arabs: A Short History*, p. 185.

6. Hitti, *The Arabs: A Short History*, p. 194.

7. Hitti, *The Arabs: A Short History*, p. 196.

## Chapter Four

1. Michael Yardley, *A Biography: T. E. Lawrence* (New York: Stein and Day, 1987), p. 28.

2. Richard Percival Graves, *Lawrence of Arabia and His World* (New York: Scribner's, 1976), p. 17.

3. Graves, *Lawrence*, p. 26.

4. Graves, *Lawrence*, p. 28.

5. T. E. Lawrence, *The Seven Pillars of Wisdom* (New York: Doubleday, 1935), p. 106.

6. Ibid.

7. Ibid.

8. Ibid.

9. Ibid.

10. Liddell Hart, *Colonel Lawrence* (London: Faber, 1938), p. 125.

11. Hart, *Colonel Lawrence*, p. 131.

12. Hart, *Colonel Lawrence*, p. 131–132.

13. Hart, *Colonel Lawrence*, p. 133.

14. Hart, *Colonel Lawrence*, p. 137–138.

15. Hart, *Colonel Lawrence*, p. 135.

16. Lawrence, *Seven Pillars*, p. 23–24.

17. Lowell Thomas, *With Lawrence in Arabia* (New York: Grosset and Dunlap, 1924), p. 114.

18. Ibid.

19. Fred J. Khouri, *The Arab-Israeli Dilemma* (Syracuse University Press, 1985), p. 9.

20. Hart, *Colonel Lawrence*, p. 169.

21. Hart, *Colonel Lawrence*, p. 171.

22. Hart, *Colonel Lawrence*, p. 172.

23. Ibid.

24. Ibid.

25. Ibid.

26. Thomas, *With Lawrence*, p. 100.

27. Thomas, *With Lawrence*, p. 104.

28. Hart, *Colonel Lawrence*, p. 170.

29. Graves, *Lawrence and His World*, p. 64.

30. Graves, *Lawrence and His World*, p. 66.

31. Yardley, *A Biography*, p. 121.

32. Ibid.

33. Ibid.

34. Lawrence, *Seven Pillars*, p. 654.

35. Ibid.

36. Sir Alec Seith Kirkbride, *An Awakening: The Arab Campaign* (University Press of Arabia, 1971), p. 91.

37. Phillip Knightley and Colin Simpson, *The Secret Lives of Lawrence of Arabia* (London: Nelson, 1969), p. 89.

38. Knightley and Simpson, *Secret Lives*, p. 96.

39. Thomas, *With Lawrence*, p. 246.

40. Humanities Research Center, University of Texas, Austin, Texas.

41. Lawrence, *Seven Pillars*, Chapter LXXX.

42. *Middle East Diary, 1917–1956* (Crescent Press, 1959), p. 32.

43. Desmond Stewart, *T. E. Lawrence: A New Biography* (New York: Harper and Row, 1977), p. 240–241.

44. Hart, *Colonel Lawrence*, p. 222.

## Chapter Five

1. Dan Kurzman, *Ben-Gurion: Prophet of Fire* (New York: Simon and Schuster, 1983), p. 74.

2. Kurzman, *Ben-Gurion*, p. 77.

3. Larry Collins and Dominique Lapierre, *O Jerusalem!* (New York: Simon and Schuster, 1972), p. 23.

4. Kurzman, *Ben-Gurion*, p. 52.

5. Ibid.

6. Kurzman, *Ben-Gurion*, p. 58.

7. Kurzman, *Ben-Gurion*, p. 56.

8. David Ben-Gurion in talks with Moshe Pearlman, *Ben Gurion Looks Back* (New York: Simon and Schuster, 1965), p. 20.

9. Ibid.

10. Ibid.

11. Leo W. Schwarz, editor, *Great Ages and Ideas of the Jewish People* (New York: Modern Library, 1956), p. 43.

12. Schwarz, editor, *Great Ages*, p. 64.

13. Kurzman, *Ben-Gurion*, p. 63.

14. Ben-Gurion and Pearlman, *Ben Gurion Looks Back*, p. 23.

15. Shabtai Teveth, *Ben-Gurion: The Burning Ground 1886–1948* (Boston: Houghton Mifflin, 1987), p. 60.

16. Teveth, *The Burning Ground*, p. 62.

17. Jehuda Reinharz, *Chaim Weizmann: The Making of a Zionist Leader* (New York: Oxford University Press, 1985), p. 13–14.

18. Reinharz, *The Making of a Zionist Leader*, p. 18–19.

19. Reinharz, *The Making of a Zionist Leader*, p. 36.

20. Chaim Weizmann, *Trial and Error: The Autobiography of Chaim Weizmann* (New York: Harper, 1949), p. 45.

21. Weizmann, *Trial and Error*, p. 52.

22. Reinharz, *The Making of a Zionist Leader*, p. 139–140.

23. Weizmann to Theodor Herzl, May 6, 1903, Weizmann Letters, 2, p. 313.

24. Reinharz, *The Making of a Zionist Leader*, p. 85.

25. Weizmann to Vera, July 6–7, 1901, Weizmann Letters, 1, p. 152–153. Italics in original.

26. Reinharz, *The Making of a Zionist Leader*, p. 79.

27. Weizmann to Theodor Herzl, May 6, 1903, Weizmann Letters, 2, p. 307.

28. Reinharz, *The Making of a Zionist Leader*, p. 174.

29. Weizmann, *Trial and Error*, p. 86.

30. Ibid.

31. Weizmann, *Trial and Error*, p. 90.

32. Weizmann, *Trial and Error*, p. 93.

33. Weizmann, *Trial and Error*, p. 109–111.

34. Weizmann, *Trial and Error*, p. 112.

35. Kurzman, *Ben-Gurion*, p. 85.

36. Kurzman, *Ben-Gurion*, p. 86.

37. Ibid.

38. Amos Perlmutter, *Israel: The Partitioned State* (New York: Scribner's, 1985), p. 44.

39. Perlmutter, *The Partitioned State*, p. 45.

40. Ben-Gurion and Pearlman, *Ben Gurion Looks Back*, p. 54.

41. Kurzman, *Ben-Gurion*, p. 54.

42. Kurzman, *Ben-Gurion*, p. 119.

43. Teveth, *The Burning Ground*, p. 121.
44. Ibid.
45. Teveth, *The Burning Ground*, p. 120.
46. Kurzman, *Ben-Gurion*, p. 196.
47. Teveth, *The Burning Ground*, p. 120.
48. Kurzman, *Ben-Gurion*, p. 122–123.
49. Kurzman, *Ben-Gurion*, p. 164.
50. Norman Rose, *Chaim Weizmann* (New York: Penguin, 1986), p. 145.
51. Rose, *Chaim Weizmann*, p. 158.
52. Weizmann, *Trial and Error*, p. 200.
53. Weizmann, *Trial and Error*, p. 194.
54. Weizmann, *Trial and Error*, p. 193.
55. Weizmann, *Trial and Error*, p. 203.
56. Weizmann, *Trial and Error*, p. 206.
57. Ibid.
58. Ibid.
59. Weizmann, *Trial and Error*, p. 208.
60. Harold Wilson, *A Prime Minister on Prime Ministers* (New York: Summit, 1977), p. 132.

## Chapter Six

1. Arthur Koestler, *Promise and Fulfillment* (New York: MacMillan, 1949), p. 4.
2. Doreen Ingrams, *Palestine Papers 1917–1922, Seeds of Conflict* (London: John Murray, 1972), p. 89.
3. Rose, *Chaim Weizmann*, p. 179.
4. Ibid.
5. Ibid.
6. Rose, *Chaim Weizmann*, p. 191.
7. Ibid.
8. Ibid.
9. Ibid.
10. Kurzman, *Ben-Gurion*, p. 129.
11. Ben-Gurion Diaries, p. 39.
12. Kurzman, *Ben-Gurion*, p. 136.
13. Kurzman, *Ben-Gurion*, p. 136–137.
14. Rose, *Chaim Weizmann*, p. 194.
15. Rose, *Chaim Weizmann*, p. 197.
16. Ibid.
17. Rose, *Chaim Weizmann*, p. 257.
18. Ibid.
19. Rose, *Chaim Weizmann*, p. 198.
20. Rose, *Chaim Weizmann*, p. 199.

21. Khouri, *The Arab-Israeli Dilemma*, p. 12.
22. Ibid.
23. Khouri, *The Arab-Israeli Dilemma*, p. 11.
24. Khouri, *The Arab-Israeli Dilemma*, p. 8.
25. Ibid.
26. Khouri, *The Arab-Israeli Dilemma*, p. 8–9.
27. Khouri, *The Arab-Israeli Dilemma*, p. 9.
28. Ibid.
29. Khouri, *The Arab-Israeli Dilemma*, p. 10.
30. Ibid.
31. Khouri, *The Arab-Israeli Dilemma*, p. 12.
32. Rose, *Chaim Weizmann*, p. 201.
33. Ibid.
34. Rose, *Chaim Weizmann*, p. 200.
35. Khouri, *The Arab-Israeli Dilemma*, p. 12.
36. Khouri, *The Arab-Israeli Dilemma*, p. 13.
37. Ibid.
38. Laqueur, *A History of Zionism*, p. 452.
39. Khouri, *The Arab-Israeli Dilemma*, p. 13.
40. Ibid.
41. Rose, *Chaim Weizmann*, p. 200–201.
42. John H. Davis, *The Evasive Peace: A Study of the Zionist-Arab Problem* (Cleveland: Dillon-Liederbach, 1976), p. 17.
43. Davis, *The Evasive Peace*, p. 18.
44. Khouri, *The Arab-Israeli Dilemma*, p. 11.
45. Henry Cattan, *The Palestine Question* (London: Croom Helm, 1988), p. 20.
46. Cattan, *The Palestine Question*, p. 20–21.
47. Dana Adams Schmidt, *Armageddon in the Middle East* (New York: John Day, 1974), p. 8.
48. Khouri, *The Arab-Israeli Dilemma*, p. 14.
49. Ibid.
50. Ibid.
51. Khouri, *The Arab-Israeli Dilemma*, p. 15.
52. Rose, *Chaim Weizmann*, p. 202.
53. Rose, *Chaim Weizmann*, p. 202–203.
54. Rose, *Chaim Weizmann*, p. 203.
55. Davis, *The Evasive Peace*, p. 19–20.
56. Davis, *The Evasive Peace*, p. 20.
57. Ibid.
58. Rose, *Chaim Weizmann*, p. 204.
59. Cattan, *The Palestine Question*, p. 22.
60. Cattan, *The Palestine Question*, p. 24.
61. Rose, *Chaim Weizmann*, p. 206.

62. Rose, *Chaim Weizmann*, p. 207.
63. Ibid.
64. Rose, *Chaim Weizmann*, p. 208.
65. Rose, *Chaim Weizmann*, p. 210.
66. Rose, *Chaim Weizmann*, p. 209–210.
67. Rose, *Chaim Weizmann*, p. 211.
68. Rose, *Chaim Weizmann*, p. 214.
69. Kurzman, *Ben-Gurion*, p. 144.

## Chapter Seven

1. See Davis, *The Evasive Peace*, p. 21, and Rose, *Chaim Weizmann*, p. 212.
2. Government of Palestine, *Survey of Palestine, Volume 1* (Palestine Government Printing Press, 1946), p. 18–25.
3. Khouri, *The Arab-Israeli Dilemma*, p. 17.
4. Nicholas Bethell, *The Palestine Triangle* (London: Andre Deutsch, 1979), p. 21.
5. Ben-Gurion and Pearlman, *Ben Gurion Looks Back*, p. 67.
6. Professor John Gerstang, *The Observer*, September 20, 1936.
7. Amos Elon, *The Israelis: Founders and Sons* (New York: Holt, Rinehart and Winston, 1971), p. 109–110.
8. Elon, *The Israelis*, p. 158.
9. Kurzman, *Ben-Gurion*, p. 149–150.
10. Kurzman, *Ben-Gurion*, p. 154.
11. Kurzman, *Ben-Gurion*, p. 155.
12. Kurzman, *Ben-Gurion*, p. 156.
13. Ibid.
14. Khouri, *The Arab-Israeli Dilemma*, p. 18.
15. Davis, *The Evasive Peace*, p. 22.
16. Khouri, *The Arab-Israeli Dilemma*, p. 19–20.
17. Khouri, *The Arab-Israeli Dilemma*, p. 22–23.
18. Kurzman, *Ben-Gurion*, p. 175.
19. Ibid.
20. Kurzman, *Ben-Gurion*, p. 176.
21. Kurzman, *Ben-Gurion*, p. 177.
22. Rose, *Chaim Weizmann*, p. 290.
23. Ibid.
24. Kurzman, *Ben-Gurion*, p. 178.
25. Kurzman, *Ben-Gurion*, p. 179.
26. Rose, *Chaim Weizmann*, p. 291.
27. Kurzman, *Ben-Gurion*, p. 179.
28. Rose, *Chaim Weizmann*, p. 292.
29. Khouri, *The Arab-Israeli Dilemma*, p. 24.

30. Harold Wilson, *The Chariot of Israel: Britain, America and the State of Israel* (New York: Norton, 1981), p. 93.

31. Khouri, *The Arab-Israeli Dilemma*, p. 24–25.

## Chapter Eight

1. Adolf Hitler, *Mein Kampf* (Boston: Houghton Mifflin, 1943), p. 57.

2. Hitler, *Mein Kampf*, p. 57–58.

3. Laqueur, *A History of Zionism*, p. 406.

4. Laqueur, *A History of Zionism*, p. 404–406.

5. Laqueur, *A History of Zionism*, p. 406–407.

6. Otto Friedrich, *Time*, August 28 and September 4, 1989.

7. Konrad Heiden, *Der Fuehrer: Hitler's Rise to Power* (Boston: Houghton Mifflin, 1944), p. 5–10.

8. H. A. Overstreet, *The Mature Mind* (New York: Norton, 1949), p. 30.

9. *Time*, August 28, 1989.

10. Sumner Welles, *The Time for Decision* (New York: Harper, 1944), p. 47–48.

11. William L. Shirer, *The Rise and Fall of the Third Reich* (New York: Simon and Schuster, 1960), p. 14–17.

12. Shirer, *Third Reich*, p. 99.

13. Ibid.

14. Otto Friedrich, *Time*, August 28, 1989.

15. Ibid.

16. Hitler, *Mein Kampf*, p. 295–296.

17. Hitler, *Mein Kampf*, p. 296.

18. Arthur D. Morse, *While Six Million Died: A Chronicle of American Apathy* (New York: Random House, 1968), p. 231.

19. Morse, *While Six Million Died*, p. 230–231.

20. Kurzman, *Ben-Gurion*, p. 182.

21. Kurzman, *Ben-Gurion*, p. 184.

22. Kurzman, *Ben-Gurion*, p. 186.

23. Ibid.

24. Kurzman, *Ben-Gurion*, p. 192.

25. Kurzman, *Ben-Gurion*, p. 193.

26. Ibid.

27. Kurzman, *Ben-Gurion*, p. 194.

28. Elon, *The Israelis*, p. 182.

29. Elon, *The Israelis*, p. 183.

30. Ibid.

32. Ibid.

32. Bethell, *The Palestine Triangle*, p. 30.

33. Bethell, *The Palestine Triangle*, p. 32.

34. Palestine Royal Commission Report, July 1937, Minutes 5648.

35. *Jewish Chronicle*, July 16, 1937.
36. Bethell, *The Palestine Triangle*, p. 33.
37. Ibid.
38. Bethell, *The Palestine Triangle*, p. 37.
39. Bethell, *The Palestine Triangle*, p. 41.
40. Ibid.
41. Ibid.
42. British Foreign Office Records, 371 21863.
43. Bethell, *The Palestine Triangle*, p. 43–44.
44. Bethell, *The Palestine Triangle*, p. 61.
45. Bethell, *The Palestine Triangle*, p. 64.
46. Foreign Office Records, 371 23232.
47. Bethell, *The Palestine Triangle*, p. 66.
48. Bethell, *The Palestine Triangle*, p. 67.
49. Teveth, *The Burning Ground*, p. 712.
50. Ibid.
51. Ibid.
52. Bethell, *The Palestine Triangle*, p. 69.
53. Ibid.
54. Ibid.
55. Bethell, *The Palestine Triangle*, p. 69–70.
56. *Manchester Guardian*, August 18, 1939.
57. Foreign Office Records, 371 23237.
58. Kurzman, *Ben-Gurion*, p. 224.
59. Kurzman, *Ben-Gurion*, p. 227.
60. Kurzman, *Ben-Gurion*, p. 228.
61. Ibid.
62. Excerpted in *Witness to the Holocaust* by Azriel Eisenberg (New York: Pilgrim Press, 1981), p. 198, 200.
63. Eisenberg, *Witness to the Holocaust*, p. 201–202.
64. Shirer, *Third Reich*, p. 970–971.
65. Eisenberg, *Witness to the Holocaust*, p. 218.
66. Foreword by Elie Wiesel from *Voices from the Holocaust*, edited by Sylvia Rothchild (New York: New American Library, 1981), p. 1–2.
67. Wiesel, *Voices from the Holocaust*, p. 4.
68. *New York Times*, March 16, 1938.
69. *New York Times*, March 20, 1938.
70. Morse, *While Six Million Died*, p. 224–225.
71. Bethell, *The Palestine Triangle*, p. 113.
72. See Bethell, *The Palestine Triangle*, p. 113, and Laqueur, *A History of Zionism*, p. 535.
73. See Arthur D. Morse for a detailed account.
74. *Jewish Frontier*, October 1943, p. 29.
75. Laqueur, *A History of Zionism*, p. 534–535.

76. Rose, *Chaim Weizmann*, p. 387.
77. Biltmore Declaration, May 11, 1942.
78. Rose, *Chaim Weizmann*, p. 377.
79. Ibid.
80. Teveth, *The Burning Ground*, p. 826.
81. Khouri, *The Arab-Israeli Dilemma*, p. 28.
82. Laqueur, *A History of Zionism*, p. 535.
83. Bethell, *The Palestine Triangle*, p. 135.
84. Morse, *While Six Million Died*, p. 320.
85. Morse, *While Six Million Died*, p. 3, 321.
86. Shirer, *Third Reich*, p. 911–913, 919–920.
87. Bethell, *The Palestine Triangle*, p. 135.
88. Morse, *While Six Million Died*, p. 48.
89. Morse, *While Six Million Died*, p. 61.
90. Morse, *While Six Million Died*, p. 323.

## Chapter Nine

1. Don Cook, *Ten Men and History* (New York: Doubleday, 1981), p. 5.
2. Cook, *Ten Men and History*, p. 1–8, 13, 17.
3. Ben-Gurion and Pearlman, *Ben Gurion Looks Back*, p. 71.
4. Wilson, *The Chariot of Israel*, p. 125.
5. Ibid.
6. Trevor Burridge, *Clement Attlee: A Political Biography* (London: Jonathan Cape, 1985), p. 252.
7. Ibid.
8. Labor Party Conference Reports, 1944, p. 9.
9. Wilson, *The Chariot of Israel*, p. 125.
10. Wilson, *The Chariot of Israel*, p. 126.
11. Cook, *Ten Men and History*, p. 24–25.
12. Cook, *Ten Men and History*, p. 24.
13. Cook, *Ten Men and History*, p. 17.
14. Burridge, *Clement Atlee*, p. 205.
15. *Look*, May 23, 1939.
16. Ibid.
17. Laqueur, *A History of Zionism*, p. 550.
18. Kurzman, *Ben-Gurion*, p. 243.
19. Ibid.
20. Ibid.
21. Ibid.
22. Kurzman, *Ben-Gurion*, p. 244.
23. Kurzman, *Ben-Gurion*, p. 246.
24. Kurzman, *Ben-Gurion*, p. 249–250.

25. Edward Tivnan, *The Lobby: Jewish Political Power and American Foreign Policy* (New York: Simon and Schuster, 1987), p. 23–24.

26. Bethell, *The Palestine Triangle*, p. 127.

27. Geoffrey Morton, *Just the Job* (London: Hodder and Stoughton, 1957), p. 144.

28. Colonial Office Records, 733 445.

29. Bethell, *The Palestine Triangle*, p. 128.

30. Bethell, *The Palestine Triangle*, p. 129.

31. Ibid.

32. Weizmann, *Trial and Error*, p. 436.

33. Bethell, *The Palestine Triangle*, p. 181.

34. Ibid.

35. Rose, *Chaim Weizmann*, p. 386.

36. Weizmann, *Trial and Error*, p. 437–438.

37. Bethell, *The Palestine Triangle*, p. 183.

38. Colonial Office Records, 733 461.

39. Bethell, *The Palestine Triangle*, p. 186.

40. Foreign Office Records, 371 41516.

41. Bethell, *The Palestine Triangle*, p. 186–187.

42. Bethell, *The Palestine Triangle*, p. 187.

43. Colonial Office Records, 733 461.

44. Bethell, *The Palestine Triangle*, p. 187.

45. Ibid.

46. Bethell, *The Palestine Triangle*, p. 188.

47. War Office Records, 169 19758.

48. Bethell, *The Palestine Triangle*, p. 190.

49. Richard Crossman, *A Nation Reborn* (London: Hamish Hamilton, 1960), p. 62.

50. Bethell, *The Palestine Triangle*, p. 201.

51. Prime Minister's Office Records, 8/89. The message does not seem to have been conveyed to Attlee personally until September 10 by Secretary of State James Byrnes. See Overdale, "The Palestine Policy of the British Labour Government 1945–1946" in *International Affairs*, July 1979.

52. Francis Williams, editor, *A Prime Minister Remembers: The War Memoirs of the Rt. Hon. Earl Attlee* (London: Heinemann, 1961), p. 189.

53. Burridge, *Clement Attlee*, p. 256.

54. Ibid.

55. Cook, *Ten Men and History*, p. 1.

56. Cook, *Ten Men and History*, p. 3.

57. Ibid.

58. Martin Gilbert, *Winston S. Churchill: Never Despair 1945–1965* (Boston: Houghton Mifflin, 1988), p. 829.

59. Rose, *Chaim Weizmann*, p. 406–407.

60. Burridge, *Clement Attlee*, p. 257.

61. Jon and David Kimche, *Both Sides of the Hill: Britain and the Palestine War* (London: Secker and Warburg, 1960), p. 22.

62. Koestler, *Promise and Fulfillment*, p. 116.

63. Rose, *Chaim Weizmann*, p. 403.

64. Dean Acheson, *Sketches from Life of Men I Have Known* (New York: Harper, 1959), p. 21.

65. Acheson, *Sketches from Life*, p. 28.

66. Rose, *Chaim Weizmann*, p. 405–406.

67. Rose, *Chaim Weizmann*, p. 403–404.

68. Eric Silver, *Begin: The Haunted Prophet* (New York: Random House, 1984), p. 65–66.

69. Silver, *Begin: The Haunted Prophet*, p. 66.

70. Bethell, *The Palestine Triangle*, p. 254.

71. Ibid.

72. Foreign Office Records, 371 52539.

73. Foreign Office Records, 371 52542.

74. Foreign Office Records, 371 52538.

75. Bethell, *The Palestine Triangle*, p. 257.

76. Ibid.

77. Bethell, *The Palestine Triangle*, p. 258.

78. Silver, *Begin: The Haunted Prophet*, p. 70.

79. Bethell, *The Palestine Triangle*, p. 258.

80. Silver, *Begin: The Haunted Prophet*, p. 72.

81. Ibid.

82. Silver, *Begin: The Haunted Prophet*, p. 73.

83. Kurzman, *Ben-Gurion*, p. 267–268.

84. Weizmann, *Trial and Error*, p. 442.

85. Kurzman, *Ben-Gurion*, p. 268.

86. Rose, *Chaim Weizmann*, p. 419.

87. Rose, *Chaim Weizmann*, p. 419–420.

88. Rose, *Chaim Weizmann*, p. 420.

89. Koestler, *Promise and Fulfillment*, p. 146–148.

90. Koestler, *Promise and Fulfillment*, p. 150.

91. See Rose, *Chaim Weizmann*, p. 425 and Koestler, *Promise and Fulfillment*, p. 150.

92. Kimche and Kimche, *Both Sides of the Hill*, p. 23.

93. Ibid.

94. Ibid.

95. Ibid.

96. Burridge, *Clement Attlee*, p. 259–260.

97. Foreign Office Records, 371 52546.

98. Ibid.

99. Herbert Feis, *The Birth of Israel: The Tousled Diplomatic Bed* (New York: Norton, 1969), p. 34.

100. Feis, *The Birth of Israel*, p. 34–35.

101. Dean Acheson, *Present at the Creation: My Years in the State Department* (New York: Norton, 1969), p. 176.

102. Feis, *The Birth of Israel*, p. 34.

103. Wilson, *The Chariot of Israel*, p. 235–236.

104. Gilbert, *Never Despair*, p. 115.

105. Burridge, *Clement Attlee*, p. 267.

106. Ibid.

107. Harry S Truman, *Memoirs by Harry S Truman: Volume One: Year of Decision* (New York: Doubleday, 1955), p. 68–69.

108. Truman, *Memoirs*, p. 69.

109. Feis, *The Birth of Israel*, p. 35.

110. Forrest C. Pogue, *George C. Marshall: Statesman 1945–1959* (New York: Viking Penguin, 1987), p. 346.

111. Pogue, *George C. Marshall*, p. 341–342.

112. Bethell, *The Palestine Triangle*, p. 336.

113. Pogue, *George C. Marshall*, p. 343.

114. Feis, *The Birth of Israel*, p. 38.

115. Jorge García-Granados, *The Birth of Israel* (New York: Knopf, 1948), p. 19.

116. Feis, *The Birth of Israel*, p. 78.

117. Ibid.

118. Pogue, *George C. Marshall*, p. 344.

119. Ibid.

120. Pogue, *George C. Marshall*, p. 346.

121. Ibid.

122. Pogue, *George C. Marshall*, p. 347.

123. Memo of conversation between Ambassador Wadsworth and Arab delegates, by Samuel Kopper, October 30, 1947, Foreign Relations of the United States 1947, V, 1177–1178.

124. Pogue, *George C. Marshall*, p. 350.

125. British Embassy to State Department, October 31, 1947, Foreign Relations of the United States 1947, V, 1227–1238.

126. Secretary of State to Austin, November 12, 1947, Foreign Relations of the United States 1947, V, 1255–1256.

127. *New York Times*, October 7, 1946.

128. Robert J. Donovan, *Conflict and Crisis: The Presidency of Harry S Truman, 1945–1948* (New York: Norton, 1977), p. 321.

129. Ibid.

130. Donovan, *Conflict and Crisis*, p. 316.

131. Donovan, *Conflict and Crisis*, p. 317.

132. Peter Grose, *Israel in the Mind of America* (New York: Knopf, 1983), p. 229.

133. Donovan, *Conflict and Crisis*, p. 319.

134. John Morton Blum, *The Price of Vision: The Diary of Henry A. Wallace, 1942–1946* (Boston, 1973), p. 606–607.

135. Donovan, *Conflict and Crisis*, p. 327.

136. Lovett to Warren R. Austin, Foreign Relations of the United States 1947, V, p. 1269–1270.

137. Donovan, *Conflict and Crisis*, p. 327.

138. Ibid.

139. Robert M. McClintock memorandum, November 19, 1947, Foreign Relations of the United States 1947, V, p. 1271–1272.

140. Donovan, *Conflict and Crisis*, p. 328.

141. Weizmann, *Trial and Error*, p. 459.

142. Truman memorandum to Lovett, December 11, 1947, Foreign Relations of the United States 1947, V, p. 1309.

143. Donovan, *Conflict and Crisis*, p. 329.

144. Ibid.

145. Feis, *The Birth of Israel*, p. 45.

146. John Snetsinger, *Truman, the Jewish Vote, and the Creation of Israel* (Palo Alto, Calif.: Stanford University Press, 1974), p. 70–71.

147. Donovan, *Conflict and Crisis*, p. 329–330.

148. Donovan, *Conflict and Crisis*, p. 330.

149. Ibid.

150. Ibid.

151. Llewellyn E. Thompson memorandum to Loy Henderson, December 18, 1947. Tab 9, Policy Planning Staff no. 19, January 19, 1948, Diplomatic Branch, National Archives, Washington, D.C.

152. Foreign Relations of the United States 1947, V, p. 1307.

153. Kurzman, *Ben-Gurion*, p. 274.

154. Feis, *The Birth of Israel*, p. 46.

155. Donovan, *Conflict and Crisis*, p. 331.

156. Feis, *The Birth of Israel*, p. 48–49.

157. Khouri, *The Arab-Israeli Dilemma*, p. 68.

158. Memorandum, Loy Henderson to Marshall, November 10, 1947, Foreign Relations of the United States 1947, V, p. 1249.

159. Donovan, *Conflict and Crisis*, p. 370.

160. Donovan, *Conflict and Crisis*, p. 370–371.

161. Donovan, *Conflict and Crisis*, p. 371.

162. Pogue, *George C. Marshall*, p. 356.

163. Pogue, *George C. Marshall*, p. 357.

164. Ibid.

165. Ed. note, Foreign Relations of the United States 1948, V, 632–633.

166. Pogue, *George C. Marshall*, p. 358.

167. Donovan, *Conflict and Crisis*, p. 372.

168. "The Department of State to President Truman," Foreign Relations of the United States 1948, V, pt. 2, February 21, 1948, p. 637–640.

169. Donovan, *Conflict and Crisis*, p. 373.

170. Donovan, *Conflict and Crisis*, p. 373–374.

171. Donovan, *Conflict and Crisis*, p. 374.

172. Donovan, *Conflict and Crisis*, p. 373–374.

173. Merle Miller, *Plain Speaking: An Oral Biography of Harry S Truman* (New York: Berkley, 1974), p. 217.

174. Donovan, *Conflict and Crisis*, p. 374–375.

175. Collins and Lapierre, *O Jerusalem!*, p. 218–219.

176. Donovan, *Conflict and Crisis*, p. 376.

177. Ibid.

178. Presidential Papers, 1948, p. 190–191.

179. Donovan, *Conflict and Crisis*, p. 376.

180. Pogue, *George C. Marshall*, p. 371.

181. Donovan, *Conflict and Crisis*, p. 375.

182. Foreign Relations of the United States 1948, V, pt. 2, p. 842–843.

183. Macatee to Marshall, March 22, 1948, Foreign Relations of the United States 1948, V, pt. 2, p. 753.

184. Donovan, *Conflict and Crisis*, p. 379–380.

185. Donovan, *Conflict and Crisis*, p. 380.

186. "Memorandum of Conversation, by the Secretary of State," May 12, 1948, Foreign Relations of the United States 1948, V, pt. 2, p. 972–976.

187. Pogue, *George C. Marshall*, p. 370–371.

188. Donovan, *Conflict and Crisis*, p. 381–382.

189. Pogue, *George C. Marshall*, p. 371.

190. Donovan, *Conflict and Crisis*, p. 382.

191. Pogue, *George C. Marshall*, p. 371–372.

192. Donovan, *Conflict and Crisis*, p. 382.

193. Donovan, *Conflict and Crisis*, p. 382–383.

194. Weizmann, *Trial and Error*, p. 477–478.

195. Presidential Papers, 1948, p. 258.

196. Donovan, *Conflict and Crisis*, p. 385.

197. Donovan, *Conflict and Crisis*, p. 384.

198. Pogue, *George C. Marshall*, p. 372–373.

# Bibliography

Acheson, Dean, *Present at the Creation: My Years in the State Department* (New York: Norton, 1969).

Acheson, Dean, *Sketches from Life of Men I Have Known* (New York: Harper, 1959).

Avnery, Uri, *Israel Without Zionists* (New York: Macmillan, 1968).

Ben-Gurion, David, in talks with Pearlman, Moshe, *Ben-Gurion Looks Back* (New York: Simon and Schuster, 1965).

Bethell, Nicholas, *The Palestine Triangle* (London; Andre Deutsch, 1979).

Biltmore Declaration, May 11, 1942.

Blum, John Morton, *The Price of Vision: The Diary of Henry A. Wallace, 1942–1946* (Boston, 1973).

British Colonial Office Records, 733, 445, 733, 461.

British Foreign Office Records, 371 23232, 371 23237, 371 41516, 317 52538, 371 52539, 371 52542, 371 52546.

British Labor Party Conference Reports, 1944.

British Prime Minister's Office Records, 8/89.

Burridge, Trevor, *Clement Attlee: A Political Biography* (London: Jonathon Cape, 1985).

Cattan, Henry, *The Palestine Question* (London: Croom Helm, 1988).

Clark, Ronald W., *Einstein: The Life and Times* (New York: World Publishing, 1971).

Collins, Larry, and Dominique Lapierre, *O Jerusalem!* (New York: Simon and Schuster, 1972).

Cook, Don, *Ten Men and History* (New York: Doubleday, 1981).

Crossman, Richard, *A Nation Reborn* (London: Hamish Hamilton, 1960).

Davis, John H., *The Evasive Peace: A Study of the Zionist-Arab Problem* (Cleveland: Dillon-Liederbach, 1976).

Donovan, Robert J., *Conflict and Crisis: The Presidency of Harry S Truman, 1945–1948* (New York: Norton, 1977).

Eisenberg, Azriel, *Witness to the Holocaust* (New York: Pilgrim Press, 1981).

Elon, Amos, *The Israelis: Founders and Sons* (New York: Holt, Rinehart and Winston, 1971).

Feis, Herbert, *The Birth of Israel: The Tousled Diplomatic Bed* (New York: Norton, 1969).

Foreign Relations of the U.S., 1947, V, 1177–1178, 1227–1228, 1249, 1269–1270, 1271–1272, 1307, 1309; 1948, V, 632–633, pt. 2, 637–640, 753, 842–843, 972–976.

Friedrich, Otto, *Time*, August 28, September 4, 1989.

García-Granados, Jorge, *The Birth of Israel* (New York: Knopf, 1948).

Gerstang, Professor John, *The Observor*, September 20, 1936.

Gilbert, Martin, *Winston S. Churchill: Never Despair 1945–1965* (Boston: Houghton Mifflin, 1988).

Gonen, Jay Y., *A Psychohistory of Zionism* (New York: New American Library, 1975).

Government of Palestine, *Survey of Palestine, Volume 1* (Palestine Government Printing Press, 1946).

Graves, Richard Percival, *Lawrence of Arabia and His World* (New York: Scribner's, 1976).

Grose, Peter, *Israel in the Mind of America* (New York: Knopf, 1983).

Hart, Liddell, *Colonel Lawrence* (London: Faber, 1938).

Heiden, Konrad, *Der Fuehrer: Hitler's Rise to Power* (Boston: Houghton Mifflin, 1944).

Heilbroner, Robert L., *The Worldly Philosophers* (New York: Simon and Schuster, 1953).

Hitler, Adolf, *Mein Kampf* (Boston: Houghton Mifflin, 1943).

Hitti, Philip K., *The Arabs: A Short History for Americans* (New York: St. Martin's Press, 1968).

Ingrams, Doreen, *Palestine Papers 1917–1922, Seeds of Conflict* (London: John Murray, 1972).

*International Affairs*, July 1979.

*Jewish Chronicle*, July 16, 1937.

*Jewish Frontier*, October 1943.

Khouri, Fred J., *The Arab-Israeli Dilemma* (Syracuse University Press, 1985).

Kirkbride, Sir Alec Seith, *An Awakening: The Arab Campaign* (University Press of Arabia, 1971).

Knightley, Phillip, and Colin Simpson, *The Secret Lives of Lawrence of Arabia* (London: Nelson, 1969).

Koestler, Arthur, *Promise and Fulfillment* (New York: MacMillan, 1949).

Kurzman, Dan, *Ben-Gurion: Prophet of Fire* (New York: Simon and Schuster, 1983).

Laqueur, Walter, *A History of Zionism* (New York: Schocken Book, 1976).

Lawrence, T. E., Lawrence Files from Humanities Research Center, University of Texas.

Lawrence, T. E., *The Seven Pillars of Wisdom* (New York: Doubleday, 1935).

*Look*, May 23, 1939.

*Manchester Guardian*, August 18, 1939.

*Middle East Diary, 1917–1956* (Crescent Press, 1959).

Miller, Merle, *Plain Speaking: An Oral Biography of Harry S Truman* (New York: Berkley, 1974).

Morse, Arthur, *While Six Million Died: A Chronicle of American Apathy* (New York: Random House, 1968).

Morton, Geoffrey, *Just the Job* (London: Hodder and Stoughton, 1957).

Nathan, Otto, and Heinz Norden, editors, *Einstein on Peace* (New York: Schocken Books, 1968).

*New York Times*, March 16, March 20, 1938; October 7, 1946.

Overstreet, H. A., *The Mature Mind* (New York: Norton, 1949).

Palestine Royal Commission Report, July 1937, Minutes 5648.

Perlmutter, Amos, *Israel: The Partitioned State* (New York: Scribner's, 1985).

Pogue, Forrest C., *George C. Marshall: Statesman 1945–1959* (New York: Viking Penguin, 1987).

Reinharz, Jehuda, *Chaim Weizmann: The Making of a Zionist Leader* (New York: Oxford University Press, 1985).

Rose, Norman, *Chaim Weizmann* (New York: Penguin, 1986).

Schmidt, Dana Adams, *Armageddon in the Middle East* (New York: John Day, 1974).

Schwarz, Leo W., editor, *Great Ages and Ideas of the Jewish People* (New York: Modern Library, 1956).

Shirer, William L., *The Rise and Fall of the Third Reich* (New York: Simon and Schuster, 1960).

Silver, Eric, *Begin: The Haunted Prophet* (New York: Random House, 1984).

Snetsinger, John, *Truman, the Jewish Vote, and the Creation of Israel* (Palo Alto, Calif.: Stanford University Press, 1974).

Stewart, Desmond, *T.E. Lawrence: A New Biography* (New York: Harper and Row, 1977).

Teveth, Shabtai, *Ben-Gurion: The Burning Ground 1886–1948* (Boston: Houghton Mifflin, 1987).

Thomas, Lowell, *With Lawrence in Arabia* (New York: Grosset and Dunlap, 1924).

*Time*, August 28, 1989.

Tivnan, Edward, *The Lobby: Jewish Political Power and American Foreign Policy* (New York: Simon and Schuster, 1987).

Truman, Harry S, *Memoirs by Harry S Truman: Volume One: Year of Decision* (New York: Doubleday, 1955).

Truman, Harry S, Presidential Papers, 1948, 190–191, 288.

U.S. National Archives, Diplomatic Branch, Washington, D.C., January 19, 1948.

Weizmann, Chaim, *Trial and Error: The Autobiography of Chaim Weizmann* (New York: Harper, 1949).

Weizmann, Chaim, Weizmann Letters, 1, 152–153; 2, 307.

Welles, Sumner, *The Time for Decision* (New York: Harper, 1944).

Wiesel, Elie, Foreword from *Voices from the Holocaust*, edited by Sylvia Rothschild (New York: New American Library, 1981).

Williams, Francis, editor, *A Prime Minister Remembers: The War Memoirs of the Rt. Hon. Earl Attlee* (London: Heinemann, 1961).

Wilson, Harold, *A Prime Minister on Prime Ministers* (New York: Summit, 1977).

Wilson, Harold, *The Chariot of Israel: Britain, America and the State of Israel* (New York: Norton, 1981).

Yardley, Michael, *A Biography: T. E. Lawrence* (New York: Stein and Day, 1987).

# Index

485

| DATE | | |
|---|---|---|
|  |  |  |
|  |  |  |
|  |  |  |
|  |  |  |
|  |  |  |
|  |  |  |
|  | 14 DAY LOAN |  |
|  |  |  |
|  |  |  |
|  |  |  |